The Wisdom *of* Coaching

The Wisdom *of* Coaching

Essential Papers in Consulting Psychology for a World of Change

Edited by

Richard R. Kilburg and
Richard C. Diedrich

American Psychological Association • Washington, DC

Second Printing, February 2011

Published by
American Psychological Association
750 First Street, NE
Washington, DC 20002
www.apa.org

To order
APA Order Department
P.O. Box 92984
Washington, DC 20090-2984
Tel: (800) 374-2721; Direct: (202) 336-5510
Fax: (202) 336-5502; TDD/TTY: (202) 336-6123
Online: www.apa.org/books/
E-mail: order@apa.org

In the U.K., Europe, Africa, and the Middle East, copies may be ordered from
American Psychological Association
3 Henrietta Street
Covent Garden, London
WC2E 8LU England

Typeset in Berkeley by World Composition Services, Sterling, VA
Printer: Edwards Brothers, Inc., Ann Arbor, MI
Cover Designer: Naylor Design, Washington, DC
Technical/Production Editor: Harriet Kaplan
The opinions and statements published are the responsibility of the authors, and such opinions and statements do not necessarily represent the policies of the American Psychological Association.

Library of Congress Cataloging-in-Publication Data
The wisdom of coaching : essential papers in consulting psychology for a world of change / edited by Richard R. Kilburg and Richard C. Diedrich.— 1st ed.
p. cm.
Includes bibliographical references and index.
ISBN-13: 978-1-59147-787-7
ISBN-10: 1-59147-787-5
1. Executive coaching. I. Kilburg, Richard R., 1946- II. Diedrich, Richard C.
HD30.4.W57 2007
658.4′07124—dc22 2006027939

British Library Cataloguing-in-Publication Data
A CIP record is available from the British Library.

Printed in the United States of America
First Edition

Contents

Contributors ix
Acknowledgments xi

Introduction: The Historical and Conceptual Roots of Executive Coaching 3
Richard R. Kilburg

Part I. Coaching Definitions, History, Research, and Commentaries 17

1. Toward a Conceptual Understanding and Definition of Executive Coaching 21
   Richard R. Kilburg
2. Executive Coaching: A Working Definition 31
   Lewis R. Stern
3. Executive Coaching: A Comprehensive Review of the Literature 39
   Sheila Kampa-Kokesch and Mary Z. Anderson
4. Executive Coaching as an Emerging Competency in the Practice of Consultation 61
   Richard R. Kilburg
5. Further Consideration of Executive Coaching as an Emerging Competency 63
   Richard C. Diedrich and Richard R. Kilburg
6. Trudging Toward Dodoville: Conceptual Approaches and Case Studies in Executive Coaching 65
   Richard R. Kilburg
7. Executive Coaching: The Road to Dodoville Needs Paving With More Than Good Assumptions 73
   Rodney L. Lowman
8. Executive Coaching: An Outcome Study 79
   Karol M. Wasylyshyn

Part II. Coaching Approaches 91

9. Executive Coaching 95
   Harry Levinson

10. Executive Coaching: A Continuum of Roles 103
Robert Witherspoon and Randall P. White
11. Coaching at the Top 113
Fred Kiel, Eric Rimmer, Kathryn Williams, and Marilyn Doyle
12. Executive Coaching at Work: The Art of One-on-One Change 123
David B. Peterson
13. Coaching Executives 133
Lester L. Tobias
14. An Iterative Approach to Executive Coaching 143
Richard C. Diedrich
15. Business-Linked Executive Development: Coaching Senior Executives 149
Thomas J. Saporito
16. The Cognitive–Behavioral Approach to Executive Coaching 157
Mary Jo Ducharme
17. Rational–Emotive Behavior Therapy: A Behavioral Change Model for Executive Coaching? 167
Jessica Sherin and Leigh Caiger
18. Action Frame Theory as a Practical Framework for the Executive Coaching Process 175
Tracy Cocivera and Steven Cronshaw
19. When Shadows Fall: Using Psychodynamic Approaches in Executive Coaching 185
Richard R. Kilburg
20. The Emerging Role of the Internal Coach 207
Michael H. Frisch
21. An Integrated Model of Developmental Coaching 217
Otto E. Laske

Part III. Coaching Challenges, Methods, and Standards 237

22. Facilitating Intervention Adherence in Executive Coaching: A Model and Methods 241
Richard R. Kilburg
23. Coaching Leaders Through Culture Change 257
Judith H. Katz and Frederick A. Miller
24. Coaching Versus Therapy: A Perspective 267
Vicki Hart, John Blattner, and Staci Leipsic
25. Multimodal Therapy: A Useful Model for the Executive Coach 275
James T. Richard
26. Executive Growth Along the Adult Development Curve 283
Steven D. Axelrod
27. Leadership Dynamics: Character and Character Structure in Executives 291
Len Sperry
28. Ideas on Fostering Creative Problem Solving in Executive Coaching 303
James T. Richard

29. Behind the Mask: Coaching Through Deep Interpersonal Communication 311
James Campbell Quick and Marilyn Macik-Frey
30. Media Perceptions of Executive Coaching and the Formal Preparation of Coaches 319
Andrew N. Garman, Deborah L. Whiston, and Kenneth W. Zlatoper
31. Executive Coaching: The Need for Standards of Competence 323
Lloyd E. Brotman, William P. Liberi, and Karol M. Wasylyshyn
32. Lessons Learned in—and Guidelines for—Coaching Executive Teams 329
Richard C. Diedrich

Part IV. Case Studies 331

33. Coaching: The Successful Adventure of a Downwardly Mobile Executive 333
John Blattner
34. A Case Study of Executive Coaching as a Support Mechanism During Organizational Growth and Evolution 343
Eugene R. Schnell
35. The Alchemy of Coaching: "You're Good, Jennifer, but You Could Be *Really* Good" 357
David B. Peterson and Jennifer Millier
36. The Reluctant President 377
Karol M. Wasylyshyn
37. Developing the Effectiveness of a High-Potential African American Executive: The Anatomy of a Coaching Engagement 389
Paul C. Winum
38. Eye Movement Desensitization and Reprocessing: Four Case Studies of a New Tool for Executive Coaching and Restoring Employee Performance After Setbacks 407
Sandra Foster and Jennifer Lendl
39. Executive Coaching From the Executive's Perspective 413
John H. Stevens Jr.

Index 427
About the Editors 435

Contributors

Mary Z. Anderson
Steven D. Axelrod
John Blattner
Lloyd E. Brotman
Leigh Caiger
Tracy Cocivera
Steven Cronshaw
Richard C. Diedrich
Marilyn Doyle
Mary Jo Ducharme
Sandra Foster
Michael H. Frisch
Andrew N. Garman
Vicki Hart
Sheila Kampa-Kokesch
Judith H. Katz
Fred Kiel
Richard R. Kilburg
Otto E. Laske
Staci Leipsic
Jennifer Lendl
Harry Levinson
William P. Liberi
Rodney L. Lowman
Marilyn Macik-Frey
Frederick A. Miller
Jennifer Millier
David B. Peterson
James Campbell Quick
James T. Richard
Eric Rimmer
Thomas J. Saporito
Eugene R. Schnell
Jessica Sherin
Len Sperry
Lewis R. Stern
John H. Stevens Jr.
Lester L. Tobias
Karol M. Wasylyshyn
Deborah L. Whiston
Randall P. White
Kathryn Williams
Paul C. Winum
Robert Witherspoon
Kenneth W. Zlatoper

Acknowledgments

We thank all of the contributors to this volume and the editorial staff at the American Psychological Association for making this collection of articles available to the reading public outside of the Society of Consulting Psychology. We are truly grateful for their efforts.

The Wisdom *of* Coaching

INTRODUCTION: THE HISTORICAL AND CONCEPTUAL ROOTS OF EXECUTIVE COACHING

Richard R. Kilburg

Did you ever wonder about the circumstances that surround the invention of a new way of doing something? Perhaps you had never heard of the product, service, or work of art before but then suddenly it seems to emerge and become a permanent feature of the human landscape. As a small example of this phenomenon, the consulting subdiscipline of executive coaching, which has gained tremendous visibility and momentum in the past 20 years, seems to have simply appeared more or less in its modern form in the 1980s. How did this happen? What were the intellectual and practice advances that led to its emergence? What is executive coaching, what are some of the problems it tries to address, and how is it done? These are some of the questions that this introduction addresses. It also provides a brief narrative describing the evolution of this book and a succinct overview of its contents.

Technological and scientific history is replete with examples of the brilliant scientist or inventor who labors away in obscurity and then makes a sudden breakthrough, and following that the world somehow changes. In the most significant cases, with creations such as the sailboat, calculus, antibiotics, gunpowder, light bulbs, radio, television, transistors, nuclear fission, and the steam and internal combustion engines, human experience was altered permanently and visibly. In other cases, the invention or creation has been influential, but the effects have been not quite so dramatic. Examples of these kinds of innovations could include cubism, postmodern logic, psychotherapy, time and motion studies, jazz, and punk rock. These changes were duly noted and did have effects, sometimes significant effects, at the time that they came into vogue, but they do not appear to have transcendent consequences for the entire species.

The modern practice of psychology has few examples of the first kind of innovation. Perhaps the invention of the first modern psychological test by Binet, the creation of psychoanalysis by Freud and his colleagues, and the discovery of conditioning responses by Pavlov could qualify as such world-changing events in the field. However, most of the literature and practice in psychology seems to evolve more gradually, with many contributing streams of ideas and people involved in the movements, shifts, and changes. Kuhn (1977) described truly significant scientific changes as involving the creation of new paradigms or ways of seeing parts of the world that profoundly alter something in the intellectual disposition of humanity or in the everyday landscape of the world. As he pointed out, most science and almost all practice does not create new paradigms. Rather, the vast majority of scientists and practitioners merely take paradigms invented by others and modify them or reapply them in different settings or with different populations. To be sure, humanity learns much and can profit greatly from these more subtle and consistent applications of well-developed paradigms, but historians rarely write about the profound effects that such work has on the entire world.

For example, the invention of antibiotics and of anesthetic agents are treated as transcendent moments in medical history, but the day-to-day applications of them in the practice of medicine around the globe and the effects of those interventions are barely noted. In fact, they are most often taken for granted. "I went to the doctor today," is something that is reported by tens of millions of people around the world. One assumes when one hears such a report that the doctor did his or her job and that the medical problem was identified and appropriately treated. On average, no human being thinks of a visit to a modern medical doctor's office as a miracle, and yet in historical terms, what happens there represents a mind-blowing collection of a number of large and small inventions and innovations. The impact on one person can certainly be profound. The collective activity of modern physicians and their colleagues in health care has created truly astounding effects on all of humanity over the past century, but most of us, most of the time, take such miracles for granted.

The fields of management and managerial consultation have experienced a similar kind of evolution over the past couple of centuries. The emergence of large-scale, formally organized, private enterprises accelerated during the Industrial Revolution. To be sure, there are many examples of family businesses extending back through centuries in both Europe and Asia. However, organizations like the Hanseatic League created in 1358 A.D. and the East India Trading Company founded in 1600 A.D. aside, capitalist enterprises with transnational reach really got rolling in the mid to late 19th century. Fueled by and contributing to the Industrial Revolution, they adopted methods of management and organization that had been created largely for the armies of the world. The principles of chain of command, division of labor, and span of control had proven themselves in military organizations over a long period of time and were simply adopted wholesale. Many others had to be invented.

In the formal sense, managerial consultation started in Europe and the United States at about the same time (Kipping & Engwall, 2002). Initially, most consulting work was technical in its focus, helping organizations with the engineering of mines, roads, and other large-scale activities. However, in the late 19th and early 20th centuries, the engineers began to become part of the formal management structures of the enterprises to which they had been consulting. With the invention of the modern production line and the subsequent creation of "Fordism," the work of Taylor, Gantt, and Fayol (see Grieves, 2000) led to the emergence of the managerial consultant who was formally recognized for providing expertise on the organization and conduct of work.

Drawing its initial breath more than 100 years ago, the first recorded psychological consultation to an industrial enterprise was provided by Walter Dill Scott when he spoke to a group of advertising executives at a meeting in Chicago. That presentation led to an offer to consult with one of the participants in the meeting, and together, Scott and his client began to apply the scientific principles that would ultimately lead to the success of modern advertising. Scott went on to establish the first consulting firm in psychology in the years after the first World War, thus becoming a principal figure in the application of the fledgling art of psychological testing to the tasks of selecting employees (Napoli, 1975). It is easy to project back to that time and to imagine the nature of Scott's exchanges with the leaders of the organizations to which he offered services. His focus was on providing scientific answers to key questions that they had about their businesses, such as "What makes for a successful ad?"; "Whom should we hire for these positions?"; and "What makes for a well-motivated employee?" Thus, it is safe to say that although it has appeared in a wide variety of forms, some variant of executive coaching probably has been a component of the practice of psychological consultation since its inception.

The 1920s and 1930s, the period between the first and second World Wars, were a time of profound social upheaval in the United States as the Industrial Revolution really took hold. The country moved the majority of its people out of agriculture and into heavy and light industry, away from farms and into cities and the original suburbs. In the 20th century, bureaucratic organization became the dominant social force in society, and these enterprises needed well-adjusted, well-trained, and well-led people to flourish. Applied psychology followed these trends in a ceaseless effort to be useful in society. Napoli (1975) described the theoretical stance of the profession of psychology at that time in this way:

> The identification of applied psychology with science included little discussion of philosophical or theoretical questions. Applied psychologists, for example, never defined psychology's special realm of inquiry. It was variously seen as behavior, habits, motives, feelings, or some combination of these. Most academic psychologists desired to come to some consensus on this issue, and they usually wrote from a clear theoretical viewpoint. The applied psychologists, on the other hand, while aware of theoretical questions, preferred to avoid them. Sometimes they presented various viewpoints; sometimes they denied the importance of the theoretical framework, arguing that their task was to "arrive at their practical goal regardless of the route taken"; sometimes they ignored such questions altogether. Applied psychologists believed that they could successfully claim to be scientists without first explaining the fundamental nature of their science. In a sense, they were forced into this pragmatic position, for they could not explain what they did not know. (p. 59)

What we have come to see as the modern practice of consultation really began to bloom after the second World War. Several major developments occurred more or less simultaneously. The partnership of Rohrer, Hibler, and Replogle (most commonly known as RHR) was formed in 1945, with offices in Chicago, Detroit, and New York, creating the first truly modern company focusing on the delivery of psychological services to corporations. Lewin (1997) and his associates initiated the modern study of human groups, which opened the path to team-building technologies and established the roots of organization development. Beginning with Arthur Anderson in the early 1950s, accounting firms began to expand their services to consult on the introduction of modern information-processing technologies in large industrial enterprises (Byrne, 2002). As more and more companies began to use and benefit from such services, the companies themselves started to create internal groups of consultants to work on a variety of challenges facing them. The investments in management development by the AT&T Corporation that led to much of the creation of modern formal personnel testing and selection and the invention of the modern assessment center were most notable during this time period (Howard & Bray, 1988). Drawing inspiration from such developments and the leadership of a small number of prestigious business schools, higher education literally exploded with the creation of educational degrees focusing on management, administration, and industrial–organizational psychology (Crotty & Soule, 1997). As practitioners and scientists who were interested in the problems of modern organizations became available in large numbers, modern consulting practice truly came of age during the 1950s and 1960s.

In one sense, what we now call *executive coaching* has been a part of the practice of consultation from its inception. In most instances, consultants must work with, through, and for the senior executives of the organizations with which they engage. Although most often providing what Schein (1988) called "expert-based" advice to leaders, consultants still communicated with the senior executives of companies and made suggestions to them about how to operate and change their enterprises. However, in my opinion, it took the confluence of several major developments in the 1980s to launch the formal subdiscipline of what is now called executive coaching.

The first of these developments consisted of the simultaneous rise of formal executive development programs within companies and those nested in higher education and other nonprofit institutions. These programs proliferated wildly after the second World War, and they tended to emphasize the integration of the highly conceptual theories taught in business schools with the mundane and practical managerial arts that companies really needed to operate in the real world (Crotty & Soule, 1997). Perhaps the best-known and most influential of the organizations devoted to executive development that is not formally attached to a university is the Center for Creative Leadership (CCL). Founded in 1970, it has devoted itself to the understanding and advancement of leadership theory and practice in the world. Emerging out of the highly energized practice maelstrom of the 1960s, it has consistently emphasized that the cornerstone of leadership development consists of preparing individuals who have enough self-awareness and understanding to change their own behavior and that of their organizations to meet the demands of highly competitive environments. CCL programs have become models for many others in the field.

The second trend that contributed to the emergence of executive coaching involved the creation of the modern corporate management assessment center. Bray (Howard & Bray, 1988) and his colleagues at AT&T were the first to merge traditional psychological assessments; information from standard performance reviews; data from interviews; ratings of performance from in-basket, small group activities, and other managerial simulations; and multiassessor feedback into a comprehensive battery that greatly added to the reliability and validity of traditional methods of executive assessments. These technologies were commercialized by Development Dimensions International (Byham, 1984), Personnel Decisions International, and other business enterprises and are in common use in the global marketplace today.

The evolution of the field of organization development (or OD, as it has come to be known) constituted the third innovation. As documented by French and Bell (1990) and others, OD emerged in a tumultuously creative process that integrated many of the findings and practices that were being created by social and clinical psychologists and others interested in the evolution and operation of small groups, the explosive interest in self-development and self-awareness that led to the proliferation of multiple approaches to psychotherapy and personal growth in the 1950s and 1960s, and the attempt to apply these concepts and practices to the operation of organizations. OD practice has continued to grow and extend to a variety of philosophies, concepts, and methods, including organizational diagnosis, team building, total quality management, strategic planning, change management, organizational culture, and the psychosocial development of leaders (Grieves, 2000). In a recent compendium describing a variety of approaches to consulting psychology, Lowman (2002) emphasized that modern educational programs must prepare practitioners to understand and constructively intervene in enterprises at the level of the whole organization, the performing managerial or production group, and the individual employee. The evolution and application of executive coaching has become one of the major components of interventions aimed at individual leaders.

The fourth major development supporting the emergence of coaching consisted of the evolution of multirater feedback systems to assess the performance of individuals in organizations. These methodologies were created in response to the long-recognized challenges of providing reliable and valid information to employees as a way of improving their work performance (Alimo-Metcalfe, 1998; Fletcher, Baldry, & Cunningham-Snell, 1998). Traditional methods of review and development relied mostly on the perspectives of the supervising manager, which were known to be limited in many ways. In the 1970s and 1980s, the research on multirater methodologies led to the creation of commercially available 360-degree review products with solid reliability, validity, and other psychometric properties that many corporations adopted as part of their overall approach to performance management. At that time, the CCL and other executive development programs began to adopt some of the approaches that evolved out of corporate assessment centers that used integrated multirater, multidimensional feedback on the performance of actual work tasks and made them part of their ongoing efforts. Advanced business simulations, such as the "Looking Glass" that was invented by CCL, integrated multirater reviews of performance in the program as well as 360-degree reviews of leader behavior in their home organizations. In the 1980s, these comprehensive examinations of leadership performance became and have remained the key components of the state of the art in the field of executive education.

The creation of behavior therapy, which emphasized using various methods to change unproductive habits and to create new approaches to human problem solving, constituted the fifth major contribution to the creation of executive coaching. Using behavioral approaches to modify existing habits or create different pathways to living, learning, and loving allowed for the beginnings of the process of "depathologizing" human development efforts. Rational emotive and cognitive behavior therapy created additional approaches that could be applied to a wide variety of human situations without the necessity of identifying someone as a patient. Recent descriptions of these and other approaches to coaching can be found in Kilburg (2004).

Despite their popularity and almost universal adoption by large corporations and other organizations around the world, executive development programs of almost every conceivable type have had demonstrable problems showing that the knowledge and skill acquired during these educational initiatives actually changed and improved the performance of participants back on the job. The identification and global recognition of what has come to be known as the problem of "transfer of training" created a sixth and major component of the stream of forces leading to the development of executive coaching (Tannenbaum & Yukl, 1992). Some of the attendees of CCL and other executive education programs began to request personalized assistance to help them apply what they had learned in their classes back on their jobs. Senior trainers thus started to continue the development work that had been confined to classrooms with leaders back in their home institutions. In the 1980s, the search for a technology or set of methods that would improve the probability that these expensive education programs would lead to better leadership led to the emergence of a set of experiments and initiatives at CCL and the creation of the first commercially available and formalized executive coaching services delivered by the staff at Personnel Dimensions International. These efforts coincided with the emergence of the Hudson Institute of Santa Barbara in 1986, which began to focus on providing services to support normal adult development and also started to use the metaphor of personal coaching to describe its approach (Hudson, 1999).

These trends culminated in the first formal research efforts to assess the impact of executive coaching in the doctoral dissertations of Dale Thompson (1987) and David Peterson (1993). Len Sperry's (1993) journal article, "Working with Executives: Consulting, Counseling, and Coaching," became the first work in the psychological literature that I could find to apply the term *coaching* to this form of developmentally oriented work with leaders. A PsycINFO search of journal articles on executive coaching for this introduction yielded 81 entries going back to Mold's (1951) article on executive development. Since publication of Sperry's article, the literature on executive coaching and the field itself have exploded (Kilburg, 2000). Indeed, a Google search of the term *executive coaching* conducted for this review yielded over 8 million hits, thus accurately demonstrating just how far the subdiscipline has come in 2 short decades.

THE EVOLUTION OF THE WISDOM OF COACHING

The initial literature on executive coaching was extremely small and widely scattered. Outside of the dissertations of Thompson (1987) and Peterson (1993), the article published by Sperry (1993), and one major book by Hargrove (1995), there had been no significant effort to chronicle what had been happening in the field. That changed in 1996, with the publication of the first special issue of the *Consulting Psychology Journal: Practice and Research* (*CPJ*) devoted solely to the emerging proficiency of executive coaching (Kilburg, 1996). In the intervening 9 years, three other special issues have been produced by *CPJ*, (Diedrich & Kilburg, 2001; Kilburg, 2004, 2005). The 27 articles published in those four volumes constitute one third of the list of articles identified as relevant to executive coaching in the PsycINFO search. Unfortunately, *CPJ*, although published by the American Psychological Association (APA), is primarily subscribed to by the members of the Society of Consulting Psychology, so the vast majority of people interested in and providing executive coaching in the marketplace have not had access to this literature. The primary purpose of the current volume is to remedy that problem and to make more widely available the collection of articles on executive coaching that have been published in *CPJ* from 1996 through 2005.

In 2004, I suggested to Dick Diedrich, the current editor of *CPJ*, that the coaching articles that have appeared in *CPJ* represent many of the best that have appeared in the literature and that making them more widely available to consultants and coaches would be a good thing to do. He agreed, and you are now holding the results in your hands.

WHAT IS EXECUTIVE COACHING?

As you will discover when working your way through the articles in this book, there are a variety of definitions of this subdiscipline. Although they vary somewhat in style and substance, the majority of them incorporate several specific concepts. First, executive coaching is a formal consulting relationship between an individual executive client and a professional coach. Second, the focus is most often on helping clients improve their performance in their roles in their organizations, although there are a wide variety of topics or issues facing leaders with which coaching can assist. Third, it is usually a time-limited engagement, although in some cases, it can and does continue over many years. Fourth, the coach and client most often set goals for the activity that are mutually defined. And finally, there is often some form of assessment that takes place which leads to both formal and informal feedback to clients about their performance.

As can also be readily seen in the articles, the methods and means of coaching vary widely depending on the practitioner, the client, and the situations that they mutually face. The most common element involves face-to-face or telephone contact between them in which some form of reflective dialogue takes place. There may be homework assignments suggested as well as specific recommendations for action or behavior change. At times, role-playing, behavioral simulations, or other methods can be used to help clients make progress toward their goals. To better understand the breadth and complexity of what happens in a coaching session, let's look at a brief case vignette to get a real feel for what can occur in an actual coaching exchange that took place between me and one of my clients. As is usual with such material, substantial changes have been made to protect the privacy of the client.

THE CASE OF COACHING UP

"He's driving me nuts," Marla Robbins said, sitting back in her chair at the conference table we shared in her office. The afternoon sun filtered through the window and frosted her brown hair with golden highlights. She wore a stylish gray, skirted suit with a blue blouse. Marla's thin, attractive face was drawn into a tight frown that I recognized as a symptom of intense concentration on her part. She was a hard-working senior vice president for sales and marketing in a large services firm who was coping with a new CEO who had joined the company less than a year before the date of our meeting. I had worked with Marla in her previous two positions in the organization, and we were familiar and comfortable with each other. Our recent coaching sessions had concentrated on how she wanted to approach the relationship with her new boss. She had no intention of leaving the company and wanted to insure that she made it onto his roster of trusted insiders.

"What has been happening recently?" I asked.

Marla leaned forward and put her arms on the conference table. "I don't know if I'm getting through to him. There are times when I think he's listening to me, but mostly, Jeffery just seems to go through the motions in our meetings and then does what he damn well pleases. It's really frustrating, because I know I can help him become a really good CEO here."

Usually at this point in a coaching session, I can see several different avenues through which to explore the situation a client faces. This one was no different. Among other things, I could ask her about the feelings that she was experiencing. We could explore more details about Jeffery Azimier, the 40-something, highly energetic, and very opinionated CEO the board of directors had brought in to reinvigorate this mainline, conservative organization. I could ask her to describe what she had been trying to do with him interpersonally or professionally or to explain more about the competitive strategy that he was trying to push into the company. However, as I often do in these situations, I chose to probe for a story that might illuminate aspects of all of these dimensions of Marla's circumstances.

"Can you give me a recent example of what you are experiencing?"

"Sure," Marla responded immediately. "I had a meeting with him last week to discuss one of our long-standing clients. Now, this is an organization I know very, very well. I'm on excellent terms with the CEO, their COO, their CFO—in fact, their whole management team. I've negotiated a succession of contracts with them over the past 5 years that have made us a bundle.

"Jeffery was meeting with the CEO for the first time at the end of the week, and I was trying to brief him on the history of the organization, our contracts, what we've accomplished, and some of the pitfalls that we've experienced over the years. I told him what we have done in the past to secure the contracts and the approach that has worked most often. I specifically told him not to mention price in the meeting with the CEO and instead to concentrate on the scope of work. These guys like to separate their negotiations, and once the CEO agrees on the main outlines of the contract, he always turns it over to the CFO to negotiate the details. Jeffery seemed to listen to me at the time, but yesterday, I got this telephone call from the CFO over there asking me if my new boss was crazy."

"What happened?"

"Apparently, Jeffery went into the meeting with the CEO last Friday and tried to sell him on an entirely new way to structure the work that we do with them and the pricing strategy for the services."

"And?"

"And, Jeffery and the board believe that we need to be more aggressive with our clients and move systematically toward higher margin services in our agreements. We've started an outsourcing component of our organization through which we can leverage aspects of our managerial specializations to really help companies do their own work in these areas more cheaply and effectively. Not only do we save them money, we make more money ourselves because our own infrastructure costs are already sunk and well distributed over several years, so with each customer we add to that business, our margins improve remarkably."

"So, what did Jeffery do?"

"He completely ignored my advice and the 7 years of working experience we have with that team. Not only did he try to sell the concepts, apparently he really went at the CEO hard on pricing strategy."

"What did the CFO say?"

"He said that his boss was ticked off and would not outsource a thing with us. He said that if Jeffery came near his organization, he'd cancel our entire deal. He said that he never wanted to talk to him again."

"Oh, my goodness. So, what did you do with that information?"

"Nothing; I waited to talk to you, coach," she said with a shy smile.

"Thanks a lot," I responded, smiling back.

"No, seriously, I have no idea what to do with this one," Marla said with a sense of urgency in her voice.

"Does Jeffery have any idea of how that meeting went?" I asked.

"Not a clue. He told me when he got back that he thought it went very well."

"Wow; either he's completely insensitive interpersonally or that CEO hides his own reactions incredibly well."

"Probably a lot of both," Marla said.

"So, what do you see as your options?" I asked.

Marla looked away for a moment or two as the frown deepened on her face. She cleared her throat and then started to talk.

"I've thought a lot about it, and there are several ways to go. First, say nothing to Jeffery and use everything in my bag of tricks to try to keep the contracts going with this client. Second, try to talk again to Jeffery to see if I can make some headway. And third, put my paper on the street and try to find a new job."

Marla smiled a little as she finished her list, which told me that she was trying hard to cope effectively with the stresses of this peculiar and difficult situation.

"And of these three, which one do you want to pursue?"

"That's easy, say nothing and save the day. But, I know that won't work."

"Why?"

"Simple. These guys aren't buying Jeffery's new strategy and approach and he needs to know. As soon as he finds out, he's going to want to go back and sell the CEO harder. If he does that, the CEO might see him or might not. In either case, the contracts are probably toast and then we're off to the races with the blame game."

"So that leaves number two?"

"You got it. And I have no idea how to talk to him about this. Do you want to do it?" she asked half seriously.

"Does he know I'm your coach?"

"I don't think so. We've never really discussed it."

"Then it's not realistic for you to introduce someone else into this right now."

"I know. I just don't want to do this," Marla said as her voice cracked a little.

These moments in the lives of leaders and of the coaches who work with them are among the most telling. The leadership literature is full of case studies of how executives did or did not do the right thing and how they tried to do the right thing but managed to botch the execution and then describe the negative consequences of their decisions or actions. Academics and practitioners alike are very good at the game of second guessing and playing "shoulda, woulda, coulda" with the leaders of modern organizations. However, there has been very little that describes the personal agonies and intense crises that most often determine just what kind of leader a person will ultimately be. When an executive faces a problem like Marla's, he or she always has the opportunity to grow, but often it simply becomes a crisis that is managed more or less effectively, and the individual moves on from there without incorporating key lessons that can help him or her master similar situations in the future. These are the moments in which a leader's character is often tested more severely than his or her ability to strategize or make a decision, and these are the moments in which emotional maturity and personal virtues serve as the bedrock for executive action.

"I know it's difficult," I said quietly. "One of the hardest things for any leader to do is try to influence his or her boss. It's even harder to try to coach up the chain of command."

"Don't tell me you expect me to coach him, for God's sake. He doesn't listen to anyone."

"That may be, but you sometimes have to coach your subordinates when they don't want to listen either."

"That's different, I can always fire them if they don't listen."

"I agree, position power can make a big difference in any exchange. But just because you don't have position power with your boss does not mean you are powerless. Part of what you are experiencing is the natural anxiety that comes with this kind of task. So, what are you afraid of when you think of talking to Jeffery about his efforts with that customer?"

Marla shifted uncomfortably in her chair. I knew she wanted to do the right thing and to perform effectively. However, everyone in leadership positions inevitably faces situations that generate strong emotional reactions or engender various forms of conflict. In such circumstances, the first job of an executive or someone who is coaching a leader is to make sure that the emotions, conflicts, and any defensive operations that are being generated in the situation get identified (Kilburg, 2000).

"Well, it's obvious that I'm afraid of losing my job."

"Anything else?" I asked.

"I know that I'll make him feel bad and that he may react poorly to what I say."

"So, when you talk to your husband about something that he hasn't done that he should have or about something that he's said that wounded you, what do you worry about?"

"That I'll hurt him."

"How?"

"It's easy to make him feel ashamed of himself, or the best is to make him feel guilty," Marla said as she smiled sheepishly.

"So, we see that strong emotions like shame, guilt, anxiety, and anger are likely to be elicited in this situation. The biggest fear is that if you approach him directly, he might become very upset and try to fire you. And we know that your boss doesn't manage such emotional states particularly well. It seems to me that we have a couple of jobs to do here. You know what needs to be said, but you don't know how to deliver it in a way that he will want to hear it. You know what he needs to do, but you also don't know whether he's likely to follow your advice."

"Yes, and I'm clueless about how to approach it."

"Marla, leaders implicitly expect their key subordinates to play many roles for them."

"Like what?"

"Here are just a few: leader, soldier, spy, analyst, coach, diplomat, follower, executioner, diagnostician, problem solver, trouble shooter, or psychic. They are expected to do all of these plus manage the technical aspects of their jobs in finance, sales, marketing, operations, research, or HR. Leaders just want to be able to turn to their team members and ask them to perform one or more of these without ever clarifying whether they really have the appropriate knowledge, skills, experience, or abilities. The implicit motto seems to be, 'Just figure it out and do it.'"

"You've got that right."

"And you probably do the same things with your own direct reports."

In response to this observation, she blushed and nodded.

"Okay, so that's the way it works most of the time. The key here is not to change the name of the game. Leaders can and must have these expectations of their team members. Rather, at a crossroad or inflection point in the history of an organization or a working relationship, it can become important to clarify those expectations and to specify what is wanted by way of performance. In this situation, we know that Jeffery is new to the organization, the industry, his role, and your customers. He doesn't take advice very well and, simultaneously, he is desperate to succeed. What would happen if you asked him if he wanted to talk further about his meeting with the customer?"

"He'd say sure. Then he'd ask me what I had on my mind."

"Have you ever asked him how he likes to get feedback from his subordinates?"

Marla shook her head again, this time more aggressively.

"What would happen if you asked him if he was willing to listen to some feedback that you had from others inside that customer organization?"

"I'd make him very nervous but he'd probably agree to it."

"What if you then asked, 'How can I do this so that you are more likely to hear it and less likely to play shoot the messenger?'"

"He might laugh or he just might shoot me."

"Okay, you see where I'm going with this. Sometimes in these complex situations you need to have a conversation about how you'll have the conversation before you leap into something very complex and potentially dangerous, or at the least, emotionally challenging. What do you think he would say if you asked him how you could give him honest information, data that he needs as the CEO, and not endanger your working relationship with him?"

Marla pondered for a moment and then said, "I don't know."

"Okay. Do you want another question you could ask him?"

"Sure," she answered, somewhat more enthusiastically.

"What do you think he would say if you asked him who he relies on to tell him the truth about himself or his organization?"

Marla smiled despite herself. "I don't know the answer to that either."

"Are you curious about the answers to those questions?" I asked.

"I sure am."

"Well, you see where I'm going with this conversation. In essence, I'm suggesting that you try to create a dialogue with Jeffery about having conversations with him. If you raise enough good questions in that exchange and do it tactfully and sensitively, he may well become more and more curious and therefore more and more desirous of the feedback. At the point at which he begins to insist that you tell him, then you can ask if he'll hold you harmless for answering his questions and telling the truth."

"And if he says no?"

"If he says no, you need to have prepared a mild-mannered version of the truth that will still get his head in the game of talking about how he did with that CEO. But if he says yes, what will you have accomplished in your working relationship with him?"

"I guess he may end up trusting me a little more."

"Is that a bad thing? You looked distraught when you said that."

Marla chuckled a little at my observation. "It's a little like that saying, 'Be careful what you wish for.'"

"Yes. Yes, it is. But if he begins to accept the feedback that you give him, what will that do for your working relationship with him?"

"Oh, it will get better. But I'm a little scared of that too, because if he starts to turn to me for advice, then I'll need to provide it and it will need to be very good indeed."

"Isn't that what leadership is all about?" I asked.

"Yes. Yes, it is," she replied calmly.

Marla did gather her courage and went on to have that conversation with Jeffery. He agreed to hold her harmless for providing the feedback and managed to hear her out. She reported being extremely nervous during that discussion, but ultimately, she was also very pleased that she managed to carry it off. After they discussed the issues together, they agreed that the best follow-up tactic would be for Jeffery to call the other CEO just to check in with him after their meeting. At some point in that conversation, he would mention that he knew that the other CEO would want their respective staffs to follow up their discussion and that he was supportive of that idea. Jeffery also agreed to make some effort to apologize to that customer if it seemed to be appropriate in the moment. Ultimately, they did not lose that customer and Jeffery started to talk a little more to Marla and other key members of his leadership group before he charged off on his own. Marla herself gained a lot of confidence as a result of her willingness and ability to tell the truth to Jeffery and created a lot of ideas about how she could better coach him in the future.

Including this case study in the introduction to this unique collection of articles on executive coaching illustrates several major issues that will become obvious to you as you make your way though this book. First, over the past 2 decades, coaching leaders has emerged rapidly to become a widespread practice throughout the world. It is used in organizations of all shapes, types, and sizes. It is done internally by leaders, human resources practitioners, organization development specialists, and peers. External coaches who make their services available to organizations now number in the thousands in the United States alone, and many major corporations have moved to centralize and organize their coaching efforts because they are spending millions of dollars on these services annually. This case study demonstrates how effective coaching can be at helping leaders develop knowledge and skill and at directly influencing organizational performance as well. In this case, Marla not only improved her ability and willingness to work with her new CEO, her intervention had the specific effect of saving the long-term client for their organization and preserving that revenue stream. As a result of her skill in working with Jeffery, coaching was also able to influence how he led his organization as well.

Second, coaching is still an emerging practice within the discipline of consulting. As I described above, you will find as you read through the articles in this book a number of definitions of *practice*, a large number of different approaches to how coaching can be done, and a variety of more elaborate case studies that demonstrate how consultants coach. There is not now and I suspect will never be one right way to do this with a leader. In this example, Marla not only needed to develop her own knowledge and skill in working up the chain of command, she also needed to take substantial personal and political risks to intervene to protect the business itself. Marla accomplished this and became better herself at coaching. In subsequent sessions with her, this became an additional focus of our work, and her coaching skills improved significantly over time.

Third, coaches never really know what they are going to encounter when they make contact with their clients. The content of coaching sessions can vary extensively as they begin with one topic but often connect to a wide variety of themes and issues. Coaches in these complex organizational settings need to be knowledgeable about a large number of subjects and issues and prepared to make the connections that their clients are sometimes unwilling or unable to make for themselves. This then ties to the personal and professional preparation to do coaching. Although formal educational programs have emerged in the field that claim to produce "certified coaches," I believe that it is highly unlikely that anyone who attends such classes will be fully competent to provide these services in these settings. As any number of the articles in this collection suggest, the field of executive coaching is still emerging, the research base for these interventions is relatively primitive, and the array of interventions being undertaken is extremely large. Individuals from a wide variety of backgrounds are coaching successfully in companies around the world, and no profession, educational program, or organization has or is likely to gain a controlling grip on this emerging field of consulting practice.

Finally, working with senior executives in organizations can be simultaneously extremely rewarding and very challenging. These leaders tend to move through their worlds with amazing swiftness and competency. They are talented, aggressive, and extraordinarily competitive. They have had to be to attain their positions. If they choose to slow down periodically to work with a coach, it represents a significant investment in time, energy, and money. These executives make their livings by delivering results to their stakeholders in very public ways. They expect to succeed, and they demand performance from their subordinates. As a result, they do not suffer fools gladly and are as hard on their coaches as they are on anyone else. When they discuss the intimate aspects of their lives with a professional, they demand to be helped as a result of the exchange. The best executive clients react to developmental feedback and exchanges with remarkable swiftness. They take in the information and begin to use it quickly and well. I have witnessed startling changes in leadership performance as a result of coaching efforts. I have also seen clients resist efforts to help them, continue to work in their familiar and comfortable ways, and sometimes fail spectacularly as a result of their inability to develop. Their organizations can fail as well, and in the worst cases, these disasters can dramatically affect the lives of tens of thousands of people. As a result, practitioners who do or want to do this work must accept a special responsibility. Not only does their work affect the lives and careers of the individual clients whom they coach, it also can create effects in the organization as a whole. The knowledge, skills, ability, and experience required to work in this way is extensive and not easily acquired. I hope that this collection of articles will help readers advance their ability to work with these types of clients.

THE PLAN OF THE BOOK

This book is organized into four sections. My coeditor, Richard C. Diedrich, has written brief introductions and summaries for each that introduce the articles. The first section contains articles that focus on definitions, history, and research on executive coaching and the commentaries that accompanied each of the issues of the journal. The second section pulls together the articles that emphasize conceptual approaches to executive coaching and contains the thinking of many of the finest practitioners in the field. The third section encompasses the articles that focus on specific challenges facing coaches, methods that can be and are used in coaching engagements, and the issue of standards of practice in the field. The final section provides all of the major case studies that have appeared in *CPJ* over the last decade or so.[1]

On the surface, it would appear that there are three major ways that any reader could approach this material. First, you could simply read it from cover to cover and address the material in each article as it appears. Second, you could browse your way through the volume, selecting articles that appeal to your curiosity or interest. Finally, you could strategically identify particular issues or problems in executive coaching that you are facing at any particular time and dive into the relevant material. Regardless of how you choose to work your way through the book, I think you will agree with me by the end that you have greatly expanded your knowledge of the field, appreciation for the depth and scope of thinking and practice that appear in these articles, and gratitude that the authors took the time to collect and express their thoughts on paper.

References

Alimo-Metcalfe, B. (1998). 360 degree feedback and leadership development, *International Journal of Selection and Assessment, 6*, 35–44.

Byham, W. C. (1984). From entrepreneur to manager. *Professional Psychology: Research and Practice, 15*, 706–715.

Byrne, J. (2002, August 12). Fall from grace. *Business Week*, 50–56.

Crotty, P. T., & Soule, A. J. (1997). Executive education: Yesterday, and today, with a look at tomorrow. *Journal of Management Development, 16*, 4–21.

Diedrich, R. C., & Kilburg, R. R. (Eds.). (2001). Further consideration of executive coaching as an emerging competency [Special issue]. *Consulting Psychology Journal: Practice and Research, 53*(4).

Fletcher, C., Baldry, C., & Cunningham-Snell, N. (1998). The psychometric properties of 360 degree feedback: An empirical study and a cautionary tale. *International Journal of Selection and Assessment, 6*, 19–25.

French, W. C., & Bell, C. H. (1990). *Organization development: Behavioral science interventions for organization improvement*. Englewood Cliffs, NJ: Prentice-Hall.

Grieves, J. (2000). Introduction: The origins of organizational development. *Journal of Management Development, 19*, 345–447.

Hargrove, R. (1995). *Masterful coaching: Extraordinary results by impacting people and the way they think and work together*. Johannesburg, South Africa: Pfeiffer.

Howard, A., & Bray, D. W. (1988). *Managerial lives in transition: Advancing age and changing times*. New York: Guilford Press.

Hudson, F. M. (1999). *The handbook of coaching: A comprehensive resource guide for managers, executives, consultants, and human resource professionals*. San Francisco: Jossey-Bass.

Kilburg, R. R. (Ed.). (1996). Executive coaching [Special issue]. *Consulting Psychology Journal: Practice and Research, 48*(2).

Kilburg, R. R. (2000). *Executive coaching: Developing managerial wisdom in a world of chaos*. Washington, DC: American Psychological Association.

Kilburg, R. R. (Ed.). (2004). Trudging toward Dodoville—Part 1: Conceptual approaches in executive coaching [Special issue]. *Consulting Psychology Journal: Practice and Research, 56*(4).

Kilburg, R. R. (Ed.). (2005). Trudging toward Dodoville—Part 2: Case studies in executive coaching [Special issue]. *Consulting Psychology Journal: Practice and Research, 57*(1).

Kipping, M., & Engwall, L. (Eds.). (2002). *Management consulting: Emergence and dynamics of a knowledge industry*. Oxford, England: Oxford University Press.

Kuhn, T. S. (1977). *The essential tension: Selected studies in scientific tradition and change*. Chicago: University of Chicago Press.

Lewin, K. (1997). *Resolving social conflicts and field theory in social science*. Washington, DC: American Psychological Association.

Lowman, R. L. (Ed.). (2002). *Handbook of organizational consulting psychology: A comprehensive guide to theory, skills, and techniques*. San Francisco: Jossey-Bass.

Mold, H. P. (1951). Developing top leaders—Executive training. *Proceedings of the Annual Industrial Relations Conference*, 47–53.

Napoli, D. S. (1975). *The architects of adjustment: The practice and professionalization of American psychology, 1920–1945*. Ann Arbor, MI: University Microfilms International.

Peterson, D. B. (1993). Skill learning and behavior change in an individually tailored management

[1] Note that references have been updated throughout the book to reflect subsequent publication of articles that were in press; references to articles that now appear as chapters in this book have been changed to cross-references to the appropriate chapters.

coaching and training program. (Doctoral dissertation, University of Minnesota). *Dissertation Abstracts International, 54*(3-B), 1707–1708.

Schein, E. (1988). *Process consultation: Vol. 1. Its role in organization development*. Reading, MA: Addison-Wesley.

Sperry, L. (1993). Working with executives: Consulting, counseling, and coaching. *Individual Psychology: Journal of Adlerian Theory, Research & Practice, 49,* 257–266.

Tannenbaum, S. I., & Yukl, G. (1992). Training and development in work organizations. *Annual Review of Psychology, 42,* 339–441.

Thompson, A. D. (1987). A formative evaluation of an individualized coaching program for business managers and professionals. (Doctoral dissertation, University of Minnesota). *Dissertation Abstracts International, 47A,* 4339.

PART I

COACHING DEFINITIONS, HISTORY, RESEARCH, AND COMMENTARIES

As Richard R. Kilburg notes in his introduction to this book, what we now call *executive coaching* has been practiced by RHR International since the late 1940s (they called it *developmental counseling* then), and Personnel Decisions International began offering a structured and personally tailored coaching program in 1981 (see chap. 12, this volume), but the definition of executive coaching is still evolving and being refined as we go. There are still no universal definitions, standards, certifications, or regulations for this explosive trend in both the workplace and psychological practice.

Four special issues of the journal *Consulting Psychology Journal: Practice and Research* have been devoted to "defining" executive coaching.[1] The 27 articles in these special issues still constitute a substantial portion of the professional literature on executive coaching. In spite of these major contributions to both the literature and practice of executive coaching, Kilburg noted in 2004 that "for all of the work that has been done to illuminate the subject of coaching in the past 15 or 20 years, what actually happens in coaching engagements remains quite mysterious" (see chap. 6, this volume, p. 65). The ongoing need of those of us in the profession to better define what we are doing, why we do this work, what the real results look like, and the necessary next steps has changed very little. The chapters in Part I document the differentiation of established facts and advocacy and continue to better "define" the field.

Kilburg sets the stage in the chapter based on his 1996 article (chap. 1), in which he reminds us of the limited empirical basis for the practice that has become known as executive coaching and shares an early, pioneering, and focused effort to conceptualize and define this emerging area of consultation. His chapter provides a brief but useful summary of the existing literature, a conceptual framework for understanding, a preliminary definition, and the encouragement for more research.

Stern (chap. 2) provides a basic definition of executive coaching, draws attention to process and methods, differentiates executive coaching from other forms of coaching, and includes several examples of situations in which executive coaching can be especially helpful. Kampa-Kokesch and Anderson (chap. 3) examine the literature of executive coaching. They comment on the history of this intervention and then critically review six themes within the practice-based literature. This review is then followed by a review of seven

[1] The first and landmark issue appeared in 1996 (see Kilburg, 1996); a second in 2001 (see Diedrich & Kilburg, 2001); and the third and fourth in late 2004 and early 2005, respectively (see Kilburg, 2004, 2005).

empirical studies (three from business management and three from psychology), a discussion of the link between these studies and the practice-based literature, and a call for additional research.

The next three chapters in Part I (chaps. 4–6) are adapted from forewords to the journal's first three special issues mentioned above. We have included them because they contain a valuable perspective regarding both the history and the status of executive coaching. The first (chap. 4) sets the stage, the next (chap. 5) reminds the reader of the continuing need for definitions of both concepts and practices, and the most recent (chap. 6) provides a current status report on the field.[2] Kilburg notes in his foreword to the first special issue of the *Consulting Psychology Journal* that "as it is currently practiced, executive coaching appears to be an eclectic mix of concepts and methods that are being applied by a variety of consultants who have accepted assignments to work with individual executives" (see chap. 4, pp. 61–62). He sees executive coaching as a specific subarea within the practice of consultation and viewed the first special issue as an opportunity to "define the core concepts and definitions of this emerging competency" (chap. 4, p. 62).

The second special issue was created to continue the efforts to define both the concepts and the practices of executive coaching. Diedrich and Kilburg's foreword (chap. 5) points out that

> from the way the field has developed in the past 5 years, it appears now that coaching has begun to make its place in the vast armamentarium of behaviorally based interventions available to psychologists and other professionals who work to help people and organizations change. (p. 63)

Kilburg's "Trudging Toward Dodoville: Conceptual Approaches and Case Studies in Executive Coaching" (see chap. 6, this volume) introduced the third and fourth *Consulting Psychology Journal* special issues on executive coaching and focuses on the current status of the scientific knowledge base for this practice. He notes that Part 1 of the two-part special issue (see Kilburg, 2004) included five "conceptual approach" articles, and he shares his delight regarding the five unique case studies and the critical review article by Lowman that were included in Part 2.

Lowman's article, included here as chapter 7, reviews the 10 theory and practice articles from Parts 1 and 2 of "Trudging Toward Dodoville." He argues that practice has exceeded research in executive coaching and reminds us that there is no substitute for the empirical validation of our practice. He suggests that the articles offer little with regard to the identification of common factors or the generation of testable hypotheses.

In the final article of Part I, Wasylyshyn (chap. 8) presents an outcome study that she hopes will cause coaches to view coaching as a major developmental tool and to think more about what it really takes to achieve positive results. The study involved 87 executives and speaks to the question, "Which executives are most likely to benefit from coaching?" Psychologists are reported to be especially effective coaches, the use of psychometric tools is recommended, and behavior change and learning are seen as key indicators of success.

Part I presents a comprehensive review of "executive coaching" as it has been defined and practiced during the past decade (1996–2006) as well as a state-of-the-art picture of what many continue to see as an evolving and illusive art form. In the chapter based on his

[2] Note that some portions not relevant to this collection have been removed for ease of reading.

1996 article, Levinson (chap. 9) notes that "in the course of executive coaching, it is particularly important to avoid becoming psychotherapeutic" (p. 95). He argues that "the word *coach* must be taken seriously, and the relationship must be one of peers, although the client is necessarily dependent on the coach for advice, guidance, insights, and even formal information" (p. 95). Laske (chap. 21), in the chapter based on his 1999 article, observes that practice theories of coaching executives are still lacking "a life span developmental perspective that would aid in making the notion of meeting the client 'where the client is developmentally' more precise" (p. 217).

Finally, Wasylyshyn, writing in 2005 (chap. 36), points out "how coaching at the top can influence organizational development—even in a culture dominated by the needs and whims of a partially dsyfunctional CEO" (p. 387). Works such as these remind us that the profession of consulting psychology and the many practitioners from other disciplines still have much to do regarding definitions, standards, and processes. In addition, as has been noted by several of the authors included in Part I, those of us in the field have only begun our efforts to conduct research and establish empirical validation for an intervention process that remains largely practice based.

References

Diedrich, R. C., & Kilburg, R. R. (Eds.). (2001). Further consideration of executive coaching as an emerging competency [Special issue]. *Consulting Psychology Journal: Practice and Research, 53*(4).

Kilburg, R. R. (Ed.). (1996). Executive coaching [Special issue]. *Consulting Psychology Journal: Practice and Research, 48*(2).

Kilburg, R. R. (Ed.). (2004). Trudging toward Dodoville—Part 1: Conceptual approaches in executive coaching [Special issue]. *Consulting Psychology Journal: Practice and Research, 56*(4).

Kilburg, R. R. (Ed.). (2005). Trudging toward Dodoville—Part 2: Case studies in executive coaching [Special issue]. *Consulting Psychology Journal: Practice and Research, 57*(1).

CHAPTER 1

TOWARD A CONCEPTUAL UNDERSTANDING AND DEFINITION OF EXECUTIVE COACHING

Richard R. Kilburg

During the past decade, consultation activities that focus on managers and senior leaders in organizations have increasingly been referred to as *executive coaching*. This term has begun to take on a technical meaning within the field of organization development, yet the area of practice has suffered significantly from a relative lack of specific attention to it in the professional literature. The purposes of this chapter are to provide a succinct overview of some of the literature available on the topic, to summarize a way of conceptually understanding the practice of executive coaching, to introduce a preliminary definition of the term as a way of beginning to clarify this practice within the field of consultation, and to encourage additional empirical research on the subject.

LITERATURE REVIEW

Accessing the current psychological literature on the topic of coaching yields literally hundreds of articles. The majority of the material focuses on the topic of coaching activities and techniques as applied to various types and levels of athletic performance. Douge (1993) provided a review of the recent literature on coaching effectiveness in athletics, and Howe (1993) specifically focused on the application of psychological techniques in sports. Pratt and Eitzen's (1989) review of the leadership styles and effectiveness of high school athletic coaches and Lacy's (1994) empirical study of various coaching behaviors in collegiate women's basketball are examples of the diverse array of articles in this field.

A second and surprisingly large number of articles covers the application of coaching techniques to change the problem behaviors of various populations. R. L. Morgan (1994) applied peer coaching methods with low-performing, young, preservice teacher trainees and demonstrated improved instruction effectiveness. Murphy (1994) reported on a study in which socially rejected fifth graders were successfully coached on improving skills to increase their ability to be liked by peers. Goldberg (1994) applied coaching techniques to help improve schizophrênics' abilities to do card-sorting tests. Hekelman (1994) summarized an effort to use peer coaching to improve the performance of residents in family medicine. A final example of this type of literature was seen in Darling's (1994) article describing the use of coaching methods by human resources professionals to help employees with difficult, work-related problems. Scanning through these articles was reassuring in that they demonstrate that if these concepts and methods can be successful with socially rejected early adolescents, schizophrenics, high school and college athletes, and a variety of other troubled and normal people who aspire to improve their performance, they can be equally successful with managers and senior executives in for-profit and nonprofit enterprises.

The recent literature on coaching in the field of management and consultation can be clustered in three related areas: research studies; articles emphasizing methods, techniques, or applications in specific situations; and efforts to modify or expand the role repertoire of managers to include coaching activities. A thorough review of this material is well beyond the scope of this chapter, but a succinct summary will be provided to the reader as a gateway to the growing body of knowledge in this field.

Most of the formal research being published on coaching in management comes in the form of graduate dissertations on various aspects of the subject. One series of studies focused on managers or leaders as coaches (Coggins, 1991; Dougherty, 1993; Hein, 1990; Spinner, 1988; Stowell, 1987). Duffy (1984), Peterson (1993), and Thompson (1987) conducted research demonstrating management skill improvements as a function of specific coaching programs. D. J. Miller (1990) and Sawczuk (1991) reported on coaching studies that enhance transfer of management and skills training into the work environment.

A variety of nondissertation research studies of coaching in organizations have also been published. R. B. Morgan (1989) published a factor analytic study of leadership behavior incorporating a scale of coaching and mentoring others. Graham, Wedman, and Garvin-Kester (1993) reported on a program that successfully improved the performance of sales representatives whose bosses became better coaches. Acosta-Amad (1992) demonstrated improved note taking and chart completion by hospital staff members who had been coached effectively. Decker (1982) showed that supervisors who were trained in coaching and handling employee complaints improved employee retention in formal programs. And Scandura (1992) demonstrated from a survey of managers that career coaching was positively related to promotional rate.

Although none of these empirical studies reported on the effects of consultants working directly with managers, they are broadly suggestive that coaching of various types is successful in improving various aspects of the performance of individuals in administrative positions. The research available and reviewed also points to a significant, ongoing problem of a lack of empirical research on the actual work of senior practitioners in the field.

By far the largest body of literature available consists of articles devoted to exhorting managers to exert themselves to add coaching to their roles to empower subordinates, solve organizational problems, and push their enterprises toward peak performance. Brown (1990); Evered and Selman (1989); Good (1993); Keeys (1994); Kiechel (1991); W. C. Miller (1984); Orth, Wilkinson, and Benfari (1987); Smith (1993); Stowell (1988); Tyson (1983); Wolff (1993); and the Woodlands Group (1980) all provided ideas, advice, encouragement, and warnings that strongly suggest that the executive who does not know how to coach effectively will suffer from poor organizational performance and stunted career opportunities. Cunningham (1991) and Knippen and Green (1990) described the use of coaching methods in the accounting and utility industries. Himes (1984) provided a case study focusing on coaching a group toward being an effective team. Barratt (1985); Leibowitz, Kaye, and Farren (1986); and Shore and Bloom (1986) specifically defined the manager's role in career development with subordinates as involving coaching them toward increased effectiveness.

A related series of articles in a variety of journals and magazines all focus on the subject of coaching subordinates for high performance. Allenbaugh (1983), Aurelio and Kennedy (1991), Bell (1987), Bielous (1994), Chiaramonte and Higgins (1993), Cohen and Jaffee (1982), Herring (1989), Lucas (1994), Rancourt (1995), and Wallach (1983) all explicitly identified one of the key roles of leaders as being people who help their subordinates to modify their behavior to improve productivity, contribute more to the growth of a company, and become what by now is the well-known "peak performers" in their organizations. These articles offer a combination of how-to tips, conceptual approaches, mini–case studies, exhortations, and rationalizations for the emphasis on coaching. Tichy and Charan (1995) interviewed the CEO of a major corporation and provided a firsthand example of how ideas about coaching have increasingly become part of the foundation of the way senior leaders are now thinking about their roles.

A series of books on the subject of executive coaching has also appeared very recently. Deeprose (1995), Maxwell (1995), J. B. Miller and Brown (1993), Peterson and Hicks (1995), Shula and Blanchard (1995), and Whitmore (1994) have all provided in-depth coverage on the topic of managers in their roles as coaches. Keep in mind that all of this literature is based on a little over a dozen recent empirical studies that just explore the role of managers as coaches.

An even smaller number of articles has appeared that discuss executive coaching from the vantage point of a consultant working with client managers. Popper and Lipshitz (1992) described coaching as containing two components, improving performance at the skill level and establishing a relationship that enhances executives' psychological development. They also provided summaries of several different types of coaching techniques. Levinson (1991) explored some of the issues and nuances of coaching and counseling top leaders in corporations. Sperry (1993) explored the relationship among consulting, counseling, and coaching with executives, pointing out the increased stresses with which these individuals live and the need for practitioners to be in tune with the inner psychological worlds of their clients. Kelly (1985) and Lukaszewski (1988) both provided some concrete examples and specific problems that consultants may face in coaching assignments with managers. O'Connell (1990) emphasized the use of process consultation with senior managers on corporate strategy using Socratic techniques in four types of interventions, including coaching. And Ferguson (1986) covered 10 types of problems that occur in organizations that organization development techniques such as coaching help resolve.

This brief review of the literature on coaching demonstrates that there is an extensive history and broad empirical base available on the general topic, especially in athletics and dealing with the problems of special needs populations. The application of coaching as a concept and set of techniques to the art and practice of management has been growing rapidly through the 1980s and 1990s. However, the scientific basis for these applications is extremely limited at this time. This is even more true for the practice of coaching in the context of consultation. Only two of the research studies covered by this review can be said to be even tangentially related to what is now being extensively marketed and practiced in the field. This lack of an empirical foundation has not inhibited practitioners or authors from advocating their approaches or publishing their views. This review also raises the question as to whether executive coaching is simply the newest label practitioners are putting on a specific focus of consultation and set of techniques that they use in their work with executives.

A CONCEPTUAL APPROACH TO EXECUTIVE COACHING

Figure 1.1 presents a 17-factor model of systems and psychodynamics introduced by Kilburg (1995). In the model, 6 system factors (input, throughput, output, structure, process, and content), 4 psychological structures (conscience, idealized self, instinctual self, and rational self), 4 internal components of individual function (emotion, cognition, defense, and conflict), and 3 types of relationships (past, present, and focal) are presented and shown to interact with the various behavioral elements of an organization from individuals through groups, subsystems, and the entire organization.

Using this model, it becomes possible to navigate through the complex world that confronts individuals who do executive coaching. It demonstrates that a consultant working with an individual manager can focus on any of the 17 factors, their subcomponents, or their interactions and still rationally call what he or she is doing executive coaching. The financial expert helping a client bring a new company forward to a public stock offering, the systems engineer assisting a manager to choose or install a new software product, and the organizational psychologist working with an executive to redesign the competitive structure of an enterprise

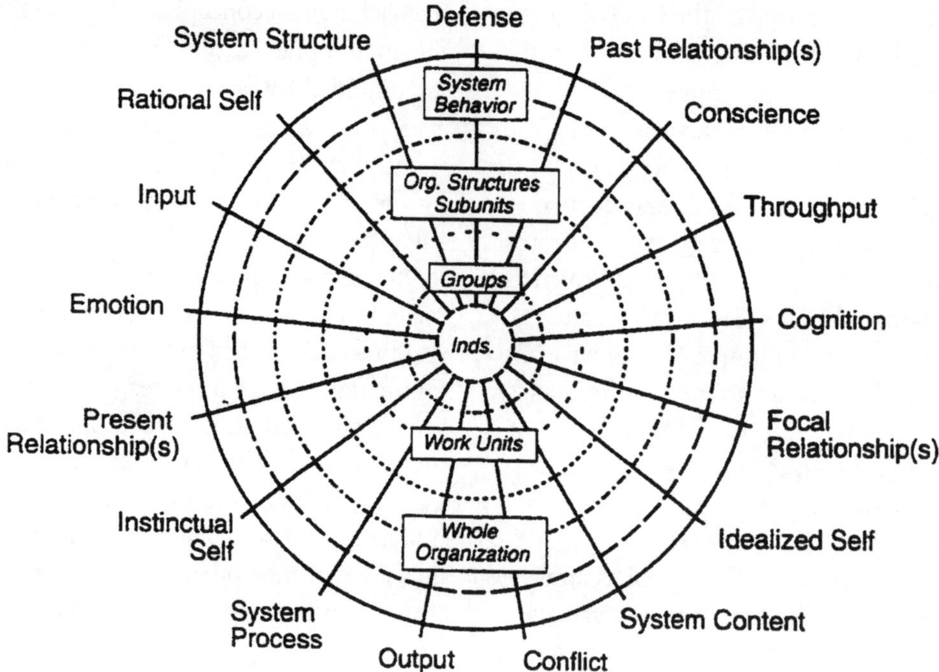

FIGURE 1.1. A 17-dimensional model of psychodynamics and organization systems. Org. = organizational; Inds. = individuals.

are all providing consultation, that is, helping services to a client manager. The focus of the effort may be radically different and the processes widely divergent, but the goals are usually to assist the person with authority and responsibility in a given organization to improve his or her performance and that of the enterprise. Within this very broad approach, it seems almost impossible to differentiate executive coaching from other forms of consultation, training, and organization development.

Figure 1.2 presents a modified version of the 17-factor model that helps to clarify this complexity and perhaps differentiate executive coaching from these other types of consultation strategies. In this figure, the 17 dimensions of the model are extended and organized into three loci: the individual executive (executive focus), the organizational systems (system focus), and the relationship and behavioral factors that mediate all interactions and activities between the manager and his or her organization (mediated focus). A consultant working with a client executive can provide assistance to an individual inside of or crossing over any of the loci. However, I would like to suggest that a more rigorous conceptual approach to executive coaching as a specific consultation service would choose the executive focus presented in the figure as the primary target of the consultation. These coaching activities would flow over into the other foci primarily as a way of helping the individual learn how to better function as a person and as a leader in a given organization.

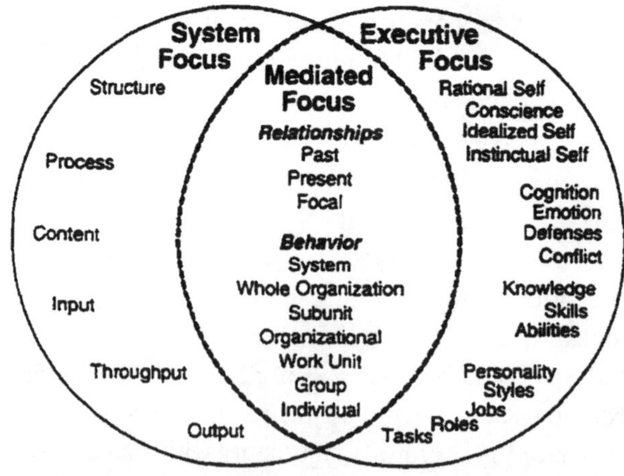

FIGURE 1.2. The foci for executive coaching.

TABLE 1.1

Components of Executive Coaching Interventions

1. Developing an intervention agreement.
   Establishing a focus and goals for the coaching effort.
   Making a commitment of time.
   Committing other resources.
   Identifying and agreeing on methods.
   Setting confidentiality constraints and agreement.
   Establishing amounts and methods of payment, if appropriate.
2. Building a coaching relationship.
   Establishing the working alliance.
   Identifying and managing transferences.
   Initiating and preserving containment.
3. Creating and managing expectations of coaching success.
4. Providing an experience of behavioral mastery or cognitive control over the problems and issues.
   Assessing, confronting, and solving problems and issues.
   Identifying and working with emotions.
   Identifying and managing resistance, defenses, and operating problems.
   Identifying and managing conflicts in the organization, in the working relationship, and in the unconscious life of the client.
   Using techniques and methods flexibly and effectively.
   Make the unsaid said and the unknown known; get the issues on the table.
   Use feedback, disclosure, and other communication techniques to maximum effect.
   Emphasize the reality principle—what will work most effectively with the best long-term outcomes.
   Be prepared to confront acting out, moral issues, or ethical lapses in a tactful way.
   Try to use and engage in yourself and your client the highest level defensive operations—sublimation, learning and problem solving, communication, curiosity, humor, creativity.
5. Evaluation and attribution of coaching success or failure—assess each of your coaching sessions together; periodically look back over what has been accomplished.

Note. From "Common Factors Aren't So Common: The Common Factors Dilemma," by J. Weinberger, 1995, *Clinical Psychology: Science and Practice*, 2(1), pp. 45–69. Adapted with permission. Copyright 1995 by Oxford University Press.

Table 1.1, adapted from Weinberger (1995), outlines five major components of executive coaching interventions. Weinberger has tried to identify the common factors in approaches to psychotherapy, and most of these, I believe, apply equally well to most relationships in which someone is playing a helping role with an individual identified as a client. These five components—establishing an intervention agreement, building a coaching relationship, creating and maintaining expectations of success, providing experiences of mastery and cognitive control, and evaluating and attributing coaching successes and failures—provide a road map of the process and content of executive coaching relationships. Exploring the details of these components in operation is also beyond the scope of this chapter, but it is in and through the implementation of these five processes that the true work of coaching takes place.

The first of these components can be further elaborated by an examination of Table 1.2, which presents a summary of many of the typical goals built into coaching contracts. These goal statements follow the emphasis of Figure 1.2 in that the first six are targeted on improving the functioning of the individual executive both as a person and as a manager. The goals use the 17 dimensions of the systems and psychodynamics model as a base from which to operate in a coaching relationship, simultaneously acknowledging and using the organizational environment in which the manager operates, selecting various aspects of the individual's behavior for tutorials, and always pushing the individual to improved levels of professional performance.

Table 1.3 presents an abbreviated listing of various coaching methods and techniques. The consultant will use these techniques during the implementation of each of the five components of a

TABLE 1.2

Typical Goals of Executive Coaching

1. Increase the range, flexibility, and effectiveness of the client's behavioral repertoire.
2. Increase the client's capacity to manage an organization—planning, organizing, staffing, leading, controlling, cognitive complexity, decision making, tasks, jobs, roles, etc.
3. Improve client's psychological and social competencies.
   Increase psychological and social awareness and understanding (see the 17 dimensions of Figure 1.1).
   Increase tolerance of ambiguity.
   Increase tolerance and range of emotional responses.
   Increase flexibility in and ability to develop and maintain effective interpersonal relationships within a diverse workforce.
   Increase the client's awareness and knowledge of motivation, learning, group dynamics, organizational behavior, and other components of the psychosocial and organizational domains of human behavior.
   Decrease acting out of emotions, unconscious conflicts, and other psychodynamic patterns.
   Improve the client's capacity to learn and grow.
   Improve the client's stress management skills and stress hardiness.
4. Increase the client's ability to manage self and others in conditions of environmental and organizational turbulence, crisis, and conflict.
5. Improve the client's ability to manage his or her career and to advance professionally.
6. Improve the client's ability to manage the tensions between organizational, family, community, industry, and personal needs and demands.
7. Improve the effectiveness of the organization or team.

coaching intervention. A consultant working in a coaching relationship has a wide array of methods available to assist the executive. Traditional "test-and-tell" approaches help the manager become familiar with various dimensions of his or her behavior and provide the coach and the client with a language and a set of concepts within which to conduct their sessions. Education, training, role modeling, simulations, and several other methods identified in Table 1.3 foster the growth of knowledge and stimulate the client to try new behaviors in the context of the coaching relationship. Traditional clinical methods of communication, clarification, confrontations, interpretations, and reconstructions can be extremely helpful when clients are struggling with significant emotional responses to their learning, jobs, relationships, or personal lives. Care and caution must be exercised when using these clinical techniques. The client must know and agree that such methods may be used and that such emotional issues may be addressed. The coach must also have the appropriate levels of training and experience to use the techniques wisely and professionally. Finally, methods such as crisis management, behavioral analysis, group process interventions, and relationship interventions with key subordinates or superiors may also be used to assist the manager in surmounting real problems encountered on the job. Choosing from this diverse array of techniques is one of the constant challenges of the coaching consultant.

In most coaching situations, at a minimum, the client gains some knowledge about himself or herself. Some experimentation with new behaviors may be attempted or resistance to change worked through. Still, in other cases, the client may improve working relationships, marital or family adaptation, or career satisfaction. In many situations, the coach provides significant assistance in helping the manager change his or her organization and improve its performance.

The final component of coaching interventions calls for the client and the coach to conduct an evaluation of the process and to assess the dimensions of success or failure. In my experience, the attributions of success by the client usually focus on the degree to which the coach provided a supportive relationship; stimulated the client to think, feel, and explore new ideas and behaviors; and assisted the individual in working through resistance to change. Recognition of the catalytic role of the coaching relationship is common. Most often, clients suggest that one of the most helpful components of coaching is that it forces the manager to

TABLE 1.3

An Abbreviated List of Coaching Methods and Techniques

1. Assessment and feedback (intelligence, leadership style, personality dimensions, interpersonal style and preferences, conflict management and crisis management approaches, knowledge, ability, skills)
2. Education
3. Training
4. Skill development: description, modeling, demonstration, rehearsal, practice, evaluation of life experience
5. Stimulations
6. Role playing
7. Organizational assessment and diagnosis
8. Brainstorming (strategies, methods, approaches, diagnostics, problem solving, intervention plans, evaluation approaches, hypothesis testing, worst case analysis)
9. Conflict and crisis management
10. Communications (active-empathic listening/silence, free association, open and closed questions, memory, translation, interpretation, analysis, synthesis, and evaluation questions)
11. Clarifications: restatements of client's communications; explanations of coaching communications
12. Confrontations (verbal interventions to direct the client's attention to issues, behaviors, problems, thoughts, or emotions that are evident to both the client and the coach)
13. Interpretations (verbal interventions to direct the client's attention in a meaningful way to issues, behaviors, problems, thoughts, or emotions that are evident to the coach but are out of the client's conscious awareness)
14. Reconstructions (attempts based on what is present in and missing from the client's communications, memories, etc., to fill in an apparently important gap in recollection of some life event along with its actual emotional and reality repercussions)
15. Empathy and encouragement
16. Tact
17. Helping to set limits
18. Helping to maintain boundaries
19. Depreciating and devaluing maladaptive behaviors, defenses, attitudes, values, emotions, fantasies
20. Punishment and extinction of maladaptive behaviors
21. Establishing consequences for behaviors
22. Behavioral analysis: gathering and assessing information
23. Group process interventions
24. Working relationship interventions (usually with key subordinates or superiors)
25. Project- and/or process-focused work on structure, process, and content issues in the organization or on input, throughput, or output problems or issues
26. Journaling, reading assignments, conferences, and workshops
27. Other interventions, using organization development or training technologies

take time to reflect on aspects of his or her performance and the performance of the organization. The value of pushing a busy manager to be more reflective on a regular basis should not be underestimated. Still, in some coaching relationships, the client, the coach, or both will judge that the interventions had little or no positive impact.

Table 1.4 presents a series of hypothesized factors in both the client and the coach that may contribute to negative coaching outcomes. These factors are adapted from Mohr (1995), who provided a succinct summary of the literature on negative outcomes in psychotherapy. I would like to suggest that executive coaching shares some but not all of the characteristics of psychotherapuetic interventions and, consequently, that some of the factors that have been demonstrated to contribute to negative outcomes in psychotherapy may cross over and generalize to coaching situations. As one can see, these factors range from severe psychopathology and resistance to change in the client to poor technique, lack of empathy, and lack of ability to clarify the coaching contract in the consultant; individuals who wish to do executive coaching would be wise to keep these suggested factors in mind as interventions are planned and, in particular, to consult the lists when and if coaching sessions do not appear to be accomplishing much for the individual or the organization.

TABLE 1.4

Hypothesized Factors Contributing to Negative Coaching Outcomes

In Clients

1. Severe psychopathology (psychotic symptoms, major character problelms, obsessive–compulsive disorder, etc., with client refusal to obtain treatment).
2. Severe interpersonal problems (client unwilling or unable to develop or maintain working relationships; significant or protracted negative transference).
3. Lack of motivation (client experiences little pressure to change from self or others).
4. Unrealistic expectations of the coach or coaching process (client expects coach or the process itself to substitute for or actually do the work of the executive; major or repeated violations of the coaching agreement).
5. Lack of follow-through on homework or intervention suggestions.

In Coaches

1. Insufficient empathy for the client (coach does not truly care about the client's well-being or future).
2. Lack of interest or expertise in the client's problems or issues.
3. Underestimating the severity of the client's problems or overestimating the coach's ability to influence the client.
4. Significant or protracted negative countertransference (coach overreacts to the client emotionally; has echoes of past significant, problematic relationships that cannot be managed appropriately).
5. Poor technique—inaccurate assessment, lack of clarity on coaching contract, poor choice or poor implementation of methods.
6. Major or prolonged disagreements with the client about the coaching process (coach believes that client's views of the agreement, problems, methods, implementation, or evaluation of the coaching efforts are flawed in major ways that become unmanageable).

Note. From "Negative Outcome in Psychotherapy: A Critical Review," by D. C. Mohr, 1995, *Clinical Psychology: Science and Practice,* 2(1), pp. 1–27. Adapted with permission. Copyright 1995 by Oxford University Press.

A WORKING DEFINITION OF EXECUTIVE COACHING

Having reviewed some basic concepts integral to the process of conducting coaching intervention with a client, I believe we can use this material to propose a working definition of executive coaching in the field of consultation. Such a definition may be helpful for practitioners and scholars alike as the field continues to evolve, clarify theory and technique, and encourage the conduct of research on these types of interventions. In the context of the concepts provided earlier, *executive coaching* is defined as a helping relationship formed between a client who has managerial authority and responsibility in an organization and a consultant who uses a wide variety of behavioral techniques and methods to help the client achieve a mutually identified set of goals to improve his or her professional performance and personal satisfaction and, consequently, to improve the effectiveness of the client's organization within a formally defined coaching agreement.

References

Acosta-Amad, S. (1992). Training for impact: Improving the quality of staff's performance. *Performance Improvement Quarterly,* 5(2), 2–12.

Allenbaugh, G. E. (1983). Coaching: A management tool for a more effective work performance. *Management Review, 72,* 21–26.

Aurelio, S., & Kennedy, J. K. Jr. (1991). Performance coaching: A key to effectiveness. *Supervisory Management, 36,* 1–2.

Barratt, A. (1985). Management development: The next decade. *Journal of Management Development,* 4(2), 3–9.

Bell, C. R. (1987). Coaching for high performance. *Advanced Management Journal, 52,* 26–29.

Bielous, G. A. (1994). Effective coaching: Improving marginal performers. *Supervision,* 55, 3–5.

Brown, T. L. (1990). Boss or coach? It's not what works for you—It's what works for your team. *Industry Week,* 239(8), 4.

Chiaramonte, P., & Higgins, A. (1993). Coaching for high performance. *Business Quarterly,* 58, 1–7.

Coggins, M. E (1991). Facilitating change through peer coaching (Doctoral dissertation, University of Georgia, 1991). *Dissertation Abstracts International,* 52(4-A), 1209.

Cohen, S. L., & Jaffee, C. L. (1982). Managing human performance for productivity. *Training and Development Journal,* 36(12), 94–100.

Cunningham, S. (1991). Coaching today's executive. *Public Utilities Fortnightly, 128,* 22–25.

Darling, M. J. (1994, November). Coaching people through difficult times. *HR Magazine, 39,* 70–73.

Decker, P. J. (1982). The enhancement of behavior modeling training of supervisory skills by the inclusion of retention processes. *Personnel Psychology, 35,* 323–332.

Deeprose, D. (1995). *The team coach.* New York: Amacom.

Douge, B. (1993). Coach effectiveness. *Sport Science Review,* 2(2), 14–29.

Dougherty, D. C. (1993). Peer coaching: Creating a collaborative environment for change (Doctoral dissertation, University of Oregon, 1993). *Dissertation Abstracts International,* 54(1-A), 71.

Duffy, E. M. (1984). A feedback–coaching intervention and selected predictors in outplacement (Doctoral dissertation, Hofstra University, 1984). *Dissertation Abstracts International,* 45(5-B), 1611–1612.

Evered, R. D., & Selman, J. C. (1989). Coaching and the art of management. *Organizational Dynamics, 18,* 16–32.

Ferguson, C. K. (1986). Ten case studies from an OD practitioner's experience: Coping with organizational conflict. *Organizational Development Journal,* 4(4), 20–30.

Goldberg, T. E. (1994). Schizophrenia, training paradigms, and the Wisconsin Card Sorting Test redux. *Schizophrenia Research, 11,* 291–296.

Good, D. J. (1993). Coaching practice in the business-to-business environment. *Journal of Business and Industrial Marketing,* 8(2), 53–60.

Graham, S., Wedman, J. E, & Garvin-Kester, B. (1993). Manager coaching skills: Development and application. *Performance Improvement Quarterly,* 6(1), 2–13.

Hein, H. R. (1990). Psychological type, coaching activities and coaching effectiveness in corporate middle managers (Doctoral dissertation, University of Bridgeport, 1990). *Dissertation Abstracts International,* 50(10-A), 3293.

Hekelman, E. R. (1994). Peer coaching in clinical teaching: Formative assessment of a case. *Evaluation and the Health Professions, 17,* 366–381.

Herring, K. (1989). Coaches for the bottom line. *Personnel Administrator, 34,* 22.

Himes, G. K. (1984). Coaching: Turning a group into a team. *Supervision, 46,* 14–16.

Howe, B. (1993). Psychological skills and coaching. *Sport Science Review,* 2(2), 30–47.

Keeys, G. (1994), Effective leaders need to be good coaches. *Personnel Management, 26,* 52–54.

Kelly, R. J. (1985). Coach the coach. *Training and Development Journal,* 39(11), 54–55.

Kiechel, W., III. (1991, November 4). The boss as coach. *Fortune, 201,* 201.

Kilburg, R. R. (1995). Integrating psychodynamic and systems theories in organization development practice. *Consulting Psychology Journal: Practice and Research, 47,* 28–55.

Knippen, J. T., & Green, T. B. (1990). Coaching. *Management Accounting, 71,* 36–38.

Lacy, A. C. (1994). Analysis of starter/nonstarter motor-skill engagement and coaching behaviors in collegiate women's volleyball. *Journal of Teaching in Physical Education,* 13(2), 95–107.

Leibowitz, A. B., Kaye, B., & Farren, C. (1986). Overcoming management resistance to career development programs [Special issue: Communications]. *Training and Development Journal,* 40(10), 77–81.

Levinson, H. (1991). Counseling with top management. *Consulting Psychology Bulletin, 43,* 10–15.

Lucas, R. W. (1994, January). Performance coaching now and for the future. *HR Focus, 71,* 13.

Lukaszewski, J. E. (1988). Behind the throne: How to coach and counsel executives. *Training and Development Journal,* 42(10), 32–35.

Maxwell, J. C. (1995). *Developing the leaders around you.* Nashville, TN: Nelson.

Miller, D. J. (1990). The effect of managerial coaching on transfer of training (Doctoral dissertation, United States International University, 1990). *Dissertation Abstracts International,* 50(8-A), 2435.

Miller, J. B., & Brown, R. B. (1993). *The corporate coach.* New York: Harper Business.

Miller, W. C. (1984). The value of nonsupervisory feedback in coaching sessions. *Supervisory Management, 29,* 2–8.

Mohr, D. C. (1995). Negative outcome in psychotherapy: A critical review. *Clinical Psychology: Science and Practice,* 2(1), 1–27.

Morgan, R. B. (1989). Reliability and validity of a factor analytically derived measure of leadership behavior and characteristics. *Educational and Psychological Measurement, 49,* 911–919.

Morgan, R. L. (1994). Effects of peer coaching on the acquisition of direct instruction skills by low-performing preservice teachers. *Journal of Special Education,* 28(I), 59–76.

Murphy, K. (1994). Coaching socially rejected early adolescents regarding behaviors used by peers to infer liking: A dyad specific intervention. *Journal of Early Adolescence, 14*(1), 83–95.

O'Connell, J. J. (1990). Process consultation in a content field: Socrates in strategy. *Consultation: An International Journal, 9,* 199–208.

Orth, C. D., Wilkinson, H. E., & Benfari, R. C. (1987). The manager's role as coach and mentor. *Organizational Dynamics,* 15(4), 66–74.

Peterson, D. B. (1993). Skill learning and behavior change in an individually tailored management coaching and training program (Doctoral dissertation, University of Minnesota, 1993). *Dissertation Abstracts International 54*(3-B), 1707–1708.

Peterson, D. B., & Hicks, M. D. (1995). *The leader as coach: Strategies for coaching and developing others.* Minneapolis, MN: Personnel Decisions.

Popper, M., & Lipshitz, R. (1992). Coaching on leadership. *Leadership and Organization Development Journal, 13(7),* 15–18.

Pratt, S. R., & Eitzen, D. S. (1989). Contrasting leadership styles and organizational effectiveness: The case of athletic teams. *Social Science Quarterly, 70,* 311–322.

Rancourt, K. L. (1995, April). Real-time coaching boosts performance. *Training and Development Journal, 49,* 53–56.

Sawczuk, M. P. (1991). Transfer-of-training: Reported perceptions of participants in a coaching study in six organizations (Doctoral dissertation, University of Minnesota, 1991). *Dissertation Abstracts International, 51*(12-A), 4195.

Scandura, T. A. (1992). Mentorship and career mobility: An empirical investigation. *Journal of Organizational Behavior,* 13, 169–174.

Shore, L. M., & Bloom, A. J. (1986, August). Developing employees through coaching and career management. *Personnel, 63,* 34–38.

Shula, D., & Blanchard, K. (1995). *Everyone's a coach.* New York: Harper Business.

Smith, L. (1993). The executive's new coach. *Fortune,* 203(12), 126–134.

Sperry, L. (1993) Working with executives: Consulting, counseling, and coaching. *Individual Psychology: Journal of Adlerian Theory, Research, and Practice, 49,* 257–266.

Spinner, E. M. (1988). The relationship between selected prescribed leadership behavior variables and self-reported measures of coaching leadership behavior (Doctoral dissertation, Temple University, 1988). *Dissertation Abstracts International, 48*(7-A), 1702.

Stowell, S. J. (1987). Leadership and the coaching process in organizations (Doctoral dissertation, University of Utah, 1987). *Dissertation Abstracts International, 48*(2-B), 589.

Stowell, S. J. (1988, June). Coaching: A commitment to leadership. *Training and Development Journal, 42,* 34–38.

Thompson, A. D. (1987). A formative evaluation of an individualized coaching program for business managers and professionals (Doctoral dissertation, University of Minnesota, 1987). *Dissertation Abstracts International*, 47(12-A, Pt. 1), 4339.

Tichy, N., & Charan, R. (1995, March–April). The CEO as coach: An interview with Allied Signal's Lawrence A. Bossidy. *Harvard Business Review,* 68–78.

Tyson, L. (1983, September). Coaching: A tool for success. *Training and Development Journal, 37,* 30.

Wallach, E. J. (1983, November). Performance coaching: Hitting the bull's-eye. *Supervisory Management, 28,* 19–22.

Weinberger, J. (1995). Common factors aren't so common: The common factors dilemma. *Clinical Psychology: Science and Practice,* 2(1), 45–69.

Whitmore, J. (1994). *Coaching for performance.* San Diego, CA: Pfeiffer.

Wolff, M. E (1993, January–February). Become a better coach. *Research Technology Management, 36,* 10–11.

Woodlands Group. (1980). Management development roles: Coach, sponsor, and mentor, *Personnel Journal, 59,* 918–921.

CHAPTER 2

EXECUTIVE COACHING: A WORKING DEFINITION

Lewis R. Stern

Executive coaching (EC) is an important method that can be applied as part of an organizational consulting intervention. It entails a coach working one-on-one with executives to help them learn how to manage and lead and to assist them to establish, structure, plan for, and lead the executives' organization. This article puts forth and exemplifies a working definition of EC: what it is, how it is similar and different from other forms of coaching, what principles should guide its practice, and what it takes for a coach to apply it successfully. In addition, this article explores the implications of this definition for the training, selection, practice, and continued development of professionals who apply EC in their consulting practices.

THE ORIGINS OF COACHING

The origins of the word *coaching* come from the Hungarian village of Kocs and the more comfortable, covered wheeled wagon or carriage (*koczi*) first developed there to carry its passengers through the harsh terrain, protected from the elements on their way from their point of departure to their ultimate destination (Hendrickson, 1987). Over the centuries, the term itself traveled along several roads of use, from academic coaching (to carry the student more safely through exams) to sports coaching (to carry the athlete through practice, the game, and the competitive season). EC is just one more evolution of the term where a coach helps to carry an executive from one point to another.

WHAT IS EXECUTIVE COACHING?

A Basic Definition

Executive coaching is an experiential, individualized, leadership development process that builds a leader's capability to achieve short- and long-term organizational goals. It is conducted through one-on-one interactions, driven by data from multiple perspectives, and based on mutual trust and respect. The organization, an executive, and the executive coach work in partnership to achieve maximum learning and impact (Ennis et al., 2003, p. 20).

Such coaching can be provided by the executive's boss, a peer, a human resources (HR) professional within the executive's organization, or an external consultant. In its most formal practice, a professional executive coach formally contracts with an executive and his or her organization to work in a collaborative partnership with the executive and others in the organization to achieve identified business results and the executive's learning objectives. Such a formal contract needs to incorporate agreed-upon ground rules, time frames, goals, and specific measures of success (Ennis et al., 2003). Regardless of the formality of the EC and who is providing it, what actually goes on in the

Reprinted from the *Consulting Psychology Journal: Practice and Research, 56,* 154–162.

coaching is driven by its objectives and the needs and preferences of the executive and the organization. It may entail any or all of the following: changing attitudes and habits; developing skills; preparing and developing for future assignments; and defining and implementing one's leadership charter, business goals, and strategies.

Structured Executive Coaching Provided by a Professional Coach

Sometimes EC is spontaneous and informally incorporated into day-to-day interactions between business associates. When provided by the professional consultant, EC is more commonly preplanned and follows a structured seven-step process: (a) initial needs analysis, (b) contracting, (c) data gathering, (d) specific goal setting, (e) coaching, (f) measuring and reporting results, and (g) transitioning to a more long-term development effort for the executive and the organization.

The Essential Systems Perspective

The professional coach needs to understand and work within the organizational system (Ennis et al., 2003; Orenstein, 2002) rather than see the executive as he or she would be seen in a traditional counseling or personal coaching relationship (with less emphasis on the organizational system within which the client works). To do so, the consultant needs to involve the executive's key stakeholders in the coaching to truly grasp and help the executive comprehend how his or her actions are affected by and impact the whole organizational system. These key stakeholders include the following: the executive's manager; the HR department; executive development professionals within the organization; and the executive's peers, employees, and others.

THE EFFECTIVE EXECUTIVE COACH

The executive coach must be versed in the business and the skills the leader needs in order to succeed. The coach must be perceived by the leader as competent, confident, independent, business savvy, patient yet action oriented, credible, trustworthy, confidential, and genuinely interested in the leader and the leader's business. The executive coach works primarily one-on-one with the leader to carry him or her through the needed changes to implement organizational strategy or transform the people or the business to a place more capable of achieving career and business objectives.

Minimum Prerequisites for Professional Executive Coaches

The needed background and competencies of the professional executive coach are determined by the goals, activities, and circumstances surrounding the specific coaching intervention, the executive, and the organization. Based on my own experience coaching executives and training, coaching, and supervising internal and external coaches over the past 25 years, as well as the experience of other experts in the field, all consultants conducting EC, regardless of their professional affiliation or background, need some basic knowledge and expertise (Hunt, 2003; Modoono, 2002; see also chaps. 9, 20, and 31, this volume):

Essential knowledge and expertise in psychology.

- individual assessment
- individual differences
- adult learning
- organizational behavior
- change management
- organizational systems theory
- leadership
- interpersonal and group dynamics
- motivation
- organization development

Essential knowledge and expertise in business.

- familiarity with the language, history, and current conditions of the executive's industry and business environment
- strategic and tactical planning and implementation
- organizational communication (employee orientation, information sharing, setting of standards, roles and responsibilities, feedback, plans, changes, customer contact, and so forth)
- business ethics
- technology

- business functions: finance, HR, marketing, research and development, manufacturing–service development, sales, and legal

Other targeted knowledge and expertise important for the coach. There are many other areas of expertise that coaches may need, depending on the specific individual coaching intervention:

- conflict mediation
- development of values, vision, and mission
- quality and process management
- team development/building
- board relations
- labor relations
- video feedback
- career development
- organization restructuring
- work–life balance
- stress management

The Characteristics and Style of the Professional Executive Coach

The diversity of executives in search of coaches (Stern, 1998) is matched by the uniqueness of each executive coach. But there are some common characteristics and stylistic inclinations of executive coaches that appear to make it easier for them to succeed and be satisfied in the coaching role. Because most executives want practical, results-oriented, efficient, and customized coaching to address their particular needs, they are less comfortable with a coach who is primarily theoretical, abstract, and lecturing rather than the more practical, concrete, and experientially oriented coach. Because most EC is time bound, with somewhere between 5 and 15 sessions in the intervention, the consultant who is right for coaching is more interested, proficient, and oriented to getting down to the real work issues in the context of the organizational system of the business. The coach needs to care about the business of the executive's organization as much as the executive himself or herself. Because most executives are smart, process information quickly, and are impatient with slow analysis that does not get to the bottom line in short order, a smart, fast-paced, practical consultant who likes to work one-on-one with leaders is best suited for the job. For executives who are slower, more careful and contemplative thinkers, another coaching style may be more relevant. Most coaching requires the coach to fluidly go from strategic issues to the micro level of tactics and interpersonal and group communication. If an executive is to be helped, he or she needs a coach who can provide live feedback, serve as a role model, and provide specific guidance on how the executive should behave and communicate to convey the right message and accomplish the goals with the highest priority. A consultant is best suited for the job when he or she is comfortable and passionate about both the strategic and the micro. Effective executive coaches have the patience to step back from day-to-day business and also dive into the moment-by-moment of what the executive could do differently for greater success. EC is not talk therapy. It is individualized leadership development, behavior modification, business planning, and organizational re-engineering. Above all, the executive coach needs to be well matched to the executive he or she coaches.

SUCCESS THROUGH PARTNERING

In most situations, EC works best when the coach does not work alone as a supplier but in partnership with the executive, his or her boss, HR professionals within the organization, and other key individuals. All of these partners, including the coach, must follow some basic guiding principles for the coaching to achieve maximum success (Ennis et al., 2003):

- a systems perspective
- a results orientation
- a business focus
- collaborative partnering for the mutual benefit of the executive and the organization
- a focus on building the competence of both the executive and the organization
- a continual emphasis on the integrity of each member of the partnership and of the coaching process

- judgment, using common sense, informed intelligence, and professional ethics to guide decisions when traditional procedures or standards do not provide the answers to unpredictable situations

DIFFERENTIATING EXECUTIVE COACHING FROM OTHER FORMS OF COACHING

In the last 20 or so years, at the same time EC evolved as a recognized practice or methodology, many other forms of coaching have also morphed into our organizational and personal lives. Personal coaching, career coaching, spiritual coaching, new leader coaching, team coaching, financial coaching, and many others have all become popular. What differentiates EC most from these other forms of coaching is its dual focus on working one-on-one to develop the executive as a leader while also helping that leader to achieve business results.

EC often incorporates some of these other forms of coaching. But it is important to differentiate the coaching methods that are often practiced separately from EC by specialists with expertise limited to one or two forms of coaching. A personal or life coach requires a very different set of knowledge and expertise than a career coach or an executive coach. The following list differentiates some of the other popular forms of coaching from EC:

Personal or life coaching primarily focuses on an individual's personal goals, thinking, feeling, and actions and how the individual can change his or her life for greater personal effectiveness and satisfaction.

Career coaching primarily focuses on the individual's short- and long-range career objectives. It helps the client to decide on career directions and then plan, seek, or change them over the short or long term.

Performance coaching focuses on an employee's specific performance potential, job requirements, deficiencies, or derailers and on how to fill performance gaps and shape the job to optimize the individual's performance.

Newly assigned leader coaching focuses on helping the leader to assimilate into a new role and successfully define and implement his or her new business charter along with key constituents and his or her team.

Relationship coaching focuses on specific relationships between individuals and helping form or change those relationships for greater productivity and satisfaction.

High potential or developmental coaching helps employees with potential for greater responsibility to develop the skills and prepare for moving into new roles.

Coaching to provide feedback debriefing and development planning helps individuals understand and use their assessment results and 360-degree feedback in the context of their personal and professional history and their career and business objectives.

Targeted behavioral coaching aims to modify specific behavior or habits (e.g., intimidation, risk aversion, nonassertiveness) or develop new behaviors to allow an individual to be more effective in his or her current or future roles.

Legacy coaching helps the retiring or winding-down leader to identify the legacy he or she would like to leave behind and to take the appropriate actions to make that legacy become a reality.

Video coaching is defined by its method of using immediate video recording and playback to allow people to become more aware of how they come across to others and to shape their verbal and nonverbal communication to convey the intended messages and achieve the desired influence.

Team coaching, different from most of the other coaching methods, provides one or more coaches who specialize in team dynamics and effectiveness to work together with the leader and each member of a team. The team coach "has an ongoing, helping relationship with both the team and the individual executives" (chap. 32, this volume, p. 329).

EXAMPLES OF CONSULTING SITUATIONS IN WHICH EXECUTIVE COACHING CAN BE ESPECIALLY EFFECTIVE

Organizational consulting takes many forms. Some are more appropriate and have greater potential than others for the consultant to incorporate EC. The following are examples of applications in which EC can be especially helpful as part of larger consulting efforts.

Executive Assessment, Development, and Succession Planning Programs

EC can be an especially effective method to develop high-potential leaders, get key players who have derailed back on track, and assimilate and accelerate the learning of leaders who are newly assigned to critical roles. It can also be effective in the development and improvement of individual skills and practices of executives at the senior level. In all of these situations, one-on-one coaching can show good results that may not be addressed as well by more traditional, group, or less intensive methods of development.

Performance Management

Executives can be coached on how to convey specific performance expectations and how to give more direct feedback. But many senior executives find it difficult to take the extra step to shape their employees' performance. The executive coach, similar to a sports coach, helps "players" to see what they are currently doing, demonstrate what they should be doing differently, and work painstakingly, through trial and error, to experiment, practice, and repractice the desired techniques until the players consistently get the desired results. By providing such coaching to an executive, the coach also serves as a role model for the executive to coach his or her employees to shape their behavior as well.

Consulting to Help Build Organizational Values, Vision, Mission, and Strategy

Many executives lack an understanding or appreciation of the importance of shared values as potential drivers of interpersonal trust, team cohesiveness, culture, and employee commitment. Others are stuck in neutral, lacking personal drive as a result of not being sure why they are working and what they care about most in leading their organization. In conjunction with consulting to help design and facilitate the strategic planning process, a coaching relationship can be especially effective in getting executives and would-be executives to think, plan, and act differently as strategic leaders.

Building and Improving the Effectiveness and Collaboration of Executive Teams

When an organizational consultant attends executive team meetings as part of the consultation process, he or she can apply EC techniques with the leader and members of the team to help them change negative behaviors (e.g., interrupting each other, making passive–aggressive comments that interfere with positive team interaction, not following established meeting agenda, or applying leadership practices that foster negative groupthink). Where some of these behaviors can be addressed publicly in the team meeting, others need repeated, private, direct feedback and practicing of alternative behaviors outside of the team before and after they are applied in team meetings.

Conflict Resolution and Mediation

Many conflicts are responsive to consultant intervention and mediation, but the conflict-related behaviors keep repeating themselves in new situations. Some executives have a tendency to provoke useless conflict or keep conflict going when other more constructive responses would be more helpful. The executive coach can use behavioral rehearsal and video feedback, replaying conflict situations with new responses, to help shape more constructive conflict management techniques.

Change Leadership and Change Management

When senior managers are barriers to organizational change, EC can help to change the managers' behaviors that create the barriers. Often the coach helps to build the senior manager's personal comfort with ambiguity, change the executive's demure announcements so they begin to show passion and conviction for needed change, and develop the manager's positive verbal and nonverbal responses when others suggest changes.

HOW TO PREPARE FOR A PRACTICE AS A PROFESSIONAL EXECUTIVE COACH

Professional executive coaches are not born. As described above, it is a specialty of organizational consultation that requires a complicated combination of knowledge, skills, and stylistic inclinations. Significant research is still needed to examine the relative truth and importance of the principles and guidelines suggested in this article (Ennis et al., 2003; see also chap. 3, this volume). If one is to accept the definitions and prescriptions as outlined in these pages, several implications need to be considered by anyone interested in preparing himself or herself for or beginning to practice EC.

What Prospective Executive Coaches Need to Do

1. Evaluate themselves honestly to decide if they have the real interest, passion, style, and propensity to work intensely, one-on-one, with executives to help them get better as leaders and achieve their business objectives.
2. Build a base of thorough knowledge in psychology, business management, organizational dynamics, and leadership development that goes beyond reading a few popular books. If they already are knowledgeable in some of these areas, they need to fill the gaps in the others through reading, course work, and mentoring from experts and through other forms of study.
3. Gain significant experience to build a strong repertoire of skills in basic business management, leadership, organizational consulting, and one-on-one coaching skills.
4. Decide what kinds of EC they want to provide: Whom do they want to coach; in what kinds of functions and organizations; in what geographic areas; toward what ends for their clients; toward what ends for themselves; applying what kinds of EC methods; and as part of a consulting organization, a network of independent consultants, or as an individual practitioner?
5. Develop a plan to gain more tailored knowledge and skills to meet the needs of the practice they have defined for themselves (industry specialization, expertise around specific targeted functions—research and development, sales, HR, marketing, etc.—specific coaching methodologies, etc.).
6. Build an infrastructure to support the EC practice they have targeted: marketing, support materials, contractual templates, a referral network for consulting needs beyond their own expertise or for collaborative consulting projects, business office technology and support, and so forth.
7. Develop a plan for their continued professional education.
8. Market themselves and develop referral sources in their target geographic, industry, and functional arenas.
9. Develop resources and outlets to manage the stresses, conflicts, and changes associated with the practice of EC. Based on the working definition set forth in this article, significant changes may be needed in the training and selection of executive coaches. Training and certification programs for coaches need to greatly increase the scope of their curriculum and the selection prerequisites for acceptance of their participants. Expecting coaches with little prior applicable knowledge or experience to be able to meet the complex demands of an executive and his or her organization is like expecting a person off the street to do eye surgery with a few days of discussion about vision and a few hours of lab work.

What Executives and Their Organizations Need to Look for in Selecting an Executive Coach

No two EC situations are alike, so each organization and executive needs to evaluate prospective executive coaches on the basis of some basic information and some specific criteria unique to their particular needs and circumstances. The following set of questions can help executives and their organizations select the right executive coach to help meet their needs:

1. Does the executive coach have the required basic knowledge and skills?

2. Does the coach have the special knowledge, skills, style, theoretical approach, and experience applicable to the goals of the specific coaching situation?
3. Is the coach familiar with the industry, business functions, market, or other environmental factors that are important to the executive to be coached?
4. Is the coach committed to follow the EC principles as described above?
5. Is there satisfactory chemistry between the executive and the coach based on how the executive perceives and responds to the coach's approach, personality, style, and professional demeanor?
6. Does the coach participate in ongoing continued education and professional development to apply EC as part of his or her consulting practice?
7. Will the contractual arrangements for the coaching fit within the preferences and limits of the executive and his or her organization (fees, time availability, flexibility of schedule, consulting policies and procedures, and so forth)?

Although it is essential to get the right coach for the EC situation, there are many other factors beside the coach that will affect the success of the coaching: the readiness of the executive, the support from the boss and the organization, the HR infrastructure, and so forth. Only through a partnership between the right coach, collaborating with the executive and his or her organization, will coaching succeed in achieving the executive's and the organization's objectives.

CONCLUSION

There is no one best way to practice EC. Only when more extensive research is conducted and validated will we have adequate data to substantiate which are the most important variables that differentiate successful training, selection, and practice of EC from less effective approaches. We have no single accepted definition of EC. Certainly, it only takes going to one conference on the topic to see that the term is used by different practitioners and clients to mean everything from life coaching, to process consultation, to psychotherapy, career coaching, and leadership development. The definition proposed and exemplified in this article is an attempt to bring us one step closer to a shared definition of EC, continuing the exploration of its value and beginning to answer questions about what makes it work better in some situations than in others.

The current state of the art of EC is in a similar situation to that of the tumultuous Medieval times in Hungary when the unknown carriage maker saw the opportunity to design the first coach. That craftsman imagined a way to carry the weary traveler along the harsh terrain to go faster, feeling fewer bumps and being protected from the dangers of accelerated travel through bad weather and around dangerous turns. Today, it is the organizational consultant who can provide the coaching to help carry the weary executive through the constantly changing and harsh environment faced by business leaders of the 21st century. Each executive coach may drive a somewhat different vehicle. We may go faster or slower, use one horsepower or another. But the essential elements of effective EC are simple: Know where the executives are starting and where they and their organizations want to end up. Then, help carry them through to their destinations so they encounter fewer bumps along the way, arrive ready to carry on, and are better prepared for their next journey!

References

Ennis, S., Stern, L. R., Yahanda, N., Vitti, M., Otto, J., Hodgetts, W., et al. (2003). *The executive coaching handbook*. Wellesley, MA: The Executive Coaching Forum (http://www.executivecoachingforum.com).

Hendrickson, R. (1987). *The Henry Holt encyclopedia of word and phrase origins*. New York: Henry Holt.

Hunt, J. M. (2003, April). *Successful executive coaching experiences: Report on a case study research program*. Paper presented at the annual meeting of the Society for Industrial and Organizational Psychology, Orlando, FL.

Modoono, S. A. (2002). The executive coach self-assessment inventory. *Consulting Psychology Journal: Practice and Research*, *54*, 43.

Orenstein, R. L. (2002). Executive coaching, it's not just about the executive. *The Journal of Applied Behavioral Science*, *38*, 355–374.

Stern, L. R. (1998). Five types of executives in search of coaching. *The Manchester Review*, 3(2), 13–19.

CHAPTER 3

EXECUTIVE COACHING: A COMPREHENSIVE REVIEW OF THE LITERATURE

Sheila Kampa-Kokesch and Mary Z. Anderson

Executive coaching as a distinct intervention has received increased attention in the literature within the past few years (see chap. 30, this volume). *Consulting Psychology Journal: Practice and Research* (Kilburg, 1996) devoted an entire issue to the topic of executive coaching. All but one article in this special issue were practice-based articles (chaps. 9–15 and 23, this volume), with the last article being a conceptual piece providing a framework and definition of executive coaching (chap. 1, this volume).

Additional writings on executive coaching cluster in three bodies of literature: the psychological (e.g., chaps. 14, 21, 25, 30, 31, and 38, this volume; Harris, 1999; Sperry, 1993; Waclawski & Church, 1999), training and development (e.g., Filipczak, 1998; Hutcheson, 1996; Kiser, 1999; Koonce, 1994; Larry, 1997a, 1997b; Ludeman, 1995; Lukaszewski, 1988; O'Brien, 1997; Olesen, 1996; Thach & Heinselman, 1999; Witherspoon & White, 1996, 1997); and management (e.g., Banning, 1997; Bertagnoli, 2000; Brotherton, 1998, Darling, 1994; Dutton, 1997; Grover, 2000; Hardingham, 1998; Huggler, 1997; Hyatt, 1997; Judge & Cowell, 1997; Machan, 1998; Masciarelli, 1999; McCafferty, 1996; Morris, 2000; Nakache, 1997; Olivero, Bane, & Kopelman, 1997; Peterson & Hicks, 1999; Smith, 1993; Snyder, 1995; Tristram, 1996). Additional articles on executives or managers as coaches can also be found (e.g., Allenbaugh, 1983; Aurelio & Kennedy, 1991; Bell, 1987; Deblieux, 1998; Good, 1993; Graham, Wedman, & Garver-Kester, 1993; Orth, Wilkinson, & Benfari, 1987; Shore & Bloom, 1986; Waldroop & Butler, 1996).

Three book chapters (Hayes, 1997; Strickland, 1997; Sperry, 1996) and four books have also been devoted to the topic of executive coaching (Douglas & Morley, 2000; Kilburg, 2000; O'Neill, 2000; Witherspoon & White, 1997). Other books that address coaching executives or managers (e.g., Deeprose, 1995; Ericsson, 1996; Gilley & Boughton, 1996; Hargrove, 1995; Martin, 1996; Maxwell, 1995; Miller & Brown, 1993; Minor, 1995; Robinson, 1996; Shula & Blanchard, 1995; Voss, 1997; Whitmore, 1994) from a general business coaching paradigm rather than a consultative one (Kilburg, 2000) can also be found.

Although there has been increased attention in the literature, there is surprisingly little empirical research on the efficacy of executive coaching. Only seven empirical studies have been reported: one investigating the outcomes of executive coaching in a public sector agency (Olivero et al., 1997); the second surveying current executive coaching practices (Judge & Cowell, 1997); the third investigating the effectiveness of executive coaching through quantitative and qualitative methods (Gegner, 1997); the fourth interviewing both executives and coaches regarding executive coaching practice, effectiveness,

Reprinted from the *Consulting Psychology Journal: Practice and Research, 53,* 205–228. Copyright 2001 by the American Psychological Association and the Society of Consulting Psychology.

and future directions (Hall, Otazo, & Hollenbeck, 1999); the fifth investigating the effects of eye movement desensitization reprocessing (EMDR) as a technique used in executive coaching; the sixth exploring the transformative effects of executive coaching on an executive's professional agenda (Laske, 1999); and the seventh examining public perceptions of executive coaching (chap. 30, this volume).

The recent increase of attention in the literature on executive coaching may be explained in part by the increased demand for executive coaching in the field (Filipczak, 1998; Koonce, 1994; Waclawski & Church, 1999). With this increased demand, however, has come increased concern regarding the definition and standardization of executive coaching as well as who is most qualified to deliver such services (chaps. 1, 4, 13, 15, and 31, this volume; Filipczak, 1998; Harris, 1999; Kilburg, 1997). Some remark about the current suspicion as to whether executive coaching is a viable intervention (see Filipczak, 1998) or simply a passing fad (see chaps. 1 and 13, this volume). There is also some concern and debate as to whether executive coaching practices resemble too closely the practices of psychotherapy (chap. 13, this volume; Filipczak, 1998).

As a way of addressing the above-mentioned concerns and organizing what has been written about executive coaching, this chapter provides a comprehensive and critical review of the existing executive coaching literature. Although Kilburg (chap. 1, this volume; 2000) has provided two reviews of the literature relevant to executive coaching, his reviews provide a brief review and summary of the development of business coaching as it leads up to executive coaching. Douglas and Morley (2000) provided an annotated bibliography of the executive coaching literature and a brief interpretation of the key issues coming from the literature. Although a comprehensive resource, the present review serves as a critique, has a different focus, and adds additional elements to the literature.

The main purpose of this chapter is to critically examine the existing literature in psychology, training and development, and management in order to determine the viability of executive coaching as a distinct intervention. References were gathered using three databases: PsycLit, ERIC, and Wilson Business Abstracts. We also consulted the references of reviewed articles and books. References were excluded if they addressed more general business coaching versus executive coaching specifically (the focus of this work). This chapter is organized into four parts. The first provides a brief summary about the known history of executive coaching. The second summarizes the main themes discussed in the practice-based literature and provides a brief overview of three recent books on executive coaching and one general coaching book that has influenced the field of executive coaching. The third part reviews the existing empirical research. The final part addresses the questions of whether executive coaching increases individual and organizational performance and whether it is a fad. This final section also further discusses the implications executive coaching has for consultation practice.

HISTORY

The history of executive coaching is difficult to track because it has only recently received attention in the literature. In reviewing the literature, it is unclear when exactly executive coaching first began. Only brief statements or speculations regarding the possible origins of executive coaching have been provided (see Harris, 1999; Judge & Cowell, 1997; chaps. 1, 4, and 13, this volume).

Tobias (see chap. 13, this volume) stated that the term *executive coaching* came into the business world in the late 1980s and was used because *coaching* sounded less threatening than other types of interventions. He argued that coaching by psychologists is a mere repackaging of practices once done under the umbrella of consultation and counseling. The "developmental counseling" conducted by RHR International since the 1940s would seem to support this observation (Flory, 1965). Kilburg (see chaps. 1 and 4, this volume; 2000) contended that for the past decade, consultation geared toward managers and senior leaders in business organizations has increasingly been referred to as executive coaching. He stated that consultants began practicing executive coaching when they gained access to the leaders of organizations. This gaining access to leaders of organizations by psychologists has been perceived by some as an attempt by psychologists to replenish their income after the damaging effects of managed care by bringing "therapy" into the workplace (see chap. 13, this volume; Filipczak, 1998).

Judge and Cowell (1997) stated that the widespread adoption of executive coaching by consulting firms began around 1990, though they acknowledged that there was a sprinkling of offerings prior to 1990. As an intervention, they believe executive coaching is currently moving from the introductory to the growth phase. One industrial–organizational psychologist practicing in the field of executive coaching and interviewed by Harris (1999) briefly mentioned three phases in the history of executive coaching. According to this psychologist, the first phase occurred between the years of 1950 and 1979, when a few professionals used a blend of organizational development and psychological techniques in working with executives. During the middle period (1980–1994), an increase in professionalism occurred as well as the beginning of standardized services (though a full standardization has not yet occurred). In the current period (1995–present), there has been an increase in publications and the establishment of a professional organization for coaching: the Professional and Personal Coaches Association, more recently known as the International Coach Federation (ICF). It is also in the current period that the demand for executive coaching has reached an all-time high.

Even though executive coaching has been dated by some as far back as the 1940s, many agree that it has only more recently come to fruition (chaps. 1 and 4, this volume; Olesen, 1996). Even though earlier periods existed, little is known about what was then practiced. It has only been during the most recent period that the practice of executive coaching has begun to be addressed in the literature. Within the most recent period, there has also been a push for a more complete standardization of services and research on the effectiveness of executive coaching.

LITERATURE REVIEW

Practice Literature

In reviewing the executive coaching practice-based literature, six themes emerged: (a) definition and standards, (b) purpose, (c) techniques and methodologies used, (d) comparison with counseling and therapy, (e) credentials of coaches and the best way of finding them, and (f) recipients of services. This section summarizes these themes and provides an overview of three recent practice-based books on executive coaching and one general coaching book. Within each theme, the psychological, training and development, and business and management literatures have been integrated. A single body of the literature is mentioned separately only if it makes a unique contribution within a particular theme.

Definition and standards. A number of authors have stated that executive coaching as a distinct intervention remains poorly defined and regulated (chaps. 1, 4, 13, and 31, this volume; Kilburg, 2000), with little training and research being conducted (chap. 4, this volume; Kilburg, 2000; Sperry, 1996). On the basis of his reviews of the existing literature, Kilburg (chap. 1, this volume; 2000) proposed the following definition of executive coaching:

> a helping relationship formed between a client who has managerial authority and responsibility in an organization and a consultant who uses a wide variety of behavioral techniques and methods to help the client achieve a mutually identified set of goals to improve his or her professional performance and personal satisfaction and, consequently, to improve the effectiveness of the client's organization within a formally defined coaching agreement. (Kilburg, 2000, p. 67)

On the basis of our current review of the literature, this definition appears to represent a fairly comprehensive view of what has been discussed and how executive coaching has been defined (see chaps. 9–13, 15, and 25, this volume; Judge &

Cowell, 1997; Olesen, 1996; Sperry, 1993, 1996; Witherspoon & White, 1996, 1997). Additional components mentioned by various authors include executive coaching as a highly confidential personal learning process that focuses not only on interpersonal issues, but also on intrapersonal ones (chap. 10, this volume; O'Brien, 1997). It has been defined as an ongoing relationship, usually lasting anywhere from a few months to a year or more (chaps. 9 and 14, this volume), in which the coach does not have any direct authority over the executive (chap. 10, this volume). As an intervention, it can be used for both developmental and remedial purposes, and it seems to occur in six stages: relationship building, assessment, feedback, planning, implementation, and evaluation and follow-up (chaps. 1, 4, 9–15, and 25, this volume; Harris, 1999; Judge & Cowell, 1997; Koonce, 1994; Lukaszewski, 1988; O'Brien, 1997; Olesen, 1996; Sperry, 1993, 1996; Witherspoon & White, 1996, 1997). These stages are consistent with other consultation models (see Caplan, 1970).

Guidelines for successful coaching have been proposed by various individuals (e.g., chap. 11, this volume), but to date, no standards or guidelines have been widely adopted. The ICF recently held a summit to better define executive coaching and develop more complete standards and practice guidelines. Although these results have not been formally published, they can be found on the federation's Web site (www.coachfederation.org/execcoachingsummit.htm). The ICF's definition of *executive coaching* is as follows:

> Executive coaching is a facilitative one-to-one, mutually designed relationship between a professional coach and a key contributor who has a powerful position in the organization. This relationship occurs in areas of business, government, not-for-profit, and educational organizations where there are multiple stakeholders and organizational sponsorship for the coach or coaching group. The coaching is contracted for the benefit of a client who is accountable for highly complex decisions with [a] wide scope of impact on the organization and industry as a whole. The focus of the coaching is usually focused on organizational performance or development, but may also have a personal component as well. The results produced from this relationship are observable and measurable. (International Coaching Federation Conference, 2000)

Regarding guidelines, the ICF is developing them; however, Brotman et al. (see chap. 31, this volume) made the argument that the American Psychological Association (APA) should set standards because psychologists possess many of the skills necessary to provide executive coaching services. What psychologists do not necessarily possess, however, is business knowledge (see chap. 15, this volume; Harris, 1999).

Purpose. There are a number of reasons provided in the practice literature for the increased use of executive coaching, including the fact that other high-performance individuals —athletes, performers, and public speakers—have used coaching as a means of improving their performance (chap. 10, this volume; Witherspoon & White, 1997). Other reasons for the increased use of coaching include the rapidly changing global economy necessitating continued development (Sperry, 1993), the lack of opportunities provided executives for growth (chaps. 11 and 15, this volume), the realization by business that poor executive leadership can lead to financial ruin (chap. 1, this volume), and the recognition that interpersonal skills are key in effectively managing oneself and those in a company (chap. 9, this volume).

In an article on leadership, Hogan, Curphy, and Hogan (1994) stated that up to 50% of executives will fail to advance in their careers. This is a high percentage according to Kilburg (1997), who suggests that organizations today do not have the tools to help their executives succeed. It should be noted, however, that not all executives can advance because the higher one is in an organization, the fewer positions there are to which one can advance. Regardless, the so-called failure rate is noteworthy and may be at least one more reason why organizations and executives are turning to outside sources for executive coaching.

By turning outward to an executive coach, executives may receive something valuable that they are missing. Lukaszewski (1988) identified the inability to gain access to people who ask questions, provide advice, and give counsel as the greatest difficulty facing senior executives. He noted that most people close to executives are afraid, or do not know how, to confront them regarding their behavior. The purpose of executive coaching is to provide these functions. An executive coach's role is to provide feedback to the executive about his or her behavior and the impact it has on others both within and outside the organization (O'Neill, 2000; Witherspoon & White, 1996). Given this type of feedback, executives gain increased self-awareness, self-esteem, and better communication with peers and subordinates (chap. 1, this volume), which in turn may lead to increased morale, productivity, and profits (Smith, 1993).

Techniques and methodologies. Unlike the previously discussed themes, in which each body of literature contributed to the summaries, the psychological literature makes a unique contribution to the techniques and methodologies theme. The special issue of the *Consulting Psychology Journal: Practice and Research* (Kilburg, 1996) reviewed a number of executive coaching models, often including case studies to illustrate key points. For example, Diedrich (see chap. 14, this volume) described a "comprehensive planning process that assesses critical competencies and guides the development of the executive" (p. 61). Katz and Miller (see chap. 23, this volume) explained an approach based on diversity and inclusion. Kiel, Rimmer, Williams, and Doyle (see chap. 11, this volume) and Tobias (see chap. 13, this volume) both took a systems-oriented approach, whereas Levinson (see chap. 9, this volume) based his approach on psychological skills and insight. Peterson (see chap. 12, this volume) adopted an approach based on five coaching strategies supported by research and experience at Personnel Decisions International, the first management consulting firm to offer a coaching program that was both structured and individually based (Hellervik, Hazucha, & Schneider, 1992). Saporito (see chap. 15, this volume) described a business-linked executive development approach, and Witherspoon and White (see chap. 10, this volume; 1997) proposed a model based on four different coaching roles: coaching for skills, performance, development, and the executive's agenda. Considering existing executive coaching models, Kilburg (chap. 1, this volume; 1997, 2000) proposed a 17-dimension model based on systems and psychodynamic theory. Additional models have since been offered, including the unpublished model of Waclawski and Church (1999) focusing on feedback utilization by means of the executive coaching process, Richard's (see chap. 25, this volume) multimodal model, and Laske's (see chap. 21, this volume) developmental approach, which integrates "agentic" and "ontic" development.

Although a myriad of approaches to executive coaching have been proposed, there is considerable overlap among them. For example, there appears to be agreement regarding the stages of executive coaching: relationship building, assessment, intervention, follow-up, and evaluation. These stages are typically consistent with most consultation interventions. There is also agreement regarding the desirable assessment techniques and instrumentation, including 360-degree feedback questionnaires, qualitative interviews, and psychological instruments, such as personality and leadership style inventories (chaps. 1, 10–15, 25, and 31, this volume; Harris, 1999). The purpose of these instruments is to gather data to present to the client.

There is further agreement that presenting data, or feedback, is a critical component of executive coaching (chaps. 10 and 14, this volume; Waclawski & Church, 1999). Kiel et al. (see chap. 11, this volume) stated that executives trust data and therefore come to trust the executive coaching process when data are provided. Waclawski and Church (1999) regard feedback as so critical to the executive coaching process that they developed a four-stage model for feedback utilization by means of the executive coaching process. They argued that it is through proper feedback that executives can come to understand patterns in the data gathered, work through their resistance to hearing the data, and identify and generate a developmental plan for behavioral change.

Though overlap exists between models, specific models are worth reading for their unique contributions to the coaching process—particularly Laske's (see chap. 21, this volume) developmental model and Kilburg's (see chap. 1, this volume) 17-dimensional model, which both provide greater contexts for understanding executive coaching and executive development. Witherspoon and White's (see chap. 10, this volume) model, which is based on four different approaches to executive coaching, is also helpful for understanding the various foci that coaching can have.

Distinguishing between counseling and psychotherapy. Because of the concern that executive coaching practices mirror too closely the practices of counseling or psychotherapy, a number of individuals have discussed the differences between the two interventions (chaps. 9, 13, 15, and 25, this volume; Kilburg, 2000; Sperry, 1993, 1996). In reviewing this literature, a number of ideas seem to repeat. For example, executive coaching occurs in the workplace with the intention of improving the executive's interpersonal skills and ultimately his or her workplace performance. It is more issue-focused than therapy is and occurs in a broader array of contexts—including face-to-face sessions, meetings with other people, observation sessions, over the telephone, and by e-mail—and in a variety of locations away from work (chap. 25, this volume; Sperry, 1993, 1996). Coaching sessions can last anywhere from a few minutes to a few hours (Sperry, 1996), whereas therapy typically occurs in a 45- to 50-minute interval. Also, unlike counseling or psychotherapy, data are collected from many sources, including the individual executive, his or her superiors, peers, subordinates, and family members (chaps. 1, 10, 11, 12, 14, 25, and 31, this volume; Harris, 1999). Other differences include being able to be more directive in executive coaching (chaps. 9 and 25, this volume) and viewing the relationship between the executive and coach as more collegial (chaps. 9 and 13, this volume) because the need for executive self-disclosure may not be as great as it is for counseling clients (chap. 15, this volume). Kilburg (2000) stated that although the principles of counseling–therapy can enhance executive coaching, the main difference is the depth to which issues are pursued and processed.

Not only are differences in the processes between executive coaching and therapy being debated, but differences between the qualifications of executive coaches and psychotherapists are also being discussed. Differences include the need for the executive coach to understand not only psychological dynamics and adult development, but also business, management, and political issues (see chaps. 11, 13, 15, and 21, this volume; Harris, 1999; Laske, 1999; O'Neill, 2000; Sperry, 1996). We would argue that possessing knowledge of leadership is also important. It has also been stated that executive coaching is measured in numerical terms, or in terms of the bottom-line performance for the executive and for the business, whereas counseling–psychotherapy is measured mainly by client self-report (chaps. 15 and 25, this volume). Data on these end results, or financial gains for business, however, are largely missing in the existing literature on executive coaching. What also seem to be missing are the more substantive ways in which executive coaching and therapy differ. The examples provided above seem somewhat logistical in nature. Even Kilburg (2000) stated that "the boundaries are not crisply drawn lines" (p. 227).

Credentials of executive coaches. The fourth point often discussed in the literature on executive coaching deals more generally with qualifications for service delivery (e.g., chaps. 4 and 31, this volume; Harris, 1999; Kilburg, 1997; Sperry, 1993, 1996). Again, the psychological literature seems to address this concern more fully than the other bodies of literature. The main issue discussed involves the myriad backgrounds of executive coaches. Currently, professionals from business, teaching, law, and sports are claiming to be executive coaches (chaps. 4 and 31, this volume). In part, this is a result of the increased demand for executive coaching, and, as such, there is concern over unqualified professionals making claims and threatening the legitimacy of executive coaching as a viable intervention (Harris, 1999; Kilburg, 2000).

Regarding qualifications, there seem to be two separate but related attitudes represented in the psychological literature. The first is the belief that psychologists already possess a large number of the skills needed to provide executive coaching and therefore are the most qualified service providers (chaps. 4 and 31, this volume; Sperry, 1993, 1996). These skills include the ability to respect confidentiality and maintain highly intense relationships with objectivity. Brotman et al. (see chap. 31, this volume) argued that psychologists are the most uniquely qualified to define what is required to be an executive coach when behavior change is the desired outcome, which inevitably is the case. The reasons behind his argument include the ability of the psychologist to do the following: establish safety in relationships, confront the executive on the reality of his or her behavior, and use the executive's developmental history and test data to identify themes in the executive's life. Furthermore, psychologists possess an understanding of psychological tests, cognitive style, managerial style, motivation, aptitude, and so forth. Kilburg (1997) also listed a number of skills psychologists possess that make them qualified to provide executive coaching services. These skills include the ability to listen, empathize, provide feedback, create scenarios, challenge, and explore the executive's world. Kilburg (2000) stated that although one does not necessarily have to be a psychologist to provide executive coaching services, having psychoanalytic knowledge (possessed by some but not all psychologists) greatly enhances the possible results from coaching.

The second attitude regarding qualifications is related to the first. Many argue that even though a psychological background provides many of the necessary skills to provide executive coaching services, it alone is not enough. Having an awareness of business, management, and political issues is also necessary to be effective (chaps. 9, 11, 13, and 15, this volume; Harris, 1999; Sperry, 1996). Again, we would argue that knowledge of leadership is also essential.

Although the business and management literature does not directly address the issue of coach credentials, this body of literature does discuss the process of finding an executive coach. According to Banning (1997) and Smith (1993), a company's human resources department, a superior, or a friend are some of the most common ways of finding a coach. Banning (1997) listed three important criteria in selecting a coach: trustworthiness, compatible chemistry, and solid reputation. Smith (1993) called attention to the focus of the executive coach, noting that some adopt a more behavioral focus, whereas others use a more psychoanalytic focus. However, he stated that most exist somewhere in between. The training and development literature also provide some helpful hints in selecting a coach. Thach and Heinselman (1999) suggested selecting coaches who have previous executive coaching and 360-degree assessment experience, knowledge of corporate environments and developmental processes, and the ability to be confrontational yet supportive while also maintaining confidentiality.

Recipients of services. Koonce (1994) stated that the consumers of executive coaching are executives who have been solid performers but whose current behaviors are interfering and putting the company at risk. A recent survey of leading companies conducted by *Fortune* presents a somewhat different view. According to this survey, the main consumers of executive coaching range from middle managers to CEOs or CEO contenders (Witherspoon & White, 1996). Witherspoon and White further stated that coaching clients are usually valued by the company because of certain skills they possess and because they are highly motivated individuals. These clients are typically looking for ways to refine and enhance their skills in order to continue in their current positions or move up into more advanced positions. Kiel et al. (see chap. 11, this volume), in the psychological literature, stated that one fourth of the executives who seek executive coaching are moving up within an organization or their career, one half are increasing their leadership responsibilities, and one fourth are having difficulties in their current job. Therefore, three fourths are using executive coaching for developmental purposes and only one fourth for remedial purposes.

Recent books on executive coaching. The rapid expansion of the literature on executive coaching has included the publication of several books. Two recent executive coaching books (Kilburg, 2000; O'Neill, 2000) are summarized here because they provide comprehensive discussions of current practice and offer practical advice for persons interested in developing an executive coaching practice. The classic, more general coaching text by Hargrove (1995) is also summarized as many of his general coaching principles apply to executive coaching, and he is often cited in the executive coaching literature (see Kilburg, 2000; O'Neill, 2000).

In *Executive Coaching With Backbone and Heart,* O'Neill (2000) proposed a systems approach to working with leaders and their challenges. She stated that the book is written for those coaching organizational leaders and focuses on the presence of coaches versus coaching techniques. She defined presence as being able to join leaders in a partnership, meeting them where they are in their struggles, and being assertive in one's position as coach while staying in a relationship with leaders. O'Neill identified presence as the most important principle and tool of executive coaching. She further identified the importance of focusing on the system of interaction between leaders and those with whom they work most closely as an additional principle that guides her approach. Applying these two principles, according to O'Neill, allows for the effective implementation of a coaching method. O'Neill's coaching method involves four phases: contracting, action planning, live-action planning, and debriefing. One chapter within the book is devoted to each phase. Additional chapters are devoted to developing a presence with clients, using a systems perspective, and how to transition into being an executive coach. Case illustrations are used throughout the book to illustrate ideas.

Kilburg's (2000) *Executive Coaching: Developing Managerial Wisdom in a World of Chaos* is probably the most comprehensive book on conducting executive coaching from a psychological and psychodynamic perspective. It is also the most complex. The author identified the purpose of this book as narrowing the gap between

> the growing understanding of the importance of complexity theory, human behavior, and the psychodynamic aspects of organizational and managerial life and the lack of practical guidance for how consultants and coaches can and should work with executives and managers on issues, performance problems, and dimensions of human behavior that have shadow [hidden] components. (Kilburg, 2000, pp. 18–19)

He fulfilled this purpose by providing a conceptual framework using systems and psychodynamic principles to understand executive character, organizational structure, and executive coaching work. He then used consultation cases to illustrate this framework and the methods and techniques used to effectively intervene as a coach or consultant. In addition, he addressed how to manage particular problems that can be elicited when working with executives' thoughts, feelings, defenses, and conflicts. Hargrove's (1995) *Masterful Coaching: Extraordinary Results by Impacting People and the Way They Think and Work Together* is a book on transformational coaching. Hargrove defined transformational coaching as a process that "shows people how to transform or stretch their visions, values, and abilities" (p. 1). Transformational coaching helps people tap their inner drive and ambition, stretch their minds and abilities, and move toward action. The author stated that this book synthesizes years of research and the practices of many coaches with the goal of helping the reader become a "masterful coach." The book is divided into three parts. Part 1 addresses the process and journey of "becoming" and "being" a masterful coach, which he sees as the key to effective coaching. Part 2 deals with group coaching and team learning, and Part 3 details Hargrove's techniques and methods for providing transformational coaching. Throughout all three sections, Hargrove interweaves theory and examples to illustrate his ideas.

EMPIRICAL RESEARCH

The above section focused on the practice-based literature. This section reviews the empirical research. The following paragraphs review the seven existing studies of executive coaching (chaps. 30 and 38, this volume; Gegner, 1997; Hall et al., 1999; Judge & Cowell, 1997; Laske, 1999; Olivero et al., 1997) and discuss the link between these studies and the practice-based literature.

The first study, conducted by Foster and Lendl (see chap. 38, this volume), was not a study on executive coaching per se but was a study investigating the effects of a specific technique less commonly used in executive coaching practice. Because it examined the effects of a specific, albeit less common, technique used in executive coaching, it is included in this chapter. However, it provides less information regarding the overall efficacy of executive coaching.

The purpose of Foster and Lendl's (see chap. 38, this volume) study was to determine whether EMDR used within an executive coaching process with four individuals could enhance workplace performance. Participants were a pilot, former CEO, office manager, and tenured professor. Three of the four participants had experienced perceived performance setbacks, and one was seeking a career change and wanted assistance reducing her anxiety regarding interviewing. Adhering to the EMDR protocol, participants were asked to (a) describe their setbacks or concerns, (b) specify the upsetting emotions tied to these incidents, (c) describe the current negative beliefs they held about themselves as a result of the setbacks or concerns, (d) identify the preferred belief about themselves in regard to the setback or concern, (e) follow the coach's fingers for a series of rapid eye movements, (f) consider again the distressing experience, and (g) repeat the eye movements until the incidents were no longer distressing and the positive belief replaced the negative belief. Results were measured by assessing physical symptoms and negative emotions pre- and post-EMDR and behavior outcomes pre- and post-EMDR. Complete pre and post scores on EMDR and behavior outcomes for each participant, however, were not given.

Results from Foster and Lendl's (see chap. 38, this volume) study suggest that EMDR can be an effective method for desensitizing distressing workplace experiences and helping participants develop more positive beliefs about themselves regarding upsetting workplace incidents to replace negative beliefs. This study also suggests that EMDR may help improve workplace performance within an executive coaching process.

The second study was conducted by Olivero et al. (1997). They implemented an action research study investigating the effects of a behavioral approach (vs. a psychodynamic approach) to executive coaching in a public sector municipal agency. The intervention was conducted in two phases and emphasized (a) goal setting, (b) collaborative problem solving, (c) practice, (d) feedback, (e) supervisory involvement, (f) evaluation of end results, and (g) presentation. Phase 1 consisted of classroom training emphasizing managerial competencies. Thirty-one trainees participated in Phase 1. Phase 2 consisted of an executive coaching process with the purpose of providing managers the opportunity to practice and obtain constructive feedback regarding the managerial competencies they learned in Phase 1. Of the 31 participants in Phase 1, 8 coaching–participants received training on how to provide executive coaching services to the other 23 trainee–participants in Phase 2. Part of the coaching experience required the 23 trainee–participants to develop a project plan to be used in coaching.

Results within each phase were measured along four dimensions: reactions, knowledge, behaviors, and outcomes. In Phase 1, participants reacted favorably to the training, giving it a mean rating of 4.87 on a 5-point Likert scale across five dimensions: usefulness of materials, instructor's knowledge, instructor's facilitation, overall instructor rating, and overall workshop rating. Knowledge of managerial competencies scores had a statistically significant increase from 71% at pretest to 88% at posttest ($p < .001$). Participants also reported that the training they received would improve their skills, but because these reports were future oriented they were not analyzed. As far as outcomes, the training phase alone increased overall productivity 22.4% as measured by the number of completed patient evaluation forms (statistical significance and p value not reported by Olivero et al., 1997).

Phase 2 included analyses of both qualitative and quantitative data. Qualitative data indicated that both coaches and coachees had favorable reactions to the coaching process. Two themes emerged from these data: coaching was beneficial to them personally and was beneficial to the overall agency. It is unclear, however, whether these themes emerged from both the coach and coachee responses or if they emerged from just the coachee responses. Reactions were not quantitatively measured. Quantitative data indicated a 20% increase in knowledge as measured by a small sample ($n = 4$) of coaches on pre- and posttest scores. The sample was too small to permit any statistical inferences, and it is unclear whose knowledge was being measured, the coaches or the coachees. Quantitative data also demonstrated a 65.6% increase ($p < .05$) in productivity during the implementation phase (Phase 2) as compared with the training phase (Phase 1) alone. These results suggest that executive coaching does increase productivity.

Regarding the limitations of this study, Olivero et al. (1997) offered several, including the fact that it was a field experiment and random assignment of participants was not permitted. They also recommended that a training-only condition and a coaching-only condition be compared with one another to distinguish more clearly between these two forms of learning.

The third study of executive coaching was a survey conducted by Judge and Cowell (1997) to better understand the practice of executive coaching. They surveyed 60 coaches regarding their qualifications and backgrounds; characteristics of the coaching industry, including fees and contractual agreements; and the process and assessments used in coaching. They also looked at the typical recipients of executive coaching, the issues most often presented by executives, and what one should look for and expect in an executive coach. Although this study provided valuable data, there was a lack of information regarding the methodology, which limits the applicability and generalizability of the findings. Therefore findings should be viewed as tentative.

Judge and Cowell (1997) reported that executive coaches come from a wide range of educational backgrounds, with undergraduate degrees ranging from drama to psychology. Of their participants, roughly 90% had master's degrees concentrated in business and the social sciences, and approximately 45% had doctoral degrees. Many belonged to professional associations, such as the American Society for Training and Development, and some were licensed to practice psychology in the state where they conducted business. Sixty percent of the coaches surveyed were male, 80% were between the ages of 35 and 55, and they averaged 24 years of work experience. Some worked for large companies employing more than 10 coaches, whereas most worked for smaller companies or worked independently. Most charged by the hour for their services, with fees ranging from $75 to $400 per contact hour, and most worked on a contractual basis. Approaches to coaching ranged from more behavioral to more psychoanalytic in nature, but regardless of orientation, the majority of coaches conducted 360-degree assessments by interviewing people close to the executive (supervisors, peers, subordinates, and, at times, family).

Recipients of executive coaching services in Judge and Cowell's (1997) study were typically mid-level to senior managers; half were CEOs or reported to CEOs. Recipients sought coaching voluntarily approximately one half of the time and were required to seek it the other one half. All recipients tended to fall within one of the following three categories: (a) individuals who were valuable but demonstrating difficulty in one or more area; (b) individuals who desired improved leadership skills; or (c) professionals other than executives, including lawyers, doctors, architects, and so forth. This last category was unexpected by the researchers. Regardless of which category recipients were in, the most common requests were to help them (a) modify their interaction style, (b) deal more effectively with change, and (c) build trusting relationships.

The fourth study was a master's thesis conducted by Gegner (1997). It was a cross-sectional field study investigating the effectiveness of executive coaching through quantitative and qualitative methods. It represents the first field study of executive coaching outcomes. Coaches (n = 47) acted as distributors of survey materials to executive participants (n = 48), who anonymously completed surveys. Gegner then conducted follow-up interviews with 25 of the 48 executives to gain additional information regarding (a) how executives became involved in coaching, (b) how a performance baseline was established prior to coaching and the resultant gains from coaching, (c) greatest obstacles to coaching, (d) most valuable learning experience, (e) whether coaching affected other life areas, and (f) any additional information executives wanted to share.

For the study, Gegner (1997) designed the Coaching Experience Survey, a 52-item measure using Likert scales. It consisted of two parts. The first asked executives to rate the effectiveness of the coaching process across eight components that were determined through the literature to be inherent in the executive coaching process: (a) goals, (b) feedback, (c) self-efficacy, (d) rewards, (e) communication style, (f) interpersonal style, (g) responsibility, and (h) awareness. The second portion of the survey gathered demographic information on the executive and coach as well as duration, frequency, and modality information regarding the coaching process.

The premise of Gegner's (1997) study was that as a result of executive coaching, executives would shift to a coaching style of management because they become more aware and take more responsibility for the actions in their organizations. The research questions were as follows: (a) Do the components (goals, feedback, self-efficacy, rewards, communication style, interpersonal style, responsibility, and awareness) of executive coaching work collectively to enhance executive performance, or are isolated components most effective; (b) does executive coaching contribute to sustained behavioral change; (c) do age, gender, and ethnicity affect the coaching process; (d) do time, frequency, and modality affect the executive coaching process; and (e) does a gender difference between the executive and coach affect the coaching process?

A total of 146 executives received surveys, and 48 (33%) returned them. Of the 48 who returned surveys, 25 were interviewed. Demographically, 14 executives (29%) were women and 34 (71%) were men. Ages ranged from 21 to 66 years (M = 44.5). Forty-four executives (95%) were Caucasian, one (2.2%) was African American, one (2.2%) was Asian, and two (4.2%) did not report their ethnic background.

To determine whether the components of executive coaching work collectively to enhance executive performance or whether isolated components are most effective, Gegner (1997) used the components of awareness and responsibility as the dependent variables measuring effectiveness. The results showed that awareness had the strongest correlations with self-efficacy (r = .55) and communication style (r = .45); had low correlations with interpersonal style (r = .24), rewards (r = .35), and feedback (r = .31); and had no correlation with goals (–.02). Responsibility had moderate to strong correlations with self-efficacy (r = .74), rewards (r = .64), feedback (r = .52), and communication style (r = .51) and low correlations with interpersonal style (r = .43) and goals (r = .32). Self-efficacy had the strongest correlations with both dependent variables: awareness (r = .55) and responsibility (r = .74). Responsibility had stronger associations than awareness with more components. Communication style had moderate associations with both awareness and responsibility, and feedback had moderate correlations with responsibility.

To determine whether coaching contributes to sustained behavior change, Gegner (1997) combined the percentages of "highly effective" and "somewhat effective" statements for awareness and responsibility (dependent variables) as these statements were considered coaching outcomes. Percentages ranged from 70.9% to 93.8% and therefore suggested that coaching contributes to sustained behavior change as defined by Gegner.

Gegner's definition, however, may not be the best measure of sustained behavior change, particularly because it is a self-rated measure and not considered over time. Whether executive gender, age, and ethnicity affect the coaching process was analyzed using Pearson's *r* coefficients to measure the strength of the associations between the demographic characteristics and the coaching components. Neither age nor gender had strong correlations (*r*s ranging from .023 to .225 for age and .001 to .139 for gender). Ethnicity could not be analyzed because 95.8% of the executives and 100% of the coaches were Caucasian. Whether duration, time, frequency, or modality influence the coaching process was also analyzed using Pearson's *r* coefficients to determine the strength of the association between these variables and the coaching components. Duration had a negative relationship with awareness ($r = -.362$), weak associations with interpersonal style and rewards (*r*s = .204 and .270, respectively), and relatively no association with responsibility, communication, feedback, goals, and self-efficacy (*r*s = .036, .080, .113, .158, and .069, respectively). The negative correlation with awareness may suggest that after a certain point in the coaching process, awareness decreases or ceases to increase. Correlations ranged from .068 to .285 for length of coaching and from .007 to .219 for modality. To determine whether gender affects the coaching process, the coach's gender was cross-tabulated against the executive's gender. The gender of the executive could not be predicted by the gender of the coach and vice versa (measured by a phi coefficient .008).

Gegner (1997) also conducted interviews with 25 of the original 48 executives. Seven (28%) reported seeking executive coaching services because of transitioning to new careers and wanting to excel in their businesses, whereas 18 (72%) became involved in executive coaching through corporate programs. Twenty-one executives (84%) reported positive feelings about their involvement in coaching. Ten executives (40%) stated that no baseline was established prior to coaching, and seven (28%) said that 360-degree feedback data, interviews, or upward feedback data were used to establish a baseline. Eight executives (32%) reported a percentage of performance improvement ranging from 10% to 100%. Eleven executives (44%) identified time as the greatest obstacle to coaching. All 25 executives (100%) reported learning more about themselves or gaining new skills as the most valuable outcome. All 25 executives (100%) also said that coaching had positively affected their personal lives by affecting their interactions with people, helping them establish balance in their lives, and helping them prioritize and make decisions about how they use their time. Regarding any additional information clients wanted to provide, 17 executives (68%) mentioned something about the coaching process itself, 10 (40%) identified personality traits or skills possessed by the coach, and 6 (24%) made comments about the growth they attained—being more open to change and possessing more self-confidence.

Gegner (1997) identified several limitations of her study. Additional limitations not mentioned by Gegner include not knowing how many coaches were contacted to participate and distribute survey materials to executives—therefore potentially limiting the generalizability of her findings—and the fact that multivariate analyses were not conducted to determine whether a combination of variables was more effective for enhancing executive performance.

The fifth study, conducted by Hall et al. (1999), consisted of interviews with 75 executives in six different Fortune 100 companies, 15 executive coaches referred by human resource (HR) personnel as leaders in the executive coaching field, and an unspecified number of HR personnel. The HR personnel were not mentioned as being interviewed in the method summary. However, they were mentioned in one part of the text.

Hall et al. (1999) were interested in the application of executive coaching, its effectiveness, and the lessons to be learned from providing services. The authors stated that understanding of interview data was also informed by the practical experience of the authors as executive coaches. No further information concerning the methodology or analysis was provided in the article. Details concerning the nature of the sample were also quite limited. Thus, the results of this study should be regarded as tentative.

The results of Hall et al. (1999) were presented in three areas: practice, effectiveness, and future directions. It was not always clear whether the information provided within each section was based on the results of the study or on the authors' theory–conceptualizations of executive coaching. Regarding practice, the authors reported that coaches could be either internal or external to the organizations and that the number of executive coaches was estimated to be in the ten thousands. Most of the seasoned coaches, however, came from psychology and the behavioral sciences and were either internal or external to the organization. External coaches were described as the most appropriate under conditions requiring extreme confidentiality, when the varied business experience of the coach is beneficial, or when "speak[ing] the unspeakable" is necessary (Hall et al., 1999, p. 40). Internal coaches were discussed as the most appropriate when possessing inside knowledge of company procedures and politics is helpful or necessary. Whether external or internal, however, coaches were described as providing feedback to executives that they had not received before. Feedback was tied to anything ranging from writing to interpersonal skills.

Regarding effectiveness, executives tended to stress that "good coaching is results oriented" (Hall et al., 1999, p. 43). Executives mentioned honesty, challenging feedback, and helpful suggestions as examples of good coaching. What they included as unhelpful were coaches who pushed their own agenda, tried to sell more consulting time, and provided only negative feedback or feedback based largely on other people's feelings rather than on data and results. Executives rated the overall effectiveness of executive coaching as "very satisfying," or a 4 on a 5-point Likert scale. Coaches agreed with the executives on what constituted good coaching but tended to focus more on the relationship and the coaching process. Coaches usually viewed the process of addressing coaching objectives as being just as important as actually meeting them (Hall et al., 1999).

The study also examined potential differences attributable to gender and race. The authors reported that gender interacted with age such that some female coaches reported experiencing difficulty coaching older high-level men, especially when providing negative feedback. They also identified multiple cultural issues that affected coaching, such as differences in eye contact, assertive communication, problem solving, and energy level. It was further reported that working with international executives sometimes required multicultural skill development. Lack of consideration of diversity issues such as age and race was identified as a limitation of current executive coaching practices.

Concerns about the future of executive coaching were categorized into three areas: managing the growth and demand for executive coaching, addressing ethical issues arising from the practice of executive coaching, and defining the scope and controlling costs. Hall et al. (1999) reported that most executive coaches have more requests for coaching than they can fulfill, and many are questioning whether this will continue or whether businesses will become more selective regarding who is offered coaching, particularly as businesses become more concerned with the cost, especially as markets tighten. One strategy the authors suggested for controlling the demand was the use of internal coaches. This practice, however, raises a potential ethical problem because it creates dual relationships. The authors further reported that some executive coaches (though which ones specifically was unclear) were concerned about the loss of control, confidentiality, and cost that may occur as a result of the increased demand by businesses. To help reduce these potential losses, they recommended that businesses establish clear guidelines for the use of executive coaching so that executive coaching is integrated into the overall development process of the organization. Doing so, they argued, would help provide for a steady demand.

The sixth study was a dissertation completed by Laske (1999). It used qualitative methods with the purpose of examining the developmental effects of executive coaching on an executive's professional agenda, with the specific focus of separating behavioral learning and ontic development.

Laske (1999) interviewed six executives identified by their coaches as experiencing developmental change because of coaching. The range of coaching was 6 months to 3 years. Each executive was interviewed twice. The first interview focused on the executives' current organizational position and functioning. The second interview, occurring 2 weeks later, focused on how executives view their world in terms of self–other object relations. Executive participation was confidential, and executive participants had final say regarding the presentation of their findings. Coach participation was also confidential. Coaches provided information regarding their executive participants' life history, themes, corporate culture, and how the corporate culture informed the coaching agenda.

The first interview, called the professional agenda interview, was based on Basseches's dialectical schemata framework (as cited in Laske, 1999) and focused on the way executives envision their work and approach their tasks. The professional agenda interview also informed the second interview by providing Laske insight into the executive's developmental stage, which was under investigation in the second interview. The first interview consisted of two global questions and numerous follow-up questions. The first question asked executives what had significantly changed in the way they perform their organizational functions as a result of coaching. Follow-up questions then dealt with specific changes in performance. The second question asked executives what aspects of their professional self-image had most notably been transformed as a result of coaching and how. Follow-up questions centered around specific changes in self-image.

The second interview was a subject–object interview, recognized by Lahey et al. and Kegan as an appropriate method for assessing stage-level of adults (as cited in Laske, 1999). This interview focused on how executives make sense of their work experiences in relationship to their ontic–developmental stage-level on the basis of Kegan's theory of adult development (as cited in Laske, 1999). The question guiding Laske in this interview was as follows: How are executives constructing their reality (personal and organizational) based on subject–object relations? The protocol for the subject–object interview included handing the executive 10 index cards with one of the following topics written on it: (a) angry, (b) anxious/nervous, (c) success/accomplishment, (d) strong stand/conviction, (e) sad, (f) torn, (g) moved/touched, (h) control, (i) change, and (j) important to me. The interviewer, in this case Laske, provided a brief explanation of the meaning of each of the 10 topics, gave the executive 5 min to think about the topics, and then asked the executive to write down memories of work experiences based on the topics of each card. Afterward, the executive and Laske conversed extensively about the cards most salient to the executive. Three to five cards were discussed. Laske stated that not all cards needed to be discussed because there is an underlying assumption that engaging in this process thoroughly for three to five cards will reveal the developmental stage of the executive.

Regarding data analysis, Laske (1999) stated that his purpose was to identify and link two sets of ontic–developmental scores. The first is a stage score, based on Kegan's developmental framework (as cited in Laske, 1999). The second is a nonstage score, based on Basseches's (1984) dialectical–schemata framework (as cited in Laske, 1999). Laske did this by analyzing the two sets of interview data, each according to its corresponding methodology. Data from the first interview were evaluated in terms of executives' endorsement of Basseches's four categories: (a) motion, (b) form, (c) relationship, and (d) metaformal schemata. Laske gave each of the four categories a weighting based on the strength of endorsements provided each category by executives.

The subject–object interview material was analyzed using Lahey et al.'s method (as cited in Laske, 1999), which provides an overall stage score based on the number of times a particular stage (or manner of making meaning) is endorsed by the executive. Laske extended this procedure by calculating two additional scores: a clarity score and a potential score index associated with the stage score. The clarity score represents the clarity with which the stage score is expressed by the executive, and the potential score represents the potential of the executive for transcending to a higher stage. These two scores could be compared to determine the risk of an executive regressing to a lower developmental level as a result of being in an unhealthy organization or under duress. The result of the analysis and interview scoring was a combined ontic–developmental score, including a level of self-awareness (stage score) and capacity for systems thinking (process score) for each executive participant.

Laske (1999) presented the results first by vignette, where he provided a comprehensive profile of each executive's present professional performance and functioning and change story, both based on the information coaches shared and the interview material. He also provided a combined ontic–developmental score. The findings of all six executives were then presented as a collective whole, and the methodology that produced these findings was discussed. Laske referred to this methodology as the Developmental Structure/Process Tool, developed as a result of his study. He provided further elaboration on the instrument, the ways in which it can be used, and the implications it has for aiding adult and executive development.

Regarding the results of his study and how well they answered the research question of whether changes that occur because of executive coaching are ontic–developmental (transformational) in nature or solely behaviorally adaptive, Laske (1999) stated that they do not completely answer the question. Therefore, he proposed two alternative hypotheses: (a) in order to experience transformative (ontic–developmental) effects of coaching, one must be developmentally ready to experience them and (b) coaching may have transformative (ontic–developmental) effect, but the developmental level of the coach must also be such that it allows the coach to co-generate these effects in the coaching relationship.

Laske (1999) summarized what he thought were the nine critical empirical findings of his work (pp. 242–244). In doing so, he focused on (a) the extent to which stage scores and process scores matched and (b) the gaps between executives' cognitive focus in their present professional performance and functioning (motion) and in their change story (metaform).

Laske found that the capacity for systems thinking tended to rise with stage score and its associated clarity–potential index such that the higher the stage score, the higher the executive's metaformal (transformational) understanding of organizational reality. Second, Laske found a discrepancy between executives' focus in their present professional performance and functioning (motion) and their change story (metaform). Second, changes reported by executives did in fact seem to be of a metaformal–transformational nature versus a merely adaptive (behavioral) one. Third, executive reports of developmental transformation reflect their ontic–developmental stage more than the impact of coaching. Therefore, executive coaching will not be beneficial unless the executive is developmentally ready (measured by the clarity–potential index) for change. Fourth, there is a corresponding relationship between stage scores and process scores, making it reasonable to assume "that the mental processes categorized in terms of dialectical-schemata analysis constitute the very processes that make attaining, maintaining, regressing from, and transcending, a particular ontic–developmental level possible" (Laske, 1999, p. 243). Fifth, the process assessment is the best way to identify and map the ontic–developmental score of a person into a particular empirical domain because the processes (schemata) individuals use for making meaning of the empirical world are more straightforward in their behavioral implications than ontic–developmental stage scores. Sixth, process and structure assessments alone are merely diagnostic; however, when combined they become prognostic. This is the case because stage scores reflect a current developmental balance ready to transform to a following one. Seventh, "a cognitive disequilibrium between critical (motion, relationship) and constructive mental tools (form, metaform), as found in the sample of executives, is not so much a deficit, but the very motor of development toward a higher ontic stage" (O. E. Laske, personal communication, June 18, 2001). Conversely, higher stages of development cannot be forced by coaching because the developmental level of the individual determines the effect coaching will have. Eighth, the current study provided a hypothesis about transformative effects of coaching; however, a longitudinal study using the same methods is necessary to provide sufficient evidence for the long-term transformative effects of coaching. Finally, because executives' change stories depend on their ontic–developmental status, the assumed truths of the theory and practice of executive development, specifically those conceptualized in terms of behavioral opinions of executive coaching, are placed in doubt (O. E. Laske, personal communication, June 18, 2000).

The seventh study, conducted by Garman, Whiston, and Zlatoper (see chap. 30, this volume), was a content analysis of publications concerning executive coaching. The purpose of this study was to describe professional opinions concerning the practice of executive coaching and the perceived relevance of psychological training for such practice. The authors identified 72 articles on executive coaching published in mainstream and trade management publications between 1991 and 1998. These articles were coded according to (a) whether they were concerned with externally provided coaching; (b) whether they were generally favorable, unfavorable, or mixed in their evaluation of executive coaching; (c) whether psychologists were specifically mentioned as executive coaching service providers; (d) whether psychologists were regarded as a distinct service provider group; and (e) whether psychologists, if regarded as a distinct group, were distinguished favorably, unfavorably, or neutrally. This coding scheme provides quantitative information concerning these dimensions but does not provide qualitative understanding of the differences between, for example, favorable and unfavorable articles. In addition, results must be regarded with some caution because of relatively moderate interrater reliabilities for some codes, as well as a lack of attention to the role of chance agreement in calculating these reliabilities.

Results from Garman et al.'s (see chap. 30, this volume) study suggest that, although executive coaching is generally viewed favorably, psychologists are not universally viewed as uniquely valuable service providers. Eighty-eight percent of the articles reviewed were coded as evaluating executive coaching favorably. In contrast, less than one third of the articles reviewed mentioned psychological training specifically, and only two thirds of those that did address it described psychologists as having unique executive coaching skills. In addition, only 45% of the articles distinguishing between psychologists and other executive coaching service providers described psychological training as an asset. An additional 36% of these articles described the unique skills of psychologists as potentially favorable or unfavorable, whereas the remaining 18% of articles directly addressing psychologists described them as potentially harmful. Although they did not directly assess it in their coding scheme, Garman et al. (see chap. 30, this volume) suggested two possible sources for unfavorable perceptions of psychologists as executive coaches: some clinical psychologists are entering the field without appropriate retraining, and some consumers perceive that psychologists use extensive assessment in executive coaching simply to increase billable hours.

LINK OF EMPIRICAL STUDIES TO PRACTICE ARTICLES

Six of the seven empirical studies (chap. 30, this volume; Gegner, 1997; Hall et al., 1999; Judge & Cowell, 1997; Laske, 1999; Olivero et al., 1997) provide some support for points discussed in the practice literature. The last study (chap. 38, this volume) provides support for EMDR as an adjunct to executive coaching. Looking at these six studies, the results of Olivero et al. (1997) support the idea that executive coaching benefits both the executive and the company. Executives experienced coaching as a positive endeavor, and they gained increased satisfaction and productivity in their work. In Hall et al.'s study (1999), executives reported being "very satisfied" with their coaching experiences as did the executives in Gegner's (1997) study. Garman et al. (see chap. 30, this volume) further reported that professional publications concerning executive coaching practice were generally positive; however, psychologists were not universally viewed as unique contributors to the executive coaching process. And the executives in Laske (1999) were chosen because they had been identified as experiencing meaningful change as a result of coaching.

A second idea discussed in the practice literature and supported by the results of Olivero et al. (1997) is the increased learning that occurs with executive coaching. Many have identified the individually tailored nature of executive coaching as one of the main reasons for its success (chap. 10, this volume; Harris, 1999; O'Brien, 1997). In Olivero et al., knowledge increased at a higher rate after training and coaching than after training alone. One point to be considered is the fact that the coaches in this study were not professional coaches. Professional executive coaches tend to have more experience than that possessed by the participants providing coaching in this study. In light of this, it seems likely that the results of executive coaching when practiced by professional and experienced coaches might be even greater.

A third idea discussed in the practice-based literature and supported by the results of Gegner (1997) and Laske (1999) is the behavioral changes that occur as a result of executive coaching. All of the executives in both studies reported behavioral changes, and Laske (1999) provided support for the hypothesis that the developmental level of the client and coach is necessary for effecting developmental change.

The results from Judge and Cowell (1997) and from Hall et al. (1999) support a fourth idea discussed in the practice literature regarding the educational background of coaches. Judge and Cowell found a wide range of educational backgrounds. Coaches interviewed had undergraduate degrees ranging from drama to psychology; however, 90% also had master's degrees in either business or social science. This, in part, supports the concern expressed in the practice literature regarding the variety of professionals identifying themselves as coaches. Although Garman et al. (see chap. 30, this volume) focused specifically on examining whether or not psychological training was regarded as an asset in executive coaching, their findings provide further support for the need to standardize qualifications and practice. The fact that Garman et al. did not find that psychologists were universally recognized as uniquely valuable challenges the idea proposed by Brotman et al. (see chap. 31, this volume) and others that psychologists are best qualified. At minimum, it challenges psychologists to articulate more clearly their significant contributions to the practice of executive coaching.

A fifth idea supported by the empirical research concerns the methods used by the coaches surveyed. Similar to what was reported in the practice articles, coaches in Judge and Cowell (1997) used a variety of approaches, ranging from behavioral to psychodynamic, yet regardless of approach included 360-degree assessments in their process. Finally, executive coaching was provided for both developmental and remedial purposes as suggested in the practice literature. One unexpected result from Judge and Cowell (1997) was the finding that many professionals other than executives (e.g., lawyers, doctors, and other professionals) seek executive coaching services. Little is known about this group of recipients, though Richard (see chap. 25, this volume) suggested that they be included as clientele for executive coaching services. If this inclusion occurs, however, what would distinguish executive coaching from general business or other types of coaching? Maybe nothing would, which suggests that *executive coaching* is a new name for a previous and long-existing consultation intervention.

CONCLUSION

The purpose of this chapter was to critically review the existing practice-based and empirically based literature on executive coaching to determine (a) what has been written and therefore what is known about executive coaching, (b) whether executive coaching is an effective tool for improving individual and organizational performance, and (c) whether executive coaching is just another business fad.

Regarding what has been written and what is known about executive coaching, the literature seems to provide some basis for understanding the definition, purpose, process, methodologies, clients, and service providers of executive coaching. The literature also provides some limited evidence that executive coaching is effective for increasing performance (Olivero et al., 1997), is viewed favorably by executives (Gegner, 1997), and has the potential to facilitate developmental change (Laske, 1999). What needs further explanation are the more substantive ways that executive coaching differs from psychotherapy and counseling. Furthermore, the type of outcomes executive coaching has in the field needs further empirical investigation.

Even though the literature provides some basis for understanding executive coaching, it also identifies concerns regarding the absence of a clear and widely accepted (a) definition, (b) standard of practice, and (c) agreement as to the appropriate service providers (chap. 31, this volume; Kilburg, 2000). Regarding the definition of executive coaching, an integration of Kilburg's (2000) definition with components of Caplan's (1970) CCAC and Kinlaw's (1997) general coaching may provide a comprehensive understanding of current practices. It is interesting to note, however, that Kilburg made the statement that consultants use "behavioral techniques" when much of his conceptualization of executive coaching is from a psychodynamic perspective. The difficulty of defining executive coaching may also be a result of the many different individuals and disciplines involved in providing executive coaching services. Regardless, however, some consensus regarding a basic definition seems important. Variants on approaches can later be addressed, as is the case in counseling and psychotherapy. Or, similar to counseling and psychotherapy, one definition may be difficult to develop and agree on.

A final note regarding definition has to do with the inclusion or exclusion of lawyers, doctors, and other professionals as recipients of executive coaching. Richard (see chap. 25, this volume) argued that other professionals should be included as recipients, and Judge and Cowell (1997) found these individuals to exist as recipients of executive coaching services. Do these individuals necessarily have managerial authority in an organization as Kilburg defines? Does making the recipients more inclusive change the executive coaching process? Is it the clientele that makes executive coaching unique, or is it the executive coaching process? Is it a combination of the two? If executive coaching is more inclusive, then how does it differ from general business coaching? To better address these questions and determine the best definition of executive coaching, the process of executive coaching may need to be better understood and researched.

Related to the definition are the standards of practice and who should be delivering executive coaching services. Although some discussion and development of standards has taken place, no set of standards has been fully developed or widely accepted. To date, the ICF has begun to develop standards; however, they do not necessarily represent the field of psychology. Brotman et al. (see chap. 31, this volume) argued that the APA should become involved in regulating executive coaching practices because psychologists possess many of the skills necessary to provide executive coaching services. If the APA were to become involved, would they do so in conjunction with the ICF or would they do so alone? What implication would the APA becoming involved have on the practice of executive coaching, particularly because the ICF represents coaches from more than one discipline? For psychologists, at minimum, it seems that the APA could provide ethical guidelines for those who are involved in providing executive coaching services.

Before one can develop guidelines, one has to address the skills and qualifications needed to provide such services. From reviewing the literature, it seems that providers need to be able to take on a feedback role (Wacklawski & Church, 1999), use the relationship as a tool (Kilburg, 2000; O'Neill, 2000), and be knowledgeable about the executive coaching context and its impact on the leader and the coaching process (chap. 14, this volume; Whitherspoon & White, 1997). Knowledge about the context probably includes awareness of business, management, and political principles, which have been identified as important (e.g., chap. 15, this volume; Sperry, 1996).

A caveat, however, and one that was previously mentioned, deals with the executive coaching process. In order to know who is best qualified to deliver executive coaching services, we need to know more about the executive coaching process and how it relates to outcomes. For example, do process and outcome look different when coaching is remedial versus developmental? What specifically about the coaching process is responsible for the desired outcomes? The relationship has been identified by many (Hargrove, 1995; Kilburg, 2000; O'Neill, 2000) as one of the most important tools in effecting change. What about the relationship facilitates change? How does the relationship as well as the coaching process and outcome vary across diverse recipients and providers, for example, gender, race, age, and so forth? Gegner (1997) found the executive coaching components of self-efficacy and communication style to be most effective for affecting executive performance, as measured by self-awareness and responsibility. Laske (1999) found that the developmental level of the client and coach are important for facilitating developmental, transformational change. Additional research along these lines would be helpful for understanding what about executive coaching effects change.

Equally important is the need to identify the different kinds of outcomes we expect and want from executive coaching. There is the bottom line of increased productivity, which has been researched in one study (Olivero et al., 1997). Provided these findings can be replicated, the viability of executive coaching will be enhanced. There are also additional outcomes that may increase the viability of executive coaching if they are identified and empirically supported. For example, the participants of Judge and Cowell (1997) identified the ability to modify their interaction styles, deal more effectively with change, and build more trusting relationships as their desired outcomes for executive coaching. Investigating whether executive coaching can produce these outcomes may be beneficial. However, these outcome variables may not be highly valued by businesses and organizations unless they can be linked to productivity and performance.

Not only is additional research needed, but also more rigorous research is necessary. Some of the research reviewed in this chapter is quite flawed. For example, Judge and Cowell (1997) and Hall et al. (1999) provided limited information regarding their methodologies and samples, which limits the applicability and generalizability of their studies. Gegner (1997) also failed to provide a response rate of coaches, which is necessary to determine the generalizability of her findings. Limitations exist in the other studies as well. Olivero et al. (1997) had design limitations in that they did not have random assignment nor did they compare a training-only and coaching-only condition; therefore, the ability to attribute outcomes to the coaching condition alone is limited. Furthermore, executive coaching was provided by employees with extremely limited training in providing executive coaching services. Though the study demonstrated improved performance, stronger results may occur if studied with professional executive coaches. The findings of Foster and Lendl (see chap. 38, this volume) are similarly limited by the absence of pre and post measures on physical symptoms and negative emotions for some participants.

Finally, regarding research, it is interesting to note that three of the seven studies conducted on executive coaching were found in the business–management literature, and three were found in the psychological literature (one a dissertation). Most of the practice-based articles, however, were found in the psychological literature. Two of the three studies that were published in the psychological literature were not outcome studies. Future research needs to be conducted drawing on all of the bodies of literature relevant to executive coaching. Also, because psychologists are heavily engaged in the practice of executive coaching and are arguing that they are best qualified (chap. 31, this volume), it seems that they hold some responsibility in conducting, supporting, and participating in the research being conducted on the effectiveness of executive coaching as an intervention.

References

Allenbaugh, G. E. (1983). Coaching . . . a management tool for a more effective work performance. *Management Review, 72,* 21–26.

Aurelio, S., & Kennedy, J. K. (1991). Performance coaching: A key to effectiveness. *Supervisory Management, 36,* 1–2.

Banning, K. L. (1997). Now, coach? *Across the Board, 34,* 28–32.

Bell, C. R. (1987). Coaching for high performance. *SAM Advanced Management Journal, 52,* 26–29.

Bertagnoli, L. (2000). One-on-one counsel for business owners. *Crain's Chicago Business, 23*(7), 8–9.

Brotherton, P. R. (1998). Making a connection: It's time for a career workout. *Black Enterprise, 28*(11), 82.

Caplan, G. (1970). *Theory and practice of mental health consultation.* New York: Basic Books.

Darling, M. J. (1994). Coaching people through difficult times. *HR Magazine, 39,* 70–73.

Deblieux, M. (1998). Encouraging great performance. *HR Focus, 75,* 13.

Deeprose, D. (1995). *The team coach: Vital new skills for supervisors and managers in a team environment.* New York: American Management Association.

Douglas, C. A., & Morley, W. H. (2000). *Executive coaching: An annotated bibliography.* Greensboro, NC: Center for Creative Leadership.

Dutton, G. (1997). Executive coaches call the plays. *Management Review, 86*(2), 39–43.

Ericsson, K. A. (1996). (Ed.). *The road to excellence: The acquisition of expert performance in the arts and sciences, sports, and games.* Hillsdale, NJ: Erlbaum.

Filipczak, B. (1998). The executive coach: Helper or healer? *Training, 35*(3), 30–36.

Flory, C. D. (1965). *Managers for tomorrow.* New York: New American Library.

Gegner, C. (1997). *Coaching: Theory and practice.* Unpublished master's thesis, University of San Francisco, California.

Gilley, J. W., & Boughton, N. W. (1996). *Stop managing, starting coaching! How performance coaching can enhance commitment and improve productivity.* New York: McGraw-Hill.

Good, D. J. (1993). Coaching practices in the business-to-business environment. *Journal of Business & Industrial Marketing, 8*(2), 53–60.

Graham, S., Wedman, J. F., & Garver-Kester, B. (1993). Manager coaching skills: Development and application. *Performance Improvement Quarterly, 6*(1), 2–13.

Grover, M. B. (2000). Preshrunk. *Forbes, 165*(6), 82.

Hall, D. T., Otazo, K. L., & Hollenbeck, G. P. (1999). Behind closed doors: What really happens in executive coaching. *Organizational Dynamics, 27*(3), 39–52.

Hardingham, A. (1998). Moments of clarity. *People Management, 4*(8), 31.

Hargrove, R. (1995). *Masterful coaching: Extraordinary results by impacting people and the way they think and work together.* San Francisco: Pfeiffer/Jossey-Bass.

Harris, M. (1999). Look, it's an I-O psychologist . . . no, it's a trainer . . . no, it's an executive coach. *TIP, 36*(3), 1–5.

Hayes, G. E. (1997). Executive coaching: A strategy for management and organizational development. In A. J. Pickman (Ed.), *Special challenges in career management: Counselor perspectives* (pp. 213–222). Mahwah, NJ: Erlbaum.

Hellervik, L. W., Hazucha, J. F., & Schneider, R. J. (1992). *Behavior change: Models, methods, and a review of the evidence.* In M. D. Dunnette & L. M. Hough (Eds.), *Handbook of industrial and organizational psychology* (2nd ed., pp. 823–895). Palo Alto, CA: Consulting Psychologists Press.

Hogan, R., Curphy, G. J., & Hogan, J. (1994). What we know about leadership: Effectiveness and personality. *American Psychologist, 49,* 493–503.

Huggler, L. (1997). Companies on the couch: Use of psychoanalysis in conflict management. *HR Magazine, 42,* 80–84.

Hutcheson, P. G. (1996). Ten tips for coaches. *Training and Development Journal, 50,* 15–16.

Hyatt, J. (1997). CEO: The zero defect. *Inc., 19,* 46–57.

International Coaching Federation Conference. (2000). *International Executive Coaching Summit: A collaborative effort to distinguish the profession: 2000.* Retrieved July 17, 2000, from http://www.coachfederation.org/ecsummit-1999.htm#b

Judge, W. Q., & Cowell, J. (1997). The brave new world of executive coaching. *Business Horizons, 40*(4), 71–77.

Kilburg, R. R. (Ed.). (1996). Executive coaching [Special issue]. *Consulting Psychology Journal: Practice and Research, 48*(2).

Kilburg, R. R. (1997). Coaching and executive character: Core problems and basic approaches. *Consulting Psychology Journal: Practice and Research, 49,* 281–299.

Kilburg, R. R. (2000). *Executive coaching: Developing managerial wisdom in a world of chaos.* Washington, DC: American Psychological Association.

Kinlaw, D. C. (1997). *Coaching: Winning strategies for individuals and teams.* Brookfield, VT: Gower.

Kiser, K. (1999). Executive coach. *Training, 36*(8), 34–35.

Koonce, R. (1994). One on one. *Training and Development Journal, 48*(2), 34–40.

Larry, B. K. (1997a). Executive counsel. *Human Resource Executive, 11*(1), 46–49.

Larry, B. K. (1997b). Now, coach? *Across the Board, 34,* 28–32.

Laske, O. E. (1999). *Transformative effects of coaching on executive's professional agenda, 1.* Ann Arbor: University of Michigan Press.

Ludeman, K. (1995). To fill the feedback void. *Training and Development Journal, 49*(8), 38–41.

Lukaszewski, J. E. (1988). Behind the throne: How to coach and counsel executives. *Training and Development Journal, 42*(10), 33–35.

Machan, D. (1998). Sigmund Freud meets Henry Ford. *Forbes, 14*(13), 120–122.

Martin, I. (1996). *From couch to corporation: Becoming a successful corporate therapist.* New York: Wiley.

Masciarelli, J. P. (1999). Less lonely at the top. *Management Review, 88*(4), 58–61.

Maxwell, J. C. (1995). *Developing the leaders around you.* Nashville, TN: Nelson.

McCafferty, J. (1996). Your personal Vince Lombardi. *CFO: The Magazine for Senior Financial Executives, 12*(11), 93–95.

Miller, J. B., & Brown, P. B. (1993). *The corporate coach.* New York: St. Martin's Press. Minor, M. (1995). *Coaching for development: Skills for managers and team leaders.* Menlo Park, CA: Crisp.

Morris, B. (2000). So you're a player. Do you need a coach? *Fortune, 141*(4) 144–146, 148, 150, 152, 154.

Nakache, P. (1997). Can you handle the truth about your career? *Fortune Magazine, 136*(1), 208.

O'Brien, M. (1997). Executive coaching. *Supervision, 58*(4), 6–8.

Olesen, M. (1996). Coaching today's executives. *Training and Development Journal, 50*(3), 22–27.

Olivero, G., Bane, K. D., & Kopelman, R. E. (1997). Executive coaching as a transfer of training tool: Effects on productivity in a public agency. *Public Personnel Management, 26*(4), 461–469.

O'Neill, M. B. (2000). *Executive coaching with backbone and heart: A systems approach to engaging leaders with their challenges.* San Francisco: Jossey-Bass.

Orth, C. D., Wilkinson, H. E., & Benfari, R. C. (1987). The manager's role as coach and mentor. *Organizational Dynamics, 15*(4), 66–74.

Peterson, D. B., & Hicks, M. D. (1996). *Leader as coach: Strategies for coaching and developing others.* Minneapolis, MN: Personnel Decisions International.

Peterson, D. B., & Hicks, M. D. (1999). Strategic coaching: Five ways to get the most value. *Human Resource Focus, 76*(2), 7–8.

Robinson, J. (1996). *Coach to coach: Business lessons from the locker room.* Johannesburg, South Africa: Pfeiffer.

Shore, L. M., & Bloom, A. J. (1986). Developing employees through coaching and career management. *Personnel, 63*, 34–38.

Shula, D., & Blanchard, K. H. (1995). *Everyone's a coach: You can inspire anyone to be a winner.* New York: Harper Business.

Smith, L. (1993). The executive's new coach. *Fortune, 128*(16), 126–134.

Snyder, A. (1995). Executive coaching: The new solution. *Management Review, 84*(3), 29–32.

Sperry, L. (1993). Working with executives: Consulting, counseling, and coaching. *Individual Psychology, 49*(2), 257–266.

Sperry, L. (1996). *Corporate therapy and consultation.* New York: Brunner/Mazel.

Strickland, K. (1997). *Executive coaching: Helping valued executives fulfill their potential.* In A. J. Pickman (Ed.), *Special challenges in career management: Counselor perspectives* (pp. 203–212). Hillsdale, NJ: Erlbaum.

Thach, L., & Heinselman, T. (1999). Executive coaching defined. *Training & Development, 53*(3), 35–39.

Tristram, C. (1996). Wanna be a player: Get a coach. *Fast Company,* 145–150.

Voss, T. (1997). *Sharpen your team's skills in coaching.* New York: McGraw-Hill.

Waclawski, J., & Church, A. H. (1999). *The 4-3-2-1 coaching model.* Paper presented at the meeting of the Academy of Management Conference, Chicago, IL.

Waldroop, J., & Butler, T. (1996). The executive as coach. *Harvard Business Review, 74,* 111–117.

Whitmore, J. (1994). *Coaching for performance.* San Diego, CA: Pfeiffer.

Witherspoon, R., & White, R. P. (1996). Executive coaching: What's in it for you? *Training and Development Journal, 50,* 14–15.

Witherspoon, R., & White, R. P. (1997). *Four essential ways that coaching can help executives.* Greensboro, NC: Center for Creative Leadership.

CHAPTER 4

EXECUTIVE COACHING AS AN EMERGING COMPETENCY IN THE PRACTICE OF CONSULTATION

Richard R. Kilburg

We begin with a key question for practicing consultants. Why do organizations fail? To be sure there are many cogent explanations that are often offered. The lack of strategic alignment between the organization and its competing environment is often mentioned. Market changes, new technologies, global competition, and financial troubles are also frequently identified culprits. However, the one answer that everyone thinks about and most often identifies is that the executive leadership of the organization was not up to the challenge. The reverse is also true; namely, when an organization is doing very well, the executive team is usually identified as the central reason for success.

For this reason, many organizations spend significant time and resources on finding and preparing people to lead. Many large corporations have built their own development infrastructures complete with faculty; a collegelike campus; and talented, full-time staff. Graded sequences of instruction, assessment centers, and performance management systems are just some of the technologies that have been developed and applied. Despite these approaches, the data and lore of executive derailment describe the carnage of careers that end too early or never blossom at all and of organizations that often suffer and sometimes die because of the inability of executives to perform in these complex, crucial roles. For these reasons, I believe that leadership development is truly a core competency of any modern organization

During the past decade, the organizational and consulting literature has continued to focus on these issues. Amid the descriptions of problems and identification of potential approaches, a few individuals have been suggesting that coaching individual executives can often help them solve major problems in their organizations and that coaching can take on specific issues in the performance, style, and even personalities of leaders themselves. As yet, there has been no focused effort to describe or define this emerging area of consultation practice, even though it has developed an initial identity known as *executive coaching*.

I believe that consultants started to practice executive coaching when they gained access to the leaders of organizations. So why, you may ask, is all of the fuss being made over what senior practitioners in the field have long recognized as a key component of their roles in organizations? I believe that there has been a subtle yet significant shift in the field, as professionals have recognized that there are some things that seem to work well when consulting with an individual executive and others that do not work at all. As it is currently practiced, executive coaching appears to be an eclectic mix of concepts and methods that are being applied by a variety of consultants who have accepted

This chapter is an abridged version of the introductory material to a 1996 special issue of the *Consulting Psychology Journal: Practice and Research, 48,* 59–60.

assignments to work with individual executives. Traditional organization development methods, adult education, management training, industrial–organizational psychology, and generic consultation skills are being blended together to define a subdiscipline. For consulting psychologists, another important development is that the theories and methodologies of clinical psychology, with its strong historical emphasis on diagnosing and changing the dysfunctional behavior patterns of individuals, are now being applied often to the other consulting approaches used with executives. These developments have led the editors of this journal to publish an issue that focuses on this emerging competency in the practice of consulting.

The purposes of this issue of the *Consulting Psychology Journal* are to focus on executive coaching as a specific subarea of practice in consultation, to review such literature that exists in the field, to identify current approaches and methods, and to provide an opportunity for leading practitioners to describe what they are doing and help define the core concepts and definitions of this emerging competency.

CHAPTER 5

FURTHER CONSIDERATION OF EXECUTIVE COACHING AS AN EMERGING COMPETENCY

Richard C. Diedrich and Richard R. Kilburg

In his introduction to the first special issue focused on executive coaching, Kilburg (see chap. 4, this volume) noted the general fascination with and the growth of coaching as a consulting intervention. That special issue "outsold" all previous issues of *Consulting Psychology Journal*. If anything, there is even more interest now than there was in 1996; therefore, we felt the field would welcome another special issue.

From the way the field has developed in the past 5 years, it appears now that coaching has begun to make its place in the vast armamentarium of behaviorally based interventions available to psychologists and other professionals who work to help people and organizations change. Life coaching (Hudson, 1999) has emerged as a counterpart to counseling and psychotherapy, and many psychological practitioners are exploring how these skills and this conceptual approach can be added to their professional portfolios. This is especially true in the face of the severe challenges faced in the traditional marketplace for mental health services, where many if not most companies now refuse to pay for life-enhancing interventions. These developments are extremely welcome in a field that has been coping for decades with the problems imposed by managed care companies. However, we believe it is crucial to distinguish between these more generic life-enhancing approaches to coaching and the services that are being provided to executives.

When a consulting psychologist is hired by an individual or by an organization to help with any of the myriad of problems and difficulties that the modern workplace can produce for a person who has managerial authority and responsibility, he or she has moved directly into the realm of executive coaching. The setting, the task and interpersonal requirements for people in leadership positions, the framework within which a practitioner must work, and the types of interventions required all contribute to demand a unique subset of knowledge, skills, and abilities from anyone who would practice with this population. Coaching executives requires knowledge about organizations, management, leadership, economics, and a host of other disciplines. Psychologists who coach executives need not necessarily be executives themselves, but they must have an in-depth feel for the lives that these most competent, ambitious, and talented people lead and how to successfully intervene with them. It is clear in this regard that executive coaching has continued on the path of becoming a unique competency in the practice of consulting psychology. Fortunately, as the practice has forged ahead, practitioners and scientists are continuing to explore and discuss the issues being encountered and do some

This chapter is an abridged version of the introductory material to a 2001 special issue of the *Consulting Psychology Journal: Practice and Research*, 53, 203–204.

research, adding immeasurably to the foundation for the field.

Much has been written, some good and more not so good, in recent years. Chapter 31 in this volume deals with the competencies of the coach, an arena of study still in serious need of further definition and clarity. Perhaps we are closer to a definition regarding "executive coaching," and perhaps we are better informed and more competent when it comes to practice; we're not sure! We hope this special theme issue will stimulate your thinking and enhance your practice.

What do we really know? Kampa-Kokesch and Anderson (see chap. 3, this volume) call attention to and review for us the considerable—and still growing—literature of executive coaching. Hart, Blattner, and Leipsic (see chap. 24, this volume), provide a helpful perspective on the perceptions among professionals regarding the distinctions between and overlaps in therapy and coaching. Interview data and narrative summaries make interesting and thought-provoking reading. Diedrich (see chap. 32, this volume) shares his experience in coaching executive *teams* rather than individuals. He suggests practice guidelines for this complicated intervention as facilitator and helper to the team.

Frisch (see chap. 20, this volume) calls our attention to the emerging role of the *internal* coach; this role is defined, and key issues are identified for further discussion and consideration. Finally, Kilburg (see chap. 22, this volume) focuses on the absence of a literature regarding intervention adherence or compliance in executive coaching. This article presents an eight-component model that addresses the outcome pathways of executive coaching assignments and suggests a possible adherence protocol.

As we continue to focus our efforts to define both the concepts and the practices of this rapidly expanding and largely ill-defined competency area of consultation, we hope to further advance your thinking as well as your practice and stimulate continued discussion, inquiry, and refinement of a practice that is still more art than science!

Reference

Hudson, F. M. (1999). *The handbook of coaching: A comprehensive resource guide for managers, executives, consultants, and human resource professionals*. San Francisco: Jossey-Bass.

CHAPTER 6

TRUDGING TOWARD DODOVILLE: CONCEPTUAL APPROACHES AND CASE STUDIES IN EXECUTIVE COACHING

Richard R. Kilburg

The history of this special issue of the *Consulting Psychology Journal: Practice and Research* really began with the work that was undertaken to support the first special issue (Kilburg, 1996). After looking through the literature available at that time, I concluded that there was very little empirical research supporting the validity or reliability of coaching interventions with executive clients. Recent reviews of the coaching literature have been provided by Kampa-Kokesch and Anderson (see chap. 3, this volume) and Kampa and White (2002). Kampa and White summarized the five known empirical studies produced in the late 1990s and early 2000s. They stated that "the studies reviewed do provide evidence that executive coaching may positively impact individual productivity at the most senior levels, and that this increased productivity is potentially leverageable for the increased productivity of the entire organization" and "that coaching results in increased learning, increased self-awareness and development, and more effective leadership" (p. 153). Most of these studies were conducted as field research projects by graduate students, but collectively they suggest that the subdiscipline of executive coaching has started to accumulate some modest empirical support for its efficacy.

In the meantime, books, training programs, and marketing initiatives by individuals and small and large consulting companies have literally exploded over the past 10 years. The interest in coaching continues to grow and coincides with the small but significant turn toward positive psychological interventions led by Seligman (2001), who stated, "I believe that a psychology of positive human functioning will arise that achieves a scientific understanding and effective interventions to build thriving individuals, families, and communities" (p. 7). Executive coaching focuses on improving the performance of leaders in organizations. To be sure, there are many situations in which clients need assistance in changing behaviors, attitudes, values, and emotions that are problematic and interfere with effective function. However, the focus nearly always remains on how to help people who have already demonstrated a great deal of competence and success get even better at what they do. This work is of necessity different in form, function, and somewhat in approach from the work with clients who appear in psychologists' offices for help with problems that create impairment and make life less than pleasant for them.

For all of the work that has been done to illuminate the subject of coaching in the past 15 or 20 years, what actually happens in coaching engagements remains quite mysterious. Coaching books and articles tend to focus on the what and how of

I thank Dick Diedrich for his ongoing editorial support and intuitive wisdom in guiding the creation of a significant part of the knowledge base for the practice of consulting psychology.
This chapter is an abridged version of the introductory material to a 2005 special issue of the *Consulting Psychology Journal: Research and Practice, 56*, 203–213.

various methods that individual practitioners are inventing, reinventing, and sometimes renaming. A review of the PsycINFO database for this article revealed 96 entries on executive coaching since 1996. Those entries focus mainly on articles published in the journals that are covered by the American Psychological Association. Virtually all of the books that have appeared in the same time frame are ignored by that database. Thus, it appears that the field is accumulating a literature composed largely of first-person accounts of coaching approaches as well as a very modest set of efforts to provide more empirical support for the entire discipline done mostly by graduate students.

As a consumer of and contributor to this growing literature on executive coaching, I have been concerned about the absence of other forms of data about coaching and particularly about the lack of detailed case studies that describe what practitioners actually do with their clients. Our clinical colleagues have a rich and storied set of cases upon which to draw for educational and research purposes. Beginning with Freud's original contributions on cases like Little Hans and Rat Man (Freud, 1909/1955), they have continuously enlivened their literature with rich narrative streams of data (Wurmser, 2000). The whole field of medicine itself has a long and storied tradition of learning from case studies. And the leadership literature is replete with biographies, autobiographies, and other forms of case summaries (Heifetz, 1994; Neustadt & May, 1986; R. Smith & Emshwiller, 2003). As an avid reader of cases, I concluded that perhaps it was time to provide our own subdiscipline with some examples of experienced coaches working with their clients. Happily, Dick Diedrich, editor of *Consulting Psychology Journal: Practice and Research*, concurred, and this special issue focusing on case studies of executive coaching was born.

DODOVILLE AS DESTINATION

In his review of perhaps the only true case study of coaching that appeared in the literature in the past 10 years, Kralj (2001), Rodney Lowman (2001) provided an extraordinary critique and call to arms within the field of executive coaching. He stated,

"In the academic enterprise, the goal is to search for universal truths, which means using microscopic and antiseptic scrutiny, and especially to identify shortcomings, perceived weaknesses, and unanswered questions" (p. 119). Staying within this metaphorical medical model, he went on to suggest that organizational consulting psychology and the subdiscipline of executive coaching are still in the process of codifying executive coaching's taxonomies of organizational ills, diagnostic procedures, and interventions. He succinctly described the well-known, logical positivist approach taken by science in the past century and a half and encouraged the production of case studies as a way of helping to create a research base for organizational assessment and intervention. He also provided a four-part framework for the construction of case studies that would help in this effort. His model included a description of the specific case events and variables, diagnostic interpretations, specific interventions made, and plausible alternative explanations of the results of the effort. He also encouraged authors of cases to discuss alternative interpretations of the data as well as limitations of the case and its methods. Thus, in the space of a few short paragraphs, Lowman advocated setting the entire discipline of organizational consulting psychology on the same paths pursued by scientific psychology as a whole and, in particular, he specifically, albeit metaphorically, embraced a medical/clinical, that is to say deficit repair, model for the theory and practice of executive coaching.

In his advocacy, Lowman implicitly endorsed the logical positivist and modernist approaches to scientific inquiry that are now the sine qua non of classic academic psychology. For the past 125 years, the fields of medicine and psychology have structured themselves around the concepts and methodologies that represent this approach. Indeed, most of modern psychology in the 20th century was devoted to the creation of this scientific foundation with its emphasis on mathematically testable hypotheses, reliable and valid controlled studies, clearly defined measures, and findings that can be challenged by colleagues who could repeat the reported experiments. The approach has yielded the vast array of theories, models, and findings that now make up the discipline.

As far as creating interventions in the lives of human beings in order to help them, clinical and counseling psychology have largely led the way in the field. Starting in the 1930s and 1940s, calls for scientific studies of treatment outcomes (M. L. Smith & Glass, 1977) ultimately led to the creation of a huge infrastructure to study clinical interventions. Over the last half of the 20th century, hundreds of controlled studies focusing on ameliorating various ills and problems were conducted in the name of science and to prove the contributions that purely psychological methods could make to the problems of human illness and well-being. These psychological studies paralleled the huge research base that has been created in the various areas of specialty medical practice. As a result, the world has witnessed the rise of modern medical practice in which clinical and counseling psychology now play a small part.

As realistic as the advances have been, they are not without their problems and controversies. In 1995, Division 12's (Clinical Psychology) Task Force on Promotion and Dissemination of Psychological Procedures and the American Psychological Association (APA) Task Force on Psychological Intervention Guidelines (1995) began to call formally for a focus on "empirically validated therapies" partly out of a firm belief in the methods and results of modernism's scientific approach and partly out of a concern that similar calls for scientifically supported treatments in medicine and particularly in biological psychiatry could leave psychological treatment out of the market for reimbursable health care services (Chambless & Hollon, 1998; Wampold, 2001; Wampold et al., 1997). These calls for empirical foundations have generated both considerable support and equally considerable controversy (Goodheart, 2004; Koocher, 2004; Levant, 2003). Interestingly, the controversies were largely anticipated by Rosenzweig (1936) in a remarkably prescient article on the common factors he identified in the various methods of psychotherapy that had arisen by then. It is not my intent, nor is it possible in the scope of this introductory article, to repeat either the controversies or summarize the literature on psychotherapy outcomes. However, as we collectively stand at the beginning of the relatively new subdiscipline of executive coaching that is implicitly embracing the scientific method as a major part of its conceptual and operational foundations, I think that it is appropriate that we pause for just a few minutes to reflect on just what over a century of science has produced in clinical and counseling psychology and then to ask whether this is the sole path that we want to pursue as we continue to develop and implement coaching interventions with leaders.

Rosenzweig (1936) organized his article around a small section of Lewis Carroll's legendary *Alice's Adventures in Wonderland* (1865/1962). In the latter part of that story, the animals, drenched by Alice's tears, are set loose in a race run in random directions with the sole goal of drying themselves off. After a time, the race itself is stopped, and the dodo bird is asked, "Who has won?" The bird responds, "Everybody has won, and all must have prizes." Within that metaphor, Rosenzweig went on to describe some of the nonspecific effects he believed were contributing to the general reported success of the variety of psychotherapies that had been invented by that time (Duncan, 2002). The psychotherapy outcome literature that has emerged during the past 70 years has largely validated Rosenzweig's observations about nonspecific factors while simultaneously trying to identify many other mechanisms that can help to account for the improvements that patients make in their lives as a result of psychotherapeutic interventions.

Beginning with M. L. Smith and Glass (1977), meta-analytic methodology has been applied to the wide variety of psychotherapy outcome studies. Generally, the findings of this and other meta-analytic studies have indicated that these interventions, regardless of their conceptual foundations and measurement methodologies, produce consistent positive effects in the lives of patients. More recently and specifically, Wampold et al. (1997) conducted an extensive meta-analytic study of the Dodo bird hypothesis that stated "when psychotherapies intended to be therapeutic are compared, the true differences between them are 0" (p. 203). As of 1995, 18 therapies had been identified as meeting the criteria for being empirically valid (American Psychological Association Task Force on Psychological Intervention Guidelines, 1995, Table 3). However, the challenge in psychotherapy is quite vast, as was suggested by Goldfried and Wolfe (1996) when they stated that there are more than 250 identified forms of psychotherapy and more than 300 different forms of disorder. Despite attempting to identify all of the known comparison studies, Wampold et al. (1997) forthrightly declared that their meta-analytic review could not be said to be conclusive with regard to the complete comparative matrix of 250-plus forms of treatment and 300-plus forms of disorder. Indeed, as extensive as the psychotherapy outcome literature has become, it is clear that only a few of the cells of the matrix have been explored and those have tended to emphasize the behavioral and cognitive–behavioral forms of therapy. Nevertheless, Wampold et al. did conclude,

> The results of our analysis demonstrated that the distribution of effect sizes produced by comparing two bona fide psychotherapeutic treatments was consistent with the hypothesis that the true difference is zero. Moreover, the effect sizes produced by such comparisons were not related to the similarity of the treatments compared, nor did they increase as a function of time. Finally, this study examined only direct comparisons between therapies so that the results are not confounded by differences in outcome measures. In all, the findings are entirely consistent with the Dodo bird conjecture. (p. 211)

Wampold (2001) reviewed these issues in a comprehensive, book-length treatment of the models, methods, and findings of the empirically validated treatment literature and expanded on the ideas and complexities introduced in the 1997 article, and a very recent parallel assessment by Gotham (2004) demonstrated that the controversy and conflict involving empirically supported treatments is not going away any time soon.

I find it somewhat ironic, intellectually puzzling, and paradoxically reassuring that after a century of trying to specify the effectiveness of psychotherapy, the field now finds itself dealing with the major empirical conclusion that the differences between approaches would appear to be nil but nevertheless positive for patients across problem conditions. One is tempted to conclude that what we are doing in psychotherapy has real and lasting value but that the conceptual and technical differences in the approaches therapists take appear to be irrelevant. However, we probably need much more research to be able to draw that conclusion safely. Interestingly enough, however, as we look at the rather meager scientific evidence currently available, those of us doing coaching interventions with leaders of organizations would appear to be facing a similar set of research conclusions without the benefit of hundreds of additional studies structured along the lines of the modernist and positivist model and conducted by three generations of academic researchers. Indeed, without the university-based infrastructure of clinical and counseling psychology to draw on and in the absence thus far of any true scientific interest in these kinds of interventions by industrial/organizational psychology that could provide the resources to begin a more thorough scientific investigation of coaching interventions, it looks like executive coaching will continue to limp along scientifically for the next decade or so entirely dependent on those few graduate students whose flairs of scientific creativity and modernist interest will illuminate our lives. I am left to conclude that whether we like it or not, practitioners of executive coaching have seemingly become more or less permanent residents of the empirical realms of Dodoville, having never consciously established that as a goal for ourselves, because it appears that the studies done to date demonstrate positive, nonspecific effects regardless of the conceptual foundations espoused by practitioners. It would also appear that the general systems principle of equifinality (Von Bertalanffy, 1968), which partially states that systems ultimately get to the same end point regardless of the starting conditions, has us firmly in its grasp.

In their recent article, Cacioppo, Semin, and Berntson (2004) further explored these issues in an effort to integrate profound differences in approaches to the methods and results of science and the philosophy of science. They concluded that psychologists should readily and actively embrace radically different paradigms in the firm belief that the true nature of any psychological phenomena will be more clearly revealed and better understood if scientists can master such multiplicity. If we follow the encouragement of Lowman (2001) implicitly, we might be tempted to conclude that Dodoville would seem to be the permanent empirical home to which we should aspire. I do not suggest this out of cynicism. It simply strikes me that what we may be seeing is the emergence of a more generalizable finding with regard to psychological interventions in human lives. You could state that overarching result in the following way: The majority of humans who welcome the influence of other people in their lives appear to achieve more or less permanent positive results as a result of those interventions almost regardless of the specific theory or techniques used by the helping agents. Admittedly, there are also consistent findings that certain forms of traumatizing interventions can produce permanent damage, such as when therapists or others sexually victimize their patients. In the end, we seem to find ourselves where Rosenzweig (1936) suggested we were heading. It would appear to be reasonable to conclude that the nonspecific aspects of helping create most of the positive leverage for change in human lives.

THE NARRATIVE CRITIQUE AND OTHER WAYS OF KNOWING

Beginning in the middle of the 20th century, modernism and logical positivism themselves began to come under critical observation (Gergen, 1999) and ultimately were attacked with an enhanced set of analytic tools that have been described as "postmodern" or "constructivist" theory. Again, it is impossible in the context of this supposedly short introduction to the special issue to thoroughly review the nature of the critique and methods used to conduct that examination. Suffice it to say that Gergen's (1999) overview of these issues provides a rather brilliant and altogether understandable synthesis of many of the problems, approaches, and issues that the postmodern assessment raises about the nature of the world itself and the nature of the scientific world as a component of the larger cosmos. At its core, postmodernism suggests that we humans construct what we see, hear, experience, and understand. That is to say, all of what we know and how we know it come to us as the primary results of our creative interaction with events, people, things, places, and so forth. Once a person is willing to accept such a premise, then it becomes possible to examine the acts that humans undertake to produce such creatively constructed realities (Polkinghorne, 1988). What is most interesting is that constructivism draws our human attention equally to what a person does not use or excludes in the creation of such realities. Indeed, one of the basic tenets of modern science is that its practitioners are ethically and morally bound to report as accurately as possible the ideas, logic, methods, and results of their experimental constructions. The very foundation of science as we learn and know it consists of the research report submitted to a jury of peers who examine the experimental construction for its integrity and merit before allowing it to be shared with the scientific community at large. The scientific edifice is now global in scope and is unlikely to be displaced as the fundamental arbiter of what is true in or about the world for some time to come. Nevertheless, the postmodern critique of science has been quite vigorous and is producing its own results. Bruner (1986) suggested a very important way of understanding the conflict between modernist and postmodernist perspectives when he stated that "there are two modes of cognitive functioning, two modes of thought, each providing distinctive ways of ordering experience, of constructing reality" (p. 11). He went on to describe these modes as the paradigmatic and narrative approaches to constructing understanding in the world:

> One mode, the paradigmatic or logico-scientific one, attempts to fulfill the ideal of a formal, mathematical system

> of description and explanation. It employs categorization or conceptualization and the operations by which categories are established, instantiated, idealized, and related one to the other to form a system. Its armamentarium of connectives includes on the formal side such ideas as conjunction and disjunction, hyperonymy and hyponymy, strict implication, and the devices by which general propositions are extracted from statements in their particular contexts. At a gross level, the logico-scientific mode . . . deals in general causes and in their establishment, and makes use of procedures to assure verifiable reference and to test for empirical truth.
>
> The imaginative application of the narrative mode leads instead to good stories, gripping drama, believable (although not necessarily "true") historical accounts. It deals in human or human-like intention and action and the vicissitudes and consequences that mark their course. It strives to put its timeless miracles into the particulars of experience, and to locate the experience in time and place. Joyce thought of the particularities of the story as epiphanies of the ordinary. (pp. 12–13)

As might be predicted, some psychological scientists have readily embraced this dualistic taxonomy and proceeded to apply the empirical paradigm to the narrative approach to constructing reality (Sarbin, 1986). It only seems fair after all that if the paradigmatic mode is to be critiqued by the narrative that the practitioners of the paradigmatic should return the favor. Thus, psychology has enjoyed the emergence of a subfield of inquiry examining narratives and trying to provide empirical support for their validity.

The narrative approach has distant roots in the empiricist 20th century. McAdams (1993, 2001) is perhaps one of the best known of the recent theorists. He suggested that human identity assumes the form of a story with setting, scenes, character, plot, and themes. He further elaborated that stories are rooted in biographical facts accumulated throughout life, but that they expand beyond the facts because humans selectively edit their experience and actively imagine their past and future in creating stories that make sense to them and to their audiences. Habermas and Bluck (2000) reviewed the literature on life stories and concluded that "as far as possible with the existing research, we have lent both theoretical and empirical support to the emergence of the life story in adolescence" (p. 764). Howard (1991) and Singer and Bluck (2001) provided additional examples of the rigorous efforts being made to explore empirically the narrative mode of cognition described by Bruner (1986).

Stepping away slightly from the narrative research model, it is also possible to view this dialogue between the paradigmatic and narrative modes of thought through the lens of qualitative versus quantitative approaches to research. Denzin and Lincoln (1998, 2003a, 2003b) did a marvelous job of illuminating the landscape of qualitative inquiry and its challenges and promises. Within the qualitative disciplines, narrative exploration is merely one of a number of methods that can be used to create understandings of life. Denzin and Lincoln explored a variety of approaches to inquiry, including ethnography and participant observation, phenomenology, ethnomethodology and interpretive practice, grounded theory, biographical method, historical method, applied and action research, clinical models, and case studies. Stake (1998) explored the subject of case studies in detail. Van Maanen (1988) suggested that there are at least seven choices of presentation styles of cases: realistic, impressionistic, confessional, critical, formal, literary, and jointly told. Stake (1998) himself reported that "case content evolves in the act of writing itself" (p. 93). He believed that "naturalistic, ethnographic case materials, to some extent, parallel natural experience, feeding into the most fundamental processes of awareness and experience" (p. 94). He called these processes "naturalistic generalization" (Stake & Trumbull, 1982, p. 94).

Through cases, "the reader comes to know some things told, as if he or she had experienced them. Enduring meanings come from encounter, and are modified and reinforced by repeated encounter" (Stake, 1998, pp. 94–95; Stake & Trumbull, 1982).

Practitioners of organizational consulting psychology and executive coaching as a subspecialty area of service within that discipline would thus seem to be faced with an interesting and somewhat daunting prospect. We have a rather nascent traditional scientific literature that suggests that we are on course in developing intervention approaches in the lives of our executive clients that produce consistent positive results. Thus, it would seem that the paradigmatic approach to understanding truth within the coaching field has begun to yield findings that parallel those that have emerged over the past 100 years of investigation of psychotherapy by our clinical and counseling psychology colleagues. If these findings continue to hold up, it would seem then that we are indeed trudging down the path toward Rosenzweig's (1936) Dodoville, a habitat in which most, if not all, coaching methods will produce positive results from a variety of difficult-to-specify but nonetheless real common causes. Dodoville would also become a home in which all coaching practitioners who produce positive results will deserve prizes and should be welcome. However, our constructivist and narratively oriented colleagues would also have us challenge ourselves to reflect on this journey, the purposes for which it is being made, the methods of meaning making that are used or not used, the findings and interpretations of the findings obtained, and the ultimate learnings derived. It would seem that the constructivists would also have us simultaneously consider collecting and validating information using more qualitative approaches such as narrative theory, participant observation, ethnographic research, and case studies. They would encourage us not to stray from maintaining reflective discipline on the forms and findings that the narrative and case approaches could shape in our ways of learning and knowing. So it would seem that as we consultants wait for the results of the correlations, analyses of variance, analyses of covariance, path analyses, and multiple regressions designed to test the efficacy of various forms of coaching to come rolling in to challenge and educate us, we could also curl up in front of our fires with some good stories of how our colleagues are entering into the worlds of their clients and trying to help them make sense and meaning of what they encounter along the roads they travel together. From such stories, case studies if you will, we can reasonably expect the modernist science branch of the field to generate more hypotheses and more empirical studies for us to consider. In the grip of this eternal dialectic between the narrative and paradigmatic modes of thought and study, we surely will continue to grow and hopefully prosper.

References

American Psychological Association Task Force on Psychological Intervention Guidelines. (1995). *Template for developing guidelines: Interventions for mental disorders and psychological aspects of physical disorders.* Washington, DC: American Psychological Association.

Bruner, J. (1986). *Actual minds, possible worlds.* Cambridge, MA: Harvard University Press.

Cacioppo, J. T., Semin, G. R., & Berntson, G. G. (2004). Realism, instrumentalism, and scientific symbiosis: Psychological theory as a search for truth. *American Psychologist, 59,* 214–223.

Carroll, L. (1962). *Alice's adventures in Wonderland.* Harmondsworth, Middlesex, England: Penguin Books. (Original work published 1865)

Chambless, D. L., & Hollon, S. D. (1998). Defining empirically supported therapies. *Journal of Consulting and Clinical Psychology, 66,* 7–18.

Denzin, N. K., & Lincoln, Y. S. (Eds.). (1998). *Strategies of qualitative inquiry.* London: Sage.

Denzin, N. K., & Lincoln, Y. S. (Eds.). (2003a). *Collecting & interpreting qualitative materials.* London: Sage.

Denzin, N. K., & Lincoln, Y. S. (Eds.). (2003b). *The landscape of qualitative research: Theories & issues* (2nd ed.). London: Sage.

Duncan, B. L. (2002). The legacy of Saul Rosenzweig: The profundity of the dodo bird. *Journal of Psychotherapy Integration, 12,* 32–57.

Freud, S. (1955). Two case histories ("little Hans and the rat man"). In J. Strachey (Ed.),*The standard edition of the complete psychological works of Sigmund Freud* (Vol. 10, pp. 153–318). London: Hogarth Press. (Original work published 1909)

Gergen, K. J. (1999). *An invitation to social construction.* London: Sage.

Goldfried, M. R., & Wolfe, B. E. (1996). Psychotherapy practice and research: Repairing a strained alliance. *American Psychologist, 51,* 1007–1016.

Goodheart, C. (2004). Evidence-based practice & the endeavor of psychotherapy. *The Independent Practitioner, 24*(1), 6–10.

Gotham, H. J. (2004). Diffusion of mental health and substance abuse treatments: Development, dissemination, and implementation. *Clinical Psychology: Science and Practice, 11,* 160–178.

Habermas, T., & Bluck, S. (2000). Getting a life: The emergence of the life story in adolescence. *Psychological Bulletin, 126,* 748–769.

Heifetz, R. A. (1994). *Leadership without easy answers.* Cambridge, MA: Harvard University Press.

Howard, G. S. (1991). Culture tales: A narrative approach to thinking, cross-cultural psychology, and psychotherapy. *American Psychologist, 46,* 188–197.

Kampa, S., & White, R. P. (2002). The effectiveness of executive coaching: What we know and what we still need to know. In R. L. Lowman (Ed.), *Handbook of organizational consulting psychology* (pp. 139–158). San Francisco: Jossey-Bass.

Kilburg, R. R. (Ed.). (1996). Executive coaching [Special issue]. *Consulting Psychology Journal: Practice and Research, 48*(2).

Koocher, J. P. (2004). Three myths about empirically validated therapies. *The Maryland Psychologist, 49*(1), 12–13.

Kralj, M. M. (2001). Coaching at the top: Assisting a chief executive and his team. *Consulting Psychology Journal: Practice and Research, 53,* 108–116.

Levant, R. F. (2003). The empirically validated treatment movement: A practitioner perspective. *The Maryland Psychologist, 49*(1), 7, 15, 18.

Lowman, R. L. (2001). Constructing a literature from case studies: Promises and limitations of the method. *Consulting Psychology Journal: Practice and Research, 53,* 119–123.

McAdams, D. P. (1993). *The stories we live by: Personal myths & the making of the self.* New York: Guilford Press.

McAdams, D. P. (2001). The psychology of life stories. *Review of General Psychology, 5,* 100–122.

Neustadt, R. E., & May, E. R. (1986). *Thinking in time: The uses of history for decision makers.* New York: Free Press.

Polkinghorne, D. E. (1988). *Narrative knowing and the human sciences.* Albany, NY: SUNY Press.

Rosenzweig, S. (1936). Some implicit common factors in diverse methods in psychotherapy. *American Journal of Orthopsychiatry, 6,* 412–415.

Sarbin, T. R. (1986). *Narrative psychology: The storied nature of human conduct.* New York: Praeger.

Seligman, M. E. P. (2001). Positive psychology, positive prevention, and positive therapy. In C. R. Snyder & S. J. Lopez (Eds.), *Handbook of positive psychology* (pp. 3–9). New York: Oxford University Press.

Singer, J. A., & Bluck, S. (2001). New perspectives on autobiographical memory: The integration of narrative processing & autobiographical reasoning. *Review of General Psychology, 5,* 91–99.

Smith, M. L., & Glass, G. V. (1977). Meta-analysis of psychotherapy outcome studies. *American Psychologist, 32,* 752–760.

Smith, R., & Emshwiller, J. R. (2003). *24 days: How two* Wall Street Journal *reporters uncovered the lies that destroyed faith in corporate America.* New York: Harper Business.

Stake, R. E. (1998). Case studies. In N. K. Denzin & Y. S. Lincoln (Eds.), *Strategies of qualitative inquiry* (pp. 88–109). London: Sage.

Stake, R. E., & Trumbull, D. J. (1982). Naturalistic generalizations. *Review Journal of Philosophy & Social Science, 7,* 1–12.

Van Maanen, J. (1988). *Tales of the field: On writing ethnography.* Chicago: University of Chicago Press.

Von Bertalanffy, L. (1968). *General systems theory.* New York: Braziller.

Wampold, B. E. (2001). *The great psychotherapy debate: Models, methods, and findings.* Mahwah, NJ: Erlbaum.

Wampold, B. E., Mondin, G. W., Moody, M., Stich, F., Benson, K., & Ahn, H. (1997). A meta-analysis of outcome studies comparing bona-fide psychotherapies: Empirically, "all must have prizes." *Psychological Bulletin, 122,* 203–215.

Wurmser, L. (2000). *The power of the inner judge: Psychodynamic treatment of the severe neuroses.* New York: Jason Aronson.

CHAPTER 7

EXECUTIVE COACHING: THE ROAD TO DODOVILLE NEEDS PAVING WITH MORE THAN GOOD ASSUMPTIONS

Rodney L. Lowman

The special series of articles on executive coaching assembled and edited by my long-time colleague and friend Richard R. Kilburg (see Kilburg, 2004, 2005) spans a number of theories and applications of executive coaching. I focus in this chapter on a few central issues raised by the series, including possible integration points and common themes among the disparate directions represented in the articles. I also attempt, to the extent the articles are representative of the field of executive coaching, to suggest directions the field needs to go next if this area aims to become something more than a practice-dominated collection of "how-to" guidance.

Kilburg, one of the psychologist-founders of the literature of executive coaching, has been a prolific contributor to this emerging literature. His writing (e.g., chap. 1, this volume; Kilburg, 2000) is both practice- and theory-based. No armchair theoretician, he and his colleagues have been very much immersed in the practice of coaching, in the challenging work of generalizing from experience to theory, and in testing theory at least against phenomenology and a pragmatic sense of what works and does not in the real-to-life work of professional practice. The consulting work he and his colleagues have done at Johns Hopkins University, presumably the archetype of the land of science, in diffusing coaching and organizational consultation approaches in a type of organization (education) that has largely been resistant to it is indeed impressive. Moreover, there are few professionals writing about coaching today who are as knowledgeable about a wide range of psychological literature as Kilburg. From this impressive base he has constructed various models and theories of coaching. These include a 17-dimensional model of psychodynamic and organizational systems (Kilburg, 2000; see also chap. 18, this volume).

The colleagues whose work is represented in this two-part special issue of the *Consulting Psychology Journal* span diverse applications. Most are practitioners rather than academics, though two are based in academic settings (where they work mostly as internal consultants rather than primarily as academics). These contributors therefore reflect the broader state of the field of executive coaching (at least of the type practiced by psychologists) that to date has caught on more as an area of practice than as one of theory or research.

STRENGTHS OF THE SERIES

There is much to positively recognize among any group of psychologists who are willing to put descriptions of their professional practice with specific clients into print for their colleagues and others to critique. Carefully described case material and identification of attempted interventions and observed outcomes are the stuff from which

This chapter is an abridged version of the introductory material to a 2005 special issue of the *Consulting Psychology Journal: Practice and Research*, 57, 90–96.

theories and ultimately empirical tests can be derived. Staying close to real-life experience enhances the likelihood that theories will ultimately be developed that have practical utility. Adding the perspectives of the person being coached (e.g., chap. 35, this volume) is especially useful because what interventionists think may be of importance to a process of change may not be what was viewed as being most helpful by the client.

There are also limits to what case study material and nonempirically derived theories can do. There are significant limits to self-reported case studies. Peterson (chap. 35, this volume), for example, charges readers to aim toward greatness in executive coaching and observes that "good, however, is the enemy of great" (p. 358). Unfortunately, he does not define the criteria of greatness in this field and leaves us therefore with an aspirational goal but little understanding of the desired end-state or the road that will take us there. Self-reports are inevitably biased by the human tendency to positive self-presentation and ego protection/enhancement.

In advocating, if that is not too strong a word, for a narrative-constructivist model of case studies as a counter as opposed to the so-called "academic" approach assumed to be based on logico-deductive empiricism, Kilburg (see chap. 6, this volume) suggests that the traditional routes that psychologists take from their scientist-practitioner models may lead us to the land of "Dodoville," in which everything is equally valid and everyone is entitled to a prize.

LESSONS FROM THE DODO

Kilburg's (see chap. 6, this volume) analogy of Dodoville reflects his apparent unhappiness with the psychotherapy efficacy literature's persistent findings (e.g., Wampold et al., 1997) that have tended to empirical support only for general rather than for specific effects for the various approaches to psychotherapy, such as those represented by various schools such as cognitive, psychoanalytic, or psychodynamic. Kilburg wonders, at least by implication, if it is worth "trudging to Dodoville" if all we find when we get there is nonspecific effects that presumably would not match the theory-driven approaches suggested by some of these articles (e.g., chaps. 16–19 and 34, this volume).

In this context, it is worth noting that Dodoville is presumably fictional, but the dodo bird was not. The dodo became, over time, a poorly designed "bird" that appears to have evolved to flightlessness by the curious happenstance of ending up in a land with much food and no predators. There was no need to travel widely or scout for new food sources and no need to be nimble and able to flee predators. According to the American Museum of Natural History (http://www.amnh.org), the dodo bird became extinct less than 80 years after its first sighting by humans in Mauritius around 1600. The flightless design worked only so long as the environment was quiescent. When the sources of food in the dodos' environment decreased because of the destruction of the forested habitat and the introduction of predators in the form of animals being imported by man, the design failed and the bird became extinct. "Fat and happy," but ultimately extinct, is one way to view that history.

CAN EXECUTIVE COACHING EVOLVE WITHOUT A SCIENTIFIC FOUNDATION?

Executive coaching has a following and not just among psychologists. It has market power, it is popular both with consumers and service providers, and it shows promise as a new outlet for psychological services, but as of this writing, as a psychological approach, it lacks a scientific base. In the absence of rigorous debate, vigorous empirical tests, and the revision of theory and practice based on those findings, intervention methodologies run the risk of either falling from their own bloatedness deriving from lack of intellectual exercise (the dodo's fate) or of becoming internally consistent belief systems, preaching faithfully to the choir if unconvincingly to those who prefer to sing from other music. Psychology's special, if no longer unique, imprint on a subject matter is the scientific study of human behavior. The field cannot have it both ways. It cannot assert it is exempt from the rules of scientific psychology while also laying claim to the mantle of psychology. (Interestingly,

Kilburg, chap. 6, this volume, while arguing for a narrative model of knowing, uses empiricism as the "gold standard" against which to demonstrate the existence of unconscious processes.)

If executive coaching puts itself in a position in which it considers case methodology to be an adequate and sufficient substitute for empirical evaluation, relying exclusively on a "constructivist narrative" approach, its days, at least as a field that potentially belongs in the house of psychology, may be as numbered as few as were those of the dodo bird. I argue instead that scientific and logico-positive approaches to evaluating the effectiveness of executive coaching are the friend, not the enemy, of effective coaching. At this time there is no basis for concluding (a) that coaching is a validated treatment; (b) if there are effects, that they are specific rather than general; and (c) that certain techniques work best with certain kinds of issues, coaches, and/or clients. Even if, after years of research (most of which has scarcely begun), it is demonstrated empirically that coaching has overall effectiveness but only because of general factors rather than because of those factors advocated by practitioners of a particular theory or approach, that is not a bad finding. For now, the psychotherapy literature demonstrating that general rather than specific factors are important in therapy cannot be the basis for drawing any conclusions about coaching because coaching is geared to a different population, with different purposes, and with different outcome criteria. Dodoville may be the destination of coaching research literature, or it may not be. Without the necessary research there is little basis currently for drawing any conclusions. And in the absence of a rich and expanding empirical literature, the theoreticians, the dodo birds of today, get fatter but not necessarily healthier. If Dodoville is the ultimate destination of such research, coaches, or at least the psychologists among them, need to know that so they do not base their practice on false presumptions. They are of course free to practice coaching from whatever perspective they want, but it cannot pretend to be validated or even psychology (at least scientific psychology) if it is not anchored in empirical research.

Coaching of course does not have to be "owned" by the profession of psychology just as the field of psychotherapy is now only partially owned by psychology. Psychologists can and have taken up coaching as their primary professional activity and in so doing join the ranks of those from many different disciplines, or lack of any professional discipline, in conducting such work. Because there is a limited empirical literature on coaching's efficacy, they may be practicing on the basis of something other than psychology. What psychology uniquely brought to psychotherapy's table was the empirical assessment of what worked and what did not. The only unique claim psychology has to the field is that which generates from its rigor in researching what works and what does not in therapy and in extrapolating from a variety of methodologies—qualitative as well as quantitative—to create better and more refined theories.

Similarly, case study reportage can be done by coaches who enter the work from a variety of professional disciplines, including those who have no professional degrees before undertaking such work. It is to fields like psychology, however, that executive coaching must turn for the evaluation of the too often extravagant claims of effectiveness. When, as in the case of coaching, practice is considerably ahead of research, there is the danger of self-assuredness and advocacy for particular methods and techniques and argument and experience being used as a basis for action. I argue that to the extent executive coaching is in the domain of psychology at all, its proponents who are psychologists must proceed with caution and must do the necessary work. Ethical Standard 2.01, Boundaries of Competence of the Ethics Code of the American Psychological Association (APA, 2002, p. 5), provides relevant guidance in the meantime: "2. *Competence*—(e) In those emerging areas in which generally recognized standards for preparatory training do not yet exist, psychologists nevertheless take reasonable steps to ensure the competence of their work and to protect clients/patients, students, supervisees, research participants, organizational clients, and others from harm."

TOWARD STANDARDS OF CASE STUDIES: DOES ANYTHING GO IN DODOVILLE?

While there are widely held consensually agreed-to standards of the scientific, or what Kilburg calls the *logico-deductive*, models of scientific research, there are few consensually agreed upon criteria for case study development or presentation (see, among others, Lowman, 2001). Thus, as in this collection of cases, there can be wide variability in terms of what cases present, whether they demonstrate the application of a particular theory or technique or simply describe factually or interpretatively a particular set of events or actions, the extent to which they are descriptive or prescriptive, the extent to which the intervention is clearly described, and the description of outcome.

The choice of case material itself is another variable that implicitly matters for the development of a field. The articles in the series, not atypically, show a positive response bias in that mostly successful cases were chosen and presented. Not very many (though some, see, e.g., Mirvis & Berg, 1977) case collections have focused more on failures than on successes. Still, case material would be more helpful if the cases were anchored in a particular context other than the consultant's own perspectives. Is the individual one of 300 seen by the coach or one of 10? To what extent are the problems represented by the case prototypical of those in a practice? What variables (age, gender, educational background, and so forth) are represented in the case, and in what way were such dimensions influential in the case? Does this coach see individuals mainly of this type?—for how many sessions on average, and in what ways was this case similar or different from those in a practice or those in a particular class or category? A little more consistency in the framework of case material presentation will go a long way in being able, over time, to aggregate across case material.

Outcome criteria in cases also vary. There will be, of course, more credibility to case outcomes when outcome criteria are established at the beginning of an intervention and when the measures are multiple and not just subjective. Readers of this series will note some variability on these dimensions.

USES AND LIMITATIONS OF THE METHOD

I raise these issues of course not to suggest that the case approach is defective but, rather, to counter an implicit suggestion by Kilburg (see chap. 6, this volume) that the logico-deductive, scientific and the constructivist-narrative models are antithetical or that one is preferred. Each has its uses and its limitations. Case studies are perhaps most useful in the early and more mature stages of an emerging area of practice. Early on they are valuable for generating empirically testable hypotheses. Later on, having hopefully demonstrated that an approach or methodology works, they can be used to illustrate the artistry of applying an empirically validated technique. However, cases are not the basis on which to draw conclusions about what works and what does not in other settings or applications without further empirical validation. For example, Wasylyshyn (see chap. 36, this volume) notes, in generalizing from a particular approach to coaching: "This is an approach that can lead to sustained results—with clients who want to learn, have the courage to change, and who perceive the need for change as one of life's continuous gifts" (p. 384). This is an interesting hypothesis that could be tested in other settings and even with other case material. As a conclusion, however, it seems premature.

FROM WHENCE DOES GOOD THEORY DERIVE?

The use of case studies as a basis for creating a sound theory and ultimately empirical research literature is perhaps a necessary, or at least a commonly encountered, stage in the initial process of developing a new field of inquiry or practice. Case studies, or what Kilburg calls the "narrative approach" (chap. 6, this volume), have the advantage of describing, one hopes factually and accurately, a phenomenon, a way of approaching an intervention, and even, at least perceived, outcomes.

The contributions of case study development can be multiple, but, I would argue, it is decidedly not sufficient basis on which to base an empirically validated theory. Too much of the executive consulting literature to date, I argue, is derivative, not original, and in that sense it rests on a slippery slope if it intends to use primarily narrative approaches to present and evaluate applications of theory or research created for other purposes and in other contexts. This approach begins not with empirical research or even with an objective description of the phenomenon at hand from which it then seeks to create a theory and literature but, rather, with a theory in psychology derived for some other purpose and rather loosely plopped down on the new phenomenon being studied. And the ethics of psychologists do demand the science—for example, Ethics Standard 2.04, Bases for Scientific and Professional Judgments, states: "Psychologists' work is based upon established scientific and professional knowledge of the discipline" (APA, 2002, p. 5).

REQUISITE CONDITIONS

Necessarily, then, I suggest this series of cases is most useful for clinical purposes—thinking about what one believes has happened and why. Unfortunately, however, there was little search in the series for common factors and little energy expended in generating testable hypotheses. What hypotheses might be generated from the series about what works and does not in coaching? I would suggest that common themes from this collection of case studies might include the following:

1. The ability to establish a relationship of trust may be critical to the success of a particular intervention.
2. Coaching must take into account the environmental context in which it finds itself.
3. The particular model (rational–emotive, cognitive therapy, psychodynamic, and so forth) used by the coach may matter less than the firmness of the conviction held by the coach as to the efficacy of the model.
4. Coaching, when effective, removes barriers to individuals' understanding or solving issues faced in the workplace.
5. Effective coaching appears to focus more on strengths than weaknesses.
6. Effective coaching appears to be anchored in multiple levels: individual, group, and organizational/systemic.
7. Effective coaching appears especially to integrate individual psychology with organizational needs.

Other reviewers of this rich and helpful series will find other hypotheses. The implied work, however—and it is indeed time-consuming, tedious work with no short cuts—is empirical. That work may require a different skill set than that which seemed to predominate in this series. Neither is superior to the other, but neither is sufficient as a stand-alone approach or basis for drawing well-validated conclusions.

CONCLUSIONS

Narrative critique and logico-positivist and "modernist" approaches to scientific inquiry are not antithetical or mutually exclusive, nor do they benefit from going their separate ways. The models can and should intersect. Each approach has its own unique contributions to make and its own limitations. Ungrounded in the phenomena that it seeks to study, the traditional scientific approach to psychology is lifeless and irrelevant. Ungrounded in scientific evaluation of its theories and claims, the narrative critique method can lead to unfounded assumptions, advocacy on the basis of argument, and a mutual admiration society. Executive coaching as a psychological approach remains, at best, in its adolescence. The growth process is perhaps necessarily slow and incremental. If, however, consulting psychology wants to claim executive coaching as part of the field of psychology, it must be more rigorous and more demanding, and it must clearly differentiate established fact and advocacy.

References

American Psychological Association. (2002). *Ethical principles of psychologists and code of conduct 2002*. Washington, DC: Author.

Kilburg, R. R. (2000). *Executive coaching: Developing managerial wisdom in a world of chaos.* Washington, DC: American Psychological Association.

Kilburg, R. R. (Ed.). (2004). Trudging toward Dodoville—Part I: Conceptual approaches in executive coaching [Special issue]. *Consulting Psychology Journal: Practice and Research, 56*(4).

Kilburg, R. R. (Ed.). (2005). Trudging toward Dodoville—Part II: Case studies in executive coaching [Special issue]. *Consulting Psychology Journal: Practice and Research, 57*(1–2).

Lowman, R. L. (2001). Constructing a literature from case studies: Promise and limitations of the method. *Consulting Psychology Journal: Practice and Research, 53,* 119–123.

Mirvis, P. H., & Berg, D. N. (1977). *Failures in organization development and change: Cases and essays for learning.* New York: Wiley.

Wampold, B. E., Mondin, G. W., Moody, M., Stich, F., Benson, K., & Ahn, H. (1997). Meta-analysis of outcome studies comparing bona fide psychotherapies: Empirically, "all must have prizes." *Psychological Bulletin, 122,* 203–215.

CHAPTER 8

EXECUTIVE COACHING: AN OUTCOME STUDY

Karol M. Wasylyshyn

As companies continue to invest heavily in—and become more discerning about—executive coaching, psychologist coaches would be wise to lead the way in exploring critical questions about the value of this costly resource. These questions include the following: What are the key credential and experience factors in selecting a coach? What are the personal characteristics of effective coaches? Of the myriad tools a coach may use, what do executives really value? What are the indications of a successful coaching engagement? What are the factors that influence the sustainability of learning and/or behavior change?

To date, there has been little executive coaching outcome research (chap. 3, this volume). In this chapter, I present findings of my research with the caveat that these results are based solely on executives whom I coached between 1985 and 2001. I hope this research enriches coaches' thinking about coaching as a major development tool and about what it takes to achieve positive results. Furthermore, I ask this somewhat disquieting question: Are companies wasting money on executive coaching? This question is not about coach credentials or coach experience or coaching methodology. Rather, it's about the people who are coached: Which executives are most likely to benefit from coaching? This question is considered in the section titled "Sustainability of Learning and/or Behavior Change as a Result of Coaching." I suggest the use of a typology for evaluating prospective coaching engagements.

DEMOGRAPHICS

An overview of the demographics is presented in Table 8.1. The unusually high response rate (82%) is attributed to strong relationships I established and maintained with many clients as well as to the persistent combination of written, phone, and

TABLE 8.1

Demographics (N = 100)

Variable	%
Gender	
Male	85
Female	15
Age	
30–40	16
40–50	79
50+	5
Company size	
Fortune 500	79
Mid-sized	19
Entrepreneurial	2
Job level	
Senior executive (senior vice president and above)	30
Officer (vice presidents)	38
Director	32

Note. Survey sent to 106 executives coached between 1985 and 2001; 94% response rate.

e-mail follow-up efforts. The great majority (79%) of the executive participants were in the 40–50 year age group, male, and held at least director-level responsibility in their places of employment. While people are motivated to learn or change behavior at any point in the life span, high-potential business people are securing (and expecting!) significant leadership positions at earlier ages than has been customary. Therefore, companies focused on bench strength need to provide employees with high-impact leader development experiences sooner. One possible and cost-effective approach would be for companies to establish interdisciplinary networks of internal coaches (drawn from interested and skilled human resources [HR] professionals, other functional staff, and line managers and leaders). These individuals could be trained and supported by consulting psychologists. (When and if companies take this idea seriously, perhaps it opens the way for a new role on the corporate roster: chief psychology officer, or CPO?)

The vast majority of participants (85%) were White men. As workplace demographics continue to change, expatriate rotations increase, and recruiting challenges intensify, companies will need to be more intentional about providing customized developmental resources to a much broader population of employees.

EXECUTIVES' REACTION TO THE IDEA OF WORKING WITH A COACH

Reactions to working with a coach were significantly positive, over 75% (see Figure 8.1). However, over one third of the sample indicated a "guarded" or a negative response. (Note that respondents had more than one choice.) These guarded or negative responses are attributed to a host of questions about what executive coaching is, how it works, what value it may bring, and—of considerable significance—how having a coach is perceived in the organization.

76%	Positive (47%)—enthusiastic anticipation (29%)
31%	Guarded—didn't know what to expect
6%	Negative—didn't expect to get anything out of it
3%	Other (curiosity, resistance)

(Respondents had more than one choice)

FIGURE 8.1. Reaction to the idea of working with an executive coach.

As widespread as coaching has become, there is still a need for organization sponsors (boss and HR professional), as well as coaches, to be explicit about *what* it is, *why* it will bring value to the executive, and *how* it works. An explicit description of methodology that includes activities, roles, and time commitments can go a long way in establishing a positive reception to coaching. Table 8.2 presents this information for one phase (data gathering) of my methodology

An experienced coach can be an invaluable resource to a senior executive—even over a sustained period of time. However, there are a few cautions. These include the following: (a) The involvement of a coach should not absolve the boss from providing frequent and frank performance management; (b) the coach should not be the only "truth-teller" on the landscape; and (c) coaching at its best is not done in isolation; rather, it's a *collaborative* process among the executive, his or her boss, and the appropriate HR professional.

The so-called internal collaborators (boss and HR) must play a major role throughout the coaching process by (a) providing ongoing feedback to both the executive and the coach regarding perceived progress or lack of same; (b) helping to influence a positive perception among others in the organization of the executive's learning/change in behavior (assuming there is change); (c) providing positive reinforcement to the executive for his or her effort to change; and (d) remaining as engaged, supportive allies after the coaching engagement has concluded. Furthermore, organizations that use executive coaching as a development resource need to manage how it's perceived in the company, that is, they need to take steps to position it as a special investment in employees. Coaches, too, must be vigilant about the perception of their work and make every effort to influence the appropriate mindset—especially when they are gathering 360 data. For example, when 360-degree feedback is gathered face-to-face (my preference), each interview is

TABLE 8.2

Executive Coaching Model: Phase I—Data Gathering

Activities	Participants	Time frame (hours)
Initial discussion/needs assessment	Senior management, human resources partner, and coach	2–4
First meeting/needs assessment	Identified executive and coach	2
Agenda-setting meeting	Senior management, human resources partner, identified executive, and coach	1–2
Post–agenda-setting meeting	Identified executive and coach	1–2
Developmental history	Identified executive and coach	3
Testing (use of psychometric tools to profile personality preferences and management style)	Identified executive	3
Customization of interview protocol (used for 360-degree feedback)	Identified executive, senior management, human resources partner, and coach	3
360-degree data gathering—interviewing of company sources (boss, peers, and subordinates)	Coach	10–14[a]
Interview of family members (optional)	Family member and coach	2
Scoring, compilation, and analysis of testing and 360 data	Coach	16

[a]Depending on number of sources in sample.

begun with a probe, such as, "What's your understanding of why we're meeting today?" If the executive has invited people into the 360 sample personally, this probe is most likely to produce an on-target response, such as, "Well, you're coaching (name) and he/she wants to have the benefit of how he/she is perceived by others." However, people are not always invited into 360s personally, they may have some ax to grind, or they may be unduly cynical about this type of development activity. When the coach gets a less than accurate response to this probe, it's essential to clarify and attempt to draw the interviewee into a more accurate perspective. Similarly, when and if the boss or HR partner is asked questions about an employee's participation, it's critical that he or she represents the work as constructively as possible. In some companies, such as GlaxoSmithKline, Rohm and Haas Company, Pfizer, and Colgate–Palmolive, coaching has been positioned as an executive perk. This perspective of *investing in the best* has obvious positive implications for both organization perception and the client–coach working alliance.

CREDENTIAL OR EXPERIENCE FACTORS IN CHOOSING A COACH

The top three credential and experience criteria for executives in choosing coaches were (a) graduate training in psychology (82%), (b) experience in/understanding of business (78%), and (c) an established reputation as a coach (25%; see Figure 8.2). Talented executive coaches must be grounded in both business and psychology. Regarding

82%	Graduate level training in psychology
78%	Experience in business/general management
25%	Coaching experience and positive reputation
15%	Experience in client's industry/knowledge of company culture
12%	Trust in judgment of person who recommended coach
8%	Other (sufficient flexibility to accommodate to executive's schedule; good communication skill; common sense)

(Respondents had more than one choice)

FIGURE 8.2. Credentials and/or experience factors in selecting an executive coach.

psychology, this finding is consistent with Van-Fleet's (1999) contention that there are certain general psychological skills essential for effective coaches. These skills include interpersonal effectiveness, listening, empathy for widely differing groups, patience, adaptability, analytical problem solving, creativity, and humor. While coaches from a range of disciplines can possess these skills, there are coaching engagements that require the specific expertise of professionals who have been trained clinically—especially if sustained behavior change is the desired outcome. Wasylyshyn (2001) wrote, "Coaches who have not had training in psychology or in a related behavior science are less likely to be successful in handling referrals where an executive must change a deeply entrenched and dysfunctional behavior pattern" (p. 17). In referring to nonpsychologist coaches, Berglas (2002) stated, "By dint of their backgrounds and biases, they downplay or simply ignore deep-seated psychological problems they don't understand. Even more concerning, when an executive's problems stem from undetected or ignored psychological difficulties, coaching can actually make a bad situation worse" (p. 87).

Regarding business, psychologists who have not held business roles must amplify their business knowledge over time and through the interplay of experiences in different companies, industries, and global sectors, and by immersing themselves in the business literature, as well as germane training experiences. There is another important consideration in this context: semantics. The language psychologists use in speaking to executives and in applying psychology-based principles to the workplace can make or break credibility. Consider, for example, the difference between describing a company president, who reports to the chief executive officer (CEO) and is having a tough time getting along with him, as having an "intense negative paternal transference" versus the president's struggle with "being told what to do." Or, consider the difference between talking to a senior executive about the company's "work–family balance problem" versus "work–family *integration* as an employee retention issue." The first depiction of the work–family dynamic would likely not engage the executive very much at all, whereas the second is a more apt representation and is more likely to evoke engagement and even support of proactive policies and practices.

Finally, regarding the coach reputation finding, experienced coaches should be able to provide references from coached executives. Although it is helpful to have strong endorsement from people in HR and line management, little is as powerful as coachee testimonials.

PERSONAL CHARACTERISTICS OF AN EFFECTIVE EXECUTIVE COACH

The top three personal characteristics of an effective executive coach were (a) the ability to form a strong "connection" with the executive (86%), (b) professionalism (82%), and (c) use of a clear and sound coaching methodology (35%; see Figure 8.3).

In terms of forming strong connections with clients, coaches who work from a perspective of the executive as the client (vs. the organization as client) are likely to form faster and more substantive coaching relationships. Seasoned coaches discover how to work from this perspective—satisfying both the coached executive and the sponsoring organization. The onus is on the consultant to manage those relationships fully and appropriately. How to orchestrate the feedback of 360 data in a manner that satisfies both the coached executive and the internal collaborators (boss and HR) is an example of walking this line. An ideal approach finds (a) the consulting psychologist providing maximum specificity to the coached executive

86%	Forms strong "connection" with client (empathy, warmth, builds trust, listening skill, engages quickly)
82%	Professionalism (intelligence, integrity/honesty, confidentiality, objectivity)
35%	Sound coaching methodology (delivers "truth" constructively, contextual grounding, unearths core issues, use of psychometrics)

(Respondents had more than one choice)

FIGURE 8.3. Top personal characteristics of an effective executive coach.

(delivered with empathy and constructive guidance), (b) the coached executive providing "headlines" from the data to his or her boss and/or HR manager, and (c) the psychologist following up with the boss and/or HR manager to discuss and clarify information they've received from the coached executive.

As psychologists, maintaining stringent ethical standards regarding confidentiality, managing psychometric or other data, and managing the boundaries of relationships are second nature. These are important facets of how psychologists can distinguish themselves from other coaches whose work is not guided by a professional code of ethical practice.

Finally, in the absence of a proven methodology, coaching engagements can flounder, be too ambiguous, and/or limp to an unsatisfactory close. Coaches must be able to both articulate their models and demonstrate how they manage engagements for maximum impact. One powerful example of this is the use of customized interview protocols with face-to-face or telephonic data gathering versus published and/or electronically administered tools. Another is the explicit presentation of all coaching phase activities, as partially shown in Figure 8.3.

PROS AND CONS OF AN EXTERNAL COACH

All respondents (100%) indicated a positive response in favor of external coaches. Predictably, there was also high negative response (76%) due to external coaches' lack of company and/or industry knowledge (see Figure 8.4).

Trust and confidentiality were the primary factors in the preference for external coaches. If external coaches are to be maximally effective, it's critical that company decision makers and coaches identify efficient and substantive steps coaches can take to get grounded in the culture. There are distinct advantages for coaches who work in companies for extended periods—assuming they maintain objectivity and build relationships with senior HR professionals and senior executives. This deepens their grasp of major culture themes and the implications of these themes for leader effectiveness.

100% POSITIVE
- Objectivity
- Confidentiality
- Breadth of experience (other companies)
- Psychological expertise; better trained
- No "political agenda"
- Trust and integrity

76% NEGATIVE
- Insufficient knowledge of the company, its culture, industry, key executives

9% NEGATIVE
- Quick accessibility, availability
- Continuity, sustaining momentum

8% NEGATIVE
- Cost

(Respondents had more than one choice)

FIGURE 8.4. Pros and cons of the external coach.

PROS AND CONS OF AN INTERNAL COACH

A majority of respondents also indicated a strong positive response (70%) in favor of internal coaches. The significant negative response (79%) was due to questions about internal coaches' potential conflicts of interest, trust and ability to maintain confidentiality, and skill level (8%; see Figure 8.5).

Clearly, knowledge of the company and its executives are primary drivers in the preference for internal coaches. Furthermore, there are many coaching indications that can be handled quite well by inside coaches (e.g., skill building, on-the-spot conflict management, new leader assimilation, and so forth). Therefore, as suggested earlier,

70% POSITIVE
- Knowledge of the company, its culture, industry, and key executives
- Accessibility (6%)
- Cost (5%)

79% NEGATIVE
- Objectivity—conflict of interest
- Confidentiality—pressure to divulge information
- Less trust with clients

8% NEGATIVE
- Skill level—"practicing without a license"

(Respondents had more than one choice)

FIGURE 8.5. Pros and cons of the internal coach.

companies may be well served by establishing inside cadres of coaches who could be trained by consulting psychologists and supported by them on an as needed basis.

FOCUS OF EXECUTIVE COACHING ENGAGEMENTS

The vast majority of coaching engagements represented in this study focused on behavior changes executives wished to make for continued career success. These changes were specified as follows: personal behavior change (56%), enhancing leader effectiveness (43%), and fostering stronger relationships (40%). Notably, 17% of the sample cited personal development as the focus of their coaching. And another 7% cited a desire for better work–family integration as a key concern (see Figure 8.6).

On the basis of this finding, it would appear that a major challenge for coaches is to learn enough about their clients so they can pull the behavior change levers quickly. In the coaching of these executives, I used multifaceted data gathering that included a developmental history, a battery of psychometrics, customized 360 interview protocol (marital partner often included as a source), and a review of career aspirations as well as of current business challenges. Typically the psychometric battery included the Watson–Glaser Critical Thinking Appraisal; Myers–Briggs Type Indicator; the Life Styles Inventory; the NEO PI–R; the BarOn Emotional Quotient Inventory; and, at a client's option, the Rorschach. Careful weaving of all these data points accelerated my understanding of the clients and deepened the clients' perceived value of the coaching through fresh or deeper insights about behavioral drivers of their leadership.

This multifaceted data gathering and weaving of the data through constructive, caring feedback into a coherent and compelling profile also enriched and anchored the coaching agenda. In other words, specificity of the coaching agenda was achieved—specific areas were identified—either strengths to leverage or developmental needs. Furthermore, clients and I crafted preliminary action plans as a beginning template of actions that launched the behavior change efforts or supported new learning. Typically, at the conclusion of a coaching engagement, the executive and I would collaborate on a master action plan (MAP), a living document that captured all of the most useful actions that helped produce new learning and/or behavior change.

Another word about specificity of the coaching agenda. It is not uncommon for initial comments from the sponsoring organization's collaborators about a potential coaching agenda to be vague, obtuse, and maybe even off the mark—especially when there is no mention or consideration of key organization culture factors. For example, there is a big difference between a coaching engagement that's based on the company's depiction of an executive "needing to increase his/her effectiveness as a leader" versus a multifaceted data approach that reveals individual behavioral issues, such as perfectionism, micro-management, strained relationships with peers, and culture behavioral norms that include second guessing, intermittent reinforcement, and lack of candid feedback. In encountering a situation just like this, I had as much work to do with the executive's boss and HR partner as with the client.

Furthermore, many clients who wanted to become better leaders had issues in one or more of the four dimensions of emotional competence as defined by Goleman (1995) and represented by my acronym, SO SMART (self-observation, self-

56% PERSONAL BEHAVIOR CHANGE (listening, tact/diplomacy, collaboration, persuasion and influence, harsh self-criticism, timidity/self-confidence, shift from tactical to strategic, customer focus, stress reduction, managing perception of "ambition")
43% ENHANCING LEADERSHIP EFFECTIVENESS (projecting confidence, inspiring and motivating others, assimilation into new role, increase in scope)
40% FOSTERING STRONGER RELATIONSHIPS (focus = cluster of "emotional competence" factors, i.e., self-awareness, self-control, attunement to others, and building relationships)
17% PERSONAL DEVELOPMENT (legacy, career management, life stage transition)
7% WORK–FAMILY INTEGRATION

(Respondents had more than one choice)

FIGURE 8.6. Focus of executive coaching engagements.

management, attunement to others, and relationship traction). Strong emotional competence requires the awareness and management of one's emotions, and numerous research studies have made the business case for the importance of emotional competence at work. These include Cherniss and Goleman (2001), Spencer and Spencer (1993), and Walter V. Clarke Associates (1996).

The self-observation (SO) dimension of emotional competence includes the accurate assessment of one's strengths and limitations, a strong sense of self-worth, and the ability to recognize one's emotions and their effects on others. Self-management (SM) includes the ability to control potentially disruptive emotions and impulses, accountability, adaptability, achievement orientation, and the readiness to act. Attunement (A) to others involves the capacity for empathy; organizational awareness; and, from a work-related perspective, recognizing and striving to meet the needs of both internal and external customers. In the work context, relationship traction (RT) involves both leading and working with others in ways that foster deep, lasting, and meaningful relationships versus superficial connection. People who are strong in this dimension can align and inspire others, influence change, and communicate clearly and convincingly, and they are generally effective at developing the people who report to them. Executives with solid relationship traction can also manage conflict effectively and build collaborative teams.

These engagements necessitated both new learning and serious commitment to behavior change. While the construct of emotional competence can be a helpful vehicle for learning and behavior change, sustained results are dependent on coaches who are well-grounded in the knowledge domains of how people learn and change. These domains are primarily psychological.

Coaching where personal development issues predominated included proactive career management, career/life transition issues, and concerns about work-related legacy. Since these data were gathered, and especially in the wake of September 11, 2001, I have experienced an increase in executive coaching clients who want to discuss the meaning of their work and the pressures of work–family integration issues as part of their overall coaching agenda. Is this a trend? Or is it a passing reaction to recent traumatic events? Although this is a difficult question to gauge, effective coaches are wise to take a holistic approach in working with senior executives—and this could mean including the executive's marital partner as appropriate.

RATINGS FOR COACHING TOOLS

Executive coaches vary significantly in terms of the methodologies, approaches, tools, and durations of their executive coaching engagements. I typically work with an executive for a number of years, and in this study I explored coachees' preferences regarding the various coaching tools I used.

On a 1–10 rating scale, the three highest rated coaching tools were (a) coaching sessions (9.2), (b) 360 feedback (9.0), and (c) relationship with the coach (8.3). Over 50% of respondents also gave high ratings to testing (7.4) and readings on leadership (7.0).

High ratings attributed to the actual coaching sessions and to the relationship with the coach suggest that frequency and face-to-face contact are essential for successful coaching outcomes—especially when sustained behavior change is the desired outcome. These ratings may raise "buyer beware" cautions about increasingly popular coaching-by-phone and other coaching methodologies that minimize the importance of the "live" coach–executive working alliance.

Good chemistry with the coach, trust, confidentiality, and coach availability are key ingredients in a strong coaching alliance. Furthermore, effective coaches maintain momentum, dispense truth constructively, and truly care about the executives with whom they work—as manifested by numerous, spontaneous reach-outs to them throughout the coaching period.

Most executive coaches provide some form of 360 feedback. And while the use of published metrics—especially those that can be administered and scored electronically—is efficient and well-established, I question whether they are as useful as a customized approach. The use of customized interview protocols that require the coach to conduct face-to-face or telephonic interviews, while more labor intensive, has the advantages of eliciting rich behavioral examples and can help minimize the likelihood of skewed data.

These data also underscore the fact that executives like data. The power of an appropriate battery of psychometrics cannot be underestimated as an efficient way to surface relevant information—and insights. Psychologists have the broadest array of psychometric tools at their disposal and a set of ethical principles that ensures such data are managed appropriately.

The strong showing for readings on leadership underscores the point that different people learn in different ways, so coaches need to focus on how their clients learn best and tap into a repertoire of tools accordingly. For some, behavioral breakthrough may be a function of what the coach models or teaches in coaching meetings. For others, it may be the fresh insight about a deeply embedded behavior pattern. And for still others, it may be the readings, books, journal articles, audiotapes, films, poems, and so forth that the coach selects as vehicles for learning and/or behavior change. Clearly, high-impact executive coaching is more art than science—customization of each engagement is key. This is why programmatic, non–behaviorally based executive development approaches are inherently limited.

INDICATIONS OF SUCCESSFUL COACHING

As indicated in Figure 8.7, the top three indications of successful coaching were (a) sustained behavior change (63%), (b) increased self-awareness and understanding (48%), and (c) more effective leadership (45%).

Two themes merit mention. The first is the importance of emotional competence as a learning and behavior change vehicle for coached executives (discussed above). In my experience, executives' abilities to change behavior, increase self-understanding, and become more effective leaders to a large degree hinged on their making progress in one or more of the SO SMART dimensions of emotional competence.

63%	Change in behavior (more emphasis on building relationships, better work–family integration, sustained progress)
48%	Increased understanding of self (personal insight regarding motivation, more accurate self-awareness, valuing importance of emotional competence, need to get proactive regarding career objectives, clarity regarding perception of others, understanding one's "fit" or lack of same with company)
45%	More effective leader (confidence, motivational ability, results, increased optimism regarding future)
29%	Credibility of coach (perception in company, trust level with coachee)
31%	Company satisfaction (shift in others' perception of coachee, retention of valuable asset)

(Respondents had more than one choice)

FIGURE 8.7. Top indications of successful coaching (as cited by coachees).

The second, less apparent, theme is the importance of coaches managing relationships with sponsors, that is, the internal collaborators (boss and HR). Beyond the financial implications of managing these relationships, there are the subtle psychodynamics of managing perception. Even the most gifted coaches are unlikely to effect a lasting change in others' perceptions of the executives with whom they work. In my experience, this is best accomplished by working in close collaboration with the boss and/or HR partner.

If coaches take seriously the axiom that perception is reality in organization life, then coaching engagements must include intentional activities focused on changing perception(s) of a coached executive. At minimum, I suggest a three-pronged approach: (a) Throughout the coaching, a coached executive conveys explicit information to the boss and key HR professional regarding status and progress of coaching; (b) throughout the coaching, the coach—while preserving appropriate boundaries of confidentiality—maintains contact with boss and HR contact for the purpose of periodic update, to gain fresh collateral data, to emphasize progress made, and when possible to provide secondary gain to these internal collaborators; and (c) at the end of the formal coaching period, coach and coachee collaborate on the creation of a MAP that captures all that was learned and actions that will reinforce those learnings. The MAP is a living document shared with integral collaborators and includes actions that require the executive to work at managing perceptions. This means the executive is proactive in sending the message that "something has changed, I'm committed to sustaining the change, and I'm more effective as a result of it."

Finally, the most positive coaching outcomes begin with executives who are genuinely motivated to learn and/or change. Therefore, sufficient scrutiny of this variable—up front at the point of referral—is key (see the following section). While coaching is a costly development investment, there are times when a company's true coaching agenda can be hidden and/or fraught with political peril. Coaches must conduct a thorough needs assessment before commencing an engagement. There will be times when the best course of action is to advise the sponsor that executive coaching is *not* the best intervention, that is, why something other than coaching appears warranted.

Recently, I was contacted by the vice president of HR for a regional bank on the east coast. He wanted to secure my services to work with the most senior woman in their organization. As we spoke, I learned that the prospective client was immensely talented but also highly defensive, rejected negative feedback, and was somewhat resistant to the idea of having a coach. She had alienated a number of people on the executive committee and had such deteriorated relationships with her peers that business results were suffering. The CEO saw executive coaching as a vehicle for being able to say, "We even tried to help her with an executive coach." Rather than initiating executive coaching, I suggested the boss first speak candidly to the woman about her flagging performance and the unlikelihood of her advancing any further in the organization. This led to a mutually satisfactory decision that she would leave the company with a hefty severance package, including individual outplacement support to help her identify a suitable career move.

SUSTAINABILITY OF LEARNING AND/OR BEHAVIOR CHANGE AS A RESULT OF COACHING

This research produced many reflective moments when I would see a rolling sea of faces—hundreds of business people whom I've had the privilege to coach. Through my own critical self-assessment, I would say many of these executives were helped immensely, some to a moderate degree, and some probably not at all. What makes the difference between great and mediocre outcomes? How effective is coaching really? These were among the questions that fuelled an exploration of the sustainability of executives' learning and/or behavior change as a result of coaching.

On a 1–10 scale, over half of these coached executives reported a sustainability level between 6 and 8; over a third were at the 9–10 level. This was a stunning finding that required closer scrutiny. Obvious factors included my experience as an external coach with an established methodology, high credibility, professional integrity, and sufficient emotional competence to form sound working alliances with clients. Reanalysis of the data suggested that tough probing about the "rightness" of a coaching referral produced a well-qualified, highly motivated group of clients.

This raises an important question that warrants further investigation: How wisely are companies investing resources in executive coaching? On the basis of this research, I offer a typology that might prove helpful to decision makers as they gauge the likely value of executive coaching for specific individuals (see Table 8.3). Surely many people can benefit from coaching, but there are also countless others who, when given this development opportunity, simply won't engage. They won't engage despite the best efforts of experienced coaches. There are personal and/or contextual issues that simply overwhelm the likelihood of forming a satisfactory working alliance with a coach. Coaches should avoid these charades; in the long run, they serve neither these executives nor their sponsoring companies well. Furthermore, such engagements do damage to the reputation of executive coaching as a substantive development tool.

TABLE 8.3

A Typology for Assessing Executive Coaching Engagements

	Three general types of referrals		
Key criteria	**Primary**	**Secondary**	**Tertiary**
Executive's motivation (for change/new learning)	High	Moderate–low	Low
Performance problems	Absent	Moderate	High
Negative perceptions of executive	Absent–low	Moderate–high	High
Climate of coaching referral	Positive (self-initiated or executive perk)	Reticent–negative (initiated by boss and/or human resources partner)	Usually negative (initiated by boss and/or human resources partner; last-ditch effort)
Executive's trust in value of coaching	High	Variable–low	Low
Likelihood of executive forming solid working alliance with coach	High	Variable	Variable–low
Impact of 360-degree feedback data	Positive	Variable (can be low if coach is first to deliver tough feedback)	Too little, too late
Likelihood of successful outcome	High	Variable	Low

In my most recent experience, corporate decision makers appear more inclined toward an "Olympian" position vis-à-vis the provision of one-on-one development services. As one senior HR executive in a Fortune 100 company stated, "We're investing most in our best." If this thinking represents a trend, it may foster more opportunity for coaching—coaching by well-qualified people of highly responsive executives that yields high value and broad impact consistently. This also leads to questions about elitist development practices—another issue that requires further investigation.

The typology categories—while still clarifying in my mind—are as follows:

Primary—successful executives and other high-potential employees. There are no performance issues. These people are genuinely interested in their development and evolution as leaders. They believe in the value of having an objective sounding board (coach), want continuous feedback, and do not get trapped or deluded by their own defensive reasoning. Sound development action = customized, one-on-one executive coaching.

Secondary—potential derailers. There *are* performance issues, but they are not so dire that the boss and/or HR manager are raising questions about retention. The executive may or may not be interested in continuous learning. He or she has failed to respond to and/or has not been given straight feedback about performance issues. Best development action = performance management abetted, if possible, by the support of an internal mentor or coach. Note that coaching by an external consultant at a later date may prove useful—assuming the individual has responded to internal performance management and coaching or mentoring efforts.

Tertiary—already derailed. There are serious performance issues and/or negative perceptions of such magnitude that no coach could salvage the situation. The company should not waste resources on a "rescue fantasy." Best development action = candor about the situation and a severance package that includes one-on-one outplacement that will assist the person in getting on with his or her career elsewhere.

CONCLUSION

Probably more questions have been raised by this study than answered. But for now there are strong indications of the following: (a) Psychologists with doctoral degrees, experience in business and/or general management, personal characteristics that abet rapid and authentic connections with executives, and who are guided by a strong set of professional ethical principles are perceived by executives as especially effective coaches; (b) executives have a desire for data and personal insight so the armamentarium of psychometric tools psychologists possess enriches their data-gathering capabilities greatly; and (c) behavior change and learning, two knowledge domains of psychology, are key indications of successful coaching. Finally, there is strong evidence that a psychologically based model that includes intense scrutiny of the appropriateness of coaching for a referred executive is likely to influence high sustainability rates of learning and behavior change.

The results of this research underscore the distinctive assets psychologists possess as executive coaches. The future appears bright. As Diedrich and Kilburg (see chap. 5, this volume) stated,

> From the way the field has developed in the past 5 years, it appears now that coaching has begun to make its place in the vast armamentarium of behaviorally based interventions available to psychologists and other professionals who work to help people and organizations change. (p. 63)

But the future will also bring heightened scrutiny of coach competencies and credentials. Commercial sources that include the International Coaches Federation (ICF) are providing training and certifications to thousands of people who are interested in becoming executive coaches.

Standards of competence or proficiency and possible certification have yet to emerge from the profession of psychology. In the meantime, psychologists are urged to conduct further outcome research that examines the value of executive coaching as a development resource and that explores whether or not psychologists—psychologists who understand business—are distinctively equipped as executive coaches. To not do so runs the risk of executive coaching fading from use because it becomes perceived as a costly fad of variable utility. If this were to happen, it would be a loss for all those executives who could benefit from coaching, a loss for all the people who report to them, and a loss for psychologists who through this work have the chance to affect thousands of lives in workplaces throughout the world.

References

Berglas, S. (2002, June). The very real dangers of executive coaching. *The Harvard Business Review,* 87–92.

Cherniss, C., & Goleman, D. (2001). *The emotionally intelligent workplace: How to select for, measure, and improve emotional intelligence in individuals, groups, and organizations.* San Francisco: Jossey-Bass.

Goleman, D. (1995). *Emotional intelligence.* New York: Bantam Books.

Spencer, L. M., Jr., & Spencer, S. (1993). *Competence at work: Models for superior performance.* New York: Wiley.

VanFleet, R. (1999, May). Diversifying psychological practice to industry: Getting started. *The Pennsylvania Psychologist Quarterly,* 15, 24.

Walter V. Clarke Associates. (1996). *Activity vector analysis: Some applications to the concept of emotional intelligence.* Pittsburgh, PA: Author.

Wasylyshyn, K. M. (2001). On the full actualization of psychology in business. *Consulting Psychology Journal: Practice and Research, 53,* 10–21.

PART II

COACHING APPROACHES

The purpose of Part II is to provide the reader with a variety of approaches and methods. The approaches and roles used by different coaches vary, and the actual processes used may appear divergent, but they all have a similar goal: helping the client executive become more adaptive in the identification of alternatives or choices, which in turn can lead to desired or necessary behavior changes and increased organization effectiveness. These authors have given every practitioner of coaching a great deal to consider, and their ideas will stimulate the field for a long time.

These chapters clearly illustrate and support the observations of Witherspoon and White (chap. 10), who state that "coaching specifics—whether by Socratic method or multirater assessment—depend on the executive and the situation" (p. 103). The selections have much to offer both the new and old coach alike if viewed as "mental maps" that can contribute to increased insight, enhanced role clarity, and better informed coaching activities. These have a broad scope but hardly scratch the surface.

Levinson (chap. 9) opens Part II with a focus on the need for the coach to understand the organization and the world of business. He then provides a well-developed presentation regarding the differences between coaching and psychotherapy and argues that coaching is a form of support, not a device for change per se. A brief but illustrative case study involving a CEO is also included. Witherspoon and White (chap. 10) define and explore distinguishing factors among a variety of coaching situations; they remind the reader that each coaching situation is different They go on to review four very different coaching roles and provide examples of a situation and the process used with each. They close by pointing out that all executive coaching involves action learning and a partnership with the executive.

Kiel, Rimmer, Williams, and Doyle (chap. 11) walk the reader through an intense 2-year-long senior executive leadership development program. An illustrative case study that describes a structured, multisystem approach to impacting the organization is included. The case allows the reader to gain a sense of lessons learned and the executive's behavioral changes and increased effectiveness. Peterson (chap. 12) describes the coaching services provided by Personnel Decisions International. He notes that this company was the first management consulting firm to offer a structured coaching program and reviews the five research-based coaching strategies used as well as the major categories of coaching that Personnel Decisions International provides. A case study describes an example of Targeted Coaching in detail.

Tobias (chap. 13) presents the Nordli, Wilson Associates coaching process and the role of the psychologist and the "psychological study" within this ongoing process. The case study about Henry provides a clear picture of the process and the resultant changes in leadership style, group functioning, and the enabling of others. Diedrich (chap. 14) outlines a 3-year structured coaching process with a difficult senior executive. This iterative process followed an initial 360-degree assessment and provided numerous "loops" of activity and ongoing feedback within a "learner-centered" developmental framework. The article also offers several practical tips for the consultant who wants his or her coaching process to be perceived as value-added by both the individual executive and the organization.

Saporito (chap. 15) shares the observation that "developmental coaching" efforts with executives must be "intimately tied to the realities of the business" (p. 149). He describes the RHR model of consulting, which deals with three fundamental questions:

1. What are the organizational imperatives?
2. What are the success factors for that particular role within the organization?
3. What are the behavioral requirements necessary to achieve these success factors?

A case study reporting a request for coaching driven by strategic realignment and a succession planning requirement completes the article.

Ducharme (chap. 16) discusses the practical value of cognitive–behavioral techniques in executive coaching given the "specific and issue-focused" nature of this approach. Strengths and weaknesses of cognitive–behavioral coaching are delineated, and situations in which this type of coaching is appropriate are identified. Sherin and Caiger (chap. 17) offer a brief review of the rational–emotive behavior therapy process and consider its applicability in the context of a coaching relationship in which the focus is executive performance. The client's explicit and implicit belief system is seen as the locus of change in this model.

Cocivera and Cronshaw (chap. 18) outline how action frame theory could be used to operationalize and apply the mediated focus of executive coaching that has been described by Kilburg (2000). They propose that action frame theory can be used throughout a coaching engagement and provide a coaching example that demonstrates its application as an analytical tool as well as a framework for planning and reviewing actions and results.

Kilburg (chap. 19) suggests still another use for psychodynamic material and methods in working with executives and reviews 15 situations in which they are relevant considerations. Developmentally oriented conflicts and attachment styles for which coaches might use a psychodynamic perspective are discussed, as is the role of interpretation. Finally, the limitations of the psychodynamic approach in the coaching engagement are outlined. Frisch (chap. 20) discusses the emerging role of the internal coach. This role is defined, and internal coaching is compared with external coaching, with the view that the two approaches complement each other. Key issues and challenges are explored, and practical guidelines and recommendations are offered. Laske (chap. 21) presents an integrated model of developmental coaching within which "the question of 'where the client is' *ontic–developmentally* is of crucial importance for conceptualizing coaching strategy as well as for determining the compatibility of coach and client" (p. 217). He argues that the view coaches hold of their own development as adults is critical in transformative coaching and that this model deals with what happens in coaching rather than how to do coaching.

Part II presents a general picture of the opportunities available to the executive coach and at least some of the concerns and issues for the profession. As noted by Kilburg (chap. 4), originally writing in 1996, "As yet, there has been no focused effort to describe or define this emerging area of consultation practice, even though it has developed an initial identity known as *executive coaching*" (p. 61). Also in 1996, Diedrich (chap. 14), in an effort to define approach, stated that "I make certain that both the executive and the organization view the coaching process as an ongoing activity that is developmentally oriented, as opposed to a 'quick fix' that is problem centered" (p. 144).

A few years ago, Wasylyshyn (2001) observed that

> in practice, requests for executive coaching take many forms; that is, the indications for this type of individual intervention can vary enormously. . . . After determining the appropriateness of such a referral, the customization of each engagement is central to a successful outcome. (p. 16)

She went on to add that "psychologists who become successful executive coaches possess an array of general and specialized skills in addition to foundational psychological expertise" (p. 16).

The chapters based on articles from 2004 by Ducharme (chap. 16), Sherin and Caiger (chap. 17), Cocivera and Cronshaw (chap. 18), and Kilburg (chap. 19) all discuss particular and different ways to approach executive coaching. These articles underscore the real differences in theoretical foundations as well as intervention processes.

Another related perspective was provided in 2004 by Quick and Macik-Frey (chap. 29). They proposed that "our health-enhancing, developmental model of executive coaching through deep interpersonal communication may serve as a form of primary prevention within an organization" (p. 312) and that "coaching through deep interpersonal communication is an enabling process through which executives may better connect their heads with their hearts" (p. 316).

Rudisill, Edwards, and Hershberger (2004) suggested 10 guidelines for becoming a "confidant." Their guidelines could serve equally well as a template that defines the behavior of the effective executive coach. Thus, the question of just how we do what we do in executive coaching remains a challenge to be actively pursued!

References

Kilburg, R. R. (2000). *Executive coaching: Developing managerial wisdom in a world of chaos.* Washington, DC: American Psychological Association.

Rudisill, J. R., Edwards, J. M., & Hershberger, P. J. (2004). Consultant as confidant. *Consulting Psychology Journal: Practice and Research, 56,* 139–145.

Wasylyshyn, K. M. (2001). On the full actualization of psychology in business. *Consulting Psychology Journal: Practice and Research, 53,* 10–21.

CHAPTER 9

EXECUTIVE COACHING

Harry Levinson

The key issues for consultants who are also coaching others have to do with broad managerial experience. I think it is impossible to coach someone about role behavior unless one has a comprehensive understanding of organizations and can be recognized by the person being coached as being authoritative with respect to the psychological and coaching process and also authoritative in his or her knowledge of the business world. Age is an advantage in many cases, for from time to time my clients will refer to me as a "wise old man."

To be an effective coach of high-level business and government executives, one must have a broad understanding of the business and government worlds, which requires that he or she be widely read and contemporarily knowledgeable. In one situation, I had to be able to demonstrate that I knew something about the world of high-level organization finance, although I am not knowledgeable about finance itself. In another situation, I had to demonstrate that I was familiar with the insurance business and its problems. In still another, I had to demonstrate that I knew something about textiles and their manufacture, and in yet another, that I knew something about the currency exchange problems of Argentina.

In addition to being knowledgeable about the business world, one also must be knowledgeable about the political world and its implications for the organization with which one is working (if the coaching is within an organization). For example, what is the important effect of the Food and Drug Administration (FDA) and breast implant litigation on the behavior of executives in pharmaceutical companies? What is the effect of the lobbying of those companies on FDA executives?

A knowledge of psychological dynamics is particularly important when trying to understand the manager–subordinate relationships in the context of adult development. An understanding of adult development is especially helpful when there are issues of prospective retirement and postretirement planning. The choice of a successor is fraught with conscious and unconscious conflicts and, once that person is in place, with the predictable ambivalence both parties experience.

In the course of executive coaching, it is particularly important to avoid becoming psychotherapeutic because executive coaching does not allow time for developing a therapeutic alliance, dealing with the transference problem, and dealing with the ambivalence engendered when the client becomes dependent on the coach. The word *coach* must he taken seriously, and the relationship must be one of peers, although the client is necessarily dependent on the coach for advice, guidance, insights, and even for real information. The executive is in his or her geographic location and is experiencing coaching as a form of support, rather than a device for changing himself or herself, although

Reprinted from the *Consulting Psychology Journal: Practice and Research, 48,* 115–123.

ideally, when necessary, some aspects of the client's dysfunctional behavior will be changed.

METHOD

A clinical psychologist by training, I have been involved in consultation on leadership, management, and organization problems for 40 years. My basic conceptual orientation is psychoanalytic, broadly encompassing the major psychoanalytic orientations with a heavy emphasis on psychological and organizational diagnosis, while appreciating the organization as an open system. Psychoanalytic theory values understanding oneself as much as possible, with an emphasis on the interdependent integrity of one's relationships to others and one's ability to use his or her capacities and resources fully in mastering his or her environment, particularly for obtaining gratification in work. When coaching executives, usually the basic task is to help the client free himself or herself from ungratifying, unsatisfying, or conflict-laden work or to help him or her plan for a new or different occupational role.

To be a successful executive (Levinson, 1980), one must be able to take charge of his or her authoritative role comfortably, to manage the inevitable ambivalence of subordinates and the rivalry of peers and superiors, and to avoid being caught up in the regressive behavior of the work group he or she leads (Kernberg, 1978, 1979). Executives must not sacrifice their authority for the need to please. Often executives must manage the troublesome behavior of customers, clients, and their own superiors or board members. They must be able to accept their own limitations and make use of the specialized contributions of others, as well as the support of their colleagues and followers. They must be able to plan ahead for periods appropriate to their role (Jaques & Cason, 1994).

With respect to individual coaching, my heavy emphasis is on interviewing and counseling with a focus on reality problems, using little interpretation or effort to deal overtly with the transference. Transference problems are those unconsciously motivated attitudes on the part of the client toward the coach that may threaten the coaching relationship. For example, if, in the course of examining the client's rocky relationship with his or her peers, the client interprets the coach as a punitive policeman, the coach cannot help the client to understand the sources of his or her projection, as would happen in psychoanalysis. Instead, the coach would confine himself or herself to clarifying his or her role and differentiating that role from the client's definition of power figures in the client's other relationships.

Although the focus of the coaching relationship is on present behavior, the coach may usefully call attention to repetitive problems that the client has not recognized (e.g., discomfort with bosses while seeking their approval). Recognizing such an issue may help the client choose a new role in which his or her prospective manager preferably is paternalistic rather than tightly controlling. Unless clients spontaneously make the comparison, or repetitively raise those experiences, usually there is little need to interpret their early relationship to their parents to illuminate their present problems.

Executive coaching usually involves coping with focal problems, mostly of maladroit executive behavior that must become more adaptive. On occasion, the negative behavior is reflected in difficulties in supervision, on other occasions in problems with peers or superiors. Sometimes coaching consists of helping a given executive to conceptualize his or her role, to prepare for retirement, or to assess new possibilities in other organizations or even upward mobility in the present one. Sometimes it involves providing counseling on family problems, even recommending psychotherapeutic resources, and sometimes it involves helping the person resolve career dilemmas.

If the coaching task is to assess a given subordinate or even the executive's own role behavior, I use a simple derivative of psychoanalytic theory as a method for analyzing problems, namely, I ask the person in question how he or she typically handles affection (the need to love and be loved), aggression (the attacking or mastery component of the personality), and dependency (the need to work interdependently with others). I also ask what is the nature of his or her ego ideal (the picture of the self at his or her future best).

For example, a client tells me she is an intense, driven securities analyst whose supervisors complain about her abrasiveness with her colleagues and about her perfectionistic practice of "going it alone." In my theoretical frame of reference, I infer that her aggression is focused not only on task accomplishment, but also on "taking it out of her own hide." Such behavior is a product of an inordinately high ego ideal. The focus of my coaching must be on tempering the angry self-demands that spill over into her relationships with other people. There is little point in trying to help her relate better to others without dealing with the source of the drivenness. If coaching proves to be insufficient to counteract the unconscious pressure she experiences, then I would recommend intensive psychotherapy.

If the task has to do with fitting a person to a role, the same questions can be asked of the role, namely, what are the behaviors required in the terms just stated? Finally, I want to help the person assess for his or her candidate or for himself or herself how far ahead the role requires the person to plan and what degree of complexity he or she must be able to master (Jaques & Cason, 1994).

I ask the counselee to give me specific examples of his or her behavior in the wide range of executive practices he or she has experienced. I ask in particular what has provided him or her with special gratification, peak experiences, or highly gratifying achievements (Czikszentmihaly, 1990). My concern is less with the specifics of achievements and more with the continuities of behavior; in short, what did he or she actually do and how? I am particularly interested in elucidating the continuities of behavior, especially if the counselee has not recognized them because the achievements themselves have obscured his or her awareness of the actual behavior. I am also interested in the client's disappointments, failures, and mode of recovery from them. I want to know when the client was not challenged in his or her roles, and also when he or she was in over his or her head. It is helpful to know when clients stumbled and how they understand their error. Of course, it is important to know how they dealt with authority figures, peers, and subordinates.

I have in mind, sometimes typed on 5-inch × 8-inch cards to be certain I have covered all of the topics, the criteria for selecting chief executives (Levinson, 1980). Others may find different sets of similar characteristics useful (e.g., Tobias, 1990). I draw from our discussion the specific data of the counselee's work history, but, more important, I infer from these words, or lyrics, the underlying melody or emotional pattern of his or her life experiences and their likely import for where he or she would like to go in his or her career trajectory and what problems he or she must solve or master to do so.

Of course, I am interested in how clients see themselves and their conscious rationale for the trajectory of their career. But I am more interested in those underlying forces of which they are less aware or even unaware that are reflected in the continuities of their behavior. These represent the compelling thrust of their adaptation and will continue to be the momentum of their vocational pursuits no matter what the specific roles they pursue.

The starting point for establishing continuities of behavior is the clients' recall of their earliest experience of pleasing their mother (or substitute). For example, the earliest such experience I can recall is learning a simple four-line part for a kindergarten play. My mother, an uneducated immigrant who knew no English, was very proud that I was going to school. As I rehearsed my part, she learned the words with me. One of my major activities, and one that I would have pursued no matter what profession I would have undertaken, is teaching and lecturing. Behaviorally, there is little difference between the earliest event I can recollect and what has been a consistently dominant aspect of my life activity since.

When I meet clients for the first time, I ask them to tell me about themselves in any way they think would help me understand them and the issues they want to deal with or problems they must surmount. Much of the time they start with where they are occupationally, which enables me to ask about their work history and then their family background, including their relationship with their parents and parental figures. I ask them to explain their educational and career choices and their varied job experiences and relationships.

For example, a CEO asked me to coach his recently employed COO who had not, it seemed, gained the acceptance of the other top executives. The COO began by telling me about his most recent managerial success, rescuing a branch of a major financial institution. Then, as we traced his work experience backward, it became clear that his lower-class parents had demanded good academic grades and that he "found himself" in graduate school after mediocre high school and undergraduate performance.

My working hypothesis was that pressure and demands from higher authority would be likely to result in passive resistance and reluctant conformity; turned loose to exercise his abilities, the COO would shine. He had demonstrated that he could take charge of a failing organization of strangers and make it profitable. His ego ideal demanded specific managerial achievements. But what was also clear was that the CEO had not differentiated the accountability of his various subordinates, nor had he prepared them for the new authority figure he was interjecting between himself and them, thus fostering resistance to their new boss. He also had not spelled out his expectations for the new COO, nor had he delineated the division of their functions.

The CEO had said that he had not yet decided how their roles should be differentiated and that he had chosen the COO on the basis of his success in rescuing his previous organization, which, like the present firm, consisted of individual professionals who operated relatively independently. To lead, I inferred, the COO would have to earn the regard of the subordinates in a relatively unstructured situation without them having clear accountability to him. He would have to take charge without seeming to do so. He would have to ingratiate himself not only to gain acceptance, but also to gain identification with himself as a leader. He could not assert control in a situation without defined accountability. Fortunately, the CEO had asked him to be sure that one of the failing operations did not indeed fail. This constituted his authority to take charge. His rescue both of the subordinate responsible for the operation and of the operation itself demonstrated to all the subordinates both his strength and his right to be their chief.

From a psychoanalytic point of view, appropriate and effective role behavior require the incumbent of a role to take charge of that role, to recognize and accept his or her accountability to the values and methods of the organization and to those to whom he or she reports. A manager or executive is also accountable to his or her own conscience (of which the ego ideal is a component), for the executive must live with himself or herself. Therefore, the executive should not violate his or her own standards even if he or she must leave the role.

Psychoanalytic thinking values openness and integrity of relationships. The consultant who uses a psychoanalytic frame of reference must help clients understand the potential destructiveness of the actions they contemplate to themselves, to the people who work with them, and to the organization. The consultant should help clients think psychologically. He or she should also help clients recognize their strengths, talents, and achievements with pride and without apology. Furthermore, the consultant should help clients recognize decisions motivated by unconscious guilt, unconscious rivalry, and other irrational behaviors that would likely invoke negative behavior in others. The consultant would wisely help clients to understand the psychology of their stage of adult development and both the problems and advantages of characteristic behavior in that life stage.

The consultant may help clients understand and come to terms with that behavior that causes difficulty for them and may teach them how to respond or how to act more wisely according to that understanding. The psychoanalytically oriented consultant would be likely to recognize symptoms of psychological distress or disturbance and to refer to appropriate clinicians. Fundamentally, psychoanalytically oriented consultants help their clients attain greater psychological freedom to make their own choices and assume responsibility for their own behavior. Unlike psychoanalytic practice, however, coaching consultants may offer suggestions, information, and guidance consistent with their understanding of the psychology of the client in his or her organizational context.

CASE STUDY

The client is a 60-year-old chief executive of a large company that makes animal feeds. He is a New England Brahmin whose family has long been involved in this business, and he himself is a product of an elite secondary school and an Ivy League university. The company's headquarters are in New England and the plants are scattered in the South and the Midwest. Following his graduation from college, the client worked for 2 years in a Wall Street financial firm before going to the Far East, where he worked in a liaison position between an American financial institution and a Japanese bank. In the course of that experience, he learned to speak Japanese and developed an effective manner of negotiating with the Japanese. He was able to build good working relationships because not only could he be congenial, but also he could await the opportune moment to close an agreement.

Although his family had been in the feed business for many years, the company had become publicly owned and was professionally managed. However, that management could not keep up with the changing demographics of the animal feed industry. As beef, pork, and chicken producers became increasingly larger, and as issues of the infusion of antibiotics and vitamins into feeds and genetic modification of the animals (e.g., to get leaner pigs) became more pressing and competition became keener, the incumbent CEO became overwhelmed. The family still retained a significant share of the company's stock (20%) and asked the client to return to manage the corporation. He did so, and in a few years increased the company's volume from $600 million to $890 million. Now he was a respected chief executive officer who was on the boards of three other major corporations. He also served on government advisory boards having to do with his business and with business in general. He did not play a significant part in the company's political efforts, except for occasionally working with the lobbyist his industry maintained in Washington, DC. His wife, who also had come from a Brahmin family and who had a similar educational background, was heavily involved in nonprofit and charitable organizations. She was prominent in local high society.

The organization faced three major problems. The first was a continuing argument about the use of antibiotics and other chemicals in animal foodstuffs in the context of a broader argument about the role of the FDA. The company was under constant pressure from environmentalists on the one hand and from producers on the other.

The second problem was whether the business should acquire another business as part of a growth strategy, allow another company to acquire it, or remain independent. There was a possibility of extending the company's reach to other animal-raising countries like Argentina and Australia. However, to do so would mean extensive travel for the CEO and more complex financial and currency arrangements, as well as the problem of political instability in South America.

A third problem, which was internal, revolved around two executive vice presidents. Each was responsible for a major part of the business, although their responsibilities were not equal in the sense of number of people managed or the volume and profitability of their respective units.

The elder of the two executives was a thoughtful PhD in animal husbandry whose conceptualization and advice had been instrumental in reorganizing the focus of the company when the CEO had started as a new chief. A conservative, well-mannered gentleman, he operated his part of the organization profitably and quietly. He was widely liked in his organization and by the board. He thought broadly about animal husbandry and the direction the company should take. The younger executive had moved up in the company by demonstrating that he could manage plants that had labor conflicts, settle those conflicts, and reduce the number of employees. A more aggressive take-charge person, he was less sensitive than his peer and somewhat more hard-nosed, which made him a more bottom-line-oriented manager and perhaps better suited to coping with the ups and downs of increased competition and conflicts with government regulators. He did not think as conceptually as his peer.

The CEO had to think about his own prospective retirement and succession. He did not want to choose one or the other of his lieutenants for fear that the one who was not chosen would leave. He also recognized that the two of them working together with him did a better job than either of them could do alone. He wanted to sustain the triumvirate as long as he could, but he knew that sooner or later he would have to choose. He agonized over that problem.

The initial contact was made by the CEO on the board of another company with whom I had been consulting. The client knew I had for some years been consulting with the chief executive of that company. His primary question had to do with his prospective retirement and succession. Although he would retire in 5 years, he might, he thought, do so even sooner. The question, then, was what kinds of options were open to him and what would he do after he retired? A secondary question involved succession and his struggle about having to decide between the two executive vice presidents, while at the same time sustaining their momentum, cooperation, and morale. Although he also had to think about the possibility of acquiring another company or being acquired, that did not seem to trouble him particularly. Those issues, it seemed, would be decided on a purely financial basis. He was not strongly attached to the family tradition of a stint in public service. The first two issues had to be addressed, and that occurred during our biweekly consultations over a period of 7 months.

The client can be described as having obsessive (in the clinical sense) personality features. Like most such executives, he was conventional in his conformity to social and business norms. He was orderly, logical, and precise: He provided stable and consistent direction to the organization. Yet he could also enjoy the social activities he and his top managers shared during their meetings in vacation resorts. He had high personal standards and had similar expectations of his staff, but he was not a prude. He attended his mainstream Protestant church regularly and served on its governing boards.

While I was at company headquarters, I also met with the two executive vice presidents, the senior vice president of human resources, and another executive who was the nominal chairman of the board to assess how things were going in the company. They knew I was concerned with their effectiveness as a team. The vice president of human resources gave me added background on the respective executive vice presidents and their relative strengths. In addition, I lectured to the larger top management group on the management of stress and change because the company had gone through successive changes and would be undergoing more.

With respect to the CEO's prospective retirement and what might come after, particularly if he were interested in a government position, I pointed out that he would have to establish himself as an authority in the field of government in which he wanted to work. That meant he would have to write for publications that provide information to those who made government appointment selections. Such articles would have to be published in professional journals related to the field of animal feeds and having to do with the economies of the industry and sometimes with the relationship of the industry to the government. I suggested also that he have public relations specialists in his company interview him to draft prospective papers for him, including one for the *Harvard Business Review* and another for *Foreign Affairs*.

I also pointed out the need to establish and sustain political contacts with appropriate people in Washington and urged that he make use of the industry lobbyist to establish such contacts for him. We talked about how he would feel about retiring and also about how he would feel about having to cope with all the rivalries, conflicts, and pressures of working in the government. He was not one to have such experiences threaten his equanimity, nor was he narcissistically preoccupied. His ego ideal included, but did not compel him to take, a government role to sustain that family heritage. He seemed to look forward to the challenge.

I suggested repeatedly that at every opportunity he address his two lieutenants with the fact that they did better collectively than they did separately and that their respective and collective track records indicated how well they were working together. He reported how he did so in their successive meetings. He was operating with them as if they were collectively an office of the chief executive.

I further suggested that he defer making a choice between the two executives until the need to choose became imperative. Part of the problem in making a choice had to do with the fact that the wife of one of them apparently presented herself as a rather helpless person when the three couples were together and therefore was not viewed positively by the other two wives. If that executive were to become CEO, then his wife psychologically would be a drag on the social network of the organization. Her helpless posture did not sit well with the CEO's Brahmin wife, whose forays in society and volunteer services were quite the opposite of that behavior. Neither she nor her husband acknowledged that she needed help. Therefore, I did not suggest psychotherapy.

The CEO was widely read and both culturally and managerially sophisticated. That proficiency enabled us to discuss business issues in their social and political context. We also talked about the importance of being able to conceptualize on the one hand and make relatively hard-nosed leadership decisions on the other. The implication was that the more thoughtful, older executive vice president probably should be the first choice as a successor. Presumably, he could formulate wide-ranging strategy and set the organizational frame of reference, which the younger one subsequently could implement. There was some risk that the younger executive vice president would not wait for that opportunity, but logically, that was the optimal way to go. When the time came to make the decision, I suggested that the CEO might do well to prepare them so that they would understand the logic behind his decision. Simultaneously, he needed to keep emphasizing their effectiveness as a team.

I experienced some uneasiness when the CEO asked me for a referral for his son, a college student who was having some academic difficulties. He obliquely referred to his wish that the therapist be one with whom upper class people like himself and his wife would be comfortable. I detected a note of anti-Semitism between the lines of that inquiry, but did not explore the transference elements of his request. Fortunately, I was able to refer him to a therapist whose background, education, and social position were quite acceptable.

The coaching sessions with the CEO went well. He made good use of my suggestions. He reviewed the ghost-drafted pieces with me and began to establish his political ties to Washington. He frequently met with the two executive vice presidents and constantly reiterated their success as a team. We talked about the probable acquisition of his company, which would enlarge it considerably. But suddenly, when I arrived one day, he told me that the prospective acquiree company, in turn, had made a bid for his company. He quickly accepted that bid, which netted him a personal gain of some $20 million, and retired. The acquiring company, unaware of my logic of conceptual development in the organization followed by operational development, and probably uninterested as well, pushed aside the older, conceptualizing executive vice president, who went on to head another company, and named the younger, operational one chief executive.

The CEO followed through with a major government position that he held for about 3 years. When the political winds shifted and he was no longer a Washington appointee, he concentrated his efforts on several corporate boards on which he served and joined another group of executives in a venture capital firm.

I do not know how the client would evaluate the coaching sessions, except to note that he had referred other executives to talk with me who were interested in business issues similar to those we had discussed. Neither of the two vice presidents, now CEOs in their own right, asked for further consultation. In all fairness, both were doing quite well in their executive roles and saw no need to do so.

CONCLUSION

All the parties involved seemed to have realized significant personal goals. I was satisfied that the CEO had consistently carried out my advice in maintaining the integrity of his team and that he carefully chose his postretirement career with excellent preparation that cleared the way for his appointment. I do not think the character of any of the people involved changed that much, nor did their respective rivalries. Nevertheless, while they were together, they were able to work congenially and cooperatively, and when the time came, they were able to go their independent ways appropriately. As a consultant, the most important thing I learned was the need to be widely informed about management issues and about what was going on politically as well as economically. Although my psychoanalytic orientation helped me understand how best to coach this client, it was equally important in enabling me to manage the professional distance between us. As a result, although I was in no way a social peer of my client, he nevertheless respected my knowledge, perspective, and professional advice. I was certainly more conscious of being a coach than was the case in most other consultations with senior corporate executives.

References

Czikszentmihaly, M. (1990). *Flow: The psychology of optimal experience.* New York: Harper.

Jaques, E., & Cason, K. (1994). *Human capability.* Falls Church, VA: Cason Hall.

Kernberg, O. F. (1978). Leadership and organizational functioning: Organizational regression. *International Journal of Group Psychotherapy, 28,* 3–25.

Kernberg, O. F. (1979). Regression in organizational leadership. *Psychiatry, 42,* 24–39.

Levinson, H. (1980). Criteria for choosing chief executives. *Harvard Business Review, 58*(4), 113–120.

Tobias, L. (1990). *Psychological consultation to management.* New York: Brunner/Mazel.

CHAPTER 10

EXECUTIVE COACHING: A CONTINUUM OF ROLES

Robert Witherspoon and Randall P. White

Imagine a professional football team that recruits the best players, puts them through training camp to hone their technical skills and learn the plays and strategies to win, and then plays the entire season without a practice session or a coach. Team owners would never expose a major investment to that kind of risk. Yet most organizations do just that. We expect people to perform key roles—lead a new project team, present financial results to outside investors, manage conflicts across departments—all in exemplary fashion, without training, practice, or coaching. Consequently, many investments in people have had mixed results, so organizations are turning to coaching. Coaching is recognized in business, teaching, and sports as a positive and empowering strategy for performance and leadership development.

Executive coaching brings out the best in people. The word *coach*, first used in English in the 1500s, refers to a particular kind of carriage. (It still does.) Hence, the root meaning of the verb "to coach" is to convey a valued person from where one was to where one wants to be—a solid meaning for coaching executives today (see Evered & Selman, 1989)!

For decades, athletes, public speakers, and performing artists have turned to coaches to help them perform better. For individuals atop their fields, the next level of performance cannot be taught, but it can be learned. To coach in these situations is to facilitate (literally, "to make easy") more than to instruct. This approach is taking hold in business, where top executives turn to coaches to reach their business and personal best.

Executive coaching enhances an organization's greatest investment by helping executives learn and make the most of that learning. Because executives are in different stages of their careers and in varied settings, coaching represents a continuum of roles. Sans role, the coaching process helps executives learn, grow, and change. Coaching specifics—whether by Socratic method or multirater assessment—depend on the executive and the situation. Coaching is situational, as captured over a decade ago by Peters and Austin (1985):

> Exceptionally talented leaders and coaches . . . make dozens of intuitive judgments daily about how to work with their people. Sometimes they focus on removing barriers. . . . Other times they immerse themselves . . . and exert a great deal of influence on the way it turns out. . . . They help people

In writing about individuals with whom we've worked, we have kept their data private by altering characteristics of each case. Condensation was necessary to fit space constraints. We consider the resulting examples to be partial composites of representative coaching situations.

We wish to thank Richard Beckhard, Teri-E Belf, David DeVries, Arthur Freedman, Mary Kralj, Nick Miles, Donna Morris, and Katie White for their comments and assistance on earlier versions of this article.

> work through personal or performance problems, and . . . provide straightforward information. (pp. 398–399)

Experience bears this out with two important exceptions. First, a coach may be external to the organization. Peters and Austin (1985) were talking about coaches as a boss or another insider. Since then, a growing number of executives have turned to professional external coaches. According to a recent survey of coaching practices at leading American companies, those coached in business these days "may be anyone from a $60,000 middle manager up to the CEO, although more commonly that person will be a leading contender for the CEO's job" (Smith, 1993, p. 126). As described by Smith, executive coaching involves a skilled outside consultant assigned to an executive on a regular basis for one or more specific functions—improving the executive's managerial skills, correcting serious performance problems, or facilitating long-term development—often to prepare him or her for a future leadership role or top corporate position.

The second exception concerns the exertion of influence. Typically, outside coaches have little or no direct influence—much less control—over the outcome of coaching. To have direct control is to manage, not coach. A coach can have considerable power, however, depending on reputation, track record, and access to other parts of the organization. This very absence of authority makes possible major internal change for the person being coached. A coach can be instrumental in encouraging and motivating, but ultimately the changes must be embraced by the executive.

Coaching is more than an event (e.g., the feedback day of a leadership development program); it is a continuous process. Good coaching requires skill, depth of understanding, and plenty of practice to deliver its remarkable potential. This article addresses the various roles of external one-on-one coaches in a business context. It does not address other settings, like personal growth seminars or "cybercoaching" over the Internet. Nor does it address group coaching functions like boardroom facilitation and team development. The focus here is on formal scheduled sessions rather than the many informal coaching opportunities that arise on a daily basis.[1]

THE ROLES CONSULTANTS PLAY

Richard Beckhard, one of the founders of organization development, remarked that he typically plays at least four roles in working with the chief executives, boards, and senior managers of organizations: (a) expert, providing solutions or action recommendations; (b) consultant, helping the client work on a problem, the responsibility remaining with the client; (c) trainer or educator, teaching the client what he or she knows, so the client can apply the learning himself or herself; and (d) coach or counselor, helping the client learn and teaching the client how to learn (personal communications, December 19, 1994, and March 31, 1995). (For a look at case examples in which these roles play out, see Beckhard & Pritchard, 1992.) The balance of this article is about this latter role, focusing on the executive coach.

THE ROLES COACHES PLAY

One way to think of executive coaching roles relates to client need. Does the executive need to learn a new skill? to perform better in the present job? to prepare for a future leadership role? Does the executive understand and acknowledge these needs? Is he or she willing to seek and accept coaching? Is the executive looking for a confidant to talk through issues and receive constructive feedback from before taking action? These questions suggest client need—or primary coaching function—as a key dimension for distinguishing different coaching roles.

[1] "Formal coaching" starts with clear contracting about specific expectations (e.g., coaching goals and roles), entered into with mutual consent. Sometimes, however, even formal coaching occurs on the fly, as when a coach shadows the executive to directly observe the client in work settings (e.g., at plant inspections and staff meetings). The coach's intent is to observe the client in action, to hear what others have to say, or both. Coaching interventions can be very valuable. For an exploration and case examples of such coaching, see Schein (1969), especially pp. 167–172.

Coaching role refers to the coach's primary function in helping an executive learn, grow, and change. The focus may be on imparting specific skills, addressing performance issues on the job, or supporting broader changes in the executive's behavior.[2] With several coaching functions possible, one must be identified as primary to avoid confusion about expectations, time, and effort.

Executive coaching roles, based on the primary function, can be described as follows: coaching for skills (learning sharply focused on a person's specific task), coaching for performance (learning focused more broadly on a person's present job), coaching for development (learning focused on a person's future job), and coaching for the executive's agenda.[3]

Early in the process, these different executive coaching roles should be clarified. It is important for both executive and coach to recognize the distinctions among the various roles, if only to foster informed choice by everyone taking part in the process—the executive (and possibly family members), the executive's boss, the human resources representative, and the coach providing the service.[4] Also, these role distinctions provide a common language about coaching for both executives and practitioners and a useful way to orient all parties to the process of assessment, feedback, and action planning. These critical distinctions represent a continuing choice through the life of the coaching relationship. The choices define behaviorally how executives and coaches work together and largely affect successful outcomes. Finally, an open discussion helps create ground rules and a feedback system.

Each of the coaching roles contributes differently to enable the executive to solve problems or seize opportunities. Role clarity is key in sizing up the situation: how to approach an opening for coaching, what to emphasize, what to leave alone for the time being, and where to start. In practice, the coaching roles may overlap. A coach contracted to help in skills building may end up working on performance issues, or a longer term relationship may be forged that contributes to the executive's overall development. Changes in role, however, should be acknowledged by all parties.

Executive coaching might be defined as a confidential, highly personal learning process: "an organized, personal learning provided over a specified period of time to bring about the possibility of effective action, performance improvement and/or personal growth" (Belf, 1995, p. 1).[5] Coaching is more personal and individualized than other forms of organized learning (e.g., workshops or traditional classrooms). In working one-on-one, there is the recognition that no two people are alike. Each person has a unique knowledge base, learning pace, and learning style. Consequently, executives progress at their own pace and are held accountable for their progress. Coaching can uncover blind spots and change one's personal style.

Coaching for Skills

Coaching for skills is typically learning focused on a specific task or project. ("Skill" is used broadly to include basic concepts, strategies, methods, behaviors, attitudes, and perspectives associated with success in business.) Sometimes the executive needs conceptual clarity—"I'm not familiar with the basic principles" or "I don't understand the

[2] Coaching may encourage executives to undergo a character shift and profound personal changes, such as by moderating a drive for perfectionism or the need to overcontrol (see Kaplan, Drath, & Kofodimos, 1991).

[3] We use the term *executive's agenda* in a sense similar to Kotter's (1982) *agenda setting.* He used this term deliberately to distinguish between the ways general managers actually determine direction and the formal strategic planning process in many organizations. The former contained "loosely connected goals and plans" addressing a range of time frames covering a broad range of business issues and included both "vague and specific goals and plans" (p. 66). In its broadest sense, this coaching might be considered "coaching for purpose." (For ideas about incorporating life purpose into coaching practice, see Belf, 1995.)

[4] We use the terms *executive* and *client* interchangeably as the primary person receiving coaching. Often this person is distinct from the *customer* or *client system,* terms used for the organization that contracts for coaching and pays for the service. It is important to clarify, disclose, and discuss in advance whose interests the coach is serving (client or customer) and to manage the process by establishing a clear contract as to the coach's role, the purpose of any assessments, the nature and extent of reporting relationships, and so forth.

[5] A related definition, adopted by the Professional and Personal Coaches Association, sees coaching as "an ongoing relationship which focuses on the client taking action toward the realization of their vision, goals or desires. Coaching uses a process of inquiry and personal discovery to build the client's level of awareness and responsibility and provides the client with structure, support and feedback" (Belf, 1995, p. 1).

need or application for these skills." Other times, the executive needs to build or sharpen a skill—"I've never learned how to do it" or "I know how, but I don't always do it well."[6] Usually the time frame for this coaching is "this week" or "this month" and is clearly identified and agreed to by the executive and others in the organization. Further coaching for skills represents little or no threat to most learners.

Coaching for skills has high clarity (goals tend to be clear and specific), high consensus (people tend to agree about the need for coaching and be strongly committed), and high control (people believe they have a good chance of achieving their learning goals). Of these three characteristics, clarity distinguishes this coaching role from other roles.

Coaching for skills helps people learn specific skills, behaviors, and attitudes and can support learning on the job (e.g., before or after a "first," such as a first customer visit or a first board meeting), traditional classroom training (by reinforcing learning and practical job applications), or job redesign (when reengineering introduces new or different roles and responsibilities).

In these cases, the coach helps the executive size up skills-building needs and recommends learning resources. Executives can apply their new skills and behaviors promptly because the needs are clear and specific. Time is often a key factor. Even if the managing partner in the following example had enjoyed the lead time to attend a course, he might have been reluctant to commit to a 3- to 5-day executive seminar on advanced presentation skills.

Example of Coaching for Skills

Situation. The managing partner of a worldwide professional services firm was called by the chairman to "pinch hit" a keynote address to roll out the "Vision 2000" program to several thousand partners at the annual meeting. The managing partner felt uncomfortable talking about a visionary topic to an audience of that size and wanted enhanced presentation skills. With the annual meeting less than 60 days away, the managing partner asked an outside coach to help sharpen his presentation skills to communicate the new vision with clarity and conviction.

Process. The coach began by encouraging the managing partner to talk freely about earlier speaking experiences. Because the coach was an outsider, the executive felt comfortable sharing that his planning usually had been the "victim" of last-minute deadlines or competing priorities. The coach and the client designed an intensive program, organized around weekly coaching sessions over a 6-week period. In the first three sessions, the executive sharpened his presentation skills and practiced until he felt comfortable. These sessions featured live videotapings of the executive in several speaking situations, along with individualized coaching, critiquing, and written feedback. At the fourth session the annual meeting presentation was developed. The executive learned a step-by-step process for planning presentations and left with an outline of his keynote address. Two final sessions allowed time to review the executive's written remarks and to critique the resulting speech rehearsal.

Results. Personal coaching helped the managing partner better prepare for and deliver the annual meeting presentation with more confidence about the quality and delivery of his message. He also felt in control of both formal and routine speaking situations in the future.

Coaching for Performance

Coaching for performance focuses on the executive's present job. Typically the executive feels the need to function more effectively at work ("I need to do a better job at . . . ") or to address other performance issues ("I'm not aware of how my actions affect others"). For executives at risk in the work-

[6] This includes competencies required at increasing levels of responsibility. For example, basic management skills might include planning, organizing, setting priorities, and so forth, whereas advanced skills associated with success in middle management could include conflict management, customer focus, and delegation of skills. Skills associated with success in the executive suite might include political savvy, strategic agility, and vision and purpose.

place, the challenge may be to correct problem behaviors before they jeopardize productivity or derail a career.[7] Usually the time frame for this coaching is "this quarter" or "this year" and is perceived as less urgent than coaching for skills. There may be less shared agreement about the need for coaching for performance and a greater threat to some learners than there is in coaching for skills.[8] For some, the experience is challenging, something like private swimming lessons for Olympic-class swimmers.

In coaching for performance situations, goals may be fuzzy. For example, the presenting problem or the business reasons ("He's not doing it the way he's supposed to") may lack clear definition of actual behavior or root causes. People may not know how to improve their effectiveness. Consequently, time to gain clarity and reach consensus about needs and outcomes characterizes coaching for performance.

Coaching for performance helps people improve their effectiveness on the job—often over several months. This coaching role can help executives to practice and apply new skills; clarify performance goals when expectations about behavior are unclear or when business goals, roles, or conditions change; or orient themselves to a new appointment or significant new responsibilities. Coaching for performance can also help change individual behaviors and correct problems by confronting ineffective attitudes or other motivational issues; alleviating performance problems when deficiencies jeopardize a person's productivity, job, or career; increasing confidence and commitment when seasoned players have experienced career setbacks and disappointments; or dealing with blind spots that detract from otherwise outstanding performance.

In these cases, the coach acts as a performance coach by helping executives assess their performance, obtain feedback on strengths and weaknesses, and enhance effectiveness.

Example of Coaching for Performance

Situation. The CEO of a diversified service firm discovered there was no performance feedback system to accurately assess his performance or that of other key players as the company grew. The short-term coaching goal was to set visible measures for executive success and apply them to all top managers. Over the long term, the CEO hoped to establish a leadership development program that would ensure the next generation of executives.

Process. A coach worked with the CEO to define a success profile of specific skills and behaviors that related to effectiveness in that organization. On the basis of this competency model, a multirater (360-degree) assessment was conducted in which the executive was reviewed by a full circle of board directors, peers, subordinates, and even outside customers whose observations the CEO thought would be valuable.

Following the assessment, this feedback was presented, along with the coach's observations, in a series of confidential sessions. The coach and the executive focused on how to learn from the data by interpreting and accepting the data, identifying performance trends and areas for improvement, analyzing reasons for major performance problems, and establishing action steps for performance improvement.

Results. The CEO described the performance feedback as revealing, accurate, honest, and useful and accepted it because it came from the combined judgment of many people with firsthand knowledge. With coaching for skills after the assessment, the executive experienced progress in managing execution, the skill set he selected to practice and apply on the job. Specifically, he was better able to delegate and coordinate work and be more effective in empowering employees. Both the CEO and others acknowledged that he had become a more effective executive.

[7] We call this related coaching subrole "coaching to correct performance" or "coaching for turnaround" ("fix-its" for short). These interventions are designed to remedy problems—often motivational or attitudinal—that interfere with job performance. The primary focus is on the present job, but the process of coaching to correct performance may involve time clarifying the problem with the executive and the boss. Unless both agree that a problem with a clear cause exists, and unless both are committed to address the issue, little is likely to be accomplished.

[8] The executive at risk may see the coaching as remedial or as a reflection on the executive's standing in the company. A less obvious scenario is that a strong performer may be ambivalent about being coached.

Coaching for Development

Coaching for development focuses on a person's future job. Typically the executive needs to prepare for advancement by strengthening leadership skills and to address long-term development needs. Others may need to "unlearn" a liability—an overdone strength turned into a weakness. The time frame for this coaching is "this year" or "next year." Because coaching for the future is involved, shared agreement about development coaching can be difficult and varies considerably. Development coaching appears prevalent in organizations with well-honed succession plans and success profiles.[9] Finally, coaching for development can be intense and analytical and therefore the most threatening to some learners.[10] Of all the coaching roles, this one focuses on executive development and personal growth. As one coach said, "This is easy for people who are introspective and enjoy root canals."

In coaching for development, clear, specific goals may be lacking or limited, and because this process customarily involves a very senior executive, there may be many relevant others involved in reaching consensus. Coaching for development involves more time—to reach clarity and consensus and to realize potentially far-reaching changes—than other forms of executive coaching.

Coaching for development helps people prepare for advancement over a year or more. Business examples include providing support for possible promotions or lateral transfers. This coaching role can enhance skills and capabilities for a future job; clarify shared goals about success when executives and their organizations disagree about the skills and perspectives needed in a future position; or encourage the long-term development of star performers by facilitating learning from challenging career experiences.

Example of Coaching for Development

Situation. A 47-year-old executive vice president of a manufacturing firm had long considered a week-long, intensive leadership development program but could never find the time. Now his boss was hinting about changes in the management committee, the executive's possible candidacy for one of two positions opening in the next year, and that better planning and communication skills would improve his current job performance and increase his chances for advancement.

Process. Because of his senior position and chaotic schedule, this executive opted for a form of development that would cater to his schedule and specific needs—executive coaching. For several weeks interviews were conducted with several superiors, including the immediate boss; about 5 peers; 6 subordinates; and his spouse, children, siblings, and friends.

Transcribed interviews were merged and comments reflected back without attribution but sorted by source category (i.e., superiors, peers, subordinates). The executive received the data in a concentrated 2-day period of reading about, discussing, elaborating on, and searching at a cursory level for coherent development themes. This process provided him with an intense but private look at strengths, developmental needs, and priorities from multiple sources.

During follow-up calls and another daylong session a month later, the coach and the executive prepared a condensed response to the data, identifying themes and issues. A later meeting was held to formalize a behaviorally-specific development plan and to agree on follow-up arrangements, including internal coaching continuity, spouse's involvement, external coaching follow-up, outcome measures, and deadlines and assessment.

Results. Changes are still in progress. This executive drove himself and everyone around him very

[9] *Success profiles* (also known as *competency models*) define sets of skills and behaviors shown by research and experience to be strongly related to effective performance in management, leadership, and executive positions.

[10] Data collection and feedback for this form of coaching go well beyond standard 360-degree assessment. This "enhanced feedback" can include data from the workplace and personal life of the executive, data on his or her behavior and motivation, and information on the executive's present as well as past history. The emphasis is on implementation. The feedback is powerful—and potentially harmful (what one person called an "emotional boot camp"). Such feedback rarely causes permanent harm, yet certain precautions should be taken to minimize risks. For a discussion, see Kaplan and Palus (1994).

hard. As a result, the people around him were wary of his next promotion, because they often saw him as having his own agenda, being either unable or unwilling to listen, and lacking in appreciative behaviors. They knew he deserved the promotion, but wondered how successful he would be given these behaviors. (This behavior played itself out at home and had gotten in the way of his relationship with his son.)

The executive had seen and heard it all before at work, but not at home. Upon seeing this, the executive was brought up short—"The proverbial 2 × 4 to the side of the head?"—and began to explore the effect his behavior had on others, both at home and at work. Through continued work with a coach, this executive continues to work on these issues.

Coaching for the Executive's Agenda

Because an executive's agenda can be broad and evolving, this type of coaching tends to involve comprehensive learning. Leading a business or a major business function can be a lonely activity. Often the executive needs a confidant to offer insight, perspective, and constructive feedback on ideas. This coaching is ongoing, and sessions evolve in response to the executive's agenda.

Goals can be broad or open-ended. Coaching may be tied to an organization's priorities (e.g., to help key people successfully implement specific change initiatives). The coach, as an objective outsider and "talking partner," questions and engages the executive on major issues, an option less open to corporate insiders. Often a coach in this role helps the executive obtain valid data to address specific issues or concerns. Consequently, the time and clarity for this coaching role can be highly variable, from a short-term contract to a long-term relationship. Coaching sessions may take place at regular intervals over a specific time period or on an on-call basis. The threat tends to be low, as the executive sets the agenda and controls its content.

Coaching for the executive's agenda deals with broader purposes—the continual life results and well-being an executive wants. The scope ranges considerably and usually goes beyond a single person or situation. Business examples include mergers and acquisitions, productivity and quality improvement, executive leadership transitions, turnarounds, and coping with explosive growth. Situations well suited to this type of coaching role include supporting better decisions when an executive needs insight and perspective, expanding options when creative suggestions could improve the chances for sound decisions, supporting change management by preparing an executive to successfully implement specific change initiatives, or guiding the executive through unknown or unexplored areas when he or she feels overwhelmed.

The coach offers feedback and suggestions. Depending on the executive's agenda, the coach may also act in other capacities, as suggested by the following example.

Example of Coaching for the Executive's Agenda

Situation. A worldwide financial services firm was rapidly losing market share in one of its business units. Once an industry leader, its competitive position was steadily deteriorating—client service was poor and quality control was marginal. To compound problems, the company's highly centralized, bureaucratic decision making was ineffective in responding to its new environment. The executive in charge realized the business unit had to change, starting with a strategic commitment to provide its clients with the very best service available. Beyond developing a specific change strategy, the challenge was to win the commitment of the employees and involve them in all levels of the change effort. The executive needed to move quickly and decisively to diffuse employee fears about firmwide downsizing.

Process. The executive engaged a coach to help her lead this change. Her own exposure to changing organizations convinced her that it was more difficult to implement strategy than to develop it. And she wanted an experienced sounding board—an objective outside resource to work through the toughest issues. The coaching began by helping the executive clarify her own goals for change, as well as the roles she wished to play in the change process.

In conjunction with the organization's human resources department, the coach helped the executive systematically assess the situation. Attitude surveys and structured interviews were used to diagnose key issues and set an agenda for change. A "balanced scorecard" was developed to measure progress on a regular basis, covering client service, cost-effectiveness, improved teamwork, and related performance ratings. The coach also facilitated a 2-day strategic retreat, a first for this business unit. In partnership, the coach and the executive designed several pilot projects to continue the changes resulting from the meeting.

Throughout the change, the executive was coached and given feedback about her performance in leading the effort, based on direct observation of her behavior in work settings and interviews of coworkers about her effectiveness. The coach remained on call to assist with the executive's change effort.

Results. In just a year, remarkable changes had occurred. "We have improved our performance substantially," said the executive, "and with lower operating costs." Senior management agreed, and the organization's board approved a major new commitment to the business unit in record time.

SOME SIMILARITIES IN COACHING

We have focused on distinctions among coaching roles. What do they have in common? First, all executive coaching involves *action research,* or *action learning* (the more user-friendly term).[11] Second, successful coaching involves working in partnership with executives. By combining a coach's observations and capabilities (especially the ability to ask effective questions) with an executive's expertise, the executive achieves better and faster results. Typically, the coaching process involves the following four steps:

1. Commitment—to a contract for coaching. Often over a series of meetings, the coach, the executive, and the executive's boss or a human resources representative lay out the parameters of the project, including degree of confidentiality for data and desired outcome.
2. Assessment—to set a goal or define a problem. The coach and the executive determine the reasons for any differences between the executive's goals and reality. Assessment can be conversations or an extensive data collection effort. No two situations are alike. This step results in a clear, realistic plan of action.
3. Action—to help change the way the executive thinks and performs by building competence, confidence, and commitment.
4. Continuous improvement—to ensure actions achieve desired results, as measured by monitoring and sustainability methods. At this stage, the boss, the human resources representative, or other internal resources personnel may again become more actively involved to sustain behavioral changes.

TOWARD A PRACTICE THEORY

Coaching is about bringing out the best in people. Good coaching begins with role clarity. Even though coaching situations differ, some role distinctions can be recognized—if only to foster informed choice by everyone involved.

Beyond informed choice, we hope this article fosters a dialogue about the roles coaches play. We see a future in which business coaching is widely available, in which coaching is informed by insights from an evolving practice theory[12] for coaching executives.

We base our practice theory on mental maps drawn up while thinking about a range of coaching cases, such as those presented in this article. Although mental maps paint an incomplete picture of coaching, our aim is to continue clarifying the respective roles of coaching, along with coaching

[11] *Action research* is research with the goal of making action more effective. Conceived as a novel form of problem solving by social psychologist Kurt Lewin, this "learning by doing" approach is now widely practiced in organizations undergoing change and development (e.g., see Shepard, 1960/1990).

[12] A practice theory resembles formal theory but is based on experience, not systematic research. It constitutes a mental map of what is important and what to do about it. We first learned of practice theory from Weisbord (1987, pp. 260–261), who attributed the concept to Peter Vaill. More recently, Vaill (1989, p. 35) said he meant something very close to the concept of "theory in use" by organizational psychologist Chris Argyris.

models, best practices, and related matters. This article, a work in progress, invites comments and contributions from readers.

References

Beckhard, R., & Pritchard, W. (1992). *Changing the essence: The art of creating and leading fundamental change in organizations.* San Francisco: Jossey-Bass.

Belf, T. (1995, Summer). In the beginning . . . on purpose. *Being in Action: The Professional and Personal Coaching Association Journal*, 4.

Evered, R. D., & Selman, J. C. (1989). Coaching and the art of management. *Organizational Dynamics, 18*(2), 16–32.

Kaplan, R. E., Drath, W. H., & Kofodimos, J. R. (1991). *Beyond ambition: How driven managers can lead better and live better.* San Francisco: Jossey-Bass.

Kaplan, R. E., & Palus, C. J. (1994). *Enhancing 360-degree feedback for senior executives: How to maximize the benefits and minimize the risks* (Tech. Rep. No. 160). Greensboro, NC: Center for Creative Leadership.

Kotter, J. P. (1982). *The general managers.* New York: Free Press.

Peters, T. J., & Austin, N. K. (1985). *A passion for excellence: The leadership difference.* New York: Warner Books.

Schein, E. H. (1969). *Process consultation: Its role in organization development.* Reading, MA: Addison-Wesley.

Shepard, H. A. (1990). An action research model. In W. L. French & C. H. Bell, Jr. (Eds.), *Organization development: Behavioral science interventions for organization improvement* (p. 102). Englewood Cliffs, NJ: Prentice Hall. (Original work published 1960)

Smith, L. (1993, December 27). The executive's new coach. *Fortune,* 126–134.

Vaill, R. V. (1989). *Managing as a performing* art. San Francisco: Jossey-Bass.

Weisbord, M. R. (1987). *Productive workplaces: Organizing and managing for dignity, meaning, and community.* San Francisco: Jossey-Bass.

CHAPTER 11

COACHING AT THE TOP

Fred Kiel, Eric Rimmer, Kathryn Williams, and Marilyn Doyle

Executives at the most senior levels present particular challenges to the development consultant. An effective coaching relationship requires that the consultant earn a level of trust sufficient to allow the executive to be open to change and willing to be influenced—a formidable task in itself. An additional challenge is helping clients recognize the value of making development a priority, when the pressures of their jobs are already so great.

KRW is a small transatlantic consultancy specializing in providing leadership development to senior executives at or near the CEO level in Fortune 500 companies and large private organizations. Fred Kiel, Eric Rimmer, and Kathryn Williams own the corporation in equal partnership and are based in Minnesota, England, and North Carolina, respectively. Two are psychologists (counseling and clinical), and the third comes from an international business background, mostly in human resources management. Marilyn Doyle is a clinical psychologist who provides psychological testing and editorial consultation to the corporation.

What follows is a description of the specialized leadership development program we have found effective with this senior-level clientele and a case example illustrating the process.

APPROACH TO SENIOR EXECUTIVE DEVELOPMENT

Over a period of more than 10 years, we have refined our approach to coaching the senior executive and have structured a program that begins with the acquisition of extensive confidential business and personal life information about the client. These data provide the core of the executive development process and reflect our belief that self-understanding is the foundation of long-lasting developmental change.

Conceptual Foundation

Our approach to understanding clients is strongly embedded in a multisystems orientation, and we view individuals as shaping and being shaped by their pasts, their personal lives, and their work environments. Because leadership ability may be enhanced or hindered by experiences in any of these life systems, we believe that the most effective development program must seek to understand those influences, generalize strengths from one setting to another, and foster an openness and readiness to change. Within this systems orientation, we draw from the frameworks of humanistic, existential, behavioral, and psychodynamic psychology and

Reprinted from the *Consulting Psychology Journal: Practice and Research, 48,* 67–77.

choose our techniques eclectically to fit the client, the situation, and the need.

Clientele

Our clientele is exclusively composed of Fortune 500 companies and large private firms. We work only with senior executives—those at, or close to, the CEO level. These clients generally fit into three major groups:

Approximately one fourth of our clients have been identified as likely candidates for advancement, and our assignment is to assist them in preparing for those positions.

Half of our referrals are seen as solid senior players, and our assignment is to increase their leadership "bench strength."

The final fourth have been identified as "'in trouble" and are possible derailment candidates. Although there are questions or concerns about their leadership, they are seen as having considerable corporate value and potential, and our assignment is to help them get back on track.

As is probably true of the executive population at large, the typical senior executive in our client population scores one or two standard deviations above the mean on measures of dominance and need for control. In our experience, few are "psychologically minded," and many even hold a fair amount of distrust or disdain for the "'soft" side of leadership. When push comes to shove, most executives habitually turn to leveraging the hard side—they focus on numbers and the bottom line and, in general, rely on the formula that worked in the past.

Method

Developing an effective coaching relationship with such individuals is not an easy task. Although trust is a necessary ingredient, it is not sufficient for a successful coaching relationship. We have found that developing an expertise about the individual client, through extensive data collection, is one of the most effective ways to build the needed relationship. Executives respect good data and generally respect people who take the time to do their homework. In our experience, in-depth databases about the client's current and former effectiveness—both in his or her professional life and personal life—meet this criterion. By interviewing broadly in the client's life, we acquire information that he or she could not get independently. Once the consultant has this depth of knowledge about the individual, a powerful coaching relationship can begin.

A second way of developing the relationship is through referred power from the organization. Ideally, this power comes by means of the client's sponsor or boss, who explicitly supports the development process and clearly states the overall goals of the coaching assignment. This organizational support also allows the consultants to focus on systemic issues within the client's portion of the organization.

Our methods are holistic. We have found that the majority of weaknesses in leadership effectiveness are the result of required skills that have never been learned. For example, many executives do not communicate their visions adequately, develop their teams effectively, or manage conflict productively. However, we have also consistently found that a significant change in workplace effectiveness is often intimately tied to the client's personal effectiveness. The interpersonal patterns we learned in childhood, as well as current family and marital distress, can often play as much of a role in ineffective leadership as can the stress of the professional position.

Our methods are also team based. It is unlikely that any one professional coach will carry a "tool kit" that contains all that is needed to provide the clients with a range of interventions from deep personal work to effective organizational interventions. Thus, our consulting teams are usually composed of two people, one of whom brings clinical skills and the other organizational development skills. In addition, two minds are simply better than one. The synergy of a team approach has often allowed a breakthrough for a client that would have been less likely without a team approach.

Finally, our methods are systems oriented. Although the individual is our primary client and the coaching and development plan is built around leveraging the client's strengths and overcoming his or her weaknesses, the organization is also our client and its needs must be addressed. Unlike individual psychotherapy, in which the goal is exclusively increased personal effectiveness, the primary goal of executive coaching is for the business itself to become more successful. This is accomplished by increasing the client's personal effectiveness, but also by using interventions to help the organizational system become more effective. Whether the success of the business is assessed as an improved bottom line, higher employee satisfaction, better labor relations, or progress in other business indicators, the organization must benefit in some recognizable way.

PROGRAM STRUCTURE

Over the course of 2 years, our senior executive development program continues through three distinct phases: fact gathering, planning and consolidation, and implementation and development.

Phase 1: Fact Gathering

Once a formal commitment to the program has been made by both the individual client and his or her sponsor (generally, a board member for clients at the CEO level) or boss, the fact-gathering process begins. The consultants interview the client in considerable depth about work life, personal history, and current personal life, and the client completes a battery of psychological tests, which may include such elements as the Adjective Checklist (ACL), FIRO-B, Myers–Briggs Type Inventory (MBTI), Minnesota Multiphasic Personality Inventory (MMPI), and a team management instrument.

With the advice of the lead consultant, the client prepares a list of those individuals who could offer information helpful to the client's development process. Up to 20 work colleagues and significant persons in the client's personal life are individually interviewed by the team following a structured data-collection format. In addition to its fact-gathering focus, this process frequently becomes a catalyst for those interviewed to develop alternative ways of viewing the organizational and family systems and to recognize the parts that they themselves play in these systems.

Phase 2: Planning and Consolidation

The second phase of the program begins with a 2- to 3-day "insight session," during which the consulting team presents all of the collected information to the client to create a comprehensive portrait. This picture pinpoints strengths and shortfalls and offers perceptions of the client's motivation, use of power and influence, decision making, expectations, handling of conflict, integrity, emotional competence, and other dimensions of personal and professional effectiveness.

The consultants work with the client to consolidate the information and target areas for development, including the leveraging of identified strengths. Both parties collaborate to produce a document that integrates the collected data and use that information as the basis for a development plan that details specific and measurable goals and action steps.

Phase 3: Implementation and Development

Implementation generally begins with the client enlisting the help of the employing organization in providing resources and support for achieving specific development goals. With the client's approval, data from the information-gathering process are shared in a meeting involving the client, the organizational sponsor or boss, and the lead consultant. The data provide the background for discussion of the client's development plan and reaffirm the importance of the organizational system in the process. Once agreement on the plan is reached, similar meetings with selected colleagues may take place as one of the developmental activities defined by the plan.

Throughout this phase, the consultants provide resources to facilitate the development process and offer coaching, counsel, support, and ongoing feedback. Regular meetings are scheduled to help the client remain focused on the goals, and assistance may be provided in acquiring specific leadership, conflict management, or team development skills. Collaboration with individuals in the client's personal and professional spheres frequently occurs to foster and support changes as they occur.

Phase 3 lasts for as long as the client continues to work toward his or her development goals—a period of up to 2 years. During this time, typically at 6-month intervals, the consulting team conducts brief spot-check interviews with selected persons to gauge progress and to retune the client's goals. After sharing these results with the client, meetings may be held with the sponsor or boss to summarize those results and keep the organization involved in the process.

The formal coaching relationship continues for about 2 years, with the involvement of the consultants being about 1 day a month during the 1st year and perhaps one half a day a month in the 2nd year. The formal process generally ends when the client has adopted an attitude toward continuous improvement of leadership abilities and has developed an organizational support mechanism for ongoing growth. Such support may include solidifying a coaching relationship with a sponsor or boss or identifying mentors within the organization. Even though the formal program may end, many of our clients seek some form of ongoing contact.

KEY ISSUES WITH SENIOR EXECUTIVES

Through our experience with senior-level executives, we have identified a number of issues and principles that guide our development approach.

Leaders need, but have few opportunities for, continuing development. It is an all too common assumption that those who reach the executive suite no longer need personal development. However, the leadership style that worked in lower level positions may not be as effective or appropriate at the senior level. Functional and technical skills need to give way to greater focus on developing others. Unfortunately, opportunities for personal growth and development to meet these new challenges are rare.

Personal development seldom gets priority. The pressures of global competition fuel a demand for ever more effective business leaders to set the tone and affect the cultural shifts of changing values and expectations. Without support, however, even those recognizing this need seldom feel able to give priority to personal growth in the face of the multiple, competing demands for their time and energy.

Development requires significant self-awareness. No organization would develop a long-term strategic plan without taking stock of its current resources and historical data, but rarely is the same care taken for the organization's leaders. An effective program provides the individual with an opportunity to stand back and take a fresh look at the experiences and assumptions of a lifetime. It advances self-understanding by identifying inner resources, targeting growth areas, and promoting the balance between career and personal life needed to sustain the vitality essential to effective leadership.

Self-understanding demands quality feedback. One major drawback of being in a senior position is isolation from meaningful feedback. An effective leadership development program must include sufficient data from a wide enough variety of sources to capture the depth and breadth of the person and provide the opportunity for significant self-understanding and change.

Positive individual change has a positive organizational impact. Organizational effectiveness is enhanced through focused individual professional development. Because senior executives have a profound effect on their organizations, their personal development also positively affects the entire system.

External support facilitates the process. Even when a leader is aware of development needs, the corporate environment may seem inhospitable to acknowledging them. Organizational norms usually call for senior-level personnel to present themselves as confident and competent, and openly addressing weaknesses can create feelings of vulnerability to the personal agendas of others. An externally led development program can provide objectivity, a safe environment in which to explore needs, and impartial direction and assistance while respecting the individual's right to choose his or her own direction.

Continuing support is essential to sustain growth. Though information and evaluation spur development, they are not sufficient to maintain change or cultivate long-term openness to continuous improvement. Lasting change requires ongoing support and coaching, reassessment, and the flexibility to meet ever-changing needs.

GUIDELINES FOR A SUCCESSFUL COACHING PROCESS

Through our work, we have identified a number of practical guides that increase the effectiveness of a coach or developer. In our experience, attention to these factors results in the most successful outcomes for the individual and the organization.

Adopt a Multisystems View

Critical to the process is recognition that the client-as-leader is only one part of the picture. The effectiveness of a development program is greatly enhanced by attending to the other systems in which the client is involved, including the organizational system and those in the client's personal life. When a client undergoes a development process and makes significant and deep changes in the way he or she responds to the world, it may have as much impact on the individual's family system and friendships as on his or her leadership style. In addition to involving the boss or sponsor, we meet with the spouse to explain the process and discuss its likely impact. In our experience, given such an approach the spouse generally becomes a positive participant and embraces the coaching process.

Establish Clear Boundaries

Establishing and maintaining clear boundaries is also crucial to the success of the coaching process. We hold strongly to the separation of social and professional roles, and we allow only one relationship: the professional relationship of coach and client. Although we may hold meetings with a client in his or her home, the tone is kept professional rather than social, and we typically decline social invitations in the interests of keeping this boundary clear.

Plan for Resistance

Over the course of our 2-year involvement, we generally encounter significant resistance at some point. Properly qualifying both the client and the organization before coaching begins and ensuring that neither has a hidden agenda are ways to reduce the possibility of resistance. For example, an executive who is presented as a solid senior player, but who is actually thought of as a potential derailment candidate, is likely to become understandably resistant when the truth becomes known.

Resistance can also occur if the client fears losing his or her "winning formula." An executive who has been amply rewarded over the years for using a particular style can be quite hesitant about tampering with it, even if it is not as effective now as in the past. By addressing this fear directly with clients or having them talk with a previous client who has had the same concern, we are usually able to reassure them that an effective coaching process helps a person expand a winning formula rather than lose it.

A client may also become resistant at some point in the coaching process simply because most people have a fear of change. Predicting such resistance and planning with the client on how to recognize and deal with it are generally effective strategies. Most clients are readily able to describe how they will behave when they are resisting the process and are willing to tell us what we should do to help them overcome their resistance.

Embrace Flexibility

Within legal and ethical bounds, maintaining a flexible approach that allows the use of "whatever works" is particularly important with this population. No manual or guide could ever spell out all the nuances of executive coaching, and creativity plays a significant role in achieving the desired outcome. One small example involves flexibility in selecting the setting used for meetings. In addition to the distraction of phone calls and other interruptions, the executive office seems to have a "hardening" effect on many clients. Meeting with clients in hotel suites or their homes frequently has the opposite effect.

Maintain Momentum

Momentum can be ensured through a number of means, including regularly scheduled sessions with the sponsor or boss, client, and consultant, and quarterly meetings with the sponsor or boss alone to obtain information about how the organization-as-client is faring. In addition, facilitated conversations between the client and key coworkers (such as peers, subordinates, or those above the client in the organizational hierarchy) or spouse and the regular collection of spot-check data about the client's progress not only serve to give the client an ongoing source of feedback but also remind the organization and family of positive change.

Preserve Confidentiality

From start to finish, the individual client must retain control of the development process. We will not talk to anyone about the client or share any data with anyone (including the sponsor, boss, or human resources staff) without the client's specific permission to do so. Although the organization pays us, the data collected and the information shared with us belong to the individual.

We generally encourage clients to be open about their development plans, in order to model such behavior to others and to be leaders in fostering positive and relevant change. As a part of the process, we require clients to give at least a verbal report to their sponsor or boss, with us in the room, about what they have discovered to be their strengths and weaknesses and describing the work-related development goals they intend to pursue. In practice, most clients find it surprisingly rewarding to be so open about themselves during these facilitated sessions.

CASE STUDY

A 40-year-old man was referred by his CEO through the head of human resources, who described him as a "star performer" with immense interpersonal problems. He was described as intimidating and needlessly competitive, and his poor peer relationships were apparently made more problematic by his identification as the "favorite son" of a very charismatic boss. Although even his strongest detractors recognized his potential, he would not be a candidate for any further promotions unless he changed the ways he interacted with colleagues.

Work Background

The client was in a senior sales and marketing role in a major international corporation and was responsible for the sales growth and profitability of his products. He was one of a small team reporting to the division CEO, along with several other "line" colleagues holding comparable responsibilities and functional colleagues in finance, human resources, and so forth. Having already enjoyed considerable success in previous sales or sales-oriented roles, he was perceived as the most heavyweight member of the team and as favored by the boss.

The client's area was a relatively small but high-profile division of the overall organization, with products outside the mainstream of the corporation's principal product areas. The division's products were highly visible, fast moving, and positioned in an extremely competitive marketplace. Most members of the division thought of themselves as in a different business than the core company, and they had relatively high day-to-day decision-making freedom. This setting was very much in tune with the client's personality, and he viewed the core organization as a large bureaucracy with which he had little in common.

Personal Background

The client and his older siblings were raised in a privileged family, attending private schools and enjoying all the luxuries of a well-to-do family while having little contact with less privileged contemporaries. His father was a business executive whose alcohol use was the basis of significant job and marital difficulties. He generally was angry, critical, and unavailable to the family, seldom displaying affection but holding very high expectations of the children. The client's mother was thoughtful and loving, very supportive of her children and involved in their lives. There was significant parental conflict in the family, but it was never dealt with directly.

Following college, the client married a professional colleague who continued to maintain a high-level position in another corporation. As a couple, they shared the responsibility of parenting their children to a greater extent than most executives.

Contract Process

The consulting team met with the client's CEO to discuss the program and to obtain his support of the process if the client himself was appropriately qualified and wanted to commit to the program. Next, the team met with the client to introduce the program and, after some initial concerns were addressed, he recognized the potential benefits and agreed to participate.

Data Gathering and Feedback

After meeting with the client's spouse to gain her support, the client and consultants prepared a list of the colleagues, family, and friends who would be individually interviewed, and the client completed a battery of tests.

When the interviews were completed, the consulting team met with the client in a 2-day session to present the interview data and test results. The test results described a bright, creative, and ambitious man with considerable personal charisma, energy, and enthusiasm. They suggested that although he could be warm, giving, and genuinely interested in intimate relationships, he was also attracted to power and achievement, which could lead him to be overly aggressive and self-focused in the pursuit of his goals. The most problematic personality traits indicated were impatience, sarcasm, a high need for control, and a tendency to become easily bored. The tests also suggested that he had considerably more personal insecurity than his outward behavior demonstrated and that to a large extent this derived from a fear of rejection.

The interview data were read verbatim to the client—while maintaining the anonymity of those interviewed—and a picture of how he was viewed began to emerge. The themes seen included a considerable number of positive characteristics. In his work life, he was described as very intelligent, creative, imaginative, and knowledgeable about the business and as having considerable drive, energy, enthusiasm, and passion in his work. He had a "great presence," with an ability to lead and motivate others and make them feel special. Many of the same strengths were repeated in his personal life, particularly those reflecting his energy, enthusiasm, forcefulness, and ability to "attract" others. Those in his personal life also reported qualities of loyalty, honesty, and devotion to family, although these qualities were not reported by those in his work life.

Significant and troubling weaknesses were noted by those interviewed in the client's work life. He was seen as antagonistic and hostile—a "vicious competitor." He was also seen as arrogant, overcontrolling, intimidating, and even "menacing" in interactions as well as moody, self-absorbed, and unapproachable. Impatience and insecurity were frequently mentioned as weaknesses, and there was a significant lack of trust, particularly by his peers. The personal data included many similar—though less strongly expressed—elements, such as impatience, a tendency to be demanding and overcontrolling, pushiness, and unpredictability. Family and friends, however, did not perceive the antagonism or hostility mentioned in the work-based data.

The client was very surprised by the interview data, as he had been unaware that others saw him as intimidating and that he was not trusted. He was also startled by the test results, but did not disagree with any of the themes. He summarized his reaction to the data in this way:

> My reactions scare people, and their fear and lack of trust lead to a blocking of information. . . . I'm surprised that the mistrust is as strong as it is across the board, but am relieved that those who know me best don't have the same mistrust. . . . I'm good at what I do—sometimes great—but I could be awesome if I dealt with the issues of control, impatience, and rigidity. Others see in me a need to win, while I see the fear of failure and the need to prove myself.

The data shared with the client allowed a strong consulting relationship to build quickly. Although initially he was quite defensive when presented with the information regarding his work interactions—as evidenced by his surprise at how he was perceived—the client used the data well in aiding his self-understanding and awareness. Although the negative data were quite harsh, the significant number of positive qualities and abilities reported allowed the client to get a more realistic and balanced picture of himself. As a result, the client was able to talk at length about what he called his "ridiculous insecurity," which was a significant breakthrough in his relationship with the consultants.

During the last half day of the session, the client's spouse attended. She had completed several of the psychological tests the client had taken and, after the team gave her the test feedback, there was an in-depth discussion of the couple's similarities and differences and how they affected their relationship. At the end of the session, the client was given a "workbook" with a series of questions that he and the consulting team would use to integrate the large amount of data, to determine the themes in both the work life and personal life, and to create a development plan.

Consolidating

At the next meeting, the client and consultants compared their responses to those in a workbook exercise and found that they generally agreed on the themes of his strengths and weaknesses and on the similarities and differences in the views of people in his work life and personal life.

The consultants asked him to create a picture of the person he would like to become. He wanted to be seen as "dedicated to developing as a person" and through this process to become "a great friend to a great many people—someone they could turn to for support, for a laugh, for a hug." He wanted to maintain his energy for everything he did and to be remembered for the people he helped and who helped him, for the businesses he built, for his family, and for the contributions he made on many levels and to many people and causes.

Using the data and his vision, the client and consultants constructed four goals for his development program: (1) to change people's perceptions about his trustworthiness and caring; (2) to build on his strengths, such as his presence and enthusiasm, while tempering those qualities so that he did not appear intimidating and arrogant; (3) to bring out at work the person he felt he was in his personal life; and (4) to reduce his reliance on negative behaviors through increased awareness of his use of them and better understanding of their origins.

Implementation of the Process

A significant step for this client came when he and a consultant held meetings with his boss, peers, and those who reported directly to him to share his development plan. These sessions were important breakthroughs for this client, as colleagues who previously had seen him as cocky and arrogant for the first time experienced him as vulnerable and concerned. They were universally open to supporting his plan and giving him continuing feedback.

In several meetings held with the client's boss, the consultants were able to help him understand the part he played in the client's difficulties within the organization, particularly in terms of the "sibling rivalry" that had grown among those who reported directly to him and the perception of the client as the boss's favored son. The boss recognized and agreed to address this perception, supported the client's development plan, and continued to give the client and consultants honest and timely feedback.

The consultants built a close, trusting relationship with the client as they explored unresolved historical issues. He became aware of the impact his childhood had on the person he had become and of early family relationships that had laid the foundation for his insecurity and reactive posture of arrogance to cover it.

The client began keeping a personal journal in which he evaluated his interactions with others, seeking increased awareness and understanding of his insecurity and intimidating behaviors. The consultants used the journal information and their personal experiences with him to aid him in recognizing verbal and nonverbal behaviors that were intimidating even to them, and they helped him develop the internal resources that would support a more patient, empathetic, and win–win approach in his interpersonal interactions. He was also encouraged to turn his competitiveness outward—to focus on competing with other companies rather than with his peers.

Among his strengths were substantial resources as a parent. The consultants worked with him to recognize these abilities and to draw from them in the work environment. As his awareness increased, he was able to transfer many of these beliefs and behaviors, such as patience and empathy, to work-related interactions. The consultants also met with the client and his spouse together and separately to help them deal with the struggles of a two-career family and with some historical issues that had not been adequately resolved.

Lessons Learned

Two assumptions were confirmed by the development team through the work with this client. First, the importance of an engaging and supportive boss was reinforced. The involvement of the client's boss, who was willing to be clear and open with the client, allowed significant growth to begin very quickly. Second, as had been expected, having consulting team members with different stylistic approaches and areas of expertise proved to be extremely effective. The combination of both clinical and organizational expertise allowed a range of interventions that promoted growth and support across environments.

Outcome

The client's colleagues experienced substantial changes in his interactions with them very quickly. Although many were initially skeptical about whether the changes would last, they remained supportive, giving him regular feedback on positive changes as well as when they experienced the more familiar competitive behaviors.

Midway through the program, the client's boss was promoted to a major new role in the core organization, and he was sufficiently confident in the development changes the client had made to recruit him into one of the most demanding sales roles in the organization—dealing with major customer–client relationships in all parts of the United States. In this new position, the client was a member of a much bigger team with a number of equally capable peers, and he needed to learn how to make things happen in a much more structured corporate environment and in the midst of major organizational and marketplace change. In this new environment with a new set of peers and a new staff, he made even more progress on his development goals. Spot-check and internal feedback data indicated that he was now seen as a real team player among his peers as well as a visionary (and even inspirational) leader of his staff. The client described his development in this way:

> I was so totally unaware of the force of my nature on people. . . . So the first way I changed was a heightened awareness of the effect I had on people. I think I became much clearer about how I wanted to be viewed as a leader and that helped me shape my behaviors more clearly. I was able to articulate the desire to be trusted and listened to as someone who could give good guidance to a team. I gained more openness—open to a more diverse and broader stripe of talent, of different ways of going about things.

After a year in that position, the client received another major promotion, as the organization decided to use his skills and accumulated knowledge in an international role based overseas. His current challenge is to completely reorganize and rebuild sales structures in a range of countries, working with a staff and their teams that are composed of people of several nationalities. He continues to do well in this new position. The consulting team maintains informal contact with him, and he occasionally uses them as a sounding board—as does his former boss.

Recently, the client was asked what he felt contributed to his development. Along with giving credit to his boss, coworkers, and family for their support and "willingness to be frank and share on an ongoing basis how they were feeling," he said,

> It definitely would not have happened on its own. Certainly [the consultants] provided both the catalyst and the ongoing support mechanisms to make the

changes. The thing that makes [KRW] special is the way you hang in and check back instead of just giving an information dump. . . .

You can't separate the product from the people. [The consultants] both are such caring and supportive people, and that really made the difference. I wouldn't be sitting . . . in this job if it hadn't been for this program. I really rate this high. There are a few life-changing events for a person—the birth of children, marriage to my wife. This fits in that category. I wouldn't be the father I am or the husband I am if it weren't for the kind of information and support I got from [KRW].

CHAPTER 12

EXECUTIVE COACHING AT WORK: THE ART OF ONE-ON-ONE CHANGE

David B. Peterson

In 1981, Personnel Decisions International (PDI) became the first management consulting firm to offer a coaching program that was both structured and personally tailored to accelerate individual change and development (Hellervik, Hazucha, & Schneider, 1992). Since that time, PDI consultants have coached over 2,500 managers, executives, and professionals around the world. Two empirical studies have shown that PDI's coaching produces significant, observable changes that are sustained at least 2 years after coaching is completed (Peterson, 1993a, 1993b; Thompson, 1986).

Coaching at PDI involves a team of people, including the participant, his or her organizational sponsor (typically his or her boss or a human resources representative), and a PDI coach. We encourage individuals and their organizations to share responsibility for development (Peterson & Hicks, 1995, 1996). This partnership requires individuals to take responsibility for investing time and effort to develop and apply relevant skills and organizations to take responsibility for setting clear performance expectations and providing the appropriate resources, support, and incentives to help individuals succeed.

COACHING STRATEGIES

We define *coaching* as "the process of equipping people with the tools, knowledge, and opportunities they need to develop themselves and become more effective" (Peterson & Hicks, 1996, p. 14). The following five coaching strategies have emerged from research and applied experience: forge a partnership, inspire commitment, grow skills, promote persistence, and shape the environment (Hellervik et al., 1992; Peterson, 1993b; Peterson & Hicks, 1993, 1996). When brought together in a well-designed coaching intervention, these five strategies help ensure that coaches gain commitment, avoid resistance, and diagnose and resolve coaching challenges as they arise. Our methodological foundation is derived from cognitive–behavioral psychology (e.g., Decker & Nathan, 1985; Mahoney, 1991) as well as from pragmatic research on individual change (e.g., Druckman & Bjork, 1991; Prochaska, DiClemente, & Norcross, 1992).

Forge a Partnership

Build trust and understanding so people want to work with you. A partnership requires that

My ongoing dialogue with Mary Dee Hicks (Hicks & Peterson, 1993, 1995, 1996; Peterson & Hicks, 1993, 1995, 1996; Peterson, Uranowitz, & Hicks, 1996) has been invaluable in helping to shape the ideas in this chapter; some of the language in the Coaching Strategies section of this chapter comes from our 1996 book. I am deeply indebted to Jan Stambaugh of Hewlett-Packard Company for her willingness to share the details of her coaching experience. All of her quotes in the case study came from the detailed notes I took on my laptop computer during sessions; she has reviewed them for accuracy. I would also like to thank Brian Anderson, Val Arnold, Michael Frisch, Cindy Marsh, Bob Muschewske, Karen Stellon, and Seymour Uranowitz for their comments on an earlier version of the chapter.

coaches earn the trust of people they work with so they can provide the right amounts of challenge and support throughout the process. If a coach fails here, people will discount the coach's perspective and will resist taking risks or experimenting with new behaviors. To build trust, coaches must learn how people view the world and what they care about. Our first conversation with new coaching participants is spent exploring their goals and how they view their work situation. As Carl Rogers (1951) said, "The best vantage point for understanding behavior is from the internal frame of reference of the individual" (p. 494). We also establish clear expectations about confidentiality and express our commitment to helping them be successful. This strategy requires effective listening skills, patience, and an understanding of the dynamics of human behavior.

Inspire Commitment

Build insight and motivation so people focus their energy on goals that matter. We have witnessed many people attempting to change someone's behavior by giving feedback. Even with willing learners, the process of giving feedback suggests a dynamic in which the coach is the expert and the learner is either ignorant or in error. To avoid the hierarchical nature of such an approach, we aim to cultivate insight during the coaching process by helping people obtain information that is personally relevant to achieving their goals. Such information comes in four categories: goals, abilities, perceptions, and standards (GAPS), as portrayed in Table 12.1.

People are motivated to work on their development when they perceive discrepancies between where they are and where they wish to go. The coach's task is to help people gather, make sense of, and act on relevant information in all four GAPS categories.

- Information on goals may come from personal reflection, a written personal mission statement, career counseling, values clarification exercises, and career interest instruments.
- Abilities information may be discovered by means of performance evaluations, professional assessments, expert observation and feedback, or through personal observation over time.
- Information about others' perceptions can be obtained from people inside or outside the organization, including peers, bosses, senior management, clients, customers, and friends. This information may be solicited through face-to-face conversation, 360-degree feedback surveys, and third-party interviews.
- Information on organizational standards and expectations may come from conversations with the organization's leaders, statements of corporate vision and strategy, competency models, job descriptions, performance evaluations, and statements of team goals.

Once the necessary GAPS information is available, coaches help people translate their new insights into action by prioritizing their development goals and developing a concrete plan for development and behavior change. All members of the coaching team, including the organizational sponsors, need to agree on the coaching plan. This contracting process increases a sense of ownership and commitment to change from all parties.

Grow Skills

Build new competencies to ensure people know how to do what is required. Helping people ac-

TABLE 12.1

GAPS Information: Goals, Abilities, Perceptions, and Standards

View	Where the person is	Where the person wants to go
Person	**Abilities:** What the person can do.	**Goals:** What the person wants to do.
Organization	**Perceptions:** How others see the person.	**Standards:** What others expect of the person.

quire new skills and new knowledge is perhaps the most straightforward of the coaching strategies. It draws on many common tools, such as formal and informal training, books, mentors, and rotational assignments. Yet the role of the coach is to find the best way for an individual to learn a specific skill. For example, the best way to develop skills in areas such as marketing, business strategy, organizational savvy, and many other aspects of leadership is through the use of case study, discussion, and analysis of real-world examples. In contrast, sales, communications, and interpersonal skills are usually best learned through role-playing, the observation of experts in action, and hands-on practice. Regardless of the learning method that is used, real-world experience is essential to deepen insight and forge sound judgment about how and when to apply what has been learned.

Two learning principles are often neglected in helping to grow new skills.

1. ***Space the practice.*** Practice often produces the best results when it occurs in regular intervals over time. A weekly piano lesson and 15 minutes of practice everyday are preferable to 1 hour of piano practice right before the lesson. Coaches help people determine the best approach to pace their learning.
2. ***Promote active experimentation.*** Coaches can also encourage people to broaden their use of new skills by applying them in different ways and in new situations. This solidifies people's understanding of the skill and how to use it.

Promote Persistence

Build stamina and discipline to make sure learning lasts on the job. When people learn something new in a training course or seminar but do not apply it back at work, it is often because the fourth coaching strategy—promote persistence—is neglected. Yet, in terms of behavior change, this is where the rubber meets the road. This is where people move from acquiring a skill to applying the skill, from learning to doing. The coach has four main responsibilities in implementing this strategy (Peterson & Hicks, 1996):

1. ***Be a talent agent.*** Help people find opportunities that require them to apply skills they have learned, to make sure their new skills do not just sit on the shelf and languish.
2. ***Manage the mundane.*** Help manage the routine and mundane aspects of development, so people stay motivated and persist in their efforts when they hit plateaus or when development activities become tedious.
3. ***Fight fear of failure.*** Support people so they feel comfortable enough with risk-taking that they do not panic or give up when things get tough.
4. ***Break the habit cycle.*** First, help people identify and anticipate specific situations in which old, ineffective habits are most likely to crop up. Second, help people learn and practice new, more effective behaviors in circumstances that gradually approximate the challenges of the actual situations. Third, work together to set specific goals about when they will use their new skills. Finally, help people reflect on their experiences so they can fine-tune their efforts for continued learning.

Shape the Environment

Build organizational support to reward learning and remove barriers. Shaping the environment moves the coach from an exclusive focus on the one-on-one relationship to the broader organizational playing field. For instance, a coach may provide guidance to the organizational sponsors so they can be better role models, or he or she may provide more feedback and encouragement to support learning in the work environment. Coaches can also help organizational sponsors identify and reduce barriers to an individual's development.

CASE STUDY

Jan Stambaugh, information technology manager at Hewlett-Packard, first called me in mid-November of 1993. Two of Jan's colleagues had independently recommended that she contact me—Mary, a peer manager I had coached previously, and Barbara, a human resources manager. Jan and I arranged to meet on December 3 for a 1-hour meeting to explore her goals and discuss the Targeted Coaching process.

As Jan walked me to her office that day, she struck me as warm and engaging. Once we were seated, she began to outline her situation. "I've been an effective manager for years. My boss says I'm good at all the typical management stuff, but I need to be a more visible, more powerful, and more strategic leader." The longer Jan and I worked together, the more I would come to recognize and respect her talent as an organized, productive, and thoughtful manager. Our conversation also covered the business pressures and strategic issues driving her current efforts. Jan was in the final stages of consolidating Hewlett-Packard's 150 independent data centers throughout the world into about I0 business-focused information technology centers.

After our discussion, we agreed to work together for four half-day sessions, scheduled about 4 to 6 weeks apart. In preparation for our first coaching session, Jan would use The PROFILOR®, a 360-degree feedback survey, to get additional input on how she was perceived by her colleagues. Our first coaching session began with a review of The PROFILOR, which confirmed Jan's impressions of her development needs and added the themes of managing conflict and being more proactive in managing upward.

We also reviewed her recent performance evaluation, which noted, "This has been a year of significant accomplishment for you," as well as, "It is important for you to emphasize new issues that may require additional skills." Those new issues included developing stronger relationships with internal customers and enhanced credibility on strategic business issues.

After about an hour clarifying and consolidating Jan's objectives, we spent the remaining 3 hours practicing the basic communications and collaborative problem-solving skills that would form a foundation for the more complex coaching areas that followed. We also identified opportunities for Jan to be more strategic in working with her organization.

Several weeks later, at the beginning of our second session, Jan reported that she continued to be consumed by tactical issues and was having difficulty finding time to work on strategic issues. As a result, we added a new area to our coaching objectives, which ended up having a profound impact on Jan's development: time management and prioritization of her work. Although Jan was extremely organized and productive, she spent a great deal of her time on urgent but relatively unimportant tasks. At management meetings, for example, she spent extra time preparing detailed and comprehensive slide presentations that went way beyond what was expected. As we looked at her priorities, we easily found opportunities for her to delegate or eliminate many tasks. However, this step brought us to the heart of the dilemma for Jan: She discovered that she had very little sense of what she wanted to accomplish as a leader. Therefore, we spent a good part of Sessions 2 and 3 exploring Jan's vision and values, both as a person and as a leader. Jan engaged in quite a bit of personal exploration between sessions as well. Her insights into what she valued and what she sought to accomplish professionally sparked an even more intense passion for her development as a leader.

In the meantime, we continued in each session to identify specific prospective situations in which she could apply what she was learning. We would diagnose the situation, analyze her barriers and old habits, and practice and provide debriefings on new ways of handling the situation. Jan could then enter those situations with a clearer sense of what she was trying to accomplish and how to do it. In the following session, we would review and fine-tune what happened.

Almost 6 months after we first met, Jan and I held a formal review meeting with her boss, in tandem with the fourth coaching session. In that meeting, I described Jan's progress as I saw it, Jan talked about the most important lessons she had learned, and we solicited her manager's feedback on her progress and any suggestions about other coaching priorities he might recommend for Jan. It was clear that he had seen little visible change in Jan's performance. So although Jan felt like she had made tremendous progress, much of that was still at the level of insight and tentative behavior changes. Following the review meeting, Jan and I strategized ways to accelerate her development and its visibility to her boss. Because her picture of herself as a leader was much clearer now, she was able to step up to her challenges much more proactively.

Although we had initially agreed to work together for four sessions, our agenda had expanded beyond the scope of our original commitment, so Jan requested that we add additional coaching sessions. We agreed, and we decided to reassess what additional coaching was needed at the end of each meeting.

As it turned out, when we met for our fifth session 6 weeks later, Jan was beginning to feel like she had consolidated her learning. She had become quite comfortable with her new behaviors and was seeing positive and tangible results from the changes she had made. Her boss had even begun to offer more favorable feedback. Here is what Jan said:

> I feel like a fundamentally different person. I do things differently. I respond to situations differently. I'm more confident about what I'm doing. I listen more. I'm more comfortable with conflict. I'm more strategic and more proactive. My relationship with my manager has changed dramatically. He's now asked me to take on some of the most difficult problems facing our department. I never expected to see this dramatic an impact on my thinking and the way I managed my life. I wasn't even looking for that kind of change. In every meeting there was something that happened that took me a giant step forward, that changed my way of thinking about what I was doing and what value I could get out of it.

I asked Jan exactly what we did in the coaching process that had the most impact. She responded,

> You let me be me, even though the me that I was in the beginning wasn't anybody that I wanted to show to anyone. You made me feel comfortable. I never felt like you were evaluating my performance; you were giving me insight and help in what was frustrating me. I felt supported in our discussions; not supported in my behaviors, but supported in trying to resolve my behaviors. You always gave me clear insight about what I could do differently. No matter what I hit you with, you always had some idea or insight that helped me on to the next phase.

She also mentioned that she was occasionally concerned because I did not rigorously structure the coaching process in each session: "I haven't always been clear where we were trying to go. I thought maybe that I could just come here and you would tell me exactly what I should do. If you'd done that, I probably wouldn't have spent as much time preparing. I appreciate that that is getting me to take ownership. It forced me to take ownership in a way that I wouldn't have otherwise."

For an external perspective on Jan's changes, here is a sample from her most recent performance evaluation, completed by the same manager. He begins by recognizing this was "another year of tremendous change and contribution for you." After listing almost two pages of her achievements for the year, he concludes,

> Perhaps the most significant common theme running through these accomplishments is your leadership of the organization in moving toward new services with a new organization structure while continuing to provide basic services that meet growing customer expectations. The organization appears to be more proactive in defining its future rather than just responding to the required narrowly focused agenda of the past. You have demonstrated the ability to complement your strong managerial skills with leadership actions that move the organization forward.

CONSULTANT'S PERSPECTIVE

Reflecting on my work with Jan, one lesson stands out: the importance of trust. Even when Jan was unsure where we were headed, she was willing to go with the flow because she trusted that I had her best interests in mind. She would accept assignments for work between sessions even when it seemed risky to her. Although we worked together to find reasonable risks, I was always walking the line between supporting Jan while still challenging and pushing her to find the limits of her comfort zone. Without trust, she wouldn't have gone as far.

Here are a few other significant factors of my work with Jan, following the framework of the five PDI coaching strategies:

Forge a Partnership

Jan already had some trust in me because I was recommended by two of her colleagues. Still, I spent most of our first hour actively listening and probing to understand how she saw herself and her challenges and what she wanted to get out of coaching. She also needed to trust that I could help her out, so once I understood her situation, I offered a few practical suggestions and shared my experiences working with people in situations similar to hers.

Inspire Commitment

Jan initiated the coaching, so it was clear she was already motivated and interested in her own development. In terms of the GAPS model, she had begun to focus on the abilities, perceptions, and standards information and was trying to improve her skills to match the expanding requirements of her job. Because she had such a clear sense of her objectives, we could begin the coaching process with a minimum of additional information. However, she had not deeply examined her own goals and values. The process of exploring her personal and leadership vision energized her change and inspired her in a new way.

Grow Skills

In every session we role-played real situations that Jan faced, helping her to learn new skills and to fine-tune and grow more comfortable with them. The first practice was straightforward, to make sure that she grasped the skill; the challenge then increased each time so that she had to stretch herself.

Promote Persistence

From the very first session, we identified specific actions that Jan would take back to the job. Most of them were simple and basic. By having some quick wins, she gained momentum for changing. In fact, she found that some relatively small changes had a more powerful effect than she expected. As a coach, I look for the changes that can be leveraged most efficiently.

Shape the Environment

We capitalized on the fact that Jan's environment was already supportive of development by discussing how she could reinforce the two-way flow of GAPS information. By seeking regular feedback on her new behaviors and by sharing her expectations and perceptions with her team, she helped to foster an atmosphere in which coaching and development can prosper.

PERSONNEL DECISIONS INTERNATIONAL'S THREE DIFFERENT TYPES OF COACHING

Jan's case study is an example of PDI's Targeted Coaching service. Targeted Coaching is one of three major categories of coaching that PDI offers. The other two are Intensive Coaching and Executive Coaching. All three are described briefly below and in more detail in Table 12.2.

- *Targeted Coaching* is a relatively focused, practical, skills-based approach to coaching that is offered to individuals who are motivated to round out their skill set in one or two key areas. It is similar to a training course delivered one-on-one, custom designed to meet an individual's needs through personalized instruction, practice, and feedback.
- *Intensive Coaching* represents a comprehensive approach for individuals who face major work challenges and who need to accelerate their learning and development to make substantial changes. It typically encompasses complex personal and organizational issues and multiple skill areas.

TABLE 12.2

Three Different Types of Coaching

	Targeted coaching	Intensive coaching	Executive coaching
Assessment	Minimal assessment, typically a 360-degree survey, personal interview, and conversation with organizational sponsor.	Comprehensive assessment that includes psychological and cognitive abilities testing, work simulations, interviews, and a 360-degree survey.	Assessment varies depending on the individual's needs.
Scope of coverage	Typically focuses on one or two key skill areas, such as communications, influencing, conflict management, or team leadership.	Focuses on a broad range of skills; addresses significant changes in role (e.g., moving from middle management to executive leadership) or major behavior changes (e.g., adapting from top-down management style to a more participative style).	Focuses on discussion of challenges, the implications of various options, and how to implement effective action once a decision is reached. Less emphasis on skill building than in targeted and intensive coaching.
Participant motivation	Participants are motivated and have a clear sense of their objectives.	The need for substantial change is evident, although specific objectives may not be clear. Participants may or may not be motivated to change at this point.	Participants generally initiate the coaching relationships with clear goals in mind.
Frequency of sessions	Four to five half-day sessions over 3 to 4 months.	Five to six full-day sessions over 6 to 9 months.	Meetings of 1 to 2 hours occur as needed or on a regular schedule (e.g., over lunch every other week).
Organizational involvement	Periodic communication with organizational sponsors.	In-depth and ongoing consultation with organizational sponsors.	The participant is often the primary communication link with organizational sponsors.
Follow-up and support	Minimal follow-up.	3- to 6-month follow-up to ensure that new behaviors endure.	Ongoing consultation is available on request.

- *Executive Coaching* is a consultative, relationship-based service provided by seasoned consultants who serve as advisors and objective sounding boards to senior executives. This type of coaching is intended for leaders who are wrestling with the implications of tough business decisions, who want to develop new strategic insights into how they can better manage the personal dynamics of their responsibilities, or who want to enhance their own development as they face greater obstacles in achieving organizational and personal goals.

TIPS FOR COACHES

In closing, here are four of the most powerful lessons that I have learned about coaching:

Go Where the Energy Is

Contrary to popular belief, people do not resist change. In fact, people are motivated to change, as long as they see a personal payoff. Therefore, coaches can take advantage of this natural motivation for change by addressing the challenges that are immediately relevant to people. Starting with their concerns builds trust and creates momentum for change. Then, coaches can look for opportunities to share new information and challenge people to new levels.

Translate Insight Into Action

Insight is a necessary condition for behavior change, but it is not a sufficient one. Therefore, we regularly ask people two questions: What have you learned? What are you going to do differently because of that? We ask these two questions to help them distill their insights and translate those insights into action (Peterson & Hicks, 1995). We continue to probe to make sure they have a clear picture of exactly what they will do and when they will do it.

Teach People to Develop Themselves

No matter what the particular coaching objectives are, we strive to teach people how to learn for themselves, including how to get ongoing feedback and GAPS information, how to determine development priorities, and how to reflect on their own experiences to maximize their learning (Peterson & Hicks, 1995). This mind-set is integral to our definition of coaching, which is "the process of equipping people with the tools, knowledge, and opportunities they need to develop themselves and become more effective" (Peterson & Hicks, 1996, p. 14).

Ask for Feedback

Coaches have at least two good reasons to ask for feedback from the people they coach. First, feedback models a useful behavior, demonstrating to the person that it can be done naturally and effectively. Second, it provides the coach with some of the most valuable information he or she can get to enhance development of his or her own coaching skills. Coaches who pay serious attention to their own development are much more likely to become great coaches.

References

Decker, P. J., & Nathan, B. R. (1985). *Behavior modeling training.* New York: Praeger.

Druckman, D., & Bjork, R. A. (Eds.). (1991). *In the mind's eye: Enhancing human performance.* Washington, DC: National Academy Press.

Hellervik, L. W., Hazucha, J. F., & Schneider, R. J. (1992). Behavior change: Models, methods, and a review of the evidence. In M. D. Dunnette & L. M. Hough (Eds.), *Handbook of industrial and organizational psychology* (2nd ed., Vol. 3, pp. 823–895). Palo Alto, CA: Consulting Psychologists Press.

Hicks, M. D., & Peterson, D. B. (1993, August). *The secrets of managing the human side of change.* Invited address presented at the 59th Annual Conference of the Human Resources Management Association of Chicago, Toronto, Ontario, Canada.

Hicks, M. D., & Peterson, D. B. (1995, December). *Hand-to-hand combat: Examining one-on-one change strategies for leaders.* Paper presented at the Business-Focused Human Resources Conference, Chicago.

Hicks, M. D., & Peterson, D. B. (1996). Half truths and real truths: How development really works. *HR Focus, 7*(5), 10–11.

Kanfer, F. H., & Schefft, B. K. (1988). *Guiding the process of therapeutic change.* Champaign, IL: Research Press.

Mahoney, M. J. (1991). *Human change processes.* New York: Basic Books.

Peterson, D. B. (1993a, April). *Measuring change: A psychometric approach to evaluating individual training outcomes.* Paper presented at the annual conference of the Society for Industrial and Organizational Psychology, San Francisco.

Peterson, D. B. (1993b). *Skill learning and behavior change in an individually tailored management coaching and training program.* Unpublished doctoral dissertation, University of Minnesota, Minneapolis.

Peterson, D. B., & Heine, D. M. (1993, October). *Can managers and executives really change?* Paper presented at the International Assessment Conference, Personnel Decisions, Inc., and the University of Minnesota Psychology Department, Minneapolis.

Peterson, D. B., & Hicks, M. D. (1993). *The foundations of management and executive development: How to get people to change.* Workshop presented at the annual conference of the Society for Industrial and Organizational Psychology, San Francisco.

Peterson, D. B., & Hicks, M. D. (1995). *Development FIRST: Strategies for self-development.* Minneapolis, MN: Personnel Decisions International.

Peterson, D. B., & Hicks, M. D. (1996). *Leader as coach: Strategies for coaching and developing others.* Minneapolis, MN: Personnel Decisions International.

Peterson, D. B., Uranowitz, S., & Hicks, M. D. (1996, August). *Management coaching at work: Survey of current practices in Fortune 250 organizations.* Paper presented at the 104th Annual Conference of the American Psychological Association, Toronto, Ontario, Canada.

Prochaska, J. O., DiClemente, C. C., & Norcross, J. C. (1992). In search of how people change: Applications to addictive behaviors. *American Psychologist, 47*, 1102–1114.

Rogers, C. R. (1951). *Client-centered therapy: Its current practice, implications, and theory*. Boston: Houghton Mifflin.

Thompson, A. D., Jr. (1986). *A formative evaluation of an individualized coaching program for business managers and professionals*. Unpublished doctoral dissertation, University of Minnesota, Minneapolis.

CHAPTER 13

COACHING EXECUTIVES

Lester L. Tobias

Somewhere around the late 1980s, the term *executive coaching* came into business parlance. As far as I have been able to tell, coaching by psychologists is simply a repackaging of certain practices that were once subsumed under the more general terms *consulting* or *counseling*. I suspect that the popularity of the term stems from the fact that coaching is perceived to be a little less threatening, perhaps because it may appear to be akin to physical fitness coaching. There is a subtle implication that coaching may not involve wrenching change and may be just a matter of fine-tuning. Sometimes, of course, fine-tuning is all that is needed, but often it *is* wrenching change that is required, so the term, although less threatening, may be slightly deceptive.

The term *coaching* has the advantage of implying an ongoing process, which distinguishes it from most seminars and workshops. Meaningful change seldom happens in one-shot interventions, so an ongoing process is potentially more thorough and lasting. Coaching is individually tailored to the person and the current issue or problem, as opposed to the "one-size-fits-all" menu provided by many seminars. Instead of stimulating one or two good ideas, coaching is continually focused and relevant. Instead of potentially wasting time and having one's mind wander, the executive can get right to the heart of the matter. The concepts and guidance a person actually needs are presented in ways that the person can immediately apply because they are personalized rather than presented to a group as vague abstractions or "laundry lists." Like a personal trainer, the coach helps the individual maintain a consistent, confident focus on tuning up strengths and managing shortcomings. Coaching allows for ongoing, continuous learning, offering support, encouragement, and feedback as new approaches are tried and new behaviors are practiced. Coaching allows for continuous learning. Thus, coaching supports change by maintaining a constant growing edge through helping the executive to challenge his or her own potentials and to confront resistance.

In its narrowest sense, coaching may help someone who has irritated others in the organization. For example, the individual may be seen as abrasive; too expressive of anger; territorial; overcontrolling; underempowering; lacking in personal insight or social, organizational, or political awareness; or a poor communicator. This definition would encompass the "diamond in the rough" who needs to soften the rough edges. A somewhat broader definition would include someone having conflictual relationships with peers, authorities, "internal customers," or others; someone having trouble adjusting to organizational or personal changes or crises; someone who is seen as lacking discipline, planfulness, or organization; someone experiencing stress at work or at home; someone having difficulty selling his or her ideas internally;

Reprinted from the *Consulting Psychology Journal: Practice and Research, 48,* 87–95. Copyright 1996 by the American Psychological Association and the Society of Consulting Psychology.

or, perhaps, someone having difficulty getting a team to coalesce.

At an even broader level, the identified problem may not be an individual but a circumstance the individual needs to manage. For example, a manager may be struggling to figure out how to confront changes that will affect his or her department, or the manager may want to do a better job at bringing out the best in his or her subordinates. Coaching can also be used when there is no specific problem that has been identified, but where an executive wishes to enhance his or her style, future options, and organizational impact. The executive may wish to take stock, to better optimize strengths, to manage shortcomings, to better align emotionally, to do career planning, or to avoid potential inadvertent consequences of his or her management style. In these senses, coaching is done less to fix a weakness than to capitalize on potentials.

Coaching is usually confidential, allowing people to freely discuss delicate issues; to let their hair down; to shed defenses; and to explore blindspots, biases, and shortcomings. To achieve lasting and fundamental change, people need to alter their perspectives, to see things in a new light, or to overcome internal resistances that may be unrecognized and habitual. Therefore, the psychologist needs to help the person get to the root causes, whether the apparent problem is organizational or one of personal style.

Depending on the circumstance, the psychologist may operate at more than one level and in more than one way. For example, the psychologist may provide feedback, help the person to elicit feedback, or manage a process in which feedback is given. The psychologist may help the person focus on specific behavioral changes as well as gain insight into the factors underlying problem behaviors. The psychologist may deal solely with the individual or may also involve others in the organization.

Although most coaching is ongoing, it may vary from just a couple of sessions to a lengthy series of meetings over a long period. Thus, the term *coaching* can be used so broadly as to encompass virtually any useful intervention that the consultant may do. I prefer using a very broad definition because it keeps one's options open and does not limit one to a prescribed sequence or narrow set of potential interventions. Therefore, if there is a distinction between what I do when I am coaching and what I do when I am consulting, it is probably best distinguished by the focus of my activity. Whereas when I am doing consulting, the focus tends to be on the entire organization, when I am doing coaching, the focus is more on a single individual. It should be pointed out, however, that in either case I tend to define the *client* as the individual with whom I am working (Tobias, 1990, 1995).

Another potential distinction between coaching and consulting is that coaching may be done both within and outside of the confines of an ongoing consulting relationship. Thus, in certain circumstances, coaching may be the only contact the psychologist has with the client organization. When coaching is done in isolation, the absence of organizational context will inevitably limit the coach's perspectives on the presenting problem. Furthermore, it may also limit the coach's options regarding interventions. For example, a creative, free-spirited, rebellious, and egocentric person can be helped to align with an organization only up to a certain point. Usually, the organization needs to give a little, too, by breaking down bureaucratic barriers, providing emotional support, tolerating failures, providing sponsors, and the like. The psychologist may have an opportunity to coach the manager to alter his or her perceptions about the organization's contribution to the individual's behavior and then to modify the eliciting conditions. If the coaching relationship is narrowly bound, these options may not be available. It is essential for the coach to keep in mind that relevant others may not only be potentially part of the solution, but that they are usually directly or indirectly a part of the problem. However maladaptive an individual's behavior may be, it never occurs in a vacuum, even though the more outrageous the behavior is, the more people will attribute it to the individual's personality.

In my experience, most diagnoses made by executives about a "problem person" are, at best, only partially correct. Seldom do they sufficiently account for the setting events that trigger the behavior. Consider, for example, a person struggling to keep his or her head above water in a job for which he or she is underqualified. The person may experience intense stress, but may label the problem as the "impossible demands" being made by his or her boss. The boss may see the problem as the inappropriate wielding of authority or as interpersonal conflicts, without attributing as its source the stress he or she has inadvertently caused. Thus, the referral may be about inappropriate social behavior when the crucial problem has to do with ill-fitting expectations. The outrageous behavior may mask the real problem and could very well effectively disappear if the person's role or the expectations are changed. Lengthy coaching with the individual about how to wield authority or reduce conflict would be counterproductive because it would add yet another problem to an already too-full plate.

In fact, perhaps the greatest danger in doing coaching with individuals from organizations in which there is no ongoing consulting relationship is the possibility that the psychologist may inadvertently participate in the scapegoating of an individual by an organization or by a boss who is unable to or does not want to look deeply enough at the ways that the environment may be supporting the conditions underlying the individual's seemingly maladaptive response. Therefore, the more removed the coaching is from the organizational context, the more pains the psychologist must take to ensure that the context is woven into the fabric of the coaching relationship with the identified individual and that the organization be persuaded that it, too, needs to play a role in defining and achieving the desired outcome. Otherwise, the psychologist may contribute to the organization's potential illusion that the referral for coaching washes its hands of its accountabilities. Thus, coaching can share with seminars the possibility of being seen as a quick fix for a labeled individual, thereby not only resulting from but also maintaining the organization's self-deception that the labeled problem is "in him or her" not "in us."

IMPLEMENTING EXECUTIVE COACHING

The coaching process typically begins with the psychologist being contacted by a human resources professional, by the person's manager, or by the person. An initial discussion can help to scope out the problem, to develop a flexible preliminary plan of action, and to discuss the extent and limits of confidentiality. Because the problem is usually described as "in" the person, this is usually a good opportunity to point out the systemic nature of most individual problems or at least to emphasize that amelioration of the problem may necessarily involve the individual's manager or other relevant people in the organization. It is also an opportunity to obtain an informal glimpse into the personalities of the other relevant people as a means of at least trying to balance the scales between the perceived accountabilities of the individual and those of the system. It is important for the psychologist to obtain as many views as possible into the nature of the problem as well as the nature of the individual and the organization as a whole.

Often the next step in the coaching process is an in-depth psychological study of the individual (Tobias, 1990) as a starting point for developing an understanding of the person. The psychological study usually involves about three hours of interviewing, including a full personal history. I normally use a number of personality and ability tests to round out the personal interview, and these may vary depending on the individual and the reasons for the referral. The specific tests used also vary among members of my firm, but often included are one or more of the following: the California Personality Inventory, the NEO-PI-R, the Meyers–Briggs Type Indicator, the Wechsler Adult Intelligence Scale (or some of its subtests), the Wonderlic Personnel Test, the 16PF, and a number of others.

The psychological study attempts to capture a person's capacities, style, direction, level of emotional maturity, and the degree to which he or she capitalizes on basic potentials. It can point out to the individual a variety of inadvertent consequences that may result from the individual's good intentions, such as how the individual's strengths, when overused, may predict the individual's weaknesses and how current successes as well as current maladaptive behaviors may sprout from roots that are embedded in the person's past. The psychological study serves not only to provide a holistic perspective, but to bring a person's strengths into the foreground, as a reassuring contrast to the usual focus on his or her shortcomings. This may be especially important because the person sent for coaching may (justifiably) be on the defensive. Pointing out strengths may soften the defensiveness; equally important, pointing out potential shortcomings may help the person realize that there is legitimacy to at least some of the feedback he or she has received. Perhaps most important, the fact that a problem has been seen fit to warrant coaching with a psychologist suggests that the problem has in some sense been viewed as intractable. Almost always, this intractability has resulted in part from defining the problem in too limiting a manner, too accusatory a tone, and too one-sidedly. The psychological study provides a framework for opening up the problem, gives the person permission to discuss it nondefensively, and helps the person take a fast step toward its resolution.

If the problem is primarily between the person and his or her manager, then the person may decide to have the psychologist share the psychological study with the manager as a means of helping the manager gain a fuller and more objective understanding of the nature of the issue and what the manager can do to enhance the individual's effectiveness. Often the problem may involve the perceptions of other key people in the organization, and a common solution is the use of a 360-degree feedback process. Such feedback accomplishes a number of goals. First, it allows the respondents to let off steam by identifying problem areas. Second, it encourages a constructive attitude on the part of respondents because it asks them to suggest constructive changes. The process assists the individual in hearing clear and consensual feedback instead of hearing vague, secondhand complaints or getting hit in the face with anger. The individual hears what constitutes a legitimate problem for others.

Nordli, Wilson's 360-degree feedback instrument contains a checklist and open-ended questions. The checklist does not rate the person. Instead, the respondent is asked to indicate if the subject should perform more or less of each of a number of interpersonal and leadership behaviors. The open-ended questions are designed to elicit constructive praise as well as constructive criticism. The respondents usually include the person's manager, relevant peers, and subordinates as well as other relevant constituencies (internal customers, senior managers, etc.). They fill out the forms anonymously and mail them to us for scoring of checklist items and for transcription of open-ended questions. The subject also completes a parallel self-feedback form before receiving respondent feedback. The psychologist meets with the individual to provide the 360-degree feedback results, to help the person understand the feedback, and to stimulate the person to plan changes as needed. We also provide a short interpretive "action guide"

A number of follow-up meetings may also be conducted

- with the respondents, to prepare them for providing clarifying oral feedback at a subsequent meeting;
- with the individual, to prepare him or her to ask for further clarification from the respondents and to signal a readiness to change;
- with the individual and the respondents, to clarify the feedback;
- to understand the past and future intentions of the person receiving the feedback;
- to open up future communication channels so that feedback becomes ongoing;
- to allow all parties to get their feelings off their chest and process the variety of emotions they may have, thereby allowing a little more vulnerability; and,
- perhaps most important, to break the negative cognitive set regarding the possibilities for change by bolstering the expectation that change will occur and by extracting commitments from each person about what he or she can do to foster change.

The meetings with the individual are often followed by discussions with the person's manager to further discuss what the manager can do with the individual as well as what the manager can do with the other interested parties to continually reinforce the changes. Because an individual's problem behavior is often hurtful to others, it is most important to involve these other people as much as possible in the change process lest they simply write the person off or stereotype the person as "incurable." Furthermore, it is important to understand why the manager was unsuccessful in facilitating change without the help of a coach. What does this say about the manager's sense of accountability to truly develop people? How does the manager really feel about the person? How much will the manager need to change to bring about a positive outcome, and how likely is such change to occur?

The coaching process may also involve a number of other potential interventions or suggestions to seek other resources. Most often, the rest of the process is one of repeated meetings aimed at helping the individual and other relevant people to overcome their resistances to change, to accomplish their goals, and to keep their commitments. Because intractable problems seldom solve themselves with one-trial learning, the fact that coaching is typically ongoing is, of course, a major advantage.

CASE STUDY: HENRY

Henry is a very bright, very hard-working, 44-year-old manager in a Fortune 100 company. The work done by the company has a technical side and a creative side. Henry has always excelled at the technical side and has been praised repeatedly for his technical proficiency; for meeting schedules and deadlines; and for his efficiency, attention to detail, and ability to control multiple complex projects. He was promoted to his position 2 years before the coaching process began. The two major functions reporting to him were technical and creative. The technical people generally appreciated his style of management, although they sometimes found him too controlling, too tight in his follow-up, and too apt to interfere. The creative people found him "impossible," "stifling," "no fun to work around or for," "unappreciative of the creative process" (although his own training was in the creative area), disrespectful of their needs for unstructured time, "one-way" in his communications with them individually and in groups, and in general "completely" insensitive and rigid. Despite this, they all acknowledged that he was well meaning and generally a "decent" person.

Upper management was somewhat conflicted about Henry. On the one hand, his record for on-time, defect-free delivery and cost containment was outstanding. On the other hand, they were deeply concerned that his area seemed to be losing its creative edge because the creative people could not flourish under him, and his reputation was such that no creative people would agree to transfer to his department to shore up the effort on the creative side of the organization.

The vice president in charge of creative work felt particularly helpless about and negative toward Henry. The creative people, who indirectly reported to her, often complained about Henry and put pressure on her to transfer them to other departments. In addition, the vice president found Henry to be "exasperating" to deal with and a "completely uncreative control freak." In fact, it was her pressure to get Henry fired that mobilized the vice president of technical work and the vice president of human resources to involve the psychologist as a means of salvaging Henry.

The psychologist had been providing a variety of consulting services to other areas of the organization for 2 years, including executive development, executive selection, and organizational change. He knew the vice presidents well and had earned a measure of their trust.

After being presented the problem by the vice president of human resources, the psychologist met individually with each of the three vice presidents. Of particular concern to the psychologist was the negative and hopeless attitude on the part of the vice president of creative work. Although the other vice presidents were much more willing to acknowledge Henry's positive attributes, it was clear from the conversations with them that they would only be willing to provide a buffer for Henry so long as his behavior showed significant change and that this change would have to be satisfactory to the vice president of creative work. Therefore, in the discussion with the vice president of creative work, the psychologist tried to determine the extent to which she would be willing to change her views about Henry, should he actually change. It was very likely that Henry was not going to come close to her ideal behavior for the manager's position, so the question was, where would she be willing to draw the line between acceptable and unacceptable leadership on Henry's part? She made it clear that she did value Henry's ability to "keep the trains running on time," but added that she could never envision herself enjoying any discussion about creative issues with him. Nevertheless, she indicated that the key to Henry's acceptability would be his providing an atmosphere conducive to creative expression so that creative people would want to work for him and eventually produce a more creative result.

The vice president of technical work and the vice president of creative work (to whom Henry dually reported) as well as the vice president of human resources were asked to provide very explicit feedback to Henry regarding his assets and liabilities as well as their agreement that he would have to change dramatically and soon if he were to retain his position. Although Henry had been given occasional feedback, it had become clear that the feedback was spotty and not always consistent. In light of the positive evaluations of his past performance, it was deemed likely that he had no idea how precarious his tenure now was, and it was felt that this had to be clarified, both in the interests of fairness and in the interests of enhancing Henry's motivation to change. The vice presidents agreed that they would meet with Henry together and then individually and that he would be offered the option of coaching with the psychologist, which he chose to take.

A psychological study was done with Henry. The study found him to be bright, planful, cautious, conservative, conventional, methodical, precise, and detail oriented. Under a calm exterior, he was worrisome, self-conscious, self-absorbed, insular, and self-inhibiting. He was competitive, achieving, striving, and purposeful. He was uncomfortable with too much disorder or lack of structure. He was much more task and goal oriented than interpersonally oriented. Although strongly oriented toward inward and outward control, he was not one who is driven to exercise power over others. Although he was introspective, he lacked perceptiveness and sensitivity; intellectualized; and was apt to look inward when encountering difficulties, thereby overlooking interpersonal cues. He maintained distance with others and tended to be impersonal and hard to get to know. Although rather sincere, honest, and well intended, he lacked skills in communicating, persuading, and engaging others. He showed himself to be very hard-working and especially effective in coordinating, organizing, and establishing policies, procedures, and guidelines.

The feedback with Henry dealt with some of the underlying dynamics surrounding his tendency toward overcontrol, his difficulties with vulnerability and intimacy, and his tendency to retreat into insularity. He had a good intellectual understanding of some of the origins of these tendencies and was able to see how they manifested themselves in his marriage and in previous jobs. He was also able to explore some of the ways his upbringing had influenced him. He was encouraged to continue these explorations and to bring them up in further sessions, which he did. Additionally, he was encouraged to look for ways of reaching out more vulnerably—to be more open, more expressive, and less stilted, and in doing so, to take more interpersonal risks—at home and at work, as a means of enhancing his intimacy with others so as to be better able to sense their feelings and reactions and to be less surprised by them. It was suggested that he guard against his tendency to be so caught up with and concerned about himself that his relationships with others may not be optimally rewarding and sharing. He was encouraged to use others as sounding boards more, as a means of testing his perceptions about other people. It was felt that he needed to be more confident in his ability to influence others so that he could allow himself to control them less. Therefore, specific ways of controlling less and empowering and communicating more were discussed with him, such as backing off more from following up; allowing more agenda-less time at group meetings; interesting himself in his people's work without a specific directive agenda; praising strengths more; and, more broadly, looking at his job less as one of accomplishing specific goals and more as one of enabling others to accomplish goals.

Importantly, Henry indicated that he had clearly gotten the message that his career was on the line and that he would be fired if he did not change quickly. He accepted the ultimatum, understood most of the reasons behind it, and strongly committed himself to changing. His greatest fear was that the vice president of creative work might be so disdainful of him that nothing he did would change her mind, and this was a concern of the psychologist, too. He also feared that he might not be able to change quickly enough to satisfy the vice presidents.

Henry agreed to share his psychological study with each of the vice presidents. He understood that much of the content would call into question his ability to retain his position; nevertheless, he felt that the situation was such that he had nothing to lose by complete openness and that by allowing release of the psychological study, he was merely confirming in less judgmental and more balanced terms what the vice presidents already knew.

The psychologist reviewed the psychological study with each of the vice presidents and discussed with them the particular ways in which each might be helpful in coaching Henry. In particular, the vice president of creative work was told in great detail about Henry's strengths, his weaknesses, and which of his weaknesses could and could not change. The psychologist felt it was essential that the vice president agree to the criteria for determining success and that she understand that to do so, she would have to accept the reality that there was no way that Henry could ever become anything like her view of the perfect manager. It was pointed out to her that it would be a waste of time to work with Henry unless she was fully prepared to eventually accept less than what her image demanded, albeit more than what Henry now achieved.

The psychologist discussed Henry's genuinely strong motivation and deep commitment, but also pointed out the significant barriers to his being able to change and the likelihood that Henry would never be naturally imaginative, fun-loving, spontaneous, or especially sensitive to or perceptive about people. It was pointed out to her that her willingness or unwillingness to accept a limited outcome would be pivotal to any attempt at embarking on a program to help Henry. After fully airing her misgivings and being encouraged to take the time to think about her decision, she agreed that the limited outcome would be acceptable. At the psychologist's strong urging, she also agreed to meet regularly with Henry to provide him feedback and to suggest ways of managing that would be helpful to the creative group. This was urged both to help Henry and to catalyze her own sense of ownership of the issue of helping Henry.

Henry also agreed to participate in a 360-degree feedback process involving all of his direct subordinates, several peers, the three aforementioned vice presidents, another vice president, and the president. The 360-degree feedback data were fed back to Henry by the psychologist and were very consistent with what he had already heard from the vice presidents and from the psychologist. The psychologist helped Henry to understand what the feedback meant and how he might translate it into concrete actions. They also discussed how Henry might react to his subordinates in an upcoming meeting with the psychologist. For example, the psychologist helped Henry phrase questions about ambiguous comments that would elicit further feedback without boxing people in or making them defensive. Most important, Henry was prompted to make clear to his subordinates his intention of changing, of loosening controls, and of making every attempt to really listen to feedback in the future.

The psychologist then met with Henry's subordinates (after obtaining Henry's permission to do so). He summarized the feedback to them and encouraged group discussion. He indicated his understanding that Henry wanted to change but also emphasized that change is a two-way street and, therefore, that Henry would require their assistance in providing him with candid feedback. Fortunately, because the group did not see Henry as particularly vengeful or threatening, they agreed rather quickly to be as candid as possible, and the psychologist helped them to think about ways of constructively providing clarifying oral feedback. Then the psychologist met with Henry and his subordinates. Although the stated goal of the meeting was to clarify feedback, the psychologist's superordinate goals were to establish some faith among Henry's subordinates so that Henry could change and to pry open more channels of communication between Henry and his subordinates so that they would not feel as compelled to complain to others but would give Henry the feedback he needed when issues arose. The meeting allowed each person to sort out some of the feelings that he or she had had about working for Henry and to make suggestions for changes he or she would need to see. Some specific changes about Henry's leadership style and the way he conducted meetings were suggested, and Henry agreed to make some immediate changes.

A subsequent meeting was held with Henry to go over the meeting and to discuss how to best implement the changes he had agreed to with his subordinates. In addition, the importance of maintaining the faith of the vice president of creative work was emphasized, and it was suggested that Henry regularly use the occasion of his meetings with the vice president of creative work to seek feedback, to open up issues, to ask for help regarding his style, and also to make her aware of his successes in changing. Thus, the importance of impression management was stressed to Henry, not to help him avoid his accountabilities but, in fact, to enable him to do a better job of communicating upward and thereby to modify old stereotypes.

The next time the psychologist came to meet with Henry, there was a giant sign on Henry's wall that read "Let go." Henry wanted to make a public statement about his intention to change as well as to remind himself of what he most needed to do. For the rest of that session, and during most subsequent meetings, Henry and the psychologist further discussed issues ranging from Henry's overcontrolled and emotionally constricted parents to his marriage to concrete issues about how to conduct a meeting and how to delegate. Although Henry caught on quickly intellectually, it took a while for things to begin to sink in, because much of the reason for these meetings in the first place was Henry's defensive way of encapsulating ideas through his intellect and thus protecting himself from confronting emotional reality. The psychologist attempted to accurately reflect Henry's feelings to him; to adopt a nonjudgmental, accepting attitude toward Henry; and to gently confront the discrepancies between what Henry knew and what he felt so as to provide just enough irritation to prompt growth and not so much as to arouse resistant defenses.

After a few months, Henry said that all this change was causing him a new problem. Now that he was not managing all the details anymore, he had the time to ask himself what it was that a manager was supposed to do when he was not managing all the details. At the psychologist's suggestion, he had been doing a lot of reading about managing and developing people, and he had attended a workshop in the area. He said he was now ready to really start thinking about his subordinates' developmental needs and wanted to spend that day's session talking about them and not himself.

Over time, Henry made small to moderate changes in his emotional vulnerability and spontaneity. He nevertheless made fairly significant changes in his management style. He loosened up a lot, took more time for pleasant small talk, concerned himself with his subordinates' performance development, delegated much more, followed up somewhat less, led more open meetings, practiced "leaving well enough alone," encouraged a freer two-way flow of ideas, and looked less tense and more relaxed. Over a 2-year period, the psychologist met with Henry 12 times. She also met with the vice president of creative work 4 more times and with the vice president of human resources twice, for the sole purpose of discussing Henry. Henry dutifully attended the meetings with the vice president of creative work and, at the psychologist's urging, encouraged her to continue them at one point when she suggested they may be unnecessary.

At the end of a year, the vice president of creative work acknowledged to the psychologist that Henry had clearly made a tremendous effort, that his group was functioning more effectively, that he was not such a "pain to be around" anymore, but nevertheless that he was still never going to "really get it," although, given what he had done, the situation was "okay." After 2 years, the vice president of creative work told the psychologist that she and Henry had toured a new facility together and that she had actually enjoyed the conversations that she had had with him for the first time ever. One month later, the group reorganized and, with the acquiescence of all of the vice presidents and the president, Henry was promoted to a position of somewhat greater responsibility.

References

Tobias, L. L. (1990). *Psychological consulting to management: A clinician's perspective.* New York: Brunner/Mazel.

Tobias, L. L. (1995). Eleven ideas that have influenced my practice of psychological consulting. *Consulting Psychology Journal: Practice and Research, 47,* 56–63.

CHAPTER 14

AN ITERATIVE APPROACH TO EXECUTIVE COACHING

Richard C. Diedrich

Corporations worldwide use psychologists to assess the "fit" between an executive and that person's role within a specific organization. The resultant idiographic profile of cognitive, affective, and social factors, when matched with the role expectations for a given executive position, is used to predict success or failure. This profile can also be used to define the developmental activities needed for that person to be able to function effectively or even more effectively.

As a Hay Group consultant, I coach executives regarding the matter of fit and developmental needs in an "executive-centered, looped, and interlaced but structured process." Three "learner-centered" principles from a recent American Psychological Association Division 15 document provide a frame of reference for my coaching activities:

> *Principle 1: The Nature of the Learning Process.* Learning is a natural process of pursuing personally meaningful goals and it is active, volitional, and both internally and socially mediated; it is a process of discovering and constructing personal and shared meaning from information and experience, filtered through each individual's unique perceptions, thoughts, and feelings, as well as through negotiations with others. (Learner-Centered Psychological Principles, 1995, p. 4)
>
> *Principle 5: Motivational Influences on Learning.* The depth and breadth of understandings constructed, and what and how much is learned and remembered, are influenced by (a) self-awareness and beliefs about personal control, competence, and ability; (b) clarity and saliency of personal and social values, interests, and goals; (c) personal expectations for success or failure; (d) affect, emotion, and general states of mind; and (e) the resulting motivation to learn. (Learner-Centered Psychological Principles, 1995, p. 5)
>
> *Principle 10: Social Acceptance, Self-Esteem, and Learning.* Learning and self-esteem are heightened when individuals are in respectful and caring relationships with others who see their potential, genuinely appreciate their unique talents, and accept them as individuals. (Learner-Centered Psychological Principles, 1995, p. 5)

The specific method of executive coaching we use involves the Hay/McBer Executive 360, a comprehensive planning process that assesses critical competencies and guides the development of the

Reprinted from the *Consulting Psychology Journal: Practice and Research, 48,* 61–66.

executive (Hay/McBer, 1992). This process helps to identify the position competency requirements that drive "star" performance and the individual competencies that a particular executive possesses. It also provides an understanding of the individual managerial style and its impact on organizational climate, and three "social motives" (achievement, affiliation, and power)—those nonconscious needs, wants, and concerns—that drive and direct the executive's behavior. Finally, this process provides a framework for planning and coaching individual development and performance enhancement (Fontaine & Burruss, n.d.). I typically supplement this basic competency-based program with an in-depth, structured, 3-hour interview; additional instruments of my choosing (often the FIRO-B or Element B and the Strength Deployment Inventory; and sometimes the 16PF); and an ongoing data collection and looped feedback process. Looped feedback refers to a process in which data are reviewed several times, with each loop becoming more specific and interactive. Feedback, coaching, and development are viewed as coupled or interlaced processes.

My assignments and the problems addressed in coaching executives most often focus on the need to

- identify, and modify, the impact of an executive's managerial style on individual effectiveness, team effectiveness, or both;
- provide practical direction for "turning around" senior people who have performance problems;
- help executives more rapidly and effectively adapt to change;
- highlight the use of key strengths;
- plan for and monitor progress regarding individual development needs;
- educate executives on key dimensions of superior performance; and
- enhance organizational performance.

I want the executive coaching process to be viewed as a "value-added" activity. The consultant must be perceived to be respectful; caring; and, from the first contact, practical. To ensure such perceptions, I work to develop and maintain an interactive learning process that focuses on the development of increased awareness and insight, the evaluation of choices or alternative behaviors, and the planning and implementation of more effective executive behavior and performance.

My efforts focus primarily on factors that are internal to the learner, while recognizing the context or social system in which the executive behavior takes place. I stress the fact that the executive needs to view behavior as a function of both role and personality; that is, his or her observed behavior exists as a proportion of two types of performance: role relevant versus personality relevant. Here, we examine the degree to which a given behavioral act is dictated by consideration for the obligations and responsibilities of a particular role, as opposed to the need-dispositions that govern his or her unique tendencies to orient and act in a certain way. We then try to define what the desired balance between the externally defined role expectations and the internally defined personality dispositions of the executive needs to look like going forward.

I also try to remind myself and other consultants that we need to deal with the executive holistically. Our feedback, stemming both from the initial assessment and from the ongoing counseling relationship, must be interlaced with our looped data gathering (Diedrich & Tepper, 1995) and be experienced as an iterative process that involves several cycles (Geirland & Maniker-Leiter, 1995). If feedback and the coaching process are to be effective, the feedback "needs to be two-way, engaging, responsive, and directed toward a desired outcome" (Lawrence & Wiswell, 1995, p. 49). Therefore, three elements must be considered: specificity, empathy, and inquiry. Feedback should be specific, accurately detailed, and refer to actual behavior. Empathy, expressed through listening and the active sharing of perspectives, builds trust. Inquiry is an open-ended process that solicits additional data and understandings and agreements regarding the feedback messages. Finally, I make certain that both the executive and the organization view the coaching process as an ongoing activity that is developmentally oriented, as opposed to a "quick fix" that is problem centered. I must remind the client, the executive, and myself that I am responsible for relating the situation as I see it, and the executive receiving the feedback is responsible for relating what he or she meant, felt, or thought. Also, I remind everyone that ongoing feedback supports growth (Karp, 1987).

PRACTICAL TIPS FOR COACHING CONSULTANTS

When contracting to do executive coaching, the consultant should make sure that the following activities are performed up front:

- engage in a very detailed discussion with the "requesting sponsor" before developing a proposal for and agreeing on a contract for coaching an executive;
- contract for an extended time line, recommend a 12-month or longer program, and do not accept an assignment of less than 6 months in duration;
- make sure all parties view the data collection, feedback, and coaching processes as ongoing activities;
- outline your process in detail and in writing, and then discuss the proposed process again before you begin, both with the sponsor and the executive;
- agree on who gets what; that is, what data are privileged versus public. Be sure you (and the executive) know what the sponsor wants to know regarding the coaching process;
- let the executive participate in defining the specific process you will use (the data to be collected as well as the structure of the tutorial process);
- make sure that all parties agree on the expectations and the format for developmental planning;
- allow for regular (perhaps quarterly) review sessions with the executive and his or her sponsor and for some three-way meetings during the process; and
- agree that you will have several opportunities to view the executive at work with his or her subordinates during the coaching process.

I have learned, often the hard way, that if all parties understand the issues outlined above, the likelihood of success is increased and the number of potential resistances and problems can be both reduced and more easily managed.

CASE STUDY

The Client

Ted is a White male who was in his mid-40s when we began the coaching process. He graduated from a public high school where he played football and wrestled and went on to earn a bachelor of science degree in marine engineering. After serving at sea as an engineering officer to meet his military obligation, he was hired into the engineering department of the company for which he continues to work. He has been with the service organization for over 25 years. Most of his career has been operations oriented. At the time we began the counseling relationship, Ted was a plant manager. He then spent 2 years in a senior staff role and recently returned to the line where, as a director, he is now responsible for several production organizations. He has been married for almost 25 years and has one child who is now in high school. He comes from a working-class family.

The Organization

Ted's employer is a large, independent, investor-owned company that provides energy and energy-related services. Company revenues exceed $1 billion annually, and in spite of recent downsizing, employees number over 4,000. The company is faced with the need for financial flexibility in the face of an increasingly competitive marketplace due to deregulation. Enormous fixed costs must be balanced with the real need to cut costs. The background and experience of senior management is changing from engineering to marketing and financing.

The Referral and Coaching Contract

The referral was initiated by a senior executive with whom we had worked over several years. He encouraged the vice president who managed the client (Ted) to seek our advice.

The presenting problems included an insensitivity to employees and their needs, an autocratic and coercive management style, and gross impatience in the pursuit of results. Ted was described as abusive in his use of power, engaging in intimidation of subordinates, and self-oriented as opposed to team-oriented. The good news was the fact that his production record was hard to beat. Although he was considered to be one of the very best technical and operations managers in the entire company, his job was on the line if he could not modify his behavior. The company chairman did not wish to receive any additional letters about Ted and his management style. Senior management wanted to "save" him if possible.

Ted's manager (the vice president), the senior vice president to whom he reported, and I agreed that the initial coaching contract would involve a 360-degree process. Ted's manager, some peers, and his direct reports would all participate. Following the 360-degree assessment, I would meet with Ted at least monthly for a 2-hour session for 12 months (Phase 1). I was also to meet with the vice president quarterly and with the senior vice president every 6 months or so. In addition to the counseling sessions, additional feedback instruments would be used when needed. It was also understood that the contract could be renewed at the completion of Phase I. The assessment interviews and 360-degree data collection took place in December 1992 and coaching began in February 1993. Formal coaching concluded in October 1995.

The coaching contract called for formal development plans with specific goals and targets; these would be reviewed and signed off on by Ted's manager. It was assumed that the development plans combined with coaching would drive behavior change. In essence, it was hoped that Ted's managerial style and his impact on his subordinates would change, and he would learn to build commitment through participation and cease to be seen as coercive. It was expected that he would also pay more attention to his personal impact and would increase his interpersonal sensitivity and self-control competencies. Finally, the team commitment dimension of organizational climate was expected to improve (increase). These goals and expectations were made most explicit and were described as essentially nonnegotiable.

Conduct and Progress of the Coaching Process

Ted participated in the Hay/McBer Executive 360 process, as did his manager, two peers, and all seven of his direct reports. All participants in the initial assessment process provided data relating to competencies, managerial style, and organization climate. In addition, Ted completed the Picture Story Exercise (a TAT-like, six-picture protocol providing self-report data regarding motives), the FIRO-B, and the Strength Deployment Inventory. I also conducted two 3-hour, in-depth, structured interviews that focused on work history, personal and managerial style, family history, career aspirations, and so forth. All data were collected between December 1992 and January 1993. I also interviewed his manager and the relevant senior vice president.

I met with Ted for 2-hour coaching sessions 16 times in 1993, 8 times in 1994, and 6 times in 1995. Over this period, I also spent many "in-office" hours planning and reviewing the ongoing coaching and met with his manager.

The initial coaching began with the first interactive feedback session in February 1993. At that time, we reviewed the FIRO-B and Strength Deployment Inventory profiles and my impressions from the two interviews. We initially compared our hypotheses and conclusions and began the process of "defining" Ted and his impact on others.

Meeting twice a month during the first 5 months, we identified and refined dominant themes from all of the assessment data. We focused on eight competencies: interpersonal sensitivity, concern for personal impact, relationship building, use of influence strategies, directing versus developing others, group management, and self-control; all but directing others were perceived by raters as very low. Ted displayed strengths in the achievement, organizational awareness, initiative, self-confidence, tenacity, and technical expertise competencies.

Ted's early self-perceptions varied greatly with those of his raters; here, for the most part, his self-ratings were high. We also looked at managerial style (the tendency to be perceived as "coercive" and "pace-setting" was high; "democratic" and "coaching" were low). Results of the FIRO-B, Strength Deployment Inventory, and Picture Story Exercise all indicated power and control needs. With regard to organizational climate, Ted was perceived as demanding unreasonably high standards of excellence, offering little flexibility and responsibility, and being only moderately concerned with team commitment. In a word or two, Ted was seen as a very tough line manager who demanded much all of the time.

Early in 1993, an opportunity arose to move Ted from the line to a very significant staff position in a large department. In this role, Ted could try different management styles because expectations were neutral. However, in this new role, Ted could not demand in the same manner as he was used to doing at the plant. Six months into this assignment, we collected 360-degree data from his five new direct reports. Managerial style, climate, and competencies looked very different and much more positive or functional; self-report and other data were much more similar than different. Ted was having a chance to behave differently, and he was liking the effect he was having on others.

Eight months into the coaching process, I collected additional leadership data as well as examples of personal bests. This information was explored for themes and for opportunities for Ted to behave in a more other-oriented and participative way. We repeatedly collected additional climate data to document the positive effect of his changing style and increasing awareness on himself and others.

Throughout the coaching process, Ted and I prepared developmental plans and reviewed and formalized them with his manager. I also regularly provided articles and books to be read and discussed.

Outcomes of the Process

Ted worked hard at defining his changing behaviors, and he learned to plan for both personal and business outcomes. He became more and more able to let go, to manage his need to dominate, and to reward and develop others as opposed to just directing them. The staff assignment made these changes much easier to implement; he could experiment and not just live up to expectations based on the past.

Ted's needs to be in charge, to win, and to outperform others lessened but did not disappear entirely. Although he now manages his reactions well, he still enjoys a "fight" and "another win" now and then. He is, however, more gentle as well as more aware of the needs of others. He is also still much more able when working with strong, achievement- and power-oriented individuals than with those who need to develop. Finally, his team or group management skills are still developing, given his pronounced desire and history to do it alone and according to his standards.

Ted was moved back into a senior line position late in 1995; he is now in charge of several units and is doing well. He has taken the behaviors he learned in the staff position to the plant setting and has discovered that they work there as well. (He is also perceived to be more interpersonally sensitive and available at home; his family relations have improved considerably.) At this point in our relationship (since December 1995), I see Ted every 2 months or so in an informal, social setting. We now meet for working lunches, at which we review what he is doing and perform some additional development planning. We are also exploring the possibility of my providing an ongoing consulting program for his new organization.

References

Diedrich, R. C., & Tepper, D. T. (1995, August). *Innovations with assessment feedback.* Poster session presented at the 103rd Annual Convention of the American Psychological Association, New York.

Fontaine, M. H., & Burruss, J. A. (n.d.). *A protocol guide to conducting individual consultations with senior executives.* Boston: McBer.

Geirland, J., & Maniker-Leiter, M. (1995). Delivering feedback: The first step, not the last. In J. W. Pfeiffer (Ed.), *The 1995 annual: Vol. 1. Training* (pp. 155–168). San Diego, CA: Pfeiffer.

Hay/McBer. (1992). *Hay/McBer Executive 360*. Boston: Author.

Karp, H. (1987).The lost art of feedback. In J. W. Pfeiffer (Ed.), *The 1987 annual: Developing human resources* (pp. 237–245). San Diego, CA: University Associates.

Lawrence, H. V., & Wiswell, A. K. (1995). Feedback is a two-way street. *Training & Development, 9*(7), 49–52.

Learner-centered psychological principles. (1995, November). *NEP/15, 19*(1), 4–5.

CHAPTER 15

BUSINESS-LINKED EXECUTIVE DEVELOPMENT: COACHING SENIOR EXECUTIVES

Thomas J. Saporito

Coaching executives at the top of an organization presents a set of issues unique in the realm of executive development. There are certain elements common to the coaching of all managers, whatever their level within an organization, but our firm's collective experience over the past 50 years of consulting to senior managers has taught us some important lessons. Probably the most important of these lessons is that if senior executives are going to view developmental coaching as being useful, it had better be evident to them that our efforts are intimately tied to the realities of the business. Chief executives, senior operating officers, and general managers are charged by their shareholders with enormous responsibility in growing their businesses and achieving new levels of profitability. With that responsibility comes the leadership challenge of building an organization; getting a group of people to perform in a consistent fashion; and, in some cases, changing the corporate culture. This is the stuff that keeps executives awake at night. And this is the stuff that is relevant to our work in developing senior executives—linking the executive development process to the realities of the business.

In seeking to make sure our consulting is relevant to the realities facing the executive, we are continually focused on trying to understand not only the work of the individual we are coaching, but also the unique context and business objectives of the client organization. There are a number of dynamics to be considered, as well as myths to be dispelled, if one is to be effective consulting in the executive suite. For example, a commonly held view is that senior executives don't need to be developed—after all, they are senior executives. "Heck—if they still need to be developed at that level, they shouldn't be there in the first place!" This myth might be summarized as "the higher you go, the less you need to be developed." The fact of the matter is, the higher an individual moves in an organization, the less feedback he or she is likely to receive. Senior executives tend to get isolated from real-time, unvarnished feedback about the impact of their individual leadership.

Senior executives tend to be skeptical folks by nature. Their training and experience have taught them to question everything, taking little at face value. This is particularly evident in their attitude toward consultants. The likelihood that a consultant could actually understand and, more important, have practical impact on issues relating directly to corporate performance and profitability is a matter for skepticism among this group. Our job as executive coaches is to get beyond the skepticism by making sure that our involvement is, in fact, extremely practical and directly related to the

Reprinted from the *Consulting Psychology Journal: Practice and Research, 48,* 96–103.

issues of corporate performance and individual effectiveness.

Senior executives have made a career out of managing personal and organizational vulnerability. Issues of control are significant, to say the least, at the top of organizations. This control issue is a dynamic, both in individual and in organizational terms, of which we must be highly aware if we are going to work in the executive suite. Senior executives aren't about to turn an executive loose in an organization, particularly if they perceive the potential for adverse effects on themselves or on the organization for which they are responsible. So where does this leave us, as consultants, in our effort to be continually effective by focusing on issues relevant to the executives with whom we work?

A few important principles emerge. First, we must be certain that the development is business based. (Later in this chapter, we will discuss one model for ensuring a high degree of relevance.) Second, understanding the unique requirements of executives at senior levels is important. This understanding can be derived, in part, from following this model. It also comes from time and experience in working with senior executives. Executives can sense very quickly whether the executives with whom they work are familiar with the subtle, but significant, aspects of the world in which they live. Being credible takes more than just using the right jargon. It has to do with understanding the influences and, sometimes, the nebulous but powerful dynamics that shape the way a senior executive goes about trying to have influence on the business and the performance of people.

MODEL

Our model of consulting, we believe, helps ensure the highest possible degree of relevance to the challenges facing the executives whom we coach. (See Figure 15.1.)

Stage 1: Setting the Foundation

We refer to the first stage of consulting with the executive as *setting the foundation.* This foundation setting requires that we work with the organization as a whole, as well as with the individual, to gain a proper understanding of the context that will dictate the needs of coaching. Understanding the needs of the individual executive is just the beginning. Developing an overall sense of the organizational requirements, culture, philosophy, and context within the industry is also essential. It is during this initial stage that we create a *Profile of Success.*™ There are three fundamental questions that must be answered to create this *Profile of Success:*

1. ***What are the organizational imperatives?*** It is important to understand the key challenges facing the organization, as well as the particular unit or division for which the executive is responsible. We think of this as the greater context within which the executive functions, and which shapes the direction of his or her development and ultimate success. Is the organization in a rapid growth mode, or is it downsizing? Is the business mature, or is it in an earlier stage of development? Is there a greater emphasis on product development, or on operational efficiency? Questions such as these and many others will help articulate the organizational imperatives driving the expectations for the individual executive.
2. ***What are the success factors for that particular role within the organization?*** Determining what this person in this particular position must do to successfully fulfill the expectations that mean the success of his or her organization is a key element of this coaching model. In establishing an understanding of these issues, we are trying to understand the particular leadership needs that define the role of the executive. Familiarity with the organization's culture and style play an important role in understanding the success factors for the individual.
3. ***What are the behavioral requirements to achieve these success factors?*** We work to clarify the personal qualities and behaviors that are relevant to the specific position, and that will also help shape a significant part of our executive coaching. For example, what are the types of problem-solving requirements an individual will be facing? What are the types of constituencies to whom he or she must relate, and what is

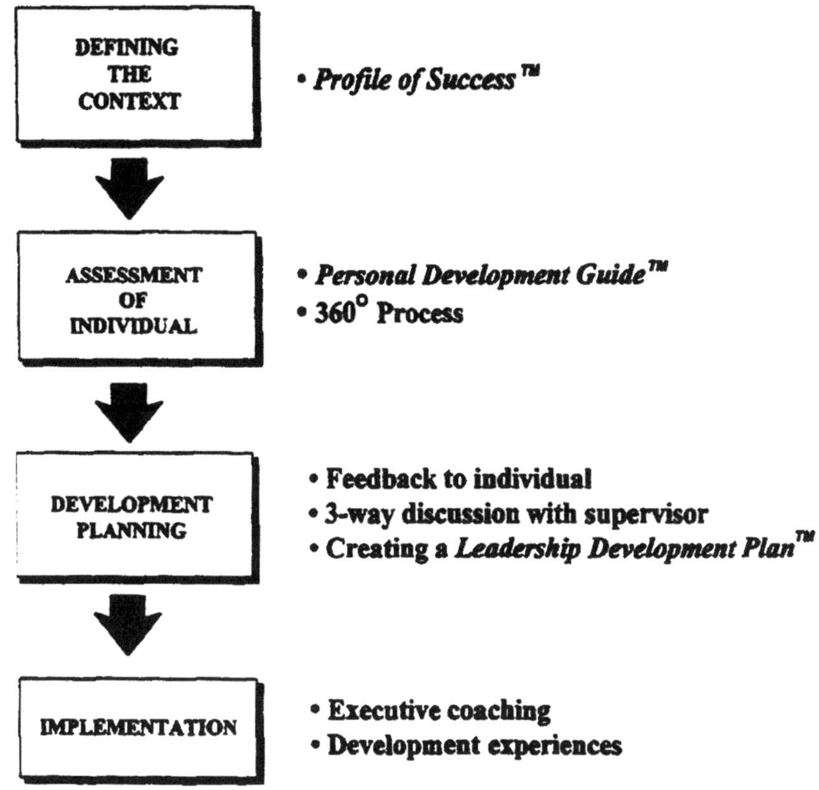

FIGURE 15.1. **Business-linked executive development model.**

the style of leadership that will be most effective in that organizational context?

This foundation is critical to making sure our coaching incorporates recommendations and personal support that the executive will recognize as being central to his or her experience. Creating this *Profile of Success* includes talking with people who have a stake in that executive's success. As our case will illustrate, this step might include talking with members of the board of directors, the senior human resources executive, the person's boss, and the individual being coached. This foundation will be key in helping to develop the degree of relevance that will encourage the executives with whom we work to allow consultants into their world. It is also during this time that we set the expectations for our work and establish the ground rules for the process.

Stage 2: Assessment of the Individual

The second stage is the assessment of the individual. With context and expectations properly defined, we are now ready to gather the data and insights that will form the individual's developmental picture. We typically engage the executive in an in-depth developmental assessment by means of a semistructured interview covering the experiences that have shaped his or her managerial philosophy and style. We take an in-depth look at the way in which the executive views his or her challenges in the current role, and how he or she is adopting a leadership posture that meets the needs of the organization. This assessment is a key component in exploring the alignment of the individual's leadership posture with the requirements identified in the *Profile of Success*. The by-product of this assessment is a summary that we call the *Personal Development Guide*™ (PDG). The PDG describes the individual and, more important, highlights the key development issues that will set the stage for our feedback to the executive, and for subsequent executive coaching.

Often, we will round out our view of the individual with a 360-degree assessment process.

Through interviews with the individual's boss, peers, and subordinates, we are able to develop a fairly comprehensive overview of the individual's development needs and coaching requirements. This 360-degree process also serves to add face validity to the process. It allows us to pinpoint the issues and circumstances that need to be addressed to help increase the openness of the executive with whom we are working.

Stage 3: Developmental Planning

The third phase is the development planning stage. This stage is composed of two parts, feedback and development planning.

Feedback. In the feedback section, we integrate our own insights into the data relevant to the particular executive with whom we are working. In-depth discussions and reviews are a critical part of helping to create the level of insight into the executive that enables him or her to see the developmental issues to be addressed. Continually referring back to the *Profile of Success* to define the central issues for that person is a powerful way to maintain relevance and move the ball forward.

Development Planning. At this stage, we typically create a *Leadership Development Plan*™, the primary objective of which is to focus on the strengths, development needs and experiences, or type of coaching that will help this person increase his or her effectiveness. This plan is usually constructed in coordination with the individual executive and his or her boss, to ensure ownership and commitment on the part of all concerned.

Stage 4: Implementation

The final stage of our executive coaching process is the implementation. This is the point in the process in which we move from determining what the needs are and how we will work on them to actually getting it done. It is at this stage that the coaching becomes most evident and concentrated, although coaching actually has been taking place from the beginning, as the developmental relationship was established and feedback was offered. So the coaching and implementation stage is really a continuation of what has been building throughout the process. What is important now is that our coaching has a foundation—a thorough assessment has been formed, and a plan has been developed that will provide continual and reliable points of reference for both the coach and the subject as they work through the process.

CASE STUDY

Our client executive, Howard, was president of a large industrial products company when we first began our work. Howard is an engineer by training. The first 20 years of his career were spent in the automotive, and subsequently the aerospace, industry. He moved steadily up through the ranks in positions of increasing responsibility. He made his mark by being a tough-minded, results-oriented line executive who generally achieved impressive financial results in his area of responsibility. Howard had been hired into this company, Amalgamated Resources, by the current chairman and chief executive officer l0 years previously as part of a plan to upgrade the management capability of the company. He joined Amalgamated as a group vice president, responsible for four divisions. Four years before we met him, he had been promoted into the position of president and chief operating officer. At about the same time, the board of directors, along with the senior management team, made the decision to strategically reposition Amalgamated Resources. This $4 billion business had been an industrial products company for 70 years. Faced with increasingly tough competition, and operating within a price-cutting environment, Amalgamated's profit margin had begun to dwindle. Top management decided to redirect the company into specialty products to establish a stronger foundation for growth. This prompted a series of divestitures and acquisitions, resulting in a "new" business and organization.

The request for executive coaching came in the midst of this strategic realignment and was driven by a succession planning requirement. The current CEO, Jim, was due to retire in 15 months. Jim, in agreement with the board, had decided to promote Howard to the position of CEO when he retired. Amalgamated's vice president of human resources,

Lynda, was familiar with our work through projects we had completed for her former company. She and Jim both recognized that not only was the position of CEO substantively different from that of chief operating officer, but also that the leadership requirements of the company were going to shift significantly as it moved into its next phase of development. They recognized the importance of Howard's being well prepared to handle an evolving set of leadership requirements, and looked to an executive coaching effort as the best way to prepare him for taking over the reigns of the company.

The first meeting was with Jim and Lynda. We discussed Howard and his future challenges and established a consulting plan that would best address the coaching required to develop him for the role of CEO. We then met with Howard to discuss the parameters of this consulting effort. He readily articulated his own recognition that the leadership challenge was going to change substantially over the next 5 years. He also seemed to be aware of the challenges that this leap in responsibility would mean to him individually. However, like most executives, he was initially skeptical as to how we might actually be effective in helping him prepare for his new assignment.

We outlined the consulting model and its various elements. We explained the creation of a *Profile of Success.* Through discussions with Howard, Jim, and the board of directors, we helped ensure a clear view of the requirements he would be facing. As he began to understand the nature of our approach and recognized the degree of familiarity we would attain with his company and his own situation, he began to be somewhat more receptive. Still, it would take months of participation and a chance to watch the process unfold before he would be entirely won over.

During the first few months, we interviewed selected board members, Jim, and Howard in creating this *Profile of Success.* The primary success factors that emerged during this phase reflected that the company's greatest need would be leadership from the top, which would provide a new vision and focus on integrating the acquired divisions into a single company with a common set of values and a unified culture. There would be an emphasis on the necessity of building a cohesive management team, the members of which would be drawn from the various acquired organizations. Howard, as the next CEO, would have the task of focusing on building a common vision around which people could rally. As well, he would have to build a company integrated by a new set of values. The acquired organizations would need to meld together. He would have to shape an organizational climate of trust and collaboration for the company to succeed.

The *Profile of Success* identified behaviors that were relevant to this task. The CEO of the future would have to be strategic in his or her thinking and broad based in his or her view of the organization. The CEO's values concerning power would have to emphasize power through people, rather than power over people. He or she would have to be psychologically accessible to people, easy to engage, supportive, and a strong communicator. Finally, his or her managerial philosophy would have to emphasize results through a managerial style that encourages participation and collaboration of effort.

With this *Profile of Success* in hand, we began our assessment of Howard. Through our own assessment, as well as the input of several people throughout the organization, a picture emerged of an executive who was respected for his ability to get results. People recognized Howard as being strategically minded, bright, and aggressive in managing toward growth. He was also seen as intimidating. He was described as "demanding," "hands-on," and "outspoken." In contrast, Jim (the current CEO) was described as being a warm and down-to-earth individual. Howard lacked the same kind of spontaneity and warmth.

The developmental questions that began to emerge with relation to Howard centered on his ability to make the transition from being a day-to-day operating manager to becoming someone able to provide broader organizational leadership. The company needed someone whose philosophy of leadership and personal style would encourage collaboration and a desire on the part of everyone concerned to form a cohesive organization. Howard's leadership challenge would be to build an organizational climate of teamwork. He had a track record of getting people to perform by means of pushing hard for results. The question was whether he could complement this results-oriented style with a more encouraging and supportive managerial posture. Given the requirements to build teamwork, trust, and collaboration, this shift in managerial style was going to be absolutely essential to his success in providing leadership from the top. Furthermore, could he influence his entire management team to exhibit the same qualifies to start pulling the acquisitions into a new single entity?

Interestingly, most of the people to whom we spoke acknowledged Howard's ascendancy to the role of chief executive, based on his track record of performance and obvious dedication to the company's future. However, they were uncertain as to whether he could provide the personal leadership needed to pull the new organization together.

Howard met our feedback with the acknowledgment of his demanding and task-oriented management style. He understood that the organization saw him in those terms, and he even understood that a shift in style was necessary. What caught his attention, more than anything else, was the doubt on the part of others in the organization about whether he could make this shift. He found this difficult to verbalize, but he was clearly worried about getting the organization to rally around him in creating the new culture. His need to achieve and his motivation to fulfill his career dream served as the fuel to work on these development issues.

After three feedback sessions over the first 2 months, we began to put together with Howard (along with input from Lynch and Jim) a development plan. Our aim was to shape a development plan with some very specific initiatives. The first element of the plan involved our working with Howard to engage the senior management team in defining the desired culture for this newly evolving organization. We worked with him to design a 3-day management retreat with the top 15 executives of the company, the purpose of which was to have them articulate the new organizational values and to establish the ground rules for the functioning of the revamped organization. The retreat, which we facilitated, presented Howard with his first significant opportunity to lay out his view of what was important and to begin practicing a new set of behaviors with this group of people. He found this difficult, because he had been accustomed to handling our objectives, reviewing results, and becoming demanding when people underperformed. The process of this retreat required him to be far more collaborative and encouraging in pulling the team together around a new vision. We encouraged Howard to be open with his management team about his intention to create a new style of organization and the difficulty he anticipated in shifting his own approach. Now, he had to deal directly with the skepticism of people on his top-level team involving his own ability to make fairly significant changes in his leadership style. Our role during this meeting was to continually encourage Howard to elicit responses from his management team and encourage debate. Continual off-line coaching, during breaks and in the evenings, helped him with this process. The biggest challenge was getting him to deal with his own impatience in having to work through the process. He would have preferred to simply tell the executives what the new values were and expect them to be adopted.

Nonetheless, the management team was able to come out of this retreat with a statement of values and operating principles for the company. More important, Howard had begun to reposition himself in a way that would ensure greater support from the 15 top managers as he prepared to take on the CEO role.

Our developmental coaching with Howard during the subsequent 6 months focused on helping to figure out exactly what he must do to adopt a broader leadership posture. For example, he began to hold monthly luncheons with people at all levels of the organization to talk about the new direction of the company, the developing cultural emphases (such as collaboration and teamwork), and the importance of their participation in making the new culture work. We made sure that the vice president for human resources, Lynda, was at every one of those lunches so that she could serve as an internal consultant in providing regular feedback. We sat regularly with the senior management members to get their input about Howard's progress and his impact on the organization. We provided continual feedback and coaching to Howard to help him in making these adjustments. Sometimes, in fact, we held "co-coaching" sessions with Lynda and Howard to combine her day-to-day feedback with our overall suggestions regarding how to continue with the progress he was making.

To suggest that the process of development was, for Howard, an easy one would be too simplistic. He continued to struggle with ways in which he could encourage collaboration and teamwork without abandoning his tradition of high expectations and demanding standards. Our challenge was to get him to recognize that these were not "either–or" postures, but rather that results would be accomplished through greater teamwork throughout the organization.

Howard's biggest shift was in moving from a top-down, one-on-one management style to a greater emphasis on managing the team as a whole through coaching and constant dialogue. Dealing with differences among his team members, given their diverse backgrounds and the various organizational cultures from which they came, and the time it would take to shape them as a team was simply frustrating and unusual for him. Howard had to learn how to manage process, not just business problems. He had to confront a traditional, top-down management style, his impatience being in learning how to build personal relationships that would allow him to encourage the organization toward a new style.

One of the consulting strategies was an attempt to engage Jim, the current CEO, in serving as another coach for Howard. This was probably one of the aspects of our executive coaching that did not go as well as we would have liked. Although Jim was warm and personal, he turned out to be a fairly ineffective coach. He disliked conflict and often found it difficult to give Howard straight feedback. He relied on us and on Lynda to carry out that task. Our efforts to pull together three-way discussions with Howard and Jim were moderately successful at best. One of the lessons we learned was that it would have been better to have engaged Jim more directly in the early stages of the consultation around his role and to consult with him throughout the process. He was involved at the front end in helping to define the *Profile of Success* and at the back end in receiving the results. We would have done better to work more actively to clarify his role in helping Howard to develop.

Nonetheless, Howard did make substantial progress. He was promoted to CEO as planned, and he had adopted enough new managerial behaviors to help him lead the new organization. He would continue to be frustrated and sometimes revert back to old behaviors, but he had made enough of a shift that the organization began to acknowledge his intentions as well as his new behaviors.

It is rare that any executive makes a complete change in his or her behavior. This would be unfair and unrealistic to expect as the outcome of any executive coaching effort. What is—hopefully—realistic is getting the individual to modify enough of his or her behavior to fit the specific behavioral requirements and success factors to a great enough degree that he or she can help the company achieve its organizational imperatives.

CHAPTER 16

THE COGNITIVE–BEHAVIORAL APPROACH TO EXECUTIVE COACHING

Mary Jo Ducharme

Since the term *executive coaching* began to appear in the literature in the late 1980s, several different approaches to this process have surfaced, including a systems perspective (see chap. 13, this volume), an iterative feedback model (see chap. 14, this volume), a multimodal therapy model (see chap. 25, this volume), rational–emotive behavior therapy (REBT) models (Anderson, 2002; see also chap. 17, this volume), a transformative–developmental model (see chap. 21, this volume), a constructive-developmental theory approach (Fitzgerald & Berger, 2002), an action frame theory approach (see chap. 18, this volume), and even an existential approach (Peltier, 2001). By far the most developed and used model of change in executive coaching, put forth by Kilburg (2000; see also chap. 1, this volume), stems from the systems and psychodynamic viewpoints.

Few authors have referred to a cognitive–behavioral perspective except as a framework for a more eclectic approach (see chap. 25, this volume), with a strictly REBT orientation (Anderson, 2002), or with a pure cognitive therapy orientation (Peltier, 2001), despite the well-known success and efficacy of the approach with clinical populations (Dobson & Craig, 1996; Hollon & Beck, 2004; Steiman & Dobson, 2002). The purpose of this article is to examine the concepts, techniques, and theoretical underpinnings usually associated with cognitive–behavioral therapy in terms of its suitability for application to executive coaching and to propose situations in which cognitive–behavioral coaching is appropriate.

COGNITIVE–BEHAVIORAL THERAPY

Assumptions

Cognitive–behavioral therapy is a broad term encompassing a wide variety of intervention techniques that range from largely cognitive to largely behavioral. Despite the diversity of approaches within the field in general, cognitive–behavioral therapy has three fundamental assumptions at its core. First, cognitive appraisals of events can affect behavioral responses to those events. How one interprets the reality of a situation or event will affect one's decision in terms of how to react to the event or situation. This assumption has found wide empirical support (see Dobson & Dozois, 2001). The second assumption of cognitive–behavioral therapy is that cognitions may be accessed, monitored, and altered. Individuals can become aware that an event or situation, such as the presence of a work-related error, has resulted in a certain thought pattern, such as thoughts regarding one's incompetence, and this awareness can aid in the subsequent monitoring and alteration of these thoughts (Dobson & Dozois, 2001). The third assumption is that changes to an individual's cognition can result in desired behavior change (Dobson & Block, 1988;

Reprinted from the *Consulting Psychology Journal: Practice and Research, 56,* 214–224.

Dobson & Dozois, 2001; Steiman & Dobson, 2002). Altering one's thought patterns in reaction to an event can result in changes to the way one subsequently behaves. For example, one's thoughts of incompetence in the face of an error can be altered to take the form of thoughts related to the potential causes of the error, thereby setting in motion ways to avoid the error from reoccurring.

Within the scope of cognitive–behavioral therapy, there are a wide variety of interventions that lie along a continuum from behavioral to cognitive. The major distinction between strictly behavioral therapies and cognitive–behavioral therapies is the assumption that internal covert processes occur and that these processes can alter behavior. This assumption of mediation of cognitions between events and behavioral outcomes is common to all cognitive–behavioral interventions. The emphasis placed on the cognitive mediator, however, may vary, depending on the orientation of the approach. For example, more behavioral approaches, while attempting to effect cognitive change, will focus on outward behavior as an index for change, whereas some more cognitive-based approaches rely only on descriptions of cognitive appraisals and evaluations as the index for change. However, most cognitive–behavioral techniques draw heavily upon behavioral principles and thus rely on behavioral assessment of change to document progress (Dobson & Dozois, 2001).

Treatment

Cognitive–behavioral treatments can be categorized into one of three categories: coping-skills therapies, problem-solving therapies, and cognitive-restructuring therapies (Dobson & Block, 1988; Dobson & Dozois, 2001). Coping-skills therapies are geared toward problems that are external to the individual and are, to some extent, beyond the individual's control. This category would include such therapies as stress inoculation training (Meichenbaum, 1985), which helps individuals build resistance to lower, more manageable levels of stress in order to build tolerance to higher, uncontrollable levels of stress. Also falling into this category of treatments is self-control therapy (Steiman & Dobson, 2002), which attempts to help individuals faced with a problem situation to be aware of their own behavior and evaluate it compared with a preset standard. Individuals are taught to use behavioral contingencies to shape their own behavior toward this preset standard.

Problem-solving techniques were developed to help individuals who have a reduced ability to manage their day-to-day problems. This category of therapies involves teaching individuals to be able to recognize problematic day-to-day situations, generate and decide among different courses of action that could be taken, and then verify that the right path was chosen (Steiman & Dobson, 2002).

Cognitive-restructuring techniques are closer to the cognitive end of the continuum and involve identifying and altering negative thought patterns. Beck (1976) proposed that individuals interpret their world through *schema,* which are defined as the basic beliefs and understanding that individuals have and use to organize their view of self and their environment. When these schemas are maladaptive, individuals develop problems coping with their lives. In general, some cognitive-restructuring techniques involve assessing and changing individuals' maladaptive schemas, automatic thoughts, and dysfunctional cognitions. These techniques were originally intended for work with depressed individuals but have also been successfully applied to anxiety, substance abuse, anger, and crisis management (see Dobson & Dozois, 2001).

COGNITIVE–BEHAVIORAL TECHNIQUES APPLIED TO EXECUTIVE COACHING

Several aspects of the practice of executive coaching are unique to interventions with this high-performing client group. Any model of executive coaching must take into account these unique aspects in order to derive substantial and lasting developmental effects from the coaching intervention. The following five unique aspects of executive coaching are particularly relevant to this discussion.

1. ***Differences between therapy and executive coaching***. Several differences between therapeutic interventions and those designed for coach-

ing have been expressed in the literature (see chap. 3, this volume) and are relevant to this discussion. Executive coaching interventions can be seen as more issue-focused, examining the specific developmental needs of the executive (see chap. 25, this volume). A unique aspect of the executive coaching alliance is that data may be collected from third parties, such as others in the organization, for both initial assessment purposes as well as to collect indexes of success (chaps. 1 and 31, this volume). Therapeutic interventions are more apt to rely on self-reports of internal states to measure success, whereas in coaching, the success of the intervention is measured in more concrete and objective terms (see chap. 25, this volume). Probably the most important difference, pointed out by Kilburg (2000), is the level of analysis: Therapeutic interventions tend to delve more deeply into issues than do typical executive coaching interventions.

Given the nature of executive coaching when compared with therapeutic interventions, it seems possible that cognitive–behavioral practices would be of great practical value in certain situations when working with executives. The results-driven micro focus of the cognitive–behavioral orientation fits well with the above description. In fact, a limitation of the cognitive–behavioral approach is that it can be seen as very specific and issue-focused, not taking into sufficient account the person as a whole or going beyond a surface level of analysis. Although this does not go so far as to say that this weakness of the cognitive–behavioral orientation should be viewed as a strength when in the context of an executive coaching situation, perhaps the level of analysis typically seen in the cognitive–behavioral orientation, as well as the results orientation, may be appropriate for some coaching interventions.

2. ***Situations in which executives typically seek coaching.*** Several different views exist in the literature regarding the reasons why executives seek coaching. One possible reason is to refine their skills so that they can progress in their careers, either by taking on more leadership responsibilities (see chap. 11, this volume) or by moving into a more advanced position (see chap. 10, this volume). In some situations, executives look to coaching to help them with maladaptive behaviors that are interfering with their work life (see chap. 11, this volume; Judge & Cowell, 1997; Koonce, 1994), such as a leadership style that is better suited to a hierarchical organization that is no longer appropriate in an organization that has an updated structure.

As such, the situations in which executives typically seek coaching seem particularly well-suited to cognitive–behavioral techniques. The acquisition of new skills to facilitate growth, as well as the elimination of maladaptive behaviors, forms the basis of basic cognitive–behavioral techniques. Kilburg pointed out that a major principle underlying coaching is to increase executives' psychological and social awareness, develop their wisdom (2000), and improve their self-awareness (1997). Although it is more difficult to see how the cognitive–behavioral techniques and orientation could achieve these more complex goals, it is not impossible. For example, in cognitive–behavioral coaching situations, executives seeking to decrease the frequency with which they act out based on their emotions in the workplace may, as part of the intervention, be asked to monitor their own feelings in such a way as to help them predict and become aware of their thoughts and emotions. Although this is perhaps a simplistic approach to self-awareness, it may nonetheless be successful for some executive clients.

Kampa and White (2002) made the point that lower-level training, such as the skill development that is the domain of cognitive–behavioral coaching, can be best obtained through training programs and workshops, and that one does not need to employ an executive coach for such lower level learning. This is an excellent point; however, in addition to the fact that for sustained behavior change the coaching situation may ensure that executives do not fall back to their old patterns of behavior, it is also true that some executives may prefer to employ a coach for a more personalized, ongoing, and private development approach.

3. ***The unique needs of the executive.*** There are several aspects of the executive lifestyle that are somewhat unique and that require special attention when considering appropriate intervention methods. First, the executive lifestyle is, for most who work at this level, associated with a high level of stress. The stressor will vary depending on the individual, but common sources of work stress are work–life balance, work-related anxiety, dysfunctional working conditions, and reactions to change in the workplace (Lowman, 1993). Other sources of stress more particular to the executive lifestyle may include procrastination, indecisiveness in decision making, reactions to criticism, and fear of confrontation. Related to the high-stress lifestyles led by many executives is the notion of Type A behavior. It is possible that a high proportion of executives could be considered Type A, a trait that is associated with competitiveness, ambition, dedication to work, thriving on tight deadlines, and rising to challenges, in addition to coronary heart disease and early death (Roskies, 1983).

Cognitive–behavioral techniques for stress management have demonstrated efficacy for high-performance individuals, such as athletes (Beauchamp, Halliwell, Fournier, & Koestner, 1996; Holm, Beckwith, Ehde, & Tinius, 1996; R. E. Smith, 1996; see also Whelan, Mahoney, & Meyers, 1991) and musicians (Kendrick, Craig, Lawson, & Davidson, 1982; Sinden, 1999). Roskies et al. (1986) demonstrated the efficacy of cognitive–behavioral techniques with middle managers who demonstrated behaviors typically associated with Type A patterns. In addition, there are a wide variety of well-established cognitive–behavioral techniques specifically geared toward stress management that are available for coaches to choose from (Hollon & Beck, 2004; Leventhal & Nerenz, 1983; Meichenbaum, 1985). Therefore, for the specific purpose of managing stress and its effects, which is a common focus of executive coaching interventions (Judge & Cowell, 1997; Kilburg, 2002b), cognitive–behavioral techniques would seem particularly appropriate and useful.

Second, as pointed out by Kampa and White (2002) and Saporito (see chap. 15, this volume), another unique need of executives is that they frequently have difficulty procuring an honest opinion of their abilities and weaknesses within the organization. Therefore, in their view, one function of executive coaching is to provide feedback that is untainted by the social desirability that exists within organizations. In addition, executives value and place trust in objective data (see chap. 11, this volume). While it can be said that feedback is an important part of most executive coaching interventions, this is perhaps even more the case with cognitive–behavioral interventions. Not only is frequent feedback a mainstay of the cognitive–behavioral orientation, objective behavioral data are often used as the index of successful change. Therefore, this aspect of executive coaching engagements, too, is highly appropriate for meeting this unique need demonstrated by executives.

Third, an aspect of the work environment that is unique to executives and managers is that they are often in a position to directly affect the development of others within the organization. In fact, it is conceivable that a significant part of their impact on the performance of the organization is through relationships with direct reports. An advantage of cognitive–behavioral coaching is that the techniques applied to the intervention are transparent and perhaps more easily comprehensible without extensive training than some other intervention approaches (e.g., psychodynamic approaches) and are therefore more easily applied by the executive to his or her other relationships. Executives who have received cognitive–behavioral coaching to develop their own skills are in a good position to apply basic behavioral and cognitive–behavioral principles to their developmental relationships with direct reports, thereby possibly impacting the performance of other members of their work units.

Finally, several authors have commented on the importance of treating the executive holistically (see chap. 14, this volume) and with consideration to the fact that they are embedded in a system (Kilburg, 2000, 2002b). Kilburg (2000) presented the complex nature of analyzing individuals in organizations as one of six major challenges that coaches must face. He emphasized the chaotic and dynamic nature of the issues presented in some coaching engagements because of the interaction of the complexities of the underlying organization and the sometimes unconscious psychological processes of individuals. Is it possible that some coaching engagements are just too complex to use the arguably simplistic approaches of the cognitive–behavioral orientation? Borrowing evidence from work with clinical populations, several complex disorders have been successfully treated using these techniques, such as depression and some aspects of borderline personality disorder (Hollon & Beck, 2004). Of course, there are serious limitations to using evidence from clinical populations and applying it to executive coaching situations; however, this may be taken as evidence of the possibility that complex issues can be dealt with by cognitive–behavioral techniques. However, even if it is concluded that cognitive–behavioral coaching can be adapted to work within the complex and dynamic situations in which many executives find themselves, the cognitive–behavioral orientation is not one that emphasizes the examination of individuals as a *whole*. Cognitive–behavioral coaching is a very targeted approach to behavioral improvement, focusing on incremental change in segmented areas of an individual's behavior. For example, an executive who suffers from frequent social anxiety would be a candidate for cognitive–behavioral coaching. The likely course of action would be to focus on the social anxiety and its associated thoughts and behaviors. Coaching sessions could involve use of systematic desensitization, gradually bringing the individual to the point where he or she is able to go into formerly anxiety-provoking social situations and have functional thoughts and behave appropriately. Although the executive client is now able to face high-stress social situations with more ease, other areas of his or her life that may involve anxiety have not been directly dealt with. Even if generalization occurs and dealing with one type of anxiety has helped the individual to better cope with other anxieties in his or her working and personal life, this is still an approach that has focused entirely on anxiety and not on the general development of wisdom or self-awareness. One could argue that a high-functioning executive would need more from a coaching situation than this very targeted microscopic approach to development.

4. ***Scope of executive coaching.*** In general, the term *executive coaching* refers to a helping relationship existing between an executive and a coach, which has as its primary goal the growth, development, and increased performance of the executive. Kilburg's (see chap. 1, this volume; 2000) definition includes an emphasis on mutually identified goals that result in increased professional performance, personal satisfaction, and improvement to the organization. Kampa and White (2002) added three points to this definition: First, a major purpose of a coach's role is to provide feedback to executives regarding their behavior and its impact on others within the organization and in their personal lives. Second, an executive coach should possess not only knowledge of psychological techniques, but also knowledge of business and organizational functioning. Finally, Kampa and White (2002) proposed that behavior change in executive coaching relationships should be measurable, and Brotman, Liberi, and Wasylyshyn (see chap. 31, this volume) indicated that results should be measured in terms of sustained behavior change. Witherspoon and White (see chap. 10, this volume) and Tobias (see chap. 13, this volume) added that most coaching situations result in ongoing relationships between executive and coach. Most other definitions of executive coaching fall within these parameters (Anderson, 2002; chaps. 15 and 24, this volume; Peltier, 2001).

As can be seen from the preceding discussion of the various elements of the definitions of executive coaching, the field is quite broadly defined. In terms of the scope of executive coaching, the cognitive–behavioral approach is a fit. The results-focused goal orientation of cognitive–behavioral techniques should at least place this approach on the table for use in coaching situations.

5. ***Efficacy of cognitive–behavioral techniques.*** The efficacy of cognitive–behavioral

interventions has been well-proven with a wide variety of clinical populations (Hollon & Beck, 2004). As was previously mentioned, there has been some evidence to suggest the efficacy of cognitive–behavioral techniques with high-performing, nonclinical populations, such as athletes (Beauchamp et al., 1996; Holm et al., 1996; R. E. Smith, 1996; see Whelan et al., 1991) and musicians (Kendrick et al., 1982; Sinden, 1999).

To be sure, some practitioners have been successfully using behavioral and cognitive–behavioral techniques in their executive coaching practices for some time (Kilburg, 2000; L. Smith, 1993), although there are no empirical studies to date that have assessed efficacy in this context. As Kampa-Kokesch and Anderson (see chap. 3, this volume) pointed out, this is an issue within the field of executive coaching in general in that very few examinations of the efficacy of coaching practices have been carried out. Although the efficacy of cognitive–behavioral techniques has been firmly established in clinical populations, there is valid concern over the efficacy of applying therapeutic techniques to work with high-performing clients. Even though cognitive–behavioral techniques have been shown to be successful with high-performance athletes and musicians, these interventions most often have to do with performance anxiety. While performance anxiety certainly comes into play in the development of some executives, this is not the main thrust of executive coaching interventions in general. Therefore, there is little or no evidence to suggest that cognitive–behavior therapy techniques would be efficacious in work with high-performing clients. However, this is a fact that is true of any of the approaches in executive coaching.

In summary, the goal of the preceding section was to itemize the unique needs of executives and of executive coaching engagements and assess whether or not the cognitive–behavioral approach is appropriate and likely to be effective in this context. Figure 16.1 contains a summary of the needs discussed in the section and an indication of whether through this discussion a conclusion was made regarding whether or not cognitive–behavioral coaching is likely to address that need.

CONCLUSIONS AND RECOMMENDATIONS

Strengths of Cognitive–Behavioral Coaching

For the pragmatically minded, results-oriented, data-trusting executive, cognitive–behavioral coaching is highly appropriate for several reasons. Cognitive–behavioral coaching (CBC) is an intuitive approach that is likely to appeal to many executives because of its transparency and simplicity. Not only is it quite likely that cognitive–behavioral techniques will be successful at developing executives in areas that are of value to executive coaching engagements, such as modifying interaction styles, improving listening skills, and improving public speaking (Judge & Cowell, 1997; Kilburg, 2002a), the results of this success are measured in obvious ways that can be demonstrated to the executive and to organizational third parties. Constant honest feedback, as with other approaches, is a vital part of CBC; however, especially in CBC the feedback is easily supported by data and objective behavioral criteria.

Stress-related dysfunction is common in organizations (Lowman, 1993; Roskies et al., 1986), and executives endure a high level of stress on a day-to-day basis. Even if they appear to be thriving on the high level of stress, it is possible that they could be categorized as demonstrating aspects of Type A behavior, a category of behavior that is associated with very serious negative health effects. In terms of managing high levels of stress and its negative side effects, cognitive–behavioral techniques offer superior efficacy (Hollon & Beck, 2004; Holroyd, Appel, & Andrasik, 1983; Roskies et al., 1986).

Weaknesses of Cognitive–Behavioral Therapy

The limitations of CBC are centered around its simplicity. While in other contexts, and perhaps even in executive coaching, simplicity can be seen as a strength of the approach, for some aspects of the executive coaching situation it may be a limitation. A high-functioning executive may be disappointed by the somewhat mechanical and seemingly unsophisticated view that is presented by the cognitive–behavioral orientation. For example, in targeting

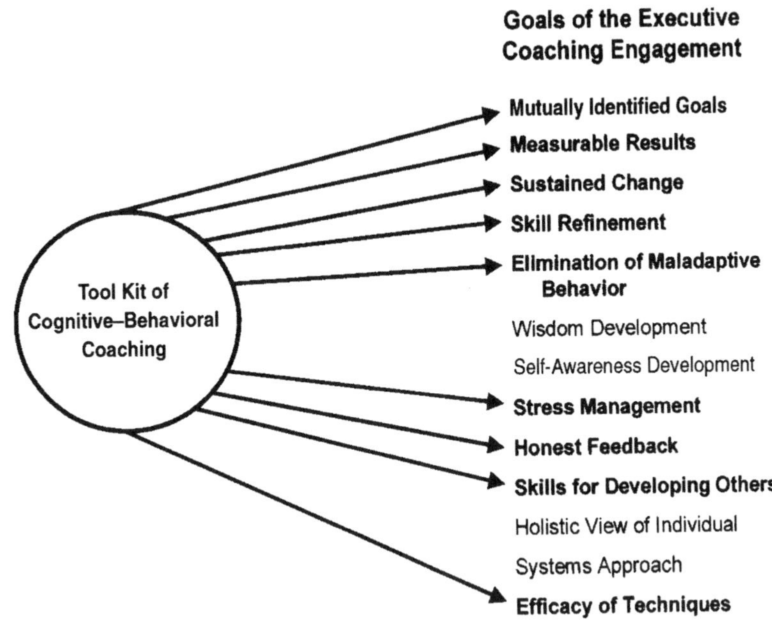

FIGURE 16.1. Goals of executive coaching that are met and not met by cognitive–behavioral coaching.

anger management as an area for improvement, a likely course of action would involve some form of relaxation training or stress inoculation. Although relaxation training has been shown to be a successful aspect of a cognitive–behavioral approach to anger management, individuals with a high degree of insight into their own thoughts and feelings may regard the simple act of learning how to relax as a giant step backward in their coping skills. In addition, beyond the actual thoughts that take place when aggression occurs, there would be little or no discussion or investigation of the origins or possible causes of the anger and little or no attempt to connect this anger with larger aspects of the individual's personality. This point leads to a second important limitation of CBC: the somewhat microscopic focus of CBC does not sufficiently allow for either a holistic view of the individual or a view of the individual imbedded in an organizational system. In fact, Kilburg (2000) warned against the use of executive coaching approaches based on models that are overly simplified, stating that it is the most common cause of catastrophic failure in coaching engagements. Given the complex nature of executive coaching in general, and of some coaching engagements in particular, careful consideration should be given to these weaknesses prior to undertaking CBC.

Recommendations

For many executive coach–client teams, there will be significant limitations to the use of cognitive–behavior techniques for the reasons pointed out above. However, it is possible that some executive coach-client teams may be drawn to the approach for the same reasons: its simplicity, ease of use, focus on results, efficacy, and goal orientation. In fact there are some situations in which it would be highly appropriate, based on the previous discussion, to use CBC.

On the basis of efficacy evidence discussed here, CBC should be an important part of any executive coaching engagement that involves the management of stress. There is an abundance of research conducted with high-performing individuals that suggests that these techniques work. Given the emotionally crippling and physically devastating effects that stress can have on an individual, and given the likelihood that executives are being impacted by the high-stress nature of their involvement with organizations, cognitive–behavioral stress management techniques should play a role in most coaching engagements.

Executive coaching engagements are commonly focused on skill development, such as learning to deal with change, clarifying goals, or improving listening skills. In these situations, the goal-oriented approach of CBC will likely prove to be a valuable tool for change. Although it is true that these skills can also be gained through cognitive–behaviorally focused training programs, workshops, or books, the one-to-one personalized nature of executive coaching increases the likelihood of success as well as the likelihood of sustained behavior change.

It would be inappropriate to use CBC in complex situations, such as those described by Kilburg (2000), where there is an interaction of the complexity of the underlying organization with the unconscious psychological processes of executive clients. When these two forces merge to create highly volatile situations, CBC would be out of its element. In addition, it would be inappropriate to use CBC when there are signs that the focus of the engagement is being negatively affected by what appear to be unconscious motives of the executive client, or as Kilburg describes the "shadow side" (Kilburg, 2000, p. 16) of human behavior. In these situations in particular, it would be important to use an approach to coaching that involves a more holistic view of the person and that goes beyond the fairly surface level of analysis that is the case with CBC.

Kilburg (1997) pointed out that some executive coaches are uncomfortable with a psychodynamic approach to executive coaching and added that as long as there is no evidence of unconscious motives or conflict affecting development, there is no reason to delve deeply into an individual's psyche. For these situations, CBC would be a highly appropriate and effective approach to change.

References

Anderson, J. P. (2002). Executive coaching and REBT: Some comments from the field. *Journal of Rational–Emotive and Cognitive–Behavior Therapy, 20*, 223–233.

Beauchamp, P. H., Halliwell, W. R., Fournier, J. F., & Koestner, R. (1996). Effects of cognitive–behavioral psychological skills training on the motivation, preparation, and putting performance of novice golfers. *Sport Psychologist, 10*(2), 157–170.

Beck, A. T. (1976). *Cognitive therapy and the emotional disorders*. New York: International Universities Press.

Dobson, K. S., & Block, L. (1988). Historical and philosophical bases of the cognitive–behavioral therapies. In K. S. Dobson (Ed.), *Handbook of cognitive–behavioral therapies* (pp. 3–38). New York: Guilford Press.

Dobson, K. S., & Craig, K. D. (1996). Preface. In K. S. Dobson & K. D. Craig (Eds.), *Handbook of cognitive–behavioral therapies* (pp. vii–xv). Thousand Oaks, CA: Sage.

Dobson, K. S., & Dozois, D. J. (2001). Historical and philosophical bases of the cognitive–behavioral therapies. In K. S. Dobson (Ed.), *Handbook of cognitive–behavioral therapies* (2nd ed., pp. 3–39). New York: Guilford Press.

Fitzgerald, C., & Berger, J. G. (2002). Leadership and complexity of mind: The role of executive coaching. In C. Fitzgerald & J. G. Berger (Eds.), *Executive coaching* (pp. 27–57). Palo Alto, CA: Davies-Black Publishing.

Hollon, S. D., & Beck, A. T. (2004). Cognitive and cognitive behavioral therapies. In M. J. Lambert (Ed.), *Bergin and Garfield's handbook of psychotherapy and behavior change* (5th ed., pp. 447–492). New York: Wiley.

Holm, J. E., Beckwith, B. E., Ehde, D. M., & Tinius, T. P. (1996). Cognitive–behavioral interventions for improving performance in competitive athletes: A controlled treatment outcome study. *International Journal of Sport Psychology, 27*, 463–475.

Holroyd, K. A., Appel, M. A., & Andrasik, F. (1983). A cognitive–behavioral approach to psychophysiological disorders. In D. Meichenbaum & M. E. Jaremko (Eds.), *Stress reduction and prevention* (pp. 219–259). New York: Plenum Press.

Judge, W. Q., & Cowell, J. (1997, July-August). The brave new world of executive coaching. *Business Horizons, 40*, 71–77.

Kampa, S., & White, R. P. (2002). The effectiveness of executive coaching: What we know and what we still need to know. In R. L. Lowman (Ed.), *The California School of Organizational Studies handbook of organizational consulting psychology* (pp. 139–158). San Francisco: Jossey-Bass.

Kendrick, M. J., Craig, K. D., Lawson, D. M., & Davidson, P. O. (1982). Cognitive and behavioral therapy for musical-performance anxiety. *Journal of Consulting and Clinical Psychology, 50*, 353–362.

Kilburg, R. R. (1997). Coaching and executive character: Core problems and basic approaches. *Consulting*

Psychology Journal: Practice and Research, 49, 281–299.

Kilburg, R. R. (2000). *Executive coaching: Developing managerial wisdom in a world of chaos.* Washington, DC: American Psychological Association.

Kilburg, R. R. (2002a). Failure and negative outcomes: The taboo topic in executive coaching. In C. Fitzgerald & J. G. Berger (Eds.), *Executive coaching: Practices and perspectives* (pp. 283–301). Palo Alto, CA: Davies-Black Publishing.

Kilburg, R. R. (2002b). Individual interventions in consulting psychology. In R. L. Lowman (Ed.), *The California School of Organizational Studies handbook of organizational consulting psychology* (pp. 109–138). San Francisco: Jossey-Bass.

Koonce, R. (1994). One on one. *Training and Development Journal, 48*(2), 34–40.

Leventhal, H., & Nerenz, D. R. (1983). A model for stress research with some implications for the control of stress disorders. In D. Meichenbaum & M. E. Jaremko (Eds.), *Stress reduction and prevention* (pp. 5–38). New York: Plenum Press.

Lowman, R. L. (1993). *Counseling and psychotherapy of work dysfunctions.* Washington, DC: American Psychological Association.

Meichenbaum, D. (1985). *Stress inoculation training.* New York: Pergamon Press.

Peltier, B. (2001). *The psychology of executive coaching.* Florence, KY: Brunner-Routledge.

Roskies, E. (1983). Stress management for Type A individuals. In D. Meichenbaum & M. E. Jaremko (Eds.), *Stress reduction and prevention* (pp. 261–288). New York: Plenum Press.

Roskies, E., Seraganian, P., Oseasohn, R., Hanley, J. A., Collu, R., Martin, N., & Smilga, C. (1986). The Montreal Type A intervention project: Major findings. *Health Psychology, 5,* 45–69.

Sinden, L. M. (1999). Music performance anxiety: Contributions of perfectionism, coping style, self-efficacy and self-esteem. *Dissertation Abstracts International Section A: Humanities and Social Sciences, 60*(3-A).

Smith, L. (1993). The executive's new coach. *Fortune, 128*(16), 126–134.

Smith, R. E. (1996). Behavioral assessment and interventions in youth sports. *Behavior Modification, 20*(1), 3–44.

Steiman, M., & Dobson, K. S. (2002). Cognitive–behavioral approaches to depression. In T. Patterson (Vol. Ed.) & F. W. Kaslow (Ed.), *Comprehensive handbook of psychotherapy: Vol. 2. Cognitive–behavioral approaches* (pp. 295–317). New York: Wiley.

Whelan, J. P., Mahoney, M. J., & Meyers, A. W. (1991). Performance enhancement in sport: A cognitive behavioral domain. *Behavior Therapy, 22,* 307–327.

CHAPTER 17

RATIONAL–EMOTIVE BEHAVIOR THERAPY: A BEHAVIORAL CHANGE MODEL FOR EXECUTIVE COACHING?

Jessica Sherin and Leigh Caiger

Today's executives are not only expected to function adequately in managing their organizations but must also excel in an increasingly competitive and demanding work context. In order to meet these challenges successfully, executives must maximize all the resources available to them. One business resource that is increasingly recognized and highly valued is executive coaching (Diedrich, 2001; Smither, London, Flautt, Vargus, & Kucine, 2003; see also chap. 24, this volume). Kilburg (see chap. 1, this volume) defined *executive coaching* as follows:

> a helping relationship formed between a client who has managerial authority and responsibility in an organization and a consultant who uses a wide variety of behavioral techniques and methods to help the client achieve a mutually identified set of goals to improve his or her professional performance and personal satisfaction and, consequently, to improve the effectiveness of the client's organization within a formally defined coaching agreement. (p. 142)

Many factors influence an executive's or organization's decision to request the assistance of an executive coach. Diedrich (see chap. 14, this volume) identified several reasons for his involvement as a coach, including the need to modify an executive's style, to help executives improve their adjustment to change, to aid in developmental efforts, and to support derailed executives. Moreover, Kiel and his colleagues (see chap. 11, this volume) suggested that roughly one quarter of their clients need assistance in preparation for advancement, another quarter have performance problems that may be rectified by increased coaching support, and the remaining group, about one half of their clients, are strong organizational players who need to increase their strengths. Levinson (see chap. 9, this volume) suggested that much of executive coaching involves assisting executives to strategically develop adaptive work behaviors.

Underlying many of these interventions is the need to effect behavioral change. Indeed, many coaching models include behavior change as a fundamental aspect of their process (e.g., chaps. 1, 9, 11, 12, and 15, this volume; Kilburg, 2000). For example, Saporito's (see chap. 15, this volume) four stages of executive coaching include effecting and monitoring behavior change as a key component of the coaching process. In order to aid clients to achieve behavior change, many coaches draw on and adapt clinical models of change to meet the needs of the coaching context. This adaptation of preexisting therapeutic models is not surprising

We would like to acknowledge Richard R. Kilburg and Serge Desmarais for their insightful comments on earlier revisions of this chapter.
Reprinted from the *Consulting Psychology Journal: Practice and Research, 56,* 225–233.

given that, although the domains and contexts of therapy and coaching are distinct (e.g., chap. 24, this volume; Sperry, 1993), behavioral change is the purview of both therapists and coaches (Rotenberg, 2000). Examples of such theoretical approaches include Adlerian (Sperry, 1993), cognitive–behavioral (chap. 16, this volume), eclectic (chap. 28, this volume), eye movement desensitization and reprocessing (EMDR; see chap. 38, this volume), psychoanalytic (chap. 9, this volume), psychodynamic (chap. 1, this volume; Kilburg, 2000), life span developmental (chap. 21, this volume), Rogerian (Goodstone & Diamante, 1998), and systems theory (see chaps. 1 and 11, this volume).

An additional therapeutic approach that has received some attention as a useful theoretical foundation for executive coaching (e.g., Anderson, 2002; Kirby, 1993; Kodish, 2002; Spillane, 1982) is rational–emotive behavior therapy (REBT; Ellis, 1971, 1994). Ellis himself believes that the REBT process holds special promise for executives, whom he perceives to be serious-minded yet imaginative and revolutionary thinkers who are committed to creating organizational change and are constantly looking for methods to improve efficiency (Ellis, 1972). According to Ellis, executives are motivated by powerful emotions, including a strong desire for success, a passion for leadership, and the need to achieve organizational goals. In his words,

> The topflight executive, moreover, is essentially logical and rational. At least, he'd better be! For although he is emotive, driving, and behavior-oriented in important ways, he is strong on thinking, imagining, planning, scheming, and theorizing. He does not merely act; he uses his head. His greatest forte, perhaps, is that where some individuals powerfully think, some heavily emote, and some pronouncedly act, he tends to engage in all three forms of behavior. (Ellis, 1972, p. 37)

REBT has already been implemented successfully in the organizational context (Lange & Grieger, 1993). It has been embedded in a number of organizational development initiatives addressing such issues as organizational change (e.g., Miller, 1992, 1993; Miller & Yeager, 1993), conflict resolution training (Timofeev, 1993), and career counseling (e.g., Klarreich, 1993; Richman, 1993). DiMattia (1993) argued that the rational–emotive behavior approach suits the organizational context because of its preventive, psychoeducational emphasis and its short-term, solution-focused orientation. When successful, the REBT process functions to increase the client's capacity for rational, critical, and psychologically sophisticated reasoning and thereby allows the client to challenge and replace any unrealistic expectations that might have negatively influenced his or her performance (Ellis, 1994). Ellis (1972) maintained that one of the subsequent benefits of the REBT process, the reduction of mental rigidity and the increase in flexible thinking, could become an executive's most powerful resource. Kilburg (see chap. 1, this volume) has described a number of the typical goals of coaching, including increasing the client's behavioral range, flexibility, and effectiveness; improving the client's social and psychological awareness and competencies; increasing the client's tolerance and range of emotional responses; and strengthening the client's hardiness and stress management skills. Given the identified outcomes of the REBT process, we believe it is possible to use the basic principles of this therapeutic approach to meet a number of these goals. In the next section, we briefly review the main tenets of REBT with appropriate references to its applicability as an instrument for change in the coaching context.

A CLOSER LOOK AT RATIONAL–EMOTIVE BEHAVIOR THERAPY

REBT resulted from Ellis's objective to better understand which specific features of personality caused people to maintain dysfunctional behavioral patterns (Ellis, 1994). Drawing on both Stoic and Adlerian philosophy, he argued that personality was best defined by how people interpret and respond to their environment. He contended that an individual's emotional and behavioral reactions are determined solely by his or her interpretations of events, not by the events themselves (Neenan & Dryden, 2000). These interpretations are, in turn, determined by the individual's core belief system. Thus, according to REBT theory, interpretations shape behavioral responses and these interpretations are determined by the individual's beliefs. Behavior is thus a result of the individual's belief system. Ellis (1994) argued that this belief system is universally shaped both by internal drives toward rationality and irrationality (i.e., self-constructive and self-defeating motivations) and by social influences, which indoctrinate individuals in their early lives (Ard, 1993; DeSilvestri, 1989). Typically, an individual's belief system will contain several of what Ellis labeled as "irrational" elements (Ellis, 1961, 1993). Some of the most pervasive elements are referred to as "core irrational beliefs," which are usually implicit and activated automatically. Furthermore, they tend to be simplistic, absolutist, and overdramatic (Ellis, 1993). Ellis identified five themes that underscore the irrational beliefs. He suggested that irrational thoughts take the form of demands (this *must* happen; Ellis & Dryden, 1987), absolute thinking (all or none, no in-between), catastrophizing (exaggerating the negative consequences of an event), low frustration tolerance (demand for ease and comfort), and global evaluations of human worth (people can be rated, and some are less valuable than others; Walen, DiGiuseppe, & Dryden, 1992). Ellis posited that if people could be prevented from indulging in irrational thoughts and beliefs, they would improve their ability to direct their energy toward self-actualization (the rational drive), which he believed could best be accomplished through reason (Ellis, 1994). For this purpose, he developed the ABCDE model of change.

COACHING WITH THE ABCDE MODEL OF CHANGE

Coaching from an REBT perspective is often referred to as *rational–emotive behavioral coaching* (REBC; Kirby, 1993; Kodish, 2002). The term *irrational belief* is reframed in the coaching context to avoid the potential negative connotation it may evoke for executives, who may be uncomfortable at being characterized as irrational thinkers (Miller & Yeager, 1993). The concept of irrational beliefs may indeed be communicated more effectively to clients by referring to such beliefs as "unreasonable" or "unrealistic" expectations clients may hold for themselves or others. When coaching from a rational–emotive behavioral model, the individual's explicit and implicit belief system becomes the locus of change. Specifically, the coach will work with clients to identify and dispute the clients' unreasonable expectations that negatively impact their performance. This is done using the ABCDE model of individual change (Ellis, 1993; Neenan & Dryden, 2000). *A* refers to the activating event, that is, the external event to which the client is responding. *B* represents the client's internal belief or expectation that is triggered by the activating event (A). This belief (B) is what leads to both emotional and behavioral consequences, or C. When the expectation or belief is unreasonable or unrealistic, the consequences tend to be unhealthy and maladaptive. When the belief is realistic or reasonable, resulting emotional responses may be negative (e.g., anger) but not necessarily unhealthy (e.g., depression), and the consequential behaviors (C; e.g., assertion) will not be maladaptive (e.g., reactivity). As part of the psychoeducational nature of REBC, it is important that this relationship is made explicit to the client. Once the relationship is understood and accepted, the coach can begin to work with the client to change those beliefs that they have identified as unreasonable and problematic by challenging and disputing them (D)—unreasonable expectations are replaced by reasonable expectations. When successful, this process results in an effective outlook, or E, wherein a client's emotional and behavioral consequences are the result of rational beliefs about activating events and thus are adaptive. According to REBT theory, this new system of identifying and disputing unreasonable expectations becomes internalized and thus provides a means for continuous improvement; it enables the client to monitor and disable irrational beliefs independently while at the same time developing and strengthening his or her rational beliefs (Ellis, 1994; Kirby, 1993).

Before the coaching process begins, it is recommended that the coach both educate the client about the REBC process and outline the procedures the coaching pair (the coach and the client) will use to dispute and replace the unreasonable expectations (Kirby, 1993). As well, Ellis (1994) suggested that the coach must attempt to instill in the client a sense of unconditional self-acceptance. This is accomplished not only through instruction and modeling, but also through the coach's own expression of unconditional acceptance of the client. If the coach does not convince the client of these tenets, progress at later stages will be difficult. The client's responsibility is to openly consider these issues.

Kirby (1993) developed a five-step process that incorporates the rational–emotive behavior model into the behavior change stage of the coaching process. The following is a modified version of this process. In the first step, the coach and client define the problem together. This process involves identifying both the activating event (A) and the emotional and behavioral consequences of the event (C). These may be clear if a distinct event or pattern of problem behavior prompted the coaching intervention, but it also may take some time to identify the target issue when the coaching intervention resulted from more ambiguous causes.

The second step in the REBC process is to identify the unreasonable belief(s) underlying the dysfunctional behavior of the client. At this point, the coach should probe for the demands being made by the client in his or her thinking—that is, exploring for "must" or "should" beliefs in the client's expectations. This procedure can be intensive and difficult. Because assumptions or beliefs (reasonable and unreasonable) are often unconscious (Ellis, 1994; Kendall & Korgeski, 1979), the coach must help the client in making them explicit; a useful technique is for clients to consciously focus on what they are saying to themselves in response to an activating event as the opportunities arise (Anderson, 2002).

The third step of REBC is where the change process is engaged (Kirby, 1993). It is recommended that a coach focus on one belief or expectation at a time until the client becomes proficient with the reasoning process taught by REBC. First, the practitioner and client must identify both the scope of the dysfunction and how it manifests itself in various situations by documenting dysfunctional behaviors at work. Next the coach should work with the client to dispute the unreasonable expectation that is resulting in the dysfunctional behavior. The coach works with the client to change his or her absolute thinking into preferential-style thinking (i.e., I "prefer" rather than I "must"). As part of this process, the client is shown how the expectation or belief can lead to maladaptive emotional and behavioral consequences. In the course of identifying these beliefs and dysfunctional thinking styles, the coach demonstrates how such beliefs preclude the attainment of long-term goals and illustrates how the consequences of maintaining these beliefs are not ultimately in the client's best interests. Having challenged and eliminated some of these unreasonable beliefs, the coach assists the client in developing more functional beliefs as substitutes. The coach and client explore potentially desirable outcomes, and the client begins to replace previously deep-seated beliefs with more reasonable alternatives. For example, imagine a client has identified that he has an issue with delegating work. Although his workload is demanding and he would benefit greatly by prioritizing his tasks and delegating those that are lower priority or could be competently completed by his direct reports, he is reluctant to give up control by delegating. The coach would work with the client to first identify the activating event (the demanding workload) and the dysfunctional consequences of the irrational belief (e.g., an inability to give tasks the attention they need, an escalating workload, a perception among the direct reports that he does not have confidence in them, and a consequent belief that only he or she can do the work as required). The client and coach would then need to identify further the underlying beliefs or assumptions that are causing the dysfunctional consequences. In this case, the client may be a perfectionist and believe that the only way to ensure the work will be completed to his specifications is for him to remain in control of it. Once the unreasonable expectations have been identified, the coach would work with the client to replace them with a more functional belief (e.g., the work can be done well by others as well as myself) by disputing the rationality of the initial expectation and using such rational–emotive behavioral techniques as rational–emotive imagery, which helps clients practice changing unhealthy emotions into healthy ones (Walen et al., 1992).

The fourth step of the REBC process involves monitoring the client's growing ability to challenge and replace the targeted unrealistic expectation with a more realistic belief. As well, the coach and client monitor the client's subsequent behavioral changes as he or she deals with the activating event. Because an individual may hold many permutations of these beliefs in several different networks, the client is often assigned homework. At this step in the change process, the client is responsible for the regular practice of REBC methods and techniques. Through practice, the process is internalized, which allows for the client to continue the process in an increasingly independent manner. Consequently, the coach takes more of a supportive role while the client directs his or her own progress. The coach meets regularly with the client and reinforces the constructive outcomes being achieved.

In the fifth and final step of the coaching cycle, the coach and client assess their success. They gather and review positive indicators that have resulted from the client's change in expectations. As well, this is an opportunity to identify other dysfunctional beliefs that are interfering with the client's job performance.

WHEN SHOULD RATIONAL–EMOTIVE BEHAVIOR THERAPY BE USED IN COACHING?

One obvious application for REBC is with executives or potential executives who are struggling with performance issues. Anderson (2002) identified a number of possible so-called derailers that would respond well to REBC. Anger management issues are often connected with "should" beliefs combined with "I can't stand it" absolutist thinking. Anderson found REBC can appreciably lengthen the time to anger and ultimately reduce the total number of anger episodes in clients who suffer from anger management issues. Another possible dysfunctional behavior for executives is fear of confrontation, as fear can create avoidance that can negatively affect a client's interpersonal relationships and job performance. Anderson (2002) noted the importance of helping the client differentiate between discomfort anxiety or low frustration tolerance versus approval-seeking ego anxiety. The unreasonable belief that failure would be unacceptable and the need for a perfect solution often underlie indecisiveness in decision making and problem solving. The need for perfectionism is often associated with these beliefs. Both problems can respond to forceful disputation, rational–emotive imagery, and positive reasonable coping statements.

We argue that there are several other reasons that may contribute to the appropriateness of REBC as a coaching intervention. Perhaps one of the most obvious advantages of REBC is its targeted nature. REBC is a short-term intervention, and it is most appropriate when dealing with discrete issues because of its underlying premise of being most effective when examining one issue at a time. Another important feature of this approach to executive coaching is that the instructional–didactic model of Ellis's REBT may reflect the format of other organizational development interventions, such as training programs. The process is also well suited to one-on-one client intervention as it requires that the client direct his or her own process, reflecting the traditional leadership role of the executive, who is accustomed to retaining power and responsibility as part of his or her organizational role. This coaching structure will be familiar to the executive, and it may reduce the client's potential anxiety or resistance to the coaching intervention.

It is important to note that the REBT literature has been criticized for providing more anecdotal evidence than empirical evidence to support its success as a therapeutic intervention (e.g., Ellis, 1996; Haaga, Dryden, & Dancey, 1991; Watson, Morris, & Miller, 2001). One main concern is that the instruments used to measure irrational beliefs have historically suffered from poor psychometrics (Kendall et al., 1995; Zurawski & Smith, 1987). Critics point out that irrational beliefs and behavioral consequences are confounded (Kendall et al., 1995) and that the scales suffer from low discriminant validity (Smith & Allred, 1989; Zurawski & Smith, 1987). Furthermore, Kendall and Korgeski (1979) questioned the self-report format of the scales, arguing that given the unconscious nature of irrational beliefs, it may be inappropriate to expect individuals to be able to indicate them on a self-report measure. However, this problem may have been resolved by the recent development of better measures that have demonstrated satisfactory reliabilities and validities (e.g., Malouff & Schutte, 1986; Malouff, Valdenegro, & Schutte, 1987; Muran, Kassinove, Ross, & Muran, 1989; Nottingham, 1992; Solomon, Arnow, Gotlib, & Wind, 2003; Warren & Zgourides, 1989; also see Robb & Warren, 1990, for a review of five leading measures of irrational beliefs).

CONCLUSION

Behavioral change is an important component of executive coaching. Coaches will often adapt preexisting therapeutic change models into their coaching process, as such models have already demonstrated some success with creating behavioral change. In this chapter, we examined the fit of REBT as a coaching intervention. REBT has already had some success in a variety of organizational development initiatives, including executive and managerial training (e.g., Anderson, 2002; Kirby, 1993). We argue that REBC would be appropriately applied to a number of issues that may impede an executive's performance, including perfectionism, anger management, and low frustration tolerance (Anderson, 2002). For clients who are very overwhelmed, REBC makes it possible to break challenges into small, attainable, sequential steps.

Arguably, this is not a model that will suit all coaches or all clients, but it is a model that will offer some individuals the tools to begin to process their workplace challenges. REBC provides coaches looking at different interventions with the possibility of integrating certain techniques into their already existing models of change. For example, it is likely that coaches often find themselves in the position of challenging clients' irrational beliefs, although the challenge may not be embedded in the broader REBC framework. REBC has the potential to challenge clients' core assumptions and provide them with a concrete system that will allow them to evaluate their maladaptive expectations and responses on an ongoing and, ultimately, independent basis.

References

Anderson, J. P. (2002). Executive coaching and REBT: Some comments from the field. *Journal of Rational–Emotive & Cognitive–Behavior Therapy, 20*, 223–233.

Ard, N. A. (1993). *A glossary and bibliography of rational–emotive therapy concepts*. San Francisco: Austin & WinField.

DeSilvestri, C. (1989). Clinical models in RET: An advanced model of the organization of emotional and behavioral disorders. *Journal of Rational–Emotive & Cognitive–Behavior Therapy, 7*, 51–58.

Diedrich, R. C. (2001). Lessons learned in—and guidelines for—coaching executive teams. *Consulting Psychology Journal: Practice and Research, 53*, 238–239.

DiMattia, D. J. (1993). RET in the workplace. *Journal of Rational–Emotive & Cognitive–Behavior Therapy, 11*, 61–63.

Ellis, A. (1961). *Reason and emotion in psychotherapy*. New York: Institute for Rational Living.

Ellis, A. (1971). *Growth through reason*. Palo Alto, CA: Science and Behavior Books.

Ellis, A. (1972). *Executive leadership: A rational approach*. Secaucus, NJ: Citadel Press.

Ellis, A. (1993). Fundamentals of rational–emotive therapy for the 1990s. In W. Dryden & L. K. Hill (Eds.), *Innovations in rational–emotive therapy*. New York: Sage.

Ellis, A. (1994). *Reason and emotion in psychotherapy*. New York: Birch Lane.

Ellis, A. (1996). Responses to criticisms of rational emotive behavior therapy (REBT) by Ray DiGiuseppe, Frank Bond, Windy Dryden, Steve Weinrach, and Richard Wessler. *Journal of Rational–Emotive & Cognitive–Behavior Therapy, 14*, 97–121.

Ellis, A., & Dryden, W. (1987). *The practice of rational–emotive therapy*. New York: Springer.

Goodstone, M. S., & Diamante, T. (1998). Organizational use of therapeutic change: Strengthening multisource feedback systems through interdisciplinary coaching. *Consulting Psychology Journal: Practice and Research, 50*, 152–163.

Haaga, D. A. F., Dryden, W., & Dancey, C. P. (1991). Measurement of rational–emotive therapy in outcome studies. *Journal of Rational–Emotive & Cognitive–Behavior Therapy, 9,* 73–93.

Kendall, P. C., Haaga, D. A. F., Ellis, A., Bernard, M., DiGuisseppe, R., & Kassinove, H. (1995). Rational emotive therapy in the 1990s and beyond: Current status, recent revisions, and research questions. *Clinical Psychology Review, 15,* 169–185.

Kendall, P. C., & Korgeski, G. P. (1979). Assessment and cognitive–behavioral interventions. *Cognitive Therapy and Research, 3,* 1–21.

Kilburg, R. R. (2000). *Executive coaching: Developing managerial wisdom in a world of chaos.* Washington, DC: American Psychological Association.

Kirby, P. (1993). RET counseling: Application in management and executive development. *Journal of Rational–Emotive & Cognitive–Behavior Therapy, 11,* 7–18.

Klarreich, S. (1993). RET: A powerful tool to turn a traumatic job termination into an enlightening career transition. *Journal of Rational–Emotive & Cognitive–Behavior Therapy, 11,* 77–89.

Kodish, S. P. (2002). Rational emotive behavior coaching. *Journal of Rational–Emotive & Cognitive–Behavior Therapy, 20,* 235–246.

Lange, A., & Grieger, R. (1993). Integrating RET into management consulting and training. *Journal of Rational–Emotive & Cognitive–Behavior Therapy, 11,* 51–57.

Malouff, J. M., & Schutte, N. S. (1986). Development and validation of a measure of irrational beliefs. *Journal of Consulting and Clinical Psychology, 54,* 860–862.

Malouff, J. M., Valdenegro, J., & Schutte, N. A. (1987). Further validation of a measure of irrational beliefs. *Journal of Rational–Emotive Therapy, 5,* 860–862.

Miller, A. R. (1992). The application of RET to improve supervisory and managerial response to subordinate survey feedback. *Journal of Cognitive Psychotherapy, 6,* 295–304.

Miller, A. R. (1993). Managing change in the workplace. In W. Dryden & L. K. Hill (Eds.), *Innovations in rational–emotive therapy.* New York: Sage.

Miller, A. R., & Yeager, R. J. (1993). Managing change: A corporative application of rational–emotive therapy. *Journal of Rational–Emotive & Cognitive–Behavior Therapy, 11,* 65–76.

Muran, J. C., Kassinove, H., Ross, S., & Muran, E. (1989). Irrational thinking and negative emotionality in college students and applicants for mental health services. *Journal of Clinical Psychology, 45,* 188–193.

Neenan, M., & Dryden, W. (2000). *Essential rational emotive behavior therapy.* London: Whurr.

Nottingham, E. J. (1992). Use of the Survey of Personal Beliefs Scale: Further validation of a measure of irrational beliefs with psychiatric inpatients. *Journal of Rational–Emotive & Cognitive–Behavior Therapy, 10,* 207–217.

Richman, D. R. (1993). Cognitive career counseling: A rational–emotive approach to career development. *Journal of Rational–Emotive & Cognitive–Behavior Therapy, 11,* 91–108.

Robb, H. B., & Warren, R. (1990). Irrational belief tests: New insights, new directions. *Journal of Cognitive Psychotherapy, 4,* 303–311.

Rotenberg, C. T. (2000). Psychodynamic psychotherapy and executive coaching—Overlapping paradigms. *Journal of the American Academy of Psychoanalysis, 28,* 653–663.

Smith, T. W., & Allred, K. D. (1989). Major life events in anxiety and depression. In P. C. Kendall (Ed.), *Anxiety and depression: Distinctive and overlapping features.* San Diego, CA: Academic Press.

Smither, J. W., London, M., Flautt, R., Vargas, Y., & Kucine, I. (2003). Can working with an executive coach improve multisource feedback ratings over time? A quasi-experimental field study. *Personnel Psychology, 56,* 23–44.

Solomon, A., Arnow, B. A., Gotlib, I. H., & Wind, B. (2003). Individualized measurement of irrational beliefs in remitted depressives. *Journal of Clinical Psychology, 59,* 439–455.

Sperry, L. (1993). Working with executives: Consulting, counseling, and coaching. *Individual Psychology, 49,* 257–266.

Spillane, R. (1982). Developing managerial talent through rational emotive training. *Journal of Integrative and Eclectic Psychotherapy, 1,* 139–149.

Timofeev, M. I. (1993). Irrational beliefs and conflict-handling orientations. *Journal of Rational–Emotive & Cognitive–Behavior Therapy, 11,* 109–119.

Walen, S. R., DiGiuseppe, R., & Dryden, W. (1992). *A practitioner's guide to rational–emotive therapy.* New York: Oxford University Press.

Warren, R., & Zgourides, G. (1989). Further validity and normative data for the Malouff and Schutte Belief Scale. *Journal of Rational–Emotive & Cognitive–Behavior Therapy, 7,* 167–172.

Watson, P. J., Morris, R. J., & Miller, L. (2001). Irrational beliefs, attitudes about competition, and splitting. *Journal of Clinical Psychology, 57,* 343–354.

Zurawski, R. M., & Smith, T. W. (1987). Assessing irrational beliefs and emotional distress: Evidence and implications of limited discriminant validity. *Journal of Counseling Psychology, 34,* 224–227.

CHAPTER 18

ACTION FRAME THEORY AS A PRACTICAL FRAMEWORK FOR THE EXECUTIVE COACHING PROCESS

Tracy Cocivera and Steven Cronshaw

Executive coaching has evolved as a practical activity undertaken to develop executive leaders and improve their functioning in highly competitive and challenging organizational environments. Kilburg (2000) proposed a holistic and integrated model to assist practitioners in their executive coaching engagements. In his seminal model, he described executive coaching as encompassing three foci: system, mediated, and executive. We believe some additional assistance helping coaches operationalize and apply the mediated focus would be useful. Kilburg (2000) described his mediated focus in general terms, whereas executive coaches must work in context with the specifics of executive action and behaviors as well as their consequences. To better make the translation from the generalities of the mediated focus to the specifics of executive behavior, we propose action frame theory (AFT) and demonstrate its application in an actual coaching assignment. In addition, we explain how AFT can be applied throughout the typical coaching process to ensure that we fully clarify its usefulness.

THE USEFULNESS OF ACTION FRAME THEORY: AN ILLUSTRATION

To better illustrate the usefulness of AFT, we begin by describing a coaching example where AFT was applied. Steven Cronshaw was recently involved in a coaching engagement with a senior leader (i.e., CEO) of a large organization, whom we will call James. The leader was experiencing ongoing problems with a subordinate at the level below vice president. This subordinate, whom we will call Robert, was working in surreptitious ways (e.g., spreading rumors and gossip mongering) to undermine James's authority and credibility in the organization.

At a surface level, the problem could be understood as resulting from Robert's personality and motivations (and indeed the fundamental attribution error would lead us to believe that the source of the problem is Robert and that any intervention should focus on changing his attitude and behavior). However, it was obvious that a more in-depth diagnosis of this problem would be useful, and AFT was able to provide the analytic tool for this purpose. By using AFT, additional critical questions about James's and Robert's past, present, and future actions could be raised that led to further discussion with James. In doing so, the intervention sought to go beyond surface-level presumptions about the personalities and motivations of Robert and James. The questions that emerged from applying AFT included the following:

- How did the organizational culture and context encourage or discourage Robert's undesired behavior?

Reprinted from the *Consulting Psychology Journal: Practice and Research, 56,* 234–245. Copyright 2004 by the American Psychological Association and the Society of Consulting Psychology.

- What skills would James and Robert need to resolve the situation?
- What past action had James taken that either encouraged or discouraged Robert's undesirable behavior?
- What future action would James be advised to undertake in his interactions with Robert?
- What results would follow from James's past behavior toward Robert?
- What results would likely follow if James changed his behavior toward Robert?
- What would the individual, team, and organizational consequences of Robert's behavior be if James left it unaddressed?
- What were the desired consequences, and how could James achieve these during the coaching process?

Using AFT, these questions were directed toward James in a purposeful and systematic manner. AFT provided the diagnostic approach taken to answer them. In other words, Cronshaw used AFT as the conceptual framework to reframe and enrich his understanding of the origin and development of the undesired behavior. He also used AFT to develop a plan with James to manage and ultimately change Robert's undesirable approach into behavior that was more acceptable to and consistent with the organizational culture. Without applying AFT, Cronshaw likely would have misdiagnosed the situation, especially the root causes, and would have seen only the negative impact of Robert's personality. He ultimately would have suggested nonproductive solutions to James, hindering the coaching process.

A FORMAL STATEMENT OF ACTION FRAME THEORY

AFT is derived from a synthesis of existing theory and research on the theory of social action (Parsons, 1937) and functional job analysis (Fine & Cronshaw, 1999; Fine & Getkate, 1995). These theories have had significant impact across the social sciences. Over the years, Parsons's work has stimulated a large and influential literature on the nature and function of human action. His work continues to carry forward in the writings of various postmodern thinkers, including Joas (e.g., *The Creativity of Action*, 1996) and Habermas (e.g., *The Theory of Communicative Action*, 1984). Fine (1989; Fine & Cronshaw, 1999) pioneered the use of work description in the organizational and social sciences. His approach has had pervasive impact on the study of work processes, culminating in national occupational classification structures in the United States, Canada, and other countries.

The core of AFT is the action frame (Cronshaw & Domanska, 2003). The action frame is diagrammed in Figure 18.1, and its elements are defined in Table 18.1. More specifically, the action frame consists of conditions, means, action, result, and consequence. We propose that by applying the action frame in a systematic manner, executive coaches can collect behavioral information helpful to the coaching assignment. As a starting point to fully illuminate AFT, we will clarify the definitions of each of the action frame elements. Then within our executive coaching example, we will highlight their interrelationships and answer the questions in the previous section, as diagrammed in Figure 18.2.

The first component of AFT is composed of the conditions under which James and Robert are presently operating. As illustrated in Figure 18.1, conditions are the first variable that the coach should analyze as part of the action frame. As outlined in Table 18.1, we defined conditions as the constraints in the situation over which James has no immediate control. In our coaching example and as diagrammed in Figure 18.2, the most pertinent conditions were related to the organizational culture in that James had established a management style where employee participation was highly valued and rewarded. In fact, James had inherited an authoritarian organization from his predecessor and had worked with Cronshaw over the previous 3 years to plan and implement participatory structures and processes within the organization. Any actions James would undertake to deal with Robert's disruptive behavior would have to be consistent with, and acceptable to, the prevailing organization culture. James would have to "walk the talk" and avoid dictatorial or precipitous actions

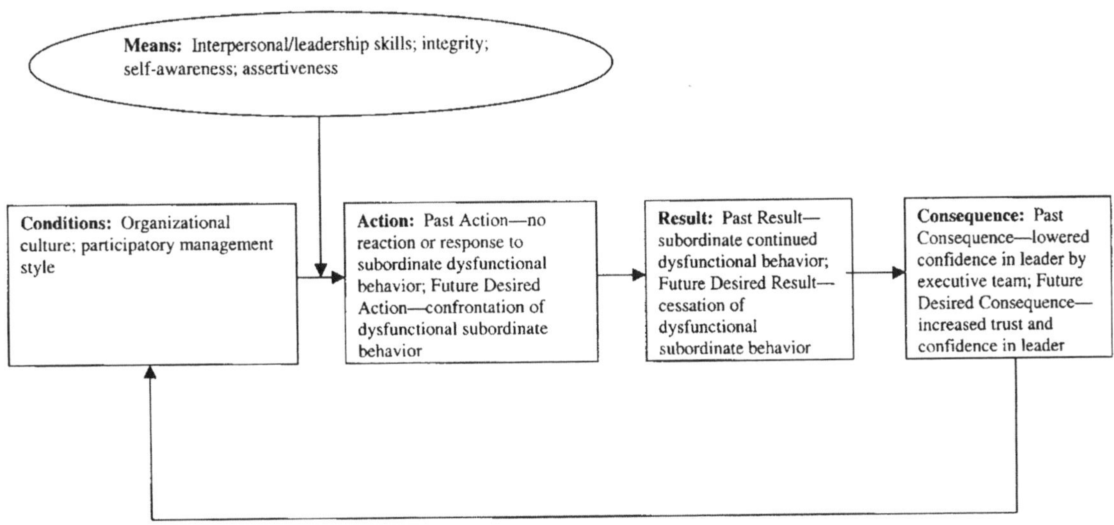

FIGURE 18.1. The structure of the action frame.

TABLE 18.1

Definitions of the Basic Components in the Action Frame Theory (AFT)

AFT component	Definition
Conditions	The constraints inherent in the situation over which the actor has no immediate or direct control and which must be considered as givens within the temporal and spatial arrangements of the unit act and the larger work-doing system
Means	The enablers within reach and control of the actor that can be brought to bear in shaping the action to achieve the result
Action	The goal-directed and voluntary movement of the actor physically, mentally, and socially toward a desired system state
Result	A systems state desired or not desired by the actor and wanted or not wanted within the work organization on completion of the unit act
Consequence	The normative evaluation of the result with respect to its present and future impact on the actor and the larger work-doing system

against Robert that would run counter to the open culture that he, himself, was espousing.

Of special concern were the perceptions of James's vice presidents, who would be closely watching his handling of the situation for clues of how they, or their subordinates, might be treated in the future. That is, if James were intemperate in his behavior to Robert in reaction to the understandably personally trying circumstances, the vice presidents would question the authenticity of James's stated values of showing respect to and consideration for his subordinates. James needed to come up with a solution (i.e., act in a way) where he would stay true to his stated values and the vice presidents would perceive that he acted in a way that was consistent with the organizational culture.

The second AFT component is composed of means. As defined in Table 18.1, *means* refer to the personal resources that James can draw on to act and resolve the situation. As shown by the first arrow in Figure 18.1, James's action is in response to the external pressure of the existing conditions. However, the vertical arrow from the means to the conditions–action linkage signifies that James also draws on freely chosen means that enable him to engage in the relevant and necessary actions.

When applying AFT in our coaching example, Cronshaw identified the most relevant means as

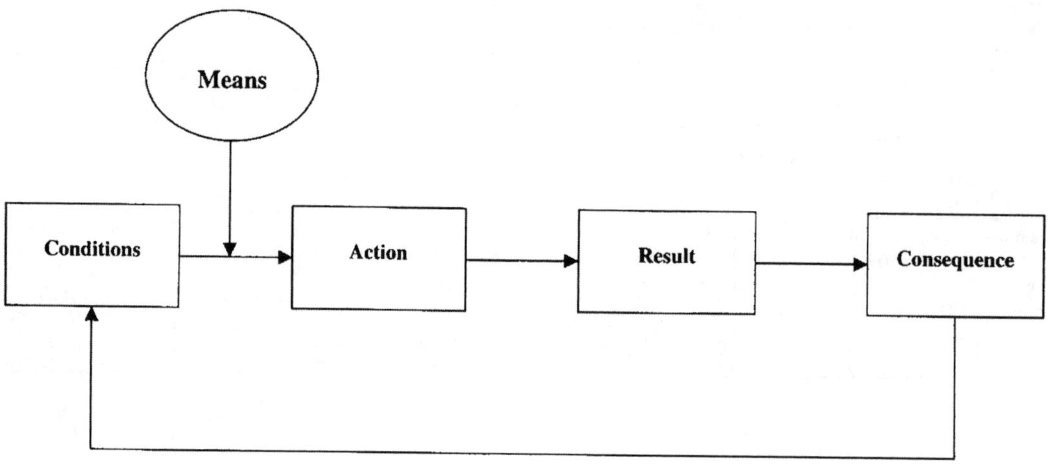

FIGURE 18.2. Application of action frame theory to the example of senior executive coaching in the education sector.

James's interpersonal skills, most notably integrity, self-awareness, and assertiveness. As illustrated in Figure 18.2, Cronshaw discussed all three interpersonal skills with James to determine the extent to which each would have to be drawn on in dealing with Robert to achieve a constructive and positive solution regarding Robert's behavior. James and Cronshaw agreed that the eventual solution would have to be, above all else, in the best interests of and for the greater welfare of the organization, its mission, and its employees and customers.

As a result of this discussion, James became aware that he would have to demonstrate his integrity by valuing the rights of everyone affected by his actions. He would have to show consistency between his behavior and his espoused values of participation and workplace democracy. James also realized he needed to separate his natural feelings of personal dislike toward Robert from his duty as head of the organization. He knew he needed to behave professionally toward Robert and act in the best interests of the organization. That is, James exercised self-awareness and reflected on his own feelings toward Robert and the admittedly unpleasant situation. James finally became aware that he needed to be assertive and directly challenge Robert's objectionable and disrespectful behavior, while taking the "high road" and refusing to engage in the kind of innuendo, rumor mongering, and subterfuge Robert was using.

The third AFT component is action. We defined action in Table 18.1 as James's goal-directed and voluntary behavior toward Robert and toward resolving the dysfunctional situation. As outlined in Figure 18.2, James had not undertaken any past actions to correct Robert's dysfunctional behavior and was in fact unsure about what he should do. As a result, fruitful discussions in the coaching sessions centered on the action that James could and should take in resolving the situation with Robert. At this point, and as is illustrated by the arrows in Figure 18.1, the conditions and means entered fully and richly into the discussion, significantly guiding and informing the action that James should undertake.

As the discussion continued, James's desired action was becoming increasingly clear to both himself and Cronshaw. We decided that James should ask Robert to attend a face-to-face meeting in James's office, where James would first review Robert's role and responsibilities within the organization. After agreement on the objective parameters around Robert's job, James would then point to the dysfunctional behaviors of concern that were inconsistent with Robert's duties and responsibilities and that might compromise the mission of the organization. James realized he needed to be open to any valid extenuating circumstances that Robert might raise but also insistent with Robert on the need for him to change his behavior.

Result is the fourth component of AFT. In Table 18.1, *result* is defined as the systems state that follows from James's actions, and in Figure 18.1 this is illustrated by the arrow from action to result. Similar to action, there are two types of result: past result and future desired result. In our coaching example, the future result that James desired was straightforward. As outlined in Figure 18.2, James wanted and would be satisfied with the cessation of Robert's dysfunctional behavior. James was well aware that Robert would not like him as a result of his actions, but James's overriding concern was to maintain and build upon the positive environment of trust that was developing in the organization. It was apparent that if James did not take action to confront his subordinate, the rumor mongering and gossiping would continue and seriously undermine the mutual respect and trust James had worked so hard to build in the organization. After James took action and met with Robert to discuss the problem, the desired result was achieved. That is, James reported in a subsequent coaching session that Robert stopped engaging in his dysfunctional behavior.

The last component of AFT is consequence. As defined in Table 18.1 and shown in Figure 18.1, consequences logically follow from results yet are often highly diffuse and play out over extended periods of time. As near as we could tell and as highlighted in Figure 18.2, the consequences of James's action further reinforced the participatory culture he had created in the organization and strengthened the trust between the vice presidents and himself. The vice presidents got further evidence that James would exercise integrity in balancing the rights and concerns of the organization with the rights and concerns of individual employees. They were also reassured that James would act assertively and in a non-self-interested way to protect the organization's interests while respecting the rights of his subordinates. That is, each subordinate would have due process and a fair hearing. These consequences would then become part of a new set of conditions (i.e., organization context) that would govern future interactions between James and other organization members. The arrow connecting consequence to conditions in Figure 18.1 shows this.

ACTION FRAME THEORY AND KILBURG'S THREE FOCI OF EXECUTIVE COACHING

Now that the reader is familiar with AFT and its application, we would like to demonstrate that AFT can be related to a widely used and respected executive coaching model. AFT can be easily and seamlessly integrated with Kilburg's (2000) model of executive coaching and is meant to augment, not replace, his approach. Kilburg (2000) developed a 17-dimensional executive coaching model to help executive coaches effectively navigate through coaching assignments, as shown in Figure 18.3. He classified these 17 dimensions into three foci of executive coaching: (a) system focus, (b) mediated focus, and (c) executive focus. AFT cuts across all three foci in Kilburg's model.

Kilburg defined his system focus on the conceptual foundation of general systems theory as applied to organizations. Using the principal elements of general systems theory described by Kuhn (1974), Miller (1972), and Von Bertalanffy (1968), Kilburg (2000) summarized the systems model in six primary dimensions: system structure, process, and content; and system input, throughput, and output. Both Kilburg (2000) and Levinson (2002) asserted that it is crucial for executive coaches to assess organizations, as well as individuals, and have a solid and sophisticated understanding of the organizational context during their coaching assignment. Integrating AFT with Kilburg's (2000) model, and specifically the system focus, systems factors translate into the conditions that must be understood as precursors to executive action.

As illustrated in Figure 18.3, Kilburg's executive focus incorporates such individual elements as rational thoughts, irrational beliefs, interpretations, and belief systems (e.g., Ellis, 1972) as well as the roles and duties a person undertakes when doing the work (e.g., tasks, knowledge). From a psychodynamic perspective, the executive focus also examines four major substructures—the rational self, conscience, instinctual self, and idealized self (Kilburg, 2000)—as well as defenses and conflicts. When the executive focus is translated into AFT, the personality and behavioral structures and dynamics represented by the executive focus

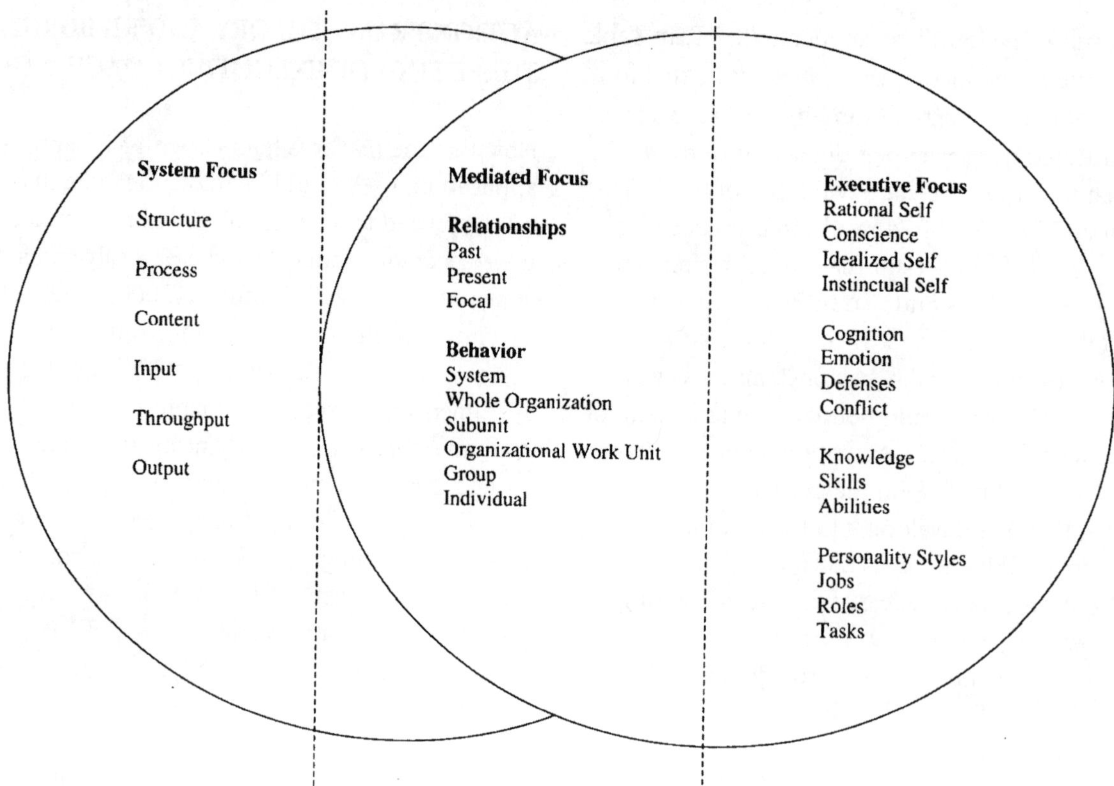

FIGURE 18.3. Kilburg's (2000) three foci of executive coaching.

become the primary means for getting executive work done.

The mediated focus, located in the center of Figure 18.3, emphasizes the relationships and behaviors that constitute the executive's more immediate interpersonal and organizational environments. The mediated focus is divided into two components: (a) relationships, conceptualized by Kilburg (2000) as the integration of executives' past and present relationships with focal relationships they are engaged in at the particular time; and (b) behavior exhibited at differing levels of aggregation, from the system level on down to the individual. When AFT is integrated into the mediated focus, the past and future desired actions become synonymous with these two mediated focus components.

Beyond the integration with current coaching models such as Kilburg's (2000), AFT points to the need to identify both the results and consequences of executive actions. The results are the systems states prevailing after the executive performs an action drawing on the means available to him or her and constrained or enabled by the given conditions. This resulting systems state may or may not be desired by the actor and may or may not be wanted within the work organization on completion of the action. The actor and others always make an evaluation of the result within the organizational system because they are continuously impacted by the action frame (i.e., consequences). This evaluation can be positive or negative, depending on what consequences flow from the result. In addition and as depicted in Figure 18.1, the consequences of an action frame may then flow back and become part of the conditions that constrain or enable a repertoire of future actions the executive may engage in.

Although we have shown how AFT is related to a current model of executive coaching, the reader may still be experiencing some trouble in seeing how AFT can apply to his or her coaching process. To assist further, we will now map the AFT components onto the typical activities that occur during coaching assignments.

TABLE 18.2

Primary Action Frame Foci to Be Identified and Assessed During Each Stage of the Executive Coaching Process

	Element in action frame				
Phase in executive coaching process	**Conditions**	**Means**	**Action**	**Result**	**Consequence**
1. Defining the job context	X				
2. Assessment of the executive		X			
3. Feedback and development planning			X	X	
4. Implementation and follow-up					X

IMPLEMENTING ACTION FRAME THEORY DURING COACHING ENGAGEMENTS

We propose that AFT can be used throughout an executive coaching assignment, and we have mapped the AFT theory components onto the usual coaching process (see Table 18.2). As outlined by Saporito (see chap. 15, this volume) and listed on the left-hand side of Table 18.2, the typical model of executive coaching consists of four stages: defining the context, assessment of the executive, feedback and development planning, and implementation and follow-up. Also depicted in Table 18.2 are the primary AFT components that are to be identified and assessed within each of these coaching stages. We will now illustrate in more detail the linkages between the specific AFT components and Saporito's (see chap. 15, this volume) coaching process.

The first stage of the executive coaching process involves defining the job context or setting the foundation (see chap. 15, this volume). This entails working with both the executive and the organization to understand fully their development needs and their organizational and business contexts. By defining the context, a performance template or set of criteria for executive performance can be established that is then used to assess executives and guide their development.

In integrating the first coaching stage with AFT, defining the job context or setting the foundation becomes synonymous with identifying the conditions. That is, to define the context, executive coaches can use AFT and identify the conditions, as shown in Table 18.2. In our coaching example, Cronshaw used AFT to determine the pertinent aspects of the organizational and business contexts (i.e., the conditions for Robert's behavior and James's response), which were the organizational culture and participatory management.

The second phase of the executive coaching process consists of assessing the individual and building a developmental picture (see chap. 15, this volume). Through the integration of the consultant's insights and observations and the collected assessment data, the executive's strengths and developmental needs are identified. When mapping AFT onto Saporito's (see chap. 15, this volume) coaching model, determining the means occurs during the second coaching phase, as illustrated in Table 18.2. During the assessment of the executive, executive coaches can analyze the means to determine what resources are within his or her control and ultimately be developed or strengthened.

In our coaching example Cronshaw drew on AFT to identify the requisite means to assess what personal skills James would need to resolve the situation with Robert. During this assessment phase, not only did AFT provide a framework for assessing executive competency, it also helped Cronshaw determine that James would need to draw on his adaptive and interpersonal skills (Fine & Cronshaw, 1999) to manage his future interactions with Robert.

The third stage of the executive coaching process incorporates two parts: providing feedback and development planning (see chap. 15, this volume). After the executives have had time to react to the feedback, the executive coach usually works with them to identify the key developmental issues that need to be addressed, while considering their personal goals and the organization's goals. Based on these key developmental objectives, a development plan is created that outlines some specific behaviors and strategies that the executives can use to achieve their goals. When merging AFT with Saporito's (see chap. 15, this volume) third coaching stage, the identification of actions and results occurs during this phase. More specifically, as shown in Table 18.2, actions and results are assessed to provide feedback and create a development plan.

In our coaching example, Cronshaw used AFT to identify the actions and results of past and future (i.e., desired) situations to provide specific and informative behavioral feedback to James and develop an action plan with him. AFT provided an analytical tool and framework to point to the past actions and results that led to the current situation as well as the specific behavioral changes that would be required by James to rectify the situation (i.e., James's future desired actions and results). It should also be noted that by using AFT, feedback could be given and a development plan could be created with proper appreciation and consideration of the system and executive foci (i.e., the conditions and means). That is, AFT enabled Cronshaw to understand the coaching situation from a broad, holistic perspective. Without AFT, these foci might otherwise have been dealt with independently and in isolation of each other or might have failed to enter the analysis entirely.

The final phase of the executive coaching process entails implementation and follow-up (see chap. 15, this volume). The primary objectives of this phase are to provide feedback to executives in terms of their behavioral changes and monitor their motivation levels as they work on the strategies outlined in their development plan. In linking AFT to this phase of Saporito's (see chap. 15, this volume) coaching process, executive coaches identify the consequences of the executives' actions during this stage, as demonstrated in Table 18.2. As the development plan gets implemented and follow-up occurs, AFT provides the analytical framework to help executive coaches determine the desired consequences and how they can be and are being achieved. In addition and as previously alluded to, the consequences identified during this phase set the stage for a new set of organizational conditions that must be understood and considered in subsequent coaching sessions, as shown by the arrow leading from consequences back to conditions in Figure 18.1.

As the final coaching phase relates to our coaching example, Cronshaw used AFT to identify the past and desired (i.e., future) consequences of James's actions as they were directed toward Robert. Understanding the consequences helped Cronshaw monitor and evaluate James's progress and provide him with ongoing feedback to ensure that James was meeting his development goals. Thus from our coaching example, it is evident that Cronshaw used AFT throughout the coaching process, as depicted by Saporito (see chap. 15, this volume).

EPILOGUE

We have integrated theories of executive coaching, action theory, and work description in proposing AFT. AFT may be considered a meta theory in that it can help integrate previous conceptual approaches in the field of executive coaching. We hope it will be useful in the practice of executive coaching, as AFT can provide a sharp conceptual and practical tool to help executive coaches navigate the system, mediated, and executive foci of the coaching relationships with their clients. AFT provides a broad, holistic view of and approach to executive coaching engagements that seamlessly meshes with existing coaching models and processes.

References

Cronshaw, S. F., & Domanska, J. (2003). *Testing an occupational theory of the impact of sociotechnical demands on worker skill.* Manuscript in preparation.

Ellis, A. (1972). *Executive leadership: A rational approach.* Secaucus, NJ: Citadel Press.

Fine, S. A. (1989). *Functional job analysis: A desk aid.* Milwaukee, WI: Author.

Fine, S. A., & Cronshaw, S. F. (1999). *Functional job analysis: A foundation for human resources management.* Mahwah, NJ: Erlbaum.

Fine, S. A., & Getkate, M. (1995). *Benchmark tasks for job analysis: A guide for functional job analysis (FJA) scales.* Mahwah, NJ: Erlbaum.

Habermas, J. (1984). *The theory of communicative action* (Vols. 1–2). Boston: Beacon.

Joas, H. (1996). *The creativity of action.* Chicago: The University of Chicago Press.

Kilburg, R. R. (2000). *Executive coaching: Developing managerial wisdom in a world of chaos.* Washington, DC: American Psychological Association.

Kuhn, A. (1974). *The logic of systems.* San Francisco: Jossey-Bass.

Levinson, H. (2002). *Organizational assessment: A step-by-step guide to effective consulting.* Washington, DC: American Psychological Association.

Miller, S. G. (1972). Living systems: The organization. *Behavioral Science, 17*(1), 182.

Parsons, T. (1937). *The structure of social action: A study in social theory with special reference to a group of recent European writers.* New York: MacMillan.

Von Bertalanffy, L. (1968). *General systems theory.* New York: Braziller.

CHAPTER 19

WHEN SHADOWS FALL: USING PSYCHODYNAMIC APPROACHES IN EXECUTIVE COACHING

Richard R. Kilburg

"How are you doing?" I asked Ron Jameson, the interim president of the northeast region of a major service company.

"Not well," he replied.

Ron had been serving in that capacity for nearly a year and had worked hard and successfully to pull together a divided and somewhat fragmented operation that was part of a larger business unit in a major conglomerate. In his mid-40s, tall, balding, and deeply tanned, Ron had distinguished himself as the executive vice president in the region for several frustrating years under his previous boss. Despite his efforts at trying to better organize and direct the operations, the organization had continued to underperform and the CEO of the enterprise had removed his boss in a fairly bloodless process earlier that year. Ron had been asked to step in and take over while the organization decided what to do with the unit he was leading. Ron had profit and loss responsibilities for the unit and had solved a number of problems that had vexed them for years.

"What's wrong?" I followed up.

"I do not know if I want to continue doing this job."

"Why?"

"The CEO cannot decide what he wants to do about the region and will not tell me what timeline he has in mind to resolve things. Truthfully, I do not think he knows what he wants to do. I cannot really clean this place up until he does because if I do, there will be too much carnage and I'll never get the permanent job."

"These situations do demand patience," I answered.

"I have patience. I just do not like to be taken advantage of," he snapped with a real note of irritation.

"How is the organization taking advantage of you?"

"Let me count the ways. I'm responsible for this place and what happens here, but I have to ask permission to do almost everything. I'm working longer hours than ever with more time away from my family, my religion, and the things I like to do. I'm doing all of this for less than a significant salary increase, and these guys cannot even tell me whether they're going to give me the job. It makes me feel like a patsy . . . just a big jerk."

The emotion in Ron's voice spilled over as he rocked back in his chair and crossed his arms. At that point so early in the coaching session with this long-term client, I knew I could push our discussion in almost any direction. The choices included exploring his efforts to influence the CEO and others in the senior leadership of the organization, his strategy to re-create the region into a full-fledged subsidiary of the company, the complete range of other operational problems that I knew

The identities of the client and organization used in the case material in this chapter have been appropriately modified to protect their privacy.
Reprinted from the *Consulting Psychology Journal: Practice and Research, 56,* 246–268.

were contributing to his frustration, or just sticking with the emotionally charged material he had so deliberately spilled for both of us to see and hear. Going on my intuition and knowledge of Ron, I chose the last course of action.

"Does this situation remind you of anything you have faced before?" I asked, knowing that this is generally a terrific way to invite people to explore the history and components of very difficult situations on their own terms.

Ron looked at me with his most appraising stare. He had always been one of my most sophisticated and reflective clients. Many of our previous sessions had produced some of the most interesting and deep exchanges I have ever had with leaders. He had an excellent working knowledge of psychology, a real commitment to a life of spiritual reflection, and an ability to observe keenly and critically the behavior of others.

Ron smiled just a little and said, "I have two responses to your question."

I gave him a head nod, and he smiled again. "Well, the first one is 'next question.'"

To this we both laughed out loud. Ron's candor, sense of humor, and ability to speak very directly about himself and his experience were truly remarkable in my coaching experience.

"You know that is your choice," I answered.

"Yeah, yeah, I know."

"Then what's the other response?"

"I do not know if I want to tell you," he replied. As he said this, his face and body seemed to gather inward as though marshalling for some sort of ordeal. To his words, I had no reply, so I simply waited in poised silence. After a quiet moment, he made up his mind and began to tell me the following story.

"When I was 6, I was living in a small town with my mom and dad and my brothers and sisters. My mom's dad was dying in the hospital in town, and sometimes I'd get in the car with her and drive over there. At that time, children were not allowed to visit patients and I had to wait in the car, which usually did not take too long. The last trip though was different. That time, she was gone for hours, and when she returned to the car, she was crying.

"She told me that my grandfather had just died and that she had been with him the whole time. I did not have any idea what to do of course because I was only 6. But I remember what she told me as if it were this morning. Through her tears, she said that her dad had been delirious and that he had kept asking for her brother. She was standing there, comforting him, but he kept asking for her brother. And you need to know that my uncle was never a nice guy. Through the whole ordeal of my grandfather's death, he never came to visit him once. My mom and dad were there each step along the way.

"Anyway, he was so agitated about wanting to see his son, that when a resident physician came in to see him, my mom asked him to pretend that he was her brother. He agreed to do that and after his examination of my grandfather, he took his hand and said, 'I'm here, Dad.' My mom was crying very hard when she told me what happened next."

"What?" I asked.

"She said that her dad smiled and squeezed the resident's hand. He seemed very comforted and at peace. Then he died."

As I listened to the story, I could only imagine the complexity of feelings his mother must have experienced. The fact that she was able to determine what her father needed and create a way for him to receive that gift was a remarkable testament to her empathy and compassion. The fact that she did not just walk out on a man who disrespected and demeaned her right up until the moment of his death was a demonstration of how much she loved him and how tightly the bonds of her commitment tied her to him. The whole story also hinted at deeper and long-standing disturbances in the family's relationships.

"Incredible story," I said after some moments.

"It did not end there. Turns out that my grandfather had been worth a considerable sum of money because of the businesses he owned. My mom and dad discovered after his death that my uncle had been bleeding my grandfather so badly for years that there was a mountain of debt to pay where there should have been a substantial inheritance. I later found out that my mom and dad decided that they needed to pay off my grandfather's debts as a matter of family honor. They could have just walked away from the obligation, but they put their whole financial future aside to make sure that they protected my grandfather's reputation in town."

"What about your uncle?" I asked.

"As far as I know, he never contributed a penny. I saw him once, years ago, when I went home to visit my folks. He was in a store, and he avoided me once he saw who it was."

"What was the impact of that decision on you and your siblings?" I asked.

"It made everything harder. My parents were not wealthy. My dad had to work two jobs at times to make ends meet. It was a constant struggle for them and for us kids. I grew up resenting my uncle and feeling that my parents, and especially my mom, had been taken advantage of pretty badly."

Ron sat quietly for a moment at that point. The strength of his feelings was readily evident on his face. I could feel the tension in him and in myself as I imagined what it must have been like growing up under a debt of honor like that one. In an era in which huge numbers of individuals, families, and businesses declare bankruptcy every year, the commitment and dedication of his parents to redeem her father's reputation was a remarkable story of conscience realized across decades of disciplined decision making.

"How do you think the story applies to your situation in the company?" I prodded Ron a little.

"Oh, that is easy now that I've remembered the story. I really hate the feeling of being taken advantage of. Cannot stand it at all. The fact that the CEO cannot make up his mind what to do and keeps me in this temporary position is just driving me crazy. I feel like I just want to quit and go elsewhere."

Ron and I spent the rest of that session talking through his options and how he could address the challenges of discussing the problem with the CEO. Through the rest of the time, he seemed much more able to consider the problems and complexities without personalizing them as much. He readily understood what his boss faced in making the decision to make the region into a full-fledged subsidiary and taking substantial time to move the organization forward to get that done. By the end of the time, he seemed determined to stick with the process and had several additional ideas that he wanted to pursue to try to help his boss get the reorganization accomplished.

When I asked him if it had helped him to tell me that story, he smiled and said, "When I remembered it, I knew immediately what was going on. I did not want to say anything, because it feels so childish in a way. But now that I know that I'm feeling that old sense of resentment about being taken advantage of, I think I can steer clear of making some bad choices."

Subsequently, Ron led a strategic planning initiative in the parent company that led to the decision to reorganize the region into an interdependent subsidiary. His boss is in the process of working through the financial and organizational implications, and a search has begun for a CEO of the subsidiary. Ron appears to have earned the true appreciation of his boss and seems to have the inside track on the job.

INTRODUCTION

The case that introduces this chapter makes the major point that events, feelings, thoughts, and patterns of behavior that are outside of the conscious awareness of executives can significantly influence what they decide and how they act. This has obvious implications for their success or failure and for the futures of the organizations that they lead. In short, unconscious material in the form of past experience, emotional responses, defensive reactions, underlying and unresolved conflicts, and dysfunctional patterns of thinking and behaving can contribute to poor leadership and consequently to decreased organizational effectiveness. Because it is unconscious, I believe this material rarely comes directly to light in the normal course of executive life and leadership activities in organizations. As a result, executives, their colleagues, boards of directors, investors, and others in stakeholder communities are often at a loss to completely explain, let alone change, patterns of decision making and action that may be full of problems for an individual leader and for the enterprise that employs him or her.

In this case example, Ron had such emotional maturity and advanced psychological development that once he told his story out loud, he was able to grasp immediately the implications that his own personal history had for how he was trying to manage a real leadership and organizational challenge. The work that we did together on strategizing his follow-up activities to incorporate the sensitivities we uncovered enabled him to both conceptualize a full array of options for himself and the organization and to set and execute a successful course of action. It was a remarkable coaching session and an even more remarkable demonstration of his leadership ability and the power that psychodynamic insight and methods can add to situations in which other, more conventional, approaches to understanding and changing behavior might have proved ineffective.

We can begin to understand psychodynamics by reviewing a couple of definitions of the term. The 5th edition of *A Psychiatric Glossary* (American Psychiatric Association, 1980, p. 112) defined psychodynamics as

> the systematized knowledge and theory of human behavior and its motivation, the study of which depends largely upon the functional significance of emotion. Psychodynamics recognizes the role of unconscious motivation in human behavior. It is a predictive science, based on the assumption that a person's total make-up and probably reactions at any given moment are the product of past interactions between his specific genetic endowment and the environment in which he has lived since conception.

Funk and Wagnall's dictionary (1975) defined psychodynamics as "the study of mental processes in action." I believe the concept can be broadened somewhat and that it can be defined as unconscious patterns of behavior, thoughts, emotions, conflicts, defenses, and relationships that influence how individuals, families, groups, organizations, and communities adapt to the circumstances, predicaments, and environments of their lives.

During the past 15 years, the scientific case for the existence of unconscious mental, emotional, and social processes has been successfully made by a number of scholars. Up until the latter portion of the last century, psychoanalysts, psychodynamically oriented therapists, and a very small handful of sympathetic researchers and scholars were the only advocates to be found for the contention that the unconscious existed and influenced the conscious behavior and experience of individuals, groups, families, and organizations. This is no longer the case.

Recent reviews of the scientific literature have solidly demonstrated that unconscious mental and emotional processes can be identified and reliably replicated in laboratories. Greenwald (1992), in a sweeping summary of lab research done on a variety of aspects of unconscious cognition, stated that the evidence for such phenomena was irrefutable. In that same issue of the *American Psychologist*, articles by Kihlstrom, Barnhardt, and Tataryn (1992); Bruner (1992); Erdelyi (1992); Loftus and Klinger (1992); and others debated the various aspects and issues involved in the laboratory results, but they all concurred that science has now reliably demonstrated that humans possess at least two information-processing systems that appear to be both dissociated and interlinked, function according to different principles and with different results, and can act simultaneously on the same material.

Even more recently, Westin (1998) summarized the research evidence that has accumulated for five key postulates of psychodynamic theory and the legacy of Sigmund Freud. Those propositions can be summarized as follows:

1. Much of human mental life, including thoughts, emotions, and motives, is unconscious and can produce behavior in people that is inexplicable to them.
2. Conscious and unconscious thoughts and feelings operate simultaneously and can be in conflict with each other in ways that require compromised resolutions.
3. Stable patterns of personality and social behavior are formed in childhood and can signifi-

cantly impact the types and effectiveness of social relationships in adult life.

4. Stable internal mental representations of the human self are formed gradually in childhood and adolescence and guide both social relationships and how individuals may become psychologically symptomatic.
5. Personality development involves learning how to regulate emotions, thoughts, and social relationships and moves from an immature, dependent state in childhood to a mature and independent state in adulthood.

Westin's (1998, p. 362) summary concluded as follows:

> On some of the central postulates of psychodynamic theory, such as the view that much of mental life is unconscious, Freud has left an important—and I believe indelible—mark on human self-understanding. As psychology moves into its 2nd century, we would do well to attend to and integrate some of these disavowed psychodynamic ideas, which need not remain, like classic psychodynamic symptoms, outside the consciousness of the scientific community.

In general, there are two main schools or conceptual approaches incorporated into the psychodynamic perspective: conflict theory and object relations theory. An effort to review both of them in depth is well beyond the intent and scope of this chapter. However, a short summary of both will be useful as a general backdrop for the discussion that follows about how they may be applied to coaching executives.

Excellent reviews of the core tenants and methods of both approaches are readily available (Auld & Hymen, 1991; Book, 1998; Brenner, 1976; Gray, 1994; Hammer, 1993; Horowitz, 1998; Langs, 1973, 1974; Safran & Muran, 2000; Levy, 1996; Rubovits-Seitz, 1998). Conflict theory forms the underlying foundation for classical psychoanalytic theory. Its major tenets can be summarized as follows:

1. Human beings have a set of unconscious feelings, thoughts, motives, and experiences that arise during the normal course of development and life and that can have a radically significant impact on how they grow and interact with others.
2. Humans also possess complex internal psychological structures that often have significantly different reactions to the same thoughts, feelings, motives, and experiences. These reactions can oppose each other and create internal psychological conflict for the individual.
3. Internal, unconscious conflict itself produces strong emotional reactions, and because of the discomfort that arises from both the conflicts and the associated reactions, people create and use a set of behaviors and feelings that enable them to keep the material out of conscious awareness. These defensive or self-protective operations can themselves become quite troubling to a person because, while they can keep the conflicts unconscious, they can also produce major symptoms of distress, such as anxiety conditions, depression, chemical dependency, and various other forms of dysfunctional behavior.
4. Efforts to change the dysfunctional behavior that incorporate activities to make the unconscious material consciously available to the person experiencing symptoms are likely to produce more complete and lasting changes for the individual than those that do not.

The object relations school arose after conflict theory had been well established. Major proponents of this approach include Ainsworth (1969; Ainsworth, Blehar, Waters, & Wall, 1978), Bowlby (1969/1982, 1973, 1980, 1988), M. Klein (1975), Mahler (1968), Safran and Muran (2000), Winnicott (1965), and others. These individuals have demonstrated that one of the most important aspects of human behavior consists of how people form and function inside of relationships. Understanding the developmental processes and history involved in each person's network of relationships brings tremendous insight and useful intervention points for practitioners. The key propositions of the object relationship approach can be summarized as follows:

1. People go through a sequence of stages in their development, from an undifferentiated and dependent infant to a fully functional and interdependent adult. These developmental stages each have their own characteristics and specific challenges. Failure to master these major challenges and dysfunctional patterns of caretaking that can be experienced in childhood can result in significantly disordered patterns of human relationships later in life.
2. These patterns of relating to others remain largely unconscious for most humans and dramatically affect the quality of their lives and the types of successes and failures they experience. These patterns have been reliably demonstrated in the first year or two of life in large numbers of laboratory studies.
3. For people with significant psychological problems, treatment should incorporate efforts that focus at least partly on these patterns of relating if they are to achieve more effective levels of functioning in their lives.

These two broad approaches to understanding the inner mental and emotional lives of people can provide anyone who is interested in or charged with changing human behavior with a wide variety of conceptual tools and intervention techniques. As demonstrated by the work of Levinson (1981), Kets de Vries (1984), Kets de Vries and Miller (1984), Czander (1993), Stacey (1992, 1996), Kernberg (1998), and Kilburg (2000), the need to understand and work with psychodynamic material also extends to leaders and the consultants who are hired to help them.

The purposes of this chapter are to review situations in which psychodynamic issues and interventions are relevant for executive coaches to consider; describe the purposes of psychodynamic approaches and interventions in executive coaching engagements; provide a succinct summary of how unconscious psychological conflict can affect executive performance; review some of the major patterns of human attachment and how they can reveal themselves in work settings; describe a variety of intervention approaches that coaches can use to approach psychodynamic material with their clients; provide a general overview of the uses for and technique of interpretation by coaches with executive clients; and finally, discuss a series of potential pitfalls and problems with the use of these concepts and methods in coaching executives.

WHEN PSYCHODYNAMIC ISSUES AND METHODS MAY BE USEFUL IN COACHING EXECUTIVES

Table 19.1 presents a series of 15 situations and circumstances that consultants may encounter in an engagement involving either systems change or coaching that suggest that they might want to consider the impact that the use of psychodynamic material and methods would make in their work. In general terms, I believe it is wise to consider psychodynamic approaches when you see patterns of dysfunctional behavior in individuals, groups, or whole organizations on which more conventional change methodologies fail to have any truly constructive effect. Similarly, when strong emotional states are encountered in clients or when they face major transitions in their personal or organizational lives, unconscious material may well prove useful to consider. Performance problems for individual executives, their groups, or their organizations often have contributing circumstances that are out of the awareness of the people involved. The nuclear families and families of origin of executives can also create major areas of unrevealed tension and conflict for a leader. Finally, the leader may be sufficiently curious and psychologically well-developed that he or she has a natural ability and willingness to explore these dimensions of human experience.

The case with which this chapter opened demonstrated several of these issues simultaneously. First, Ron was experiencing some ongoing and unresolved problems in relating to the senior leaders of his organization. His coping efforts in trying to manage those challenges were failing by his own estimates, and he was having very strong emotional responses that he was finding difficult to control.

TABLE 19.1

Situations in Which Psychodynamic Issues and Interventions Are Relevant Considerations

Situation in which a client

1. continues to misbehave or underperform, despite the consciously stated intention and desire to improve and do well.
2. suffers from powerful disorganizing and disruptive emotional experiences and reactions for which there are no obvious explanations.
3. faces repeated situations and problems in families, groups and organizations that are incomprehensible and destructive and for which there are no obvious answers or previous intervention efforts have failed.
4. seeks to understand his or her history, goals, motives, and behaviors with a greater degree of psychological sophistication.

Or when

5. things are not happening in the executive's organization that should or should not be happening.
6. conflict, overt or covert, conscious or unconscious, is possible, impending, detected, or explicit.
7. major life course changes are possible, impending, or explicit in the executive, the executive's group, or the executive's family.
8. when transitions in human relationships in the organization or the family are possible, impending, detected, or explicit.
9. when normal or abnormal crises, regressions, or failures in the group, organization, or markets are possible, impending, detected, or explicit.
10. knowledge, ability, or skill may be insufficient to master a challenge or solve a problem.
11. an executive's spouse, key family member, close friend, or significant other is in trouble or experiencing problems.
12. performance problems or an inability to do a job are impeding an executive's career.
13. relationship disturbances are imperiling an executive's career, ability to do a job, or a group or organization's functional capacities.
14. a trauma or catastrophe strikes an individual executive, the executive's group, or the executive's organization.
15. a coach detects significant emotional, cognitive, or behavioral responses in him- or herself to a client or a client's situation.

Finally, he was sophisticated and curious enough that when encouraged to explore how his past experience might be impacting his current job situation, he rapidly and effectively discovered developmentally relevant conflict and relationship material that proved very helpful to him. Based on his discoveries, he was willing and able to broaden and deepen his awareness of his current situation and then create a much more constructive and creative approach that he implemented successfully.

Table 19.2 reviews a variety of purposes that psychodynamic concepts and methods can serve in executive coaching engagements. In general terms, these approaches can and will help leaders improve their awareness of a wide variety of relevant ideas and experiences that can help them increase their personal and professional effectiveness. Job performance, work relationships, organizational change initiatives, and family problems can all be helped when individuals improve their knowledge of their motives, feelings, thoughts, and past relevant experiences that contribute to problems or patterns of dysfunctional behavior. The table demonstrates that there are a wide variety of situations in which coaches can profitably use psychodynamic concepts and methods.

TABLE 19.2

Purposes of Psychodynamic Approaches and Intervention in Executive Coaching

Psychodynamic approaches and interventions when used effectively by coaches promote and improve

1. self-awareness, family, group, and organizational awareness and savvy.
2. emotional containment and management.
3. executive performance.
4. behavioral flexibility and creativity.
5. human resiliency.
6. psychosocial development.
7. professional, personal, and social relationships.
8. mental abilities.
9. capacity for spiritual growth.
10. family, marital, and intimate relationships.

PSYCHODYNAMIC CONFLICT AND OBJECT RELATIONS—SOME USES IN COACHING

Table 19.3 presents a summary of the six basic types of developmentally oriented conflicts that Wurmser (2000) identified as having major psychodynamic implications for individuals. These major areas include conflicts over emotions and their management, the desire to see the world clearly and creatively through the exercise of curiosity, basic identity issues, control over oneself and one's environment, competition and triangular relationships, and finally, the complexities involved in addressing various loyalties that people have in their lives, especially to important people, values, and moral principles. These six types of conflicts arise in the normal course of human development and are faced by nearly everyone in our society. In accordance with the principles of conflict theory, each of us will have more or less success in dealing with these issues as they first arise in our lives. We will remain more susceptible to reexperiencing conflicts of similar types later in our lives if we did not have the ability to appropriately master them the first time we confronted them. Each of these areas of conflict can become even more problematic through the course of our lives if we have had what could be experienced as a trauma associated with them. For example, exposure to invasive, overcontrolling, and punitive parenting as a toddler, when sensitivity to issues of autonomy, self-esteem, and self-efficacy is extremely high, could establish a dysfunctional pattern consisting of real problems with accepting legitimate authority and inappropriately deviant behavior in the workplace. In another example, difficulties in learning basic moral principles of fairness early in the school years can lead to significant problems in making ethical business decisions later in life. Coaches need to be alert to evidence for such conflicted behavior in their clients.

Table 19.3 also demonstrates that these core developmental conflicts for individuals can be reflected in their families, executive groups, and whole organizations. As the seniority and authority an executive has in an organization increase, the risks of recapitulating these individual conflicts in broader environments increase. Table 19.3 presents some suggested patterns of behavior in these larger domains that can reflect these individual conflicts. Thus, an executive who has had difficulty mastering the complexities of emotional management can exhibit a pattern of emotional outbursts, aggressive and injurious episodes of criticism with key subordinates, or even difficulties with controlling sexual impulses. These individual problems can then manifest in dysfunctional and abusive family situations, executive groups that experience core "fight-flight" dynamics (Bion, 1961), and entire organizations that become hostile work environments. Again, coaches are wise to examine such presenting workplace and interpersonal problems from a psychodynamic perspective to determine whether any of these core developmental conflicts are manifesting themselves in this way. Kernberg (1998) has illustrated that groups and organizations can often present these kinds of challenges to their leaders and to the consultants and coaches who work with them. Developing a diagnostic sense for the presence of these core conflict areas and how they can manifest in organizations and groups can greatly enhance a coach's ability to work with executive clients in very difficult situations that often arise in these larger behavioral settings.

As noted in the introduction to this chapter, object relations theory constitutes the second major approach to extending psychodynamic knowledge. Table 19.4 presents a summary of five basic attachment styles and how they manifest in seeking help under stress as a way of demonstrating that this approach to understanding psychodynamics can have significant usefulness to coaches in their engagements. These attachment styles reflect the work of Ainsworth (1969; Ainsworth et al., 1978); Bowlby (1969/1982, 1973, 1980, 1988); Lyons-Ruth, Bronfman, and Atwood (1999); and Solomon and George (1999), among others. The styles are as follows: secure-approaching and supporting, insecure-tenuous, insecure-avoidant, insecure-ambivalent, and insecure-disorganized. Research has demonstrated that these patterns of human relating emerge from the approaches to parenting people experience as infants. The most desirable pattern provides consistent, attentive, and noninvasively responsive parental support to infants. It

TABLE 19.3

Equivalents of Developmental Conflicts in Executive, Group, Family, and Organizational Life

Type of developmental conflict	Executive manifestations	Family manifestations	Group manifestations	Organizational manifestations
Emotional management	Emotional overcontrol of the self, unregulated emotional outbursts with others, sexual harassment, self-control, joy, job satisfaction, emotional containment	Unregulated anger, physical abuse, verbal violence, shame–blame dynamics, emotional detachment and isolation, depression, unexpressed fears	Fight–flight dynamics, shame–blame dynamics, fears of retaliation, fears of expression, inhibitions, emotional contagion, joy, curiosity, job satisfaction	Hostile workplaces, pass the buck, covering up, retaliation dynamics, shame–blame dynamics, violence in the workplace, joy, and job satisfaction
Wishes for self-expression and curiosity, conflict with fears of intrusion, control, exposure, empathic misalignment	Creativity, empathic resonance, assertive communications, exhibitionism, risk taking, defensive communications, coldness and lack of emotional resonance, sterility and lack of invention, paranoia	Creative exchanges, encouragements to achieve and explore, empathic resonance, individual differentiation, physical or emotional abuse, soul blindness, soul murder, paranoia	Exploration, new product and service ideas, problem solving, defensiveness, not invented here, not in my backyard, scapegoating, discrimination, paranoiagenesis	Good advertising, clear organizational identities in the market place, good market position, poor customer relations, poor product or service design, scapegoating, discrimintion, paranoiagenesis
Maintaining an independent sense of self or identity	Role clarity, good limits, good work habits, self-confidence, security, the reverse of them	Good and respectful boundaries, sense of "family," good morale, acceptance of diversity within the family, lack of respect for or insufficient boundaries, xenophobia, disrespect, no limits, acting out	Good and respectful boundaries, sense of "group identity," good morale, acceptance of diversity within the group, inclusion, lack of respect for or insufficient boundaries, xenophobia, disrespect, no limits, acting out	Good brand image and management, name recognition, inclusive workplaces, good morale, respect for individuality, lack of respect for or insufficient boundaries, xenophobia, disrespect, no limits, acting out, discrimination
Wishes for self-control and fears of control or intrusion by others	Acceptance of or difficulties with authority, micromanagement or abandonment, power sensitivity, needs for and respect for autonomy, good or poor delegation skills	Insufficient differentiation from the family, anxious performances, trouble with or respect for boundaries, control fights, acting out, support for independence and differentiation	Constant forming and storming in groups, insufficient or informal and fluid norms, boundary violations and fights, poor coordination and collaboration, lack of communication, power fights	Differentiation and decentralization; fights over resources, control, and direction; influencing and political jungles; grapevines; good brands; good development initiatives; respect for the boundaries, roles, and duties of others

(continued)

TABLE 19.3 *(Continued)*

Equivalents of Developmental Conflicts in Executive, Group, Family, and Organizational Life

Type of developmental conflict	Executive manifestations	Family manifestations	Group manifestations	Organizational manifestations
Competitive strivings and triangular relationships	Ambition striving and achieving, political wheeling and dealing, climbing the ladder, triangulated communications and relationships, promotion of the self and others, self-development	Conflicted relationships, pecking orders, competitive strivings and achievement, support for competition or supression of same, failure, open and under-the-table conflict, triangulated communications and relationships	Triangulated communications and relationships, conflicted relationships, pecking orders, competitive strivings and achievement, support for competition or suppression of same, failures, open and under-the-table conflict, paranoiagenesis, group successes, group failures	Grapevines, end runs, political wheeling and dealing, triangulated communications and relationships, market victories and failures, internal and external intelligence systems, paranoiagenesis
Questions and challenges to loyalty	Work–family conflicts; ethical dilemmas; conflicts of interest; spiritual challenges; self, group, and organizational conflicts of loyalty; power fights at senior levels; policy conflicts; conflicts of conscience; illegal acts	Work–family conflicts, ethical dilemmas, spiritual challenges, illegal acts	Work–family conflicts; ethical dilemmas; conflicts of interest; spiritual challenges; self, group, and organizational conflicts of loyalty; power fights in the group; policy conflicts; conflicts of conscience; illegal acts	Work–family conflicts; ethical dilemmas; conflicts of interest; spiritual challenges; self, group, and organizational conflicts of loyalty; power fights at all levels; policy conflicts; conflicts of conscience; illegal acts

TABLE 19.4

Human Patterns of General Attachment and Obtaining Help Under Stress

Pattern of attachment	Description
1. Secure–approaching and supporting	The person actively seeks contact or closeness and uses parent, superior, or peers as a secure base from which to explore the world, ideas, emotions, or manage stress or trauma. The individual can provide a secure foundation for others and is sensitive and responsive to human needs as they arise and are perceived. As a leader or a follower these people will tend to have, set, and respect boundaries; encourage and support others; delegate but not abandon subordinates; and be thoughtful about working relationships. The person typically received this kind of caretaking as a child.
2. Insecure–tenuous	The person tends to be disorganized in approaching others for support or help. They often display overt signs of distress and longing for contact yet seem oblivious to those who could provide assistance. They appear to recognize that they need connection and can even identify from whom that might come but are often ineffective in making anything happen. As supporters or leaders, they struggle with knowing what to do and how to do it even when they know that something should be done. People come away from interactions with them feeling unfulfilled, frustrated, and not really helped.
3. Insecure–avoidant	The person typically avoids parents, superiors, and peers and does not actively seek support or comfort from others. The individual tends to be a loner and does not usually offer assistance or contact to others. As children, these people were often rebuffed by their own caregivers and learned to fend for themsleves. They may avoid positions of responsibility, have troubles with accountability to others, have a tendency to delegate or dump a lot on subordinates and then leave them by themselves, and avoid what they experience as stressful, difficult, or challenging relationships and exchanges.
4. Insecure–ambivalent	The person forms attachments but may have difficulties being steady in them or consistent in how they relate to others. They will experience difficulties with exploration and managing stress and challenges, and may complain about how difficult relationships are to develop and maintain. They often experienced inconsistent and unpredictable patterns of caregiving. As supporters and leaders, they will often be difficult to pin down and get a steady supply of nurturance from, and may seem dismissive and really unavailable despite appearances to the contrary.
5. Insecure–disorganized	The person appears to have no consistent pattern or strategy of relating to others. At their worst, these individuals will be experienced by others as invasive, hostile, and nonsupportively controlling. They will often be impervious to feedback from others about their behavior, which can and often does frighten others. They received similar caregiving, usually from traumatized, grieving, helpless, depressed, or truly hostile parents. As leaders and supporters, they will often drive people without mercy, achieve varying degrees of success, and not be the kinds of people that others would ever approach for help, support, or comfort.

most often results in children and adults who can behave in a similar fashion to others around them even in stressful circumstances.

Table 19.4 also describes four patterns of less functional attachment, all of which are labeled "insecure." Those individuals with tenuous styles usually want to relate to others, approach them consistently, but often do not seem to know what to do or how to do it with any degree of grace or competence. Relationships with these people as leaders are often difficult and dissatisfactory despite good effort on the part of everyone involved.

The person with an avoidant style tends to be a loner, preferring solitary activities and having difficulties imagining the kinds of support others might need. As leaders, they will be great delegators, especially for equally avoidant subordinates or very well-developed and independent professionals. However, these individuals are often seen as the kind of managers who dump things on their people with a complete lack of support or sympathy for the difficulties that such abandoning delegation can create for them.

The ambivalent attachment style appears in leaders who both want to form relationships with others and are able to do so. However, the relationships they form are often troubled and full of difficulties as expectations are created and then remain unfulfilled. Subordinates will often complain about how difficult these individuals are to work with and that they struggle to understand what they are supposed to do in their delegated tasks and in managing the relationship because the supervisor often seems to change opinions, directions, and emotional states. They are difficult coaching clients because nothing ever seems to please them for long and they have difficulty in consistently following a course of action.

Finally, individuals with the disorganized style are characterized by a lack of consistency in the ways in which they relate to others. They are extremely difficult people with whom to form working relationships. As the table illustrates, at their worst, these individuals are invasive, overcontrolling, and often very critical. The style is quite typical in individuals who have been traumatized through either abuse or neglect as infants and children. As coaching clients, they often are referred as derailing executives that may have significant knowledge and technical skill that the organization needs. However, they have frequently left a record of broken relationships, interpersonal wounds, and bad feelings wherever they have served in an organization. As they move higher and higher in management, their interpersonal skills are increasingly called upon and the primitive nature of how they relate to others very often gets them into trouble. Whenever coaches confront clients about whom others complain vigorously about how difficult they are to work with, they should seriously consider that this form of attachment style may be expressing itself in the relationships in the organizational unit.

Thus, we can see that object relations theory as expressed in the complexities of attachment styles and relationship development can have great usefulness in understanding patterns of leadership and followership in organizations. Coaches who have a working knowledge of these patterns can be in an excellent diagnostic position when beginning their work with clients. They can also benefit enormously from understanding these concepts when they encounter difficulties in the working relationship with an individual. Insecure patterns of attachment readily open themselves to exploration with coaching clients in both current and historical terms.

In one sense, the opening case study provides an example of some of the transgenerational relationship (object relations) issues that can manifest in work situations. Ron's struggle to accept his organization's slow-footed response to settling the leadership and organizational issues in his unit reflected the historically ambivalent attachment between his mother and his grandfather and the underlying resentment that was created in his family. Surfacing this pattern and the associated, powerful emotional conflicts produced in him subsequently enabled Ron to manage his emotional states fairly well; consequently, he was able to stay in a difficult situation that otherwise might have forced him to depart from the organization prematurely. This would not have been in either his or the organization's best interests.

WORKING WITH PSYCHODYNAMIC MATERIAL

Once a coach becomes aware that psychodynamic material and issues may be influencing a client's behavior or the behavior of the people he or she lives or works with and identifies the general nature of what may be happening, the next issue that coach faces is how to intervene in the situation to try to be helpful. Table 19.5 presents a listing of 19 methods that coaches can use to either elicit or work with psychodynamics. Examining each of these in depth is far beyond the scope of this chapter. However, I want to highlight several of these methods and then spend more time explicitly reviewing some of the complexities in the use of interpretation with coaching clients.

Table 19.5 begins with perhaps the most simple and most powerful of all of the tools available to coaches: storytelling. Seeking permission to go exploring with the client and asking another human being to tell a part of his or her personal story starts an enormously complex cognitive and emotional process in motion. I firmly believe that we do most

TABLE 19.5

Coaching Methods to Elicit and Work With Psychodynamic Material

1. Seeking permission
2. Storytelling
3. Listening
4. Empathic resonance
5. Pattern recognition
6. Mental simulations
7. Types of inquiry, questions
8. Intuition
9. Creating theories of mind about others
10. Rational analysis
11. Identification of and education about emotions, defenses, thoughts, conflicts, life span developmental agendas and issues, compromise formations, and other dynamic issues, such as transference, countertransference, trauma, character traits, interpersonal dynamics, attachment styles, sadomasochism, and repetition compulsion
12. Invitations, hypotheses, challenges
13. Silence
14. Clarifications
15. Supportive interventions–suggestions, directives, depreciation and devaluation of ineffective, inappropriate, destructive, or other acting out behaviors
16. Confrontations
17. Interpretations
18. Reframing
19. Reconstructions

of our best work as coaches when we are able to facilitate the storytelling of our clients. To hear about the struggles and victories of their lives educates us and them and allows us to discover how they might improve either their situations or themselves. Respectfully asking to enter into their lives this way often provides coaches with most of the information they need to do their work.

Once the story is underway, empathic resonance, intuition, pattern recognition, inquiry skills, and listening strengthen and deepen our understanding of what has been happening and how our clients are managing their lives and circumstances. We use these skills to expand our appreciation of the story and to probe for additional levels of meaning and understanding. Once the data come to light, coaches can turn to mental simulations, rational analysis, and creating theories of mind of others (TOMO; G. Klein, 1998) to generate hypotheses and complex models of what is happening. The use of these techniques constitutes what we can think of as the diagnostic process of psychodynamic interventions in coaching.

When a coach reaches an understanding of what may be happening in the psychodynamic realm of an individual, family, group, or organization, he or she will need to decide whether any further intervention is necessary. In our opening case study, the simple elicitation of the very significant story in Ron's history proved almost completely sufficient to help him understand the origins of his emotional responses to his real organizational situation. Because he understood the historic parallels between the situation he faced at work and what his mother and father had managed through the years of his childhood, he immediately became aware of the differences in the circumstances as well. Independently, he leapt quickly to differentiate his work situation from the family history and came quickly to a more mature emotional response and leadership strategy for handling the succession and reorganization problems in his organization. Such cases, difficulties, and clients are not unique in my experience. Senior leadership clients who are successful often possess very high levels of self-awareness and psychological insight.

But what happens when a client is not like Ron and cannot immediately draw the connections between the discovery of psychodynamic material and the current work situation? The rest of Table 19.5 consists of methods, mostly developed for and used in psychodynamic psychotherapy, that coaches can use to help a client. Let me say here to be clear, I believe that coaching can have therapeutic value for our executive clients. However, coaching is not, and should not be considered, a form of psychotherapeutic intervention. I keep in mind at all times that the executive client did not contract for psychotherapy, has not presented himself or herself as someone who suffers from a psychological disorder, and does not want to be treated as a patient. Rather, I believe the coaching process is aimed mostly at improving the client's ability to do the work of leadership and management. To be sure, improvements in self-awareness and knowledge of how their minds and emotions work parallel what happens in good therapy. It pays to have a solid, healthy, observing ego at work or in life in general, and I believe that most good coaching actually strengthens and deepens the effectiveness of this most important psychological structure. However, the improvements in self-reflective and self-management abilities made through coaching are not aimed at the amelioration of diagnosable disorders.

Of the extensive range of interventions available to work with psychodynamic material, I believe that coaches will make the most frequent use of psychoeducational interventions to explain the nature of conflicts, defenses, emotions, and relationship issues to clients. Reframing, clarifications, and silence are used very often as well. Supportive interventions, which can take the form of suggestions, directives, homework, and reading assignments, are also very helpful. When faced with a very challenging situation, coaches can find themselves using certain forms of confrontation and interpretation with clients. However, I think it would be extraordinary for coaches to move into reconstructions. Much more detailed information on psychodynamic interventions can be found in Brenner (1976), Gray (1994), Langs (1973, 1974), and Kilburg (2000).

Interpretations constitute the most complex and challenging of the methods that coaches may choose to use with clients. Again, it is impossible to review a subject in a few short paragraphs about which many books have been written. Extensive discussions are available in Auld and Hyman (1991), Book (1998), Brenner (1976), Hammer (1993), Langs (1973, 1974), Levy (1996), and Rubovits-Seitz (1998). However, I believe it is useful to summarize some of the very basic issues involved in the delicate matter of interpreting the material that the coaching process may uncover.

Table 19.6 presents 10 types and four foci for interpretations in coaching work. It expands on the basic taxonomy of interpretations offered by Harway, Dittmann, Raush, Bordin, and Rigler (1955) by arraying the different forms that an interpretation can take against whether it is made about the individual executive, the executive's current family or family of origin, the executive's immediate work group, or the executive's home organization. At the most basic levels, interpretations consist of merely restating client's communications in the present or past and increasing attention to those communications. From there, a coach can move to suggesting that there may be thoughts, feelings, or experiences that are implied in current situations or communications but are immediately unavailable to the client without specific work to bring them to light. In the case study involving Ron, I initially worked at these levels and finally asked a question as to whether something else might be working in the situation. This yielded an instantaneous response that was directly applicable to the leadership challenge with which he had been struggling for months.

At the fourth level, one invites a client to be aware that two or more issues, events, people, or situations under discussion may have a previously unrevealed or unexplored type of relationship. This can be thought of as an exercise in creative or out-of-the-box thinking. In this form, a coach can simply invite a client to attend to the matters at hand and suggest a different way of seeing, relating, or investigating them. This is very common in coaching situations when the material being examined is not explicitly psychodynamic in origin or focus. Promoting such a focus definitely steers the dialogue into a deeper exploration of unconscious material.

In Levels 5 through 7, a coach works with the client's behaviors in a session to identify potentially hidden processes, issues, or challenges. Helping individuals look at the metacommunicative aspects of what they say or do, assisting them with looking at how different aspects or components of a session might relate to each other, and helping them to reformulate their understanding of the behaviors displayed in a coaching session are all pretty common activities in coaching sessions, even if coaches not trained clinically do not call what they are doing interpretation.

The activities involved in Items 8 through 10 are those more routinely thought of as the interpretations done in psychodynamic psychotherapy and psychoanalysis. In these activities, coaches would be stretching awareness much more deeply into unconscious material. Efforts are made in these in-

TABLE 19.6

Types and Foci for Interpretations in Executive Coaching

	Foci for interpretation			
Type of interpretation	**Individual executive**	**Executive's current family or family of origin**	**Executive's work group**	**Executive's parent organization**
1. Restatements of the content/material of the client's present communications				
2. Restatements of content/material of which the client is already aware				
3. Implied focus on material with which the client may be unaware (thoughts, emotions, defenses, conflicts, compromise formations, transferences)				
4. Connections between two or more aspects of the client's previous and/or current communications				
5. Reformulations of the client's behavior in a coaching session in a way that is new				
6. Comments on aspects of the client's nonverbal or metacommunications that may reflect thoughts, emotions, defenses, conflicts, compromise formations, transferences about which there may be no awareness				
7. Using a client's previous statement to identify or reflect upon a process that has been occurring or gathering momentum in a coaching session				
8. Speculations or hypotheses by the coach about developmental experiences that may relate to the current situation about which there may or may not be awareness				
9. Speculations, hypotheses, explorations of the implications and inferences of material that is completely out of the client's awareness (thoughts, emotions, defenses, conflicts, compromise formations, transferences)				
10. Speculations, hypotheses, explorations of the implications and inferences of material that examine connections between the past or present relationships and the relationship with the coach				

Note. From Harway et al., 1955.

terventions to speculate, create hypotheses, and draw attention to connections that are developmental in nature, that are completely outside the individual's awareness, or that involve present or past relationships, including the relationship with the coach. It is in these types of interventions that coaching might most closely resemble psychotherapy. Yet there are circumstances in which these types of depth interpretations are definitely usable in coaching. For example, if a client is acting in an invasive, demanding, demeaning, and controlling way with you as a coach during a session, it could be perfectly appropriate to invite that person to be aware of how you are experiencing the behavior and to speculate on who might have treated him or her in a similar fashion. Similarly, a coach in that

TABLE 19.7

Stages of a Behavioral or Psychodynamic Interpretation in Executive Coaching

1. Coach and client possess substantial knowledge, skill, and abilities about (a) the work of leaders; (b) the process of changing human behavior; (c) individual, family, group, and organizational dynamics; and (d) the current challenges in their lives.
2. The coach possesses a solid set of concepts that guide his or her work with executive clients.
3. Client and coach generate a diverse and extensive base of information and experience related to both the current and past relevant situations.
4. Coach and/or client become aware that there may be a thought, feeling, defense, conflict, compromise formation, or past or present relationship that is having an adverse impact on performance and about which there is limited information about how it is working in the client's mind.
5. Coach constructs tentative hypotheses based on the data collected, the analysis undertaken of the data, and the explicit or implicit underlying models, theories, and concepts he or she uses in this work.
6. Coach requests permission to intervene and invites the client to a mutual exploration of aspects of the data that have accumulated.
7. Coach selects the type and foci of the interpretation (see Table 19.6).
8. Coach delivers the interpretation in an astringent and tender fashion and invites the client's response and participation in making it relevant, meaningful, and helpful.
9. Client responds immediately or through time, consciously and unconsciously, verbally and nonverbally, providing data to validate or invalidate the content, structure, and timing of the interpretation.
10. Coach and client mutually explore, collaborately reformulate, and modify the interpretation to make it more meaningful and useful in the client's life.
11. Coach and client reflect individually and collaboratively on the interpretation and its effectiveness in helping the client in his or her work and use the information to further refine and define the coaching work they are doing together or, if necessary, the coaching agreement.

situation could profitably draw the client's attention to parallels between what was happening between them and how subordinates or existing family members might experience such behavior. Again, I do not think that any of these types of interpretive interventions are completely out of bounds in coaching, but I do believe that coaches must be careful to be clear about why they choose a particular intervention and how they think it contributes to the goals jointly established with the client.

Table 19.7 highlights 11 identifiable stages or components of a behavioral or interpretive intervention in coaching. The process begins with the knowledge bases of the coach and client about the organization, group, family, leadership, current adaptive situation, client history, strengths, and developmental edges and the underlying conceptual frameworks available to both of them. In most situations, it would be useful for the coach to do some education with the client about the nature of unconscious mental, emotional, and social processes and how they can impact executive work and life.

Next, the client and/or the coach becomes aware that there may be something going on in the realms of thoughts, feelings, motives, relationships, or experience that may be relevant to the situation currently being confronted. Hypotheses are formulated in tentative form (there may be some connections, hidden meanings, or previous history that are relevant to the life and work circumstances of the client), and then the coach, or much more rarely, the client, issues an invitation to go exploring together. This is one of the most critical and easiest ways to increase the likelihood that these types of interventions will be successful. Creating a sense of partnership, a joint will toward exploration in the interests of growth, and providing support and shared courage in the work are crucial to helping clients who want to do this kind of self-development.

The coach then has to select the level and focus for the interpretation. The choices arrayed in Table 19.6 are a good place to start to consider what will be addressed. Having chosen what to target, the coach states the interpretation, as Hammer (1993) says in a way that is "astringent in content and tender in manner" (p. 34). This involves telling the client tactfully what one thinks without sugarcoating it while simultaneously resonating to and helping the individual incorporate and cope with the emotional impact that the intervention creates. As we discussed above, at the minimal levels, these interventions can consist of simple restatements of a client's words or helping him or her put several pieces of a coaching session together in a more meaningful fashion. In their deepest form, they can invite a client to open doors into their thoughts, feelings, conflicts, or relationships that they may never have known existed before the interpretation was made.

From that point forward, the coach and client engage in a mutual process of exploration, determining if the interpretation has validity in the client's life, extending and deepening the meanings that might be involved, broadening the range and extent to which what was observed and experienced might be useful especially in the client's work. At its best, this effort is extremely collaborative even though the client ultimately must own it. In the end, the client and coach must develop a mutual way of understanding and explaining what is going on so they can use it to help improve the client's performance and life. Finally, in the best circumstances, the coach and client are able to step back and look at the work that they are doing together and gain additional levels of perspective and insight into what has been happening. This will usually involve Schon's (1987) second and third levels of reflection. It requires the ability to examine what has been learned and how the client and coach have accomplished the learning. It may lead to subsequent changes in how they work together and, in some circumstances, even to modifications in the coaching agreement. I want to make it clear that not every interpretation follows this precise sequence or works exactly as planned. However, the stage model outlined here is presented as a template of sorts to help coaches understand the complexities that are involved and some of the issues to which they should attend when they try to interpret behavior and psychodynamic material.

Table 19.8 presents a set of more concrete principles that can guide the formation and execution of interpretations. They roughly follow the guidance provided by Hammer (1993), who tried to succinctly summarize how to use interpretations in psychotherapy. I think most of these principles do apply if one keeps in mind the caveats mentioned above about goals and limits. In general terms, if a coach finds him-or herself working far more on client reactions to early trauma events, relationship issues outside of work, defensive and emotional reactions not specific to the goals of the coaching agreement, or unconscious conflicts that seem only tangentially related to work, then I think the activity has in all probability slid inadvertently into therapy. In this situation, referrals for treatment are definitely in order.

Table 19.8 makes several other major points I would like to highlight. First, I believe that psychodynamic issues are present in coaching work from the time of the initial contact. However, I do not think it is safe or appropriate for this material to be directly accessed or worked with until the coach and client establish a solid alliance in the service of the goals they establish. Examining these types of issues can be very taxing on both the coach and client, and a good deal of trust and empathy should be built between the parties before moving into areas that may well be threatening or difficult in some other way. To be sure, there may be emergency situations that represent exceptions to this recommendation, but they will be few and far between for the average coach.

I also think it is very important for coaches to retain a sense of humility about this work. It is all too easy to see the flaws in someone else and to come to believe that you know what is best for others. Our abilities to collect data, to use our experience and knowledge, and to see others clearly when they find it difficult to see themselves are open invitations to pride, hubris, and narcissism for us as practitioners. We must remember that the true expert in any coaching engagement is the client. He or she has most of the knowledge about the organization, the challenges, and the experiences and abilities that led to his or her executive appointment. Always remembering that coaching is a helping activity and that fundamentally all helping activities are partnerships can help to avoid situations that lead to blown assignments,

TABLE 19.8

Some Principles Underlying Interpretation

1. Provide interpretations when the client is nearly ready to understand the material or issues by him- or herself.
2. When in doubt, interpret in this order: emotions, defenses/resistances, conflicts, transference.
   - What are these feelings? What are they about, directed toward, arising from?
   - Are you trying or do you need to protect yourself in this situation? Against what? How does it work?
   - Might there be a conflict here? What is involved? How does it work? Work against or for the client?
   - Is this behavior, feeling, pattern that has appeared in our relationship like or unlike what you may have experienced in the past that has been troubling to you?
3. Be sparing in the use of interpretations and insofar as possible make them a collaborative process.
4. Develop and use your own style in constructing and delivering interpretations—what you say, how you say it, the meaning of what and how. The manner of it can radically affect the matter and effectiveness of it (concise, clear, simple, "astringent in content and tender in manner" [Hammer, 1993, p. 34]).
5. Convey the material in a working partnership and allow for possibilities (Could it be? Perhaps it is? There are several options or ways of thinking about this.).
6. Use the client's words when possible, except when the client is blurring, avoiding, or ducking a point; then try to be tactfully direct.
7. Minimize the use of technical words. This should be a conversation between two long-time friends who understand each other.
8. Don't be afraid to use stories, metaphors, aphorisms, proverbs, examples, and so on, to make the point immediate and more accessible.
9. If possible, point out the timing or sequence of events, reactions, emotions, thoughts, defenses, conflicts, behaviors, transferences.
10. Don't interpret until a reliable and effective relationship is established.
11. When coaching, interpret transference cautiously when resistance to change increases, when the client does not seem free to express him- or herself, and by asking about feelings the person might be having toward the coach.
12. Stick close to the data, be humble, and be very careful about telling clients what they should do.
13. Clients should be encouraged and enabled to take the credit for their own discoveries, changes, and improvements. Coaches need to regulate their desires to be seen and experienced as
    - wizards, sages, oracles, wise old people, detectives;
    - friendly advisors, God, omnipotent observers, scientists or physicians studying an interesting specimen or case;
    - secretly discovering the hidden flaws in people;
    - inflating oneself or feeding one's self-esteem or narcissism at the expense of a client by taking credit for the work;
    - basking in the positive transference and appreciation of the client;
    - being threatened by the negative emotional reactions of clients toward themselves, the work of change, the coaching process;
    - maintaining client dependencies;
    - being the benevolent, omnipotent, perfect parent; and
    - being the insecure, impotent, invasive, controlling, abusive, soul blind, or soul murdering parent.

Note. From Hammer, 1993.

damaged professional reputations, and reduced incomes.

LIMITATIONS OF USING PSYCHODYNAMIC APPROACHES IN COACHING

For all of their power and usefulness, I do not believe that the more extensive aspects of psychodynamic methodologies should be commonly used in coaching engagements. Table 19.9 presents a series of pitfalls and limitations to using these approaches. To begin with, many successful coaches are completely unprepared to work in these ways. The vast majority of people who are trained in these concepts and skills are psychotherapists. Although I personally am often kidded by clients for being their "shrink," both they and I discuss and know that there are radical differences between coaching and psychotherapy. For those of us therapeutically trained, it is all too easy to work with material with which we are familiar and comfortable. If we find ourselves pushing clients to talk more about families of origin, intrapsychic conflict and defensive operations, and transference issues in our coaching relationships, I think we are most likely avoiding the much more important and rele-

TABLE 19.9

Pitfalls and Limitations in Using Psychodynamic Approaches in Coaching Executives

1. Insufficient data and inability to confirm observations, intuitions, and hypotheses.
2. Lack of interest in the information by clients.
3. Lack of knowledge, skill, or ability in the coach to identify or work with psychodynamic material.
4. Improper execution of methods and concepts.
5. Lack of motivation to do psychological work by clients.
6. Conflicts of interest between the needs of the individual to do long-term self-development or remediation work and the needs of the organization for rapid improvement in executive performance.
7. Intensification of potentially destructive transference and countertransference issues in the client and coach.
8. Increased defensiveness in the client to the work of personal or organizational change.
9. Increased defensiveness in the client's executive team or organization to the work of personal, group, or organizational change.
10. Increased mental and emotional disequilibrium in the executive, the executive's team, the executive's family, or the parent organization.
11. Incomplete, ineffective, or incorrect psychodynamic interventions leading to injuries, disruptions, decreased performance, and rejection of coaching or consulting services.

vant examination of the work of the executive and how it is or is not being done. If we do discover that this is the case in a given situation, shadow consultation should be sought to get some help with unraveling just why the more relevant work-centered material is being avoided.

In addition, when the client has no real interest in doing such work, when there is insufficient data to confirm that psychodynamic processes are interfering with the executive's performance or the work of coaching, and where there may be conflicts of interest between the need to do long-term development as opposed to quickly solving behavioral, performance, or organizational problems related directly to work, I believe that psychodynamic material and work must be put aside. Furthermore, there are circumstances in which the examination of these kinds of issues can, in fact, make situations much worse, especially in the short run, for individual executives, their families, work groups, or organizations. This is especially true in coaching engagements that are of the time-limited variety. The strong feelings that can be elicited and expressed can produce wounds that are difficult to manage, particularly in the heat of the supercharged and lightening fast business organizations in which many coaches work. If such reactions are thought to be likely, and if the coach cannot reasonably anticipate that he or she will be around or have the time to help work through the aftermath of such interventions, then, I believe they are best avoided completely.

CONCLUSIONS

In summary, I think several points can be made about working in the shadows of organizations and individuals. First, and most important, the research and practice evidence for the existence of unconscious mental, emotional, and social processes and for their ability to influence conscious behavior has been well established. The nature and complexity of these structures, processes, and contents have been widely explored both clinically and scientifically. I think that professionals who work with executives in organizations are foolhardy in the extreme to approach their work as if such forces did not exist and did not affect the people with whom they work. Second, both the conflict and object relations approaches to understanding psychodynamics have high degrees of relevance for working with executives. Knowing what happens to people when they are in conflict and how they are likely to form and struggle in human relationships is of central importance in being able to help leaders do their work better, because they are always in conflicted situations and always accomplishing their tasks through other people. Third, many methods developed largely for use in psychotherapy are transferable to coaching situations. Knowing which ones to use and why you are choosing to use them at a particular time are crucial competencies for coaches to have if they are going to try to work at these levels and in this way with clients. Fourth, many coaches are not able to do this type of work competently, and many coaching engagements do not call for these approaches to be used. Diagnostic acumen and professional judgment are central to determining whether the shadow realm of psychodynamics should be entered. Finally, it is very possible to make a situation worse by using these concepts and methods. This is especially true in the short term. For the most part, coaches are not hired to make things worse for their clients. Above all else, in this work with very responsible people who are typically very demanding of themselves and those whom they hire, we must try to be helpful and retain a dignified humility about what it is that we can truly accomplish in any given assignment. If we can do that, then I believe it is safe and effective to use psychodynamic concepts and methods in our work with many clients.

References

Ainsworth, M. D. S. (1969). Object relations, dependency, and attachment: A theoretical review of the infant-mother relationship. *Child Development, 40,* 969–1025.

Ainsworth, M. D. S., Blehar, M., Waters, E., & Wall, S. (1978). *Patterns of attachment.* Hillsdale, NJ: Erlbaum.

American Psychiatric Association. (1980). *A psychiatric glossary* (5th ed.). Boston: Little, Brown & Company.

Auld, F., & Hyman, M. (1991). *Resolution of inner conflict: An introduction to psychoanalytic therapy.* Washington, DC: American Psychological Association.

Bion, W. R. (1961). *Experiences in groups and other papers.* London: Tavistock.

Book, H. E. (1998). *How to practice brief psychodynamic psychotherapy: The core conflictual relationship theme method.* Washington, DC: American Psychological Association.

Bowlby, J. (1973). *Attachment and loss* (Vol. 2). New York: Basic Books.

Bowlby, J. (1980). *Attachment and loss* (Vol. 3). New York: Basic Books.

Bowlby, J. (1982). *Attachment and loss* (Vol. 1). New York: Basic Books. (Original work published 1969)

Bowlby, J. (1988). *A secure base.* New York: Basic Books.

Brenner, C. (1976). *Psychoanalytic technique and psychic conflict.* Madison, CT: International Universities Press.

Bruner, J. (1992). Another look at New Look 1. *American Psychologist, 47,* 780–783.

Czander, W. M. (1993). *The psychodynamics of work and organizations: Theory and application.* New York: Guilford Press.

Erdelyi, M. H. (1992). Psychodynamics and the unconscious. *American Psychologist, 47,* 784–787.

Funk & Wagnalls. (1975). *Standard college dictionary.* Pleasantville, NJ: Reader's Digest Association.

Gray, P. (1994). *The ego and analysis of defense.* Washington, DC: American Psychological Association.

Greenwald, A. G. (1992). Unconscious cognition reclaimed. *American Psychologist, 47,* 766–779.

Hammer, E. (1993). Interpretive technique: A primer. In E. F. Hammer (Ed.), *Use of interpretation in treatment: Technique and art* (pp. 31–42). Northvale, NJ: Jason Aronson.

Harway, N. I., Dittmann, A. T., Raush, H. L., Bordin, E. S., & Rigler, D. (1955). The measurement of depth of interpretation. *Journal of Consulting Psychology, 19,* 247–253.

Horowitz, M. J. (1998). *Cognitive psychodynamics: From conflict to character.* New York: Wiley.

Kernberg, O. F. (1998). *Ideology, conflict, and leadership in groups and organizations.* New Haven, CT: Yale University Press.

Kets de Vries, M. F. R. (Ed.). (1984). *The irrational executive: Psychoanalytic explorations in management.* Madison, CT: International Universities Press.

Kets de Vries, M. F. R., & Miller, D. (1984). *The neurotic organization.* San Francisco: Jossey-Bass.

Kihlstrom, J. F., Barnhardt, T. M., & Tataryn, D. J. (1992). The psychological unconscious: Found, lost, and regained. *American Psychologist, 47,* 788–791.

Kilburg, R. R. (2000). *Executive coaching: Developing managerial wisdom in a world of chaos.* Washington, DC: American Psychological Association.

Klein, G. (1998). *Sources of power: How people make decisions.* Cambridge, MA: MIT Press.

Klein, M. (1975). *"Envy and gratitude" and other works.* New York: Delacorte.

Langs, R. (1973). *The technique of psychoanalytic psychotherapy* (Vol. 1). New York: Jason Aronson.

Langs, R. (1974). *The technique of psychoanalytic psychotherapy* (Vol. 2). New York: Jason Aronson.

Levinson, H. (1981). *Executive.* Cambridge, MA: Harvard University Press.

Levy, S. T. (1996). *Principles of interpretation: Mastering clear and concise interventions in psychotherapy.* Northvale, NJ: Jason Aronson.

Loftus, E. F., & Klinger, M. R. (1992). Is the unconscious smart or dumb? *American Psychologist, 47,* 761–765.

Lyons-Ruth, K., Bronfman, E., & Atwood, G. (1999). A relational diathesis model of hostile-helpless states of mind: Expressions in mother-infant interaction. In J. Solomon & C. George (Eds.), *Attachment disorganization* (pp. 33–70). New York: Guilford Press.

Mahler, M. (1968). *On human symbiosis and the vicissitudes of individuation.* New York: International Universities Press.

Rubovits-Seitz, P. F. D. (1998). *Depth-psychological understanding: The methodologic grounding of clinical interpretations.* Hillsdale, NJ: Analytic Press.

Safran, J., & Muran, J. C. (2000). *Negotiating the therapeutic alliance: A relational treatment guide.* New York: Guilford Press.

Schon, D. A. (1987). *Educating the reflective practitioner.* San Francisco: Jossey-Bass.

Solomon, J., & George, C. (Eds.). (1999). *Attachment disorganization.* New York: Guilford Press.

Stacey, R. D. (1992). *Managing the unknowable: Strategic boundaries between order and chaos in organizations.* San Francisco: Jossey-Bass.

Stacey, R. D. (1996). *Complexity and creativity in organizations.* San Francisco: Berret-Koehler.

Westin, D. (1998). The scientific legacy of Sigmund Freud: Toward a psychodynamically informed psychological science. *Psychological Bulletin, 124,* 333–371.

Winnicott, D. W. (1965). *The maturational process and the facilitating environment.* New York: International Universities Press.

Wurmser, L. (2000). *The power of the inner judge: Psychodynamic treatment of the severe neuroses.* New York: Jason Aronson.

CHAPTER 20

THE EMERGING ROLE OF THE INTERNAL COACH

Michael H. Frisch

Coaching has become a mainstream offering in management and executive development functions. Engaging professional coaches to work with managers on their development is a regular occurrence in most large corporations in the United States (Kilburg, 1996; Morris, 2000; Peterson, Uranowitz, & Hicks, 1996; Tyler, 2000). Gone is the stigma of needing a coach to help with an individual's development, to be replaced by the opposite—the status of being important enough to the enterprise to deserve the investment of individual attention (Buss, 1998; Nobel, 1994; Stern, 2001). As with the explosion of popularity of personal trainers to guide and maximize physical development, management and executive coaches these days build their efforts on a ubiquitous interest in professional development. The role of the executive coach has evolved from its roots as the organization's agent on performance remediation to the present focus on the upside of an individual's potential (Zemke, 1996). There are still performance improvements to be made, but almost always as investments in the organization's future, rather than a "fix it" ultimatum.

At the same time, other trends have been facilitating the growth of coaching. People development as a broad topic has become much more routine in most organizations (Tichy & Cohen, 1997; Toomey, 1994). Managers these days are expected to foster the development of their staff as well as to be prime movers of their own growth. Individual development planning has graduated from being a two-line entry on an appraisal form to being an on-line template that managers and their direct reports are expected to actually write and implement (Hicks & Peterson, 1997). In addition, various feedback processes, such as 360-degree and multirater feedback, have become widespread inputs to those development plans. Many more managers have gotten used to interpreting varied information about themselves in shaping well-founded and actionable development plans (Peterson & Hicks, 1995). Finally, to keep pace with the increased sophistication of the entire development function, organizations have hired individuals with commensurate skills and upgraded the skills of existing staff (Tobias, 1990). This process has brought into organizations levels of expertise about development that were previously available only by going to outside consultants.

What has not changed until recently is the fact that executive coaches were always external to the organization (Tyler, 2000). This fact made sense given the original requirements of the role: counseling skills focused on behavior change, knowledge of organizational functioning, confidentiality,

I would like to thank consultant colleagues and editors at Personnel Decisions International—both New York and Minneapolis headquarters offices— for reviews of earlier drafts, especially Victoria Hall and Tracy Anderson. In addition, I would like to thank several of the internal coaches who extended my thinking by generously taking time to describe their work: Nick Amadori, Ted Bililies, David Gilbert, and Karen Metzger.

and, to varying degrees, an overarching professional identity (e.g., relevant advanced degree, license, or certification) that elevated the coach's credibility for both the individual and the organization. Given the older agenda of remedial, or "must-fix" coaching, these requirements were essential in quickly instigating a developmental focus and reducing defensiveness of the participant. Along with the normalizing of coaching and development planning, these requirements also have eased. Reaching outside the organization to screen and contract with a professional coach became less important than making rapid progress on a development plan, especially because similar, if not identical, resources were increasingly likely to exist within the organization. It was inevitable that internal coaching resources would be matched up with managers who wanted, or needed, to implement their development plans. For some coaching needs and for some participants, the clout of engaging an external consultant became less important than getting coaching mobilized.

Into this maturing arena comes the predictable, but not entirely obvious, emergence of the internal coach. Although many human resource (HR) generalists would say that coaching had always been part of their jobs, it was informal and transactional. Quietly and without fanfare, the role of the internal coach has achieved recognition in some large organizations as valuable in its own right. It may not represent a professional's full-time responsibilities, but, where it exists, the role itself has achieved enough legitimacy to elicit a developmental commitment essentially the same as what would be expected with an external coach.

The numbers of internal coaches or of organizations employing them is unknown at this point, but their presence is clear. At a recent coaching conference at the University of Maryland's University College ("The Art and Practice of Coaching Leaders"), some attendees identified themselves as internal coaches and, in some cases, as part of an internal coaching department. When asked, they proudly talked about the growth of their services and were clearly energized to absorb all they could to take back to their organizations. Examples of their backgrounds included an HR generalist who overtly dedicates part of his time to coaching, an external consultant who accepted a part-time role as an internal coach, and a sales manager whose prowess as a coach brought her to seek to have an impact beyond her immediate work group. Although discussions with these internal coaches were informal and no tally was attempted, subsequent conversations and interviews have confirmed their growing presence. In organizations such as Teletech in Denver; IBM, Scudder Kemper, and TIAA/CREF in New York; State Street Bank in Boston; and US Tobacco in Connecticut, internal coaches have established themselves and proven their value in providing coaching services from their unique perspective.

This chapter is an attempt to formally recognize the role of the internal coach, define it, and highlight some key policy and practice challenges that internal coaches, or internal coaching departments, need to resolve to successfully deliver their services. This content is derived from approximately 10 structured interviews I was able to conduct with internal coaches as well as my own perspective as a highly experienced coach with both internal and external consulting experience. I hope that this article will both provide practical guidelines to internal coaches and stimulate discussion and research about this newly emerging role.

WHAT IS INTERNAL COACHING?

Internal coaching as a role is derived from the longer history of external executive coaching, with one important and obvious difference: The internal coach is a fellow employee of the same organization as those he or she coaches. The implications of this difference are explored later in this chapter, but it is useful to summarize elements of the role in totality.

Executive coaching has been defined variously (Buss, 1998; Hargrove, 1995; Kilburg, 1996; Morris, 2000; Peterson & Hicks, 1996; Zemke, 1996), but a common theme is that it is anchored by a one-on-one relationship of trust aimed at fostering learning and professional growth. (The focus here is exclusively on professional development; comments are not intended to apply to personal coaching that has emerged as a counseling and therapy model.) Most definitions emphasize the coaching relationship as providing the impetus for professional breakthroughs, which applies equally well to internal and external coaching. Other parallel factors include an emphasis on the organizational context, such as maintaining relationships with sponsors of the coaching (i.e., boss and HR contact), and collaboration on a development plan that all of those involved can use as a guide.

The simplest definition of internal coaching may be a tautology: being formally viewed by organizational coworkers as a coach makes it so. The clarity and strength of the label, formalized under a job title, may be all that is needed to operate as an internal coach. However, wanting to be more descriptive here, and in keeping with the attempt to delineate the emerging role, the following definition is offered: Internal coaching is a one-on-one developmental intervention supported by the organization and provided by a colleague of those coached who is trusted to shape and deliver a program yielding individual professional growth.

From the standpoint of setting standards, however, there are several implications of this definition that should be made explicit. Internal coaches should be outside of the usual chain of command of those they coach, to differentiate it from the job coaching that all effective managers do. Also, whereas external coaches usually use a standardized assessment at the beginning of coaching applicable to the wide range of situations, internal coaches can often be more flexible. They will know extensive background information about the situation and have access to the results of organizational processes, such as performance appraisals and multirater feedback surveys. They can therefore shape an assessment that targets the key development issues without overmeasuring. Finally, derived from both the importance of a trusted relationship and the presence of a development plan, multiple coaching meetings are assumed. A single chat may be interesting and useful but should not be defined as a coaching relationship.

(Note: No attempt is made at this point to delineate professional backgrounds of those delivering internal coaching services. Suffice it to say that as with other newly emerging roles, responsibilities and activities determine qualifications. Suggested competencies are listed later in this chapter. Over time, however, a dialogue about requisite experience, education, degrees, or even certifications would be a useful endeavor.)

WHAT IS NOT INTERNAL COACHING?

Because there are activities that are similar to internal coaching, it is useful to highlight their differences. In particular, the general advisory role often provided by HR professionals and other internal consultants should not be construed as internal coaching. Even though both advising and coaching involve discussing sensitive topics, considering alternatives, and making recommendations, their goals and targets are different. Advising on topics such as recruiting, compensation, morale, and so forth leverages an HR professional's technical expertise in those fields for the best interests of the organization. Internal coaching is focused at the individual level, aiming to maximize a specific manager's effectiveness. Internal coaches often have insights about the organization, but those insights are plowed back into assisting individual growth. For example, even if a manager and an internal coach are discussing that manager's staffing plan, the focus would be on the developmental opportunity that resides within those challenges rather than on any specific staffing decision.

Team builders, organization effectiveness consultants (internal), and trainers may also engage in activities similar to those of internal coaches. Not only might the topics under discussion overlap with coaching, but those professionals may have one-on-one meetings as a component of their efforts. However, because they work with groups and define their goals in terms of organizational improvement, they do not fit the definition of internal coaches. Many internal coaches may have experience in, or currently do, organizational development projects, but a clear distinction should be maintained between the roles.

Finally, mentoring is sometimes used as a synonym for coaching but will not be so used here. Although mentoring involves a one-on-one relationship and repeated meetings, its focus has evolved to emphasize career advising and advancement (Murray, 1998). Mentors are most frequently viewed as internal sponsors, helping to make key introductions that can lead to career opportunities, especially for high-potential managers from underrepresented groups. To the extent that internal coaching includes career discussions, one could say that all coaches do mentoring as part of their assignments. The converse, however, is not true; in general, mentors need not delve into the specifics of skill building or behavior change that a coach would.

INTERNAL AND EXTERNAL COACHING: TWO SIDES OF THE SAME COIN

There are many benefits of internal coaching that are fueling its growth. An obvious one is cost savings as compared with the fees for external coaching programs. Internal coaching resources can be applied more widely than more expensive external coaching. More important, internal coaches often can use their existing insights about the organization and its players to make faster initial progress in suggesting a developmental agenda. Similarly, an internal coach is more likely to be able to observe or hear about how those being coached are doing and fold those observations back into the coaching. Finally, internal coaching is a tangible manifestation of the "learning organization" (Senge, 1990). For those organizations that have made efforts to embrace that identity, internal coaching can model it as well as help individual managers make the transition.

Although these benefits are compelling, external coaching has advantages as well. It does not require any in-house resources or additional staff. Also, traditionally external coaches with impressive degrees and broad coaching experience are likely to engender more immediate credibility (Tobias, 1990). This credibility can be essential with a resistant or defensive manager who is being paired with a coach. Furthermore, external coaching relationships are "cleaner"; internal coaches may have multiple roles and interactions, both formal and informal, with those they coach. This situation can be confusing or even raise concerns about trust and confidentiality if not handled with sensitivity and forethought.

Given their mutual trade-offs, even where an internal coaching function exists, however, there always will be managers and executives for whom external coaching is the best choice. This may have to do with the complexity of the personality involved, coach credibility, concerns about confidentiality, or other factors. Organizations should view these two faces of coaching as complementary, both supporting the objective of managerial growth and development but for somewhat different audiences. They should not be viewed as competitive with each other; doing so could actually inhibit the effectiveness of both by making one appear inherently superior to the other, which is not necessarily the case.

KEY CHALLENGES IN SHAPING AN INTERNAL COACHING PROGRAM

Because no definitive guidelines exist about how to design and implement an internal coaching program, the goal here is to highlight the key challenges that such programs must address. These challenges are interdependent; an iterative approach is necessary in determining how they would apply to a specific organization. Suggestions are offered with the hope of stimulating dialogue about best practices in dealing with these challenges.

Internal Coaching Selection and Training

Those who may be interested in providing internal coaching services and those who are likely to be successful in the role may not always be the same. Just as with any other function, competencies should be identified that directly contribute to success in the role of internal coach, and these should be objectively applied to candidates. A process could be designed using a board or panel of knowledgeable professionals, possibly including a trusted external coach, to evaluate candidates against the required competencies. Rather than a yes or no decision, evaluations could highlight both strengths and gaps for the role, allowing development plans to be implemented for those truly motivated to ready themselves.

Training for internal coaches is too large a topic to be treated here, but a few suggestions are offered. Assuming a foundation of relevant courses (or a degree) in counseling, organizational behavior, and individual psychology, internal coaches need to have a thorough grasp of the coaching guidelines applicable to their organization. These guidelines should be written for easy distribution, possibly evolving with changes in the program, describing coaching services and dealing with key issues likely to confront coaches. A reading list for coaches as well as any required organizationally sponsored leadership or management courses is also useful. Furthermore, because tutorials on communication and interpersonal skills are often part of coaching, standardized modules on these topics should be assembled. Once coaches are trained to deliver these modules, they will provide a consistent foundation that can be flexibly applied within the context of the coaching. Similarly, training or certification in the use of organizationally preferred 360-degree or self-insight questionnaires should be provided. Finally, ongoing in-service training and case supervision should be offered on a regular basis.

Creating a consensus about key competency requirements for internal coaching is an excellent opportunity for interorganization benchmarking and cooperation. For the present, however, the list below is offered to guide both selection and training. Effective internal coaches do the following:

- Build trusting relationships with colleagues focused on their professional growth and development;
- Understand a model for a coaching process and execute it flexibly but dependably;
- Derive deep satisfaction from making discoveries about why others behave as they do—they have psychological curiosity;
- Articulate insights about behavior in ways others understand and find useful on the job;
- Understand a model of how adults change and grow and use such a model to guide coaching efforts;
- Approach job challenges with optimism and creativity—they are a source of ideas and suggestions for on-the-job learning;
- Have expertise in a variety of managerial topics and are able to provide just-in-time guidance on those topics;
- Are superb listeners, both as role models and information seekers;
- Balance the dual commitment to individual colleagues and the organization—they are able to transition smoothly between multiple organizational roles;
- Are constant students—they model how to learn from experience and expand their effective range in coaching;
- Have the maturity and ego strength to seek help with complexities outside of their expertise, accept help if it is provided, and refer to other coaches or professionals if it is in the best interests of a colleague; and
- Feel gratified with strengthening the organization one manager at a time.

General Expectations and Program Design

Coaching is an activity deceptive in its apparent simplicity. Most managers would believe they understand it but in fact would be hard pressed to list steps in a coaching process. Internal coaches must anticipate the need for clarity and set general expectations about roles and milestones. They can publish, or have available by e-mail, a description of the types of issues that can be addressed with internal coaching, the steps in a typical coaching process, and how one would explore initiating the process.

For internal coaches, it is likely to be useful to describe, or even label, specific coaching programs tied to organizational events—for example, coaching tied to specific outcomes of performance appraisals or development recommendations. Coaching could be applied in support of multirater survey feedback and development planning. Transition to a new role is another event that could be used to trigger a specific coaching program. Descriptions of such programs may be quite similar, but interested participants are more likely to be able to commit when a program's structure is spelled out.

Just as external coaches have moved away from "black box" characterizations of their programs, internal coaches should be descriptive of what happens, when, and with whom. A typical structure might be organized around several steps or phases: (a) development planning, (b) contracting, (c) skill building, and (d) follow-up. Each could be described in terms of players, actions, outcomes, and time frames, with variations reflecting different types of coaching programs. General expectations could also be summarized for issues such as sponsor roles and confidentiality limits. These descriptions, although challenging to draft, would yield ongoing benefits in promoting services internally and keeping delivery consistent, especially when multiple internal coaches are operating in the same organization.

Confidentiality

Although confidentiality is typically less of a concern when participants voluntarily request coaching, it must be clearly addressed in structuring an internal coaching program. Strictly speaking, complete confidentiality in any type of coaching is impossible. Organizational sponsors always know that an employee and a coach are working together and usually know what is in the development plan. The issue, therefore, is to clearly identify what is confidential and what will be shared. A simple but useful guideline is to structure the process so that all sharing of information with the organization is done jointly by the coach and the person being coached. Development planning and progress review meetings would include that person, the coach, the boss, and potentially an HR representative and would be the only time information would be provided to the organization. Of course, the coach would be free to gather information at any point but would be precluded from giving any independently. (Note: Legal precedent supports breaching confidentiality if physical harm to anyone is perceived by the coach to be a threat.)

With internal coaching, however, it is important to recognize that this simple guideline, or any other, would be tested much more frequently than with external coaching. Both formal and informal interactions are likely between the coach and organizational sponsors. Innocent hallway questions about how the coaching is going or what the coach thinks of the issues represent challenges to confidentiality. Internal coaches need a diplomatic way to avoid answering such inquiry. More complex challenges to confidentiality are likely when a coaching client posts for a new position and when a coach also covers HR generalist duties. How should the coach handle situations in which promotions, salary, succession, and so forth are discussed for those being coached? There may not be a definitive answer to this question, but the safest approach would be to officially opt out of the discussions. Although useful input may be lost, it should be viewed as a sacrifice in order to keep internal coaching viable. Internal coaches need to anticipate these and other pressure points on confidentiality, plan appropriate responses, and, to the extent possible, clarify expectations about confidentiality up front for all concerned.

Contracting

Contracting aims to establish clear commitments between the coach and the person being coached. External coaches have an advantage in setting and having others follow these commitments because of the tangible nature of fees. Missing paid-for appointments or squandering an allocated budget amount brings rapid attention to the issue of commitment. It is therefore more important that internal coaches establish mutual expectations at the beginning of a coaching engagement. These should include specific points about scheduling, respect for each other's time, and procedures for changing appointments. Better than just discussing such points is also providing them in writing, possibly as a foreword to a folder or log that can be used throughout coaching to record ideas, keep track of progress, and be a repository for articles or handouts.

One document that is key to the success of coaching and represents the most specific contract is the development plan. Effective development plans are targeted and short term rather than broad, general, or comprehensive (Peterson & Hicks, 1995, 1996). They focus on just two or three developmental objectives, including specific examples of on-the-job behaviors that support those objectives, and identify others involved and time frames (Davis, Skube, Hellervik, Gebelein, & Sheard, 1996; Gollwitzer, 1999). A motivating development plan is a significant work product of the early collaborative efforts of the coach and person being coached. Even when someone begins coaching with a development plan already drafted, the coach always needs to explore it, test its meaning, and refine it to a point where it is clear, actionable, and on target for what needs to be developed. Making it a joint effort and a living document that can be revised and adjusted is one of the best ways to heighten commitment to what is to be accomplished through coaching.

However, coaches should avoid the tendency to push for tighter contracting as a means to assure commitment. There are no guarantees for commitment, least of all in a process like coaching. The emphasis should be on the internal coach delivering consistent value, and lapses in commitment should therefore trigger questions more than contract waving. When coaches perceive that commitment is waning because of missed, shortened, or postponed appointments or other cues, they need to act quickly to explore those perceptions. Asking questions of themselves and their client may expose the problem: What progress have we made, and what have we still to accomplish? In what ways does the development plan need to be revised at this point? What new or different pressures exist in the client's work life? Although it might feel risky to raise such questions for discussion, it models a much healthier approach than becoming offended or seeking recourse with sponsors of the coaching. In their best use, contracts provide a basis to identify and discuss variation in commitment rather than as an illusory guarantor of compliance.

Sponsor Roles

Sponsors are those colleagues designated as overtly supporting a coaching program. They routinely include a boss and an HR generalist responsible for the business or department in which the participant works, but others could be enlisted as well, including career mentors, past bosses, or dotted-line bosses. Sponsors are important players in coaching programs for many reasons. They inform both the coach and the person being coached about performance issues and perceptions before, during, and near the end of the program. They are excellent reviewers of a draft development plan, both vetting its practicality and clarity and serving as witnesses to the commitment that it embodies. Of course, they offer support and encouragement, and possibly feedback, as new behaviors are tried. Also, they offer both the coach and the person being coached informed listeners to discuss the progress of the coaching effort, especially if obstacles occur or commitment wavers. Finally, they offer a means to bookend coaching so that gains can be openly acknowledged.

For all of their value, sponsors are often underused. In self-initiated coaching, as internal coaching is likely to be, their value may be overlooked in the desire to move ahead. Coaches should include them, for all the reasons stated above, even if the person being coached may not feel the need. Sponsor roles are not time consuming or complex. Especially for a boss, sponsoring the coaching is a natural extension of people management responsibilities. Being a sponsor simply formalizes coaching as a developmental intervention that adds to, but does not replace, the usual developmental commitments in a reporting relationship. Behavior change is much more likely to take hold if support, feedback, and praise are available from the existing management structure, represented by the sponsors, as well as from the coach.

Setting and Logistics

Although it is a relatively simple topic, the setting in which to deliver coaching is a particular consideration for internal coaches. The ideal setting for coaching is a quiet, comfortable room, free from distractions, with modest equipment available, such as a flip chart or whiteboard and a video camera and monitor for playback. These requirements are unlikely to be met in a typical office, so the coach should have his or her own office or conference room set up to maximize the use of coaching time. Meetings can be scheduled with no ambiguity about where to meet and with confidence that no phones, e-mail beeps, or knocks on the door will interrupt the coaching.

The right setting can support a variety of developmental activities. Coaches need to be prepared to teach listening, communication, and interpersonal skills as well as models of management and leadership that are often the underpinnings of developmental plans. Internal coaches can draw on appropriate modules from the organization's in-house curricula, also including ideas for exercises and role-plays. Videotaping and playback is a valuable tool for trying new approaches safely and providing feedback. Having it readily available makes it more likely to be used rather than having to make special arrangements for it to be set up.

Internal coaches have the distinct logistical advantage over external coaches in the ready opportunity for real-world observation. Internal coaches can much more easily slip into a presentation or meeting, either as part of another role they perform in the organization or just as an interested colleague. They are therefore in an excellent position later to provide feedback to the manager being coached and brainstorm alternatives with concrete knowledge of the players and dynamics of the situation. Similarly, internal coaches have extensive shop floor awareness of organizational culture, business pressures, frustrations, leadership challenges, and anticipated change, which significantly adds to the immediacy and value of their counsel.

Assessment Tools

Although external coaches may be deeply experienced with specific assessment tools, internal coaches have the advantage of being able to select from an often wider range of feedback tools and insight builders. Never to be underestimated, interviewing can have surprising value and should not be overlooked by internal coaches (Miller & Rollnick, 1991). For paper-and-pencil measures, they can scan the marketplace of vendors and select those instruments best suited to their organizational culture and coaching needs. Organizations are usually very willing to fund internal coach certification in such tools. Popular ones include the range of 360-degree surveys that are available, anchored to specific organizational levels or job types, interpersonal and communication style inventories, and values or motivational profile tests (Frisch, 1998). In some cases, organizations have customized tools or purchased the rights to use them without limitation, which provides opportunities for internal coaches to become experts in their application.

Such tools can be useful early in coaching to help both the coach and the person being coached gain insight into behavioral tendencies and preferences. These insights can then be used to guide and inform the development plan. However, internal coaches need to apply standards for the use of these measures just as external coaches would. Test scores, survey results, and feedback reports should be confidential, available only to the coach and the person being coached, and should be stored under lock and key. Even though results are usually descriptive and emphasize insight, they can easily be misinterpreted or overgeneralized by untrained or inappropriate users. Handling such instruments is somewhat easier if multiple internal coaches are operating in the same organization. Standards and procedures can be established as policy and included in statements descriptive of coaching programs. In addition, such policy can also allow for the coach to seek counsel from other coaches—bound by the same rules of confidentiality—in interpreting unusual or especially complex results.

CONCLUSION

The goal of this chapter was to highlight and validate the emergence of a formal, organizationally sanctioned role for the internal coach. In doing so, key aspects of that role have been identified, defined, and contrasted with other HR roles in the organization. Awareness of key challenges that the role faces were also explored with the hope that such awareness will aid in their resolution. The internal coach role is still too new to offer definitive guidelines on these key challenges, but recommendations have been offered. More important, however, the hope here is to stimulate a dialogue about this emerging role. Best practices can then accumulate as the dialogue progresses, benefiting all internal coaches and those organizations planning on offering such services. There is every expectation that the roster of internal coaches will continue to expand. External coaching will expand with it, bringing greater appreciation for how the two approaches complement each other. Eventually, as internal coaching catches up and defines its practices more clearly, internal and external coaching will be viewed as two sides of the same coaching coin, realizing greater benefit for organizations committed to the development of their human resources.

Appendix 20.1

Bibliography

Boynton, R. S. (1989). Doctor success. *Manhattan, Inc, 6*(8), 52–59.

Clay, R. A. (1998). More clinical psychologists move into organization consulting realm. *APA Monitor, 29,* 28–29.

Filipczak, R. (1998). The executive coach: Helper or healer? *Training, 35*(3), 30–36.

Hyatt, J. (1997). The zero defect CEO. *Inc., 19*(6), 46–57.

Kizilos, P. (1991). Fixing fatal flaws. *Training, 28*(9), 66–71.

Lary, B. K. (1997). Now, coach? *Across the Board, 34*(6), 28–32.

Smith, L. (1993, December 27). The executive's new coach. *Fortune, 128,* 126–134.

Wheeler, C. (1995). Could your career use a coach? *Executive Female, 18*(5), 49–51, 81.

References

Buss, D. B. (1998). Enlisting a coach to boost your game. *Nations Business, 86*(12), 36–40.

Davis, B. L., Skube, C. L., Hellervik, L. W., Gebelein, S. H., & Sheard, J. L. (1996). *Successful manager's handbook*. Minneapolis, MN: Personnel Decisions International.

Frisch, M. H. (1998). Designing the individual assessment process. In R. Jeanneret & R. Silzer (Eds.), *Individual psychological assessment: Predicting behavior in organizational settings* (pp. 135–177). San Francisco: Jossey-Bass.

Gabriel, T. (1996, April 28). Personal trainers to buff the boss's people skills. *The New York Times* [Business section], p. 10.

Gollwitzer, P. M. (1999). Implementation intentions: Strong effects of simple plans. *American Psychologist, 54*, 493–503.

Hargrove, R. (1995). *Masterful coaching*. San Diego, CA: Pfeiffer.

Hicks, M. D., & Peterson, D. B. (1997). Just enough to be dangerous: The rest of what you need to know about development. *Consulting Psychology Journal: Practice and Research, 49*, 171–193.

Kilburg, R. R. (Ed.). (1996). Executive coaching [Special issue]. *Consulting Psychology Journal: Practice and Research, 48*(2).

Miller, W. R., & Rollnick, S. (1991). *Motivation interviewing: Preparing people to change addictive behavior*. New York: Guilford Press.

Morris, B. (2000, February 21). So you're a player. Do you need a coach? *Fortune, 141*, 144–154.

Murray, B. (1998). Mentoring: No longer just for students. *APA Monitor, 29*, 34–35.

Nobel, B. P. (1994, April 24). In praise of executive coaching. *The New York Times* [Business section], pp. 23–24.

Peterson, D. B., & Hicks, M. D. (1995). *Development FIRST: Strategies for self-development*. Minneapolis, MN: Personnel Decisions International.

Peterson, D. B., & Hicks, M. D. (1996). *Leader as coach: Strategies for coaching and developing others*. Minneapolis, MN: Personnel Decisions International.

Peterson, D. B., Uranowitz, S. W., & Hicks, M. D. (1996, August). *Management coaching at work: Current practices in Fortune 250 companies*. Paper presented at the 104th Annual Convention of the American Psychological Association, Toronto, Ontario, Canada.

Senge, P. M. (1990). *The fifth discipline: The art and practice of the learning organization*. New York: Currency/Doubleday.

Stern, L. (2001). A new standard for executive coaching. *The Industrial Organizational Psychologist, 38*(3), 135–137.

Tichy, N. M., & Cohen, E. (1997). *The leadership engine*. New York: HarperBusiness.

Tobias, L. L. (1990). *Psychological consulting to management: A clinician's perspective*. New York: Brunner/Mazel.

Toomey, P. J. (1994, July 4). Grace under fire. *The Hackensack Record*, pp. B1, B3.

Tyler, K. (2000). Scoring big in the workplace. *HR Magazine, 45*(6), 96–106.

Zemke, R. (1996). The corporate coach. *Training, 33*(12), 24–28.

CHAPTER 21

AN INTEGRATED MODEL OF DEVELOPMENTAL COACHING

Otto E. Laske

Most "practice theories of coaching executives" (see chap. 10, this volume) conceive of the client in a cognitive–behavioral manner, as a habituated mechanism whose organizational functioning can be improved. At times (Martin, 1996), this conception is extended to include psychodynamic assumptions, with a concomitant increase of attention to defensive mechanisms (Kaplan, Drath, & Kofodomis, 1991). What is presently lacking is a life span developmental perspective that would aid in making the notion of meeting the client "where the client is developmentally" more precise. Such a perspective requires a widening of the time window within which coaching is conceived and practiced, as a means of locating the coaching experience at some point along the trajectory of the client's life span development. It is this deepening of the developmental perspective for the purpose of "developmental coaching" that is at issue in this chapter.

When seeing coaching in the context of the life span development of executives, two notions of development spring to mind. One is based on the metaphor of making development happen and, as a result, on human agency; thus, I refer to it as *agentic*. The other notion is based on the metaphor of a human organism experiencing developmental changes over its lifetime as a matter of course, and thus I label this notion *ontic*. In my view, much of the complexity of coaching assignments involves the constant and deep interaction between these two modes of human development, on the side of both the coach and the executive. Therefore, the question of "where the client is" *ontic–developmentally* is of crucial import for conceptualizing coaching strategy as well as for determining the compatibility of coach and client.

In my practice as a developmental psychologist as well as researcher (Laske, 1999), I have found it helpful to conceptualize the topology of the mental space in which coaching takes place in terms of two "houses" called the Professional House and the Company House (Haber, 1996). As shown in Figure 21.1, coach and executive are thought to inhabit a Professional House whose "floors" embody their particular issues of self, work context, professional agenda, and personal culture. In addition, both coach and executive reside in a Company House in which issues of the workplace (rather than personal issues) are topical. Given the telos of coaching and the complexity of the workplace, I distinguish two related Company Houses and, consequently, two types of coaching. In first-order coaching (First Company House) the coach assumes a structural–political perspective on the executive's organization, while in second-order coaching (Second Company House) the coach models the ability to take multiple perspectives on organizational matters, as required in a leadership position. In the integrated model of developmental

Reprinted from the *Consulting Psychology Journal: Practice and Research, 51,* 139–159.

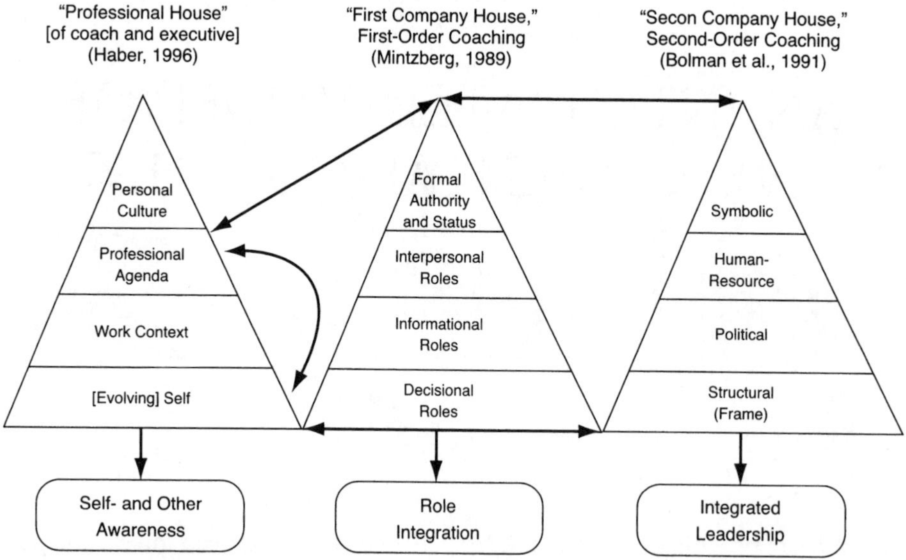

FIGURE 21.1. The mental space of coaching activity.

coaching, such thinking is cast as the reframing of organizational matters in terms of four different perspectives, as outlined by Bolman and Deal (1991). Each of the three houses comprises four floors (or levels) representing the topics that can emerge and be "worked on" in the coaching relationship. These three houses define the mental space in which coach and client mentally reside at any moment during their partnership. In fact, executives often report their experiences of coaching in terms of where in these three houses and their floors they have predominantly resided over the lifetime of a specific coaching relationship. In short, Figure 21.1 indicates the scope of coaching activity as well as the framework in which coaching is experienced by executives.

Before entering into greater detail regarding the houses and levels outlined, it is in order to draw attention to the fact that the "bottom floor" of the Professional House, of self, is construed differently in each of the three approaches I have mentioned. (Equally, cognitive–behavioral, psychodynamic, and constructive–developmental theories differ in their conception of what constitutes an organization, a topic that is beyond the scope of this chapter.) The way in which the level of self is construed, both theoretically and practically, determines the telos adopted for the coaching and the kind of coaching that is actually done. For example, in a cognitive–behavioral conception of executive self, performance and skill issues tend to be paramount in the coaching. In a psychodynamic approach, self is seen as a system of defenses, or "character," with the consequence that life history, especially attachment history, enters the coaching and is considered instrumental in how the executive functions organizationally. Finally, when the self is construed as "evolving" over the life span, emphasis is placed on the fact that at any point during their existence, individuals make meaning of their experiences in a more or less complex fashion; accordingly, they can be said to be at a particular "stage" of development that can be empirically assessed (Kegan, 1982, 1994; Kohlberg, 1984; Kohlberg & Armon, 1984; Lahey, Souvaine, Kegan, Goodman, & Felix, 1983; Loevinger, 1976; Piaget, 1970). While nonstage approaches to development are equally relevant (Basseches, 1984), and are particularly important for distinguishing psychological and epistemological aspects of human development (Basseches, 1989; Laske, 1999), for simplicity's sake I am restricting myself to dealing with stage theories of life span development and their impact on the practice of coaching. The reader should keep in mind that executive development is, after all, adult development in the workplace.

Constructive–developmental theories, of whatever ilk, introduce two fundamental ideas:

(a) that not every change represents *development* and (b) that what is learned and experienced by an individual depends on the *ontic–developmental position*, or *stage*, of that individual. In other words, along the life span, qualitative changes in what is experienced as reality are thought to occur. The shortest way to render the first idea was well formulated by Loevinger (1976, p. 38):

> If development consists of structural changes, any new structure constitutes a break from the old one. It cannot be obtained by adding or subtracting [i.e., in a mechanistic way], but only by establishing a new principle governing the relations among the parts.

The "structure" referred to here defines the particular worldview of a person at a particular time point along his or her life span trajectory. This structure is thought to determine, more teleologically than causally, how the person conceives of what, for him or her, is "self" and what is "other." Consequently, the structure determines how the person's psychological boundaries are drawn and where in the scheme of things that person finds himself or herself and takes action. The understanding of structure as a principle governing relations among parts refers to a principle of meaning making, sometimes conceptualized as a "stage" of cognitive–emotional development (Kegan, 1982). "Stage" refers to an equilibrium of the cognitive–emotional capabilities of a person. Equally, in a nonstage conception of "structure," the overriding idea is that over the life span, qualitative changes take place in the way a person construes his or her world, each of which represents a particular developmental equilibrium associated with a particular worldview.

The second idea, that of qualitative changes in experiencing the world (including the world of work), is equally fundamental. Constructive–developmental theories redefine organizational cognition, that is, the way in which organization members make sense of what is going on in and around them (Kegan, 1994; Weick & Bougon, 1986). These theories support novel ways of conceptualizing "agentic" change efforts meant to promote executive development. (The question these theories ask regarding such efforts is a critical one, namely, "Is it really *development*?") They also suggest the elaboration of new assessment methods for purposes of coaching and mentoring. Finally, constructive–developmental theories give rise to a novel conception of the nature of coaching, in that they shed light on the ontic–developmental *preconditions* and *outcomes* of coaching (in contrast to adaptive changes occurring in an executive's organizational performance). These theories suggest that the effect of coaching depends on the ontic–developmental preconditions that determine where an executive is when entering a coaching relationship. They further suggest that coaching potentially has ontic–developmental effects (i.e., lasting effects on the complexity of executives' personal as well as professional meaning making).

A MODEL OF DEVELOPMENTAL COACHING

As shown in Figure 21.1, coach and executive can, at any time, dwell in one of the three houses that together define the topology of executive coaching. Each of the houses is focused on a different developmental telos: self-awareness and awareness of others in the Professional House, role self-integration in the First Company House, and integrated leadership capability in the Second Company House. The hypothesis grounding the topology of coaching is that the potential and the limits of coaching are defined by the ontic–developmental stage or equilibrium of cognitive–emotional capabilities instantiated by coach and executive at any given time. As a consequence, the relationship between coach and executive—and thus issues of compatibility—is seen as having to do with the ontic–developmental maturity of the two parties. The hypothesis entails that issues pertaining to an executive's unique psychological organization (and therefore "clinical" issues of character and pathology) require a distinct mode of intervention. In short, ontic–developmental insight is indicative of, but not per se therapeutic for, clinical issues an executive might struggle with, nor can such issues be reduced to stage concepts (Laske, 1999). For example, a developmentally highly complex individual may present with severe clinical issues, since complexity of meaning making does not guarantee mental health. Rather, it only defines mental growth (Rogers & Kegan, 1990).

The integrated model of developmental coaching makes the assumption that coach and executive dwell in two different but related mental domains: first, their own sphere as professionals and, second, the organizational sphere. Given that the evolving self is seen as the basis of what happens in both houses, what is topical in developmental coaching is not the organization per se but, rather, the way executive and coach make sense of, or construe, the organization and their relationship to the organization. In short, the organization is seen as constructed by them. The specific way in which the organization is constructed by both parties is reflected in each party's interaction in the houses. It is, in particular, both parties' professional *agenda* (Professional House) that determines their relationship to work. This relationship, in turn, is thought to differ between individuals at different ontic–developmental levels, whether they are seen as stages or not.

Here I have adopted a metaphoric language for conceptualizing how a coaching relationship may promote executive development as adult development. To this end, I have introduced the metaphor of three houses as a means of observing where and how the executive intervenes in his or her organization and what are his or her whereabouts and limits in the houses. The perspective on coaching adopted in the present model is that of looking at the executive's actions within the organization in the way a clinical supervisor might look at how a supervisee therapist intervenes with a client system. In the present case, the client system is the executive's organization. After all, it is the mandate of the coach, as well as a supervisor, "to amplify, partner with, utilize, and redirect the executive's resources" and to prevent him or her from "becoming bogged down in stereotypical roles in the different rooms and floors" of both houses (Haber, 1996, p. 33). The coach can help the executive—just as the supervisor helps the counselor—"to work in the floors and rooms that are foreign, emotionally provocative, difficult, overwhelming, or simply uncomfortable" (Haber, 1996, p. 34), starting in the Professional House and expanding into the floors of the Company House.

Also, depending on the executive's level of personal development, the executive may tend to dwell more intensely in one or the other of the two houses, in which case a switch of focus may be in order. Being in that position, the executive may not dare to enter certain floors and rooms of either house and may need new skills and emotional and/or conceptual support to do so. Coaching is thus a multidirectional ability to observe executive–organization interactions in the houses, for the purpose of refining the executive's interventions with himself or herself and with the organization. Coaching provides time and space "to reflect on a broad picture of the . . . [executive's] professional relationships in the houses . . . without the immediate pressure to react" (Haber, 1996, p. 34). Being external to the organization, the coach is at leisure to assume a meta-perspective.

The mandate of coaching is to develop a cognitive–emotionally and behaviorally more flexible professional whose activity in the organization shows greater perspicacity and self-awareness, resulting in a more balanced approach to his or her job performance. The extent to which this mandate succeeds depends on the ontic–developmental maturity and compatibility of both executive and coach. Although he or she is "joining" (identifying with) the client system (in the Company House), the executive also needs to preserve his or her distinctness from the organization (in the Professional House). The reason is that an executive who "is" his or her professional agenda, rather than "having" an agenda, is incapable of taking a truly systemic view of the organization. The extent to which such a view can be created depends on the executive's ontic–developmental position, since that position informs his or her notion of authority and self-authoring (Hodgetts, 1994). Ideally, a combination of changes on the floors of the Professional House and professional growth in the Company House leads to greater differentiation and flexibility of moving about in both houses.

TABLE 21.1

The Executive's and Coach's Position in the Professional House

Bottom floor (self)
▪ Personal characteristics (sex, ethnicity, physical appearance, intellectual ability, communicational style, etc.)
▪ Personal life cycle phase
▪ Structural–developmental position
▪ Family history and family allegiance
▪ Life ambitions and themes
Middle floor (work context)
▪ Parameters of work context (position, rules, roles, relationships)
▪ Support systems at work (executive team)
▪ Perceived culture of the organization
▪ Relationship with coach
Top floor (professional agenda)
▪ Relationship to work
▪ Personal mission (mandate)
▪ Construence of job description (objectives)
▪ Translation of theories, methodologies, professional ethics, and values into professional performance
▪ Goal formulation
▪ Approach to task
Attic (personal culture)
▪ Value system
▪ Moral standards
▪ Priorities
▪ Preferences

Note. From Haber (1996).

Professional House

The floors of the Professional House are mainly linked along "psychological" lines, whereas those of the Company Houses are linked along "organizational" lines. I start with the Professional House. In Table 21.1, I specify in more detail the coach's and executive's positions in the Professional House.

Self

As indicated in Table 21.1, the bottom floor of the Professional House of both coach and executive comprises all of the internal experience, personal history, and characterological idiosyncracies of the two individuals. In Haber's words (1996, p. 20): "The self lives within the confines of the professional role. Our uniqueness—personal history, personal style, strengths and weaknesses, gender and cultural perspective, emotional responses, physical and characterological capabilities and limitations—comprises our singular version of humanness."

In coaching, the relationship of the self to its professional role(s) is of particular salience. These two dimensions of a professional identity are typically distinct in their social manifestation:

> The role receives more credence than the self. . . . The self is frequently left to manage on its own and consequently is more primitive, unconscious, unconventional, and mysterious than the professional role. The self uses the language of dreams, metaphors, feelings, symbols, intuition, and physiological responses to represent its reality. (Haber, 1996, p. 21)

Optimally, self and role coexist "in an acknowledged, functional, creative, and respectful union" (Haber, 1996, p. 21). However, such a union is an achievement of maturation over the life span. For this reason, a clinical notion of self needs to be amplified by a developmental one, to encompass life span development. One can then view the coaching experience within an expanded, adult-developmental time window that comprises not only the professional's past but his or her developmental status quo and future. Stage and nonstage theories of adult development are equally capable of conceptualizing professionals' developmental status quo and telos. Here I choose R. Kegan's (1982, 1994) stage theory of self to illustrate the ontic–developmental point of view.

According to Kegan's constructive–developmental theory, human beings are engaged, throughout their life span, in a ceaseless process of meaning making. This process leads them from being embedded in their own subjectivity (as is an infant) to an increasingly stronger and refined ability to take the world, including themselves, as an object. In the context of Kegan's theory, "taking as object" entails being able to transcend embeddedness in one's subjectivity, that is, being able to take responsibility for, and to be in relationship with, what is "other than me" (object), including parts of oneself, rather than being embedded in (subject to) one's subjectivity. Along the life span, different subject–object equilibriums emerge that determine where the boundaries between self (me) and other (not me) are being drawn. This subject–object dialectic manifests itself in the degree to which humans can balance the opposites of a yearning for inclusion and self-authored independence. It determines the way they construct, at any point, their world, both cognitively and affectively. As a consequence, at different ontic–developmental positions (stages), different rules of meaning making "govern," as it were, an individual's relationship to self, role, work, and the social world in general. In Kegan's words:

> Subject–object relations emerge out of a life-long process of development: a succession of qualitative differentiations of the self from the world, with a qualitatively more extensive object with which to be in relation created each time; a natural history of better guarantees to the world of its distinctness; successive triumphs of "relationship to" rather than "embeddedness in." (1982, p. 77)

Kegan's theory does not emphasize stages per se as much as the transitions between pivotal stages. Because his theory is teleological, not causal or clinical, it makes transparent the meaning of developmental struggles and their telos. His theory provides 21 ontic–developmental positions at which individuals can find themselves along the trajectory of their journey. Of these positions, about 11 apply to professional life. Kegan's theory is helpful for understanding differences in individuals' professional functioning. It provides information on the self–role relationship an individual actualizes in an organization, as well as his or her relationship to work.

In light of Kegan's theory, the self being addressed at the bottom floor of the Professional House is an evolving self engaged in a ceaseless reworking of its subject–object equilibrium. Therefore, the link between self-agenda and professional agenda cannot be severed (see the arrow linking them in Figure 21.1). Rather, the content and form of an executive's professional agenda are determined by the developmental position of the self. (The developmental position is not, as in phasic theories [Levinson, Darrow, Klein, Levinson, & McKee, 1978], strictly aligned with age, although age functions as a limiting variable.) This means that an executive's professional agenda is "mature" to the extent that he or she has sufficiently emerged from embeddedness in subjectivity to *have* an agenda (Kegan's Stage 4) rather than *being* (i.e., being embedded in) the agenda (Kegan's Stage 3). In a further step, an executive may transcend his or her own agenda and thus become capable of integrated leadership (Kegan's Stage 5).

In terms of Figure 21.1, the evolving self of the Professional House teleologically determines the content and form of executives' professional agenda. It is the task of constructive–developmentally informed coaching to observe executive–client interactions in the houses and decode their ontic–developmental "signature" (i.e., the subject–object equilibrium underlying such interactions) to assist change efforts. A coach who is expert in this practice is able to determine what organizational demands an executive can and cannot fulfill given her or his ontic–developmental status quo, and in what manner. The expertise to formulate constructive–developmental hypotheses adds another dimension to the ability of the coach: that of guiding the executive in making transitions to a subsequent developmental equilibrium.

For instance, a certain maturity is required if an executive is to emerge from embeddedness in his or her organization (which is essentially embeddedness in the subjectivity of his or her own role in the organization). An executive who cannot take this embeddedness as an object will find it difficult, for instance, to reframe organizational matters. He or she cannot make the transition from a single perspective on the organization to a more complex view. Similarly, the developmental position of the coach is ideally one that lies "beyond" that of the executive being coached. However, there ought to be enough compatibility between the developmental positions of coach and executive so that a dialogue between them is provocative and challenging. The precise nature of this compatibility remains a topic of empirical research.

Work Context

The "work context" floor (see Figure 21.1) regards the parameters of the executive's work situation, including his or her relationship with the coach, viewed from the perspective of the self. (In the First Company House, the work context is spelled out objectively, in terms of the roles the executive plays in the organization.) The work context is an articulation of how the executive construes his or her relationship to the organization in practical, action-oriented terms. It is equally determined by where in the organizational hierarchy an executive is stationed (in the sense of Mintzberg, 1989) and by the subject–object equilibrium an executive is instantiating in his or her interactions with the organization. Consequently, topical on this floor are the rules and conventions (as construed by the executive) that inform an executive's professional agenda and the support systems that sustain or fail the executive in carrying it out.

The executive's relationship with the coach is also topical on this floor. For instance, it makes a difference how the executive conceives of the coaching (i.e., whether he or she views it as affecting skills, performance, development, or agenda; see chap. 10, this volume). Clearly expressed expectations of the coaching relationship will clarify the roles and responsibilities of the partners in the coaching relationship. The coach must carefully consider the culture of the executive's workplace. "It may be necessary for the . . . [coach] to challenge bureaucratic constraints that have an impact on . . . [the coaching] relationship. On this floor, we are also dealing with the images of sponsor, boss, and colleagues" (Haber, 1996, p. 22). Thus, in taking organizational culture into account, the coach goes far beyond the triangle of sponsor–coach–executive, dealing with a cast of characters he or she may never see in person.

Professional Agenda

According to Haber's clinical point of view (1996, pp. 22–24), the top floor of the Professional House represents the "ideology of the . . . [executive] in the context of the . . . [organization]." I would add to this issues having to do with how the executive construes his or her mission and job description and how, consequently, he or she sets goals, approaches assignments, and pursues tasks. In cognitive science terms, the professional agenda is a set of "theories in use" (Argyris, Putnam, & McLain Smith, 1987), that is, a set of assumptions the executive makes about his or her work. The agenda is an implicit theory of where the executive stands with regard to the organization, along with his or her mission in the Company Houses, viewed from a specific ontic–developmental position. The relationship between professional agenda and the two Company Houses is entirely reciprocal. The professional agenda is determined by the executive's formal authority and status as much as by his or her ontic–developmental status (see the two-directional arrows between the houses in Figure 21.1).

It is important to keep in mind that the coach, too, is at a particular ontic–developmental stage of self and situated in a particular work context. The coach has knowledge of the organization largely in terms of how the executive conceptualizes the organization in the Company Houses. The professional agenda of the coach has to do with how he or she approaches the coaching assignment (i.e., the theoretical perspective in terms of which the coaching task is conceived). Making use of research on the determining variables of successful outcome in psychotherapy (Luborsky, Crits-Christoph, Mintz, & Auerbach, 1988), one can speculate that the approach taken by the coach—whether cognitive–behavioral, psychodynamic, or constructive–developmental—is ultimately less important than the quality of the working alliance he or she establishes with the executive. This entails that a coach who is coaching from a strictly cognitive–behavioral perspective may unwittingly achieve ontic–developmental results, although he or she will probably be amiss in regard to interpreting them correctly.

Equally, a coach working from a psychodynamic perspective may misconceive development as deriving from the executive's attachment history and be tempted to reduce developmental issues to early childhood problems instead of seeing them in terms of the wider time window of a life span trajectory. However, the coach's ontic–developmental position may be more influential in defining the quality of the coaching alliance and its outcomes than any of the specific techniques he or she may be using. Since the coach is in a "meta-position" relative to the executive, it is the coach's responsibility to become aware of the executive's ideological position, as well as the values he or she stands for. This means that the coach must be able to take himself or herself and his or her own coaching philosophy as object, which normally entails a more advanced developmental position than that held by the executive. As Haber (1996) stated in regard to the case of supervisors:

> As a supervisor in a "meta" position, I have a good vantage point to make process interventions that are relevant and collaborative even if I do not define the process in the same terms [as the supervisee]. However, if I cannot use the language from my supervisee's model, I would ask him or her to define it. [In this way I] would explore the triangle between my supervisee, his or her ideology [professional agenda], and my approach in order to explore ways to work together as a team. (p. 23)

Personal Culture

The topic of culture appears twice in the houses, as *personal culture* in the Professional House and as *organizational culture* in the symbolic perspective of the Second Company House. On this floor, I would include the ethics and the value system adhered to by both the executive and the coach and the way in which their personal idiosyncracies express themselves in their style. One might also include the "cognitive fingerprint" of both coach and executive and their particular style of learning. Since, as a leader, the executive is the bearer of organizational culture (Schein, 1992), the intangible link that binds his or her personal culture to the organizational culture is a topic of great relevance in coaching. One might also include on this floor what is sometimes called "charisma," although the developmental substrate of this ascription remains unclear.

FIRST COMPANY HOUSE

In making the transition from the Professional House to the Company Houses, the emphasis in coaching shifts from the personal to the organizational and from the ontic–developmental to the systemic aspect of the executive's functioning. In focus now are the executive–organization interactions associated with the executive's day-to-day functioning (First Company House), on one hand, and the leadership capabilities of the executive (Second Company House), on the other. Accordingly, it makes sense to distinguish two types of coaching, first- and second-order coaching, associated with the First and Second Company Houses, respectively. Second-order coaching is not so much a "higher" form of coaching as it is a different kind of coaching that emphasizes leadership issues. By contrast, first-order coaching regards the executive's role functioning and role integration. In the present model, the First Company House is shaped after Mintzberg (1989), and the Second Company House is patterned after Bolman and Deal (1991). Both Company Houses together comprehensively render the executive's systemic interactions with the organization, the first from a more technical point of view and the second from an ideological point of view

In contrast to the executive who is expert in the Company House, the coach develops knowledge of the organization in an indirect way, by interacting with the executive. This holds especially in stand-alone coaching not tied to more wide-scoped consulting work. In both situations, the coach operates on a meta-level relative to the executive, who tends to be embedded in her or his subjectivity as a manager. The executive therefore tends to "act out" her or his ontic–developmental position in a fashion that can be scrutinized by a schooled observer. In what follows, I discuss the First Company House in some detail.

First-order coaching deals with the executive's situation in his or her organization and with the thoughts, feelings, defenses, metaphors, and ideas evoked by the executive's formal authority and status. The executive's status gives rise to a set of interpersonal, informational, and decisional roles (Mintzberg, 1989). First-order coaching is primarily concerned with how the executive assumes the roles that status and formal authority bestow on him or her. These roles take on different forms depending on the way in which the executive's organization is structurally configured. As Mintzberg (1981, 1989) has shown, companies differ in how the universal building blocks of strategic apex, midline management, technostructure, support staff, and operating core are put together, as it were, and how historical change modulates this composition over time:

> Effective organizations achieve a coherence among their component parts . . . they do not change one element without considering the consequences to all of the others. Spans of control, degrees of job enlargement, forms of decentralization, planning systems, and matrix structure should not be picked and chosen at random. Rather, they should be selected according to internally consistent groupings. (Mintzberg, 1981, p. 103)

Executives who are invested in the specific configurational status quo of their organization cannot be leaders of change in, and culture bearers of, that organization. They are not attuned to the shifts occurring in organizational development. To begin with, functioning as an executive in a "simple structure" organization is something quite different from serving as an executive in an "adhocracy," for example. In a simple structure, the manager is part of a small group consisting of one or two individuals directly supervising the work of the operating core. Conversely, in an adhocracy, she or he may be the leader of a project group "that fuses experts drawn from different specialties into a smoothly functioning creative team," a fluid structure in which "power is constantly shifting and coordination and control are by mutual adjustment through the information, communication, and interaction of competent experts" (Mintzberg, 1981, p. 111). As a consequence, the executive is part of a configuration in which the functionality of middle management is highly reduced. That functionality becomes distributed among project teams that make up the operating core of the company, which is supported by an enlarged administrative support staff. In such a structure, the experts are no longer concentrated in the operating core, but "they tend to be dispersed throughout the structure according to the decisions they make—in the operating core, middle line (management), technostructure, strategic apex, and especially support staff" (Mintzberg, 1981, p. 112). These configurational determinants of the executive's work context form the framework within which his or her roles are actualized.

As empirical studies conducted by Mintzberg (1989) and others have shown, one can usefully distinguish four aspects of executive role performance in an organization: (a) formal authority and status, (b) interpersonal roles, (c) informational roles, and (d) decisional roles (Mintzberg, 1989). This is detailed in Figure 21.2.

> All [managers] are vested with formal authority over an organizational unit. From formal authority comes status, which leads to various interpersonal relationships, and from these comes access to information. Information, in turn, enables the manager to make decisions and strategies for his or her unit. (Mintzberg, 1989, pp. 15–16)

These four categories of role performance have a twofold relevance for coaching. First, they determine the executive's goals, tasks, and performance. Second, as much as they are determined by the executive's professional agenda, they in turn exert a strong influence on that agenda. On the "work context" floor of the Professional House, the coach is primarily concerned with how the executive's environment is represented by his or her mental maps (Weick & Bougon, 1986), while in first-order coaching the coach focuses on the executive's specific role performance and repercussions in the larger organizational environment. As Mintzberg (1989) has emphasized, executives must "have insight into their own work," since "their

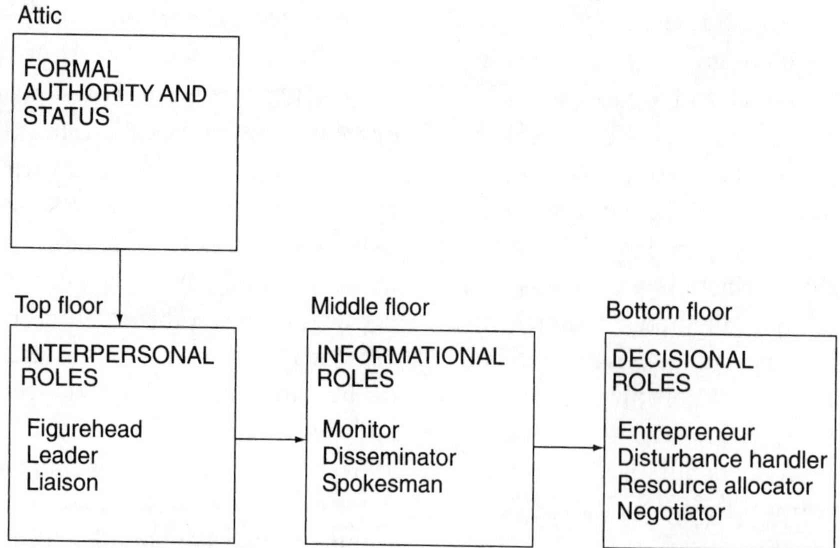

FIGURE 21.2. Executives' roles as floors of the First Company House (Mintzberg, 1989).

performance depends on how well they understand and respond to the pressures and dilemmas of the job" (p. 22). From an ontic–developmental perspective, the executive must be able to take organizational structure, as well as the roles it provides, as object, rather than being embedded in either. This ability presupposes an emergence from his or her own professional subjectivity. Assessing an executive's ontic–developmental status quo involves looking for what the executive can and cannot take a perspective on (i.e., what he or she is subject to and thus cannot have a relationship with). If the coach is also "subject" in the same way, "it becomes problematic to make a developmental assessment, because there is little ability to take a perspective on the development" of the executive (Pratt, 1993, p. 58). In question here is the developmental compatibility of coach and executive, a topic still lacking a research base.

I have assumed (see Figure 21.1) that the floors of the First Company House are coincident with the executive's roles (as seen by Mintzberg, 1989, pp. 15–24) and that these roles differ according to the compositional structure to which a particular organization adheres (Mintzberg, 1989, pp. 95–115). Accordingly, first-order coaching pays primary attention to the actual functioning of the executive within a specific organizational structure. As shown in Figure 21.2, executive roles are predominantly interpersonal, informational, or decisional in nature.

Among the interpersonal roles, the executive functions as (a) figurehead, (b) leader, and (c) liaison. On the top floor of the First Company House, executives are concerned with (a) their position as head of an organizational unit, (b) their role as a leader responsible for the work of individuals in their unit, and (c) making "contacts outside [their] vertical chain of command" (Mintzberg, 1989, p. 17). These contacts may range along a broad spectrum: "subordinates; clients; business associates, and suppliers; managers of similar organizations, government and trade organization officials, fellow directors on outside boards, and so on" (Mintzberg, 1989, p. 17). Liaison contacts go far beyond the compositional structure of the organization. They presuppose that the executive can take her or his particular organization as object and has the ability to reframe organizational matters.

The executive's position on the middle floor of the First Company House is that of "the nerve center of his or her organizational unit" (Mintzberg, 1989, p. 17). To a large extent, roles performed on this floor have a political flavor, while cognitively they involve predominantly information-processing tasks. On this floor, the executive functions as

(a) monitor, (b) disseminator of information, and (c) spokesperson for his or her organizational unit (see Figure 21.2). In specifying these informational roles, Mintzberg (1989) placed primary emphasis on cognitive rather than political aspects:

> As *monitor,* the manager . . . scans his or her environment for information, interrogates liaison contacts and subordinates, and receives unsolicited information, much of it as a result of the network of personal contacts he or she has developed. . . . Managers must share and distribute much of this information. In their *disseminator* role, managers pass some of their privileged information directly to their subordinates, who otherwise would have no access to it. . . . In their *spokesman* role, managers send some of their information to people outside their units . . . every manager must inform and satisfy influential people who control his or her organizational unit. (pp. 18–19)

In short, in their position on the middle floor of the First Company House, executives monitor, disseminate, and "broadcast," as it were, information vital for the functioning of their unit and the organization at large.

On the bottom floor of the First Company House, the executive is in the role of decision maker. The capacity to make decisions is a natural characteristic, as it were, of a person who has formal authority, lives in the center of a complex web of interpersonal contacts, and takes in as well as disseminates vital information. As Mintzberg (1989) put it: "As its formal authority, only the manager can commit the unit to important new courses of action; as its nerve center, only the manager has full and current information to make the set of decisions that determines the unit's strategy" (p. 19).

As a decision maker, the executive functions as (a) entrepreneur, (b) disturbance handler, (c) resource allocator, and (d) negotiator for his or her unit (see Figure 21.2). The executive's functioning on this floor requires more of his or her capacity for cognitive flexibility than is the case on the other floors of the First Company. House. As an entrepreneur, the executive seeks to adapt her or his unit to the changing conditions in the environment (Mintzberg, 1989, p. 19). This often takes the form of promoting and maintaining a large number of development projects, not by way of single decisions or "unified clusters of decisions but as a series of small decisions and actions sequenced over time" (Mintzberg, 1989, p. 19). Accordingly, the executive "juggles" a large number of such projects. The executive is also the person who deals with unforeseen contingencies (disturbance handler), attempting to produce a seamless performance by containing the unforeseeable. This contributes to a more political than structural liability, to the executive being the person who determines "who will get what in the organizational unit" (Mintzberg, 1989, p. 20). As resource allocator, too, the executive entertains various action frames that have political consequences beyond his or her unit. Finally, on this floor, the executive is engaged as a negotiator: "Only the manager has the authority to commit organizational resources in 'real time,' and only he or she has the nerve center information that important decisions require" (Mintzberg, 1989, p. 21)

In summary, first-order coaching scrutinizes the executive's ability to take a perspective on where in the First Company House he or she preferentially resides: in the interpersonal role, the informational role, or the decisional role. How does the executive juggle the 10 roles outlined in Figure 21.2? Is the executive overinvested in interpersonal roles to the detriment of decisional roles? Does the executive perform decisional roles with insufficient input from the informational roles? How is the executive integrating self (Professional House) and role (First Company House)? Is the executive's professional agenda expert matched to the floors of the First Company House, and does it contain resources for integrating different roles in a seamless performance?

While the executive is the expert with regard to interacting with the organization, the coach has the obligation to monitor the executive's performance in the First Company House. Clearly, she or he can do so only to the extent that she or he understands

TABLE 21.2

Positions in the First Company House, Highlighted by Questions Asked by the Coach

Executive's position

- Where in the organizational hierarchy is the executive "at home"—the operating core, technostructure, support staff, middle line, or strategic apex—and what, consequently, is his or her formal authority and status?
- How does the executive relate to different, possibly shifting, strata of the organization?
- What, on account of his home base, are the executive's interpersonal, informational, and decision-making roles?
- What, for the executive, are the privileged floors and rooms of the First Company House (where he or she spends most of his or her time)?
- Is the executive's decision about where to spend most of his or her time in keeping with his or her mission?
- What rooms of the floors of the First Company House (e.g., gender, ethnicity) does the executive find hard to acknowledge existence of or enter?
- How far can the executive take the organizational configuration "as object," thus having a perspective on his or her situatedness?
- In what roles does the executive function deficiently, given his or her general mandate in the organization?
- What defenses, or lack of analytical skills, hinder the executive from functioning efficiently in one or more of his or her roles?
- On what floor, or floors, of the Professional House does the executive's "stuckness" (regarding role performance) originate?
- What parallel processes—between executive/organization and executive/coach—are at work in the coaching relationship?

Coach's position

- Where in the organizational structure does the coach find him- or herself, as defined by his or her assignment, and the type of intervention he or she is asked to perform?
- What is the coach's formal authority and status in the organizational unit and the organization at large?
- Is there a "personal agenda" that hinders the coach to attend to the whereabouts, manner of intervention, and limits of the executive and, if so, on what level of the coach's Professional House does his or her "stuckness" originate?
- Which of the executive roles does the coach pay primary attention to, and at what point in time?
- How compatible ontic–developmentally are the partners of the coaching relationship, as evidenced by their position in the Professional House?
- Is the coach's personal culture compatible with that of the executive?
- In what way does the coach's sponsor restrict the potential of the coaching relationship?
- What transformation of the coaching relationship is required to improve developmental compatibility in the Company House?
- What kind of supervision does the coach need to improve his or her shaping of the executive's role performance?

the executive's organization structurally and politically, as seen by the executive. To be capable of such understanding, the coach must draw on prior organizational experience and on her or his knowledge from within the executive's Professional House. The issues the coach may come up against in this endeavor are summarized in Table 21.2.

It is clearly impossible for a coach to have proficiency and expertise on all floors and rooms of the First Company House and with regard to all issues engendered by the structural composition of a particular organization. However, ideally the coach has experience with variously configured organizations. Depending on his or her organizational experience as a schooled observer and change agent ("psychologist"), the coach may prefer to dwell on certain roles of the executive more than others (e.g., interpersonal roles). Therefore, the coach himself or herself may benefit from (peer) supervision. As holds true for a clinical supervisor, the coach needs to develop "a proficient methodology, theory, and personal ability to work in a variety of environments inhabited by culturally and configurationally diverse people" (Haber, 1996, p. 34). In the era of multinational corporations, bilingual or trilingual expertise and multicultural expertise are in especially high demand.

SECOND COMPANY HOUSE

There is more to an executive manager's career than being a performer of roles. The executive is also a thinker-in-action. More precisely, "Organizational reality is a socially constructed one, forged out of a consensus of vision and action that exists largely or completely in the minds of the organization's members" (Gioia & Sims, 1986, p. 384).

The way in which executives conceive of their organization and their capability of shifting perspective from one vantage point to another are crucial preconditions of integrated leadership. As pointed out by Bolman and Deal (1991), managers who cannot "reframe" organizational matters are failing in their task of developing a vision. Bolman and Deal exemplified one way in which to make the cognitive dimensions of executive functioning transparent. These authors distinguished four qualitatively different perspectives, or "frames," from which to conceptualize organizational events: (a) structural, (b) political, (c) human resource, and (d) symbolic. Since these frames underlie executive action, they are not only thought forms, but they define alternative action scenarios. Each organizational event has a structural, political, human-resource, and symbolic (i.e., cultural) implication. It is up to the executive to determine which of these implications is paramount in a given situation and the aspect or aspects to which he or she should pay primary attention.

When conceptualizing the organization in terms of a structural perspective, executive and coach adopt the viewpoint of rational systems theorists who emphasize organizational goals, roles, hierarchy of control, and division of labor in an organization. In and of itself, this perspective is highly limiting. It neglects the fact that the organization is a storehouse of human resources and that these resources raise issues of "the fit between people's needs, skills and values, on the one hand, and their formal roles and relationships, on the other" (Bolman & Deal, 1991, p. 9). Adding to this complexity is the fact that organizations often are divided into coalitions focused around issues of power and scarce resources. In this political perspective, "organizations are like jungles in which cooperation is achieved by managers who understand the uses of power, coalitions, bargaining, and conflict" (Bolman & Deal, 1991, p. 9). Finally, as Schein (1992) has demonstrated, the way in which an organization learns to solve its problems—that is, the organization's value system and rituals ("the way we do things around here")—is a powerful determinant of the executive's inner and outer task environment. In this fourth perspective, executive and coach are dealing with organizational culture. In terms of this mostly implicit symbolic sphere of organization, an executive must rely on images, drama, magic, and ritual to be effective (Bolman & Deal, 1991, p. 10).

As a leader, an executive cannot remain ensconced in any single one of these four perspectives. Rather, he or she must be able to deal with structure (structural frame), need (human-resource frame), conflict (political frame), and present loss or future success (symbolic frame) simultaneously (Bolman & Deal, 1991, p. 420). Each of the four frames gives rise to different scenarios, schemes of action, and interpretations of where the organization stands with regard to its employees and the outside world. Especially in "turbulent" market environments (Hall & Associates, 1996), the capability of refraining is in high demand as a leadership quality. First-order coaching, especially when carried out exclusively from a cognitive–behavioral perspective, is insufficient to safeguard an executive's creativity, since it does not account for his or her ability to use different, often mutually exclusive, cognitive maps. One might say that while first-order coaching deals with where the organization presently is from the executive's point of view, second-order coaching has more to do with where the executive needs to take the organization in the near or remote future. The coach extends not only the number of dimensions to deal with but the time window through which organizational matters are viewed. As a consequence, the executive's ability to generate integrated leadership (see Figure 21.1) is the major focus of coaching in the Second Company House.

A developmental difference between first- and second-order coaching also exists. Considering that the executive's ontic–developmental position informs his or her professional agenda, which in turn informs his or her interactions with the organization in the Company Houses, the executive may be more or less developmentally prepared to realize integrated leadership. Whether conceptualized in stage or nonstage terms, executives' developmental equilibrium must qualify them for transcending their own self-system (Kegan's Stage 5). Even if they are exquisite performers in the First Company House (roughly Kegan's Stages 3 and 4), they may fail as leaders. In fact, the First Company House and the Second Company House are somewhat antithetical in that they tap different developmental resources. While one can fine-tune a leader as a performer, one cannot always turn a performer into a leader. For this reason, what decisively matters in executive coaching, especially when undertaken for the purpose of succession management, is to be able to assess a performer's capability in terms of the Second Company House, where integrated leadership is topical. (At present, a constructive developmental theory of leadership does not exist.)

An optimal way in which to characterize second-order coaching is to see it as bringing about what Lewin called "reeducation" (Benne, 1976, p. 274). What is required in reframing is not only learning something new, but unlearning something overlearned:

> Lewin's analysis assumed that effective reeducation must affect the person being re-educated in three ways. The person's *cognitive* structure must be altered. And for Lewin, this structure included the person's modes of perception, his ways of seeing his physical and social worlds, as well as the facts, concepts, expectations, and beliefs with which a person thinks about the possibilities of action and the consequences of action in the phenomenal world. But re-education must involve modifying his *valences* and *values* as well as his cognitive structures. Valences and values include not alone his principles of what he should and should not do or consider doing—which along with his cognitive views of himself and his world are presented by his beliefs. They include also his attractions and aversions to his and other groups and their standards, his feelings in regard to status differences and authority, and his reactions to various sources of approval and disapproval. Re-education finally must affect a person's motoric actions, his repertoire of behavioral skills, and the degree of a person's conscious control of his body and social movements. (Benne, 1976, p. 274)

This encompassing view of reeducation seems to me most germane to what is required in second-order coaching. As Lewin implicitly made clear, second-order coaching aims at changes that originate in the self and move to all floors of the Professional House. Reeducation calls for cognitive, axiological, and behavioral changes simultaneously. However, neither Lewin nor Bolman and Deal took a developmental perspective on the abilities required for reeducation. They were unaware of the ontic–developmental constraints that restrict an executive's ability to be reeducated or the coach's ability to reeducate at a particular juncture along the life span trajectory.

The issues emerging in second-order coaching all regard the executive's readiness for transcending his or her own self-system and for taking new and multiple perspectives. Since individual frames are incomplete mental maps that, when used in isolation, distort reality, such cognitive flexibility is a requirement of leadership. As shown in Figure 21.3, different frames are based on different realities in an organization; they emphasize different aspects of its functioning. They also have varying degrees of salience in different situations. The structural perspective's emphasis on the organization's vertical and horizontal command structure is most salient in situations in which goals and information flow throughout the organization are clear, conflict and ambiguity are low, and there is legitimate authority. However, in times of conflict or turbulence, when scarce resources are at stake, and enduring differences between different coalitions in the organization emerge, the political frame is more apt for viewing the organization. In that situation, the executive is dealing with goal and value conflicts and possibly diffuse and unstable power. Other situations (e.g., downsizing) put in focus the fulfillment of human needs in the organization. The

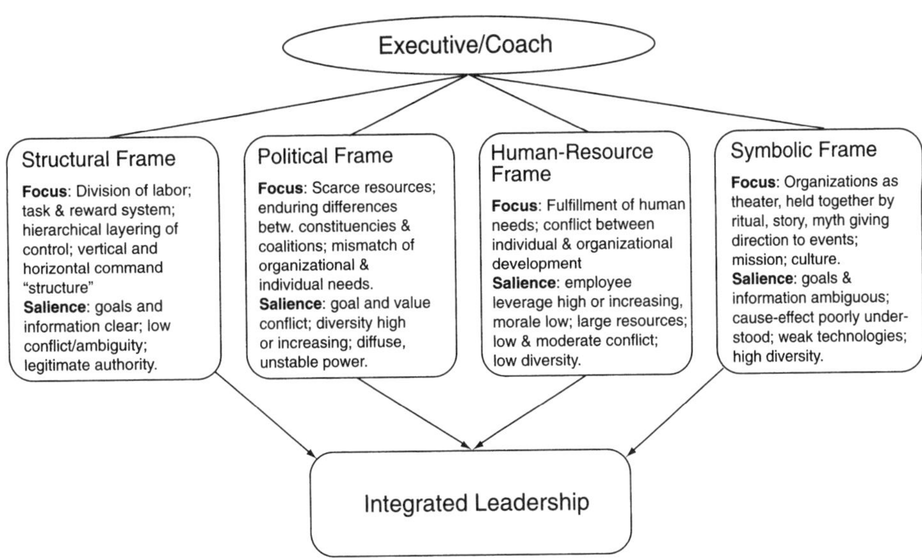

FIGURE 21.3. Incomplete maps as floors of the Second Company House (Bolman & Deal, 1991).

company is experiencing conflict between individual and organizational development, and employee morale is low. In such a situation, the most salient perspective for an executive to take may be the human-resource frame. This is again different from a situation marked by high diversity and lack of transparency of cause and effect, when goals and information are ambiguous and diversity is high. In that case, the executive as a culture bearer might benefit from taking a symbolic perspective and from using mission, symbol, ritual, or story to give direction to events in the organization.

Cognitive flexibility is also required for defining policy. As shown in Figure 21.4, it is the task of executive management to synthesize salient frames into an integrated change policy. Each frame, once adopted, suggests a different approach to solving organizational problems. In order to ascertain the salience of a frame, certain key variables need to be scrutinized (Bolman & Deal, 1991). According to Bolman and Deal, such variables might be (a) motivation and commitment to the company, (b) technical quality of the required decision, (c) uncertainty and ambiguity experienced in the company, and (d) conflict and diversity in determining organizational functioning. As Figure 21.4 indicates, executive actions flowing from the structural frame have to do with realigning and renegotiating formal patterns and policies in order to establish clarity in organizational roles and relationships (i.e., the

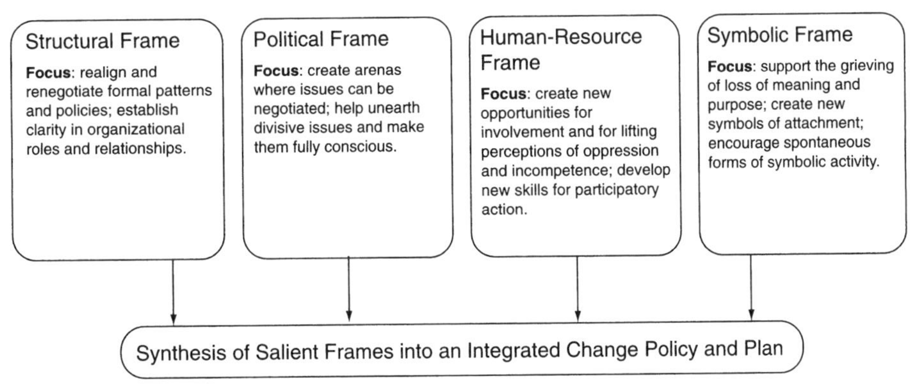

FIGURE 21.4. Initiatives for reframing organizations in the Second Company House (Bolman & Deal, 1991).

TABLE 21.3

Positions in the Second Company House, Highlighted by Questions Asked by the Coach

Executive's position

- Which frame is the "home frame" of this executive?
- Why is the executive ensconced in this limited way of seeing company matters (look at floors in the Professional House, especially the professional agenda)?
- How does the executive's home frame limit his or her effectiveness in the Company House?
- What action scenario is suggested by the frame that is most salient in the situation the executive finds him- or herself in?
- How does the executive's home frame give rise to the parallel process experienced by the coach in the Professional House?
- How would a different frame, or set of frames, help the executive enter rooms and floors of the First Company House that are presently difficult to access or locked?
- What changes in self and professional agenda (Professional House) have to occur for the executive to become reeducated to a more integrated type of leadership?
- What are the basic cognitive, emotional, axiological, and/or behavioral limitations that hinder the executive from realizing integrated leadership as evidenced in the Professional House?
- What organizational experiences (including failure) could prepare the executive for lasting reeducative changes in his or her Professional House?

Coach's position

- How can I demonstrate to the executive the limitations of his or her preferred frame without offending his or her authority and sense of expertise?
- How can I empower the executive to try out a different frame?
- How can I stop defensive parallel processes of the executive by attending to the executive's home frame that lends him or her energy?
- How does my own personal culture and coaching strategy reinforce the executive's blind spots in the Professional House, making multiperspectival thinking impossible?
- How can I myself become reeducated to model integrated leadership for the executive (e.g., through supervision)?
- Am I a sufficient ontic-developmental match for this executive with regard to his or her position in the Second Company House? (It is here that questions of professional ethics come in.)

floors of the First Company House). A political frame suggests that management should create arenas where issues can be negotiated and divisive issues unearthed and made fully conscious. By contrast, adopting a human-resource frame entails the creation of new opportunities for involvement and the development of new skills for participatory action. Finally, executive endorsement of a symbolic frame would suggest the creation of new symbols of attachment (as in a family), the introduction or reinforcement of ritual, and support for grieving loss of meaning and purpose (e.g., after downsizing).

This is the arena of second-order coaching. In Table 21.3, I enumerate some of the questions to be asked by the coach in order to assist the executive in learning to reframe his or her organization for the sake of realizing integrated leadership.

In sum, in second-order coaching, reeducation is the primary responsibility of the coach. As indicated by Lewin, the questions in Table 21.3 pertain not only to changes in cognitive structure but equally to changes in the axiological viewpoints and behavioral stance of the executive in both houses.

CONCLUSION

In this chapter, I have defined coaching as the multidirectional ability to observe executive–organization interactions in two related mental spaces called the Professional House and the Company House, for the purpose of bringing about not only adaptive but transformative change. My main question has involved not *how to do* coaching but *what happens* in coaching from a cognitive–science point of view. I have not posed as a coaching guru: Within the present model, any number of how-to approaches can be elaborated, depending on the knowledge and ontic–developmental position of coach and executive. I have conceived of coaching in analogy to clinical supervision, asking "How does the executive interact with his or her client system, the organization?" As a consequence, I have viewed coaching as "professional leadership that monitors, assists, redirects, and amplifies an . . . [executive's] work . . . and promotes the conceptual, intuitive, personal, and methodological skills necessary for professional development" in the workplace (Haber, 1996, p. 34). I have amplified the classical supervisory view of coaching by integrating it with the adult-developmental literature in conceptualizing the Professional House (especially Kegan, 1982, 1994) and the theory of organizational cognition in conceptualizing the Company Houses (especially Bolman & Deal, 1991; Mintzberg, 1989).

On the basis of this theoretical foundation, I have introduced a model of executive coaching as a set of cognitive maps for describing, analyzing, understanding, and tuning coaching activity. I have conceived of these maps as tools for observing executive–organization interactions in the cognitive–affective domains called the houses. Implicitly, I have criticized cognitive–behavioral and psychodynamic approaches to coaching for failing to recognize the life span developmental dimension of executive development. Two links have been the focus of my discussion: the link between self-agenda and professional agenda in the Professional House and the reciprocal relationship between the Professional House and the Company Houses (which is built on the first link). I have emphasized the fact that coach and executive inhabit their own Professional House and Company House and that it is the developmental compatibility of the two parties to the alliance that guarantees lasting, in contrast to merely adaptive, change.

Several caveats are in order. I am aware that I have neglected a host of issues pertaining to the organizational logistics of strategic executive development, especially succession management (McCall, 1998; Sloan, 1998). However, many of the requirements of coaching defined by the present model equally pertain to the issues neglected here. Furthermore, the model, while it attempts to transcend "practice theories of coaching executives" (see chap. 10, this volume) in the direction of cognitive science, is in need of empirical validation (to a small extent, this validation has been attempted in Laske, 1999, on grounds prepared in Laske, 1977).

Referring back to my distinction between "agentic" and "ontic" development in the workplace, it seems to me that the ontic–developmental model of coaching outlined earlier is valuable for two reasons. First, it deepens the theoretical discourse about coaching from a psychological as well as an organizational perspective. Second, it defines ontic–developmental constraints on agentic change efforts as well as on coaching effectiveness. From my point of view, most of the competency models used in present-day coaching, however "strategically" matched to board-certified business requirements, read like wish lists without any developmental foundation whatsoever. Equally, present uses of 360-degree feedback are developmentally blind in that they neglect the fact that an executive's acceptance and processing of feedback depend on his or her ontic–developmental status quo (developmental grasp). For example, in cases in which an executive's self-identity is made up of internalized valuations of others, as in Kegan's Stage 3, use of a 360-degree feedback instrument (reinforcing that developmental position) could easily promote developmental arrest. From my constructive–developmental vantage point, I also question the utility of the notion of "executive talent" that is substantiated by nothing other than previous performance results couched in the adevelopmental language of personality traits and that neglects the executive's developmental status and potential.

Lack of developmental know-how, which may be tolerable in coaching for performance (First Company House), is inadmissible in coaching for succession management (Second Company House), in which integrated leadership is central. For second-order coaching, then, neither a cognitive–behavioral (strictly performance-oriented) nor a psychodynamic ("personality"-oriented) strategy suffices per se. Rather, a constructive–developmental approach to coaching is a prerequisite for any wide-scoped coaching strategy aiming at both Company Houses and cognizant of the level

TABLE 21.4

Topics of Research Issuing From the Present Model

- The way in which the developmental status quo of executive and coach manifests itself in their professional agenda (see Laske, 1999).
- The relationship between stage and nonstage conceptualizations of executive development as adult development.
- The notion of (ontic–)developmental compatibility of coach and executive.
- The way in which integrated leadership (Second Company House) depends on self- and other awareness (Professional House), on one hand, and role integration (First Company House), on the other.
- The way in which executive performance profiles (First Company House) are associated with the frame(s) privileged by an executive (Second Company House).
- The nature of developmental recommendations that can inform optimal coaching strategies and their adjustment to what is ontic-developmentally possible for an executive at a given time.
- The ontic-developmental fingerprint of an organization's culture, strategic business requirements, and change policy.
- The attunement of strategic business requirements to the ontic-developmental profile of the executive team.
- The elaboration of constructive-developmental assessment methods (stage or nonstage) that can be integrated with existing methods of executive assessment before, during, and after coaching.
- The ontic-developmental prerequisites and implications of cognitive–behavioral (agentic) development plans.

of evolving self in the Professional House. My critique does not entail, however, that cognitive–behavioral and/or psychodynamic approaches to coaching are inferior to a constructive–developmental approach. Not only are there situations in which one or the other approach is pragmatically optimal. More important, scientifically validated coaching practices will emerge only once coaches versed in all of the three approaches have reached a level of clinical–developmental expertise sufficient to indicate to them when and with whom to use what approach (Havens, 1987). At such time, professional standards for coaching will also emerge.

The uniqueness of the present model lies in the fact that it deals with what happens in coaching (not with how to do coaching) and is thus foundational (practice independent). The model is also not bound to stage theories of adult development (e.g., Kegan, 1994) but equally allows for nonstage approaches (e.g., Basseches, 1984). The model assumes an intrinsic link between self-agenda and professional agenda; it sees all three coaching houses as being ontic–developmentally determined. Coaching is conceived as a personal and professional relationship that is not simply informative (promoting learning) but potentially transformative (promoting adult development).

At present, a constructive–developmental theory of coaching as applied adult development does not exist. Without such a theory, developmental coaching will remain at its present stage of infancy. Table 21.4 lists some of the topics in need of empirical research. In addressing some of these topics, the "agentic" and "ontic" streams of executive development could cease to be polarized, and a developmental science of human resources could be established. Clearly, the lack of ontic–developmental thinking in coaching, and in executive development generally, says something about how practitioners conceptualize adulthood, including their own. The barrier to making coaching a developmentally transformative enterprise may therefore lie in the limited view practitioners hold of their own development as adults.

References

Argyris, C., Putnam, R., & McLain Smith, D. (1987). *Action science.* San Francisco: Jossey-Bass.

Basseches, M. A. (1984). *Dialectical thinking and adult development.* Norwood, NJ: Ablex.

Basseches, M. (1989). Toward a constructive–developmental understanding of the dialectics of individuality and irrationality. In D. A. Kramer & M. J. Bopp (Eds.), *Transformation in clinical and developmental psychology* (pp. 188–209). New York: Springer.

Benne, K. D. (1976). The processes of re-education: An assessment of Kurt Lewin's views. In W. G. Bennis, K. D. Benne, & R. Chin (Eds.), *The planning of change* (4th ed., pp. 272–283). Fort Worth, TX: Holt, Rinehart & Winston.

Bolman, L. G., & Deal, T. E. (1991). *Reframing organizations: Artistry, choice, and leadership.* San Francisco: Jossey-Bass.

Commons, M. L., Demick, J., & Goldberg, C. (Eds.). (1996). *Clinical approaches to adult development.* Norwood, NJ: Ablex.

Gioia, D. A., & Sims, H. P., Jr. (1986). Introduction: Social cognition in organizations. In H. P. Sims, Jr., & D. A. Gioia (Eds.), *The thinking organization* (pp. 1–19). San Francisco: Jossey-Bass.

Haber, R. (1996). *Dimensions of psychotherapy supervision.* New York: Norton.

Hall, D. T., & Associates. (1996). *The career is dead—Long live the career.* San Francisco: Jossey-Bass.

Havens, L. (1987). *Approaches to the mind.* Cambridge, MA: Harvard University Press.

Hodgetts, W. H. (1994). *Coming of age: How male and female managers transform relationships with authority at midlife.* Unpublished doctoral dissertation, Harvard Graduate School of Education, Cambridge, MA.

Kaplan, R. E., Drath, W. H., & Kofodomis, J. R. (1991). *Beyond ambition.* San Francisco: Jossey-Bass.

Kegan, R. (1982). *The evolving self.* Cambridge, MA: Harvard University Press.

Kegan, R. (1994). *In over our heads.* Cambridge, MA: Harvard University Press.

Kohlberg, L. (1984). *Essays on moral development: Vol. 2. The psychology of moral development: Moral stages, their nature and validity.* San Francisco: Harper & Row.

Kohlberg, L., & Armon, C. (1984). Three types of stage models used in the study of adult development. In M. L. Commons, F. A. Richards, & C. Armon (Eds.), *Beyond formal operations: Vol. 1. Late adolescent and adult cognitive development* (pp. 383–394). New York: Praeger.

Lahey, L., Souvaine, E., Kegan, R., Goodman, R., & Felix, S. (1983). *A guide to the subject–object interview: Its administration and interpretation.* Unpublished manuscript, Harvard Graduate School of Education, Cambridge, MA.

Laske, O. (1997). Four uses of self in cognitive science. In P. Pylkkanen, P. Pylkko, & A. Hautarnaki (Eds.), *Brain, mind, and physics* (pp. 13–25). Amsterdam: IOS Press.

Laske, O. (1999). *Transformative effects of coaching on executives' professional agenda.* Unpublished doctoral dissertation, Massachusetts School of Professional Psychology, Boston.

Levinson, D. J., Darrow, C. N., Klein, E. B., Levinson, M. H., & McKee, B. (1978). *The seasons of a man's life.* New York: Ballantine Books.

Loevinger, J. (1976). *Ego development.* San Francisco: Jossey-Bass.

Luborsky, L., Crits-Christoph, P., Mintz, J., & Auerbach, A. (1988). *Who will benefit from psychotherapy?* New York: Basic Books.

Martin, I. (1996). *From couch to corporation.* New York: Wiley.

McCall, M. W. (1998). *High flyers.* Cambridge, MA: Harvard Business School Press.

Mintzberg, H. (1981, January–February). Organization design: Fashion or fit? *Harvard Business Review,* 103–115.

Mintzberg, H. (1989). *Mintzberg on management.* New York: Free Press.

Piaget, J. (1970). *Structuralism.* New York: Basic Books.

Pratt, L. L. (1993). *Becoming a psychotherapist: Implications of Kegan's model for counselor development and psychotherapy supervision.* Amherst: Department of Psychology, University of Massachusetts.

Rogers, L., & Kegan, R. (1990). Mental growth and mental health as distinct concepts in the study of developmental psychopathology. In D. Keating & Rosen (Eds.), *Constructivist approaches to psychopathology* (pp. 103–147). Hillsdale, NJ: Erlbaum.

Schein, E. (1992). *Organizational culture and leadership* (2nd ed.). San Francisco: Jossey-Bass.

Sloan, E. (1998). *Succession management briefing.* Boston: Personnel Decisions International.

Weick, K. E., & Bougon, M. G. (1986). Organizations as cognitive maps. In H. P. Sims & D. A. Gioia (Eds.), *The thinking organization* (pp. 102–135). San Francisco: Jossey-Bass.

PART III

COACHING CHALLENGES, METHODS, AND STANDARDS

Part III offers well-articulated explanations of the challenges, methods, and standards of executive coaching—a rich and varied collection of chapters that has already inspired and guided the work of the consulting psychologist who has decided to coach. The reader has the opportunity to learn what coaching is and is not and will discover a wealth of ideas and examples that should advance his or her knowledge of and skills in the arena of executive coaching.

Kampa and White (2002), in summarizing some known empirical studies of coaching, reported that "coaching results in increased learning, increased self-awareness and development, and more effective leadership" (p. 153). Perhaps the chapters in this section will aid in efforts to better understand how or why; this material may also help address the fact that "there remains a great deal of confusion and mystery as to what actually happens behind closed doors when executives engage with a coach" (chap. 39, p. 414). Almost a decade ago, Kilburg (1997) reminded us that "executive coaching is one of the most challenging assignments for the consultant, and it is difficult at best" (p. 298). This condition has not changed, and the concepts, methods, and techniques described in this collection should be most helpful to the many practitioners of executive coaching.

Kilburg (chap. 22) gets Part III started with a report on the dearth of psychological literature that speaks to intervention adherence in executive coaching. In this search, no references were found, so he turned to the health care literature that is relevant to coaching; this literature was used to frame the article. His chapter offers a model of coaching effectiveness, and he addresses in detail components of an effective adherence protocol (p. 249). Major problems coaches encounter that contribute to nonadherence are discussed.[1]

Katz and Miller (chap. 23) call attention to the role that the executive coach can play in assisting senior leaders in learning new competencies as they are faced with organizational culture changes. They identify partnership competencies, key focus areas for leaders and their coaches, and ground rules for senior learning groups. A brief case study is included.

Hart, Blattner, and Leipsic (chap. 24) share the results of a seven-question study regarding the distinctions and overlaps of therapy and coaching; 30 professionals were

[1] This chapter was chosen by the *Consulting Psychology Journal: Practice and Research* editors and editorial review board as the "Most Outstanding Article: 2001," and a citation was presented to Richard R. Kilburg in 2002 at the 110th Annual Convention of the American Psychological Association, Chicago.

interviewed, all of whom practiced coaching, therapy, or both. Issues that warrant further exploration were identified and discussed.

Richard (chap. 25) makes a case for using Lazarus's multimodal therapy model to ensure a holistic approach in executive coaching. The coach would use the seven dimensions of this model to guide an assessment and set the stage for developmental coaching interventions. A brief case is used to illustrate the application of the model in executive coaching. Axelrod (chap. 26) summarizes general principles of adult psychological development that appear to have broad applicability in consulting with executives. Two case examples, one dealing with midlife transition and another with late middle age, are used to show how adult development core issues and themes inform leadership functioning and can provide guidance for the executive coach as well as the executive.

Sperry (chap. 27) describes six commonly noted character structures in executives that are particularly relevant for coaches, given that character is largely learned and therefore can be changed. A case example is used to illustrate consultation implications.

Richard (chap. 28) proposes that the expanding role of the psychologically oriented executive coach include fostering innovation. The coach is seen as a helper who deliberately teaches the skills of operationally defining problems and of rational creative problem-solving techniques. Examples are provided.

Quick and Macik-Frey (chap. 29) propose a health-enhancing, developmental model of coaching that is anchored in a process of deep interpersonal communication. They argue that this model is neither superficial nor therapeutic in approach. Instead, they outline a two-tiered model of executive communication that speaks directly to the executive's need to deal with his or her more complex, emotional, and conflicted nature. They feel that much of executive coaching fails to get behind the role or "mask" of the executive and misses the opportunity to work with the authentic human being behind the mask.

Garman, Whiston, and Zlatoper (chap. 30) present the results of a study analyzing 72 articles on executive coaching. Their review of the literature reported that favorable views of executive coaching far exceeded unfavorable ones. The perspectives of nonpractitioners, the extent to which psychologists have an identified role, and the nature of the perceptions of psychologists as executive coaches are discussed. The ongoing need for definitions and standards is flagged.

Brotman, Liberi, and Wasylyshyn (chap. 31) provide what still represents a unique contribution to the literature—a first-class effort to define and discuss the essential skills, competencies, and experiences of the psychologist who practices executive coaching. They observe that

> despite its growing importance, executive coaching remains an unregulated, poorly defined arena. With no licensing, credentialing, or professional designation for executive coaches to achieve or maintain, the retaining party or organization would be aided by a set of guidelines to identify competent, ethical professionals when searching for an executive coach. (p. 324)

They then provide a solid first step with the identification of 12 core competencies and go on to suggest requisite tactics, tools, and training.

Diedrich's brief chapter (chap. 32) ends Part III and speaks to the coaching of executive teams rather than of the individual executive. He reminds us that the primary role of the coach is still the facilitation of understanding and learning even with the client as a team. Practice guidelines are included.

Part III presents chapters that address coaching challenges, methods, and standards. The media perception study by Garman et al. (chap. 30) reminds the reader that although media attention has been increasing rapidly in recent years, the results of their study suggest that "psychology training is neither regularly nor universally recognized as useful or even relevant to practice in the field of executive coaching" (p. 320). They go on to note that "the typical article on executive coaching does not identify any particular skill base, outside of some business content knowledge, as in any way essential to effective practice, regardless of the nature of the engagement" (pp. 321–322).

Other recent literature reviews report additional concerns. Kilburg (chap. 22), in a search for relevant literature dealing with adherence or compliance phenomena, notes that "the silence of the empirical literature on most subjects related to coaching executives remains one of the most stunning characteristics of the field" (p. 244). Diedrich (chap. 32) voices another concern in sharing his observation that the literature of consulting seldom "offers any guidance with regard to another subarea or specialty—the coaching of executive teams" (p. 329).

Hart et al. (chap. 24), in describing the controversy of coaching versus therapy, speak to key categories of inquiry that warrant further consideration in the field of coaching: concerns about legality and accountability, the importance of adequate training, and the need for supervision.

So where are we? In their conclusion, Brotman et al. (chap. 31) suggest that

> psychologists have a duty to define the competencies required to achieve sustained behavior change through the medium of executive coaching and to be proactive in conveying these standards of competence to the public. Only in this way can this fast-developing realm within psychology reach its full potential as an invaluable resource for business executives. (p. 327)

These observations appear to describe appropriately and accurately the continuing need to better define standards within the field, further inform and educate our clients, and be more accountable for our behavior in the still-emerging arena of executive coaching.

References

Kampa, S., & White, R. P. (2002). The effectiveness of executive coaching: What we know & what we still need to know. In R. L. Lowman (Ed.), *Handbook of organizational consulting psychology* (pp. 139–158). San Francisco: Jossey-Bass.

Kilburg, R. R. (1997). Coaching and executive character: Core problems and basic approaches. *Consulting Psychology Journal: Practice and Research, 49*, 281–285.

CHAPTER 22

FACILITATING INTERVENTION ADHERENCE IN EXECUTIVE COACHING: A MODEL AND METHODS

Richard R. Kilburg

THE CASE OF THE DEMORALIZED OPERATIONS DIRECTOR

"I almost canceled this appointment," Jennifer Wilson, the stately, 30-something, African American director of operations for a professional services firm said as she entered the conference room and sat down across from me.

"Could you tell me why?" I responded, feeling the rising threat of a coaching assignment about to blow up in my face.

"Quite frankly, I have a job interview at another company this afternoon. I'm exhausted from all the work around here. I can't get any help despite asking repeatedly because Charlie has no appreciation for what I do around here. I'm doing the job of a chief operations officer but I have the wrong title and I'm being paid like a line manager. He talked to me about a promotion last year, but has taken no action."

"Have you approached him?"

"No, coach, I haven't talked to him and I'm not going to. If he doesn't value me enough to follow through on his promises and our well-respected and very visible CEO, Mr. Watson, doesn't care enough to hold him to the commitment, I see no reason to pursue it. Honestly, at this point, I don't think I want Charlie to have anything to do with my career."

Jennifer and I had been working together on her role in the subsidiary and her relationship with the president, Charles Piedmont. I consulted with him and the company CEO, James Watson, as well. Jennifer's relationship with Charlie had never been good. He was reserved, intellectual, and too busy with his own work in an understaffed and highly successful subsidiary of the company. Charlie had been pushed by James to promote Jennifer to the position of director of operations 2 years previously, based partly on an organizational review that he had conducted of the subsidiary and partly on my quiet recommendation to him. Charlie wanted to hire someone from the outside but couldn't fill the position in time. Jennifer was moved into the job with virtually no change in her previous duties and no significant increase in salary or resources. At the time, she saw it as a good career move. She also knew that her interpersonal skills, attention to detail, and ability to see the big picture of how all the elements of the operation interacted would make the company perform better and improve the quality of work life for everyone, including herself. She had, in fact, significantly improved the flow of work and the quality of teamwork, and, with the cooperation of her colleagues, she had solved some long-standing logistics nightmares for the organization. She did this by working very long hours, pulling the resources of other key players in the organization together to focus on bottlenecks and problems, and fending off the least productive and most intrusive members of the management team.

These efforts had left her drained, angry, and increasingly cynical about the company in general and Charlie in particular. We had discussed her promotion in our coaching session the month before, and it was then that she had first said that she did not want Charlie involved. At that time, she was unsure about the value of an additional appointment with me. I pursued the matter with her and made sure that the meeting stayed on both of our calendars. I was quite concerned that her experience of burnout was real, and I encouraged her to go to both Charlie and James with her concerns. Instead, she had started to conduct a job search.

"Would you tell me about the job interview?" I asked.

"It's with a small competitor of ours across town. They are nice people. Their company makes money but is far less visible and successful than us. They are interviewing me to be the president of the same type of operation that we run here. It's smaller, slower, but it would pay more and I'd have a social life again."

I could hear her discouragement and the anger in her voice. I had been and remained concerned that she would act out these feelings by leaving the company. I wasn't sure that she really wanted to do that, and I had the sense that it would not be good for her career in a number of ways.

"You've worked a long time to become a president in this company. Do you think that leaving now is in your best interest?"

"I don't know. I just feel that I can't stand it here anymore. I've had it."

We spent the remaining portion of the hour talking about what she would be looking for in the interview. Occasionally, she would express her continuing discouragement with her existing position and the treatment she had been receiving. At the end of the appointment, I felt a strong need to confront the potential self-destructive element of this action.

"I'm really concerned that your feelings right now may be clouding your judgment. I'm especially worried that you've made no attempt to talk to Charlie or James, and that you really don't know what the company's leadership wants to do about your promotion."

"If they want to promote me, they can. I'm not going to go in there and beg that man."

"I rarely suggest such a step, but in this case, what do you think about me going to talk to James about the situation? I think that it's very unlikely that he knows how you feel or about the potential for losing you. I'm sure if he knew, he would take appropriate action."

I watched Jennifer struggle with her answer. She took her time as she often did with complex issues.

"What would you tell him?" she asked.

"I'd simply describe the situation as I see it. You are burning out, discouraged in your working relationship with Charlie, disappointed that neither Charlie nor James have followed through on their commitments to promote you, and seriously thinking about leaving the company very soon. With your permission, I'd strongly encourage James to contact you directly to hear from you and to explore the issues in the promotion."

I knew this would not be an easy thing for Jennifer. She carried herself with a lot of pride and had very high standards. She constantly held herself to impossible expectations and met them far more often than not. As a result, she could be very hard and critical of others whom she saw as lacking in similar dedication and commitment. After an aching silence that stretched for a couple of minutes, she answered.

"You can call James and give him that message. I don't know what good it will do, but you can call him. In the meantime, I have a job interview to go to."

Jennifer stood and held out her hand. I shook it, and we both walked to the door of the conference room in which we had been meeting. As we exited, she said, "I'm glad I didn't cancel this appointment."

Later that day, I succeeded in getting a telephone call through to James. He was both surprised to hear from me and concerned about losing Jennifer. He said that he would take immediate action and thanked me for coming to him with the situation. Several days later, Jennifer called me and reported that James had called her personally and spent over an hour on the phone with her. He had made a commitment to directly and personally support her promotion in the next subsidiary presidency to open, which he expected within the year. He had also encouraged her to talk yet again to Charlie about his difficulties in listening to her, and he said that he would do so as well. Jennifer thanked me for calling James. She said that she felt relieved because she did not really want to leave the company. She told the competitor that she was grateful for their offer but that she would be staying where she was. When I got off the phone, I too felt relieved that my additional intervention with James had worked to everyone's benefit. It is very unusual for me to take such action, but in this case it was both needed and proved to be the right thing to do. I'm happy to report that Jennifer is now in the process of being promoted in her company and seems quite pleased with the situation that she will be going into in the very near future.

This case is one of several that I could have chosen to open this chapter on intervention adherence in executive coaching. They all have similar characteristics, namely, that because I took specific action to ensure the continuation of the coaching relationship and the coaching process, the client either made constructive gains in his or her job or avoided serious and potentially long-term problems. During the course of the past several years, I have become increasingly interested in this phenomenon. It almost goes without saying that the lives of executives are frequently overwhelming, complex, and difficult. There are daily opportunities for significant failures in their job performance and personal situations. Most of them muddle through with little or no external assistance except that which is available from colleagues, friends, or family members. Those few who choose to pursue coaching provide themselves with an additional safety net, yet there are myriad opportunities for that very net to fail.

In this situation with Jennifer, my simple insistence in keeping a regularly scheduled appointment provided an opportunity for a pivotal moment in her career. Discovering the depth of her discouragement, confronting the potential misjudgment that she was considering, offering an additional supportive intervention, and following through on that commitment will lead to her being promoted in her company. This outcome is positive for her, for Charlie (her boss), for the CEO of the company, and for the organization itself. I believe that we as coaches and consultants often misapprehend how important and powerful simple interventions can be in the lives of our clients and their organizations. Careful attention to intervention adherence as an issue in consulting and coaching will play a major role in increasing the long-term effectiveness of our efforts on behalf of our clients.

The purposes of this chapter are to provide a brief review of the intervention adherence literature as it seems relevant to executive coaching, present a definition of intervention adherence in executive coaching and a model of coaching effectiveness, examine some of the potential elements of an adherence protocol that can be used by practitioners, and succinctly explore some of the major problems that may adversely affect the adherence process in coaching.

INTERVENTION ADHERENCE IN EXECUTIVE COACHING—SOME RELEVANT LITERATURE

In earlier works (Kilburg, 1996, 2000), I noted the general lack of empirical literature in support of approaches to executive coaching. Despite the inattention to research, new books on coaching seem to arrive on a regular basis (Bergquist, Merritt, & Phillips, 1999; Dotlich & Cairo, 1999; Hargrove, 2000; Hudson, 1999; O'Neill, 2000). Each of them promises to help consultants assist their executive clients in managing their jobs, careers, and organizations. Each of them quite rightly speaks to the experience base of the author or authors. Each of them offers suggestions for methods and suggests ways to overcome problems that coaches encounter with clients and that clients have in their organizations. None of them speaks specifically to the issues of client adherence to coaching interventions or the long-term outcomes of coaching activities. In an effort to review the literature for this chapter beyond the latest books available, no references to adherence or compliance phenomena addressed to coaching work with managers or leaders were found in the psychological literature. With the exception of a few recent dissertations by graduate students (Colvin, 1997; Galley-Eggeman, 1997; Johnson, 1997; Meyer, 1997), the silence of the empirical literature on most subjects related to coaching executives remains one of the most stunning characteristics of the field.

Undeterred by these findings, I pushed into the health care literature, where I found a virtual cornucopia of references on treatment adherence. In fact, the literature is so extensive that it has reached a point where excellent books that summarize the general findings and approaches are available. Because the focus of this chapter is on adherence and coaching executives, I make no effort to summarize this extensive research base. However, in the desire to point to empirically grounded results that have proven useful in a related service arena, I provide some references to research that I believe are extremely relevant to the work of consultants with their clients. This literature is then used to help frame the subsequent sections of this chapter, in which I offer some reasonable advice to practitioners who are coaching executives.

Blackwell (1997) stated that "over 12,000 articles have been published on the topic of compliance in the past 25 years" (p. 9). He went on to describe five major models that have been developed to study and understand the challenges of adherence in health care. These include the biomedical, operant behavioral, educational, health beliefs, and self-regulatory systems models (Leventhal & Cameron, 1987). Of particular relevance to work on coaching, the two best-studied areas of adherence research have consistently focused on pediatrics and psychiatry, both involving the most difficult single subject in the entire literature, namely maintaining changes made in human behavior.

Some of the most challenging human problems to treat involve alcoholism and other forms of substance abuse. Marlatt and Gordon (1985) reported studies demonstrating that 90% of alcoholics treated for the problem relapse within 2 years of treatment. They reviewed a wide variety of approaches to take with addicted individuals to assist in the maintenance of sobriety. Similarly, Daley and Zuckoff (1999) in a more recent book offered an excellent summary of counseling approaches that can be used to help this population comply with the long-term demands of treatment for addictive disorders. Irvin, Bowers, Dunn, and Wang (1999) provided a meta-analytic review of the relapse prevention literature for substance abuse disorders and suggested that these methodologies generally had shown positive results with these difficult populations and that there were several mediating variables of note. I believe that these studies are of extreme relevance to coaching executives. For after decades of research and practice with these most difficult problems in human behavior, it has been clearly demonstrated that relapse prevention and adherence methodologies are crucial to maintaining therapeutic and behavioral gains. The implications for those of us working with relatively normal clients who are trying to change problem behaviors or develop new skills are that adherence issues must become a core component of the planning of coaching interventions and that long-term, positive outcomes of our coaching work will ultimately depend in large measure on the strength and sophistication of our own adherence knowledge and skill.

In a parallel line of research on psychotherapy, a significant number of studies have focused on the problem of patients who prematurely drop out of psychotherapy treatment. Wierzbicki and Pekarik (1993) completed a meta-analysis of 125 studies of this type and found an average of 47% of patients leave treatment prematurely. Reis and Brown (1999), in a complex review of the issue of premature termination, found that 30% to 60% of patients drop out of treatment before it is completed, and they offered a serious and insightful look at a large number of variables that appear to be related to this problem. The literature reported is very contradictory, with a number of methodological difficulties, but studies of the working alliance between therapist and clients, patient satisfaction with treatment, and patient likeability have demonstrated that these issues are critical to preventing the dropout problem. Results suggest that reducing the difference between therapist and client perspectives regarding treatment would help reduce premature termination. Brogan, Prochaska, and Prochaska (1999) and Piper et al. (1999) echoed these suggestions in recently reported studies in this area.

After spending a number of months reading in this extraordinarily extensive area of research and practice, I continue to feel like a relative novice when considering the enormous array of variables associated with whether coaching clients actually benefit long term from services delivered to them by well-intentioned and extraordinarily well-trained professionals. At the most bewildering times, it has felt to me as though long-term, positive outcomes of coaching activities might well be merely a form of random chance. One does one's best with a client and then lets nature take its course, figuring that somewhere between one third to one half of the people one has provided services to will continue to benefit from the work years later and that the rest will not. This was not exactly an exhilarating prospect, yet work with my own clients such as Jennifer strongly suggests that such probably will be the case if I do not begin to pay closer attention to the adherence problem. The complexity and extent of the adherence literature in health care also contributed to my bewilderment. Just where could a practitioner who was reasonably motivated to address this issue begin to change his or her own behavior?

The best current answer to this question can be found in Meichenbaum and Turk's (1987) guidebook on treatment adherence. This was the best organized and most comprehensive resource found in my examination of resources available on this subject. They successfully reviewed most of the literature up to the time of publication, but even more important, they presented it in easy-to-access and understandable tables. In addition, they took great pains to organize the material in ways that are most meaningful to practitioners. In reading their book, I found a remarkable number of practical ideas and suggestions that come straight from the empirically based research of hundreds of other scientists and practitioners who have struggled with the issue of trying to ensure that their investments in helping their clients would actually pay off in the long term. This resource is highly recommended to anyone who is doing coaching or consulting with organizational clients as a way of developing one's thinking about the long-term outcomes of behavioral interventions.

A MODEL OF COACHING EFFECTIVENESS

As I thought about the issues involved in the role of adherence in coaching executives, it slowly dawned on me that compliance was but one of a number of components that contribute to whether a coaching assignment has an effective outcome. This pushed me to consider what goes into making a good coaching intervention. As I pondered the large and diverse number of variables that probably contribute to overall effectiveness, they slowly organized themselves into a set of eight key elements: client commitment to the path of progressive development, the coach's commitment to the same path, the characteristics of the client's problems and issues, the structure of the coaching containment, the client–coach relationship, the coaching interventions used by the practitioner, the adherence protocol, and the nature of the coach's and client's organizational settings. Figure 22.1 illustrates the overlapping and interpenetrating characteristics of

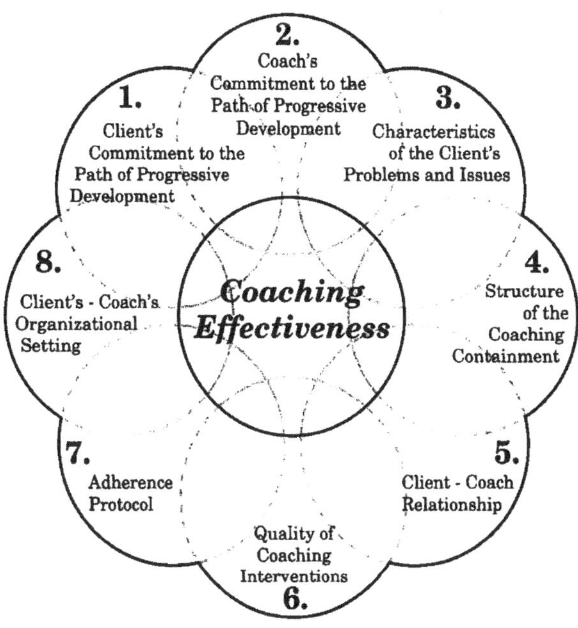

FIGURE 22.1. A model of coaching effectiveness.

TABLE 22.1

Key Elements in a Model of Coaching Effectiveness

1. Client's commitment to the path of progressive development; levels of
   - Self-awareness and understanding of problems and issues
   - Adherence behavior
   - Competence–cognitive complexity
   - Psychosocial development
   - Curiosity, ability, and willingness to learn; sufficient inquiry and communication skills
   - Courage
   - Diversity dimensions
   - Development drive and motivation
2. Coach's commitment to the path of progressive development; levels of
   - Self-awareness and understanding of problems and issues
   - Adherence behavior
   - Competence–cognitive complexity
   - Psychosocial development
   - Curiosity, ability, and willingness to learn; sufficient inquiry and communication skills
   - Courage
   - Diversity dimensions
3. Characteristics of the client's problems and issues
   - Frequency
   - Intensity
   - Duration
   - Degree of jeopardy present
   - Degree of defensiveness present
   - Degree of conflict present
   - Degree of emotionality present
4. Structure of the coaching containment
   - Clarity of the agreement
   - Goal specificity
   - Resources committed
   - Roadblocks and barriers identified
5. Client–coach relationship
   - Sufficient trust and mutual respect
   - Accurate empathy
   - Warmth
   - Nonpossessive positive regard
   - Tolerance for interventions
   - Tolerance for defensiveness and conflicts
   - Diversity dimensions
   - Playful challenge
   - Tactful exchanges
   - Authenticity and genuineness
6. Quality of coaching interventions
   - Constructive use of levels of reflection
   - Wise choice of interventions
   - Client openness to technique/method chosen
   - Interventions are necessary and sufficient
   - Interventions are accurate and timely
7. Adherence protocol
   - Anticipates client resistance and adherence problems
   - Adherence methods are necessary and sufficient
   - Techniques are customized to client needs
   - Anticipates coach's resistance and adherence problems
   - Makes appropriate use of client motivators
   - Makes appropriate use of client and coach strengths
8. Client's and coach's organizational setting
   - Support for coaching
   - Degree of resilience or regression

these complex variables. Each of the variables contributes in major ways to whether a coaching assignment achieves its long-term goals. In addition, each of these eight key elements can be thought of as consisting of a number of significant components that coaches must consider throughout the course of a coaching assignment. Some of these subcomponents are identified in Table 22.1.

The model is based on the assumption that both the client and the coach have an intensive and complex commitment to the path of *progressive* development (Freud, 1965). Translating this abstract term into useful language remains difficult, for I believe such commitment has many different aspects. In general terms, it involves the psychological motivation and associated behaviors that are necessary to move a human being toward defined goals over a reasonably extensive period of time. The inclusion of "progressive" adds the expectation that development takes place over time in phases or stages. The layering of experience, learning, and deliberate efforts to change the self through time in the context of social roles and occurring in the complexity of the inner biopsychological life space of the participants represents the hallmark of progressive development. Both the client and the coach must possess this commitment, and it seems to me to be composed of such elements as the levels of self-awareness and understanding of problems and issues, adherence behavior, competence and cognitive complexity (Jaques & Clement, 1991), level of psychosocial development, curiosity, ability and willingness to learn, sufficient inquiry and communication skills, courage, diversity dimensions, development drive, and motivation. Each of these elements deserves treatment in depth, but such coverage is well beyond the scope of this chapter.

Assuming that sufficient commitment to development is present, then the nature of the problems and issues faced by the client move to center stage for consideration. Coaches experience enormous variation in the challenges their clients bring to be addressed. The depth of emotional responsiveness and psychological conflict that are interwoven into the problems also vary widely. The more complex, frequent, intense, emotionally demanding, and conflict ridden the challenges, the greater the pressure on both the client and the coach to perform well if positive outcomes are to be achieved.

In an earlier work (Kilburg, 2000), I explored the importance of the containment that coaches must construct to hold the work relationship with the client. Of crucial importance to the issues of effectiveness and long-term intervention adherence is the ability of the coach and client to reach a clear understanding about the nature of their agreement and the goals that are to be pursued in the coaching assignment. Similarly, efforts to identify barriers and roadblocks to goal attainment can be critically important to long-term success.

In all the literature on helping human beings with their problems and issues, the single most important item repeatedly identified as contributing to positive outcomes is a meaningful, lasting, and effective working relationship. Accurate empathy, positive regard, authenticity and genuineness, playful challenge, tactful exchanges, tolerance for interventions made, and the dimensions of diversity for both clients and coach can make or break a coaching assignment. Some of these variables are within the power of the coach to create, whereas others emerge from the complex and, at times, mysterious interactions created in the behavioral field that exist between the client and the coach.

Once an intervention is underway, the coach uses a wide variety of techniques and methods to help the client reach the goals that have been established. The collection of evaluation data from instruments and interviews, the creative and effective use of levels of reflection and methods of inquiry, and the application of such techniques as role playing, reframing, simulations, confrontations, and interpretations in a timely, sensitive, and tactful fashion constitute the heart of executive coaching (Kilburg, 2000). Practitioners demonstrate their maturity and professional mastery through the use of these methods. Steady client progress toward the goals that have been established constitutes the evidence that the coach is choosing methods wisely and implementing them well.

Critical to the long-term impact that coaching has on the client is the development and implementation of an adherence protocol by both parties. Some explicit ideas for what can be included in such a protocol are presented below. The protocol should be designed with the client and should address the specific goals and likely long-term barriers and resistance to maintaining intervention compliance that the coach and client can identify for themselves. It should also take appropriate motivators into account. Finally, it should be based on the strengths of both the coach and the client.

The eighth element in the model of effectiveness consists of the organizational environments of both the coach and the client. Participants in a developmental process must have a minimum level of support for those activities, including commitments of sufficient time and financial resources to make the coaching possible. In addition, the organizational environment of the client must provide sufficient room for him or her to experiment with behaviors and approaches and give feedback on the progress being made. Organizations with average to excellent levels of resilience, described by Kilburg, Stokes, and Kuruvilla (1998) and by Kernberg (1998), usually are capable of doing this. In organizations with significant levels of regressive behavior, coaching efforts may have limited impact because of the chaos, lack of consistent attention to developmental activities, and potential for acting out by individuals and groups. In such regressed situations, behaviors that might ordinarily be seen as attempts at change and growth can be viewed as acts of deviance that must be punished rather than rewarded. Significant time and attention should be

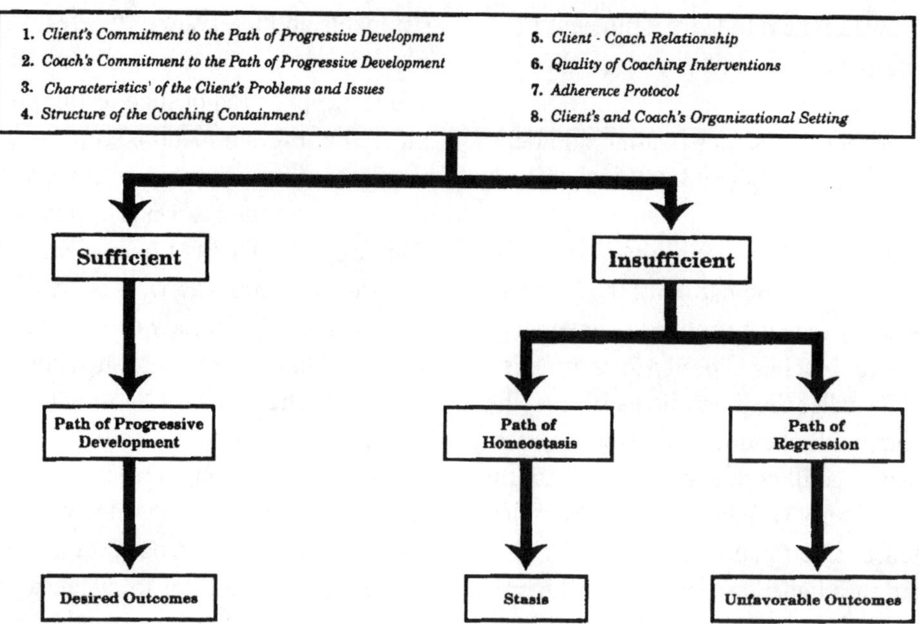

FIGURE 22.2. Outcome pathways of executive coaching.

taken by coaches and clients to adequately assess the developmental status of the home environments and then to make appropriate modifications in the goals, intervention plan, and adherence protocol.

Figure 22.2 illustrates the effectiveness model with a flowchart. When all eight of the key components are present to a sufficient degree, clients typically do follow the path of progressive development and achieve the majority of the outcomes they sought through their coaching agreement. If one or more of the eight elements is flawed in some major way, two other pathways may be followed. In the least troubling one, the client merely maintains the behaviors, attitudes, values, beliefs, skills, knowledge, and so forth that he or she possessed before coaching began. In other words, the client remains in a homeostatic state for better or worse. The most difficult pathway occurs when the client actually gets worse. Behavior, values, skills, knowledge, and performance can regress, leading at times to truly dangerous results, such as loss of job and career derailment. I have had a number of clients follow this regressive path, and the effect on them and often their families can be devastating. As with Jennifer in the opening case study, individuals often find themselves facing and making decisions about their lives with insufficient preparation or consideration. As Jennifer noted after the coaching intervention, our work together prevented her from making what she came to see as a large mistake in her life. Although coaching sessions rarely have such dramatic specific outcomes, the example does illustrate the model and the issues quite nicely. Without my insistence on the session, a form of following the adherence protocol, the results for her might well have had negative impacts throughout the rest of her life.

DEVELOPING AN ADHERENCE PROTOCOL

Following Meichenbaum and Turk (1987), adherence in an executive coaching assignment can be defined as "an active, voluntary, collaborative involvement of the *client* in a mutually acceptable course of behavior to produce a desired preventative or *ameliorative* result" (p. 20). Thus, adherence assumes that the client is actively involved in the design and implementation of the intervention. I have come to see the enormous value in raising adherence issues very early in the coaching process. Approaching the coaching assignment in this way assures to some degree that both client and coach will approach and address resistance to learning

TABLE 22.2

Components of an Effective Adherence Protocol

1. Clarity in the coaching agreement
2. Goal clarity
3. Adherence assessment process
   - Client's and coach's barriers to adherence
   - Client's and coach's attitudes toward adherence
   - Identification of likely patterns of nonadherence behavior
4. Necessary and sufficient adherence awareness
5. Client-specific and sensitive adherence methods
   a. Mutually adopted adherence measurements
      - Keeping appointments
      - Completing homework assignments
      - Preparing for coaching sessions (topics, issues, challenges, examples, reactions, thoughts, feelings)
   b. Relationship enhancement techniques
      - Accurate empathy
      - Appreciative inquiry used beyond work topics
      - Taking advantage of other settings and opportunities
   c. Client education techniques
      - Reading assignments
      - Other developmental experiences (workshops, classes, action learning experiences, travel, conferences)
      - Mentors
      - Tapes
      - Use of effective communication methods—Inquiring for understanding/comprehension
   d. Customization of intervention for the individual client—Immediate and long-term foci
   e. Exploring the client's theory-in-use, model of performance, understanding of current situation, developmental needs
   f. Addressing forgetfulness
      - Identify cues for remembering
      - Reminders
      - Appointment reminders
      - Follow-up e-mail, notes, letters, calls
      - Reinforcement sessions
   g. Teaching self-regulation
      - Self-awareness
      - Problem solving
      - Decision making
      - Emotional management
      - Conflict management
      - Diversity awareness
      - Diversity management
      - Communication skills—Appreciative inquiry, feedback, self-disclosure, listening
      - Relapse management
      - Identification and management of vicious circles of defensiveness and conflict
   h. Behavior modification methods
      - Self-monitoring
      - Goal setting
      - Corrective feedback
      - Behavioral contracting
      - Reinforcement techniques
      - Commitment enhancement techniques
   i. Other
      - Visits to client's office
      - Emotional inducements
      - Rewards
      - Psychotherapy
      - Health care

and behavioral change before it is actually encountered. An early discussion of adherence allows this to happen in a far less defensive atmosphere in which both parties are already engaged actively in a process of exploration. It also creates a tremendous anchor point to which the parties can return when and if actual resistance or nonadherence begins to occur.

Table 22.2 presents some suggestions for creating an effective adherence protocol. I believe client compliance begins with the process of developing a coaching agreement that includes real goal clarity. I usually spend the first and second sessions trying to develop an understanding of the client's situation and what he or she is trying to accomplish at work and in life in general. I work with the person to identify specific goals, and then, in most situations involving a longer term coaching relationship, I commit these goals and the other components of the coaching agreement to writing so that both of us can review them. In the majority of situations in which I coach formally, I seek the client's written acknowledgment of the terms of the agreement and the goals.

In this initial process of inquiry, I have now found it easy to begin to address the issue of adherence directly by trying to identify the client's attitudes toward compliance, history of deliberate change, and examples of situations in which the client did not adhere to agreements, failed to achieve goals, or did not follow through on commitments. Following Meichenbaum and Turk (1987), a variety of questions can be asked:

1. What do you think led to your choosing these goals to pursue?
2. Have you tried to develop these skills or solve these problems before? If yes, what happened? If no, why not?
3. Does anything worry you as we begin this coaching effort?
4. How effective do you think this coaching will be?
5. Can you think of any problems that we might encounter in following through on the coaching agreement?
6. How likely to occur are these problems in follow-through?
7. Have you ever stopped trying to accomplish something once you've started? What happened? Why do you think that occurred?
8. Is there anything that we can do to increase the likelihood that you will follow through?
9. When you've been able to achieve something or change in the past, how did you best accomplish that?
10. What would you describe as the major strengths you usually apply to any effort you make to develop yourself or change something in your life?
11. When you've encountered problems in changing something in the past, what has worked best for you to overcome those problems?

Once I complete an adherence-oriented history with a client, he or she almost automatically increases the level of awareness of the issues involved in ensuring compliance. It is also easier to return to elements of the history when and if resistance to change is encountered during the coaching process. Using this base of awareness, I can then move on to work with the client in choosing specific adherence methods that will address the issues identified in the assessment and support the coaching effort. Table 22.2 describes some of these methods in an abbreviated fashion. Meichenbaum and Turk (1987) also provided in-depth coverage of a variety of these methods along with detailed references of resources to consult for additional information.

Following Table 22.2, identify mutually agreeable measurements of adherence, use traditional methods to strengthen and deepen the working relationship with the client, and push the client education process along as rapidly and fully as possible. I often provide reading material and references to issues that I discuss with clients. I will help them find workshops and conferences to attend and debrief such learning experiences with them. Several of my clients prefer to obtain taped versions of books I recommend because they want to invest the time spent in the car while commuting in professional development. I work very hard with the client to customize the intervention to their issues, strengths, weaknesses, threats, opportunities, and goals. I push to help the client understand his or her theory-in-use (Argyris, 1993), developmental needs, and understanding of the current situation.

As identified in the table, I also help the client address forgetfulness by providing reminders of work that we did together and upcoming appointments. I often e-mail a client after a session to reinforce key learning points or highlight what I believe may be barriers in implementation. Phone calls can also accomplish the same thing. For the clients whom I coach over the phone, I often need to pursue them in order to ensure that we stay in reasonable contact. In my experience, the pace of the lives of many executives tends to overcome their best intentions to focus on change and development. I often work with clients on self-regulation issues, such as decision making, problem solving, diversity management, communication skills, conflict management, defensive operations, and areas of conflict. I have found behavior modification methods useful in some situations. Behavioral contracting, goal setting, self-monitoring, corrective feedback, and reinforcement for positive efforts to change and adhere to commitments to change can be very helpful to many clients.

Finally, there are a variety of other techniques that can help a client to adhere to the coaching interventions. Visiting clients in their offices can be very helpful both in understanding them and in making sure that they actually follow through on a visit. Encouraging clients to keep up good work and discouraging dysfunctional behavior patterns can often assist them in maintaining positive momentum. At times, I have worked with clients and their supervisors to arrange rewards such as raises or promotions if goals are obtained. In extreme situations involving clients who experience real trouble changing or who seem like they are really struggling with emotional, relationship, or other physical issues, I will refer them for treatment to well-qualified mental health or health care professionals. I have often assisted executives obtain marital or family treatment for problems that are identified in coaching sessions. On rare occasions, I have had to work with supervisors to design and conduct an intervention for an alcohol or drug problem that was undiagnosed or untreated. All of these methods can be very helpful in the effort to ensure adherence. I am now more aware of the use of these methods not only for helping a client initiate change, but also for maintaining those hard-won gains. The key involves recognizing that creating and executing a unique and client-specific adherence protocol must become an explicit part of the planning and conduct of a coaching intervention. It is now my strong believe that failure to do so can jeopardize the extensive investment that clients and coaches make in their work together.

MAJOR PROBLEMS CONTRIBUTING TO NONADHERENCE

The final topic addressed in this chapter consists of some of the major problems that coaches encounter that contribute to nonadherence to intervention by clients. Any experienced practitioner understands that there are a huge number of variables that contribute to the success of a consulting assignment and that only some of them can be influenced directly. We have already discussed the requisite conditions for success in the model of effectiveness. If all eight of those components are present in sufficient amounts, coaching will usually enable the client to accomplish part or all of the goals outlined in the original agreement. However, several particularly troubling situations that are encountered fairly frequently and that inhibit adherence and success warrant attention.

Table 22.3 identifies six separate problems that contribute to nonadherence. These are listed in no particular order or priority. The first one, insufficient agreement or goal clarity, often serves as the root cause of a failed consulting or coaching assignment. Clients seek assistance with their work and for themselves for a wide variety of reasons, and it is absolutely crucial that practitioners use their assessment skills in the opening phase of an assignment to determine what is needed. It is equally critical that the client and coach reach a mutual understanding of the goals and logistics of the effort. Without such clarity and agreement, any problem that arises almost automatically can be attributed to a poor contract, even if the real issue is something else. More problems in consulting and coaching assignments stem from lack of goal clarity than any other single cause. Sackett (1979) suggested that there are three crucial questions that service providers should ask themselves: Have I made an accurate assessment? Will my intervention regime do more good than harm? and Is the client a free, informed, consenting participant in the intervention? I believe the most important question is the first, because it forms the foundation for all that follows in any service intervention and therefore shapes the agreement that the client and consultant or coach reach regarding goals, resources, methods, and the other fundamentals of any engagement.

The second major problem coaches confront in nonadhering clients is their lack of commitment to the path of progressive development. Assessing

TABLE 22.3

Major Client and Coach Problems Contributing to Nonadherence

1. Insufficient agreement or goal clarity
2. Lack of commitment to path of progressive development
3. Insufficient client competence–cognitive complexity
4. Insufficient coaching competence–cognitive complexity
5. Client–coach defensiveness, conflicts, emotionality
   a. Addictions
   b. Psychopathology
   c. Sadomasochism
6. Regression in coach's or client's organizational environments
   a. Racism, sexism, ethnocentrism, heterosexism, and so on
   b. Poor performance
   c. Downsizings, mergers, acquisitions
   d. Paranoiagenesis
   e. Bankruptcy

motivation must be a key part of the opening phase of an assignment, but it is very complex. As we well know, what clients say they think or do often varies from reality. It is fairly easy to get some idea of the ongoing level of development hunger and activity by asking potential clients questions such as what meetings or conferences they routinely attend, how much time they set aside for reading, what they are currently reading, where they see their career progressing over the next 5 years, and what developmental activities they routinely find most helpful. Clients who respond in the negative to such questions—"I haven't gone to a meeting in years; I don't have time to read; I haven't thought about where my career is going"—would seem to be at fairly high risk for coaching failure. In addition, clients who are referred for coaching because they are in danger of career derailment in an organization because of performance problems are also likely to have some motivation problems. Coaches should be prepared to identify and manage such problems early in an assignment. Careful attention to the design of an adherence protocol in the opening phase of coaching can be a very important step in helping these clients not only see the benefits of development, but also take the necessary steps to create an ongoing program to do so.

The third and fourth problems go together. At times, both coaches and clients might find themselves in an assignment for which they are poorly equipped. The absence of key components of competency can be professionally fatal in a world that increasingly demands virtually instant results. Similarly, levels of cognitive complexity required for various jobs vary widely (Jaques & Clement, 1991). The ability to process various types of information in increasingly sophisticated ways against longer time lines is a hallmark of executive-level positions in organizations. The inability to function at these levels of complexity may not be coachable in some clients. Rather, this may be seen as a prerequisite for assuming the responsibilities of such a position. At times, executives who hire or promote fail to critically evaluate these kinds of abilities in candidates. Similarly, coaches considering assignments at higher and higher levels in organizations must be willing to challenge themselves on whether they truly have the levels of knowledge and skill required to assist people who work in these positions. Coaches who cannot think and perform as effectively as a CEO of a major corporation will have real difficulty with clients in these positions. Senior executives eventually do determine whether a consultant or coach has what it takes to help them develop. A coach without the necessary abilities to work at senior levels will find significant problems in client nonadherence. Mature coaches can use such problems diagnostically to determine whether there is a correct match between client needs and their professional capacity. If a coach is unwilling to do so in a forthright and unflinching fashion, he or she may find an assignment being brought to a premature end by the client. Even more troubling, coaches in this position may not know the significant long-term damage that can occur to their reputations. The social connections of executives in various industries are quite rich, and competitors do talk to each other at very high levels. Coaches must keep this in mind when they evaluate the pros and cons of taking on a client who might represent more than a significant stretch.

The fifth problem listed in Table 22.3 can also represent an extremely difficult nonadherence challenge. Although some coaches may have backgrounds in the mental health professions, these assignments and clients do not readily open themselves to such interior scrutiny. Some coaches routinely administer batteries of psychological tests to clients, conduct interviews with family members, and pursue in-depth interviews that probe into such issues (Kilburg, 1996). Some clients who have contracted for such intensive levels of assessment may expect explicit feedback that they have a mental health or interpersonal problem that must be confronted. I believe it is more often the case that coaches discover such challenges in the course of an assignment. When these problems are encountered, they must be confronted forthrightly and with extreme sensitivity. Appropriate referrals to highly effective treatment resources can significantly aid a coaching assignment succeed.

Confronting addictions in executives presents a special challenge that often requires a coach to involve the supervising executive and, if available, the employee assistance program of the organization. Depending on the policies, attitudes, and history of the enterprise in managing these kinds of difficulties, intervention plans may well need to be modified. For example, many organizations still routinely fire people with addiction problems. In these situations, coaches must be very savvy in how they can help a client proceed with treatment and recovery without jeopardizing the client's employment. Coaches must be aware that addictions and mental health problems often present work-related symptoms, such as lack of follow-through on assignments, interpersonal conflict on the job, and general incompetence. Careful exploration of these situations can alert a coach that an underlying problem may be contributing to normal developmental or work-related challenges.

Table 22.3 also identifies the problem of sadomasochism in this category. Novick and Novick (1996) presented a detailed consideration of this most difficult challenge in human behavior. I raise it here explicitly because one of the underlying features of this pattern of behavior in some individuals is that they may explicitly seek help from supervisors, coaches, or other professionals in a simultaneous desire to solve the problems they are experiencing and, at an unconscious level, to cause the person helping them to fail in those efforts. Such individuals can be exceptionally frustrating to work with as clients because they can say all of the right things in actual coaching sessions and then consistently manage to behave in ways that inevitably lead to their individual failure, thus dooming the coaching assignment. Careful attention to such contradictions can alert a coach that these difficulties may be present and to the need for a referral to a highly qualified professional. Knowing how to find such resources in the home cities of coaching clients should be a key part of the basic knowledge and skill set of practitioners who work with executives.

Coaches are equally susceptible to these problems, for we are all too human. I suggest that coaches should have a shadow consultant (Kilburg, 2002) or supervising consultant available to them to provide assistance when an assignment develops problems. It is equally important that coaches should be prepared to seek treatment themselves if signs of depression, anxiety disorders, or addiction become more than transitory. The lives of consultants are full of rewards and challenges. The stress of travel, the stress of work at high levels in organizations and under conditions of extreme scrutiny, and the difficulties in getting one's own psychological and physical needs met during consulting assignments often leads to family problems, emotional and behavioral disorders, and addictive behaviors (Pinault, 2000). Consulting and coaching professionals are not immune to such problems. It can be very useful for practitioners to have an ongoing working relationship with a mental health professional to whom they can routinely turn for assistance when problems arise. Having such an alliance with someone who comes to know both one's work and psychology can serve to prevent problems from rising to overwhelming and, at times, career-threatening levels.

The final problem identified in Table 22.3 elaborates on another of the components of the model of coaching effectiveness. If the organization of the client or that of the coach suffers from any of these problems—poor performance, downsizing or merger and acquisition challenges, paranoiagenesis (Jaques, 1976; Kilburg, 2000), bankruptcy, racism, sexism, or other forms of discriminatory behavior—it is quite likely that the coaching effort will become consumed with assisting the client in managing the particular problems confronting the organization. Kilburg (1996, 2000), Levinson (see chap. 9, this volume), Hargrove (1995, 2000), and many others have pointed out that such challenges are often quite rightly the focus of coaching assignments. Learning to manage these problems can provide very rich and deep learning opportunities for executives that can affect them profoundly throughout their professional lives. However, it must be said that such situations can also create career-threatening environments in which, as noted above, mature and developmentally appropriate activities can, if carried out incorrectly or in a mistimed fashion, lead to job loss or contribute to organizational failure. In such circumstances, client defensiveness is often quite high, and this should be seen by coaches as often justifiable. Coaching methods and the nature of the containment that the coach creates in the situation must reflect these organizational realities.

Similarly, if a coach finds himself or herself working in a severely regressed organization, he or she can become preoccupied with those circumstances to the detriment of consulting engagements. Human development best proceeds where there is an atmosphere of trust and a willingness to take appropriate risks. If a coach is feeling inappropriately defensive because of a lack of professional support or because the home organization has become dysfunctional, it becomes increasingly difficult to take risks and engage in the kind of creativity that high-level coaching often requires. Having external supports, such as shadow consultants and one's own therapist, in such situations can enable coaches to help both themselves and their clients adhere to coaching contracts and remain on the path of progressive development instead of falling victim to the regressive pull of the environment in which they find themselves.

As executive coaching continues to emerge as a major subdiscipline of consultation, practitioners will confront the need to address many new and old problems. Intervention adherence in situations requiring ongoing maintenance of behavioral changes has been well documented in the health, mental health, and addictions literature as one of the most significant ongoing problems of high-quality, effective practice. It is time that executive coaches start to discuss this issue and take appropriate steps to modify their practices to ensure that clients have the opportunity to do their best work and maintain the gains that their hard work has brought them. More attention to the key components of coaching effectiveness and in particular to creating collaboratively negotiated agreements and adherence protocols will, I have come to strongly believe, increase the likelihood that coaches and their clients will achieve their goals and pursue the path of progressive development.

Failure to pay attention to the concepts, scientific literature, and behavioral technologies of intervention adherence poses a significant risk to the development of coaching practice. Increasingly, many companies are asking hard questions about the resources that they deploy for managerial and leadership development. In the past 2 months, I have had conversations with several colleagues who described organizational policies that limit development investments to a small cadre of people who they really believe have the potential to lead their organizations in the future. In these focused development approaches, other managers receive little or no attention or are simply cast aside at the convenience of the enterprise. Coaching interventions are expensive in real dollar terms to the organizations that use them, and eventually this fact alone will lead to increasing calls for outcome accountability for these practices. In that context, the literature on adherence developed in the last 30 years can provide consultants who coach with many ideas and approaches to improve the likelihood that their clients will achieve long-term benefits from the investments that they make in these experiences.

References

Argyris, C. (1993). *Knowledge for action: A guide to overcoming barriers to organizational change.* San Francisco: Jossey-Bass.

Bergquist, W., Merritt, K., & Phillips, S. (1999). *Executive coaching: An appreciative approach.* Sacramento, CA: Pacific Soundings Press.

Blackwell, B. (1997). *Treatment compliance and the therapeutic alliance.* Amsterdam: Harwood Academic.

Brogan, M. M., Prochaska, J. G., & Prochaska, J. M. (1999). Predicting termination and continuation status in psychotherapy using the transtheoretical model. *Psychotherapy, 36*(2), 105–113.

Colvin, R. E. (1997). Transformational executive leadership: A comparison of culture-focused and individual-focused leadership modalities (Doctoral dissertation, Virginia Commonwealth University). *Dissertation Abstracts International, 57*(10-A), 4536.

Daley, D., & Zuckoff, A. (1999). *Improving treatment compliance: Counseling and systems strategies for substance abuse and dual disorders.* Center City, MN: Hazelden.

Dotlich, D. L., & Cairo, P. C. (1999). *Action coaching: How to leverage individual performance for company success.* San Francisco: Jossey-Bass.

Freud, A. (1965). *Normality and pathology in childhood: Assessments of development. Writings.* New York: International Universities Press.

Galley-Eggeman, R. J. (1997). Touchstone mentoring: A multiple mentor model that mirrors women's career development needs (Doctoral dissertation, The American University). *Dissertation Abstracts International, 57*(9-A), 3824.

Hargrove, R. (1995). *Masterful coaching: Extraordinary results by impacting people and the way they think and work together.* Johannesburg, South Africa: Pfeiffer.

Hargrove, R. (2000). *Masterful coaching fieldbook.* San Francisco: Jossey-Bass/Pfeiffer.

Hudson, F. M. (1999). *The handbook of coaching: A comprehensive resource guide for managers, executives, consultants, and human resource professionals.* San Francisco: Jossey-Bass.

Irvin, J. E., Bowers, C. A., Dunn, M. E., & Wang, M. C. (1999). Efficacy of relapse prevention: A meta-analytic review. *Journal of Consulting and Clinical Psychology, 67,* 563–570.

Jaques, E. (1976). *A general theory of bureaucracy.* Portsmouth, NH: Heinemann & Cower.

Jaques, E., & Clement, S. D. (1991). *Executive leadership: A practical guide to managing complexity.* Arlington, VA: Cason Hall.

Johnson, J. B. (1997). An exploratory study of teachers' efforts to implement cognitive coaching as a form of professional development: Waiting for Godot (Doctoral dissertation, University of St. Thomas). *Dissertation Abstracts International, 58*(4-A), 1250.

Kernberg, O. F. (1998). *Ideology, conflict, and leadership in groups and organizations.* New Haven, CT: Yale University Press.

Kilburg, R. R. (Ed.). (1996). Executive coaching [Special issue]. *Consulting Psychology Journal: Practice and Research, 48*(2).

Kilburg, R. R. (2000). *Executive coaching: Developing managerial wisdom in a world of chaos.* Washington, DC: American Psychological Association.

Kilburg, R. R. (2002). Shadow consultation: A reflective approach for preventing practice disasters. *Consulting Psychology Journal: Practice and Research, 54,* 75–92.

Kilburg, R. R., Stokes, E. J., & Kuruvilla, C. (1998). Toward a conceptual model of organizational regression. *Consulting Psychology Journal: Practice and Research, 50*(2), 101–119.

Leventhal, H., & Cameron, L. (1987). Behavioral theories and the problem of compliance. *Patient Education and Counseling, 10,* 117–138.

Marlatt, G. A., & Gordon, J. R. (Eds.). (1985). *Relapse prevention.* New York: Guilford Press.

Meichenbaum, D., & Turk, D. C. (1987). *Facilitating treatment adherence: A practitioner's guidebook.* New York: Plenum Press.

Meyer, J. L. (1997). Leadership perceptions and achievement motivation in sport (Doctoral dissertation, Gonzaga University). *Dissertation Abstracts International, 58*(1-A), 0119.

Novick, J., & Novick, K. K. (1996). *Fearful symmetry: The development and treatment of sadomasochism.* Northvale, NJ: Jason Aronson.

O'Neill, M. B. (2000). *Executive coaching with backbone and heart: A systems approach to engaging leaders with their challenges.* San Francisco: Jossey-Bass.

Pinault, L. (2000). *Consulting demons: Inside the unscrupulous world of global corporate consulting.* New York: Harper Business.

Piper, W. E., Joyce, A. S., Rosie, J. S., Ogrodniczuk, J. S., McCallum, M., O'Kelly, J. G., & Steinberg, P. I. (1999). Prediction of dropping out in time-limited, interpretive individual psychotherapy. *Psychotherapy, 36*(2), 114–122.

Reis, B. F., & Brown, L. G. (1999). Reducing psychotherapy dropouts: Maximizing perspective convergence in the psychotherapy dyad. *Psychotherapy, 36*(2), 123–136.

Sackett, D. L. (1979). A compliance practicum for the busy practitioner. In R. B. Hayes, D. W. Taylor, & D. L. Sackett (Eds.), *Compliance in health care.* Baltimore: Johns Hopkins University Press.

Wierzbicki, M., & Pekarik, G. (1993). A meta-analytic review of psychotherapy dropout. *Professional Psychology: Research and Practice, 24,* 190–195.

CHAPTER 23

COACHING LEADERS THROUGH CULTURE CHANGE

Judith H. Katz and Frederick A. Miller

In today's organizations, diversity is a business issue, not just an issue about political correctness, public relations, or legal liability. How an organization deals with the diversity of its workforce, markets, and suppliers will have a major impact on its strategies, productivity, market penetration, customer service, recruitment costs, turnover rate, and many other aspects of its day-to-day operations.

If they are to avoid the pitfalls and cap the potential of their workforce, executives need a new set of competencies for communicating with, partnering with, and leading a diverse group of people. To fully leverage diversity and maximize performance, they need the ability to build and sustain an inclusive work culture. For many executives, the need to capitalize on diversity and create inclusion therefore becomes an issue of professional development as well as an organizational necessity.

But too often, organizations fail to provide support or opportunities for the development of their senior executives. They seem to assume that senior executives must already be fully developed. Few leaders can afford to make the mistakes associated with on-the-job training, which makes learning and applying new skills very risky. And few have reliable access to honest feedback or a regular peer review process. People seem to expect the leaders' every action to be their desired level of performance, and they believe that, having risen to the top, the leaders have nothing more to learn. In reality, like anyone on a path of growth and development, leaders, too, need mentors—partners and coaches who can assist them in developing the necessary skills to lead culture change and facilitate an understanding of the linkage between an inclusive culture and organizational success.

Whether done formally or informally, senior executives and the top leadership group need support for their development and success. They need training for skill enhancement and safe opportunities for practicing new skills. Although it is critical to find coaches with the appropriate skills for coaching senior leaders through the process of building an inclusive work culture, that coaching will be useless unless the leaders see the need for the change process.

POSITIONING DIVERSITY AS A MEANS TO ORGANIZATIONAL SUCCESS

The Organizational Imperative for Diversity and Inclusion

The Kaleel Jamison Consulting Group was founded in 1970 to help organizations engage and use the full talents of all their people by developing high-performing and inclusive work cultures. In our practice as strategic change and management consultants, our work often begins with senior executives. In many cases, our first task is to help the

Reprinted from the *Consulting Psychology Journal: Practice and Research*, 48, 104–114.

same leaders who hired us redefine their reasons for hiring us.

Often, a leader brings us in to help the organization address perceived problems with diversity. The problems may be identified by high turnover rates, low employee morale, poor public image, stagnant productivity, concerns raised by women and minorities regarding the lack of upward mobility, lawsuits, or any number of other visible issues. Frequently, the leaders ask us to provide diversity training to fix the problem. However, experience has taught us to avoid the kind of isolated, programmatic involvement often associated with diversity training. Instead, we seek to engage the leadership in examining how diversity can be harnessed in pursuit of the organization's overall business strategy.

Our first act of coaching is very often to help the leader see the diversity of the workforce not as a problem but as a valuable resource waiting to be tapped, and how a strategic culture change that emphasizes inclusion can help the organization achieve its core goals. In most cases, the problem is not the diversity of the organization's workforce but an organizational culture and systems that prevent the use of the full range of skills, talents, and energies of the workforce.

To truly engage senior executives in the strategic culture change required to create a high-performing and inclusive organization, it is vital to build a framework from which they can see how diversity fits with the organization's goals and strategies. In fact, we often find it useful to develop with the organization's leaders a formal document or position paper detailing the strategic reasons why a diverse workforce and an inclusive work culture are imperative for the organization's survival and success. Unless diversity and inclusion are tied inextricably to the successful achievement of the organization's goals, any diversity or inclusion efforts will be temporary—seen as just another passing fad or one of the many "flavors of the month." But there are a lot of ways people resist establishing this organizational imperative for diversity and inclusion. This is a critical time to help leaders understand the differences among terms like equal employment opportunity (EEO), affirmative action, diversity, tolerance, acceptance, and inclusion.

EEO refers to laws that prohibit discrimination on the basis of sex, color, race, religion, national origin, age, or physical ability. Rarely mandated by law, affirmative action has been a historic effort to address past and present factors that have systematically disadvantaged individuals on the basis of group identities such as gender and race. Under affirmative action, among equally qualified candidates, those from underrepresented groups might be aggressively pursued, hired, or promoted. The focus is on recruitment, retention, and upward mobility.

Diversity is the range of human differences, including differences of gender, race, nationality, sexual orientation, physical and mental ability, health, stature, age, religion, class, education level, job level, and function. Inclusion is the practice of embracing and using differences as opportunities for added value and competitive advantages in teamwork, product quality, and work output.

The distinctions among tolerance, acceptance, and inclusion may not be easy to see for people in the dominant culture of an organization, but for members of previously excluded groups they can be significant. When your differences are tolerated, you can feel the hostility in the prevailing culture even though it is being held in check. When your differences are accepted, you can often feel the unspoken "but not as good as" that comes with that acceptance. But when your differences are included, encouraged, and used, you truly feel welcomed, valued, and invited to contribute—and better able to do your best work.

A great many people still define diversity as affirmative action—diversity by the numbers. Many undertake diversity efforts out of moral values—the right thing, the politically correct thing, or the mandated thing to do—but see little connection to the ultimate success of the organization. In addition, many see the organization's diversity work as something that gets in the way of the real business of the organization. As coaches, we need to assist leaders to see the diversity initiative as critical to the organization's success. We need to help them see the cost in not addressing diversity issues and the profit to be gained from tapping a broader pool of talents, skills, perspectives, styles, and energies.

We believe that the issue of profitability should be applied to all strategic change initiatives. The most effective and sustainable way to approach any change effort is as a bottom-line issue. Each effort should be defined in terms of how it can enhance the implementation of the organization's goals. Assisting leaders in seeing how a change effort is in their own best interest and the best interest of the organization is the real key to gaining their commitment.

An important part of the coach's role is helping leaders fully grasp the notion that some people in the organization have been given advantages that other, equally worthy people have been denied. These advantaged people often come from the same cultural, ethnic, or educational background as the founders of the organization—people the founders feel most comfortable with. The members of the advantaged group may never even realize that they are routinely given preference or that others are routinely blocked—it is very hard to notice barriers to inclusion until you bump into them. And unless they clearly understand the cost of those barriers to the organization, the advantaged people of the organization will have no investment in seeing or removing those barriers.

In most organizations, the barriers to inclusion are rooted in the structures, culture, and institutional dynamics of the organizations and may be reinforced by the wider society. One of the key concepts for coaches to get across is that these systemic barriers cannot be removed by training sessions, awareness programs, politically correct speech, retooled mission statements, or cultural appreciation days. The very culture of the organization must be changed—its systems, structures, practices, rewards, norms, and accepted behaviors—and that requires learning new skills and new ways of behaving, managing, interacting, partnering, and doing business.

The Path From Exclusion to Inclusion

As change agents and coaches, we use cognitive frameworks and models to help leaders understand the characteristics of their organizational culture and to develop strategies to achieve desired results. One of the most valuable models is one initially developed by Bailey Jackson, Rita Hardiman, and Mark Chesler (1981), which we have adapted. The model "The Path From a Monocultural Club to an Inclusive Organization" (Katz & Miller, 1995a) identifies different stages of development along a continuum between exclusive and inclusive organizational cultures (see Figure 23.1).

The premise of the "Path" model is that organizations must go through a predictable developmental process in changing from a culture of exclusion to one of inclusion. The model helps illustrate graphically that the process of culture change is not like turning on a light switch—that a diversity seminar or an ethnic foods week are not sufficient to achieve inclusion.

The Path model provides a framework from which we coach leaders to prepare them for leading change. One of the Path model's values is in identifying the need for different leadership strategies and actions at different stages along the continuum, including what to expect at each stage, what to communicate to the organization, what behaviors and attitudes to exhibit, what skills are required, and what structural changes will be needed. The stages consist of exclusive clubs, passive clubs, symbolic difference organizations, organizations at critical mass, organizations at acceptance, and inclusive organizations.

Exclusive clubs. Exclusive clubs are organizations that actively or passively pursue monocultural norms and values; they are open only to those who are willing and able to fit in. Active, discriminatory exclusion, especially as practiced by hate groups, is easy to identify. Much more difficult to identify is exclusion that is practiced passively, often without malice or forethought—for example, by people who are just comfortable with each other.

To move an exclusive organization toward inclusion, leaders must start by addressing the culture that supports the exclusive makeup and practices. An aggressive recruiting program for the "absent" groups would be counterproductive—where there is little or no tolerance for differences, aggressive recruitment invariably leads to conflict,

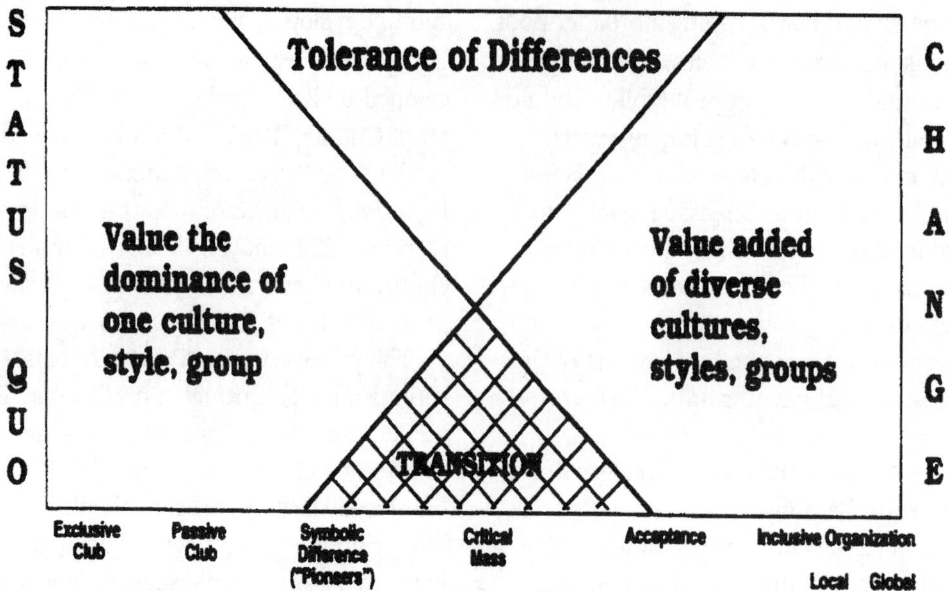

FIGURE 23.1. The path from monocultural club to inclusive organization. Adapted from a model referred to as *multicultural organization development* (MCOD; Jackson et al., 1981).

hostility, resentment, and high turnover. Most likely the people already in the system feel stifled themselves. These organizations are better served by internal programs to widen the bandwidth of acceptable behavior for current personnel areas such as organizational effectiveness, problem solving, and communication styles (Miller, 1988). Effective culture change requires significant changes in human resources policies, management practices, and reward systems—the infrastructure that reflects, reinforces, and guides the organization's culture (Katz & Miller, 1988).

Symbolic difference organizations. Symbolic difference organizations are those organizations that tolerate differences in appearance but not in behavior; they are often self-described as "bias-free" or "blind to differences." Pioneers from different identity groups are often called "tokens" in these organizations. In many cases, the accepted difference is in appearance only—hence the term symbolic difference. The new people may look different, but they are expected to act the same as everyone else.

Leaders need to recognize the difficult yet critical role of pioneers in the change process. Effective leadership actions at this stage can be to support the organization's pioneers and minimize their isolation while educating the wider organization about obstacles that limit or prevent the full contribution of all people. Gathering committed individuals and including champions from the original culture as well as new culture pioneers into organizationally sanctioned networks can provide needed support and build "pockets of readiness" that can help move the organization to the next stage along the path.

Organizations at critical mass. These are organizations with a growing core of people who are committed to a diverse workforce and an inclusive work culture. This is a key transition point: the old rules no longer work, but the new rules have not all been created. This is the stage at which most organizations turn back, stop where they are, or move on to other initiatives.

Critical mass is a time of stress for everyone in the organization, especially leaders. They face charges and countercharges of chaos and conflict, backlash, and reverse discrimination. It often seems like they must develop new competencies, new procedures, and new internal structures overnight. Amid the conflict, chaos, and upheaval of culture change, the "good old days" look particularly good.

A key leadership strategy at this point is visible support for the change effort. It is crucial for leaders to establish, communicate, and model how the mission, vision, and values of the organization are served by diversity and inclusion.

Organizations at acceptance. These are organizations in which people are beginning to be seen as multidimensional, unique, and belonging to several identity groups and in which they are included because of these qualities. There is no longer the question of an organizational imperative for diversity and inclusiveness. The organization experiences the payoff on a daily basis.

With broad acceptance that inclusive practices are critical to business success, closer scrutiny of all aspects of the organization becomes easier. People start to identify more and more structures, procedures, and norms that need to be changed to further the process of inclusion and eliminate oppression of "one-down" groups and individuals. More people step forward to describe how they have been harassed, oppressed, or excluded because more people are willing to listen and champion their causes.

Leaders will find that this is an ideal time for redefining competence throughout the organization and for providing education to impart and improve competencies required for working effectively in diverse partnerships and teams. They will also find increased demand and acceptance for establishing informal reentering opportunities and networks to support all the people of the organization.

Inclusive organizations. These are organizations that actively include, value, and use the wide range of perspectives, opinions, and skills offered by different individuals, identity groups, and functional specialties. Inclusive organizations are oriented to and geared for constant change, continuous improvement, and a constant search for 360-degree vision (Miller, 1994). They are constantly widening their bandwidth of human resources and human potential, and they are eager to gain from the synergy that can be tapped when those differences are brought together

The leadership actions and strategies that will be most effective in inclusive organizations reflect the skill sets and behavior patterns that will be required of all members of high-performing organizations in coming years. Such actions and strategies include the following:

- using organizationwide training and encouragement to facilitate clear, direct, authentic communication;
- using organizationwide training to address, work through, and recognize the value of conflict as a way to enhance outcomes;
- ensuring that processes are in place so that the right voices are in the room, especially voices of potential disagreement;
- challenging and supporting each individual, partnership, team, and group to continuously learn, grow, develop new skills, behave inclusively, and do their best work;
- empowering each person to maximize his or her ability to contribute and add value;
- expanding the conceptual boundaries of the organization to include its stakeholders, communities, customers, and suppliers; and
- recognizing that learning new skills and working through change can be frightening and therefore constantly searching for new ways to reward courage.

Keep in mind that strategic initiatives and culture change interventions that might be effective at one stage along the continuum might be disastrous at other stages. Problems can be even greater when using many "off-the-shelf" diversity programs, like the ones that are used with exclusive clubs.

AN INCLUSIVE APPROACH TO COACHING

Partnering With Leaders

Implementing an effective culture change intervention is virtually impossible without the active support and participation of senior executives. Not only do they need to approve of the direction and commit the necessary resources, but also they need to model the required behaviors and attitudes of the culture change. In that framework, helping senior executives make a strategic assessment of the skills they need to learn becomes an intervention in itself. Therefore, coaching the senior executives becomes a cornerstone of the culture change effort—

much more than a potentially profitable extra to add to a menu of a consultant's services.

Our partnering with senior executives in the process of designing and leading the change effort must start before any active education or training begins, and this involvement is also an act of coaching. As a diverse partnership ourselves—a Jewish woman working with an African American man—we model important skills and attitudes they will need to learn. And as we engage them in the partnership effort, we provide a relatively safe forum for learning a key competency of a high-performing and inclusive work culture—partnering across difference (Buntaine & Miller, 1995).

Partnership Competencies

So many of today's performance initiatives focus on empowerment, training everyone to be a leader. But very few pay any attention to what it means to be a partner. Too few organizations train their people in the key competency of knowing how to join somebody else—how to let somebody else take the lead, how to stand beside and behind instead of above or out front. Just as we coach leaders on how to include the people of their organizations, we coach the leaders' staffs on how to become partners with the leaders (see Table 23.1).

A key to partnership is understanding that there are many routes across an ocean. A leader's role is to choose one of them and to recruit other people for the journey. Often, the act of choosing is more important than the actual choice. With the cooperation, competence, and enthusiasm of good partners, any number of different choices can yield excellent results. But second guessing, bickering, and apathy can turn even the best possible choice into a fiasco.

The unthinking chorus of "yes men" has become a comic strip icon of the monolithic organization. But an occasional chorus of "yeses" can do wonders for a leader's effectiveness and an organization's success. This is not a blind following, but an informed agreement and a committed partnership, with the understanding that all have a role to play in achieving success.

TABLE 23.1

Five Key Partnership Competencies

1. The vision to see leaders, followers, and peers as partners who each have essential and differentiated roles.
2. The self-assurance not to feel diminished by following another's lead.
3. The ability to see a delegated task as part of the process of implementation and not as a put-down
4. The ability to contribute information, opinions, and wisdom to the decision-making process without requiring that they be used.
5. The ability to listen effectively and to ask questions for clarification as part of a process of joining, not as a means to nibble, discount, tear down, or destroy.

The Need for an Outsider's Perspective

One of the odd ironies of diversity training is that leaders often need a fresh point of view to see the value of different points of view. Despite decades of affirmative action initiatives and EEO mandates, the boardrooms and senior leadership structures of major corporations in the United States remain 95% White and male, so senior executives have little exposure to differences. This lack of exposure can cause them to fail to understand the issues and the advantages presented by different perspectives, skill sets, and problem-solving styles. It also offers them little opportunity to become comfortable in dealing with such differences. By using outside consultants as coaches, sounding boards, and practice partners, leaders can gain valuable experience and a greater understanding of the potential benefits to be gained from inclusive practices.

Leading Change

Maximizing the potential of a diverse workforce and an inclusive culture requires greater competencies than managing a monocultural organization. And before an organization can expect the new, inclusive competencies to be valued and practiced by its general population, its senior executives must be able to model them. That makes the coaching of the senior executives vital to the change effort.

The kinds of competencies tomorrow's executives will need are reflected in the changing roles of executives in organizations. Until fairly recently, the standard industry model reflected straight-line thinking regarding leadership—put the best accountant in charge of all the financial people, the best chemist in charge of all the chemists, and so forth.

However, in recent years it has become clear that simply promoting the best technicians does not achieve the leadership needed for success. Organizations are realizing that they need to develop and promote people who can lead—who can get things done through others—as opposed to taking the best person at a specific technical task away from that task and asking that person to watch others do the task.

This is a major shift from the traditional military-style model of many organizations, in which the leaders were supposed to be able to do everything each person in their unit could do. In today's multidisciplined, high-tech organizations, the leader cannot be expected to know it all. More and more, the leader's role is to be an enabler—assisting, guiding, coaching, nudging, and inspiring people who know more about specific tasks to get all the things they need to do those tasks and enabling them to do their best work (which may well be better than the leader could have done).

Today, a leader also has to be a partner (Buntaine, 1994), but in a partnership in which power, authority, and responsibility move back and forth, not one in which one person has all the power and the other has none. The paradox of leadership is that the more power a leader gives away to others, the more powerful he or she can become.

For a culture change effort to be successful, leaders must perform a number of specific and critical roles—as models of behavior, champions of change, definers of mission and vision, and enablers of high performance. In addition to coaching them in their roles, the leaders' coaches must also make sure the leaders know the rationale behind the roles. Coaches must help leaders understand

- why the culture change is important to the organization (i.e., the organizational imperative for diversity and inclusion; Katz, 1995; Katz & Miller, 1995b);
- that culture change is required to leverage diversity (i.e., inclusive norms and values, human resources systems and benefits, and management styles and practices); and
- that the change process is ongoing—not like turning on a light switch.

Creating a Safe Environment for Learning

A key for any coach trying to teach new skills is creating opportunities for learners to practice those skills even though they may feel awkward and uncomfortable. The challenge is to expose leaders to new skills and situations without leaving them exposed. One of the advantages offered by outside consultant coaches is the comfort level they can bring to senior executives who need a confidential and supportive forum for practicing new behaviors before "taking them public." In addition to acting in this role in our consulting practice, we provide a sounding board for leaders to discuss potential actions and strategies. Because we are not a part of the organization and our future career paths do not hinge on our relationship with the executive, we can offer honest and objective feedback that can be accepted or rejected without job-threatening consequences or public embarrassment (Katz & Jimerson, 1993).

Some Keys for Coaches

There is no one right way to achieve an inclusive corporate culture. The landscape is constantly changing. To navigate through the change process, an organization needs visible leadership, and its leaders will need ongoing coaching so they can model the necessary skills, behaviors, and attitudes effectively and with authenticity.

If leaders are given the opportunity to practice and improve, the results will come. The following are some key areas for leaders and their coaches to focus on:

- develop an organizational imperative that aligns inclusive behaviors with the organization's ultimate success;
- find the strategic linkage to the organization's goals;
- create a safe environment that encourages people to learn and grow and engage in ongoing dialogue;

- look for learning and synergy, not perfection;
- fine-tune all the time;
- avoid using labels and stereotyping;
- learn to reject myth, rumor, innuendo, and incomplete facts;
- remember that change in the middle looks like failure;
- look at real issues that create barriers to achievement;
- understand and use models like the Path;
- find learning partners for senior executives from all levels of the organization;
- learn and teach the skills required for tapping diversity;
- start with the people in the room;
- preach to the choir, and spread outward by example;
- coach carefully and gently, but honestly;
- remember that learning takes courage—offer encouragement and rewards for being brave; and
- remember that change is constant—the process never ends.

CASE STUDY

Good Leadership Requires Good Partnership

After being surprised and embarrassed by the findings we presented at a briefing session about his organization's diversity initiative, the chief executive of a large division of one of the largest corporations in the United States started yelling furiously at one of us during a consultation meeting. "Don't take it personally," we were told. "He yells at everyone."

The leader was yelling out of anger, frustration, fear, and vulnerability. People did not brief the leader on upcoming issues, give him feedback, or help prepare him for meetings. His people and his organization's culture were often setting him up to look foolish and uninformed. No one wanted to be the bearer of bad news. People did not share their concerns with him. They looked out for their own hides by lying low and playing it safe. His people and his system were keeping him incompetent. His expressions of anger were covering his sense of being out of control.

After identifying the processes in action, we worked with the leader to develop a more inclusive work environment. We provided the leader with two coach mentors from our consulting group, a White woman and an African American woman. They were selected because of the different perspectives they could provide—from each other as well as from him. He met with them together and separately on a regular schedule over a period of several months. They were also available to him virtually around the clock by telephone to discuss immediate or emerging issues.

Over time, he learned that it was okay to not have all the answers. He learned how to facilitate discussions and address problems without laying blame. He learned to treat mistakes as opportunities for learning, not as something requiring punishment.

Perhaps just as important to his success, we also coached his entire team on how to practice inclusive values and behaviors, especially good two-way communication and "Learning Community Behaviors" (see Table 23.2). Now his team helps to prepare him before meetings, helps him understand newly emerging key issues, and keeps him clear on how he can best add value as a leader. The team helps him be a better leader, and the entire leadership group gains in effectiveness.

Leaders may find an external coach's "objective" view of their organization valuable, but good coaching regarding inclusion needs to go beyond that. Leaders need access to a full range of external and internal perspectives. We find that providing leaders with a secure source of internal perspectives offers profound and lasting benefits.

As we have done in several large organizations, we established a learning group for the senior executive. The group was carefully selected from a pool of people identified as current and future leaders of the organization who did not report directly to the leader.

As coaches, we established a set of ground rules for these learning groups, which we call "Learning Community Behaviors" (see Table 23.2). The ground rules also parallel the new skill set required of leaders who wish to create an environment of

TABLE 23.2

Learning Community Behaviors

1. *Provide and create safety—a safe zone.* Learning requires safety and respect. Leaders must make it safe for themselves and others to risk, to experiment, to make mistakes, to grow, and to change.
2. *Be self-responsible and self-challenging.* Leaders must be honest with themselves so they can be honest with others. They must model the practice of giving grace when mistakes happen, combined with a supportive challenge to do better—to be gentle with themselves and others, but not self-indulgent. The focus is for each to be committed to her or his own learning—challenging to self, supportive of others.
3. *Listen, listen, listen, and respond.* Accepting a learning posture requires more patience and more active listening skills than most people are used to. The tendency is to challenge and give one's own opinion early and often. As role model as well as learner, a leader must try to absorb and appreciate the information being presented, including its context, then restate his or her understanding of the information to be sure no miscommunication took place. THEN, the leader can respond.
4. *Lean into discomfort.* Just as pain is a sensory message that something is wrong, so is discomfort. Ignoring it may cause people to avoid situations, behaviors, or relationships that could enrich the individual and the organization. Leaders should model the use of their own discomfort as a possible indication of opportunity to learn something new.
5. *Experiment with new behaviors in order to expand one's range of response.* Leaders and partners gain new perspectives as well as increase their skills. Today's changing world calls for all to learn new interactive behaviors and skills.
6. *Take risks, be raggedy, make some mistakes—then let go.* Try to feel the exhilaration instead of feeling foolish. Leaders must give themselves and their partners permission to make the necessary mistakes to learn.
7. *Accept working through conflict to its resolution as a catalyst for learning.* People have more to learn from those with a different point of view than from those who agree with them. Leaders must model sticking with the interaction until they work through the conflicts to find the potential points of learning for all people involved.
8. *Be crisp and say what is core.* Leaders must not beat around the bush, sugar-coat, or "dissemble" for fear of causing hurt or conflict. They must give the other person credit for being able to handle their honest feelings or observations. They must be direct, but not abusive or overpowering.
9. *Be open-minded.* No one has all the answers. Even what seems like the most completely off-base comment or idea usually contains some nuggets of value. Leaders must not let the weakest parts blind them to all the other parts. They must learn to see from the eyes of the presenter as well as from their own.

inclusiveness and continuous improvement within their organizations.

In this case, the group became a safe place for the leader and the other group members to learn and improve communication skills, to engage in offering clear and honest feedback, to practice inclusive behaviors and attitudes, to internalize the organizational imperative for diversity and inclusion, and to become fully competent in their roles in creating a high-performing and inclusive organization.

The group's original purpose was to provide the senior executive with a group of internal coaches who could voice a variety of internal perspectives and keep the leader in touch with the true pulse of the organization. In practice, the group also became a cadre of leaders of change throughout the organization—people who not only understood and supported the senior executive's strategies and plans, but also had input into them and could transfer them to the different constituencies within the organization. Although the group had been established as a temporary task force, the senior executive found it so valuable that he has turned it into a permanent advisory group with a rotating membership.

In each of the organizations in which we have established these groups, they have become miniature learning communities, supporting the leader's development as well as the development of the other participants. Through participation in these groups, senior executives have seen the broader value of their roles as enablers of learning and skill development throughout their organizations.

References

Buntaine, C. S. (1994). Developing cross-gender partnership competencies: Exploring the 7 C's. In E. Cross, J. Katz, F. Miller, & E. Seashore (Eds.), *The promise of diversity* (pp. 259–266). Washington, DC: NIL Institute, and Burr Ridge, IL: Irwin.

Buntaine, C. S., & Miller, F. A. (1995). *Competencies for an inclusive workplace*. Unpublished manuscript.

Jackson, B., Hardiman, R., & Chesler, M. (1981). *Racial awareness development in organizations*. Unpublished manuscript.

Katz, J. H. (1995). Leveraging diversity: The business imperative. *Cultural Diversity at Work, 8,* 4.

Katz, J. H., & Jimerson, P. (1993). Executive development for managing diversity. In *Proceedings of the Executive Development Roundtable*. Boston: Boston University School of Management.

Katz, J. H., & Miller, F. A. (1988). Between monoculturalism and multiculturalism: Traps awaiting the organization. *OD Practitioner, 20,* 1–5.

Katz, J. H., & Miller, F. A. (1995a). Cultural diversity as a developmental process: The path from a monocultural club to an inclusive organization. In W. Pfeiffer (Ed.), *The 1995 annual* (Vol. 2, pp. 267–281). San Diego, CA: J. Pfeiffer.

Katz, J. H., & Miller, F. A. (1995b). *Inclusiveness: The new organizational imperative*. Unpublished manuscript.

Miller, F. A. (1988). Moving a team to multiculturalism. In W. B. Reddy & K. Jamison (Eds.), *Team building: Blueprints for productivity and satisfaction* (pp. 192–197). Washington, DC: NIL Institute, and San Diego, CA: University Associates.

Miller, E A. (1994). Forks in the road. In E. Cross, J. Katz, F. Miller, & E. Seashore (Eds.), *The promise of diversity* (pp. 38–45). Washington, DC: NIL Institute, and Burr Ridge, IL: Irwin.

Olesen, M. (1996). Coaching today's executive. *Training and Development, 50,* 22–27.

CHAPTER 24

COACHING VERSUS THERAPY: A PERSPECTIVE

Vicki Hart, John Blattner, and Staci Leipsic

Although the origins of coaching began back in the 1940s, it wasn't until the 1980s that the field really came into its own (chap. 13, this volume; Hudson, 1999). As the world of work and organizations changed, so did the needs of the individuals within them. Services—such as succession planning, leadership training, and outplacement, to name a few—became more common. We also witnessed societal changes, with many aspects of our lives being more unpredictable, turbulent, and fragile. Because of these dynamics and the increasing frequency and speed of associated transitions, coaching has evolved as a methodology to fill a need for growth as well as continuity in our lives.

Counseling and therapy also assist individuals in need and have their own rich traditions of helping and social influence. Much overlap currently exists between therapy–counseling and coaching, including the fact that many former therapists have switched to coaching or practice both coaching and therapy concurrently. Both coaching and therapy are based in similar theoretical constructs, and similar practitioner–client issues may arise in each. Both professions are based on an ongoing, confidential, one-to-one relationship between the therapist or coach and his or her client. "Clients come to therapy or coaching wanting change, and both professions assume that significant change will occur over time" (Hayden & Whitworth, 1995, p. 1). These overlapping characteristics between therapy–counseling and coaching raise issues and, in some cases, foster controversy among professionals in both arenas. In an effort to articulate, clarify, and further discern these issues, we conducted face-to-face and telephone interviews with 30 geographically dispersed participants. The participant pool was composed of professional colleagues as well as random, self-selected respondents to an Internet-based request for participants. All participants met the criteria of (a) holding a clinical master's or doctoral degree and (b) having either active or former practices in both coaching and therapy. Participants' demographics are summarized in Table 24.1.

TABLE 24.1

Demographic Data of Participants

Demographic data	Male	Female
Educational training		
MA or MSW	6	9
PhD or EdD	9	6
Type of coaching		
Generic (i.e., personal)	8	10
Executive	7	5
Description of practice		
Currently practicing coaching and therapy	8	7
Has practiced both, but not concurrently	7	8
Description of clients		
Individual	7	6
Organization	2	1
Individual and organization	6	8

The experience and opinions drawn from these interviews provide the basis for our inquiry and are categorized and summarized below.

QUESTION 1: FROM YOUR EXPERIENCE, WHAT DO YOU THINK IS THE CRITICAL DIFFERENCE BETWEEN COACHING AND THERAPY?

Participants identified between one and six critical differences between coaching and therapy. Their comments emphasized the distinction in focus of attention, time orientation, level of activity, and type of conversation between themselves and their clients.

In therapy, the focus is often on interpersonal health and an identifiable issue, such as acute depression or relational discord, that interferes with the client's level of functioning and current psychodynamic or psychosocial adjustment. The focus is typically retrospective, dealing with unconscious issues and repair of damage from earlier experiences, according to numerous interviewees. It may even involve medication, adjunct therapies, and coordination of services. Discerning and treating pathology and relieving symptoms through behavioral, cognitive, or analytic intervention is the domain of the psychotherapist.

The coach's orientation is prospective, focusing on goals, untapped potential, and critical success factors in a whole person who seeks to maximize his or her fulfillment in life and work. Although both approaches involve developmental issues and focus on awareness, therapy encourages awareness of past injuries in order to promote insight and healing, whereas coaching focuses on untapped present possibilities in order to link awareness to action.

Regarding level of activity and types of conversation, coaches are more likely to initiate topics for discussion and to step into a session with ideas and suggestions. They portray their coaching interactions as more active, informal, and self-disclosing, often perceiving their coaching clients as experts in their own right. According to most interviewees, conversations in coaching are tied to business and work objectives. Whereas therapy may be an undefined, wandering process of uncovering and discovery, coaching interactions were described by participants as more structured and task focused, often involving concrete action plans designed to move clients toward their defined goals. Therapeutic dialogue is seen as more often involving the expression of feelings and emotional processing. The exploration of depth issues is perceived as outside the boundaries of coaching for nonclinically trained coaches.

Participants also articulated the overlap between coaching and therapy. In particular, they highlighted the similar methods of inquiry, propensity for advice giving, boundary issues, and potential power differentials that exist in both. Several participants stated that the grayness between these two approaches to social influence and the current lack of regulatory standards of practice for coaching create critical issues for both professions.

QUESTION 2: HOW DO YOU RELATE TO COACHING CLIENTS VERSUS THERAPY CLIENTS?

Overall, there is a profound difference in relating while conducting coaching versus therapy with clients. All of the participants agreed that coaching is more goal directed, action based, and outwardly defined. When coaching clients, participants reported themselves as "self-revelatory," "having a skilled friendship," and "in partnership." Other common themes were having looser boundaries, being more relaxed, using the self as a vehicle for change, and not addressing transference issues. Participants reported using more humor, being more actively engaged, and having greater flexibility within the coaching relationship. There is not the same need to "protect" the relationship, and as a marriage and family therapist from Montana put it, "You can admit that you know them in the grocery store." Almost all of the participants interviewed for this study admitted that they expect more from their coaching clients. They indicated that they can adopt less of a caretaking role with their coaching clients and are not responsible for emotional fragility and looking out for them. A master's-level therapist from British Columbia who is now practicing only coaching stated that "coaching is not such a tender zone as therapy is."

Most of the participants interviewed for this chapter relate to therapy clients in a traditional psychotherapist–client manner. A clinical psychologist in New Jersey who is practicing both therapy and coaching stated,

> In coaching, once the coach opens the door, the client walks through with little, if any, difficulty. In therapy, the client is more likely to be reticent, not "seeing the door" or feeling afraid to find out what is on the other side.

In therapy, the emphasis is on past relationships, problems, and behavioral patterns. Participants reported that they are "distant" and "protective" and do not develop friendships with their therapy clients. Self-disclosure is minimal unless it is considered beneficial to the therapeutic process. There is an assumption that the therapy client is damaged, lower functioning, or in crisis. Boundaries are usually rigid and impermeable in therapy relationships. Another major difference is the use of transference issues in therapy, which is virtually ignored in the coaching relationship. In therapy, the therapist is viewed as the "healer" in the relationship, whereas coaching implies more collaboration between coach and client. The extensive clinical training and education that the therapist has experienced compounds this position, primarily because for some time psychotherapy has aligned itself with the medical model. When a client comes to therapy, he or she has the expectation that the therapist is the so-called expert who knows more about the diagnosis or problem than he or she (the client) does. This is different than when a client comes to the coach with the expectation of a more collaborative model.

QUESTION 3: WHAT WOULD YOU DO OR NOT DO WITH A COACHING CLIENT VERSUS A THERAPY CLIENT?

Perhaps the biggest difference between executing coaching versus therapy for the participants we interviewed is the emphasis (or lack thereof) on the client's past. A psychologist from Washington State who no longer practices therapy reported, "Coaches have to stay in the here and now; they do not go into the past to try and figure out why a person is behaving in the way that they are." A PhD psychologist from Massachusetts who practices both coaching and therapy delineated between the two by "not taking up issues pertaining to one's family, not dealing with depression, and referring out if symptoms of pathology are present" while he is doing coaching.

Flexibility and duality appear to be overriding differences between maintaining coaching versus therapy relations. An EdD who is the president of a national coaching training program for therapists stated, "The coaching client can also be in other relationships with you [golf, social, etc.] if boundaries are respected. Dual relationships are taboo in therapy relationships." Coaching does not carry the same stigma that therapy has in the past. People are even inclined to publicize the fact that they are receiving coaching. "I would meet a coaching client in Starbucks for a session while I would never meet a therapy client in a public place," exclaimed a clinical social worker from California.

Looser boundaries allow the coach much more latitude than the therapist. An example of this difference was elucidated by a licensed clinical social worker in Florida who practices both therapy and relationship coaching:

> If a coaching client asks me my birthday, I'll tell them, and even accept a card. If my therapy client asks me the same question, I'll ask them why they want to know or what do they want to hear.

Participants reported much greater flexibility in the delivery of coaching methods but tended to rely on the traditional means of conducting psychotherapy. Participants interviewed for this chapter reported relating to coaching clients by means of telesessions (over the phone), the Internet, video conferencing, and in-person meetings. Therapy relations existed largely on a face-to-face basis, relying on telesessions for an emergency basis only.

Participants reported a greater feeling of dependency from their therapy clients. The expectation is that the coaching relationship will not foster the same level of dependency and that there will be a more egalitarian relationship. A master's-level therapist from California reported, "A lot of therapy can be coaching but not vice-versa." A psychologist from Indiana stated, "Coaching can be used by a therapist as a situational application when the circumstance requires him to act as a coach, as an adjunct approach. A coach, on the other hand, is not equipped to act as a therapist."

Among participants there was a strong consensus that when providing therapy, remaining distant is always a concern. However, this concern is not there in coaching relationships. One therapist–coach from Maryland reported that he "talks more" in coaching: "I am more likely to offer something that might catapult them in some direction."

QUESTION 4: WHAT DO YOU CONSIDER "RED FLAGS" FOR COACHES WHO ARE NOT TRAINED THERAPISTS?

Responses to this question clustered around two areas of concern: (a) the specific client characteristics and issues that a coach needs to be able to recognize as danger signals requiring referral and (b) the issues surrounding people acting as coaches who are not professionally trained clinicians. Starting with the first, the red flags most often mentioned as indicators of deeper client issues include signs of depression, anxiety attacks, alcohol or drug addictions, personality disorders, and paranoia. A psychologist who trains therapists to be coaches feels that "if the client is stuck in a victim role or emotional drama, not showing up, not following through, has serious emotions in more than one session, or [is] expressing that they cannot go on," a coach should beware. He stated, "A tight feeling in your gut is a red flag, and don't dance around it."

A master's-trained therapist from Maryland said,

> Watch out for low affect, high degrees of chaos, and the inability to take action and move forward on a path. If you feel you have to be overly responsible, this is not a good sign for a coaching situation.

A clinician trained in organizational behavior warned that when the "mood of the client is a prominent feature of the interaction" and "it takes on the character of an overarching belief system that you know may not have anything to do with the reality of the present-day situation," the coach should beware. When the client tells the coach, "You are the only one who cares about me," there is cause for concern. Other red flags suggesting the need for referral include persistent anger or aggression, suicidal ideation, self-destructive impulses or behaviors, and extreme dependency.

These issues lead into the second area of concern held by many participants, starting with whether nonclinicians are able to identify a mental or emotional problem that lies beyond the realm of coaching. "You must know how to identify, how to ask the right question to assess, and how to manage the problem," stated a psychologist from the San Francisco Bay area. A blind spot for coaches who are not trained therapists is that "their paradigm keeps them ignorant and myopic in that they approach everyone as if they are whole and complete. They do not recognize pathology, nor have a skill set to manage or treat it," according to a psychologist in Oklahoma who is authoring a book on the subject. "They themselves may demonstrate their own pathology or unresolved issues within the context of the coaching relationship without recognizing it."

Boundary issues constitute another area of concern related to coaching without clinical training. As the psychologist from Oklahoma stated, "Coaches may surface powerful pockets of transference and countertransference through establishing highly intimate dialogues that create a power differential, without any clear parameters or articulation of that process." "One of the advantages of coming from a therapy background is knowing the distinctions, knowing where not to go, but helping people find a good clinician," said an executive coach practicing with multinational corporate clients. A number of interviewees raised yet a third concern involving ethical behavior and issues of confidentiality in coaching given there are currently no licensing or governing boards. As one participant pointed out, "Protecting confidentiality and keeping agreements are important in coaching but are legally required in therapy."

QUESTION 5: ALTERNATIVELY, WHAT DO YOU THINK IS UNIQUE ABOUT COACHING THAT A TRAINED "THERAPIST-TURNED-COACH" NEEDS TO BE AWARE OF WHILE COACHING?

Perhaps the biggest obstacle that the therapist-turned-coach needs to be aware of is that coaching is not for every therapist. Coaching models seem best suited to goal-oriented therapists who prefer to enable clients to take responsibility for their own process and outcomes, rather than to "fix" the problem (Steele, 2000). Participants strongly stated the need to stay away from psychodynamic issues. The coach's intention is to keep the process moving forward, and discussion of the past should be avoided: "You may want to 'visit' the past, but don't spend time analyzing it." In coaching, one does not focus on symptoms or draw conclusions. As one participant stated simply, "Don't do therapy."

In therapy, one "works to achieve wellness," whereas in coaching one focuses more on increasing capacity and reaching goals. The coach is there to help the client achieve results. As one participant stated, "People want you to help them, and just listening is not enough." This often translates into a necessity for the coach to demonstrate business savvy and achieve business results. Coaches must understand how business organizations function and have a grasp of different industries and their particular needs. Having a business mindset is important when making the transition to coaching.

Participants raised other distinctions between coaching and therapy that therapists should be aware of related to timing, scheduling, and setting an agenda. In coaching the time frames are not as rigid as in therapy. A session may be broken up into half-hour time blocks and may be weekly or monthly, depending on the contract between the coach and the client. So coaching would vary from the traditional 50-minute hour. The coach needs to guide the process and not direct it. The client, not the coach, should establish the agenda for the coaching. Also, many participants agreed that the client is in charge of the process as opposed to therapy, where the therapist is often in charge.

In reference to executive coaching, it was suggested that the concept of and training in leadership roles is helpful. A coach should be familiar with different styles of managing others. Coaches need to appreciate the role of the individual in the context of the organization. Overall, the executive coach should maintain a focus on achieving results for both the client and the organization.

Finally, participants indicated that therapists desiring to become coaches would greatly benefit from a formal coaching program. One study participant suggested that "therapists may need to 'unlearn' therapeutic techniques" in which they were previously trained and instead learn what is required to be an effective coach. This may also necessitate that therapists-turned-coaches "let go of the ego of their title." One participant offered this comment: "Being a therapist does not [by definition] make you a good coach."

QUESTION 6: WHO WOULD YOU SAY IS "IN CONTROL" IN COACHING AND IN THERAPY?

The participants responded in a variety of ways to this question. A few participants indicated that in therapy the therapist is in control of the process. This may be attributable to the therapist's experience in dealing with mental health issues or the perception that the particular therapist has of a client. Also, the influence of professional training and orientation may play a role in how the process is managed. One participant stated, "The issue of control is about 80% of the therapy."

Another group of participants classified control for coaching as a comutual or cocreative process. Coaching is seen as a more collaborative process and more straightforward than therapy. It appears to be an activity that is shared by both parties and not controlled by the coach. The coach will guide the person being coached but will not directly assume responsibility for the outcome. These participants indicated that in coaching, the person being coached would know that he or she is in charge.

Other participants suggested that the issue of control rests with the client. Whether it is coaching or therapy, they maintained that control is always in the hands of the client. One participant stated, "The client is always in charge; in coaching the client knows this, and in therapy, it is something that has to be taught."

QUESTION 7: HOW ARE CONTRACTING AND CONFIDENTIALITY HANDLED IN COACHING VERSUS THERAPY?

Participants reported mixed responses to this question. Contracting in coaching appears to be more formal than in therapy. A PhD from California confided that

> in coaching, there is a clear contract—it is explicit: "Where are we going, where do you want to be?" In executive coaching, the organization comes to the coach and says, "We have this guy who is really messed up."

Other aspects that seem to make coaching contracts more formal than therapy contracts are quarterly reviews, fixed time lines, open discussions of clients' expectations, outcomes, payment made up front, and requirements to demonstrate targeted results.

According to some participants, contracting in therapy appears to be looser and less defined. A clinical psychologist from California stated that he does not do much contracting in therapy and that he "may use it very loosely around what it is we need to work on, but do not ratchet it down to specific behaviors or goals." Contracts in therapy appear to be verbal or left to the insurance companies. At the opposite end of the spectrum, a psychologist from Oklahoma stated that "in therapy, the implied contract is rooted in national standards for ethical practice to which therapists are held accountable, are reviewed, monitored, and can be sued."

Approximately one third of the participants interviewed for this study reported no difference in contracting. A master's-level clinician from Illinois who is concurrently practicing both therapy and coaching sees contracting in both "as the same process— dealing with fees, goal setting, logistics, time and place." Another psychologist from Indiana reported "no real difference—different psychologists use different contract models. It depends on the individual."

Confidentiality is a critical aspect of any helping relationship. An EdD from Colorado reported, "Confidentiality is a little looser in coaching, although I do not share who my client is or any details without their permission. Coaching clients, however, love to tell people who their coach is!" Others reported that there is a lack of monitoring in coaching and that there are not any actual rules pertaining to confidentiality. A PhD from Georgia confided, "In coaching, there is not legal protection. In coaching you could 'blab' to anyone, whereas you are not able to do that in therapy." Obstacles to confidentiality in coaching include instances when you are working as an external consultant for a company and when the company is your client.

Overall, most of the therapists who are also practicing coaching appear to take confidentiality very seriously and are skeptical that other coaches without the clinical training are doing the same. Most therapists who are doing coaching seem to adhere to the therapist guidelines and to practice under their oath as a psychotherapist. A psychologist from Illinois stated, "Confidentiality in coaching must be cleared with the client first. In therapy, there are laws governing what can be said and how. You must follow the law."

Managed care has caused the notion of confidentiality in therapy to take an interesting turn. One master's-level therapist from Arizona stated,

> There is actually more confidentiality in coaching. People do not realize that when they submit their bills to their insurance company [for therapy], their information is public knowledge. They can access that information at any

> time. There are also clearinghouses that a savvy person can call to get the addresses of people with certain diagnoses from their insurance companies. Most people don't know this.

CONCLUSION

This chapter has documented some of the thoughts and concerns expressed by 30 professionals who practice coaching, therapy, or both. In summary, participants identified several distinct differences between coaching and therapy, including the focus of attention, time orientation, level of activity, and types of conversations between themselves and their clients. They also articulated the overlap between coaching and therapy; in particular, they highlighted the similar methods of inquiry, propensity for advice giving, boundary issues, and potential for power differentials that exist in both. Second, participants reported that they relate to coaching and therapy clients differently and described coaching as more goal directed, action based, and outwardly defined. By contrast, there is an assumption that in therapy the client is often "damaged," lower functioning, or in crisis. Third, participants reported overriding differences in flexibility and duality between coaching and therapy relations: Dual relationships are taboo in therapy, whereas looser boundaries allow the coach much more latitude than the therapist. Participants reported that they have much greater flexibility in their coaching relationships and that they tend to rely on a more traditional expert–subject relationship with clients while conducting psychotherapy. In addition, they reported a tendency to stay in the here and now rather than delving into the past in order to determine why a person is behaving as he or she is.

A fourth area of response clustered around the specific client characteristics that a coach needs to recognize as danger signals requiring referral, with coaches who are not professionally trained clinicians often failing to recognize these red flags. Hallmarks of danger include signs of depression, anxiety attacks, alcohol or drug addictions, personality disorders, and paranoia. At the same time, participants also identified that a therapist-turned-coach must have business knowledge in addition to clinical experience (i.e., a business mindset) and be able to achieve business results. Therapists may need to avoid using certain therapy techniques or, more to the point, realize that being a good therapist does not necessarily make one a good coach.

Some participants reported that the therapist is in control of the therapy process; another group classified control in coaching as a comutual or cocreative process. There were also mixed responses to questions about contracting and confidentiality in coaching versus therapy. In general, contracting in coaching appears to be more formal than in therapy, where it appears to many to be looser and less defined. However, approximately one third of the participants reported no difference in contracting. Confidentiality was also reported by some to be a little looser in coaching. However, most of the therapists who are practicing coaching appear to take confidentiality very seriously and were skeptical as to whether nonclinically trained coaches are doing the same.

ISSUES FOR FUTURE CONSIDERATION

The experience and opinions summarized above give rise to issues that warrant further exploration. Key categories of inquiry suggested here include concerns about legality and accountability, the importance of adequate training, and the need for supervision.

Concerns About Legality and Accountability

Issues of ambiguity that arise for therapists who are transitioning to coaching include licensing accountability for practicing as a therapist while coaching, governing laws, and future legislation. As of now, coaching is an unregulated field. There are some who think this may change in the future, and they are waiting for the first coach to be sued in court. An example of this uncertainty exists in the state of Washington, where a coach must be registered as a counselor. The law includes the following definition, which has been interpreted by some as including coaching:

> (5) "Counseling" means employing any therapeutic techniques, including but not limited to social work, mental health counseling, marriage and family therapy, and hypnotherapy, for a fee that offer, assist or attempt to assist an individual or individuals in the amelioration or adjustment of mental, emotional or behavioral problems, and includes therapeutic techniques to achieve sensitivity and awareness of the self and others and the development of human potential. (Revised Code of Washington, 1987)

Many coaches practicing in Washington have interpreted this definition to include their profession and have registered in order to be safe. The likelihood of other states following Washington's lead is unknown at this time.

Importance of Adequate Training

A second issue for future consideration relates to the need for nonclinicians to receive training to address red-flag issues. A number of our participants offered advice in this arena. In the words of an Olympic coach who became an executive coach and authored a coaching book: "A coach is not a therapist and should focus on the issues that the client brings. If he (she) is aware of anything that interferes with these issues, that could be a cue for a referral." Another psychologist recommended that coaches have a statement they make for themselves and others as to what their limits are and that they verbalize it with examples of what they do and what they do not do in coaching:

> Elucidating their coaching processes—such as defining the issues, the goal, the plan of action, and the deliverables—gives the client some perimeter or a container to put her/himself into. Then the assumption is that [if the coach] does these things and the client does not change, there may be a clinical issue going on.

Need for Supervision

A third issue and recommendation that several participants voiced is that a coach should have a coach in addition to adequate training. One reason is to ensure that the coach understands the coachee or client experience. Our participants suggested that ongoing supervision for coaching is important for professional development, just as a practicum or internship is usually required in clinical training. Another purpose of this mentoring relationship is to provide a context for working through issues that cross the boundary between coaching and therapy as they surface in one's coaching practice. A final reason relates to the variety and complexity of organizations. Although ideally a coach has experience with various organizations and industries, "it is clearly impossible to have proficiency and expertise with regard to all issues" (chap. 21, this volume, p. 228) that may arise with clients. A coach's aptitude is inherently limited by his or her prior exposure to specific cultures and professional experiences. Peer supervision can enable coaches to develop "a proficient methodology, theory and personal ability to work in a variety of environments inhabited by culturally diverse people" (Haber, 1996, p. 34).

If the field of coaching continues to expand, as its current popularity suggests, future research will no doubt find these and other issues worthy of further inquiry. It is likely that, as more scientifically validated coaching practices and their applications are identified, "professional standards for coaching will also emerge" (chap. 21, this volume, p. 234).

References

Haber, R. (1996). *Dimensions of psychotherapy supervision*. New York: Norton.

Hayden, C. J., & Whitworth, L. (1995). Distinctions between coaching & therapy. *The Coaches Agenda, 1*, 1–2.

Hudson, F. M. (1999). *The handbook of coaching*. San Francisco: Jossey-Bass.

Revised Code of Washington c 183 §1 (1995) ; c 3 §27 (1991); c 512 §13. (1987).

Steele, D. (2000, March/April). Professional coaching and the marriage and family therapist. *The California Therapist*, pp. 54–55.

CHAPTER 25

MULTIMODAL THERAPY: A USEFUL MODEL FOR THE EXECUTIVE COACH

James T. Richard

Recently, Diedrich (see chap. 14, this volume, p. 144) exhorted consultants "to deal with the executive holistically." To meet this challenge, Arnold A. Lazarus's multimodal therapy is suggested as a useful model to improve the performance of executives. This model can add value to tools and models currently in use by industrial/organizational (I/O) psychologists in the workplace. It also can easily be used by counseling/clinical psychologists who wish to escape the confines of managed care by adding psychological executive coaching to the services they offer. In this way, psychologists are able to broaden the scope of their practice. In addition to a discussion of this model, the present chapter presents a case study to illustrate how the model can be used by the eclectic psychologically oriented executive coach.

LAZARUS MODEL

Lazarus (1976, 1989), a much-heralded innovator in the field of cognitive–behavioral therapy, views personality as encompassing seven dimensions. By addressing all of these aspects, the consultant is able to facilitate the improvement of an executive's performance. The dimensions are easily remembered via the acronym BASIC I.D.: behavior, affect, sensation, imagery, cognition, interpersonal relationships, and drug/biology modality.

Following this model, the executive coach/psychologist, in the initial assessment session and the subsequent counseling sessions, asks the following continually:

1. What behaviors need to increase or decrease?
2. What is the dominant feature in the makeup of the executive's affect (e.g., anger, anxiety, guilt, depression)?
3. What sensations does he or she mention that are associated with the problem (e.g., stomach distress, tightness in the neck or shoulders)?
4. What mental pictures or images are revealed in the client's language (e.g., "I'm a weasel," "I'm David against Goliath," "I see myself being humiliated by my boss")?
5. What are the typical cognitions or internal sentences the executive is repeating over and over to himself or herself (e.g., "I won't be able to meet those quarterly sales goals," "The vice president shouldn't have given me these new territories; I'm stretched already")?
6. How does the client get along with significant others in terms of daily interpersonal relationships (e.g., relating to superiors, peers, and reports)?
7. Within the drug/biology modality, are there any factors that may affect the client's job performance and/or influence any of the other six

I wish to thank Arnold A. Lazarus, Ruthmary Richard, Susan Richard, William Ford, and Ronald Goldstein (deceased) for their helpful comments on earlier versions of this chapter.

modalities (e.g., taking excessive amounts of over-the-counter medications, using illegal drugs, untreated physical illness)?

After completion of the initial assessment, the consultant can begin to strategically plan the interventions within each of the seven modalities. For example, if the client's employer has complained that the client is missing project deadlines (behavior modality), we can quickly see how some of the modalities influence each other. We can briefly explain to the client that procrastination (behavior modality) is often preceded by feelings of dread or anxiety (affect modality), which are themselves accompanied by thoughts (cognitive modality) such as "If I screw up, I'm going to look like a fool." This didactic intervention in the context of a specific counseling interaction might be further coupled with the suggested use of the "Premack principle" (rewarding oneself for doing an unpleasant task).

Continual updating of the BASIC I.D. profile is congruent with Diedrich's (see chap. 14, this volume) contention that executive coaching is an ongoing process within a developmental context. He advises against attempting a "quick fix" to a glaring problem. Through conscientious completion of the profile, the consultant may discover that the executive is viewed as an inattentive listener who uses intimidation as a way of gaining consensus. In addition, the coach may also find that the executive's lifestyle is inordinately out of balance (e.g., he or she does nothing but work). By discovering these traits, the coach is able to select appropriate interventions.

Over the years, I have learned, based on my clinical experiences, to add some atypical questions in helping to determine appropriate interventions. For example, I have noticed that a number of professionals harbor numerous fears or anxieties (affect modality) over financial matters. I frequently ask the following questions: Do you have a formal retirement plan? Do you have a will? Are you up to date on filing your tax returns? Based on the responses to these questions, I may make referrals to accountants, certified financial planners, and/or lawyers.

KINDS OF INTERVENTIONS

What interventions can be used with the multimodal therapy model? While it may seem at first glance that this model is appropriate solely for the cognitive–behavioral consultant, this is not the case. Lazarus (1985, 1997), in the evolution of the model, made repeated appeals for what he calls "technical eclecticism." Thus, the consultant can confidently employ strategic interventions based on family therapy concepts, organizational development models, or creative problem-solving techniques. This is also consistent with another notion that Lazarus has repeatedly promulgated in his writings: The consultant needs to bring specific strategies and techniques to each of the seven modalities.

To further support technical eclecticism, a review of Kilburg's "Abbreviated List of Coaching Methods and Techniques" (see chap. 1, this volume, Table 1.3) illustrates a wide variety of behavioral techniques that consultants can use in a coaching relationship. Education, training, reading assignments, role modeling, simulations, brainstorming, and journaling fit easily into the multimodal model.

MULTIMODAL THERAPY ADDS VALUE

Introduction of the multimodal model can add value to the use of contemporary assessment instruments. While the 16 Personality Factor Questionnaire (16PF; Cattell, Cattell, & Cattell, 1993) and Myers–Briggs Type Indicator (Briggs & Myers, 1977) provide valuable broad developmental perspectives, the multimodal model can focus on more specific behaviors or problematic issues.

In addition to being more specific, contextual, and problem focused, the multimodal model can highlight possible conflicts between personal traits and job demands. It also aids in measuring or mapping the developmental aspects of the client's progress.

A review of two executive coaching instruments, the 16PF and The Attentional and Interpersonal Style (Nideffer, 1995), reveals that both measure level of comfort in confronting troublesome employees as part of their array of scores. While these data are part of the long-term developmental goals of executive coaching, a follow-up BASIC I.D. assessment can add specifics of how the executive perceives an impending confrontation. This practice can also yield worthwhile cognitive correlates of this confrontation, such as "I want to avoid a lawsuit" and "I hate head-on confrontations, but this manager is like a spreading cancer in that plant."

Checklists represent another area in which Lazarus's model and common assessment techniques are complementary. Checklists yield professional and personal behavioral tendencies in dealing with time management, physical exercise, and so forth. The actions that the client wants to increase or decrease conveniently fit into the behavior modality. The checked items offer an excellent starting point for the process of establishing specific coaching goals. If the behaviors are operationally defined, progress is more easily mapped.

In addition to producing specific and contextual data, the BASIC I.D. may highlight incongruities with measured broad factors and job demands. For example, an executive may appear to be decisive on the commonly used instruments, to be a good problem solver, and to possess excellent insight into people but may be very reluctant to confront a subordinate. A BASIC interview might reveal an uncharacteristic cognition (e.g., "I don't know why, but I'm intimidated by him") or affect (e.g., "I feel nervous about how this is playing out").

Because coaching typically takes place over a period of time, the multimodal profile can map the journey of the executive and coach. The profile is not a static instrument. Over the course of counseling, it is constantly being revised and developed depending on the client's specific problem, issue, or goal.

MULTIMODAL THERAPY AND 360-DEGREE FEEDBACK

In addition to being used with other frequently employed instruments, the multimodal approach can be integrated into a 360-degree assessment. Special attention should be paid to the cognitive and interpersonal modalities. The primary purpose in using the profile is to conduct individual interviews or coaching sessions. While it is a one-on-one guide, the model can be used in doing 360-degree work via conducting interviews with superiors and peers and compiling reports on competencies, managerial style, interpersonal skills, and overall corporate climate. Interviewees' responses can then be categorized according to the seven modalities.

VALUE ADDED: THREE PERSPECTIVES

A review of some of the popular assessment tools used in executive coaching, such as the 16PF and the Myers–Briggs, revealed that they provide excellent developmental perspectives (e.g., "confronting problem employees," "compassion and sensitivity," and "introvert vs. extravert"). These perspectives are broad and general in nature. The BASIC I.D. approach adds value because it provides a problem-focused profile of the executive as he or she deals with present stressors such as changing industrywide trends, human resources issues, personal and corporate performance goals, and possible career moves.

Three constantly shifting perspectives seem to be operating within the executive coaching paradigm. The time-honored Gestalt principle of reversibility may provide the theoretical frame of reference to explain this dynamic process. First, sketch the executive's view of the specific elements of the problem or issue using the BASIC I.D. interview. Second, view the issue in the context of the more stable personality traits of the executive. Finally, view the issue in the context of the corporate culture.

SHORTCOMINGS OF THE PROFILE

The sine qua non of doing successful coaching is understanding the background or corporate culture of a particular workplace. One of the limitations of the BASIC I.D. is that it does not give the executive coach an immediate and direct, systematic idea of the business imperatives the executive is facing (e.g., workforce reduction, facility closing, possible bankruptcy). As a means of overcoming this deficit, questions should be added that are specifically directed at the business environment, anticipated challenges from competitors, cyclic features of the industry, or major fundamental changes occurring in the industry.

In addition, structured interviews and opinion/attitude surveys are the traditional ways of systematically filling in parts of the mosaic that is the corporate culture. While the BASIC I.D. does not directly address this, some pieces of the corporate landscape may unintentionally emerge. Especially rich areas to be attuned to are the cognitive and affective modalities.

In the process of establishing individual coaching or in focusing on problematic areas, the following growth-impeding cognitions about the corporate culture have been heard: "This plant has always been the stepchild of this company," "This company never has the guts to get rid of the dead wood around here," and "Working your butt off around here doesn't pay; it's who you know." On the affective dimension, more explicit emotional clues about the prevailing corporate culture are often voiced: "I'm afraid they are going to eliminate my job if there is a merger; they won't need two CEOs" or "I'm worried that with this corporate restructuring I may have to relocate my family, and I'm within 3 years of full retirement!"

Regarding the drug/biology category, a caveat must be made. Because direct questions about this area can be viewed as invasive, it is best to avoid direct, probing questions about alcohol or drug use. In addition, details regarding health history should not be discussed unless special circumstances warrant it or they are spontaneously volunteered. I am not aware of any commonly used executive coaching tools that contain questions about this sensitive area. In most situations, it is probably not pertinent if there is no evidence to the contrary. But it can be a difficult situation for a coach if evidence of abuse is gained either informally or from direct observation. Do you confront or ignore? The question is best answered by the coach, taking into consideration the level of rapport with the client, who did the referring (self or employer), the purposes for which the assessment will be used, and whether questions in this area violate federal and/or state laws.

COACHING VERSUS THERAPY/COUNSELING

Since the multimodal model derives from the domain of clinical psychology, and it is suggested here that the model can be integrated into the process of executive coaching, the following question arises: How does one distinguish between coaching and therapy/counseling? First, clinical work is focused on diagnosis-bound behavior, while coaching is centered on improving work or job performance. Second, clinical work is patient centered and process oriented, while coaching is more direct and may involve more prescriptive approaches (e.g., advising and information giving). Third, in counseling progress is measured mainly by patient self-reports, while in coaching performance is measured in more concrete numerical terms. Fourth, therapy is traditionally done face to face; coaching can also include telephone sessions and even e-mail correspondence. The final difference is how compensation is received. In therapy, the patient or health insurance company pays. In consulting, in most cases, the client company is billed.

CASE STUDY

A case involving a woman who was a senior executive in a health care corporation further illustrates the application of the multimodal therapy model in an executive coaching context.

Ms. L, a 50-year-old divorced woman who had a PhD, was actively recruited, along with her former boss, to rebuild a department. To her surprise, she learned after her arrival that she was expected to change the "culture." Her typical style of leadership in her previous job was one of consensus building; in her new position, she was immediately confronted with the fact that she had a staff that was not competent, in her estimation, and could not be brought up to industrywide standards in a short period of time. The goal was to conduct the replacement process with the least amount of legal flak. She was experiencing stress over the anticipated number of personal confrontations that had to take place and the number of dismissal letters that had to be written. While she felt that she had the support of her boss, she was not sure senior management liked the way the housecleaning was progressing.

To her pleasant surprise, she was totally affirmed in both what she was accomplishing and the speed with which change was occurring. Over the period of 10 months when most of these changes—some planned, some unplanned—took place, she had a number of unpleasant confrontations with professional employees and support personnel. The client reported that as a result of the support of her psychologist coach, she survived very well and was now concentrating on making the department more productive by overtly encouraging creativity from the new staff and a few incumbents, which is more consistent with her anticipated goals at the time she accepted the new position.

In terms of her personal life, the client did extremely well in establishing new relationships. On family-gathering occasions, she was vigilant about not sliding back into being controlled or manipulated by her impaired former husband. On reflection, she was very proud of this personal accomplishment.

Table 25.1 contains a profile of the multimodal approach used with this client. The case involved dealing with some stressors that are the traditional domain of the clinical/counseling psychologist and other issues that fall within the scope of the executive coach. Analysis of the case notes shows that the percentage of time spent at each session on personal issues and work problems varied from 20% to 80% (never on one area exclusively).

This approach can easily be used by the traditionally trained I/O psychologist, as seen in the case profile. The multimodal model can also be practical for clinical and counseling psychologists who wish to include executive coaching within the scope of their practices. This may be prompted by the desire to expand one's practice and/or to escape the control of managed care (i.e., billing sponsoring companies/institutions for consulting services directly as opposed to insurance companies).

NEW MARKETS

It seems incomplete to propose a paradigm shift in the use of a popular clinical approach while not addressing a paradigm shift in "marketing," particularly as it concerns the clinical/counseling psychologist wanting to expand his or her consulting practice.

I propose expanding the target populations for executive coaching. The scope of the traditional market has been executives in large corporate settings and, to some degree, small corporate enterprises. It has been my (unintended) experience to work with many professionals, especially attorneys, accountants, physicians, and small company entrepreneurs. These solo practitioners represent untapped markets of individuals in need of someone to complain to, to bounce ideas off of, and from whom they can receive practical feedback. Other possible market niches, in addition to the professionals cited earlier, are men and women who work alone (or perceive themselves as working alone), university administrators, and religious leaders. Professional sports executives, managers, and coaches are other possibilities. One could also help these latter clients build a financial, social, and psychological survival kit for the day when they are no longer involved in sports.

How do you reach these solo practitioners? How do you penetrate these markets? One way the clinical/counseling psychologist can effectively do this is to suggest executive coaching to a spouse or other family member who has described an executive, professional, or entrepreneur who is unhappy in his or her work, whose efficiency or productivity has obviously declined, or who feels static but has no clear goals. I have found that the "executive coaching" label is much more palatable than the terms *counseling* and *therapy* because it has a more positive connotation and focuses on outcomes (e.g., increasing the client's job performance).

ACCEPTANCE OF COACHING

I have seen a wide variety of responses to psychologically oriented coaching. At one end of the continuum, some executives are very resistive and distrustful of the idea of having someone not in their field help them improve their performance. Others view having a coach "to bounce ideas off of" as a status symbol. I observed the latter at a charity

TABLE 25.1

BASIC I.D. Profile of Executive With a New Position and Going Through a Divorce

Modality	Problem	Intervention
Behavior	Replace some staff and support personnel.	Develop time chart.
	Restructure jobs and redefine goals.	Seek corporate legal advice.
	Adjust to recent divorce from alcoholic spouse.	Develop strategies for future meetings.
Affect	Guilt over firing of personnel.	Use rational emotive therapy.
	Anxiety over ability to turn around organization.	Challenge cognitions: *shoulds* and *oughts*.
	Depression over dealings with children and ex-spouse.	Suggest counseling for adult children.
	Anger with ex-spouse and impact on children.	
Sensation	Neck pain and muscle tension in shoulders.	Encourage to see family chiropractor.
Imagery	Sees herself as doing four different jobs.	Discuss job duties with boss.
	Has difficulty seeing self as a successful executive.	Supportive therapy that she has education, experience, and maturity to succeed.
Cognition	"This job is incredibly good. I hope it can last until I retire."	Opportunity to affirm.
	"With increase in income, I have more to invest, but I don't know where to put it."	Discuss retirement plans and suggest seeing a financial planner.
	"I know I have to fire a number of people following the policies and procedures."	Frequently call human resources department.
	"I can't let my former husband control me anymore."	Anticipate social situations and rehearse responses.
Interpersonal	Received good feedback at corporate retreat.	
	Annoying rumors from former employer.	Discuss possible responses and lack of control over rumors.
	Dealing with problem employees.	Behavioral rehearsal of encounters.
	Would like to meet eligible men.	Encourage to go to social and professional settings.
Drug/biology	No medical problems or excesses in lifestyle concerning eating or drinking.	Affirm her good diet and exercise practice of walking 3 miles daily.

affair while listening to a principal in a small but very profitable accounting firm loudly extol the skill of his executive coach and how much more efficient he was as a result of this experience.

SUMMARY

Lazarus's multimodal model meets the challenge of dealing with the executive holistically. It is systematic, allowing the psychologist to use favorite strategies and tests to pinpoint potential areas of growth. Since coaching usually covers a period of weeks or months, this model represents a developmental as opposed to a quick-fix orientation. The multimodal BASIC I.D. model also enables the consultant to continually assess the progress of coaching. Adopting Lazarus's model can not only fulfill Diedrich's (see chap. 14, this volume) mandate that executive coaching be more holistic and integrated but also advance Kilburg's (see chap. 1, this volume) goal to "help the client achieve a mutually identified set of goals to improve his or her professional performance and personal satisfaction and to improve the effectiveness of the client's organization" (p. 28).

References

Briggs, K., & Myers, I. B. (1977). *Myers–Briggs Type Indicator.* Palo Alto, CA: Consulting Psychologists Press.

Cattell, R., Cattell, K. A., & Cattell, H. (1993). *16 Personality Factor Questionnaire* (5th ed.). Champaign, IL: Institute for Personality and Ability Testing.

Lazarus, A. A. (1976). *Multimodal behavior therapy.* New York: Springer.

Lazarus, A. A. (Ed.). (1985). *Casebook of multimodal therapy*. New York: Guilford Press.

Lazarus, A. A. (1989). *The practice of multimodal therapy*. Baltimore: Johns Hopkins University Press.

Lazarus, A. A. (1997). *Brief but comprehensive psychotherapy: The multimodal way*. New York: Springer.

Nideffer, R. M. (1995). *The Attentional and Interpersonal Style (TAIS)*. New Berlin, WI: Assessment Systems International.

CHAPTER 26

EXECUTIVE GROWTH ALONG THE ADULT DEVELOPMENT CURVE

Steven D. Axelrod

Executive coaching is a powerful developmental activity that influences both work behavior and overall personal well-being. As such, the effectiveness of coaching can be enhanced if it is based on a model of adult development that encompasses both career and personal life. In the course of coaching executives in more than 20 organizations, I have found that core concepts of adult psychological development provide such a model, informing my interventions and helping me better understand their impact.

In this chapter, I summarize some general principles of adult psychological development that have broad applicability to consulting work with executives. I focus on two developmental inflection points that drive and define effective functioning in senior management roles. Characteristics of the "midlife transition" (Levinson, Darrow, Klein, Levinson, & McKee, 1978) are important in understanding the generic senior vice president (SVP) role while the psychological qualities associated with the transition to late midlife are important in understanding the executive vice president (EVP) role. Although these roles do not correlate perfectly with either age or level of psychological development, I try to show that there is a developmental progression during adulthood that may be productively aligned with increased and broader responsibility in the organization. (Alternatively, developmental processes may occur strictly *within* one role, such as the SVP, enriching and improving performance within that role.) Illustrative case materials are presented to show how psychological competencies and leadership competencies can be interrelated by developmental stage. Finally, some broader implications for organizational growth and development are discussed.

ADULT PSYCHOLOGICAL DEVELOPMENT

Development in adulthood is an ongoing dynamic process influenced by the childhood past, the adult past, and present-day experiences (Colarusso & Nemiroff, 1981). Although early experience is very important in forming the personality, the psychology of the adult cannot be reduced to childhood factors. Early conflicts and deficits can be reworked or rendered less disruptive by adult experience. Experiences in adulthood have their own imperatives that offer opportunities for personality growth. This is especially true of landmark events, such as marriage, parenthood, illness, aging, and trauma. Work life is particularly important in providing experiences for growth and development of the personality in adulthood (Axelrod, 1999).

Erik Erikson (1950, 1958, 1968) pioneered the understanding of adult psychological development by describing how core psychological issues or tasks define the different epochs of adulthood. Erikson elaborated the psychosocial implications of

Freud's stages of childhood and extended them to adolescence and adulthood. He defined adult stages by the key psychological challenges posed, and he described the outcomes in terms of a polarity. Thus, most famously, "identity versus identity diffusion" characterized the outcomes of adolescence. "Intimacy versus isolation" described young adulthood, "generativity versus stagnation" characterized adulthood, and "integrity versus despair" was seen as the critical polarity in later adulthood.

Other theorists have added to Erikson's contribution, focusing on the psychological dynamics of the transition to midlife and of midlife itself. Jaques (1965) argued that confronting the death anxiety associated with the midlife transition can precipitate a restructuring of the personality, with a strengthening of a sense of life's continuity and a deepening of awareness, understanding, and self-realization. Modell (1989) noted that middle age brings with it a mourning of lost illusions, which is actually a precondition for continuing psychic aliveness. Auchincloss and Michels (1989) suggested that one of the most important psychological tasks of middle age is the vigorous and conscious reexamination of life goals. Ideals and ambitions formed under the influence of childhood fantasy must be updated in the face of new, overriding realities. Neugarten (1975) noted the growth of "interiority" during middle age and further observed that men become more receptive to affiliative and nurturant promptings and women more responsive to and less guilty about aggressive and egocentric impulses. Overall she observed a decrease in personality complexity over time with an increased dedication to a central core of values and habit patterns. Gould (1972) agreed that in midlife, with resignation to the finite time of one's life, there is a decrease in illusions about the self; increased self-acceptance; and for men, especially, a mellowing and warming up of the personality.

The adult development framework is a good fit with executive coaching in that it furnishes a dynamic perspective on personality growth without privileging the childhood past. While the coach might have some understanding of an executive's early life issues and conflicts, these phenomena become the backdrop against which the all-important struggles of adulthood play out. The coach is more likely to focus on issues of the adult past and to be aware of how landmark adult developmental tasks are being negotiated by the client. The coach then adds to the mix an understanding of how career progress, success and failure, goals and values, leadership style, interpersonal relationships, communication skills, self-management skills, and so forth have affected the development of the personality in adulthood.

Coaching is guided by an understanding of how the imperatives of psychological development in adulthood play out in the here and now. Erikson's (1950) stages, or any of the other important concepts identified by the adult developmentalists, provide broad psychological themes that can help the consultant better assess the developmental challenges facing a particular executive. The coach adds value by examining specific decisions and choice points in terms of their impact on the core psychological tasks of a particular stage. At the same time, awareness of the general thrust of development during adulthood can aid the coach in identifying emerging capabilities that are critical for job performance and personal growth.

The next sections of this chapter describe how some of these psychological themes and capabilities inform leadership functioning in early and later midlife.

THE EXECUTIVE REACHES MIDLIFE

My most common assignment as an executive coach has been to guide the development of the hard-charging middle manager. These are executives who are typically, but not always, men[1] and are usually in their mid-30s to early 40s. They are long on drive and ambition and rather short on people skills such as active listening, persuasion, consensus building, and conflict resolution. They tend to be results-oriented, project driven, and highly focused. They admit that they "do not suffer

[1] Because the majority of my clients have been men, I use the masculine pronoun in this chapter.

fools gladly" and have difficulty tolerating divergent opinions when the solutions to problems seem so obvious. These executives are typically abrasive, and in remedial cases, abusive. They are often "all business" and don't show enough of their more human (and humorous) side.

In my experience, this aggressiveness comes to light as a problem, and the coaching assignment is frequently initiated on the cusp of a promotional opportunity. The organization values the executive's contributions, but there is a sense that he is not yet ready for the broader responsibilities of SVP or managing director. In some cases, organizational sponsors may point to the kinds of so-called soft skill gaps noted above. In others, there may be a more global sense that the executive lacks polish.

I like to think of the coach's role with these executives as helping them "ride the wave" of development from early to middle adulthood. Some are natural born surfers, but others need help spotting the wave and riding it. Understanding the normative developmental challenges of this era can help the coach guide the executive through the "transformational task" (Gould, 1993) represented by the promotion.

The anthropologist David Gilmore has described group rituals in traditional cultures that allow young men to demonstrate their fearlessness and physical prowess, thereby proving their manhood (Gilmore, 1990). In our culture, the emphasis in the mid-20s to the mid-30s is on the acquisition of technical skills and their application through activity, initiative, and assertiveness. This is typically what I would call the manager as hero role. The executive prides himself in being able to do what hasn't been able to be done before and on doing it faster, better, and cheaper. From an organizational perspective, this provides a critical infusion of energy into the enterprise.

Levinson et al. (1978) have described a midlife transition ushered in by the awareness of aging and death or by signal experiences of limitation or failure in some sphere of functioning. (This was brought home to me during an offsite team-building activity when several executives on the cusp of this transition described very personal encounters with death and failure as critical events that made them the persons they are today.) The result of the midlife transition, as described by Axelrod (1997), Jaques (1965), Neugarten (1975), and Gould (1972), is a restructuring of the personality, with increased emphasis on awareness, insight, and affiliation. The pleasures of being, experiencing, and understanding become as important as the excitement associated with striving and reaching. Gender polarities are less sharply drawn. Growing children and aging parents help foster a sense of generational continuity as well as a deepening sense of both limitation and responsibility.

Under optimal circumstances, as executives develop, they add characteristics of role functioning that mirror the changes of the midlife transition described above. A shift in cognitive functioning is a critical driver of this change in role functioning, but interpersonal and work style characteristics are also important. The following are some of the so-called soft skills that define effective functioning as the executive moves into an SVP level position:

- longer time frame and increased capacity for strategic thinking;
- increased propensity for reflective thinking;
- increased ability to acknowledge, understand, and integrate the meaning of personal and career failures;
- increased tolerance of ambiguity and paradox;
- increased ability to listen to and appreciate different points of view;
- increased ability to reconcile differences based on an understanding of underlying trends and causes;
- shift from a work style based on brute strength or endurance to one based on prioritizing and leading broad efforts; and
- increased ability to look broadly across the organization and identify with the larger mission.

CASE EXAMPLE 1

Jerry was a vice president in his mid-30s in a major financial services company when his coaching was initiated by his boss, Kathy. She respected Jerry's intellectual firepower, project management skills, and his aggressive, can-do attitude, but she was concerned about his tendency to make others feel excluded, blamed, and dominated. Jerry had focused on "managing up," but now Kathy would not feel comfortable promoting him unless he became better at fostering collaboration on a larger scale in this matrixed organization. Kathy and others had concluded that the wunderkind would have to grow up.

The results of a 360 assessment were painful for Jerry. He had to face the degree to which his hard-driving, impersonal, and abrupt style had alienated his peers and some of his direct reports. His confidence was shaken. He wondered if he should limit himself to an individual contributor role and felt adrift without his characteristically aggressive management style. A coaching plan was built around Jerry's reaching out more actively to both peers and direct reports and taking the time needed to forge consensus. He met with participants in the 360 survey to share the key results and solicit help in changing. He learned how to listen more effectively to others and to tune in more to their needs, motivations, and constraints. His needs to be the smartest and the one who was always right were identified as problems, and he learned to tone them down.

Jerry had grown up fast in his lower middle class family. He felt the wound of his father's financial setbacks during his adolescence and was intent on reaching a position of security that would protect him against anything of the kind ever happening again. In his career, he had been promoted rapidly and ahead of his peers. Not getting the SVP promotion "on schedule" was the first time Jerry had to confront failure in his work life. Simultaneously, he was being faced with setbacks in his personal life. His son had begun to show behavioral problems in school, and he and his wife were at odds over the best way to respond to these difficulties. Jerry had begun to reflect on his own childhood and his similarities to his son. He was also beginning to sort out his own values and approach to raising children.

Eventually, Jerry began to examine his close relationship with his boss, Kathy. He had become overly involved in gaining the approval of this volatile woman and embroiled in her power struggles in the organization. We began to work on differentiating his own style, values, and goals from Kathy's and to stake out a more independent position in the organization. He became aware of the collateral damage caused by his need to be the boss's favorite and learned how to rebalance the needs of his boss, peers, and subordinates. While Kathy fumed and at times berated Jerry for being disloyal, she promoted him. Jerry moved from a project management role to become the leader of a 100-person organization.

In the final phase of executive coaching, our focus was on Jerry's leadership of his organization. He worked on bringing more of himself personally to the leadership role, demonstrating a better sense of humor about himself and more forgiveness of others' shortcomings. He guided the leadership team toward developing a vision for the organization and working more effectively with each other. He became strongly committed to developmental activities for his entire organization and began to meld his drive for results with a commitment to meaningful change and growth.

THE EXECUTIVE AT LATE MIDLIFE

Executive coaching assignments at the executive vice president (EVP) level bring with them a very different set of developmental challenges. In my experience, coaching at this level often means addressing issues of personal integrity and continuing commitment to work and organizational life. These executives must draw on their technical competence and history of managerial effectiveness in order to be successful; however, they must also leverage a sense of self as it has developed over time in the organizational context. Flaws or derailments in this core sense of self have profoundly adverse consequences for the executive's all-important stewardship and modeling functions for the organization.

To be effective with executives at this level, the coach must work at a deep level of "self in the world," as the executive confronts dilemmas of growth versus stagnation of the self. The EVP is typically concerned with meaningfulness—not only of his own career, but also of the enterprise's overall mission. He commonly wrestles with whether he can continue to passionately commit himself to work in the organization or whether he should leave the organization altogether to pursue more personally meaningful activities. The executive is typically thinking about his legacy as well as opportunities not taken, both personal and professional. In remedial cases, the coach is confronted with alcoholism, marital dissolution, and workplace relationships poisoned by narcissism.

These coaching assignments may be given special urgency by issues of succession and retirement that are on the horizon. The executive is of great value to the organization but only if he is committed to his role and its core competencies. He needs to work out a constructive relationship with the leadership of the organization and to identify himself with the organization's future and the development of its people.

Erikson (1950, 1958, 1968) and Gould (1972) have emphasized the centrality of a sense of authenticity and integrity in late middle age. The growth of the personality in the late 40s and 50s is built on resilience in the face of setbacks, increased concern with the meaning of life and the process of taking stock, and greater self-acceptance. There is a deepened sense of the core self, with fewer illusions and a beginning appraisal of the career legacy. More clearly than ever before, the individual in late middle age grasps the flow of generations and feels a sense of responsibility for the generations to come. Optimally, he is both more separate and centered in the world and more deeply attached to others.

The attainment of authenticity carries with it an increased sense of what is truly important, a capacity to assess and accept what is real in both the external and internal worlds regardless of the consequences. Authenticity in late middle age entails a more penetrating sense of what is intrinsically important over time in relationships, work, and the life of an organization.

Healthy development at this stage carries with it a strong sense of life as a journey and adventure, complete with joy, grief, success, setbacks, love, and death. Healthy development in late midlife strongly defines the core competencies of the EVP role. Authenticity is evident in the following key elements of role functioning:

- ambition for the organization and its mission rather than for the self;
- ability to communicate an understanding of the intrinsic rewards of work, especially the work that defines the particular organization;
- ability to take positions and chart a course of action based on integrity and a long-term perspective;
- ability to see what is most important in the life of the organization without illusion, cynicism, or despair; and
- development of managerial and leadership talent.

Just as he helps the younger executive catch the wave of midlife development, the coach working at the EVP level helps the executive leverage the strengths and opportunities of late middle age. Healthy, effective organizations are critically dependent on the vital functioning of these leader–managers, on their capacity to serve as steward of the organization and models of personal and career development. The ability to foster meaningful development of managerial talent based on insight into the dynamics of their own development and that of people more generally is one of the most important functions they can provide.

In my experience coaching these executives, I have often had to help them grapple with whether they want to continue working and how they can best contribute to the organization. This has meant helping them find a balance between building on previous strengths and successes and trying new things. In the course of coaching, stagnation, inauthenticity, and an unwillingness to loosen control are some of our most potent adversaries. Measured against the criterion of what an organization needs from an executive at this level, the coach may be most helpful in supporting the executive's decision to resign the role and pursue more fulfilling activities.

CASE EXAMPLE 2

As the chief operating officer (COO) of a financial services firm, Jack was very supportive of a coaching initiative that was being implemented for a group of junior executives. Wanting to lead by example and needing a forum to discuss some of his concerns about his career, Jack requested a coach for himself.

After decades rising through the ranks to become a practice leader in a large organization, Jack had left to join this relatively small, dynamic firm. He had wanted to take a more active hand in deal making, but agreed first to lead the effort to improve the organization's infrastructure. After limited success in that role, Jack was ready to step down as COO and devote himself to broader strategic management and deal making. However, he was getting mixed signals from Bill, the young CEO of the firm, about how to define his new role. Jack was frustrated with Bill, whom he felt constantly changed direction and undermined others' autonomy.

Colleagues at all levels viewed Jack as a man of substance, honesty, and integrity. He was considered an independent thinker and a caring person behind his gruff exterior. Highly valued for his decades of industry experience and breadth of contacts, he was seen as just what the organization needed. But people seemed to want more of Jack and more from him, and there was an undertone of frustration and disappointment in the 360 interviews. If only he would decide what role he wanted to play and commit to it!

Jack did indeed seem weary and listless. He was particularly frustrated with Bill and vented his frustration by reminding people that he did not need the money and could retire at any time. While he had taken an interest in the development of some of the junior members of the organization, he was seen as rather uninvolved with others whom he had hired. He tended to expect some of the key players in the organization to come to him and found it difficult to reach out and develop these relationships.

Executive coaching focused on what his colleagues needed from Jack and how he could best define his role. We were searching for what could energize Jack and how his knowledge, advice, and guidance could be made available to the firm. On paper, we developed a role description that would give both Jack and the organization what they needed. But a combination of a deteriorating economy and Jack's relative inexperience in this area of investment prevented his project from getting off the ground. Jack was stuck, and the coaching seemed stalled. He no longer seemed interested in building on past strengths and successes and could not really focus on improving his interpersonal and communication skills. He had been unable to move forward into new areas of interest, and he was increasingly preoccupied with the destructive aspects of Bill's leadership.

It became apparent to both Jack and me that the sense of stagnation he felt could be remedied only by exiting the organization. A sense of burden eventually lifted as Jack began to plan the next chapter of his life. He began to focus more on the impact he had had in his industry and how he could still draw on that with a sense of pride as a consultant. He would focus more on his board memberships and a few mentoring relationships. Most important, he would be able to devote himself more fully to some of the leisure pursuits that meant so much to him.

EPILOGUE

In this chapter, I have suggested some of the ways in which the core issues of adult development can serve as a template for evaluating executive competencies and fostering both personal and professional growth. As consultants and executive coaches, our interventions focus on leadership behavior, but we will be most effective if we incorporate an understanding of where our clients are on the curve of adult development. We need to be mindful of both what an executive is trying to accomplish in terms of his leadership and what he needs to accomplish more broadly as a person. We can be most helpful to the extent that we can bring the leadership role into alignment with the specific tasks of his stage of life, challenging him to grow in ways that are specific and personal. Our interventions with an executive also become more powerful when we understand what the organization needs from him, not only in terms of role responsibilities and hierarchical rank, but also in terms of developmental level. These are expectations that go beyond the performance of individuals to encompass the factors that lend vitality to the enterprise as a whole.

Over the course of an executive's career, who he is as a person becomes as important as his technical and business knowledge in determining his effectiveness as a manager and leader. The executive self is in part a social role but one that is a function of stable personality characteristics, developmental factors, and self-awareness. Executives move at varying rates and with different degrees of self-awareness along the adult developmental curve. Understanding the impact of broader adult developmental factors on the managerial role can be an effective tool for the executive himself to coach and lead others.

Finally, I believe that the model of executive growth put forward in this chapter is particularly germane in our post–September 11th world. The terrorist attacks were a signal event that heightened the awareness not only of our mortality but of the limits of our work lives. As consultants and coaches, we are being challenged to respond to clients who are reexamining their relationship to their work and their commitment to their organizations. They may be less willing to do high endurance work, even if it is highly rewarded, in the absence of a sense of meaning and personal growth.

In underscoring our vulnerability and limitations, the September 11 attacks represent a traumatic version of more typical life events that propel movement along the developmental curve of midlife. We are being challenged by our clients to engage their efforts to restructure their executive selves and to provide tools for the kinds of growth described in this chapter. Now more than ever there is a premium on mature leadership that is attuned to the imperatives of personal development. Our most senior executives play a critical role in this regard, for even during normal times their effectiveness draws on a deep understanding of the need for meaningfulness, an ability to distinguish between what is important and what isn't over the long term, and an appreciation of the complexity and sometimes the tragedy of life's journey.

References

Auchincloss, E. L., & Michels, R. (1989). The impact of middle age on ambitions and ideals. In J. M. Oldham & R. S. Liebert (Eds.), *The middle years: New psychoanalytic perspectives* (pp. 40–57). New Haven, CT: Yale University Press.

Axelrod, S. D. (1997). *The evolution of masculine ideals in adulthood.* Paper presented at the spring meeting of Division 39 (Psychoanalysis) of the American Psychological Association, Denver, CO.

Axelrod, S. D. (1999). *Work and the evolving self.* Hillsdale, NJ: The Analytic Press.

Colarusso, C., & Nemiroff, R. (1981). *Adult development.* New York: Plenum Press.

Erikson, E. (1950). *Childhood and society.* New York: Norton.

Erikson, E. (1958). *Young man Luther.* New York: Norton.

Erikson, E. (1968). *Identity: Youth and crisis.* New York: Norton.

Gilmore, D. (1990). *Manhood in the making: Cultural concepts of masculinity.* New Haven, CT: Yale University Press.

Gould, R. L. (1972). The phases of adult life: A study in developmental psychology. *American Journal of Psychiatry, 129,* 521–531.

Gould, R. L. (1993). Transformational tasks in adulthood. In G. H. Pollock & S. I. Greenspan (Eds.), *The course of life: Vol. VI. Late adulthood* (pp. 23–68). Madison, CT: International Universities Press.

Jaques, E. (1965). Death and the mid-life crisis. *International Journal of Psychoanalysis, 46,* 502–514.

Levinson, D., Darrow, D., Klein, E., Levinson, M., & McKee, B. (1978). *The seasons of a man's life.* New York: Ballantine Books.

Modell, A. (1989). Object relations theory: Psychic aliveness in the middle years. In J. M. Oldham & R. S. Liebert (Eds.), *The middle years: New psychoanalytic perspective* (pp. 17–26). New Haven, CT: Yale University Press.

Neugarten, B. L. (1975). Adult personality: Toward a psychology of the life cycle. In W. C. Sze (Ed.), *The human life cycle* (pp. 379–394). New York: Jason Aronson.

CHAPTER 27

LEADERSHIP DYNAMICS: CHARACTER AND CHARACTER STRUCTURE IN EXECUTIVES

Len Sperry

Leadership and *character* are words that have special meaning in the public's consciousness. Somehow the American public wants and needs to believe that the two are closely and positively related. Unfortunately, many stories seem to suggest just the opposite, that is, that leaders appear to "lack" character. Two recent examples involve corporate greed in the guise of the multimillion dollar salaries of CEOs of national HMOs and the admission by a cigarette manufacturer that the tobacco industry has consistently lied about the cancer risks and addictive potential of cigarettes. The general public tends to view character in terms of limited number of traits, and dichotomously: integrity versus dishonesty, altruism versus greed, courage versus cowardice, and diligence versus laziness. For instance, Gail Sheehy's (1988) book, *Character: America's Search for Leadership*, was a "character analysis" of the eight candidates in the 1988 presidential primaries. Sheehy's journalistic analysis focused primarily on such traits. Needless to say, this view is much narrower than that of clinicians, organizational consultants, and behavioral scientists. This chapter addresses the following questions: What is the current theoretical and scientific status of character, what is its relationship to personality, and what are the practice implications of character for organizational psychologists and others who consult with senior executives? Because character has recently been "rediscovered" by personality researchers, an overview of this empirical research is presented along with brief descriptions of character structures commonly noted in executives. Finally, a case example illustrates some consultation implications of focusing on character structure.

THEORETICAL PERSPECTIVES ON CHARACTER AND PERSONALITY

The origin of the word *character* is the Greek root meaning "engraving." As applied to humans, character refers to the enduring, unique marks that life etches on the psyche. These marks are etched by parental and religious imprinting and by early interactions with siblings and peers, as well as with authority figures. The effects of social class and subculture along with the experiences of traversing various life transitions in early adulthood also leave a lasting impression. In short, character refers to the learned, psychosocial influences on personality.

Because character is essentially learned, it follows that it can be changed through such processes as psychotherapy. Largely due to the influence of Freud and the subsequent psychodynamic revolution, psychotherapy focused primarily on the dimension of character to the point at which personality essentially became synonymous with character. Before 1980, personality was often conceptualized in "character language," such as the oral character or obsessive character. Descriptions of

Reprinted from the *Consulting Psychology Journal: Practice and Research*, 49, 268–280. Copyright 1997 by the American Psychological Association and the Society of Consulting Psychology.

personality disorders in the first and second editions of the *Diagnostic and Statistical Manual of Mental Disorders* (*DSM* and *DSM–II*; American Psychiatric Association, 1952, 1968) reflected this emphasis on character and psychodynamics. Within the psychoanalytic community, character reflected specific defense mechanisms. Accordingly, the defense of isolation of affect, intellectualization, and rationalization were common in the obsessive character.

Character has a long and venerable tradition in the study of personality (Millon, 1996). Although there was a biological tradition in the study of personality that emphasized temperament, the psychological tradition that emphasized character was in vogue for the first two thirds of the 20th century.

Currently, personality is being conceptualized in a broader perspective that includes both character and temperament. Neurobiological and biosocial formulations of personality have attracted considerable attention and have generated a considerable amount of research. Millon (1996) and Cloninger (Cloninger, Svrakic, & Pryzbeck, 1993) hypothesized that temperament and neurotransmitters greatly influence personality development and functioning. Like many others, both Stone (1993), a psychoanalyst, and Cloninger (Cloninger et al., 1993), a neurobiological psychiatrist, described personality as the confluence of both character and temperament.

Another way of specifying the characterological component of personality is with the term *schema.* Whether in the psychoanalytic tradition (Horowitz, 1988; Slap & Slap-Shelton, 1991) or the cognitive therapy tradition (Beck, 1964; Young, 1990), schema refers to the basic beliefs individuals use to organize their view of self, the world, and the future. While the centrality of schema has historically been more central to the cognitive tradition and the cognitive–behavioral tradition than to the psychoanalytic tradition, this apparently is changing (Stein & Young, 1992). While classical psychoanalysts focused on libidinal drives, some modern analysts have focused instead on relational themes, emphasizing the self, the object, and their interaction, while a number of ego psychology and object relations theorists have emphasized schema theory. Many have contributed to the development of schema theories in the psychoanalytic tradition (Eagle, 1986; Horowitz, 1988; Inderbitzin & James, 1994; Slap & Slap-Shelton, 1991; Wachtel, 1982).

A representative example of these theories is the model described by Slap and Slap-Shelton (1991). They described a schema model that contrasts with the structural model devised by Freud and refined by the ego psychologists and that they contend better fits the clinical data of psychoanalysis than the structural model. Their schema model involves the ego and sequestered schema. The ego consists of many schemas, which are loosely linked and integrated with one another and relatively accessible to consciousness. These schemas are based on past experience but are modified by new experience. This process forms the basis of adaptive behavior. Sequestered schemas are organized around traumatic events and situations in childhood that were not mastered or integrated by the immature psyche of the child. These schemas remain latent and repressed. To the extent these sequestered or pathological schemas are active, current relationships may be cognitively processed according to these schemas rather than treated objectively by the more adaptive schemas of the ego. Essentially, current situations cannot be perceived and processed in accordance with the reality of the present event but rather as replications of unmastered childhood conflict.

Treatment consists of helping the client to describe, clarify, and work through these sequestered, pathological schemas. These schemas are exposed to the client's mature, adaptive ego in order to achieve integration. Clients are helped to recognize how they create and recreate scenarios that reopen their pathologic schemas. The repeated demonstration and working through of the traumatic events that gave rise to the pathological schemas engenders a greater degree of self-observation, understanding, and emotional growth.

Beck and his coworkers (Beck, 1964; Beck & Freeman, 1990) have pioneered schema theory within the cognitive–behavioral perspective. Beck introduced the schema concept with reference to depression and more recently to the treatment of personality disorders. Early developments in cognitive therapy focused on two levels of analysis: cognitive distortions and dysfunctional beliefs specifically as they to related depressive and anxiety disorders. But cognitive therapists pursued a third level of analysis, schemas, to aid in the understanding and treatment of personality disorders that proved to be impervious to the treatment methods based on the first two levels of analysis.

EMPIRICAL STUDIES OF CHARACTER

While the theoretical and clinical literature on character is quite extensive, the empirical literature is not. Two important research initiatives are described in this section. These include the work of Cloninger and his colleagues (1993) and Millon (1996; Millon, Millon, & Davis, 1994).

Cloninger

On the basis of extensive interview studies, Robert Cloninger and his colleagues (Cloninger et al., 1993) concluded that individuals with mature personalities tend to be self-reliant, cooperative, and self-transcendent. In contrast, those with personality disorders were noted to have difficulty with self-acceptance, were intolerant and revengeful toward others, and felt self-conscious and unfulfilled. This suggested that the presence or absence of a personality disorder could be defined in terms of the character dimensions of self-directedness, cooperativeness, and self-transcendence. These three dimensions of character were subsequently incorporated into Cloninger's seven-factor model of temperament and character and can also be measured by the Temperament Character Inventory (Cloninger et al., 1993). Healthy personality reflects positive or elevated scores on these three character dimensions, while personality disorders reflect negative or low scores on them. Furthermore, individuals with low scores on one or more of the character dimensions and increased dysregulation of one or more of the temperament dimensions typically experience either considerable distress or impairment in life functioning or both. For example, the borderline personality disorder would likely rate high in two temperament dimensions but low in character dimensions of self-directedness and cooperation.

The following sections further describe these three character dimensions.

Self-directedness. The basic concept of self-directedness refers to self-determination, which is an individual's ability to control, regulate, and adapt behavior in accord with one's chosen goals and values. Individuals differ in their capacity for self-determination. Individuals with moderate to high levels of self-determination are considered to be mature, effective, and well-organized. They tend to exhibit high self-esteem, are able to admit faults and accept themselves as they are, feel their lives have meaning and purpose, can delay gratification in order to achieve their goals, and take initiative in overcoming challenges. On the other hand, individuals with lower levels of self-determination have low self-esteem, blame others for their problems, feel uncertain of their identity or purpose, and are often reactive, dependent, and resourceless.

Self-determination can be thought of as having various subcomponents such as internal locus of control, purposefulness, resourcefulness, and self-efficacy. Individuals with an internal locus of control tend to believe that their success is controlled by their own efforts, whereas individuals with an external locus of control tend to believe their success is controlled by factors outside themselves. Research on locus of control has indicated that those with internal locus of control are more responsible and resourceful problem solvers, whereas others are more alienated and apathetic, tending to blame other people and chance circumstances for problems. Purposefulness and meaningful goal direction is a motivating force in mature people. Viktor Frankl (1984) suggested that man's main concern is to fulfill meaning rather than to gratify impulses and avoid conflicts. Such purposefulness varies widely between individuals. Initiative and resourceful problem solving, which define effective executives, are important aspects of mature character. Self-efficacy is also related to resourcefulness and initiative in goal-directed behavior.

Self-esteem and the ability to accept one's limitations unapologetically without fantasies of unlimited ability and ageless youth are crucial aspects of the development of mature, self-directed behavior. Individuals with poor adjustment and feelings of inferiority or inadequacy are often reactive and deny, repress, or ignore their faults, wishing to be best at everything always, whereas well adjusted individuals are able to recognize and admit unflattering truths about themselves. Such positive self-esteem and ability to accept individual limitations is strongly correlated with responsibility and resourcefulness. The absence of self-directedness is the common characteristic of all categories of personality disorder. Regardless of other personality traits or circumstances, a personality disorder is likely to be present if self-directedness is low.

In short, self-directedness is a developmental process with several dimensions. These include acceptance of responsibility for one's own choices versus blaming other individuals and circumstances, identification of individually valued goals and purposes versus lack of goal direction, development of problem-solving skills and resourcefulness versus apathy, self-acceptance versus self-striving, and congruent second nature versus personal distrust (Cloninger et al., 1993). Generally speaking, successful executives tend to exhibit a high degree of self-directedness (Hogan, Curphy, & Hogan, 1994; Quick, Nelson, & Quick, 1990).

Cooperativeness. The character factor of cooperativeness was formulated to account for individual differences in identification with and acceptance of other people. This factor is a measure of character that is related to agreeability versus self-centered aggression and hostility. Low cooperativeness scores contribute substantially to the likelihood of a concomitant personality disorder (Svrakic, Whitehead, Pryzbeck, & Cloninger, 1993). In individuals who are high or only moderately low in self-directedness, the probability of a diagnosis of personality disorder was increased by low cooperativeness. All categories of personality disorder are associated with low cooperativeness. Cooperative individuals tend to be socially tolerant, empathic, helpful, and compassionate, while uncooperative individuals tend to be socially intolerant, disinterested in other people, unhelpful, and revengeful. Cooperative individuals are likely to show unconditional acceptance of others, empathy with other's feelings, and willingness to help others achieve their goals without selfish domination. It is not surprising that social acceptance, helpfulness, and concern for the rights of others are correlated with positive self-esteem. Empathy, which is a feeling of unity or identification with others, facilitates improved communication and compassion. Helpful generativity and compassion are frequently noted as signs of maturity in developmental psychology. For instance, such compassion involves the willingness to forgive and be kind to others regardless of their behavior rather than to seek revenge or to enjoy their embarrassment or suffering; it involves feelings of brotherly love and the absence of hostility. Effective and mature executives are more likely to seek mutually satisfying, "win–win" solutions to problems than to indulge personal gain (Kurtz, Boone, & Fleenor, 1989; Quick et al., 1990). Finally, religious traditions also emphasize the notion of "pure-hearted" acceptance of principles that cannot be broken without the inevitability of grave consequences for individuals and society.

In summary, cooperativeness is a developmental process with several dimensions. These include social acceptance versus intolerance, empathy versus social disinterest, helpfulness versus unhelpfulness, compassion versus revengefulness, and pure-hearted principles versus self-advantage (Cloninger et al., 1993). With regard to executives, uncooperative ones tend to see the world and others as hostile and alien to them. In contrast, cooperative executives tend to believe they are synergistic components of a mutually supportive and helpful community that is motivated by compassion and reciprocal respect.

Self-transcendence. Self-transcendence and character traits associated with spirituality are typically neglected in systematic research and omitted from personality inventories. Nevertheless, observations about self-transcendence and self-actualization abound. Specifically, the subjective experiences and changes in behavior of people who attain the state of self-transcendence as a result of insight and meditation techniques have been well documented in the transpersonal psychology literature (Underhill, 1911; Wilbur, 1985). The stable self-forgetfulness of self-transcendent individuals has been described as the same as experienced transiently when individuals are totally absorbed, intensely concentrated, and fascinated by one thing, such that they may forget where they are and lose all sense of the passage of time. Such absorption often leads to transpersonal identification with things outside of the individual self. The person may identify or feel a sense of spiritual union with anything or everything

Self-transcendence is considerably lower in psychiatric inpatients than in adults in the general community. Except for individuals with schizoid and schizotypal personality disorder, self-transcendence is not a distinguishing factor between patients with and without personality disorders. Self-transcendence can be particularly useful in distinguishing schizoid from schizotypal patients, because the latter tend to endorse questions about extrasensory perception and other aspects of self-transcendence. Also, individuals with schizoid personality disorder tend to exhibit low self-transcendence. In contrast, self-directedness and cooperativeness are low in all personality disorders (Cloninger et al., 1993).

Considered as a developmental process, self-transcendence has various dimensions. These dimensions can be simplified to some basic experiences and behaviors that have been described in a broad spectrum: self-forgetful versus self-conscious experience, transpersonal identification versus self-differentiation, and spiritual acceptance versus rational materialism. Thus, it seems to me that psychologically healthy and mature executives tend to score appreciably higher as self-transcendent than less mature executives.

Millon

Another noteworthy empirical approach to character is that developed by Theodore Millon. Since the 1970s, he has developed and refined a set of instruments that have become widely accepted by clinicians and psychological consultants, particularly the Millon Clinical Multiaxial Inventory—III (Millon et al., 1994). The MCMI–III is considered an objective psychodynamic instrument in that it is administered in a standardized manner but interpreted by examining scale score interactions, as well as clinically established relationships among cognitive processes, interpersonal behaviors, and intrapsychic forces (Millon, 1996). Millon's goal in developing this instrument was to use the MMPI as a model but minimize its limitations and introduce theoretical and psychometric advances in its construction. Millon integrated his personology system (Millon, 1990) with the fourth-edition *DSM* (*DSM–IV*; American Psychiatric Association, 1994) Axis II categories. It is a 175-item true–false personality inventory with 24 clinical scales, including some Axis I scales as well as scales for all *DSM–IV* personality disorders, including self-defeating/masochistic, sadistic, and depressive personality disorders. Underlying Millon's system and instrument is a unique biosocial view of character and personality. Millon articulated his model on a continuum ranging from healthy and normal to pathological. For instance, he described the continuum from the healthy type, confident personality, to the pathological type, narcissistic personality disorder (Millon & Everly, 1985).

EMPIRICAL STUDIES OF SCHEMAS

More than 40 years ago, Beck (1964) first described the cognitive triad of depression as negative views of the self, the world, and the future. He described schemas by types: cognitive, affective, motivational, instrumental, or control. Of these, the most clinically useful are the cognitive schemas regarding self-evaluation and worldview or evaluation of others. Other cognitive therapists (Bricker, Young, & Flanagan, 1993; Young, 1990) have described several types of schemas. Young has developed a 123-item self-report inventory called the Schema Questionnaire that has been widely used in clinical practice as well as in research studies of the outcomes of cognitive therapy. The psychometric properties of this instrument possess adequate test–retest reliability and internal consistency (Schmidt, Joiner, Young, & Telch, 1995). Of particular note for organizational consultants is that this instrument has been used with both clinical and nonclinical samples and shows promise as an assessment measure in both populations.

CHARACTER STRUCTURES OF EXECUTIVES

Currently, there is considerable interest in the character structure and personality dynamics of executives. Kets de Vries (1989; Kets de Vries & Miller 1987) has written widely about the personality dynamics of senior executives. He believed that individuals with narcissistic, controlling, paranoid, and aggressive styles or combinations of these styles tend to gravitate toward top leadership positions, whereas individuals with histrionic, dependent, passive-aggressive, and masochistic styles do not. He also noted that a combination of healthy narcissism and control creates a complementarity that is quite effective and successful in business, whereas the paranoid and detached styles are a poor combination for effective leadership. A perusal of Kets de Vries's description of unhealthy executive character structure suggests that, while the trait of self-directiveness may be high, the traits of cooperativeness and self-transcendence are low.

While these clinical and pathological characterizations of executive character structures are valuable, many executives and consultants are uncomfortable with the use of such clinical designations to describe healthy, adaptive workplace functioning. Needless to say, management has considerable interest in identifying individuals with healthy character structure. Thus, they tend to be quite receptive to typologies and assessment systems that focus on the positive and healthy aspects of character, as well as to systems that describe positive as well as negative aspects of character. Unlike personality tests that have been normed primarily on clinical populations—such as the MMPI–2 and MCMI–II—instruments like the California Personality Inventory (CPI), which have been normed primarily on nonclinical populations, continue to prove their value in the workplace. One subscale on the CPI, Dominance, has been consistently shown to accurately differentiate leaders from nonleaders (Gough, 1969). However, the way in which leaders exert influences over others is greatly influenced by another factor measured by the Responsibility subscale. When dominance and responsibility are both high, leaders tend be described as progressive, conscientious, and ambitious. But when dominance is high and responsibility is low, leaders tend to be described as more aggressive, rigid, and destructive (Gough, 1969).

The following descriptions of six executive character structures use the nonclinical designations suggested by Millon and Everly (1985), Oldham and Morris (1990), and Sperry (1996). Basic to these descriptions of healthy executive character structure are relatively high degrees of the traits of self-directedness, cooperativeness, and self-transcendence.

Self-Confident Character Structure

Executives with this character structure are energetic, outgoing, and competitive. They can be visionary, hard-working, and decisive. In addition, they can set priorities, plan, delegate, and galvanize commitment of subordinates. They present themselves as interested, interesting, and impassioned. They possess considerable political savvy in that they can size up the power structure and informal networks within a group or organization and will proceed to establish power alliances that are personally advantageous to them. Generally, they can work comfortably and productively with others. Nevertheless, they view others as the means to the successful ends they constantly seek. While they may be deferential and cooperative to those in authority or to whom they seek gain, they can be generous in their financial and persistent support to loyal subordinates. In short, they can be extraordinarily effective and efficient persons and make excellent leaders (Millon, 1996).

As executives, they will allow subordinates sufficient autonomy and leeway to get the job done or accomplish a shared vision. They are quite skilled at team building, of which they must be clearly the source and center. They demand loyalty to the job and team goals, as well as to themselves (Kets de Vries, 1989). Furthermore, they can be jealous of those in power and can be quite skillful in unseating an "opponent." They are innately competitive and relish staying one step ahead of their nearest competitor. While they are the acknowledged leader when things are going as planned, they seldom insist on a hierarchical structure. And, as long as no one criticizes, competes, or attempts to share their glory, they can be encouraging, supportive, and fun to work with and for. However, if this unwritten agreement is breached, they can react with vengefulness. Finally, they can function effectively in the mentor role provided that those under their tutelage are perceived as loyal and noncompetitive. The *DSM–IV* clinical counterpart to this character structure is the narcissistic personality disorder.

Adventurous Character Structure

Executives with this character structure reflexively seek out challenges. When they perceive work to be such a challenge, they are likely to approach it with excitement and anticipation. They will then function in a disciplined, focused, and responsible manner. Their efforts are not only energetic, but can also be resourceful and innovative. In time, however, they may become bored with the task, and if no longer finding it stimulating and challenging, are likely to drop it and move on to another project, or even another job. However, if this style is combined with sufficient compulsivity, these individuals are more likely to preserve and see the task through to completion. They do not particularly like authority figures and may resist those who attempt to control them. Not surprisingly, these individuals tend to gravitate to occupations that combine risk and challenge with skill. They tend to see themselves as "top guns" whether they are fighter pilots, ski instructors, heart surgeons, trial attorneys, salespeople, or venture capitalists. They energize themselves by thinking of ways to outwit the conventional wisdom and standards. Being inner-directed, they may bend rules for expediency if they do not believe the rules make sense or apply to them.

As executives, they may build corporate empires through wheeling and dealing. They can function exceedingly well as entrepreneurs, but when it comes to professionalizing an organization they often have neither the skills nor the desire to attend to such managerial functioning as initiating strategic planning and management systems, budgeting and control systems, and the like. Generally, they prefer to operate on ingenuity and instinct rather than on the basis of rational thinking and long-range planning. Because of their tendency to resist authority and external constraints and regulations, they may run aground of state and federal regulating agencies or even their board of directors. The *DSM–IV* clinical counterpart to this character structure is the antisocial personality disorder.

Dramatic Character Structure

Executives with this character structure tend to avoid repetitive, routine jobs and technical careers. Instead they are attracted to exciting and creative work settings and careers. These individuals tend to be broad-stroke idea people who operate on hunches and intuition rather than being reasoned, deductive-thinking, and detail persons. They tend to be creative, emotional, persuasive and energetic, and fun to be around. Not surprisingly, they can promote, sell, and wheel and deal when it comes to a product line or service. They may have difficulty following strategic plans, instructions, and protocols. Staying on budget and keeping accurate records is alien to their free-spirited approach to life, and thus they look for others to take care of administrative details. They seem to be happy and content in job settings that can accommodate their creative flair in terms of work habits, dress code, and working hours. Accordingly, these individuals often choose careers in teaching, sales, marketing, and the various entertainment industries.

As executives, dramatic individuals tend to be strong managers. They can be inspiring bosses to work with and for, and they are usually appreciative and generous in rewarding the efforts of their subordinates. Likewise, they can show their anger and displeasure at a subordinate's shortcomings. They may be gruff, make threats, and be uncommunicative one day, only to forget it all and be enthusiastic and cheerful the next day. Successful managers with this character structure may be able to assemble a strong organization to complement their creative flair. Usually this means hiring assistants and staff members who are more compulsive to handle finances, legal issues, regulations, and paperwork. The *DSM–IV* clinical counterpart to the dramatic character structure is the histrionic personality disorder.

Leisurely Character Structure

Executives with this character structure approach work for purely financial reasons, such as paying bills, ensuring a pension, or financing their hobbies and recreation. Rather than being attracted by the possibilities of fame or success, they are attracted by security. These individuals can be good workers and adequate team players, but they are quick to draw the line between work time and personal time. They will not take work home with them, they do not worry about job matters in off hours, and they will refuse to do more than is required of them. When the job demands efforts beyond their stated responsibilities, they balk. They have little need to please their bosses or coworkers or to feel better about themselves for being altruistic and dedicated. Rather, they will meet their stated job requirements but not allow themselves to be exploited by anyone. Generally, they seek meaning or fulfillment not in their jobs or in the workplace but in their personal lives. Not surprisingly, these individuals are not driven or achievement oriented. While they work slowly and comfortably, they tend to chafe when deadlines are imposed. When it comes to authority figures, they are likely to be mildly suspicious and wary. When asked to work faster or do more, they are likely to feel they are being treated unfairly. These individuals are keenly aware of their rights and avenues of redress for perceived wrongs or exploitation. Consequently, if their supervisor insists and demands, they are likely to threaten to file a grievance. Furthermore, they can tolerate a considerable amount of routine and tedium. Individuals with leisurely work personalities are likely to be found in a wide range of job classifications and careers, but because of their need for security, they gravitate toward jobs in union shops, the military, civil service, and other bureaucracies. They may achieve promotions but are unlikely to achieve the top slots.

Because they are not inherently ambitious in their careers, they do not usually gravitate to top management. Their reluctance to sacrifice personal time, energy, and effort appears to be incompatible with corporate demands on executives. Nevertheless, consultants occasionally come across individuals with this character structure in executive suites. As executives, these individuals may have no higher expectations of their subordinates performance than they have for themselves. Consequently, they expect their staffs to follow protocol and meet quotas, but they do not make unreasonable demands. At best, they are average and competent managers but not leaders per se: They do not or cannot develop and hold up a vision of how things could be, galvanize motivation and support for it, or muster the dedication and energy to achieve it. But they are able to keep the wheels of industry turning. The *DSM–IV* clinical counterpart to this character structure is the passive–aggressive personality disorder.

Conscientious Character Structure

Executives with this character structure like to do things the right way, compared with individuals with obsessive–compulsive personality disorder who must do things perfectly. The need of those with the conscientious style to do things right is likely to result in uncompleted or delayed projects because the finished product may not be good enough. Thus, the conscientious individual who is writing a report will edit and reedit sentences, laboring under the belief that there must be a better way to say it. These individuals figuratively drown themselves in a sea of never-ending possibilities and details, doubts that cannot be stilled, and decisions that seldom seem to get made. They can become so obsessed with minor details that they can leave the most important tasks to the end, when time is a premium. All sense of priority is lost. Having misplaced a list of things to be done, they spend an inordinate amount of time looking for the list rather than taking a moment or two to reconstruct it. Or they may expend an inordinate amount of time and energy filling out reminders and schedules that could better be directed toward completing the scheduled task. These individuals avoid opportunities to relax. They invest the vast majority of their energy in their work, but over time lose most of their enthusiasm for it. They are tense, anxious, and overwhelmed by the amount of work before them, whether it involves their job, their profession, or their hobbies and vacations.

Conscientious executives tend to be critical, demanding, and even tyrannical in the face of small errors made by subordinates. They demand more attention to small detail, neatness, and perfection than executives with other personality styles. Conscientious executives cannot recognize that their staff admirably completed a rush job because they keep spotting minor imperfections—a few minor typographical errors or a computer terminal that was not turned off. Furthermore, they tend to equate overtime with job commitment and loyalty. Thus, they are likely to believe that subordinates or colleagues who leave the office at the regular quitting time are leaving early. Though these executives may be rigid and lack interpersonal skills and political savvy, they tend to be extremely competent. They expect tasks to be accomplished thoroughly and following standard protocol. They frown on creative and innovative approaches. They expect loyalty and consistent performance but may find it difficult to offer reassurance and praise. They are likely to form quick judgments of others that are long lasting and difficult to change. And they may hold grudges. They tend to dress conservatively and conventionally. As mentors, they may be quite talented and knowledgeable but tend to be emotionally distant, proper, nonspontaneous, and only minimally encouraging. The *DSM–IV* clinical counterpart to this character structure is the obsessive–compulsive personality disorder.

Vigilant Character Structure

Executives with this character structure tend to gravitate to work settings and careers where there is a good "fit" with their talents and style. They tend to be perceptive, alert, sensitive to subtle cues, and not easily misled. Their ability to attend to a variety of cues and multiple levels of meaning and communication suggests an exquisite sensitivity to people and situations. They tend to be ambitious and hardworking. But the degree to which they are successful in their work is often a function of their relationship with bosses and coworkers. These individuals are likely to be sensitive to an organization's power structure. Furthermore, they dislike and are uncomfortable with subordination to and dependence on others. And because of their belief that power can be used against them, they can find it hard to trust authority figures and feel comfortable within particular organizations. Accordingly, they may work best in careers and occupations in which they can operate with considerable leeway and independence or with limited oversight from a superior. Many individuals with this style may be able to tolerate their boss and peers but are quite aware of inequities in corporate policies and practices and may be quick to point these out. It should not be surprising that corporate watchdogs and whistleblowers tend to have this character structure. These individuals may be excellent investigative reporters, diagnosticians, critics, and researchers. Others may prefer to work with technologies rather than with people, being well served by their unique ability to concentrate. Although some individuals with this personality covet the rise through the ranks, others choose to function more independently and gravitate to roles in which they can perform their duties without worrying about managing subordinates.

As executives, these individuals require the assurance of loyalty from their subordinates. When they suspect disloyalty, they can be angry, unforgiving, and ungrudging. In some instances they may mistake a subordinate's ambition for disloyalty and subsequently thwart that subordinate's movement within the company. Generally, these managers tend to take particularly good care of their staff. In certain situations, these managers may even protect their subordinates against corporate policies or actions they perceive as demeaning or unfair. Since they need to feel in complete charge of their unit, they may find delegating important—especially politically sensitive—responsibilities most difficult. They do not mind putting in longer hours or being out "among the troops" as this provides them an opportunity to closely monitor people and the situation. The *DSM–IV* clinical counterpart to this character structure is the paranoid personality disorder.

IMPLICATIONS FOR CONSULTATION: A CASE EXAMPLE

At 32, Kirk Kendrick had become one of the youngest CFOs of any Fortune 100 corporation. Prior to that he had helped a relatively obscure biotech start-up catapult into the big leagues largely due to his vision, cunning, and risk-taking acumen. Now at the age 36 he also held the title of executive vice president of strategic initiatives, and it was rumored that he had the inside track on succeeding the current CEO when he retired in 18 months. Kendrick was clearly a rising star, or at least that was what a feature article in a business journal had recently noted. Kendrick grudgingly agreed to an executive consultation at the behest of the CEO, who was concerned about the CFO's increasingly hostile jibes at other members of the executive team over the past month and because he feared that Kendrick might endanger the succession plan. Kendrick's wife demanded that he get help or she would divorce him. He had been married for 7 years to his current wife, and prior to that was briefly married while completing MBA studies at the London School of Economics. Recently, his wife had complained that she would no longer tolerate his constant need for attention or his increasing rage and verbal abuse, which consisted of blaming, insults, and name calling. Lately, their time together had been marked by either destructive conflict or cold distancing for days to weeks. In addition, the CEO had also warned him that if he did not adopt a "more consultative management style," he did not stand a chance of succeeding him as CEO, since the chairman of the board had also began expressing some concern. Apparently, Kendrick had increasingly alienated a number of his administrative staff over the past year by his arrogant, demanding style and because he had recently fired two staffers for "insubordination." The corporate grievance committee that reviewed the firings found that due process was not followed and recommended that the employees be reinstated. Kendrick was furious with the committee's recommendation and demanded that it be rescinded. It was then that CEO gave him the ultimatum. The CFO's rage turned to depression manifested by dysphoria, insomnia, and some loss of energy. Although he had refused his wife's demand for couples therapy, he reluctantly agreed to meet with a consulting psychologist.

At their first meeting, the consultant noted that the CFO was narcissistically wounded and mildly to moderately depressed. Kendrick announced during this session that he was there against his better judgment and that he had no problems except for a wife who was a "bedeviling shrew" and a boss who was a "wimpish idiot." Reluctantly, he admitted that he was embarrassed and hurt by recent events, particularly at the company, but said these would pass. Mainly, he was concerned about his mood, which seemed to have worsened over the past 2 weeks, and by difficulty in maintaining an erection. He quickly dismissed the consultant's suggestion that he talk with his personal physician about a medical evaluation of his concerns. By the second session, his sleep was normalizing and he was more energetic but still quite wounded. He responded positively to the consultant's mirroring and attentiveness and agreed to return for a third session. Freeway construction delayed the consultant, which resulted in him being about 6 minutes late for the third session. The CFO immediately launched into an attack on the consultant's character and competence and stated he should never have agreed to this psychobabble nonsense. The consultant successfully soothed Kendrick and apologized for the delay. Later that session, the CFO announced that he had gotten "control" of his moods and sexual performance and that he would no longer need consultation. The consultant commented that it might still be in the CFO's best interest to consider some alternative ways of dealing with his wife, colleagues, and CEO that would ease the current situation and prevent their recurrence. Kendrick agreed it was in his best interest to "do some damage control" and committed to at least four additional sessions. Coached on alternate ways of dealing with interpersonal issues, work team conflict, and personal disappointment, Kendrick's functioning improved considerably.

CASE ANALYSIS

Kendrick clearly manifested a self-confident character structure. This was evident in his self-view of specialness and his view of the world that had others catering to his needs. This character structure was evidenced by his capacity to take the risks necessary to achieve the rather lofty goals he envisioned for himself and the corporation. It was clearly manifest in the characteristic way he experienced disappointment and hurt.

Had the consultant not recognized this character structure and responded with efforts to soothe the CFO's narcissistic injury or to "mirror" him, Kendrick might have left the session early, never to return. Similarly, because the consultant understood this character type, he was able to strategically phrase statements (i.e., "it might be in your best interest to"), which not only ensured that Kendrick felt understood by the consultant, but also facilitated a commitment to the change process.

CONCLUDING NOTE

At the same time that leadership dynamics and character issues are of keen interest to the general public, current formulations about character described in this chapter are of increasing interest and value to clinicians and organizational consultants. It is particularly noteworthy that empirical research on character and schemas is gaining prominence. Such research holds the promise of more sophisticated assessment measures and more focused intervention strategies for executive evaluation, coaching, and consultation.

References

American Psychiatric Association. (1952). *Diagnostic and statistical manual of mental disorders.* Washington, DC: Author.

American Psychiatric Association. (1968). *Diagnostic and statistical manual of mental disorders* (2nd ed.). Washington, DC: Author.

American Psychiatric Association. (1994). *Diagnostic and statistical manual of mental disorders* (4th ed.). Washington, DC: Author.

Beck, A. (1964). Thinking and depression: II. Theory and therapy. *Archives of General Psychiatry, 10,* 561–571.

Beck, A., & Freeman, A. (1990). *Cognitive therapy of personality disorders.* New York: Guilford Press.

Bricker, D., Young, P., & Flanagan, C. (1993). Schema-focused cognitive therapy: A comprehensive framework for characterological problems. In K. Kuelwein & H. Rosen (Eds.), *Cognitive therapies in action: Evolving innovative practice* (pp. 88–125). San Francisco: Jossey-Bass.

Cloninger, R., Svrakic, D., & Pryzbeck, T. (1993). A psychobiological model of temperament and character. *Archives of General Psychiatry, 50,* 975–990.

Eagle, M. (1986) The psychoanalytic and the cognitive unconscious. In R. Stern (Ed.), *Theories of the unconscious* (pp. 155–190). Hillsdale, NJ: Analytic Press.

Frankl, V. (1984). *Man's search for meaning: An introduction to logotherapy* (3rd ed.). New York: Simon & Schuster.

Gough, H. G. (1969). *Manual for the California Inventory* (rev. ed.). Palo Alto, CA: Consulting Psychologists Press.

Hogan, R., Curphy, G., & Hogan, J. (1994). What we know about leadership: Effectiveness and personality. *American Psychologist, 49,* 493–504.

Horowitz, M. (1988). *Introduction to psychodynamics: A new synthesis.* New York: Basic Books.

Inderbitzin, L., & James, M. (1994). Psychoanalytic psychology. In A. Stoudemire (Ed.), *Human behavior: An introduction for medical students* (2nd ed., pp. 107–142). Philadelphia: Lippincott.

Kets de Vries, M. (1989). *Prisoners of leadership.* New York: Wiley.

Kets de Vries, M., & Miller, D. (1987). *Unstable at the top: Inside the troubled organization.* New York: New American Library.

Kurtz, D., Boone, L., & Fleenor, C. (1989). *CEO: Who gets to the top in America.* East Lansing: Michigan State University Press.

Millon, T. (1990). *Toward a new personology: An evolutionary model.* New York: Wiley.

Millon, T. (1996). *Disorders of personality:* DSM–IV *and beyond* (2nd ed.). New York: Wiley.

Millon, T., & Everly, G. (1985). *Personality and its disorders.* New York: Wiley.

Millon, T., Millon, C., & Davis, R.(1994). *Millon Clinical Multiaxial Inventory—III.* Minneapolis, MN: National Computer Systems.

Oldham, J., & Morris, L. (1990). *The personality self-portrait.* New York: Bantam Books.

Oldham, J., & Morris, L. (1995). *The new personality self-portrait* (Rev. ed.). New York: Bantam Books.

Quick, J., Nelson, P., & Quick, J. (1990). *Stress and challenge at the top: The paradox of the successful executive.* New York: Wiley.

Schmidt, N., Joiner, T., Young, J., & Telch, M. (1995). The schema questionnaire: Investigation of psychometric properties and the hierarchical structure of a measure of maladaptive schemas. *Cognitive Therapy and Research,* 19, 295–321.

Sheehy, G. (1988). *Character: America's search for leadership.* New York: Morrow.

Slap, J., & Slap-Shelton, L. (1991). *The schema in clinical psychoanalysis.* Hillsdale, NJ: Analytic Press.

Sperry, L. (1996). *Corporate therapy and consulting.* New York: Brunner/Mazel.

Stein, D., & Young, J. (1992). Schema approach to personality disorders. In D. Stein & J. Young (Eds.), *Cognitive science and clinical disorders* (pp. 272–288). San Diego, CA: Academic Press.

Stone, M. H. (1993). *Abnormalities of personality within and beyond the realm of treatment.* New York: Norton.

Svrakic, D., Whitehead, C., Pryzbeck, T., & Cloninger, R. (1993). Differential diagnosis of personality disorders by the seven factor model of temperament and character. *Archives of General Psychiatry, 50,* 991–999.

Underhill, E. (1911). *Mysticism: A study in the nature and development of man's spiritual consciousness.* London: Methuen.

Wachtel, P. (1982). *Resistance: Psychodynamics and behavioral approaches.* New York: Plenum Press.

Wilbur, K. (1985). *No boundary: Eastern and Western approaches to personal growth.* Boston: Shambulu.

Young, J. (1990). *Cognitive therapy for personality disorders: A schema-focused approach.* Sarasota, FL: Professional Resource Exchange.

CHAPTER 28

IDEAS ON FOSTERING CREATIVE PROBLEM SOLVING IN EXECUTIVE COACHING

James T. Richard

At recent American Psychological Association conventions and in the professional literature, the clarion call has been made that psychologists should focus more on applying clinical psychology and organizational development theory to enhancing business performance (Brickey, 1999; Foxhall, 2002; Haas, 1999; Newman [as cited in Clay, 1998]; Perrott, 1998). Many psychologists in independent practice are looking to add executive coaching to their menu of services as a strategy to counter the negative thrust of market factors, such as managed care (Fox, 1999).

Some of the areas currently being emphasized by executive coaches are stress management, time management, career planning, interpersonal relationship enhancement, and management style and leadership analysis. Being consistent with the adage that the major functions of management are marketing and innovation, deliberately focusing on innovation could prove to be a significant addition to this list.

The proposed ideas are intended primarily for counseling and clinical psychologists who are retooling and who ask, "How do you do executive coaching?" For the experienced consulting psychologist, it provides a review about some basic concepts even though they may frequently use variations of them.

In addition to reviewing some creative problem-solving techniques that have been in the literature for years, this chapter reminds practitioners of the applied scientific backdrop of coaching. This is accomplished by the use of the scientific method as a general frame of reference and the use of operational definitions to enhance fidelity of communication and to aid in assessing the outcomes of coaching.

RESEARCH

Stevenson, Busemeyer, and Naylor (1990) observed that there was a distinction between research on problem solving with emphasis on construction of new and novel options versus research on decision making. This chapter focuses only on the generation of options and does not include discussion of issues related to decision making.

In recent years, theory and research in the burgeoning field of executive coaching have focused on various dimensions. They include history (Perrott, 1998); definition of the role (chap. 4, this volume); the goals of skill development, performance, and development (chap. 10, this volume); the effectiveness of coaching (chap. 12, this volume); and practice theory (chap. 4, this volume). Practice theory includes process issues, such as trust (chap. 12, this volume), agreements of coaching time and length (chap. 14, this volume), use of multimodalities (chap. 25, this volume), and confidentiality

I wish to thank Ruthmary Richard, William Ford, and Susan Richard for their helpful comments and editorial suggestions in an earlier version of this chapter.

(chap. 11, this volume). In a broader view, the phases of coaching have been postulated and the relevance of chaos theory has been examined (Kilburg, 2000).

Witherspoon and White (see chap. 10, this volume) observed that coaching practice theory is still evolving and is a work in progress. Peterson (see chap. 12, this volume), in defining coaching, underscored the teaching function by noting that coaching "is the process of equipping people with the tools, knowledge, and opportunities they need to develop themselves and become more effective" (p. 123). The conscious inclusion of problem-solving techniques was encouraged by Kilburg (see chap. 1, this volume), who in listing behavioral techniques that coaches use included brainstorming, worst case analysis, problem solving, and hypothesis testing.

Kilburg (see chap. 1, this volume), a supporter of creativity, described successful coaching as "stimulat[ing] the client to think, feel, and explore new ideas and behaviors" (p. 26). This catalytic role of coaching is fostered by the skillful interjection of strategic questions by the coach.

From a management perspective, Drucker (1998) noted that innovation is the responsibility of every executive and it begins with a conscious, disciplined seeking of opportunities—looking for simple, focused solutions to real problems. He observed that grandiose ideas designed to revolutionize an industry seldom work. Effective innovations start out simple and small.

Recent research on creativity in business pushes the frontiers of the problem-solving model from generating options to selecting options and trying them out on simulators. Thomke (2001) noted that these technological advances enable companies to practice "enlightened experimentation," which is to test on a low-risk, low-cost basis various options before they are adopted.

COACH AS TEACHER

The psychologist is deliberately teaching throughout the coaching process. Whether stress management, time management, or creativity strategies, the executive coach teaches these techniques and the rules for using them in the context of meaningful examples from the executive's industry.

As with all teaching assignments, motivation of the learner must be considered, thus the question: What is the benefit of learning rational problem-solving approaches? The answer in the short term is to aid the executive and his or her company to be more efficient and profitable. In addition, the creative process can be very satisfying for the executive and for the coach when they witness it. In the larger context, being creative and dynamic are the quintessential ingredients to survival in the global marketplace. While companies need and appreciate intelligence data about their position in the marketplace, the growth challenges still remain: generating new services, products, and processes; developing creative ways to finance them; and responding creatively to human relations issues. The answers to these questions are the keys to progress.

TEACHING APPROACHES—WHEN TO POP THE QUESTIONS?

Asking questions is an ongoing component of any and all coaching The coach can artfully integrate the following strategies into the coaching process by interjecting questions when problems arise or can include these lessons on a things-to-do coaching list. A third option is to purposely teach the techniques and then integrate them by underscoring examples as they spontaneously occur in future sessions.

The long-range pedagogical goals would be to teach the executives to appreciate rational problem-solving techniques; to recognize when they "see" the invisible reality of these techniques taking place in personal conversations or meetings; and, finally, to associate reflexively items they see, read, or hear about to problems that they face. In short, the goal is to increase executives' use of the phrase, "It's like . . ."

THE ROLE OF QUESTIONS—COMFORTABLY VAGUE OR RESPONSIBLY SPECIFIC?

Executive coaching, like psychotherapy, often consists of a series of strategic questions. Kilburg

(2000) suggested "requesting permission to ask questions, explore issues, challenge or push the client" (p. 116). The process takes on an even more Socratic style when he adds metaphors and stories to help clients build their own models and methods.

Essential to the coach's "mental map" (chap. 10, this volume) is control over the direction of the level of abstraction: specific to general or vice versa. Isaksen, Dorval, and Treffinger (1994) noted that by asking "Why?" questions, the discussion spirals into a more abstract, philosophical realm, whereas asking "What?" forces the responders into generating more concrete, specific options.

The coach's strategic questions could be instrumental in fostering innovation by what Drucker (1998) referred to as "systematically managing where and how to look" (p. 149).

As an aside, if the executive coach feels uncomfortable in asking strategic questions based on these techniques, it might be worthwhile to reflect on the issue of intimidation by the client's job title or academic degree. Because the client has studied these techniques doesn't diminish their usefulness, especially if they are couched in strategic questions that are not prefaced by any psychological category label.

SCIENTIFIC METHOD

The process of creative problem solving in executive coaching usually follows the general scheme of the scientific method that was espoused by Sir Francis Bacon and other medieval thinkers (c. 1603). He argued that the scientific method could be applied to the study of human affairs and that knowledge was dynamic (attributed to Bacon, cited in Knapp, 1999, p. 4). It is the scheme that most people use when developing a rational methodology. Even though the scientific method does not match the cognitive style most people use to solve problems, it is a universally accepted way of progressing.

Traditionally, the five steps of the scientific method include the following: state the problem, generate options, select and implement options, measure results, and follow up results. Although the executive coach focuses seriatim on all five steps, this chapter concentrates on stating the problem and generating options.

STATE THE PROBLEM

As the adage goes, a problem well-stated is a problem half solved. Teaching clients how to state a problem in operational terms is a crucial part of the executive coaching process. Spending time showing executives how to focus on specific, observable, measurable actions or events—as opposed to using sports or military metaphors—can accelerate the practical aspects of the creative problem-solving process. For example, trying to increase gross sales by 8% in the next quarter is a more focused goal than "put up better numbers on the scoreboard," or "reduce our casualties in the field."

A caveat for the coach is that an operational definition of a problem offers only one perspective. Different executives can look at the same troublesome phenomenon and give varying operational definitions—"I think the real problem is. . . ." Whose perception of the problem is most accurate is not the issue. There are pluses and minuses to insisting on operational definitions. Granted they are narrow and do not include subtle factors, such as attitudinal aspects, but, unquestionably, they do increase fidelity of communication. Because operational definitions include measurable, quantifiable behavior, executives know when and if they have achieved their goals (Kaufman, 1979).

GENERATE OPTIONS

Once the problem has been defined, the executive is guided to generate solution options using rational techniques. The goal of this process is to produce a quantity of ideas for future evaluation.

Brainstorming—The More, the Merrier

The executive coach can teach the client the precepts of Osborn (1963) on how to conduct brainstorming sessions as a consultant or group leader. Contrary to widespread belief, brainstorming is more than just free association. Osborn's original model serves as a reminder of his specific guidelines:

- criticism is ruled out, judgment is deferred;
- freewheeling of wild ideas is encouraged to produce a large quantity of ideas—the greater the number of ideas, the greater the likelihood of useful ideas; and
- combining and improving of ideas are sought, thus producing new ideas.

Lists were a part of Osborn's process. Osborn (1963) developed a number of so-called idea spurring questions. Some examples are the following: Modify? Substitute? Rearrange? Reverse? Combine? Copy? Magnify? Minify? Put to other uses? Eliminate? (pp. 175–176).

Interestingly, Osborn developed the general checklist not only to improve objects or processes, but also to be used to address personal, social, and educational problems (Raudsepp, 1982).

Avoiding immediate evaluation ("that's dumb" or "that will never work") may be the most difficult mandate to follow because educated people are taught at an early age to critique everything. Consequently, some executives are notorious idea killers. Not postponing evaluation was one of the factors that Amabile (1998) pinpointed in her research on how some companies have unwittingly killed creativity.

IDEA CHECKLIST: SEARCHES AND SOURCES-LISTING DEVICES

The Idea Checklist (Isaksen et al., 1994) stimulates nonhabitual, nonobvious idea combinations. When seeking someone to head a new project, read a roster of company employees. If searching for just the right word, consulting a thesaurus may help immensely. When shopping for employee recognition awards/gifts, glancing through catalogs may trigger just the right one.

A number of items can qualify for a list. As an example, the following is a partial list of strategic options developed by the author for companies looking to increase profitability. These are based on reading business periodicals, such as *The Wall Street Journal*, *Barrons*, and *Business Week*: cut successful but low-margin product lines, increase advertising budget, downsize the number of employees, sell high-overhead divisions, and so forth. Additional strategic alternatives are easily drawn from business literature. The combining of ideas could result in a newer, more comprehensive strategic plan.

The lesson to be taught is that when a situation arises, consider consulting a predeveloped list of options. It must include options from outside sources, rather than relying on the heuristic leanings of the executive, that is his or her favorite two or three solutions that have worked in the past. Also, the coach must point out a possible herd effect. This is demonstrated by the herdlike movement companies have toward employee downsizing despite evidence that it does not always result in immediate return to profitability.

While working out a checklist of possible options, the coach's role might be to develop a starter idea checklist for the client. The coach can also develop a checklist geared specifically for the executive, his or her industry, or specific problems. It can be an ongoing customizing process to which both the client and coach contribute.

The predeveloped idea checklist is especially useful when the idea-generating process is stalled. Also, under stress or in crisis situations, many people cannot come up with new ideas on demand. If the situation allows, using the old construct of incubate or "let me sleep on it" may prove productive (Osborn, 1963).

A useful book, *201 Great Ideas for Your Small Business*, by Applegate (1998) expanded on the idea checklist technique and has great potential for eliciting new ideas from the reader and for making a host of new associations when coaching executives.

If the session becomes arid, Adams (1974) suggested the use of a so-called bug list—the client names as many unsolved problems that bug him or her as possible. It can be an excellent starting point for brainstorming sessions.

Attribute Listing: Another Point of View

Attribute listing (Adams, 1974; Isaksen et al., 1994) involves isolating and carefully listing the major characteristics of a product, object, or idea.

The next phase is the consideration and modification of each characteristic. The final phase is evaluating all of the combinations according to the limitations of the problem, that is, civil laws, laws of chemistry, availability of machinery, or contemporary fashion. For example, if a client manufactures men's suits, different fashion aspects such as color, material, and single- or double-breasted cut might be considered. The following might also be evaluated: cost, the availability of skilled or semiskilled workforce, and the availability of raw materials.

Morphological Synthesis: Use a Matrix

Morphological synthesis (Adams, 1974; Isaksen et al., 1994) requires the blending of two or more dimensions of a problem. It is helpful to develop a matrix, especially if the client is visually oriented. For example, to develop new frozen yogurt products, list 20 flavors down one vector and 30 goodies (chocolate chips, marshmallows, nuts, and so forth) that can be added to each flavor, thus producing 600 potential new products. Although these can be produced in theory, the final selection options are narrowed by taste, chemistry, equipment, or engineering hurdles.

The above example is relatively easy to visualize because there are only two dimensions to the matrix. For multidimensional synthesis, individual sheets of paper can be used for each vector and can be moved up and down to form different options. For example, some "cafeteria" employee benefit programs consist of different forms of compensation, such as medical insurance, dental insurance, life insurance, profit sharing contributions, retirement plan contributions, and so forth.

Metaphorical Approaches: Like, Like, Like . . .

The key word with metaphorical approaches (Gordon, 1961) to creative problem solving is *like*. What links or associations can clients draw from their storehouse of experiences? Personal, direct, and fantasy make up these different forms of analogy. They are part of a method whose purpose is to frame problems using analogies in new and previously unthought of ways.

Personal analogy encompasses a personal comparison: "Like I experienced once when I was working at . . . " The powers of imagery can be harnessed by having the client imagine himself or herself to be the problem. A pharmaceutical executive illustrated this when he discovered a contaminant by adopting an "if I were an organism, how would I get in" frame of reference and found the cause was miniscule cracks in the wall of a sterile room.

Direct analogy is used to compare parallel facts, knowledge, or technology. This technique requires drawing on personal experiences and knowledge that have similar relationships with the problem. Ironically, comparisons that are too close a parallel are not as useful as those that are more remote. Over the years, engineers have found that biology has been a rich source of practical parallels (Papanek, 1969). Confronted with design problems, mechanical engineers might look for parallel solutions already existing in other living beings. They might ask, "How do birds function aerodynamically?" or "How do chameleons change their color to match the environment?"

Fantasy analogy presses for ideal or farfetched solutions; it may involve wish fulfillment. A helpful question or perspective might be, "How can a problem solve itself?" Self-defrosting refrigerators, self-sealing tires, and self-cleaning ovens illustrate this thinking pattern. Most people can relate to pumping fuel at self-service gas stations, satisfying banking needs at ATM machines, or checking themselves out at the supermarket by passing barcodes over the sensor. In what may seem to be a far-fetched alliance, the United Nations and Coke will develop AIDS-awareness billboards. Coke will use its big red trucks and existing distribution routes in Africa to deliver condoms and flyers (McKay, 2001). By working together, they are helping to stave off an overwhelming health disaster. (For more details on these techniques, consult Isaksen et al., 1994.)

MARKETING: DOES COACHING ADD VALUE?

The notion that the ideas presented add value to the executive coaching process is partially based on research done with front-line employees, managers, and senior executives. Solomon (1990), examining case studies at Frito-Lay, DuPont, and Texas Instruments, found that these companies were all supporters of creative problem-solving training activities. Frito-Lay reported that trainers using the Osborn–Parnes Creative Problem Solving Program, a variation of the scientific method, saved millions of dollars in production costs during the first 6 years. Solomon (1990) also reported favorable results from public school employees, college administrators, and medical school attending physicians. Rose and Lin (1984), using a meta-analysis, assessed the long-term impact of training in creativity dating back over 30 years. They concluded that education and training stimulated the innate creative problem-solving ability of individuals.

Recent research on creativity and innovation in business that has implications for coaches points to appreciating, recognizing, and trusting ideas generated by intuition (Hajiski, 2001). This attitude balances the rational techniques and is buttressed by the research on left and right brain functioning.

Regarding the overall effectiveness of executive coaching, Kilburg (2000) noted that research is broadly suggestive that the performance of individuals in administrative positions is improved. He also, however, highlighted the ongoing problem of the lack of empirical research regarding the actual work of senior practitioners in the executive coaching field.

EXPANDING MARKETS

To broaden their marketing horizons, clinical and counseling psychologists who are adding executive coaching to their services should focus their efforts to include not only senior executives of large organizations, but also professionals—physicians, lawyers, architects, accountants, and clergy—small business owners, and mid-level executives. Many of these untapped populations report they have no one to talk to or bounce ideas off of. Many of these come from traditional clinical referral sources: spouse, significant other, and bosses.

Beinhocker and Kaplan's (2002) discovery of corporate discontent with annual strategy meetings points to a possible market niche that psychologists might fill. The frequent sessions with an executive coach could make real-time strategy planning an attainable reality. Exchanging the annual meeting or supplementing it with more frequent coaching ones to examine corporate goals and strategies is a more realistic approach to the rapid changes caused by terrorism, financial market shifts, currency fluctuations, legal decisions, emerging technology, and so forth. These sessions could prepare clients for strategic uncertainties and encourage more immediate creative problem solving to occur.

IMPLICATIONS FOR CLINICAL/ COUNSELING PSYCHOLOGISTS

In general, some of the implications of these ideas for fostering innovation for the retooling clinical/ counseling psychologist are that he or she must do the following:

1. Learn a new language using terms that reflect the appreciation of such basic concepts as profit, loss, cost, marketing, and legal precedents.
2. Stay abreast of state licensing laws, ethical standards, and liability insurance coverage as they apply to executive coaching.
3. Stay current by reading newspapers and periodicals, watching TV financial news shows, and attending educational seminars that focus on business issues.
4. Adopt different methods of preparing by formulating pertinent idea-stimulating questions with the client's organization and industry as the backdrop and by constantly developing lists of possible strategies and matrices.
5. Be more active in structuring and in interacting in the sessions than in traditional counseling or therapy.
6. Present at times competitive intelligence information drawn from diverse business readings that may have eluded the client.
7. Incorporate consciously these rational techniques into one's mental map that guides the problem-solving process that is coaching.

SUMMARY

It is suggested that the expanding role of the psychologically oriented executive coach include fostering innovation. For the retooling clinical/ counseling psychologist who wants to offer executive coaching services, this can be a significant marketing feature. To achieve this objective, the coach focuses on teaching the skills of operationally defining problems and of rational creative problem-solving techniques in the context of the scientific method, whether it is interpersonal or business oriented. To generate a list of options, the coach must ask strategic questions based on these rational techniques, such as "What conditions can impact your market?" or "What have other groups done with problems like this?" And finally, the psychologist must maintain the perspective that even though he or she may have made substantial suggestions, the client executive is the agent of innovation.

References

Adams, J. L. (1974). *Conceptual blockbusting: A guide to better ideas.* San Francisco: W. H. Freeman.

Amabile, T. (1998, September/October). How to kill creativity. *Harvard Business Review, 76,* 76–88.

Applegate, J. (1998). *201 great ideas for your small business.* Princeton, NJ: Bloomberg Press.

Beinhocker, E., & Kaplan, S. (2002). Tired of strategic planning? *The McKinsey Quarterly, 2,* 1–7.

Brickey, M. (1999). Traditional and innovative views of coaching: Interview with Marilyn Puder-York and Ellen McGrath. *The Independent Practitioner, 19*(3),110–111.

Clay, R. (1998, July). More clinical psychologists move into organizational consulting realm. *Monitor, 29*(7), 28–29.

Drucker, P. (1998, November/December). The discipline of innovation. *Harvard Business Review, 76,* 149–156.

Fox, R. E. (1999). Clinical psychologists as executive coaches. *The Independent Practitioner, 19*(3), 121–123.

Foxhall, K. (2002, April). More psychologists are attracted to the executive coaching field. *Monitor, 33*(4), 52–53.

Gordon, W. J. (1961). *Synectics: The development of creative capacity.* New York: Harper & Row.

Haas, W. (1999, August). *Balancing work and family—Findings and implications for consulting psychologists.* Paper presented at the 107th Annual Convention of the American Psychological Association, Boston, MA.

Hajiski, A. (2001, February). When to trust your gut. *Harvard Business Review, 79,* 66–75.

Isaksen, S. G., Dorval, K. B., & Treffinger, D. J. (1994). *Creative approaches to problem solving.* Dubuque, IA: Kendall-Hunt.

Kaufman, R. (1979). *Identifying and solving problems: A system approach.* La Jolla, CA: University Associates.

Kilburg, R. (2000). *Executive coaching: Developing managerial wisdom in a world of chaos.* Washington, DC: American Psychological Association.

Knapp, S. (1999, November). Francis Bacon and the future of psychology. *The Pennsylvania Psychologist, 59*(11), 4, 6.

McKay, B. (2001, June 20). Coca-Cola, Gates help step up assault on AIDS. *The Wall Street Journal,* pp. B1, B4.

Osborn, A. (1963). *Applied imagination.* New York: Scribner's Sons.

Papanek, V. (1969). Tree of life: Bionics. In S. Parnes (Ed.), *Source book of creative problem solving behavior* (pp. 372–379). Buffalo, NY: Creative Education Foundation Press.

Perrott, L. (1998). Business psychology: A new specialty. *The Independent Practitioner, 18*(1), 30–33.

Raudsepp, E. (1982). *How to create new ideas for corporate profit and personal success.* Englewood Cliffs, NJ: Prentice Hall.

Rose, L., & Lin, H. (1984). A meta-analysis of long-term creativity training programs. In S. Parnes (Ed.), *Source book for creative problem solving* (pp. 124–131). Buffalo, NY: Creative Education Foundation Press.

Solomon, C. (1990). What an idea: Creativity training. In S. Parnes (Ed.), *Source book for creative problem solving* (pp. 473–485). Buffalo, NY: Creative Education Foundation Press.

Stevenson, M. K., Busemeyer, J. R., & Naylor, J. C. (1990). Judgment and decision-making theory. In M. D. Dunnette & L. M. Hough (Eds.), *Handbook of industrial and organization psychology* (2nd ed., pp. 283–374). Palo Alto, CA: Consulting Psychologists Press.

Thomke, S. (2001, February). Enlightened experimentation, the new imperative for innovation. *Harvard Business Review, 79,* 66–75.

CHAPTER 29

BEHIND THE MASK: COACHING THROUGH DEEP INTERPERSONAL COMMUNICATION

James Campbell Quick and Marilyn Macik-Frey

Executives, especially chief executives, can be egocentric, action-oriented, competitive risk takers with above average anger and hostility (J. D. Quick, Cooper, Gavin, & Quick, 2002). Power is a prime motivator for executives, who are not typically introspective personalities (Nelson, 2003). Therefore, an executive's role can become a mask that traps him or her into communication and behaviors that come from neither the heart nor the soul. Communication and behavior that fail to originate in the core of who we are and what we believe lack personal integrity and fail the test of authenticity. Luthans and Avolio (2003) traced the historical roots of authenticity to ancient Greek philosophy ("To thine own self be true"). For them, authentic leadership best represents a confluence of positive organizational behavior that emerges from positive psychology, transformational leadership, and ethical and moral perspective taking. Executives and leaders who are authentic display good character, personal integrity, optimism, and a sense of direction.

To develop fully and grow healthy, to transcend simple physical and psychological health, we suggest that executives must work and live with character and a deep sense of personal integrity (Gavin, Quick, Cooper, & Quick, 2003; J. C. Quick, Gavin, Cooper, & Quick, 2004). So what we are suggesting is that to reach for that spirit of personal integrity requires executive coaching through deep interpersonal communication. We find that in deep interpersonal communication a dialogue occurs in which executives are able to enhance their health and further approach greater authenticity. Furthermore, deep interpersonal communication is the key to building healthy, supportive, positive relationships in the workplace and is essential to working together (Macik-Frey, Quick, & Quick, 2005).

Wasylyshyn (see chap. 8, this volume) showed us that executive coaching can focus on personal behavior change while enhancing leadership effectiveness and fostering stronger relationships, personal development, and/or work–family integration. As she well knows, some executive coaching reaches for a deeper level of clinical and therapeutic intervention. We are proposing a health-enhancing developmental model of coaching anchored in a process of deep interpersonal communication. This approach is neither a surface approach nor a therapeutic approach. It is an

An earlier version of this chapter was an invited address given by James Campbell Quick to the Society of Consulting Psychology of the American Psychological Association (APA) in August 2003 in recognition of his 2002 Harry and Miriam Levinson Award. While the authors crafted this title in December 2002, they found the main title (*Behind the Mask*) sadly ironic in light of the SARS health scare in Toronto leading in to the 111th Annual Convention of the APA (2003). James Campbell Quick would like to especially thank past Division 13 President Anne M. O'Roark for her nomination, Harry and Miriam Levinson for their generosity to the American Psychological Foundation, Division 13 Awards Committee Chair Sharon Robinson Kurpius for her encouragement in the development of this work, and Division 13 members for their informal hospitality over the past 2 years. We thank Harry Levinson, Joanne Gavin, David J. Gavin, Sheri Schember Quick, and Karol Wasylyshyn for comments on earlier versions of this chapter.

interpersonal approach focused on safe, secure communication in which difficult, complicated issues are addressed and crucial conversations occur (Patterson, Grenny, McMillan, & Switzler, 2002). Through this process, the executive is approached as a person, one who stands behind the executive mask or facade.

EXECUTIVE COMMUNICATION

We propose a two-tiered model of executive communication. The outer tier is one in which the executive engages in functional, organizational communication through a wide variety of channels and mediums. The inner tier is one in which the executive engages in much more personal and intimate communication; this is where deep interpersonal communication occurs. At the organizational level, the executive is a communicator and source of information in a variety of roles, originally etched out by Mintzberg (1973) in his classic, *The Nature of Managerial Work*. Communication in these various roles, such as the interpersonal role as leader or the informational role as spokesperson, is performance related and is separable from the executive's need for a much deeper form of personal, intimate dialogue. Although executive coaching may be done at the performance level with a focus on the executive's roles or mask, that category of executive coaching does not get at the deeper level of the executive as an authentic human being. Behind the mask is an authentic human being in the process of development (Fosdick, 1943; Luthans & Avolio, 2003). Few executives are very clear about this distinction between the roles they fulfill as executives and their performances related to these roles and who they are as persons apart from the role. This is due in part to their lack of introspection, yet self-awareness born of introspection is a key element of emotional competence (Nelson, 2003).

At a deep interpersonal level, the executive must deal with his or her more complex, emotional, and conflicted nature (Levinson, 1985). It is at this deeper emotional level that emotional toxins may accumulate within the executive ranks, having adverse health effects both on the individual executive and on the larger organizational system as emotional pain spreads (Frost, 2002). One important source of emotional pain is unresolved inner conflict and tension. Resolving inner conflict and tension through emotional expression has consistently been found to have health-enhancing value (Pennebaker, 1997). Furthermore, the processes of confession and expressive writing outlined by Pennebaker (1995, 1997) enable the person to develop a deeper understanding of his or her complex emotional life.

Our health-enhancing, developmental model of executive coaching through deep interpersonal communication may serve as a form of primary prevention within an organization (J. C. Quick, Quick, Nelson, & Hurrell, 1997), which complements Schein's notion of organizational therapy (J. C. Quick & Gavin, 2000). Primary prevention is aimed at addressing the source of the stress and pressure that create the risk for distress, strain, and dysfunction. Because executives are a central driving force for many employees within organizations, their actions or lack thereof may serve as positive or negative forces for employees. Thus, the influence of top leadership on the organization impacts the organization's work climate and morale of employees as well as individual and organizational performance. When the health of one executive is enhanced, that can have positive, health-enhancing effects for tens and hundreds and possibly thousands of others within the organization who are in varying degrees influenced by that senior executive. Likewise, we suggest that when an executive does not effectively deal with emotional conflict and expression, but rather acts out anxieties, anger, and/or frustrations within the work environment, the resulting negative consequences affect not only the health of that executive, but also the health of the entire organization.

BUSINESS AS PUBLIC SERVICE

What is our common view of business, in contrast to our common view of the professions? One colloquial stereotype suggests that men and women go into business to make money, whereas individuals are "called" into the professions, such as the ministry to care for the distressed, psychology to strengthen the talented and help the traumatized, or medicine to heal the sick. We suggest that an executive may be called, too, and that, like Solomon (1999), business might better be thought of as public service that contributes to the common good when it is practiced in a positive, healthy manner. Focusing only on the short-term issue of making money can lead to behavior and performance that lacks personal integrity and is at variance with the common good. Some of the more recent negative examples in this regard come from Enron, HealthSouth, and MCI (formerly WorldCom) and strike at the heart of this issue. While Xerox paid a significant penalty of $10 million during 2002 for accounting irregularities, MCI's penalty from the Securities and Exchange Commission (SEC) was a quantum move above that, amounting to $500 million for a misstatement of earnings in the amount of $11 billion.

When health status is considered, there is a positive correlation between one's socioeconomic status and health status, as indicated by morbidity and mortality (J. C. Quick, Gavin, Cooper, & Quick, 2000). We find this same positive relationship at the level of national economies. Specifically, those national economies with the highest economic (read business) markers, such as domestic product and economic activity, also are the ones with the highest health status markers, again considering morbidity and mortality. These data suggest to us that good business and economic activity is in the collective best interest of people. These data seem to us also to stand in contrast to the notion that people and profits are in conflict. Although we can accept that such a conflict may exist in the short term, we further believe that the rationale and logic for a conflict between people and profits breaks down in the long term.

While accepting the notion that business can be framed as a public service in the common good is not central to either our model of deep interpersonal communication or to an understanding of executive health, we view the notion of business as public service as a useful contextual framework. This is because the process of working together connotes both a sense of personal integrity and integration as well as a cooperative and collaborative model of collective activity that stands in contrast to the strictly competitive, free enterprise economic model that emphasizes survival of the fittest (J. C. Quick et al., 2004).

THE MASK(S): THE ROLES OF THE EXECUTIVE

According to Boettinger (1975), management is an art form, essentially a science of the artificial (Simon, 1969/1996), which relies on three essential skills of the artistic process. These are craft, vision, and communication. For Boettinger, one of the responsibilities of senior executives is to teach, guide, and mentor. As an art, management relies on dynamic interaction and examination of the results of one's actions; that is, one must learn from experience. These notions are consistent with Luthans and Avolio's (2003) developmental ideas concerning authentic leadership, which requires both optimism and direction. The managerial skill of communication to which Boettinger refers is the same organizational communication to which we referred earlier. It has little to do with the personal and intimate and everything to do with the capacity of the executive to project positive power and influence through the organization he or she leads.

Mintzberg (1973) found that managers enact their positions through a set of 10 roles in which communication is integrally involved. These 10 roles are organized as follows.

- *Interpersonal roles*
  Figurehead
  Leader
  Liaison
- *Informational roles*
  Monitor
  Disseminator
  Spokesman
- *Decisional roles*
  Entrepreneur
  Disturbance handler
  Resource allocator
  Negotiator

While the increasing complexity of the 21st-century business environment resulting from the new era of globalization has dramatically changed much of the nature of managerial work, there is still merit in the core of Mintzberg's conceptualization. The 10 roles he identified do rely heavily on organizational and formal communication. The forums, venues, and mediums through which managers communicate in these roles have been transformed by the revolutions of information technology and the information age.

These managerial roles, or *masks*, to use our terminology, are part of a facade through which others view the manager. Levinson's (1985) notions of an executive's deeper complexity attributable to the conflicts of his or her emotional life are very much alive behind this facade. Although the facade may be functional, have utilitarian value, and not necessarily be directly in conflict with the executive's deeper emotional life, the authentic person of the executive does require a deeper, more personal, and more intimate dialogue to be healthy. That dialogue must come through deep interpersonal communication. This can happen in a long-term relationship or a longer term coaching engagement in which there is a role shift from executive coach to trusted advisor (chap. 36, this volume).

DIALOGUE THROUGH DEEP INTERPERSONAL COMMUNICATION

In addition to the need to communicate through his or her various formal roles, the executive has a deeper interpersonal need for communication and relationship that is seated at the limbic or emotional level of the brain. This deep interpersonal communication is the target of our coaching model as it reaches beyond the superficial mask of control, drive, and competition and develops within the executive an awareness, understanding, and management of the emotions that are fundamental to his or her being. This level of communication functions at a deep level of trust and requires open, nonthreatening exchange. Operating in a relatively isolated realm, with limited opportunities to express this deep emotional communication need, leaves the executive vulnerable to suppressed emotional anxiety, conflict, and expression. Kets de Vries (1989) wrote eloquently about the problem of loneliness of command, and Lynch's (2000) clinical evidence on the medical consequences of loneliness for executives and others is compelling. Hallowell (1999) suggested that the human moment at work is the antidote to this experience of human isolation and loneliness. To be healthy is to be connected. This is one of psychology's gifts to the world.

What may be a more insidious, yet important, active problem is that of toxic emotions and emotional pain in the workplace (Frost, 2002). Executives are not typically well versed in the complexities and dynamics of emotions and emotional life. Yet the damage that toxic emotions and emotional pain can do to an organization's bottom line is real and substantive. For executives interested in the health and vitality of their organizations, partly reflected in bottom-line results, there is an incentive to address these deeper issues, within themselves if not within others. Schein has talked about addressing toxic emotions at work through organizational therapy (J. C. Quick & Gavin, 2000). In this framework, executive leaders may serve as homeopathic agents within the organization to metabolize toxic emotions and serve as therapeutic agents. However, the process of metabolizing toxic emotions also places the executive who is acting in a healthy way at risk in terms of his or her own health. Thus, executives need coaches who help them metabolize, through a process of deep interpersonal communication, any toxic emotions they may have absorbed.

A complicating issue in the executive coach's attempt to reconnect the executive to his emotional foundation is the executive's poor introspection abilities, a trait correlated with the emotional competency dimension of self-awareness (Cherniss & Goleman, 2001). Self-awareness has been consistently identified as crucial in identifying higher success in managers and leaders (Bar-On, 1997; Goleman, 1995, 1998), and it is felt to be the cornerstone of emotional intelligence (Boyatzis, Goleman, & Rhee, 2000). Sala (2001) found that higher level executives tend to overrate themselves by 15% on the self-awareness cluster compared with lower level executives. That is, they rated themselves 15% higher in this dimension than others in their work environment in a 360-degree assessment. He also found that there was a significant positive relationship between level of management and self-misperception of this ability (Sala, 2001, 2003). Perhaps as the executive rises in the ranks, the feedback from others is decreased sufficiently enough to impact the executive's ability to accurately assess his or her emotional awareness. Regardless, the inability to appreciate their relative weakness in this area may contribute to a reluctance to remove the mask and engage in deep interpersonal communication.

Executive coaches can play a health-enhancing role with executives by establishing a dialogue that characterizes deep interpersonal communication. In dialogue we talk about the most important aspects of our lives and drop the mask(s) that the larger world often sees. The work of psychologist James Pennebaker (1995, 1997) showed us the health-enhancing value of talking about the most troubling, painful, and important issues in open and expressive ways. Coaches can help executives do just that to resolve tension, conflict, and emotional pain. This is heartfelt communication, and it may even open a pathway between the executive head and heart (J. C. Quick, Gavin, Cooper, & Quick, 2004). Here, the coach is an immunizing agent, an antibody for the organization. In this regard, the coach needs a coach to keep himself or herself healthy and in balance, defended against any emotional toxins from the system.

To do this work, the executive coach needs a coach. We need our own coach to help us to metabolize the emotional toxins of upset, disturbance, and concern as we work through deeper emotional issues that are our own response to the emotional toxins and pain executives express to us. Harry Emerson Fosdick (1943), the minister of John D. Rockefeller Jr. in the early 1900s, learned this firsthand when he stepped out of the pulpit as a great preacher and into the pastoral counseling role. The first time he opened his pastoral office to his parishioners, he was overwhelmed with parishioners talking about suicide and other deeply disturbing issues in which he had no expertise. However, by reaching out to the psychological community in New York City, Fosdick learned to grow deeper in his life as a pastor and counselor and coach.

In our professional work with executives, general military officers, and university presidents, we may be characterized as psychiatrists, consultants, "the stress doctors," and ministers in addition to psychologists. What has struck us as important is the need great men and women have for a deeper personal connection in which they can feel safe and secure to express and metabolize their deeper emotions and pains. While there is clearly catharsis in the moment, this is not a quick fix approach to executive coaching. Pennebaker (1997) found that revisiting emotional traumas is an ongoing process of a lifetime. To coach through deep interpersonal communication is not necessarily to intervene therapeutically or psychoanalytically. We are not talking about psychopathology or mental illness. We are suggesting that these normal, healthy human processes of communication and relationship are essential to the health and well-being of executives, whose psychological health has benefits for all those with whom they work in organizations.

CONCLUDING THOUGHTS ABOUT HEALTHY EXECUTIVES

We have discussed executive coaching through deep interpersonal communication as a vehicle for executive development and for enhancing the organization's health. This model aims to complement existing models of executive coaching evaluated by Wasylyshyn (see chap. 8, this volume). While much of executive coaching has been viewed as remedial in nature, Wasylyshyn (2003) showed us that coaching the superkeepers is aimed at the top high-potential executives for the purpose of long-term development and contribution. This moves us away from the therapeutic and remedial intervention toward developmental and preventive work. To the extent we make this move, we are in sync with the zeitgeist in positive psychology, whose emphasis is building on individual strengths and abilities, rather than correcting shortcomings and limitations.

Although coaching through deep interpersonal communication may have therapeutic value to the extent it drains toxic emotions from the executive ranks, its aim is to build relationship and enhance personal integrity. Our observation has been that healthy executives do build relationships, with coaches and experts as well as with employees throughout their organizations. Such was the case for Joseph M. Grant during the great Texas banking crash of the mid-1980s, the most difficult and trying period in his life (Grant, 1996). As chairman and chief executive of Texas American Bankshares, he reached out to coaching resources, he built a management team to take the bank through the closure process, and he closed the bank and turned over its charter to the U.S. government with dignity and integrity. He exhibited an excellent example of authentic leadership (Luthans & Avolio, 2003). Today, Grant is chairman and chief executive of Texas Capital Bancshares in Dallas, a bank that has just completed a highly successful initial public offering.

Coaching through deep interpersonal communication is an enabling process through which executives may better connect their heads with their hearts. What is behind the mask? Behind the mask of every executive is an authentic person who has deep feelings, emotions, values, beliefs, and character. We are suggesting that the role of the executive coach in our model is to enable that authentic person to become an authentic leader who exhibits personal integrity and great character for his or her own well-being, for the health of those around him or her, and for the health of the organization.

References

Bar-On, R. (1997). *The Emotional Quotient Inventory (EQ–I): Technical manual*. Toronto, Ontario, Canada: Multi-Health Systems.

Boettinger, H. M. (1975). Is management really an art? *Harvard Business Review, 53*, 54–64.

Boyatzis, R., Goleman, D., & Rhee, K. (2000). Clustering competence in emotional intelligence: Insights from the Emotional Competence Inventory (ECI). In R. Bar-On & J. D. A. Parker (Eds.), *Handbook of emotional intelligence* (pp. 343–362). San Francisco: Jossey-Bass.

Cherniss, C., & Goleman, D. (2001). *The emotionally intelligent workplace: How to select for, measure, and improve emotional intelligence in individuals, groups and organizations*. San Francisco: Jossey-Bass.

Fosdick, H. E. (1943). *On being a real person*. New York and London: Harper & Brothers.

Frost, P. J. (2002). *Toxic emotions at work: How compassionate managers handle pain and conflict*. Boston: Harvard Business School Press.

Gavin, J. H., Quick, J. C., Cooper, C. L., & Quick, J. D. (2003). A spirit of personal integrity: The role of character in executive health. *Organizational Dynamics, 32*, 165–179.

Goleman, D. (1995). *Emotional intelligence*. New York: Bantam Books.

Goleman, D. (1998). *Working with emotional intelligence*. New York: Bantam Books.

Grant, J. M. (1996). *The great Texas banking crash: An insider's account*. Austin: University of Texas Press.

Hallowell, E. M. (1999). *Connect: 12 vital ties that open your heart, lengthen your life, and deepen your soul*. New York: Pantheon Books.

Kets de Vries, M. F. R. (1989). Leaders who self-destruct: The causes and cures. *Organizational Dynamics, 17*, 5–17.

Levinson, H. (1985). *Executive stress*. New York: New American Library.

Luthans, F., & Avolio, B. (2003). Authentic leadership: A positive developmental approach. In K. S. Cameron, J. E. Dutton, & R. E. Quinn (Eds.), *Positive organizational scholarship* (pp. 241–258). San Francisco: Berrett-Koehler.

Lynch, J. J. (2000). *A cry unheard: New insights into the medical consequences of loneliness*. Baltimore: Bancroft.

Macik-Frey, M., Quick, J. C., & Quick, J. D. (2005). Interpersonal communication: The key to unlocking social support for preventive stress management. In C. L. Cooper (Ed.), *Handbook of stress, medicine, and health* (2nd ed., pp. 265–292). Boca Raton, FL: CRC Press.

Mintzberg, H. (1973). *The nature of managerial work*. Englewood Cliffs, NJ: Prentice Hall.

Nelson, D. L. (2003). *Competencies of the stars: What leads to success?* (Executive briefing). Stillwater: Oklahoma State University.

Patterson, K., Grenny, J., McMillan, R., & Switzler, A. (2002). *Crucial conversations: Tools for talking when stakes are high*. New York: McGraw-Hill.

Pennebaker, J. W. (Ed.). (1995). *Emotion, disclosure, and health*. Washington, DC: American Psychological Association.

Pennebaker, J. W. (1997). *Opening up: The healing power of expressing emotions*. New York: Guilford Press.

Quick, J. C., & Gavin, J. H. (2000, February). The next frontier: Edgar Schein on organizational therapy (interview). *Academy of Management Executive, 14*, 30–44.

Quick, J. C., Gavin, J. H., Cooper, C. L., & Quick, J. D. (2000, May). Special issue: Executive health. *Academy of Management Executive, 14,* 1–134.

Quick, J. C., Gavin, J. H., Cooper, C. L., & Quick, J. D. (2004). Working together: Balancing head and heart. In R. H. Rozensky, N. G. Johnson, C. D. Goodheart, & W. R. Hammond (Eds.), *Psychology builds a healthy world* (pp. 219–232). Washington, DC: American Psychological Association.

Quick, J. C., Quick, J. D., Nelson, D. L., & Hurrell, J. J., Jr. (1997). *Preventive stress management in organizations.* Washington, DC: American Psychological Association.

Quick, J. D., Cooper, C. L., Gavin, J. H., & Quick, J. C. (2002). Executive health: Building self-reliance for challenging times. In C. L. Cooper & I. T. Robertson (Eds.), *International review of industrial and organizational psychology* (Vol. 17, pp. 188–216). Hoboken, NJ: Wiley.

Sala, F. (2001). *It's lonely at the top: Executives' emotional intelligence self (mis)perceptions.* Retrieved October 2003, from http://www.eiconsortium.org/research/executive_emotional_intelligence360.htm

Sala, F. (2003). Executive blind spots: Discrepancies between self- and other-ratings. *Consulting Psychology Journal: Practice and Research, 55,* 222–229.

Simon, H. A. (1996). *The sciences of the artificial* (3rd ed.). Cambridge, MA: MIT Press. (Original work published 1969)

Solomon, R. C. (1999). *A better way to think about business.* New York: Oxford Business Press.

Wasylyshyn, K. M. (2003). Coaching the superkeepers. In L. A. Berger & D. R. Berger (Eds.), *The talent management handbook: Creating organizational excellence by identifying, developing, and positioning your best people* (pp. 320–336). New York: McGraw-Hill.

CHAPTER 30

MEDIA PERCEPTIONS OF EXECUTIVE COACHING AND THE FORMAL PREPARATION OF COACHES

Andrew N. Garman, Deborah L. Whiston, and Kenneth W. Zlatoper

Executive coaching is perhaps most clearly distinguished from other management consulting interventions in that the service is directed toward an individual, and the organizational benefits are accrued indirectly through the development of that individual. The history of executive coaching can be traced back to the applied psychological sciences (Hall, Otazo, & Hollenbeck, 1999), and many executive coaches have advanced training in psychology in their backgrounds. However, although coaching may have arisen from psychological roots, there are currently no universally recognized standards of expertise in executive coaching related to training in applied psychology—or any other facets of the practice, for that matter. This lack of recognized credentialing has continued despite, or perhaps because of, a strong and apparently growing demand for coaching services (Thach & Heinselman, 1999).

Because there are no recognized standards, currently the only real entry criterion for the profession is a practitioner's ability to solicit clients. Concerns of quality inevitably arise with any unregulated commercial activity, and executive coaching is apparently no exception. Several recent trade publications in management and human resources have openly criticized inadequacies in certain coaching professionals and practices, although usually still speaking highly of the practice as a whole (e.g., Filipczak, 1998; Thach & Heinselman, 1999; Williams, 1997). The purpose of the present study was to examine this public perception in order to ascertain the general ways in which coaching is viewed in mainstream and trade management publications. Through this review, we sought to understand (a) nonpractitioners' perspectives on coaching; (b) the extent to which psychologists have an identified role in providing these services; and finally, (c) the nature of these perceptions of psychologists as executive coaches.

First, however, the definition of coaching needs to be clarified. The widespread use of "coaching" in common business parlance has led to its describing any of a variety of activities geared toward improving staff relations and/or performance. For the purposes of this chapter, we refer to *coaching* as one-on-one consultation, provided by outsiders (individuals who do not have organizational ties), regarding the consultee's individual performance as it relates to a specific organizational context or contexts. Note that this definition comprises three parts. First, coaching is defined as a service delivered in a one-on-one format. This distinguishes coaching from services such as classroom-based training in supervisory skills. Second, the coachees are not direct reports of the coaches. This distinguishes the day-to-day coaching expected of effective managers from the services we are describing, which are typically focused, time limited, and contracted from a source outside of the formal chain of authority. Finally, the focus is on performance improvement within the context of a specific organization, which distinguishes our definition from that of career counseling, psychotherapy, and other interventions having individual improvement as their goal. Our definition, we believe, captures the spirit of executive coaching as typically practiced by psychologists and therefore provides the most meaningful context for our review.

METHOD

The articles reviewed were identified through searches using a variety of electronic abstract databases, including WinSPIRS, Proquest, Carl Uncover, and First Search. Initial searches were conducted during May 1998; a second round of searches was then conducted in August 1999 to cover the remaining months of 1998. Articles were identified containing the keywords "coach" and "coaching" and then refined by means of permutations of the following keywords: "management," "executive," "leadership," and "business." This list was then examined for relevance to executive coaching, defined as one-on-one consultation provided by nonsupervisors on individual performance occurring in an organizational context.

Articles were content analyzed according to the following dimensions: (a) relevance to the subject at hand (externally provided coaching services); (b) general tenor (favorable, unfavorable, or mixed); (c) whether the article specifically mentioned psychologists in executive coaching roles; (d) whether psychologists, if mentioned, were viewed as a distinct group; and (e) if they were distinguished, whether the distinction favored, disfavored, or remained neutral about their roles. Additional coding was conducted for type of publication, date, and type of author (editorial staff, freelancer, professional coach).

RESULTS

The content-analytic approach yielded interrater reliabilities averaging .82; reliabilities ranged from .76 (for author type and general favorability) to .90 (for mentions of psychologists). As anticipated, absolute numbers of media stories on executive coaching grew steadily across the period studied, as shown in Figure 30.1. Of the 72 articles representing the initial pool, 40 were rated as relevant to externally provided coaching services, and the remaining 32 were relevant only to internal coaching issues. Of these, a majority (67%) were authored by editorial staff or freelance journalists. The remaining 33% were written by individuals who identified themselves either as executive coaches or as working for firms offering these types of services; of these individuals, 15% had psychology backgrounds, 15% had business backgrounds, and 70% did not report specific background data. The greatest number of these articles (44%) appeared in trade publications from a breadth of industries not related to human resources, including manufacturing, insurance, and information systems. The next most frequent source (23%) was general monthly business publications (e.g., *Fortune, Inc.*), followed by trade human resource publications (15%), daily business publications (10%), and general newspapers (8%).

The majority of the articles reviewed (88%) presented coaching very favorably. However, fewer than one third of the articles (31%) provided any mention of psychologists or individuals with training in psychology/counseling in executive coaching roles. As a percentage of the total articles published in any given year, mentions of psychology dropped steadily, from 67% for 1993–1994 to 30% for 1997–1998. When psychological training was mentioned, 61% of the time it was discussed in terms of providing a unique and different skill base. This skill base was viewed as having clear added value in 45% of these articles, as potentially favorable or unfavorable in 36%, and as potentially harmful in 18%.

DISCUSSION

Our results suggest that media attention to executive coaching has been increasing rapidly in recent years. In addition, they show that psychology training is neither regularly nor universally recognized as useful or even relevant to practice in the field of executive coaching.

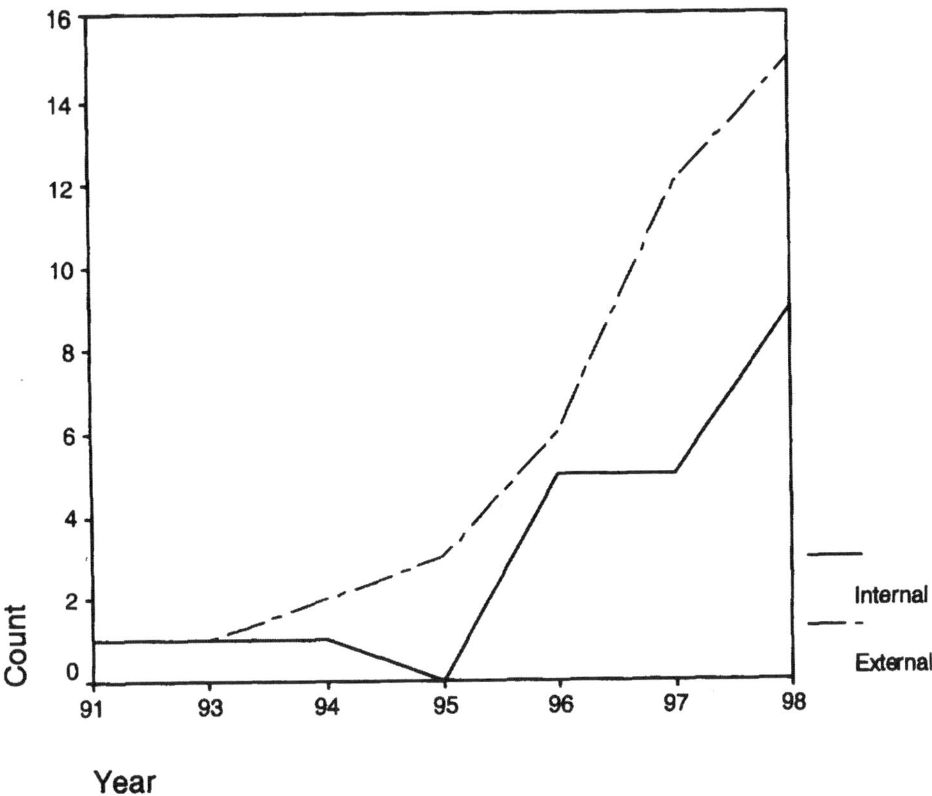

FIGURE 30.1. Trade journal articles on executive coaching: 1991–1998. *Internal* refers to articles focusing on an internal manager's coaching role. *External* refers to articles focusing on external consultants in coaching roles.

Unfortunately, quantitative reviews such as this one are limited in their ability to provide a depth of understanding on topics as complex as the present subject matter. Qualitatively, however, several trends were noted with regard to psychologists as coaches. First, a number of the articles presenting mixed or unfavorable reviews provided accounts of the recent trend for some clinically trained therapists to enter this market with inadequate retraining (Lowman, 1998; Somerville, 1998). For example, Filipczak (1998, p. 35) noted the appearance of "therapists with no corporate experience," a group thought to enter the field by having "a sister-in-law who is head of [human resources] at a corporation, and they worm their way in." Second, there was occasional skepticism as to the value of a thorough precoaching assessment (e.g., 360-degree interviews). These practices were occasionally viewed as unnecessary, thrown in only to increase the number of billable hours on a project (e.g., Williams, 1997).

Many of the articles reviewed provided lists of questions to consider when hiring a coach. Some lists did recommend asking about training in psychology or behavior (e.g., Wheeler, 1995) or asking questions that one would expect to favor psychologists, such as "Does the coach conduct reliable and valid assessment activities?" (Judge & Cowell, 1997, p. 77). However, most guidelines stressed past experience in coaching and a good interpersonal "fit" with the coachee over specific types of formal training.

CONCLUSION

This review suggests that media coverage of executive coaching has been growing—and that assuming the current trend continues, it will continue to grow at a rapid pace. At the same time, the typical article on executive coaching does not identify any particular skill base, outside of some business content knowledge, as in any way essential to effective practice, regardless of the nature of the engagement. Furthermore, the use of psychological methods such as 360-degree assessments was at least occasionally viewed as a mere profitability ploy by the authors of these articles. What can we conclude from this? For one, there may be value in psychologist coaches initiating efforts to enhance public awareness of the value of psychological training in providing coaching and related services, as well as to more formally continue the process of defining standards of practice. The former could be accomplished through the development of accessible information about executive coaching from a psychological perspective and through the scientific method. Research supporting a psychologically oriented approach to manager performance improvement could also be cited (e.g., Olivero, Bane, & Kopelman, 1997; Walker & Smither, 1999). The latter could be accomplished by expanding our role in encouraging graduate and postgraduate research demonstrating the effectiveness of coaching and related services.

Granted, many psychologists do and will probably continue to make comfortable livings as coaches without formal support of the profession. Clearly, however, "coaching" of managers is a concept that is starting to attach itself to a tremendous breadth of professions, much the way "advisor" eventually began appending "psychic" and "consultant" began appending "wardrobe." A collective examination of standards, although perhaps not as immediately lucrative as spending the same amount of time doing actual coaching, may provide a much-needed differentiation of what psychological approaches have to offer above and beyond unprocessed experience.

References

Filipczak, B. (1998). The executive coach: Helper or healer? *Training Magazine, 35,* 30–36.

Hall, D. T., Otazo, K. L., & Hollenbeck, G. P. (1999). Behind closed doors: What really happens in executive coaching. *Organizational Dynamics, 27,* 39–53.

Judge, W. Q., & Cowell, J. (1997). The brave new world of executive coaching. *Business Horizons, 40,* 71–77.

Lowman, R. L. (1998). Consulting to organizations as if the individual mattered. *Consulting Psychology Journal: Practice and Research, 50,* 17–24.

Olivero, G., Bane, K. D., & Kopelman, R. E. (1997). Executive coaching as a transfer of training tool: Effects on productivity in a public agency. *Public Personnel Management, 26,* 461–469.

Somerville, K. (1998). Where is the business of business psychology headed? *Consulting Psychology Journal: Practice and Research, 50,* 237–241.

Thach, L., & Heinselman, T. (1999). Executive coaching defined. *Training & Development,* 55(3), 34–39.

Walker, A. G., & Smither, J. W. (1999). A five-year study of upward feedback: What managers do with their results matters. *Personnel Psychology, 52,* 393–23.

Wheeler, C. (1995). Could your career use a coach? *Executive Female, 18,* 49–51, 81.

Williams, M. (1997). How a coach can help you be a better manager. *Executive Female, 20,* 24–25.

CHAPTER 31

EXECUTIVE COACHING: THE NEED FOR STANDARDS OF COMPETENCE

Lloyd E. Brotman, William P. Liberi, and Karol M. Wasylyshyn

Executive coaching has been identified as "an emerging competency in the practice of consultation" (see chap. 4, this volume). However, the explosive growth of this consultative specialty has been somewhat random, as coaches from various disciplines and backgrounds, with myriad competencies, identify themselves to organizations as appropriate resources to guide the development of leadership. A search of the World Wide Web with Infoseek (Infoseek, 1995–1997) identified more than 300 links with the key words *executive coach.* Former business executives, MBAs, attorneys, human resource specialists, sports coaches, and teachers, as well as psychologists, all claim to have the necessary competencies and proven approaches to address organizational needs for leadership development. And so the label "executive coach" may be defined in many ways, depending on the orientation of the coach and the needs of the organization seeking such a consultant. We believe that psychologists are uniquely qualified to define what is required to be an executive coach when sustained behavior change is the desired outcome. As psychologists, we have an obligation to delineate those required competencies both to protect the integrity of this emerging field and to provide clients with criteria for evaluating the skills of coaching candidates.

Consulting Psychology Journal devoted an entire issue (Kilburg, 1996) to executive coaching in an effort to clarify and define this specialty. The articles discussed models using 360-degree feedback (chap. 14, this volume); the use of relationship building, insight, and competency development (chap. 12, this volume); a systems-based, contextual approach (chap. 13, this volume); a highly structured, intense systems-based approach (chap. 11, this volume); an approach that focuses on the need for culture change and the promotion of diversity in the workplace (chap. 23, this volume); and an approach that provides support to executives based on the power of the coach, a politically savvy, psychoanalytically oriented psychologist (chap. 9, this volume). Saporito (see chap. 15, this volume) pointed out that successful coaching can take place only when it is clear to organizational leaders that the process of coaching is consistent and aligned with business realities. Witherspoon and White (see chap. 10, this volume) suggested that coaches may play four different roles that need to be clarified early in the coaching process. They identified coaching (a) for skills focused on specific tasks; (b) for performance, more broadly focused on the executive's present job; (c) for development, with the focus on the executive's future role or job; and (d) for work focused on the executive's agenda.

Kilburg's (see chap. 1, this volume) review of the literature reveals that numerous articles have been written in the general area of coaching, especially as it pertains to athletics and special-

Reprinted from the *Consulting Psychology Journal: Practice and Research, 52,* 201–205. Copyright 2000 by the American Psychological Association and the Society of Consulting Psychology.

needs populations. However, as applied to the art and practice of management, limited empirical data are available to support the techniques and approaches coaches have used with business leaders. He defines *executive coaching* as

> a helping relationship formed between a client who has managerial authority and responsibility in an organization and a consultant who uses a wide variety of behavioral techniques and methods to help the client achieve a mutually identified set of goals to improve his or her professional performance and personal satisfaction and, consequently, to improve the effectiveness of the client's organization within a formally defined coaching agreement. (p. 28)

Regardless of the coach's background or discipline, or which set of techniques or methods is used, some behavior change on the part of the senior executive is usually the goal of an executive coaching engagement.

Teal (1996) stated that "Management is not a series of mechanical tasks but a set of human interactions" (p. 36). In a similar vein, Goleman (1995) maintained that the demands of globalization and the explosion of information technology strain even the best leaders and that the most successful executives are likely to be those who possess strong "emotional intelligence" as well as innate depth. In this context, emotional intelligence encompasses candid self-awareness, openness to learning, and competencies that foster interpersonal effectiveness.

It is not surprising, then, that executive coaching work is often focused on the interpersonal sphere. Typical assignments involve talented executives whose future success necessitates their relating to people more effectively. Although they may have risen steadily in their companies, the strengths used to achieve early success can become liabilities or weaknesses given the demands of executive leadership. Continued success necessitates that targeted behavior(s) be modified.

Despite its growing importance, executive coaching remains an unregulated, poorly defined arena. With no licensing, credentialing, or professional designation for executive coaches to achieve or maintain, the retaining party or organization would be aided by a set of guidelines to identify competent, ethical professionals when searching for an executive coach. Given the costly nature and high profile of executive coaching work, corporate decision makers must be fully informed to be able to hire competent consultants. This is especially true because sustained behavior change is frequently the desired outcome of an executive coaching assignment. Psychologists who practice in this area are in a strong position to educate and guide decision makers in this important selection process.

In this context, *sustained behavior change* is defined as follows: The executive displays a change in the targeted behavior(s). This change is consistent even under pressure or stress. The new behavior is sustained by (a) the internalization of deeper psychological insights about undesirable behavior(s) and (b) targeted coaching that converts the insights into pragmatic action steps.

We believe psychologists must assume a more proactive role in educating corporate decision makers about whom to hire for this work. If psychologists are not accountable in this way, an important application of psychology could be diminished and undermined.

Psychologists who coach executives must strive to promote a more complete understanding of the coaching process by articulating the necessary skills, experience, and competencies. In this way the emerging competency of executive coaching will be established as a respected consultative process, adding real value to corporate leadership development strategies.

CORE COMPETENCIES

On the basis of our collective experience, we have identified a number of core competencies that executive coaches—coaches hired to help bring about lasting behavior change—must possess. These competencies, adapted from Career Architect

(1992), constitute a skill set weighted toward being a "trusted and approachable person" who can establish long-lasting relationships with a variety of people throughout an organization. The necessary competencies include the following:

1. *Approachability:* Is easy to approach and talk to; spends the extra effort to put others at ease; can be warm, pleasant, and gracious; is sensitive to and patient with the interpersonal anxieties of others; builds rapport well; is a good listener.

2. *Comfort Around Top Management:* Can deal comfortably with senior executives; understands how top executives think and process information; can talk their language and respond to their needs; can craft approaches likely to be seen as appropriate, efficient, and positive.

3. *Compassion:* Genuinely cares about people; is concerned about their work and nonwork problems; is available and ready to help; demonstrates real empathy with the joys, frustrations, and pain of others.

4. *Creativity:* Can formulate new and unique ideas, easily makes connections among previously unrelated notions in ways that yield novel problem solving and/or plans for the future.

5. *Customer Focus:* Is dedicated to meeting the expectations and requirements of internal and external customers, establishes and maintains effective relationships with customers and gains their trust and respect.

6. *Integrity and Trust:* Is widely trusted; is seen as a direct, truthful individual; can present the unvarnished truth in an appropriate and helpful manner; keeps confidences.

7. *Intellectual Horsepower:* Is bright and intelligent; deals with concepts and complexity comfortably; described as intellectually sharp, capable, and agile.

8. *Interpersonal Savvy:* Relates well to all kinds of people: up, down, and sideways, inside and outside the organization; builds appropriate rapport; listens; builds constructive and effective relationships; uses diplomacy and tact; truly values people.

9. *Listening:* Practices attentive and active listening, has the patience to hear people fully, can accurately restate the opinions of others even when he or she disagrees.

10. *Dealing With Paradox:* Is very flexible and adaptable; can act in ways that seem contradictory; can be both tough and compassionate, empathic and objective; can be self-confident and appropriately humble; is seen as balanced despite the conflicting demands of a situation.

11. *Political Savvy:* Can maneuver through complex political situations effectively and quietly, is sensitive to how people and organizations function, anticipates where the land mines are and plans his or her approach accordingly, views corporate politics as a necessary part of organizational life and works to adjust to that reality.

12. *Self-Knowledge:* Knows personal strengths, weaknesses, opportunities, and limits; seeks feedback; gains insights from mistakes; is open to criticism; isn't defensive; is receptive to talking about shortcomings.

Our collective experience as executive coaches, spanning more than 20 years of work with Fortune 100 to entrepreneurial business environments, underscores the fact that executives have enormous difficulty achieving and sustaining behavior change, despite strong cues from their organizations regarding this need. We believe this resistance or barrier is primarily psychological in nature. Lasting behavior change is frustrated, eluded, and resisted by a confluence of habitual scripts, core misperceptions, unconscious defenses, and an individual's subjectivity and internal dialogue.

Therefore, executive coaching, where specific sustained behavioral change is the goal, must be psychologically based. The effective executive coach will (a) identify habitual scripts and learn how the adverse elements of these scripts erode leadership effectiveness; (b) reveal truth and fresh insights about what drives the executive; (c) convert insights into observable behavior change; (d) distinguish between higher level, healthy defenses and those that are more primitive and damaging to both the self and others; and (e) objectify the executive's subjective reality and internal dialogue by anchoring them in candor and a self-actualization pattern congruent with business objectives and organizational priorities as well as with an executive's aspirations.

When the desired outcome of an executive coaching assignment is sustained behavior change to improve an executive's effectiveness, the effort must be based on sound psychological principles. We agree with Tobias (1990):

> While some change is possible in the absence of an explicitly intrapsychic focus . . . in its complete absence, the consultant will just walk blindly through a mine field of psychological resistance. (p. 88)

In our view, executive coaching that fails to focus on intrapsychic factors produces a shallow result, a recapitulation of the obvious with minimal guidance for behavioral change. Although other specialists may bring important talents to the task of coaching, there are three major factors that make psychologists uniquely qualified as executive coaches. These factors are coaching tactics, psychological tools, and graduate training leading to licensure. This combination of professional tactics, tools, and training, or "Triple T" proficiency, enables the psychologist to penetrate the executive's resistance and to provide sufficient learning and structure to ensure sustained behavior change.

TRIPLE T PROFICIENCY MODEL: TACTICS, TOOLS, TRAINING

Tactics

In his study of how smart people learn, Argyris (1991) concluded that the "defensive reasoning" of intelligent people posed the most significant impediment to new learning:

> Because many professionals are almost always successful at what they do, they rarely experience failure. And because they have rarely failed, they have never learned how to learn from failure— They become defensive, screen out criticism, and put the "blame" on anyone and everyone but themselves.
>
> In short their ability to learn shuts down precisely at the moment they need it most. (p. 100)

Successful executive coaching must swiftly neutralize the inevitability of defensive reasoning. In our experience, the most powerful tactic is the executive–coach relationship. This working alliance is characterized by mutual trust and respect, stabilized by confidentiality, and deepened by the coach's overt recognition of the executive's successes and strengths. It is axiomatic that little or no new learning can take place in the absence of adequate affirmation of an executive's "gifts," both intrapsychic ones and others that are skill based and experiential in nature. To ignore these gifts, or to allow them to become contaminated by an exclusive focus on what needs to change, compromises the success of executive coaching.

Another essential coaching tactic that reinforces the likelihood of new learning and change is the coach's courage to convey and confront the core reality of an executive versus his or her well-protected persona. The effective consultant can illuminate the unsettling mix of an executive's fears, anxiety, vulnerability, and defenses. This tactic requires considerable clinical skill, exquisite timing, and patience; it potentially produces the most learning and direction for change. Executives who are helped to understand and integrate this level of self-discovery ultimately transform it into another source of personal power, that is, enhanced leadership effectiveness.

Using the developmental history and testing as primary tools, competent coaches identify the themes from the executive's life stories. Together, executive and coach make linkages among the choice and crisis points in a life span. For many executives, breakthrough learning is a function of understanding how emotionally congruent and incongruent prior choices were made and then applying this knowledge to both present and future circumstances. Coaching fosters greater personal clarity and authenticity, providing a sturdy foundation for action planning and sustained behavior change with important ramifications for executives' personal and business lives.

Tools

The professional tools of the psychological consultant compose the second "T" of Triple T coaching proficiency. Through the ethical use of carefully selected tools, including developmental history and tests of intelligence, personality, motivation, cognitive style, managerial style, interests, and aptitudes, the consultant provides a psychological study that honors the whole person and pinpoints fruitful avenues for developmental exploration. Many psychologists also use other tools, such as appraisal forms, self-development guides, attitude surveys, and 360-degree feedback instruments. The weaving of all these data points into an integrated and meaningful exposition distinguishes the true psychological study. As Tobias (1990) stated,

> The psychologist helps the manager become better attuned to his own subjective experience of himself, of others, and of situations, in order to better manage his inner emotional life, to free himself of subjective distortion, and to broaden his transparent consciousness of the experience of living. (p. 11)

When providing feedback, it is crucial that psychologists link psychometric data with the contextual realities of the executive's work group and organization culture. The product is an interactive loop between intrapsychic causation and outward manifestation, that is, the grist for the coaching phase of an executive coaching engagement. The coach must remain focused on how the client's personal growth can result in behavioral shifts as well as initiate and facilitate organizational change.

Training

The graduate training and subsequent licensure of psychologists compose the third element of Triple T coaching proficiency. The philosophical foundation of this graduate training, internship rotations, and hundreds of hours of rigorous supervision prepares psychologists for distinctive, results-driven work as executive coaches. This foundation includes the following:

1. Clarity about psychologists' fallibility as change agents.
2. Inner scrutiny in an attempt to maintain objectivity, guarding against the projection of the psychologist's issues onto the client.
3. Control of the urge to deliver insight rather than facilitating the courage it takes for clients to use discovered insights in the service of behavior change.
4. Maintenance of appropriate boundaries with clients, that is, avoiding dual relationships.
5. Appropriate timing for delivering the interpretive material that constitutes new learning for the client.
6. An appreciation of the critical nature of confidentiality.
7. The belief that the individual is always the client and that the needs of the organization will be met through an executive's personal growth and sustained behavior change.

CONCLUSION

Executive coaching has been identified as an "emerging competency" in the practice of psychological consultation to business organizations. Psychologists throughout the world are assisting talented business executives in making behavioral changes that produce stronger leadership and equip them to develop their successors. In the absence of credentialing, the practice of executive coaching needs defined standards of competency to preserve the integrity of the field and the confidence of the consumer. Because the end goal of executive coaching frequently is sustained behavior change, this is best achieved through the application of established psychological principles. Psychologists have a duty to define the competencies required to achieve sustained behavior change through the medium of executive coaching and to be proactive in conveying these standards of competence to the public. Only in this way can this fast-developing realm within psychology reach its full potential as an invaluable resource for business executives.

References

Argyris, C. (1991, May–June). Teaching smart people how to learn. *Harvard Business Review,* 99–109.

Career Architect (Version 2.2B) [Computer software]. (1992). Minneapolis, MN: Lominger Limited.

Goleman, D. (1995). *Emotional intelligence: Why it can matter more than I.Q.* New York. Bantam Books.

Infoseek [Computer software]. (1995–1997). Sunnyvale, CA: Infoseek Corporation.

Kilburg, R. R. (Ed.). (1996). Executive coaching [Special issue]. *Consulting Psychology Journal: Practice and Research, 48*(2).

Teal, T. (1996, November–December). The human side of management. *Harvard Business Review,* 35–44.

Tobias, L. L. (1990). *Psychological consulting to management: A clinician's perspective.* New York: Brunner/Mazel.

CHAPTER 32

LESSONS LEARNED IN— AND GUIDELINES FOR— COACHING EXECUTIVE TEAMS

Richard C. Diedrich

The fact that executive coaching has arrived and is growing at what many consider to be an alarming pace has been well documented in recent years (chaps. 3 and 4, this volume; Stern, 2001). This competency or practice in consultation is established but still largely ill defined. What concerns me even more is how seldom the literature of consulting offers any guidance with regard to another subarea or specialty—the coaching of executive teams.

Years ago, Brouwer (1964, p. 156) shared the view that "as a member of a firm of consulting psychologists to management, I can report . . . that no one can tell managers exactly how to grow. Rather, the most one can do is to help managers understand themselves in their own situations, and then trust them to find the best directions themselves." Also, "People are masters of their own destiny in the sense that they take charge of their own development if they want to grow. Nothing can be done to them to make them grow; they grow only as they want to and as their own insights enable them to" (Brouwer, 1964, p. 162). These basic concepts seem to apply equally well to teams. When coaching teams, our primary role is still one of facilitating understanding and learning.

In my mind, the coaching of an executive team is *not* the same as team building or team development. The coaching of a team is a process where the consulting psychologist has an ongoing, helping relationship with both the team and the individual executives; that is, he or she has time with the team as well as one-on-one coaching contacts with the team members over time. Coaching a team is an iterative process for both the team and the individual that is developmentally oriented as opposed to being a problem-centered quick fix for the team (chap. 14, this volume, pp. 144–145).

GUIDELINES

How can we be more effective? As a foundation for thinking about coaching executive *teams*, I suggest that the consultant needs to do the following:

- View team coaching as a natural occurrence—the opportunity is there; just watch for it while remembering how complex and demanding this intervention can be.
- Engage in process consultation with the team and the individual members, keeping in mind that the task is one of helping to establish and maintain a relationship that provides the freedom to learn.
- Know a lot about the development and functioning of small groups, to include task and process issues; if not, one needs to work with a knowledgeable and group-experienced colleague.

Reprinted from the *Consulting Psychology Journal: Practice and Research*, *53*, 238–239.

- Focus on the here and now; what does the current situation look like for the team and the consultant?
- Represent team coaching as an ongoing, jointly defined learning process; be sure the team defines and understands roles, responsibilities, and the timelines up front.
- Remember that the client is the team, not the senior client executive or the team members, and that the team owns the problems as well as the potential solutions.
- Spend time with each and every team member before discussing or agreeing to any specific initial process or intervention.
- Learn the mind-set or frame of reference of the responsible team leader regarding impact, influence, and flexibility; then help the team to interact most effectively within these boundaries or seek change.
- Help the team to do a few things well; keep the coaching agenda simple and focused.
- Nurture the ability of individuals (and the team) to both observe and then share what they have observed.
- Keep the focus on *team* tasks and processes and the ability of the team member and team to address these issues when coaching the individuals.
- Think long and hard before the team collects any 360-degree *peer* data: What is needed, why is it needed, and what impact will this process and data have on people's inclination and ability to work with each other?
- Have a specific plan before working with the team regarding how the team (and the consultant) will manage the transition from the task to the relationship arena.

References

Brouwer, P. J. (1964). The power to see ourselves. *Harvard Business Review, 42*(6), 156–165.

Stern, L. (2001). A new standard for executive coaching. *The Industrial–Organizational Psychologist, 38*(3), 135–137.

Part IV

CASE STUDIES

Even though our colleague Rodney L. Lowman (chap. 7, this volume) argues that coaching practice has greatly exceeded research and that changes in theory and practice rely on empirical evaluation and restructuring on the basis of that research, he suggests that

> the use of case studies as a basis for creating a sound theory and ultimately empirical literature is perhaps a necessary, or at least commonly encountered, stage in the initial process of developing a new field of inquiry or practice. (p. 76)

If we believe, as he does, that executive coaching is, at best, in its adolescence, we might try to view case study methodology as a desirable supplementary step along the way rather than "an adequate and sufficient substitute for empirical evaluation, relying exclusively on a 'constructivist narrative' approach" (chap. 7, this volume, p. 75). Lowman also notes that "adding the perspectives of the person being coached . . . is especially useful because what interventionists think may be of importance to a process of change may not be what was viewed as being most helpful by the client" (p. 74).

We could more often go directly to our clients for the validation of outcomes (see Diedrich, 2003, 2004, as well as several of the cases in this section). Fortunately, we have three rare examples of case materials in this section that allow the client to report and share his or her perspective (see chaps. 33, 35, and 39). In addition, we owe thanks to four additional authors (see chaps. 34, 36, 37, and 38) for their contributions to the limited literature reporting actual examples of practice rather than another theory or conceptual model. Part IV opens with a chapter by Blattner—and his client—(chap. 33) that describes a 2-year coaching engagement with a global corporate executive, Terry. The process and content are reported in detail, and we are treated to the outcome summaries provided by both the coach and the *client*! Schnell (chap. 34) writes about a system consultation conducted by an internal coach–consultant over a period of 5 years. We are treated to an accounting of lessons learned during the growth and evolution of an organization and the challenges of growth for both the leadership pair and the long-term coaching relationship involving an internal provider.

Peterson and Millier (chap. 35) present the opportunity to experience a rare and rich verbatim report by the client across two "rounds" and many conversations of coaching over several years. David and Jennifer each share in detail their perspective regarding coaching highlights, process observations, specific and candid advice for coaches, and conclusions regarding personal learnings and perceived outcomes of the coaching engagements.

Wasylyshyn (chap. 36) provides a look at the impact of a data-driven, insight-oriented coaching methodology used with a CEO candidate. The contributions of three meta-principles (traction, trust, and truth telling) and the role of four methodological factors (holistic approach, deep behavioral insight, involvement of top executives, and sustained relationships) are reviewed in terms of value in a coaching engagement that focused on the retention of a top succession candidate.

Winum's case study (chap. 37) reminds us of the importance of the interaction between the person-specific attributes and capabilities of the client executive and the context in which the executive is operating. Coaching needs to focus on both the executive and the context (key stakeholders) in which he or she leads. Specific recommendations regarding diversity issues are also included as is a general sequence outline for the design and implementation of coaching programs.

Foster and Lendl (chap. 38) describe how sets of eye movements were used to "install" envisioned goals with four individuals coping with work productivity impairments. This technique, eye movement desensitization and reprocessing (EMDR), was integrated into executive coaching and used to desensitize upsetting events; the participants were then able to shift negative views to more positive ones, and work performance improved. EMDR was reported to be an innovative method that operates more directly on mental processing than verbal coaching alone.

Finally, the chapter by Stevens (chap. 39) should be viewed as seven cases studies, because we are given the actual ideas and voices of seven senior executives as they describe how they experienced and define executive coaching. This case material is anchored in the client rather than the practitioner. Stevens provides a thematic summary that has many implications for the preparation and practice of coaching with top-level executives.

Our purpose in Part IV is to present a unique and comprehensive collection of chapters describing the complex practice of executive coaching. This coaching case material is unavailable any other place in the literature. Until this material became available, probably the only true case study of executive coaching in the 1990s was that reported by Kralj (2001). The observations and recommendations contained in the cases clearly document the potential impact of the case study to the field of executive coaching. They are to be viewed as both an expansion of the literature and as a significant contribution to the further development of theoretical models and the quest for testable hypotheses and future treatment validations of the process and structure of coaching interventions.

References

Diedrich, R. C. (2003, August). *Let's talk with our clients.* Division 13 presidential address presented at the 111th Annual Convention of the American Psychological Association, Toronto, Ontario, Canada.

Diedrich, R. C. (2004). In the eye of the CEO! *Consulting Psychology Journal: Practice and Research, 56,* 129–131.

Kralj, M. M. (2001). Coaching at the top: Assisting a chief executive and his team. *Consulting Psychology Journal: Practice and Research, 53,* 108–116.

Chapter 33

COACHING: THE SUCCESSFUL ADVENTURE OF A DOWNWARDLY MOBILE EXECUTIVE

John Blattner

In recent years there has been a focus on assisting managers and senior leaders to achieve maximum personal and professional growth. This type of consultation has been referred to as *executive coaching*. Coaching in corporate America began to take hold in the 1980s. The thinking was that coaches would consult over a period of time with individuals to promote more resiliency and increase performance (Hudson, 1999). A major focus was to help individuals deal more effectively with rapid change and ever-increasing complexity in the inherently unstable atmosphere of today's business world. Thus, a coach may be a guide to the executive who is facing increasing demands to do more in less time. As consultants, we still do not know how the process of coaching actually works. Kilburg (2000) noted, "This area of consultation has suffered significantly from a lack of attention in the professional literature." This case study is an attempt to illuminate some of the issues and processes of executive coaching. There are many models of coaching, and it is important to keep in mind that there is more than one way to coach, just as there is more than one way to consult (chap. 12, this volume; Hudson, 1999; Kilburg, 2000). This case is provided to offer some insights into one process and to create or stimulate ideas for the professional currently engaged in such activity.

BACKGROUND

Terry was president of a business unit for a global organization headquartered in Asia. A colleague referred him. Terry at that time was experiencing considerable anxiety and tension. Our initial session was spent in establishing contact and discussing the parameters of coaching. He indicated he had an interest in pursuing a career change and improving his personal life. At that point, I suggested that we agree to a 3-month coaching contract and evaluate the need after that period of time. During our second session, I suggested taking an assessment to get a baseline on his strengths and barriers to success. He agreed and then completed the DISC. The DISC model merely analyzes behavioral style, that is, a person's manner of doing things. Style analysis is based on *The Emotions of Normal People* (Marston, 1979).

GOALS

The first step in the engagement was to determine goals and objectives. Terry filled out a questionnaire regarding what brought him to coaching and his goals for the initial phase. I then asked him what might be his goals for 3, 6, and 12 months. He identified the following goals:

Reprinted from the *Consulting Psychology Journal: Practice and Research*, 57, 3–13.

What brings you to coaching?

- Lack of fulfillment in current position
- High anxiety—mild depression
- Unable to enjoy time away from work

What do you want?

- Improved level of gratification
- More freedom
- Product, service, or company I can be excited about motivating me to do well

Three-month goals:

- Clarify work possibilities
- Increase my courage and confidence
- Explore "balance"
- Examine my financial tendencies—possible effect on work, family
- To feel better—mentally, physically

Six- to 12-month goals:

- New job
- Increased energy level
- Ability to sleep
- Have more fun

Skills to work on:

- Leading others
- Delegating
- Balance
- Celebrating
- Discovering my purpose
- Having courage

ASSESSMENT

DISC measures the natural and adapted style of an individual (Bonnstetter, Suiter, & Widrick, 1993). The acronym represents four characteristics: D = dominance, I = influencing, S = steadiness, and C = compliance. Scores range from 0 to 100, with 50 being the midrange. Score differences between the natural and adapted that are less than 20 points are not significant. Score differences of 20 points or more on corresponding scales are significant and warrant further exploration. Terry's scores are given in Table 33.1.

TABLE 33.1

Terry's DISC Scores

Scale	Natural score	Adapted score
Dominance (D)	21	34
Influencing (I)	84	71
Steadiness (S)	84	65
Compliance (C)	52	65

Results from the natural and adapted scores indicated that there were no scales with 20 points or more difference. A difference of 20 points or more would have suggested that there was a decrease or drain on Terry's behavior. Thus, his scores suggested that there was not a significant energy drain—Terry was not experiencing significant stress or fatigue. His steadiness and compliance scores suggested an ability to deal with situations and to maintain a sense of balance in life and energy. Also, the scores provided feedback regarding Terry's behavioral style. Some of the positive findings indicated that Terry was people oriented—building confidence in others; he was service oriented—a dependable team player, and he was cordial and helpful when dealing with new clients or customers.

Other DISC results suggested that he would appreciate some of the following: a stable and predictable environment, an environment that allowed time to change, assignments with a high degree of people contact, and little conflict between people. Also, he needed personal attention from his manager and compliments for each assignment well done.

Additional DISC results suggested the following areas for improvement based on his tendencies to

- be so enthusiastic that he can be seen as superficial;
- make decisions based on surface analysis;
- trust people indiscriminately if positively reinforced by those people;
- be unrealistic in appraising people—especially if the person is a "friend";

- be optimistic regarding possible results of his projects or his people;
- be too verbal in expressing criticism; and
- overestimate his ability to motivate people or change others' behavior.

This assessment was the starting point for our coaching engagement. Terry felt clear about his stated goals. His reaction to the assessment data yielded more agreement than not. He did concur with the stated areas for improvement. With this mutual understanding, we launched into our coaching process.

START OF COACHING

Terry had been a successful individual when I met him. He approached work and life from a practical viewpoint. He had worked for the same global organization based in Asia for approximately 18 years. The global organization served several markets, from consumer products to manufacturing equipment. Terry started out in sales and worked his way up through the organization, being promoted to manager, then director, which led to a promotion to president of a business manufacturing unit in 1990. At the time of his presidential appointment, that unit was grossing approximately $20 million in annual sales. His business, while profitable, was a small component in the billion-dollar parent corporation. Year after year, Terry's unit met or exceeded its financial goals while successfully overcoming problems and issues in the marketplace. Terry's business unit in 10 years had grown from $20 million to $60 million in sales with 125 employees. During this period, Terry worked for a dozen managers and senior executives in the parent organization. He stated that he consistently received positive feedback from the executives in Asia.

INITIAL PHASE

Our initial coaching sessions were biweekly and were spent reviewing his history; outlining what occurred in the organization, on the job, and in his personal life; and building a relationship based on trust. He was open from the beginning and easy to converse with. He was highly motivated as most executives are; however, Terry was clearly frustrated with his increasing inability to achieve even small amounts of satisfaction in his professional life. This had been ongoing for a number of years, and at peak levels of anxiety, he would typically compensate by expending more energy toward the job.

Approximately 1 year before I met Terry, his organization was directly affected by reorganization due to the acquisition of another business. The two businesses were merged into one. The senior manager from the acquired company was appointed to the top position, creating yet another new reporting structure for Terry. The new reporting structure, and specifically his new boss, created an environment that Terry found extremely oppressive to his work style.

Up to then, Terry had been afforded a certain freedom to run his day-to-day business without regular and continuous involvement from his superiors. This freedom had been earned on the basis of a successful track record and his unique knowledge of the business markets in manufacturing. This changed dramatically with the new boss, who required Terry to provide seemingly endless reports, presentations, and business justifications. Terry reported receiving countless e-mails on a daily basis from his boss that required action on his part. Meetings and conference calls were scheduled on an increasingly frequent basis. To Terry the meetings seemed to have unclear objectives and did little for the business other than another meeting being scheduled or the need for yet another report to be generated. As a result of the new reporting structure and pressure from senior management in the parent organization to grow the business, an increased workload, and a never-before-experienced isolation from the rest of the organization hierarchy in Asia, Terry felt exhausted and frustrated.

Our first few meetings occurred at the end of the year. Although he was tired and discouraged with his situation, he had resolved to understand it better and expressed a desire to improve it. In parallel, Terry had begun the initial phases of a search for a new job. He stated repeatedly that the job search activity alone was emotionally gratifying, and even though his campaign was in its infancy, he felt encouraged by the process. The holidays gave Terry a chance to rest and take a break from the daily anxiety, tension, and stress of his work.

As the new year began, we re-reviewed in detail the results of the initial assessment. It provided him with a frame of reference to understand the possible sources for his current difficulties. It was also intended to help him acknowledge his accomplishments. The results were more positive than negative, and he appreciated them even more. As a result of the review, he understood clearly the areas that needed improvement.

The first 3 months of coaching in the new year were spent supporting Terry while his situation worsened. Having a coach at this particular time probably provided a stabilizing effect. Armed with his assessment information, he was able to create some clarity in this complex situation. We discussed his work environment in great detail. He was not able to trust his boss, and the business situation was changing rapidly. Senior management expected greater sales and profits since the acquisition and merger. Terry's workload continued to grow, seemingly to him at a higher rate than that of his peers. The politics became extremely intense. The new boss did not seem to understand the business market and discouraged Terry from communicating with senior management. Terry experienced isolation from the senior managers more than ever before and did not feel supported by the new boss, whom he thought of as a micromanager.

During this time, Terry learned much about his boss as well. He had come from a high-ranking government career followed by senior management positions in industry. He had an autocratic, rank-and-file management style hidden beneath an outward veneer of openness and collaboration. He was keenly aware of corporate politics and a skilled practitioner. Knowing Terry's tenure with the company, he would regularly quiz Terry about members of the senior management and use the information to his benefit. Terry felt his boss's use of this information was isolating him from the company management, especially in the area of accountability. It seemed to Terry that if the results were good, his boss was in line for credit. If the results were not good, it was Terry's responsibility. This atmosphere fostered a lack of trust between Terry and his boss.

During our early sessions, Terry related one incident in particular that clearly illustrated the challenges he encountered. As a president, he was responsible for defining the annual business revenue and profitability goals together with the measures needed to accomplish them. This was always a complicated task given that his plan had to satisfy two organizational entities within his company: the American organization that he reported to and the parent Asian organization regularly asserting control over his business. The primary goals of these two reporting entities were at odds with each other, that is, they consistently differed on their objectives for sales growth, profitability, and the opportunities within the marketplace to support their respective expectations of Terry. This situation was now further complicated by Terry's new boss, who was clearly positioning himself as the new business leader and the one capable of meeting the challenges of both organizations.

Terry's approach to the annual business plan had evolved into an ongoing fact-based assessment of the market and related indexes that afforded a solid foundation to establish revenue forecasts. It is worth noting that this practical, fact-based methodology was how Terry had always approached and evaluated important matters. In the past, this methodology and effort had been highly regarded by Terry's management in the United States and very useful in establishing realistic goals with senior management in Asia.

Terry's boss was confronted with the Asian management's high expectations early in his tenure. The boss informed Terry that he and the Asian management did not believe that his market assessment was correct and instructed him to do more research that would indicate that the answer should be a larger market with more opportunity. Although frustrated with his boss's reaction, Terry delved into this assignment, expending tremendous energy on conclusively defining the market. At the end of the assignment, his research showed that his original assumptions and estimates were correct. His boss could not dispute his findings and indicated his concurrence with the results.

In a subsequent presentation to the Asian and American management, Terry reviewed his market analysis and revenue plan. The Asian management rejected his sales forecast, independent of the research, and requested a more aggressive plan. Terry professionally disagreed with this request on the basis of his exhaustive research. He received no support from his boss in the meeting. After the presentation, he was instructed by his boss to reevaluate the market once again and provide a more aggressive sales plan as instructed by the senior management in Asia. He questioned his boss on why he had not been supportive in the meeting and expressed concern regarding the dangers of being held to an unreachable goal. His boss replied that the Asians were the customers in this matter and it was Terry's job to satisfy them. Nothing more.

It was becoming clearer that a change was imminent. Terry had thought and stated that a job change was inevitable prior to our coaching. The concept of change was a challenge. He had consistently been successful. Now he was beginning to see himself in an unfavorable way. Terry at times was self-critical and hard on himself at this time. His sense of well-being in the past had come from dealing with difficult issues head-on, most often very successfully and regardless of the energy drain it had on him. He was becoming increasingly self-critical because this proven approach was now not working. He questioned his abilities to improve on his current situation. He was fearful that a change might lead to a compromised position or poorer work environment or even potential failure at another job. He was also concerned with what others might think of him should he leave his current position and fail in another. We discussed this at great length. I encouraged him to look for his strengths. Encouraging Terry was very important at this time in our relationship. He also agreed to continue coaching for another 3 months.

During the second quarter of that year, Terry decided to leave the organization. Throughout the separation period (a month), he was contacted by several of the high-ranking managers he had worked with over the years. These managers encouraged Terry to stay with the company. However, as it became clear to them that Terry was leaving, they offered their assistance and support. These gestures were reassuring and proved to Terry that the company placed high value on his contributions and wanted to keep a door open for future possibilities. Several current and past managers acknowledged his work. They separated on positive terms.

As previously mentioned, prior to and throughout the first phase of our coaching engagement, Terry was searching for a new career. As difficult and consuming as his work environment had been, he had a certain awareness and clarity about himself and what he wanted in a new position. The number of opportunities available encouraged him as his job campaign progressed. He received several offers, leading to a new position as a sales manager for a high tech manufacturer of biomedical equipment. He secured this prior to leaving his old job. Finding and landing a new job greatly raised his confidence and self-esteem.

There was the usual apprehension in starting a new position. Terry, although nervous, was also very excited about getting back to work after having a month off. He became very focused on his new management position in an entirely different industry. At this time, as his anxiety became more overt, he was more self-critical. This was new and unfamiliar, and he lapsed back into previous negative self-talk. This lapse was more reflective of his historical pattern and enduring in nature. His concerns focused on orientation to the company, its structure and leadership, and his new manager. We discussed in much detail how to approach his sales people, and we brainstormed several scenarios about how he would introduce himself to them. Simultaneously, we began discussing emotional intelligence (Goleman, 1995), at first in a conceptual way; however, we quickly explored practical applications as Terry readied for the challenges of his new job.

In a coaching session prior to Terry's new job start, he volunteered that the first staff meeting would occur during his first week with the company. Eager to make a positive impression and in line with the way he had done things in the past, he planned to prepare a detailed PowerPoint presentation on his background, his management style, and his vision for the team. As he continued describing his plan, it appeared to me that he was offsetting his anxieties with activity and energy. He was not fully grasping the likely emotional state of the new staff during this first meeting and was underestimating the potential impact this approach might have on them. We discussed this at great length and determined that perhaps the meeting goal should be to establish some initial rapport with his new team and that a more open, less structured forum might be a better approach. Terry embraced this quickly and was eager to engage his new staff this way. He later reported a very successful meeting. He personally felt positive and energized as a result.

Terry now found himself realizing and further developing skills that he had not been aware of previously. In his prior position as a president, he had become quite skillful at dealing with mid- to high-level management personnel. He possessed tremendous industry knowledge and an ability to present ideas in a manner that often led to quick approval by management and subordinates alike. Although he was under continuous pressure for higher levels of productivity, his familiarity with the business kept his confidence high and enabled him to complete jobs successfully. However, this created extreme energy drain for him in the process.

In his new position, he was introduced to an unfamiliar work environment. He was in a new field, learning how to develop others from a totally different perspective. He was confronted with several human resources issues immediately, one of which required him to fire a staff member within his first 30 days on the job. His administrative tasks were time-consuming and included running an office, forecasting, reporting, and answering up to 60 internal e-mails per day. Sales levels in the unit were significantly lagging behind business plan projections. In addition, Terry was forced to adapt quickly to his new boss's style and methods of work. Terry was further pressured by his concern about how customers and staff viewed him given his lack of highly technical product and industry knowledge and his self-perceived inability to participate competently in business meetings.

In one coaching session, I asked Terry how his relationship was developing with his new boss. He became reflective. He reported that he liked his new manager and was anxious to please him. However, Terry was concerned that his productivity was not progressing quickly enough. He cited one instance where he felt overwhelmed by the new job and shared his feelings with his new boss in a positive, yet honest way. The pressure to improve sales in a difficult year, both immediate and longer term, was the common topic of seemingly every one of the conversations. His boss was reassuring during this time, stating that Terry's analytic ability and business experience were contributing to and motivating his team and peer group in ways he could not see himself. His boss also indicated that 90% of Terry's experience and skill applied to his new job and perhaps all he could see was the 10% that was new. This open, collaborative, and encouraging work environment was clearly having a positive effect on Terry. He reported that his boss liked many of his ideas, and when he used them, he made sure everyone knew it was Terry's idea. Also, Terry reported that he was learning new sales techniques from his new boss. For the first time in a long while, he felt he was getting positive feedback in exchange for his contributions versus the endless research, reporting, and presentations of the past that provided no tangible return.

Coaching at this time assisted Terry in remaining focused. It lessened his anxiety. At times, we would go back to the assessment data as a check. It helped Terry to stay on track. Having data and an objective frame of reference was extremely important for him. As our process continued, he grew more comfortable. He began to see how coaching was allowing him to think, to reflect, and, more important, to grow.

After 3 to 4 months on the new job, Terry reported he was not enjoying the administrative tasks it involved. It was clear to me in this conversation that the "fear of failure" syndrome was reemerging. Terry struggled with his perceived inability to participate in customer meetings because of his lack of technical product knowledge. In addition, he felt a certain degree of inadequacy in collaborating and managing the technical staff who reported to him. He expressed doubts about his ability to learn the technical aspects of the job easily in his self-imposed time frame.

His self-doubt was magnified by the actions of one direct report who compared him with his predecessor in a condescending way, especially when discussing technical matters or customer problems. This had a negative impact on Terry, causing him to question his ability to continue the job and, even worse, consider prospects for other employment. Part of him was trying to determine a practical, fact-based approach to overcome his self-perceived deficiencies even as his self-confidence and assuredness were surfacing regarding his own emotional well-being and that of those around him.

Reverting to methods he had used in past, he decided that he needed to devote evenings and weekends to studying the technical aspects of the industry. He knew that this would not be easy. He feared that immersing himself in study would lead to frustration; however, he was concerned that anything less would be irresponsible on his part. I suggested that instead of pursuing what we both realized would be an energy drain, he focus on the numerous strengths that he brought to the position. I recommended that in customer situations he might try to be more comfortable with listening and learning while his staff did their jobs. I suggested that he could consider clarifying with each of his staff members what their personal and professional goals were in order to better understand what motivated his people. We discussed using this same method to determine the goals for the customer meetings he would attend with his staff. He adapted this concept to his daily work and quickly reported feeling better about himself, his confidence, and his ability to contribute in positive ways. Perhaps for the first time in a while, Terry began to have some fun on the job.

I was encouraging Terry at this time. I felt that trust was significantly established and that this would allow us to go even further in pursuing his goals, values, and beliefs about himself. Terry explored in a rather open fashion with me at this point. He looked forward to our coaching sessions. He was more patient with the process. It should be noted that in the beginning of our work together, Terry—being a "bottom line" kind of guy—had just wanted me to roll out a formula, give him the answers, and "that would be that." I had resisted that approach and responded by repeatedly reframing his questions and asking thoughtful and clarifying questions in return. Now that Terry understood more about coaching, he was using the same method quite effectively with his sales people. He was able to generate ideas about their styles and develop strategies to better approach them for more effective individual communication. This is an area that we worked on for several sessions.

Simultaneously, Terry agreed with my suggestion to read *Emotional Intelligence* (Goleman, 1995). He found that it fit very nicely with the work that we had done. It was as if a gestalt had formed and Terry was seeing a bigger picture. In addition to his historic fact-based approach to situations, Terry now had a much clearer internal awareness about himself and the emotional states of others. This awareness allowed him to see and evaluate situations in more comprehensive ways than he had in the past. He was becoming more aware of his staff as individuals: their strengths, weaknesses, hopes, and desires. Increasingly, Terry and I discussed how he was handling his sales staff and his boss. Terry, bright and technically skilled, now was armed with the additional understanding of the emotional lives and styles of his colleagues at work.

These new skills assisted him in the development of his staff. He connected with most of them, knew the ones who were not performing, and realized what he needed to do. After a period of about 4 months, the pressure from his superiors to perform even better continued relentlessly. He again allowed this pressure to hinder him because he felt he did not have the industry-specific knowledge that most of his customers and all of his coworkers did. This was extremely frustrating for him and caused anxiety. During this time, we spent time in coaching surfacing his assumptions and beliefs and relating them back to previously learned patterns. Terry's self-doubt was slowly diminishing, and he was more energized and working hard with the staff and the customer base. Coaching helped him to relax and not take himself too seriously. He became comfortable with his skills and his newly developed sense of emotional self-awareness.

That year, 2001, was a significant learning year for Terry from many perspectives: fresh team, new management, different industry, and, above all, self-discovery. From time to time, we re-reviewed his original assessment. It aided in keeping a focus on his progress. At this point, Terry saw how much he had developed and wanted more. His sense of "impending failure" was lifting and being replaced by a fresh sense of optimism. During one session, he volunteered that he clearly felt that his previous job was contrary to his natural interests. His ongoing progress and success on the new job supported this recently acquired understanding. He recapped situations in which his opinion may have been considered at odds with his boss. On each of these occasions he conveyed confidence that did not exist 2 years ago. That year was filled with learning experiences. The self-knowledge gained was rewarding, and it directly improved his performance and strengthened his self-confidence. At this time, he was also managing his boss rather constructively and would "push back" when appropriate. He did not shy away from his responsibilities. He was now able to be less anxious most of the time, resulting in having energy left over for himself.

MIDDLE PHASE

As 2002 opened, Terry stated that he was more comfortable with his sales team. He had had a year to work with them and to understand their individual behavioral styles. This armed him with an ability to keep them on task to significantly exceed the sales projections for the year. Terry was able to communicate on an individual level and manifested positive energy to that end. He initiated novel approaches with various individuals on his staff to reach a desired result, each time learning more about himself and the person involved. This continuous learning provided Terry with additional satisfaction on the job. The fulfillment was added to his confidence. He communicated with his direct boss more effectively. We even role-played what might be his boss's behavioral style.

Later in the year, Terry again faced having to terminate a staff member. During our session, he was bothered by the situation, and the impending need to act was causing him anxiety. After a few questions, it became obvious that Terry had effectively worked to clarify the staff member's responsibilities and had repeatedly received unfulfilled commitments to change from the employee. Just discussing the situation with Terry calmed him down. He later reported that the termination meeting came as no surprise to the staff member, and they parted in a professional manner, once again reinforcing the fact in Terry's mind that he was dealing with these situations very effectively. It was clearly apparent that Terry's confidence continued to grow, with him feeling more competent not only on the job, but in his personal life as well. The self-limiting, self-critical feelings of the past were becoming much less prominent.

Terry's relationship with his boss also continued to develop. On one occasion, his boss asked him to create a new position to penetrate a vertical industry segment. Terry was troubled with this assignment, stating concerns about reporting structure, position expectations, and performance measurement. Using his analytical skills, he carefully reviewed the issues and opportunities this position would encounter. In the end, he advised his boss that he could not envision that the position could be successful under the given parameters. During that discussion, the two shared many of the same concerns, causing them to mutually agree to abandon the project in its current form. This continued ability to collaborate on a professional level with his manager proved extremely rewarding to Terry.

Terry reported to me that the company again had increased the yearly sales quotas for 2003, and once again, he was challenged to raise the bar. When on sales calls, his anxiety level continued to be elevated, despite the fact that his technical knowledge had increased, which reduced his level of distress. We reviewed many scenarios on how he could become more secure with the technology. We discussed what the possible reasons would be for this current experience of distress. As a result, he was able to keep it in perspective. From his report, he was slowly developing more trust and understanding with his sales team.

At this point, our coaching sessions became more focused on specific situations that were causing Terry difficulty. For example, we explored the dynamics with a particular customer who had been troublesome since the start of his new job. The manner in which the customer communicated caused anxiety before, during, and after Terry's calls. We discussed this specific situation in detail, and it became clear that he feared not having all the answers, worried about what the customer would think of him, and worse, what his company would think of him should a negative report on him surface. By now, though, Terry had overcome many issues that had previously bothered him, and this was no different. Armed with the positive results from his team, his sales productivity, and his increasing product knowledge, together we were able to put this issue into perspective and deal with it in a positive way.

In one coaching session near the end of our engagement, we reflected on his previous occupation as a president and what was different and positive in Terry's professional life currently. He elaborated that in the past he, in many instances, avoided customer contact, collaboration with peers, and regular interaction with staff. Looking back, he identified this behavior as stemming from a feeling of inadequacy, lack of energy, and no passion for the job or the company. As a result of coaching and subsequent experience, he saw himself proactively engaging customers and peers with the objective of learning from each encounter. He felt that learning could occur more naturally without the energy drain and had a powerful, renewed sense of self-confidence.

FINAL PHASE

As 2002 drew to a close, we reviewed Terry's progress and his key milestones. Upon reflection, Terry had learned—but, more important, had incorporated—significant appreciation for the emotional component of personal interaction and how he could use it advantageously in his work with the staff, customers, and his boss. There were even reported improvements with communication in his marriage. It appeared that we had arrived at a place to start working on closure for our coaching sessions. At this point, we more actively talked about a stop date. It was a mutual conclusion and from my perspective felt right. Terry had worked very hard, made some important progress, and was actually practicing what we worked on. We revisited his anxiety, and that was neither as pronounced nor as distressing to him. He was able to monitor and keep his reactions in a better perspective.

CONCLUSION

In my view, the coaching engagement, which lasted just over 2 years, allowed this client to prosper and develop in ways that he might not have otherwise. In our initial meeting, I found Terry more fact-based than emotionally informed in his approach to leadership. Appealing to his logical side seemed to be the best approach to help in developing our relationship. My challenge was to balance giving Terry facts without just answering all of his questions and providing him with a "formula" instead of his learning how he could develop his own answers. Keeping him focused on his goals and allowing him to experience himself in a different manner was one of my objectives as a coach. Assisting him to expand his awareness was a part of our work together. Generally, Terry came to our sessions with an agenda. I was constantly checking to keep the focus of his agenda and be attentive to his distraction or diversions. Timing was an important part of our process. I wanted to establish rapport with Terry before proceeding; thus, I spent considerable time solidifying our relationship in the beginning. It was important to understand his assumptions and beliefs to better construct interventions that would have an impact. Toward the middle of our process, a shift had occurred for Terry. He connected to his emotional self. There was an energy shift and a sense of excitement that accompanied it. From that pivotal point, Terry made significant connections to his emotional self. As he practiced with this enhanced aspect of himself and reported on it, there was usually a big smile of enthusiasm on his face. This reinforced the newly acquired behavior and integrated it into his personality. As the termination date came closer, it was relatively easy to tell we had accomplished his initial goals.

I asked Terry to review our work and reflect on his experience with the process. The following section gives some of his comments.

TERRY'S PERSPECTIVE

Having a coach provided me with an unbiased third party to discuss difficult career- and work-related issues. Furthermore, as the trust and relationship was built over time, I was at ease discussing my work-related fears, problems, and possible resolutions that I would otherwise have been unable to explore with friends, colleagues, or family members. Over time, I often felt I had a private business tutor giving me a significant edge over my contemporaries.

In our coaching sessions, I was given a much broader perspective on the possibilities that are available to me in my professional and personal life. I knew for a long time I was miscast in my earlier career and struggled with how to understand and change it. By focusing on my strengths and the limitless opportunities available, raising my courage and self-esteem to effect positive change became reality.

I specifically struggled with fear and anxiety in certain aspects of my professional life. By continually visiting this issue during the coaching sessions, I am now much more satisfied with doing my best and accepting the outcome versus doing my best and worrying if it is good enough.

My personal life is now much more satisfying as I have energy left over to enjoy it. I've learned that energy drain is not synonymous with being responsible for a job or task. I've learned how to recognize energy drain and avoid it while getting the job done to a high standard. And if that is not good enough . . . tough sh*t!

References

Bonnstetter, B. J., Suiter, J. I., & Widrick. R. J. (1993). *The universal language DISC: A reference manual.* Scottsdale, AZ: Target Training International.

Goleman, D. (1995). *Emotional intelligence.* New York: Bantam Books.

Hudson, F. M. (1999). *The handbook of coaching.* San Francisco: Jossey-Bass.

Kilburg, R. R. (2000). *Executive coaching: Developing managerial wisdom in a world of chaos.* Washington, DC: American Psychological Association.

Marston, W. M. (1979). *The emotions of normal people.* Minneapolis, MN: Persona Press.

CHAPTER 34

A CASE STUDY OF EXECUTIVE COACHING AS A SUPPORT MECHANISM DURING ORGANIZATIONAL GROWTH AND EVOLUTION

Eugene R. Schnell

Much of the extant literature about executive coaching (e.g., see Kilburg, 2000; Fitzgerald & Garvey Berger, 2002; Goldsmith, Lyons, Freas, & Witherspoon, 2002) implies that the coaching consultation has several features: that the coach is external to the client system; that the client is an individual (vs. a pair or a group); and that the leaders' organization system, while perhaps turbulent, is either in a start-up or maturation phase. This case provides description of a successful coaching experience contrary to those assumptions: the coach was from an "internal" source, the primary client for much of the consultation was a pair of leaders, and the organizational system was undergoing a phase shift from a start-up operation to a mature organization. In addition, the client organization was part of an academic medical center at a public university and therefore subject to interesting dynamics of university and public funding politics. The case is provided as a means to illustrate the rich contexts in which a coaching intervention can be used. In order to protect the confidentiality of the coach and clients, specific identifying information has been appropriately changed, but other descriptors are provided that maintain the integrity of the leadership and organizational dynamics.

BACKGROUND

Coaching Practitioner and Context

The primary consultant, Eric H., was an internal consultant working for a large state-funded university system in the midwestern United States. Eric was supported in this work by a small team of practitioners based in the human resources department that served the university's medical school and hospital. The group jointly reported to the director of human resources (within the organizational structure for the vice president for business and administration) and the university's vice president for medical affairs. The vice president, who oversaw health care operations and had joint responsibility for the medical school, was a strong advocate for quality improvement approaches in health care. He stimulated the creation of the Organization Development (OD) unit in 1993 with a vision that it would provide support for strategic planning, improvements in business processes, and participatory management.

Eric was the leader of the OD unit. A White male with an MBA and doctoral preparation in industrial–organizational psychology, he had come to the university in 1983 while his wife was in medical school. At the time the consultation began, he was 35 years old and had worked as a

Reprinted from the *Consulting Psychology Journal: Practice and Research*, 57, 41–56.

department business administrator for 10 years. In 1993 he was recruited by the vice president to accept this new position as the leader of the OD unit. The OD unit was funded so that it could provide free consultations to individuals and groups throughout the university and medical center.

Eric had little experience in OD but understood its academic underpinnings via his graduate work. While an administrator, he had successfully led several universitywide task forces and was one of the pioneers in demonstrating the effective use of quality improvement approaches within an academic department. He established the OD unit and its credibility in a very short period of time and hired two additional training and OD specialists to assist him in accomplishing the mission of the new unit. During this evolution of this case, I (Eugene R. Schnell) served as shadow consultant and coach to Eric to assist with his transition and development as an OD practitioner.

Client Description

In late 1994, Eric received a consultation request from the Center for Minority Health (CMH). The CMH had functioned since 1983 as an interdisciplinary unit reporting to the dean of the medical school. The CMH conducted health education outreach programs for teens and young mothers, and their routine programs were centrally featured in the university's publications regarding community engagement. The founder of CMH was Gloria C., a White 45-year-old daughter of a highly prominent state politician. After completing doctoral studies in the sociology of health, Gloria had worked at the highest levels in a federal health institute and was well known for her circle of personal connections in the state capital and in federal government.

Eric was aware that Gloria had a reputation for visionary ideas and controversial interactions with university leadership. She was viewed as an underproducing scholar, and, indeed, she had remained on the faculty with a teaching contract after her tenure was not recommended by the department years before. Her outspoken opinions about minority health needs were routinely featured in the local print and TV media, and she had pressed university leadership in public forums for more community outreach. Eric had heard from other department chairpersons that she "only was kept around" because of personal connections that she had used to pressure leaders during her tenure decision. Eric understood from the vice president for medical affairs that Gloria had been allowed to continue with the university, over the strong objections of the medical school dean, as long as she could attract funding to support her position.

Eric also discovered that Gloria was an asset to the university. She was called upon selectively when political contacts were needed by the university. During election campaigns, Gloria arranged for candidates to visit the university, and she facilitated very positive collateral press coverage of medical center accomplishments. Her courses were popular electives, and her teaching was highly regarded by students. CMH programs attracted media attention, and Gloria's circle of influential acquaintances supported her publicly. Unable to obtain seed funding for her programs, Gloria had even successfully lobbied for direct funding of the CMH from the state legislature.

Gloria's vision and success in networking continued for several years. By 1989, the CMH was relatively established in the community and among medical staff who volunteered annually to help with its programs. The CMH had maintained approximately $2 million per year in sponsored funding and employed a staff of 5 full-time employees (FTEs) for 10 years. In 1993, the CMH applied for and began to receive several multimillion dollar grants from private foundations. The grants were to be used to create a national clearinghouse for minority health education programs, to unite minority health scholars, to organize minority health education practitioners, and to begin a monograph series. With these successful grants in hand, the CMH awards grew in 1 year to $22 million annually, and the staff had grown from 5 to 42 FTEs by the end of 1994. During the 5 years of this consultation, the CMH would continue to add approximately $5 million per year in new awards and a concomitant growth of about 10 FTEs per year.

Gloria's national networks served the CMH well as it faced the need to rapidly recruit and hire staff. As leaders for each of the projects, Gloria hired friends and colleagues who did not prevail in 1994 local and Congressional elections. This brought several well-known political celebrities to the CMH, though few of them had direct experience with the scholarship behind minority health research and even fewer with grant management experience. Many of the individuals hired spent little time as staff members in organizations, but each one was hailed with much media fanfare when he or she joined the CMH.

Privately, the dean of the medical school continued to express concerns for the CMH, its demands for space and other infrastructure, and its lack of integration with other research or clinical activities in the medical school. When he criticized Gloria for the lack of any serious academics, she personally persuaded one of the most distinguished scholars from another prestigious institution to lend his name to the center and to be acknowledged as a scholar in residence. Gloria arranged for the scholar to deliver a lecture series and personally organized a series of private dinners for him with some of the most active researchers in the medical school.

The staggering rate of growth for CMH created great stress for Gloria and the talented office manager she had relied on for over 10 years. Aware of her own disinterest and skills in management, Gloria called Anne H., a 36-year-old doctoral student in nursing from Latin America whom she had met while guest lecturing in a community health course. Gloria had been impressed with Anne's passionate questions and curiosity about leadership. Gloria asked Anne if she might consider functioning as CMH's chief operating officer to oversee the management and reporting requirements of the different CMH grants. Anne readily agreed and saw the job as leading to wonderful personal growth, mentorship, and access to the national scene she felt most lacking in her own professional background.

THE CONSULTATION PROJECT

Initial Request

Eric was contacted by Gloria approximately 6 months after Anne had been hired as chief operating officer for CMH. Gloria lamented to him, "I miss the family culture that was our trademark and helped me come to work every day. Can't we find a fluid way to structure ourselves that would get the job done while still encouraging innovation and quality?" Gloria was delighted with Anne's performance and wanted to empower her to run as much of the organization as Anne felt comfortable doing. Gloria was supportive of quality improvement methods and hoped to become a model within the medical school for the vice president's interest in this management approach. She forthrightly stated that obtaining the support of the vice president might off-set the ongoing criticism of the CMH from the dean of the medical school. Gloria suggested to Eric that she and Anne might benefit from leadership coaching in their pursuits to grow the center and be one of the university's best examples of using quality improvement methods.

As was customary, Eric established an initial meeting with Gloria to discuss her request. He asked that she bring key documents about the organization (e.g., job descriptions, organization charts, plans, and so forth). When Gloria arrived for the meeting, she announced that she had brought Anne in place of all the documents that had been requested. Despite the surprise addition of Anne to the meeting, Eric was impressed with their candor about the CMH, their own strengths and weaknesses, and their receptiveness to consultation. When asked about their working relationship, they described several instances where they had experienced conflict, surfaced the issues, and successfully resolved their differences. Prior planning and OD work had been provided by a friend of Gloria's who was also an organization consultant. Although pleased with her work, they both felt it was time to engage a more objective practitioner. The consultant had arranged for Gloria to attend some of the premier self-awareness and leadership development programs in the country, and Gloria indeed demonstrated a strong appetite for improving self-awareness and for reading management literature. Gloria had already begun Anne on a track of taking the same development workshops and planned on continuing that effort as part of her ongoing mentorship.

Gloria and Anne described their enterprise as one that was struggling to organize itself. The CMH had worked primarily in the first 10 years as the only program of its type in the state and built itself around several core programs. The organization lacked a formally stated mission or vision, did not have an organizational chart, and prided itself on having no formal reporting lines. They also did not have written strategic objectives, and when asked how they had obtained so much grant support without them, it was revealed that each was the result of a series of personal appeals from Gloria via political connections with little documentation or promised deliverables. Much of the day-to-day work was coordinated by project directors, who were a mix of people in part-time and full-time roles working on-site, off-site locally, and off-site from long-distance locations. No formal role delineation had been made between Gloria and Anne, and the two functioned nearly as coleaders. Gloria and Anne talked each morning about priorities and ideas. The only other regular meeting in the organization was a meeting of the whole conducted each Wednesday morning, starting at 8 a.m. over breakfast and concluding "when no one wanted to stick around any longer." Aside from the dean's lack of financial support and concerns about lack of academic rigor, Gloria and Anne were frustrated by repeated inquiries from the dean's office and central administrative units (like human resources, payroll, facilities planning, and so forth) that the center was violating numerous policies and procedures. When asked about staff concerns, Anne shared that she thought they were frustrated by a lack of colocated office space, poor computing support, lack of connection between programs ("We do not know the other new programs or what they are doing"), and difficulty with access to the part-time and off-site project directors.

With so many basic management elements under development, Eric suggested that pursuing a traditional quality improvement approach (e.g., using quality circles, customer feedback, and process improvement) might be more cumbersome than helpful. He proposed instead to meet weekly with the pair to coach them about the basic "floorboards" needed to organize the CMH so that improvement teams, measurement, and other elements from quality improvement could be introduced. Both Gloria and Anne were highly receptive and thought the weekly coaching to the pair would be exactly the type of reflective space needed for them to get above the daily fray of requests and complaints. As was customary in place of consulting fees within the university, a short memo of agreement was drafted that assured support from Eric and his office for 6 months. The agreement included the following goals: "to address core management needs in the CMH associated with rapid growth; to clarify roles and duties for all levels of leadership in the CMH; to identify gaps in skills needed to manage the new scope of the CMH; to guide the growth of Gloria and Anne's leadership skills."

Coaching the Leadership Pair

At first, the agenda for each weekly coaching meeting with the pair was shaped by Gloria and Anne in response to the most difficult crises facing the CMH at the moment. The pair would usually present Eric with "what should we do" types of questions, having exhausted all their known options for action. Some of the questions were very basic and surprised Eric so much that he felt compelled to draw on his 10 years as a university administrator to quote a procedure or provide a technical answer. Gloria and Anne responded with enthusiasm with this format for the meeting.

Eric began to feel that that the coaching had evolved into an ad hoc supervisory relationship, particularly after he received a call from the associate dean of the medical school about some advice he had given to the pair that was later quoted to the associate dean. The associate dean did not agree with the advice and raised concerns that the pair was redirecting their management issues to Eric instead of placing them in the normal supervisory chain of command at the medical school. In accordance with their confidentiality agreement, Eric raised the concerns with Gloria and Anne at their next meeting.

Eric entered the next meeting with a two-column chart showing on one side how he had responded to their question and what had unfolded in their leadership actions (i.e., compliance to advice) and on the other side how he might have used more questioning and inquiry with the same issue and what he hoped would unfold in the future (i.e., reshaping leadership behaviors and assumptions). Gloria and Anne found the chart quite useful, and it objectified the nature of the coaching relationship. The format also allowed Eric to explain that an inquiry-based approach might be more frustrating in the short run but more beneficial as future leadership actions unfolded in the future.

Eric's change in approach provided great stimulation for interesting exchanges during the coaching sessions. His questions would generate an initial response from Gloria or Anne and then a counter-response from the other in the pair. Eric observed that Gloria and Anne had great tolerance for long discussion and deliberation (often continuing after Eric had left for another appointment). Gloria and Anne's exchanges often typified some of the issues being raised for coaching, and their active dialogue often gave Eric added data to help them reflect on the nature of their own exchanges.

Over time, Eric observed that the pair were not coming to coaching prepared and did not complete homework between sessions. As the issues presented by the pair began to repeat from prior sessions, Eric would query the pair about a root cause, which usually created more theoretical discussion (often with the two sharply but supportively disagreeing) about the state of the organization. Anne seemed to behave in the discussions as if the coaching sessions were more like graduate seminars. Gloria too remarked that the sessions were helping her to mentor and develop Anne. Although the sessions were intellectually stimulating for himself as well, Eric became concerned that they were captured by their own reflective process while ignoring their critical role as agents of action for the organization.

A Transformative Crisis

Approximately 3 months into the consultation, Gloria and Anne reported that the dean had requested a management audit of the unit. The pair's first reaction was characterized by guilt and shame for having unwisely ignored Eric's questions about the need to act on pressing business issues at the CMH. They asked Eric to intervene with the dean's office and report their good intentions with the coaching sessions, which Eric declined to do, but he encouraged them to raise this as a positive point directly with the auditors. Privately, Eric was encouraged by the audit and knew it would yield some useful management advice. Eric was accustomed to the audit process and was only mildly concerned about any political or personal embarrassment that might come from audit findings.

When the preliminary audit report was released, the findings were more embarrassing than Eric had expected, and very strong language accompanied recommendations for an overhaul of financial practices and core accountability mechanisms at the CMH. Gloria exploded over the harsh tone of the audit, and several coaching meetings were required simply to help her contain her anger and avoid taking rash action. Eric's strategy during these sessions focused on redirecting Gloria's attention to how the audit findings might be helpful to the organization. Eric had hoped to use the audit agenda as a baseline for increasing accountability for the coaching sessions.

Gloria decided to respond to the audit with her own written observations and by generating letters of support from external sources. As part of this process, however, Eric suggested that he privately interview the project directors about their experience in the organization and help Gloria prioritize the audit recommendations. The project directors strongly supported the audit findings (though usually by identifying how the audit findings were relevant to other units, not their own). Eric presented Gloria and Anne with the data from his interviews during one of the coaching sessions.

Gloria was devastated by the concurrence of findings between "her people" and the "dean's inquisitors." She had expected the project directors to reject the audit findings and to defend the accomplishments of the organization. Gloria's anger then extended to Eric, whom she accused of "long being on the side of the dean" and "being an agent of the dean to force her to accept the audit recommendations." Over protests from Eric and Anne, Gloria left that meeting abruptly.

Eric requested a private meeting with Gloria to help her sort through her emotional reactions. At that session, she quickly apologized for her outburst and the accusations she had made about Eric's motives, and then she lapsed into inconsolable weeping. She was unable to remain composed and vacillated between rage and harsh self-criticism. Unable to contain Gloria's reaction, Eric suggested they leave the building and the reminders of frustrations for a walk on the campus. The physical movement and new sensory inputs calmed Gloria enough for Eric to reflect on her reaction and ask if it was reminiscent of another time in her life. Gloria nodded and welled up with tears. Eric suggested that it might be wise to work that time through with a mental health practitioner for whom he provided contact information.

Anne called Eric several days later to report that Gloria had not returned to work the day of his meeting with Gloria. She had left a message with Anne that she was going to use unspent vacation leave for 3 weeks and asked that Anne continue to meet with Eric to work through a response to the audit findings and the feedback data. During the vacation period, Gloria called Eric to thank him for the mental health referral and reported satisfaction with a new regimen of psychotherapy and treatment with antidepressants. Eric had not remembered to seek Gloria's permission to disclose their conversation with Anne, so his first meetings with Anne were awkward. This was a dimension of the pairs coaching he had not anticipated.

When Gloria returned to work from vacation, she would only meet with Anne at their regular morning meeting and then leave to work from home for the rest of the day. She cancelled most of her public engagements or asked that Anne attend in her place. Gloria maintained this pattern for 2 months (which was facilitated by the summer) until one morning she bluntly reported to Anne that she had been diagnosed with breast cancer subsequent to a physical examination suggested by her new psychotherapist. Gloria stated that she would be undergoing surgery and other possible treatments and that she had asked the dean to appoint Anne as acting director for the foreseeable future.

Settling on a New Management Approach

During Gloria's medical leave, Gloria and Anne maintained regular e-mail, phone, and individual contact. Gloria supported Anne in making a flurry of changes suggested by the audit: conducting regular meetings of a management team, constructing new offices, hiring a budget analyst, clarifying roles between Gloria and Anne, delineating authority lines, creating a new marketing plan for the center, incorporating a separate nonprofit organization for the professional network groups, and publishing their first center monograph. Eric continued with the regular coaching sessions with Anne and remarked on her energy and follow-through. The coaching sessions themselves also changed, providing more closure on issues. Anne used the sessions to propel her own focus and accountability for action.

Reports from Gloria, however, were not as favorable. Initial surgery was not completely successful, and necessary radiation and chemotherapy treatments would require daily appointments. As further surgeries were scheduled, Gloria turned over most, but not all, of her projects to Anne. Anne reported some anxiety problems during the early individual coaching sessions, mostly focusing on anticipatory grief for Gloria's possible death and guilt for enjoying the dean's repeated praise of her performance in Gloria's absence.

Transforming the Consultation Request

Eric's role during Gloria's long medical leave shifted from being a coach to the two leaders of the organization to becoming an organization consultant to the acting director. A number of OD interventions were required to fully implement the changes Anne was introducing (with Gloria's support), such as role negotiations, political strategy development, management team retreats, project planning sessions, collection of customer feedback, and team-building with specific work groups.

The additional focus on the organization required several delicate shifts. First, because Gloria was still handling large issues and projects, it was not uncommon for Gloria to still make phone contact with Eric and request guidance with specific issues that were unfolding in the organization. His contacts with her were clearly coaching in nature, though it was necessary in several instances for him to ask if Anne should be brought into the discussion if the issue being raised was one that Gloria was working on alone or if she was looking for Eric to critique or praise Anne's performance. Gloria clearly preferred that Eric serve as a pair of eyes and ears for her to check on how Anne was performing. This issue required the development of several ground rules for coaching sessions, including the following: starting each session with "clearing the air" about Gloria's current feelings about her health and absence from the work, asking how the conversation would be different if Anne were present on the call, clarifying how the coaching was aimed at improving Gloria's capacity for leadership, resisting questions where she already seemed to have an answer, and summarizing the topics of conversations in an e-mail that Eric copied to Anne.

The second shift involved a change in emphasis with Anne from capacity building for her leadership to improving Anne's capacity building for the organization as a whole. Anne and Eric were accustomed to talking one-on-one, and this additional focus required postponing some conversations until other parties could participate in the exchange. In a few instances, this shift was more readily achieved through the introduction of new consultants. This became particularly important in situations when Eric believed his prior leadership coaching predisposed him to a solution or to an evaluative perspective of another staff member's performance. The selective involvement of additional consultants from Eric's unit was also managed by agreeing how to brief them, what information to share, and in what sequence to share that information. Eric also realized that the presence of new consultants in the client system allowed new questions to be raised that had not been raised before. For example, Eric was predisposed to be fairly goal-directed with Anne, given the prior difficulty achieving closure between Gloria and Anne on issues. A consultant from Eric's office did not have that experience and treated the closure problem as an issue of organizational readiness and asked questions about resistance to explore the problems of decisiveness when they arose.

Finally, Eric discovered that Gloria and Anne had been discussing some of the coaching sessions with staff and that rumors had developed in the organization about his role in Gloria's "personal leave." These events caused staff to assume that Eric was an enthusiastic supporter of Anne and had stood behind each of the decisions she and Gloria had made. The introduction of a new consultant allowed a new air of objectivity and safety to be established for the staff, especially during a time of disjointed communications and "mysterious" events.

The Return of Gloria

After 18 months of medical leave, Gloria began to reenter the organization on a part-time basis. Most staff in the organization commented on the dramatic changes in her physical appearance (i.e., a dramatic loss of weight, thinning and loss of hair, change in skin tone) and her demeanor (i.e., less reactive to comments, more open to ideas, more even in her mood). She received helping responses and tenderness from staff who had previously not been present in the organization. Project directors who were highly devoted to the opportunities she had created now felt less need to prove their worth or compete with her on the sharpness of their ideas. Gloria did not respond well to any sense of pity or treatment of her as frail, but she expressed appreciation for the acknowledgment of her contributions and the renewed connection with the many talented people she had recruited.

As Gloria gained in health and put more time in the organization, she also began to hear complaints from project directors about Anne's management style that had been harbored and hidden for 18 months. Many of the project directors found Anne to be micromanaging and overly cautious about university rules and procedures. Some project directors thought she was condescending and did not allow the project directors to save face when their content knowledge was not as good as Anne's. Some felt Anne was dismissive of the important role the project directors' reputations and connections played in the ongoing visibility and funding of the CMH. As had been the case throughout their relationship, Gloria brought each of these concerns directly to Anne. Gloria was supportive of Anne and mentored her in finding a way of thinking through the concerns and responding effectively.

During the same period of Gloria's return to CMH, Anne was busily focused on requests for program evaluation from the private foundations. More foundations were becoming interested in CMH's work and asking questions about the impact of programs and projects. Three elite universities had shown renewed interest in minority and urban health problems and had criticized the CMH in competition for grants for lack of outcome evaluations. Eric and Anne discussed how to handle such criticisms publicly while also making the needed changes. The leadership issues discussed during these coaching sessions focused on Anne's struggle with the high degree of public visibility, having too much success too soon in her career, and her management of competing demands.

At the end of one coaching session, which were then held monthly without Gloria (who had insisted they continue without her, due to her reduced schedule), Eric asked Anne if the sessions were helpful to her. With a teary response Anne revealed that the sessions were the only time she had for reflection and that Eric was the only person who seemed to care about her well-being. Anne reported that she personally felt attacked in those grant progress reports and was underappreciated by "everyone" at CMH for having to carry the burden of the organization's leadership. Anne worried that she had not made significant progress in her doctoral studies and was under pressure to finish her dissertation. When asked about support from Gloria, Anne reported that she did not want to burden Gloria with more stress or "she might never come back full time." Anne perceived that she had tried to engage Gloria in a few problems but that Gloria seemed to only want to advise and coach her, rather than step back into the fray of the organization.

Anne was also very angry with Gloria for appearing to "side" with the project directors. Anne felt that Gloria would just "dump" the issues on her and then not work with her to improve relations with the project directors. Anne also believed that Gloria was holding back some of what had been said by the directors. When asked if she might share that anger with Gloria, Anne erupted in a confused storm of emotions. Anne felt her anger was so strong that she might cause Gloria to get sick again. She also said she had come to really love the job and privately had hoped that Gloria would not return. Finally, demonstrating a lot of guilt for the paradoxical nature of her emotions, Anne expressed her deep loyalty and gratitude for Gloria and the opportunities she had created. At a subsequent session, Eric tried to normalize the complexity of the emotions Anne felt. Eric asked Anne if the emotions of this situation were familiar to other experiences from her life, and Anne shared that it seemed related to the period after her mother died shortly after she had arrived in the United States from Latin America. Eric and Anne discussed the unresolved grief and Anne's sense that she had "made" her mother ill by coming to the United States. The parallels between that difficult moment in her life and the present situation were explored in the coaching session, and Anne reported a sense of relief and new energy from the insights.

Eric and Anne worked through a script for a conversation between Anne and Gloria. At first Anne wanted Eric to be present, fearing that the intensity of her emotions and the similarity to her family situation would cause her to lose control. The coaching session explored the value of those emotions and the contribution they would make to an authentic exchange. However, when she decided to not have Eric present, Anne revealed that her instinct was to "dump" on Gloria the way she felt that she had been "dumped on." Eric's support of the decision to not be present allowed Anne to look at her motivations more carefully and choose a strategy to inquire about the changes in their relationship, to explore what Gloria wanted to do next with her role at the CMH, and for both parties to be engaged in the problem of helping Anne find time to finish her dissertation.

Differentiated But Connected

The exchange between Anne and Gloria was successful. Gloria reported her ambivalence about returning and her deep support for Anne to take over permanently as director. Anne was able to express her loyalty but also draw boundaries so that she would no longer feel dumped on and so that she could find additional time to work on her dissertation. Anne confronted Gloria about needing to face the problems of the CMH more directly as well as deal with a few protected favorites that might be holding the organization back. Gloria confronted Anne about the need to acknowledge the importance of politics and the need to bend the rules to be innovative. Together they agreed to have Gloria take over several key areas of center management for 8 months so that Anne could complete her dissertation.

The months of the dissertation work were silent for Eric in the consultation. Anne eventually invited him to a celebration of her dissertation defense where Anne reported to him that Gloria had held up her end of the bargain. Anne and Gloria had decided that with a doctorate in hand, Anne would be given the title of director and Gloria would become founding director and focus her efforts on fund-raising and corporate connections. The dean approached Anne at the same celebration and expressed support for her permanent role and let it be known that he would rather Gloria move on to new projects.

First Tests as Director

During Anne's first semester as director, the dean called her and reiterated his earlier commitment. He also shared that something had to be done immediately regarding the scholar in residence that Gloria has supported for several years. The dean, citing changes in provosts and presidents, revealed that he could no longer support what he believed was an unethical relationship costing the university more than twice Anne's salary, involving less than 1 month on campus, and producing no scholarship. He expected Anne to handle the situation during the upcoming contract negotiations in December.

Anne returned and immediately told Gloria of the dean's concerns. Gloria later met with the dean, who stood his ground. Anne called Eric after the dean expressed disappointment with Anne in an e-mail that she had involved Gloria. With Eric's help, Anne constructed a negotiation process and review of budgets that allowed the scholar a chance to do more with the center (e.g., teach a course) and slowly have the relationship curtailed over several years. The negotiation process also allowed the dean to learn indirectly that Anne believed this test of her loyalty was unwarranted and extracted from the dean more public support and financial resources to enable the CMH's fund-raising activities to off-set the loss of a scholar's reputation as a fundraising anchor.

The process of renegotiating the scholar's contract reignited Gloria's anger and resistance to authority. Even while supporting Anne's negotiation process, she had several personal meetings with the dean and his staff regarding the issue. During this time, Anne contacted Eric again to help with leadership coaching. Together they identified that Anne's position in this conflict was contaminated by her lack of differentiation from Gloria and her own career path options. Anne stated that she felt vulnerable professionally, having invested in only one mentor, and she had not thought through her career alternatives.

Differentiation as a Leader

Eric worked with Anne to develop two forms of differentiation from Gloria. First, she would design a process for reconstructing the CMH's board of governors, replacing members who had a primary relationship with Gloria with people who were recruited by Anne. Where appropriate, relationships with members of the board and the work of board subcommittees would serve as substitutes for her mentoring from Gloria. She involved the dean and other leaders in the medical center and community to help her build her own base for political and personal support. In this pursuit, she also engaged the dean's director of development, who also became a mentor and source of professional support.

The second means of differentiation from Gloria was to launch a strategic planning process for the CMH. The steps of this initiative were interwoven with her reconstruction of the board. For example, when completing their stakeholder analysis, Anne made sure to make contact with leaders in the city and state governments and in her profession to ask for input. She drove the strategic planning process with a combination of internal and external working committees that reviewed every project in the center; studied potential alignments with medical center, medical school, and university goals; compared the CMH with similar centers at other institutions; and cultivated the ideas of influential medical school faculty. Eric and his staff provided consultation support for the planning effort.

These two steps proved to be quite essential for Anne and the CMH. Gloria's exchanges with the dean became both more heated and more personal once the dean's opinion surfaced that he thought the prior CMH relationship with the scholar was unethical. In response, Gloria attempted to publicly expose the dean's weaknesses among her circle of influential political contacts and in the media. Despite repeated attempts to build bridges with Gloria, Anne's efforts to differentiate herself were viewed by Gloria as disloyal and ungrateful. During this time, she accused Anne of siding with the dean and threatened to ruin her career.

Thinking Though Succession

Anne responded positively and was excited about Eric's idea of thinking through her career. She had originally enrolled in her doctoral program with vague ideas of working in public health administration and policy development. The usual process of weeding through ideas for future jobs in the later years of doctoral study was interrupted by Gloria's recruitment of her to the CMH. From there she relied heavily on Gloria's career advice, much of which was highly nontraditional and valuable, but it was not balanced by other perspectives. In fact, Anne had thought her only career goal might be to become the permanent director of the CMH.

During several coaching sessions, Eric used an appreciative inquiry approach with Anne. Eric asked Anne to map the best moments of her career experiences, both before and after working at CMH. Eric used an easel to map the moments she suggested and asked her to complete the map by adding other personal and professional activities at the time of each period of peak performance. Anne found the process revealing, and it tapped her preference for a visual mode of learning. She shared the map with trusted friends and colleagues, who added data she had forgotten and also asked questions about her experiences. She found the experience very grounding, and it allowed her to tell and retell the story of her professional development.

Using the map, Anne identified three other individuals with jobs she thought contained all the elements she desired. In interviewing them about their work lives, she realized more about what she enjoyed in her job with CMH and what she needed to change. For a short period, she made changes in her job duties to match more of her interests. It sharpened her ability to listen to colleagues' work experiences and to consider positions outside of health care. Most important, it provided an option set for those days when the director's job at CMH did not seem particularly satisfying or were sullied by the increasing tensions between Gloria and the dean.

Executing Plans and Developing Others

Ultimately, Anne decided to stay in the stormy weather created around the CMH by Gloria and the dean. She completed the strategic planning process and boldly changed the direction of the CMH toward new funding streams and collaborations. She worked to configure her job to those elements she knew were exciting to her. Gloria publicly criticized the plan, but the coaching process appeared to provide the distance Anne needed to not overrespond to Gloria's reactions to her thinking. Anne kept Gloria at a distance and used support from the dean and the others she had interviewed about career options to guide her decision making. The exercises about career options and her own experience with Gloria stimulated Anne to examine leadership succession plans within the CMH. As the organization had grown more complex, several staff had been promoted to advanced positions. Gloria worked with Eric to devise a process for writing career development plans for these senior staff. The coaching sessions also focused on how she could use patterns in the career aspirations of staff to shape her strategic plan and to assign new projects or restructure roles and duties when required by staff departures, maturation of programs, and termination of grants.

KEY LEARNINGS

Evolution of the Coaching Relationship

This case demonstrates how coaching can be used to assist leaders and their organizations over an extended period of time. Critical to the evolution of coaching in this case was the regularity of meetings. While ordinarily relegated to a logistical issue, the scheduled weekly and then monthly meetings provided a mechanism for Eric and the clients to find the best ways to use the coaching format and for Eric to stay updated on a rapidly changing, complex situation. A regular schedule also prevented long periods of noncontact when the inevitable list of legitimate reasons for cancellation came up (sickness, travel, vacations, schedule conflicts, and so forth). It is important to note in this situation that because Gloria and Anne met daily, a lower frequency of coaching meetings at the start of the consultation would have made it difficult for Eric to find a significant place in the rapidly evolving learning and decision making with the two leaders.

One downside of such regular meetings was that at times, Eric thought that the coaching seemed to be used as a means to prolong deliberations or even stall closure on issues. If the meeting with Eric did not yield a change in perspective rather immediately, both Gloria and Anne would assume they had exhausted all options in understanding a situation. This pattern continued when Anne was meeting with Eric by herself, when she seemed to raise only intractable problems rather than sharing patterns of struggles and learning in her leadership. A final caution about regular sessions is to observe that the coach may be having more exchanges with a leader than subordinates in the leader's regular chain of command. As demonstrated in this case, the coaching sessions began to deflect issues away from their natural homes in the supervisory chain of command. Gloria and Anne often reported that getting help in the coaching sessions often led them to not provide status communications up the chain of command. Once this issue was identified in coaching, a benefit of the process was a renewed deliberateness and clarity about upward communications and the appropriate use and increased engagement of senior leadership in organizational problems.

Recontracting

A key to success in this long-term relationship was the continual use of service contracts and explicit goal setting. All parties were tempted to slide into the comfort of their compatibility, lamenting intractable problems. Formal agreements established annually forced all parties to examine progress and increased vigilance on goal accountability. Given the high volume of events and the amount of interpersonal drama that unfolded in this case, repeatedly returning to the service agreement also reminded the client and provider of root issues that continued to repeat as leadership and relationship challenges. The recontracting also permitted the coach to blend in the need for organizational consultation and to consider explicitly whether and how to use additional consultation resources. Over time, it was also Eric's observation that the practice of relationship and service contracting for coaching became a leadership skill Gloria and Anne began to use in other settings. The pair demonstrated improved capacity to engage and supervise outside vendors on their work and to conduct internal role negotiations as needed with staff for short-term projects and initiatives.

Coaching Provided by an Internal Practitioner

This case highlights several advantages and disadvantages of being a coach inside the same overarching organizational system as the clients. Some of the advantages include the following:

- the ability to bring in expert knowledge about university policy and procedures,
- a larger nexus of relevant contacts in the organization for Gloria and Anne to use in solving problems,
- a shared experience base to refer to when examples of alternative modes of leadership or organizational processes were needed,
- an understanding of the broader organizational goals when needed to encourage alignment,
- alternative sources of information for initial

background regarding the contracts and for testing the accuracy of Gloria and Anne's perceptions of their leadership and of the organization's reputation, and
- ease of making contact for meetings and taking advantage of chance encounters while conducting other business in the university.

Several disadvantages can also be seen in the case. The primary drawback was the need for fastidious maintenance of confidentiality. Eric had to be careful not to share what he knew of the CMH from other confidential contacts in the university and not to disclose sensitive information he had learned from Gloria and Anne to others who inquired. This also required deliberate exchanges in which Eric had to assure Gloria and Anne that he was maintaining confidentiality because some of Eric's other university clients were viewed as nonsupporters of the CMH. In addition, as the incident with the associate dean demonstrated, once the work with the CMH was known to the dean's office, regular inquiries were made to Eric as a more "objective" and "trusted" source. Given his multiple responsibilities, Eric negotiated a fuller understanding of his role and developed a procedure for limited disclosure to the dean's office with Gloria and Anne.

Another major disadvantage was Eric's very knowledge of "right" answers to problems and dilemmas facing his clients, given his own command of university administration. This was initially an issue regarding the nature of the coaching but persisted throughout the years when Eric became aware of problems via the coaching or when Anne would ask Eric to help him find "quiet" ways of resolving sensitive problems. Gloria and Anne's awareness of his knowledge often created pressure on Eric to leave a coaching posture in the consultation to become an expert. The availability of this knowledge also created a sense of comfort with Gloria and Anne that they did not need to learn this material on their own.

Coaching to a Leadership Pair

Eric found this work with a pair somewhat easier than some of his other individual executive coaching clients. Eric felt that the presence of a third person encouraged and provided professional distance for him to examine underlying patterns and assumptions. Gloria and Anne's readiness to engage in lively debate with Eric as an observer also repeatedly provided him with the opportunity to ask the two leaders to reflect on their working relationship. Given the centrality of the pair to the overall functioning of the CMH, Eric was able to get a very good firsthand experience with how others might experience problem solving and leadership from them.

Coaching to the pair presented enormous difficulties after Gloria no longer attended the coaching meetings and attempted to triangulate separately with Eric about Anne. Eric reported his conversations to both parties, but his inability to stop the exchanges contributed to hesitancy in all interactions and an eventual cooling of the intensity of the coaching. Most of this period was conveniently "covered up" by Anne's need to protect time while finishing her dissertation and the agreement for her to become the permanent director when it was completed. When the coaching restarted after completion of the dissertation, Eric experienced Anne's desire to win his approval. Eric reflected to me that his skill in managing the pair was familiar to his own family dynamics and that he was more comfortable working with the triangles rather than intercepting or putting limits on them. He also observed that the gender differences contributed to his posture as an alternating brother or father figure mediating between conflicting sisters or daughters. This, too, reflected an earlier family dynamic, including a sense of superiority he often felt in watching the two female members of the pair engaged in an emotional relationship battle. Most of this awareness was not formally realized by Eric until the writing of this case and supports the need for ongoing shadow consultation for coaches themselves (Kilburg, 2002).

Leadership and Organization Development

One useful way of reflecting on this case is to understand the transition in states of growth of CMH from an entrepreneurial organization, with challenges to meet basic financial and reputational needs, to an organization that must fulfill routine expectations and deliverables. Greiner (1998) outlined these stages of organizational evolution as well as the predictable crisis issues that arise at each stage. In Greiner's typology, the CMH would be characterized as having crises of leadership, stimulating the need for basic management structures such as those finally put in place by Anne. Eric used this model with Anne while he helped her prepare the response to the management audit findings. The model helped to depersonalize the problems and identify them as ones that are normal and not the direct result of any generalized incompetence. The model also helped Anne recognize that her difference in leadership style was the difference needed by the CMH at this stage of growth.

Another important organizational phenomenon to observe is the founder's syndrome (McNamara, 1998). The founder's syndrome is characterized by loyalty to a start-up executive with failure to confront the need for a different type of leadership at the next stage of the organization's growth (due to both organizational and leadership characteristics). While Gloria's strong reaction to the management audit was likely amplified by fatigue, episodic or reactive depression, and her character structure, it is important to note that she had received little specific feedback about her leadership from the dean or other university leaders. Aside from tensions with the dean, her experience had much in common with other founders who receive much admiration and public praise for their accomplishments, often developing a certain sense of untouchability from having overcome long odds in surviving the start-up phase and bringing the organization to the next level of achievement. Eric introduced the concept of the founder's syndrome to Gloria upon her return from medical leave. The concept normalized the reluctance of staff to follow Anne, allowed Gloria to recognize the need to play a different role in the organization, and dissipated much of the personalized aspects of the disagreements between Gloria and Anne about the CMH's new strategic plan.

Just as the organization was learning to differentiate itself from the reputation and ideas of its founder, Anne's core leadership development agenda was to differentiate herself personally from Gloria. In this way, the case demonstrates how the evolution of the organization and the leader were interdependent. The tasks needed to develop the organization, such as a strategic plan, became a major tool for Anne to explore and establish her own identity as a leader. The agenda for differentiation is also consistent with other ideas about the stages of evolution in a close mentoring relationship (see Daloz, 1986).

SUMMARY

This case study of providing coaching to Gloria and Anne's leadership of the CMH provides an interesting examination of a long-term coaching relationship and providing services to a pair of leaders. More case studies are needed that take this longer time horizon and contribute to our understanding of how coaching can be a valuable element in the support provided to individuals and systems as they grow and change. This case study also illustrates some of the challenges of being an internal provider of coaching services as well as some of the unique formats where coaching can be an exciting intervention in organizations. In this case, the value of having a forum where leaders were able to decompress emotionally and contain difficult personal and professional events is clear. Fast-growing organizations place inordinate demands on the boundaries and capacities of leaders, and dramatic events are predictable correlates of start-up organizations. Coaching provides the reflective space needed by leaders in these situations to realize their options and maintain a healthy degree of psychological detachment from events. During these periods of exceptional demands, leaders are likely to feel unprepared, and coaching provides an opportunity for skill development that is directly linked to new actions needed to make the organization succeed.

References

Daloz, L. A. (1986). *Effective teaching and mentoring: Realizing the transformational power of adult development experiences.* San Francisco: Jossey-Bass.

Fitzgerald, C. R., & Garvey Berger, J. (Eds.). (2002). *Executive coaching: Practices & perspectives.* Palo Alto, CA: Davies-Black.

Goldsmith, M., Lyons, L., Freas, A., & Witherspoon, R. (Eds.). (2002). *Coaching for leadership: How the world's greatest coaches help leaders learn.* San Francisco: Jossey-Bass.

Greiner, L. E. (1998, May–June). Evolution and revolution as organizations grow. *Harvard Business Review,* 55–64.

Kilburg, R. R. (2000). *Executive coaching: Developing managerial wisdom in a world of chaos.* Washington, DC: American Psychological Association.

Kilburg, R. R. (2002). Shadow consultation: A reflective approach for preventing practice disasters. *Consulting Psychology Journal: Practice and Research, 54,* 75–92.

McNamara, C. (1998, November–December). Founder's syndrome: How corporations suffer (and can recover). *Nonprofit World, 16*(6), 38–42.

CHAPTER 35

THE ALCHEMY OF COACHING: "YOU'RE GOOD, JENNIFER, BUT YOU COULD BE *REALLY* GOOD"

David B. Peterson and Jennifer Millier

As a coach and the first author of this chapter, I (David B. Peterson) have been interested in ensuring that the voice of the client is heard. I invited Jennifer to participate with me on this particular chapter for several reasons. First, we worked together on two separate occasions, which provides the opportunity to demonstrate her progress and illustrate how we collaborated in different ways on different topics at different points in time. Second, Jennifer is perceptive and articulate, so her comments about the coaching process are interesting and insightful. She has a lively, dynamic personality and an entertaining style, evidenced in this comment from our first conversation: "I'm so good at what I do that I've been pigeonholed. I'm like Meg Ryan—she's always cast to play the Meg Ryan part. I need to tell them, I'm no longer Meg Ryan. Today, I'm the wicked witch of the west."

THE COACH: DAVID B. PETERSON

I began working at Personnel Decisions International (PDI) in 1985, the same year I started graduate work in psychology at the University of Minnesota. I quickly gravitated to the coaching business, and in 1990 was promoted to lead PDI's worldwide coaching practice. In synergy between work and school, I spent 5 years gathering outcome and follow-up data on 370 coaching participants for my dissertation (Peterson, 1993; see also Peterson & Kraiger, 2004) and then received my PhD in counseling and industrial/organizational psychology in 1993.

My coaching practice began with local companies in Minneapolis, such as 3M, Honeywell, and General Mills. Today, I work in a diverse range of industries and organizations (such as Shell, Deloitte & Touche, Daimler Chrysler, and the Mayo Clinic) but gravitate toward technology companies, such as Hewlett-Packard and Medtronic. Most of my coaching is with general managers and senior executives, although I work with midlevel managers in two or three companies where I have a long-standing relationship. The topics that come up most frequently include strategic thinking, executive leadership, leading change, and time management (everyone seems besieged by the challenge to get more done in less time with fewer resources). Over the years, I've worked with people on virtually every aspect of leadership, interpersonal and communications skills (e.g., Peterson, 2003), decision making, and other managerial skills. Nonetheless, my true expertise is in the process of learning and development—helping people actually implement the changes that make them more effective in the real world—which is discussed in more detail below (see also Hicks & Peterson, 1997; Peterson & Hicks, 1995, 1996).

We would like to thank Bobbie Little and Jeffrey Janowitz for their comments on earlier versions of this work.
Reprinted from the *Consulting Psychology Journal: Practice and Research, 57,* 14–40.

My coaching is guided by two overarching principles:

1. Be the kind of coach that I would like to work with. This principle, which I adopted in 1990, led me to many insights. I shifted my coaching away from activities such as giving feedback and dealing with resistance and toward mutual exploration and helping each person clarify and achieve what is most important to him or her. I began each coaching conversation by asking, "What would you most like to get out of this?" (which was followed by, "What does your organization expect and require of you?"). Instead of following the same routine process with everyone, I began partnering with people to design the coaching process from start to finish. For example, instead of subjecting them to a so-called objective assessment, we would discuss what data would be most helpful and agree on a process that would be fair and credible for all stakeholders. I stopped referring to people as "coachees," which makes them sound like passive recipients, and started talking about them as the people I work with in coaching. All these changes in my style, and many more, started with a few simple questions: "How would I like to be treated if I were in coaching?" and "What kind of coach would I choose to work with?"

2. Aim to be a great coach; do not settle for being a good coach. After working with hundreds of coaches from virtually every background of training and experience, I've concluded that it is relatively easy to be a good coach. With a core set of tools, some basic interpersonal skills, and a desire to be helpful, you can provide genuine benefit to others. At the same time, I've seen good coaches become complacent by concluding that since what they are doing works, they will stick with it. Good, however, is the enemy of great, and I've tried to live by the principle of striving to become a great coach (see Peterson, 2002; Peterson & Hicks, 1999; Peterson & Sutherland, 2003). I operationalize this by continually asking myself, "What is the most positive and powerful thing I can do right now?" Of course, the answer to that question must take into account the person's goals, values, capabilities, personality, and specific learning objectives as well as the expectations from their organization. So I keep searching for ways to achieve better results in less time.

THE PARTICIPANT: JENNIFER MILLIER

I earned my degree in electrical engineering and joined Hewlett-Packard (HP) in 1983. Most of my early career was in research and development (R&D) for the personal computer (PC) business, although I worked several years in technical marketing and spent 3 years as a sales person for Europe. After another stint in R&D, I moved back into marketing as the manager of the value delivery chain, which involved extensive cross-functional and cross-divisional work. Finally, I moved into a new business for HP, working on direct-to-customer sales for HP products. Historically, we have always sold through indirect channels, so this new area was a challenge to the status quo.

I have been fortunate to work for managers who have always been willing to let me run with the job and exercise my judgment and who have given me the freedom to lead large programs. However, I found that I was repeatedly handed projects and programs that met my need to work on something important to the business while only drawing on the same set of skills and problem-solving approaches that I had already developed. I was not being stretched. I no longer felt that I was sharpening the tools that would take me to the next level of growth and opportunity.

By early 2000, I had led a series of successful programs and people discovered that I was quite good at solving gnarly problems that had stymied others. After progressing up the management chain into second-level management, I was facing different business challenges on each project while still being viewed the same old way. I was so good at my job that my manager's major suggestion for my development plan was simply to clone myself so I could do more of the same. But I craved new challenges so I could stretch and grow beyond what I had always done. Unfortunately, I was told I was too critical to the program I was working on to move on, even for a promotion.

That summer, I decided to leave HP and accepted a job with another company. When senior management found out I had resigned, they began an intense campaign to keep me. They had underestimated how serious I was about needing a new opportunity, just as I had underestimated how much they valued me. After a series of conversations with my boss and his boss, I found myself in Duane Zitzner's office, the group general manager three levels up from me. Surprisingly, Duane offered me a job working directly for him. Here I was asking for development and challenge, and he was willing to create a special job just to keep me.[1] Although everyone thought I was a fool for not taking it, I did not want special treatment—I wanted to work in an organization that would take my development seriously. I was not looking for the money or the stock options but the challenge and the learning. As part of our discussion about my development, I was offered a 360 feedback survey and a coach. I knew that in order to find new challenges and advance my career I needed to work on financial skills, how to manage managers, political savvy, and leadership in the broader business context. But I was curious to see what the 360 would tell me.

COACHING BEGINS, 2000–2001

David: On Friday, August 18, 2000, Jennifer and I walked into a small conference room at HP's site in Cupertino, California. Jennifer was anxious to talk about her 360 results. After she told me about her background and her goals for coaching, we went over the survey. Jennifer scored above average on virtually every dimension. Her highest ratings were on results orientation, energy and enthusiasm, motivation and commitment, teamwork, relationships, networking, communications, and business acumen. Her lowest ratings—which were still very strong—were on systems and processes, and there was a clear message that people would welcome more delegation and coaching from her.

Jennifer: After we went over the feedback, David asked me what I wanted to work on. I immediately focused on the lowest ratings from my 360 survey. At one point, I grabbed the 360 report, opened up to the weakness page, and started listing each weakness as a development need. David reached over, shut the book, and again asked what I wanted to work on. I flipped back to the page of my weaknesses. David shook his head, shut the book and then moved it away from my reach. He asked me again, and I thought it was some kind of test or that he was trying to prove some point. As we talked, I realized that I automatically focused on my weaknesses. That is how I'd always gotten better in the past. What I began to realize now was that I needed a different approach. We started to talk about where I wanted to go and what I wanted to do next. I was already good at what I was doing—the 360 told me that if I did not already know it. Getting better at those things would just keep me pigeonholed. The way I was doing things had always served me well, but I needed to shift my focus to the future. From that moment on, for the rest of our coaching, David's message to me has always been, "You are good, but you could be really good." I'm a stubborn case, but that was the most helpful thing he ever did—help me realize that I needed to start learning a new set of tools and build a bigger tool box.

David: One of the most helpful tools in coaching is the Development Pipeline (Hicks & Peterson, 1999; Peterson, 2002). As a diagnostic of the five necessary conditions for development, it helped me identify the greatest leverage for Jennifer's learning. Here's what I saw, presented in the order in which they became clear to me (see Figure 35.1):

Motivation: Defined as people's willingness to invest the time and energy it takes to develop themselves: Incredible motivation and commitment to learning; eager for challenge; she was willing to spend her time and energy on development.

Capabilities: Defined as the extent to which people have the skills and knowledge they need: Bright, talented, and with the raw capabilities to be

[1] I have always attributed much of my success to good fortune in having had a string of great managers and supporters. Even with talent and hard work, having the advantage of mentors and advocates such as Duane Zitzner, Scott Stallard, and Xuan Bui would have measurable impact on anyone's career.

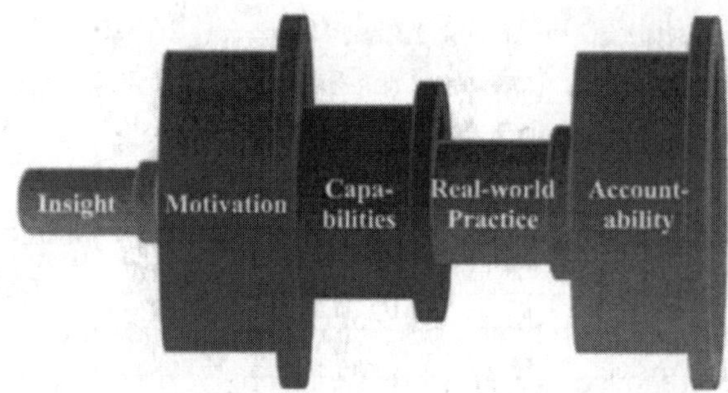

FIGURE 35.1. Jennifer's development pipeline. Motivation and accountability are strong. Insight is most constrained.

successful at almost everything she put her mind to, though she would need to develop additional new skills in several areas.

Real-world practice: The extent to which people have opportunities to try their new skills at work: She was stuck in a rut, doing the same old things. Even though she was eager for new challenges, it was not apparent that she had opportunities at hand to stretch herself and try new things, so this was clearly a constraint.

Accountability: The internal and external mechanisms that drive people to internalize their new capabilities so they actually improve performance and results: Jennifer was already holding herself accountable for high levels of learning and performance.

Insight: The extent to which people are aware of what they need to develop to achieve greater personal and organizational success: In many ways, Jennifer was very insightful. In others, she was surprisingly unaware. It took me a while to realize that this was actually the main constraint to her successful development. She would throw herself at problems and find a solution, but she rarely stopped to reflect about what she could do differently. Although I never used this language with Jennifer, I started using a technique I call *clear goals, conscious choice* (Peterson & Sutherland, 2003). In each of our four meetings, we spent some time working on clear goals: getting a clear sense of what matters to her, what motivates her, what values she wants to live by and lead by. And then we worked on how she would use those goals and values to make conscious choices about what she did and where she spent her time. As a starting point, and to help her gain insight for her development, I encouraged Jennifer to reflect every single day on two things—what she wanted to accomplish that day and what was the best way for her to do that.

Jennifer: Just asking myself those questions forced me to stop and think. I was always running so fast that I did not connect the dots. I needed to look at the broader system—if I stood back, what picture did the dots paint? Was that the picture I wanted it to be? Where was the Monet rather than just the individual dots? In fact, I began to realize that I was the painter and I could start painting the picture I wanted.

In the past I had graded myself on how fast I moved toward the end goal on a project. I got all kinds of validation from my managers that I was doing important things for the business. After I started reflecting on what was important, it felt like I could make greater progress on even bigger things. I had to develop some discipline to think strategically about what I wanted to do and not just paint single dots on the canvas. I had to ignore the distractions to get to the bigger picture. David was challenging me to go further, to choose my priorities and focus on them. Now I saw that I could set a higher standard and go in to learn as well as go in to do a good job.

It sounds so simple, but it had a profound impact at the time. With my priorities clear, I began to spend my days gathering gold instead of pyrite. I felt a greater sense of accomplishment, because I ended each day with a small sack of gold instead of an impressively heavy bag of rocks. I was able to focus on what had the greatest value, ignoring the distractions and walking the 10 miles to the riverbed where the gold nuggets were sitting.

David: At the time, Jennifer was tackling whatever problems were put in front of her. Her managers knew that she was so talented and motivated that they could point her at something and she would take care of it. But for Jennifer to get where she wanted to go, she had to start choosing where she spent her time. Knowing that she liked to keep score of her progress by checking things off her lengthy to-do list, we started talking about using a point system for how valuable something was. Spending the entire day just to complete half of a critical project may not have allowed her to cross one thing off her list for the day, and she might have felt discouraged. But now, she could count that as 25 points on her scale of how important the project was and feel far more productive than she would if she had just crossed off 10 tasks that were worth only 1 or 2 points each.

Jennifer: In each meeting, David always asks me what I learned. I distinctly remember two things from this meeting that have stayed with me ever since:

1. I need to be more reflective and develop the voice that is constantly asking, what's the next move I need to make? I have to keep the goal in sight for everything I do—even my own development.
2. This is a different ballgame, and I need to learn to play the new game. I was a pro at program management but I needed a new set of skills for the new game I wanted to play, which is strategic, not tactical.

David: We spent the last half hour talking about what Jennifer learned and what specific actions she would take. Building on the key theme from the day, four of her six action steps related to insight and reflection:

1. Every day, ask "What is the most important thing I need to accomplish today, and what is the best way to do that?"
2. Identify the hot buttons and issues that distract me from staying focused on the most important. Reflect at the end of the day on what I accomplished and what got in my way.
3. Before every important meeting, identify the most important thing for me to do in this meeting:
   - Assume that getting the job done will take care of itself and figure out what more strategic agenda I need to be tackling.
   - Work on the internal voice that reminds me to pay attention to the task at hand and the strategic task.
4. After every important meeting, ask myself how well I did.

My notes from the session show that we also discussed political savvy and several other topics in the 4 hours that we spent together, but these are clearly the highlights. As a coach, one of my most critical tasks is to find leverage: What is the most positive and powerful thing that I can do to help Jennifer achieve her objectives? Spending more time on the 360 survey and digesting other people's comments clearly had little value for Jennifer in the grand scheme of things. Instead, we focused on the one area of the development pipeline that was most constrained: Jennifer's insight into what matters most to her—her own goals and values. Until she was clear on what exactly she was trying to accomplish, she was going to keep spinning her wheels.

OUR SECOND COACHING CONVERSATION

David: We met for another 4-hour session about 6 weeks later, on October 3rd. I asked Jennifer how things were going, and she launched into a whirlwind of updates on all the changes at work and her progress on her assignments.

Jennifer (comments taken from David's notes)[2]: Things are changing so fast at work that I feel like I cannot make progress on anything. But I'm making progress on the things we talked about, and it is fun. You asked me to reflect, to be conscious in the moment, but my brain is going all over. I'm thinking about what to do next. I have a friend who wears a rubber band on her wrist to help her quit smoking. I flicked myself every time I caught myself drifting. I flicked myself a lot. But I found I'm much better at reflecting afterward, rather than planning beforehand. I do not think about the purpose ahead of time.

We had a futurist come talk to our group. He was saying the same thing—you have to get out of

[2] It is important to point out that David takes detailed, often verbatim notes on his computer during coaching sessions, so these comments are direct quotes captured at the time.

the mode of looking in your rearview mirror to define your future. You have to stop operating out of habit. You have to figure out first where you want to go.

I remembered something you said last time, that I was working so hard on performing that I did not have time for learning and improving. As long as I keep getting As on all the same old things, I will not have time to take new classes. I need to get some Bs and Cs. It is like Tiger Woods. He had to slow down, give up some short-term wins to work on his swing. He spent a whole year working on it and gave up some good tournament winnings for the sake of winning more later. And he came back stronger than ever. But he had to slow down to move ahead. That is what I need to do.

David: Once Jennifer saw how important this was to her, we shifted our focus, in terms of the development pipeline, from insight to capabilities and real-world practice. We began working on specific skills Jennifer could use to stay focused, to clarify her goals ahead of time, to negotiate expectations with herself as well as the people she worked with, and to let herself be satisfied with earning a B instead of an A. As she got better at those skills, she would be able to focus more effectively on the other skills that she wanted to work on. For example, using the clear goals, conscious choice technique, Jennifer and I would pick specific instances of situations that would distract her from her priorities. One of the hot buttons she had identified was letting herself get distracted by people asking for her time. In her complex, fast-paced world, someone was always asking for something. And because she would quickly volunteer to help, she was continually reinforcing other people for interrupting her. Here's what the conversation looked like (reconstructed from detailed notes):

Clear Goals

David: So when someone interrupts you to ask for a few minutes of your time, what do you want to do? What are your goals?

Jennifer: See if it is important or not. Help them if I can.

David: What else do you care about?

Jennifer: Well, I want to manage my time. Not get drawn into something that will distract me from my priorities.

David: What else?

Jennifer: Make sure they feel OK about the conversation. I do not want people to think I'm treating them poorly.

David: What else?

Jennifer: I think that is about it.

David: What's most important?

Jennifer: I need to work on saying no. Actually, I need to work on giving them the appropriate amount of time, given my priorities.

Conscious Choice

David: OK, so next time someone interrupts you to ask for a few minutes of your time, what are your options?

Jennifer: Just say, come on over. Like I always tell them now. [David writes her responses on a flipchart.]

David: What else could you do?

Jennifer: Ask what they want to talk about. . . . Ask them how important it is. . . . Tell them I'm booked; I just do not have any time available. Of course, if it is Scott I'll say yes. But otherwise, I could just say no. . . . Ask them if it can wait until tomorrow. And hope that it goes away.

David: What else could you say?

Jennifer: Ask if they could give me a quick e-mail on it so I can look at it later . . . Ask them if there's someone else that could help them with that. . . . Ask them what they need and then together figure out if someone else could help them . . . [long pause]. That is all I can think of.

David: OK, let us work with that list for now. Given your goals, which of these responses comes closest to giving you what you want?

Jennifer: Probably some combination. If it is Scott, I'll say yes. If I'm totally swamped, I could ask them to send me a short e-mail. And if I have a minute, I could ask them what they need so we can find a solution together.

David: How well would that work for you?

Jennifer: The first two are easy. But on the last one I think I'd get all wrapped up in it as soon as they started talking.

David: So what can you do to help them but not get caught up in helping them?

David: Jennifer did not have a clear answer, so at this point we began to practice a typical conversation. I played the role of one of her direct reports who tended to need a lot of hand holding. I would ask Jennifer for a few minutes to talk over a situation. She would respond by asking if we could spend a minute discussing what I needed and then try to find a solution that did not involve her. My role as the coach was to find all the ways to hook Jennifer into a long conversation. Each time she got hooked, we'd stop, debrief what happened, and generate a new plan for avoiding that hook. We practiced the same basic conversation over and over again until Jennifer had responses that she felt comfortable with—meaning that they helped her accomplish all of her goals from above and that she could remember in the heat of the moment. This completed the third part of the clear goals, conscious choice technique—effective action. Now Jennifer could walk into this situation, knowing what she wanted to accomplish (clear goals), understanding her options (conscious choice), and being able to skillfully implement whatever she chose (effective action).

Jennifer: The practice with David was almost always helpful in showing me exactly how I could hold an effective conversation—how I could protect my time and still be responsive. What I remember most vividly from this meeting was that just because I was the manager and strategic owner of a topic did not require me to always be there on demand. If I set the agenda for people, I also need to trust they will do a good job. I do not need to be involved at every single step.

David: Even though we were working explicitly on building her capabilities (using the development pipeline again), she was also continuing to gain better insight. With visible progress in both of these areas, we turned our attention to the next constraint—real-world practice. How would she remember to actually use what she had learned when she faced the real situation? A coach can help people prepare for real-world practice in at least two ways (part of an overall process I call *fanatical transfer*; Peterson & Sutherland, 2003). The first is by practicing specific situations in as realistic a way as possible (Druckman & Bjork, 1991, chap. 3). We had done this by having me play the part of a real person discussing real topics as well as by keeping the pressure on Jennifer. Every time she got a little better at what she was doing, I'd throw in a new curve. I'd get irritated that she was not helping me, add a new topic out of the blue, interrupt her, or go off on tangents myself. In other words, I made our practice conversations just as messy, unpredictable, and complex as the real-world situations that she would face. In the real world, she would not have the luxury of a coach reminding her to stop and use her skills.

The second way a coach can help transfer skills to the real world is through bulletproof action steps (Peterson & Sutherland, 2003). Using the same example, here's what this might have looked like with Jennifer.

David: So what will you do with this new skill? How will you actually use it?

Jennifer: Every time someone asks me to help, I'll either tell them to send me a short e-mail or ask them what they need and try to find a solution that does not involve me.

David: Every time?

Jennifer: Yes.

David: How often does this happen?

Jennifer: Maybe 5 to 10 times a day.

David: So every single time someone asks, this is how you'll respond?

Jennifer: Yes.

David: So when I ask you in 4 or 5 weeks how you did on this, you'll tell me that every single time someone asked for your help, you did this?

Jennifer: Well, probably not every time.

David: OK, so tell me exactly what you want to commit to. It does not matter to me if it is one time a day or every time, but I want you to be perfectly clear on what you are aiming for.

Jennifer: There are two or three people where this is a real issue. So every time one of them asks me for help I'll do this.

David: Two people or three people?

Jennifer: Two.

David: So how will you remember to do this every time they ask?

Jennifer: I just will.

David: You have already told me that you often get so wrapped up in things that you forget to plan ahead. Why will this be different?

Jennifer: You are right. I'll probably forget.

David: I'm not saying you will or will not. I'm just trying to get you to be clear and help you anticipate obstacles. So what will help you remember to do this every time?

Jennifer: I need to write it down. I'll put it on the top of my to-do list so I think about it every day.

[The conversation continues in a similar vein . . .]

David: So you, the reader, should be getting a sense that this is a rigorous and perhaps even tedious process. I continue to ask questions such as the following to make sure that we've thought through all the ways her intention might get derailed (see the discussion of fanatical transfer in Peterson & Sutherland, 2003).

- What else do you need to do to make sure you remember this every time?
- What else will get in the way of you doing this? What might prevent you from doing what you want?
- Once you have done it, how will you reflect on your actions, learn from them, and improve what you do the next time?
- How will you get feedback from these two people to see how it is working?
- What else do you need from me, yourself, or anyone else, to make sure you are successful at this?
- Now that we've worked through this, is this still a realistic commitment?
- Will you really do it?

Jennifer: Sometimes this process was annoying, but after the first couple of times I could really see the value. There were so many things that could lead me away from my purpose. David helped me anticipate them and have a plan. It is not about the detail of each specific obstacle; it is about making sure that I stick to my higher purpose.

David: In addition to knowing what is important to Jennifer, clear goals and conscious choices requires that she prioritize things so she can choose where to spend the majority of her time. We began to work on a priority grid, starting with three basic categories.

A: Your job depends on it.
B: Someone will be irritated, annoyed, or upset with you if you do not do it.
C: Everything else.

Because you simply have to do the A priorities and you should just throw away the C priorities, the B priorities are the only place where you really have a choice about what you do. Jennifer, like many people, found that it was often she, herself, or her family who was losing out. She was so responsive to others that she did not prioritize her own goals high enough on the list. So she was putting off some of her own less urgent, long-term priorities to respond to other people's short-term priorities. Together, we worked out a priority grid that was grounded in what mattered to Jennifer and what mattered to the business.

Figure 35.2 does not represent Jennifer's actual grid but a sample similar to one I showed her. Key people are listed in columns from left to right in relative order of importance, and then their priorities are listed in each row in relative order of importance. Reality is never this cut-and-dried or simple, and the grid is most useful as a thinking and clarification tool rather than as an actual decision-making tool. Each individual has to determine where people and projects fall. Some will place themselves, family, or senior management higher or lower on the grid. There is no right or wrong here, as long as the ranking reflects the individual's values as realistically as possible.[3] The rows need to reflect the projects and business objectives and tasks that potentially take up one's time.

Once the priorities are laid out in order, it is relatively easy to assign an A, B, or C rating. Obviously, the A priorities will cluster in the top left of

[3] The relative ranking of the columns of different people does not necessarily reflect how much the person values or respects them as individuals. For example, someone may not have a strong affinity for his or her boss but may still rank his or her manager high in priority because of the manager's importance in achieving overall career objectives or of making sure that the work environment is positive.

	Boss	Project Manager for critical project	Senior Management	Self	Direct reports	Peers and others I interact with frequently	Colleagues I don't interact with much
Strategic business priorities; key projects	A	A	A	A	A	B	B
Customer Issues	A	A	A	A	A	B	B*
Team issues (motivation, morale, development, teamwork)	A	A	B	A	A	B	C
Strategic planning	A	A	A	A	B	B	C
Skunk works project	B	B	B	B	B	C	C
Other projects and priorities	B	B	B	B	B*	C	C
Pet projects and personal interests	B*	C	B*	B*	C	C	C
Etc.	C	C	C	C	C	C	C

FIGURE 35.2. A sample priority grid for illustrative purposes. (Note that this does not reflect Jennifer's actual priorities.) The columns represent key people, ranked in relative order of priority (it could also include family, customers, shareholders, and so forth). The rows represent key priorities for each person or group; a more detailed analysis would rank each person's or group's own priorities from top to bottom. A = highest priority; B = medium priority; C = lowest priority; B* = B item that could be moved to C category.

the grid, and the C priorities will cluster in the bottom right. It is only in the B priorities where there is real leverage for time management, usually starting with the ones along the diagonal boundary between the Cs and Bs. In this example, the B items marked with an asterisk are where the person might choose to free up his or her time. Essentially, this involves moving the B* items into the C category. This comes at a price, because the inevitable result is that these people will be annoyed when their requests or expectations are no longer met. So that is where negotiating skills, political savvy, risk taking, and a willingness to pay the price—trading some short-term pain for important long-term gains—come in. As Jennifer pointed out, Tiger Woods had to make short-term sacrifices to move forward. If you do not proactively choose whom to annoy, you end up annoying yourself or someone else when critical things slip through the cracks. This is a tool to be more proactive in managing your priorities and making sure that you focus on the most important areas.

Jennifer: The goal, of course, is not to annoy people, but to have a clear focus on where they fit in your priorities and the overall strategy. At the time, this discussion pointed out some low-hanging fruit, where I was taking on relatively low-priority tasks for people on the right-hand side of the grid just because they asked.

OUR THIRD COACHING CONVERSATION

David: In our first two sessions together, Jennifer and I spent only about 20% of our time working on the topics that she originally said she wanted to work on. Most of our work had actually been on dealing with the things that kept her from learning at the level she needed to, including understanding the rules of the new game she wanted to play and setting the stage for building her new tool kit. We had planned to focus our third session more explicitly on building those new skills. However, when Jennifer showed up to that meeting in mid-January 2001, she had other plans.

Jennifer had recently been offered a new job, which would have involved a significant promotion and given her the opportunity to explore a totally new part of the business. She was tempted. We spent most of this meeting talking about this specific job in the context of her long-term plans. We clarified Jennifer's long-term career goals and used the conversation to deepen our understanding of what really mattered to her, a topic we had examined in each of our previous meetings. Jennifer concluded that, although the new job would meet two of her critical short-term priorities (advancement, opportunity to learn), it did not move her forward on her long-term priorities. As she said at the conclusion of our meeting,

> I'm too easily seduced by the temptation in front of me. I often choose the challenge that is sitting in front of me—to prove I can do it or because it looks like fun—rather than choosing the one that meets the most important criteria for me.

In many ways, this discussion consolidated the issues we had been working on so far.

We also spent time planning how Jennifer could find, and even create, the opportunities that would meet more of her criteria. We discussed networking, influence, and organizational savvy as skills that she could use to be more strategic in managing her career. We also practiced conversations that she could potentially have with key leaders who might have positions she would be interested in. We ended with a specific action plan for whom she would go talk to and what she wanted to accomplish in each conversation.

It is often in sessions like this, where we set aside the standard agenda to work on a live issue, that the greatest learning occurs. That is one reason why I'm always looking for immediate challenges that the person is going to face where they can apply what we are working on. It increases both motivation (people are more willing to try new things when they know their old approaches are not sufficient) and real-world practice (it gets people using the skills relatively quickly, so there is less chance of the new skill or approach fading away).

Jennifer: David gives a good overview of this meeting, but he left out the most important moment. I was talking a mile a minute about this job offer and all the other things going on around me at work. I have so much energy that people have told me they can get a contact high just listening to me sometimes, and I was probably bouncing all over. Maybe an hour into our meeting, David looked at me and said, "Jennifer, you are not using me very well." I stopped flat in my tracks. I felt like I was getting a lot of value, and I was shocked when he said this. I asked him to explain. In response, he just asked me a few questions.

David: I think it was something like this:

- What percentage of time are you listening versus talking?
- What percentage of time would you like to be listening versus talking?
- What do you want to accomplish in our meeting today?

- What do you want from me and from our time together?
- What will you do to make that happen?

Jennifer: I realized that I was just using David as a sounding board, and I was not focusing on what I really wanted to accomplish. Ironically, at that moment, I had been very conscious about why I was telling this story, "David, I'm going to tell you about a situation and I want your reaction." Other times, I was conscious about saying, "David, I have a difficult situation and I need you to walk me through this." I run very fast at times—I get excited about the moment in front of me and I do not always hold myself accountable for how I use my coach. And David called me on it.

This single comment from David, that I was not using him well, is where I truly started to understand the importance of slowing down in order to go fast. I had so much to talk about that day, but I was not covering it in any kind of structured way. David's comment has stayed with me for years now—how do I want to use my coach, how do I want to use my time, how do I want to use the opportunity in front of me? It reinforced the message from our last meeting—I need to focus on what is most important.

So I learned how to work better with my coach, but I also learned how to work better with me. I'd start to ask myself, "So, Jennifer, this is all very interesting, but is it going back to what you really want to accomplish and what you really want to be?" I learned there are some things I have to shed over time, even if those are the things that came so naturally and helped me be successful in the first place. If I was going to grow, I had to focus on the next set of things. Focus, focus, focus. Without David constantly holding that mirror up for me, I would naturally gravitate in a direction that I was used to. I'd find myself saying, "Wow! I have a whole bag of cool rocks!" But do I have the gold nugget? That is the real question.

OUR FOURTH COACHING CONVERSATION

David: We met again 2 1/2 months later. Jennifer had worked with her manager, using the approach we put together last time, to create a new, larger role for herself. It was actually quite exciting to see what they had come up with. She would now be working in a more strategic, cross-functional capacity on a critical part of the business. This was the perfect role to explore the topics Jennifer had wanted to work on from the beginning, and by this point the foundation had already been laid. Jennifer came in to this session with a clear picture of what was most important for her and what she wanted to get from me. When she laid out her agenda, including a description of what she wanted from me, I broke into a huge grin.

Jennifer: It actually made a physical difference for me. I felt much clearer and calmer to have my priorities identified, not just for this meeting, but for all my important meetings. In fact, I put time for reflecting and planning on my calendar every day, from 5:00 to 5:30, where I'd think about my goals and the most important things I needed to accomplish tomorrow to get there.

That day, with my coach, I wanted to work on navigating the politics of the new world I was entering and figure out how to establish credibility and good working relationships with some of the key people, especially Xuan Bui. I was moving into a newly established lab manager role, and Xuan was the head of the organization I'd be working in. He had a reputation for being brilliant and demanding, and I was a bit intimidated. I really wanted David's help on figuring out what to do. Actually, I was not too good with politics, and I was hoping he could just tell me what to do. Instead, he did his usual thing of asking me questions to get me to think it through for myself.

David: There is a school of thought in coaching that says people have all the answers within themselves. I do not necessarily accept that, but I do think it is the best place to start. Let us find out what Jennifer already knows and build on that. But more important, the questions that I ask can serve as a framework for helping Jennifer think similar problems through for herself in the future. My role as a coach is not to teach people skills (although that is part of what I do); I see my role as to help people become better learners. By asking Jennifer a set of systematic questions, across a range of different scenarios, she would start to internalize the process. One of the simplest set of questions is also one of the most profound (this approach is elaborated in Peterson, 2003):

- What is your goal? What do you care about?
- What does the other person care about? What are his or her concerns?
- Where can you find the win–win so you both get your needs met?

We applied these questions to Jennifer's next meeting with Xuan. As is typical for Jennifer and many others, her immediate responses addressed the short-term, tactical matters at hand. By continued probing, and occasionally offering other possibilities, Jennifer expanded her list of objectives to include "build a better relationship, learn more about his priorities, convey my commitment to his organization's success, and so forth." When I probed about her view of Xuan's goals and priorities, she had a very narrow, tactical list as well. To help broaden her perspective, I suggested other items that are often important to senior leaders, such as "not waste time, be seen as an expert, be seen as a credible leader, and so forth." The list may seem obvious, but it is remarkable how easily people violate those expectations when they fail to consciously include them as criteria in how they work with others. In fact, politics is often as simple as keeping in mind the personal priorities and concerns that people have (e.g., feeling respected, feeling important, not looking foolish, increasing or maintaining their power) as well as the business priorities (see Peterson, 2003).

I believe that most managers are good problem solvers, and Jennifer is extremely talented in this area. When we took the time to map out the full agenda (i.e., goals, values, concerns) that she and Xuan brought to their meetings and treat each aspect as an important criterion, she was quick to find a solution that made sense. Given that we did not have a clear and accurate picture of what was really important to Xuan, she would still have to explore this area during the actual meeting and consider various solutions along the way. But this conversation helped Jennifer feel much more confident that she could manage the politics, to a great extent because it was easy for her to tune into what people cared about.

Jennifer: I also wanted to get up to speed quickly on strategy, since this was a key part of my new job. David pushed back, saying I did not need the class. This is actually a topic that we still talk about today—my need to feel like an expert. I feel like I should know the technical details of any area that I work in. David has pushed me to rely on my skills as a leader and project manager to add value and then to be more systematic in learning from those around me. His idea was that, instead of taking a class, I should spend more time with a range of people, talking to them about how they viewed strategy. In essence, I could use this both to build relationships and learn at the same time. I actually learned a lot from this, not just about strategy, but about how people saw the business. I saw that some people could look at the business very strategically, as a whole business, and others might be more focused just on the technology or on their particular functional perspective. And, to my surprise, admitting some of my ignorance actually helped build my credibility with people—they liked the fact that I came and talked to them about their perspective.

OUR FIFTH AND FINAL COACHING SESSION IN THE FIRST ROUND OF COACHING

David: My typical engagement is four half-day sessions with people, although that is very flexible depending on the needs of the person I'm working with. In Jennifer's case, mainly because she took on a major new role, we continued for one additional session where we strategized how she would use what she had learned in this new environment. We practiced a number of upcoming conversations in order to fine tune and solidify what we had been working on. We closed our final session with a detailed summary of what we had covered and what Jennifer had learned so far.

Jennifer: When I started working with David, I thought I knew exactly what I wanted. He helped me see a whole new perspective on what I needed. David's big coaching to me has always been, "You are good, Jennifer, but you could be *really* good." That is the Zen of what we worked on. How to be great when being good is actually good enough—how to go beyond where you are.

At a certain point in everyone's growth, you have to transition from the standard set of tools you have always been using to a different set of tools. You have to learn to use different parts of your brain and stretch your comfort zone. That is what David did for me: It was that realization—that I needed to reflect and go outside my comfort zone to jar myself out of how I had always done things. I had created my own snare; I was blaming my management for never giving me new opportunities, but the reality was that I was not creating them for myself. I was not allowing myself to move forward.

I learned a lot of other things from David, too, but when I try to put the important lessons into words, it is actually quite short and simple:

- Be clear on my goals. Think about what I want to do strategically.
- Keep the goal in sight, so I do not get distracted by the *good* things that I can do but focus on doing the *great* things. Make that discipline a habit.
- Slow down to go fast. I had to learn to reflect on what's important and what I want to do. I did not need to improve because something was broken but because I needed to flex new muscles.
- Manage the interaction rather than just go with the flow. Take responsibility for achieving what is most important.

I learned a lot of skills and techniques as well—how to be a better listener, strategic thinking, influence, managing politics, and so forth, but they did not transform me. The magic was in David continually pointing out where a few simple habits were leading me down one path when—whether I knew it or not—I really wanted to go down another. He was gentle but incredibly persistent in holding me accountable. That is what made the difference. That is the alchemy of coaching.

David: That is often the case with people in coaching. The list of what they learned is rarely impressive in and of itself. It often consists of simple principles that everyone already knows at one level. What makes coaching effective is that it makes these simple insights tangible and visceral at the precise moment they matter. It takes the lesson from a trite principle to a specific choice and a specific action at the moment of truth. Coaching is about cultivating a deeper level of insight that leads to the right action at the right time.

OUR SECOND ROUND OF COACHING, 2002–2003

Jennifer: A year and a half later, I had been promoted to a director-level position back in R&D and was now working directly for Xuan Bui. The manager that I had been so intimidated by 18 months ago was now taking me under his wing. He saw something in me that was a direct outcome of my work with David. Instead of merely doing a great job with the assignments I was given, I had become a "white space manager." In addition to my formal job, I would seek out the sticky issues that fell between the cracks. Instead of waiting for someone else to give me a big assignment, I was now creating my own challenges to stretch and grow. Xuan had a tendency to throw big challenges at people anyway, so he seemed to appreciate my willingness to step in. Wow, was I getting stretched now. I called David in August 2002 to see if he could help me with the next generation of learning. Partly I just needed an advanced version of what we had worked on before, but I also needed to be better at setting strategy and leading others who did not necessarily want to be led. I was responsible for many projects where I had no direct authority and yet I had to get alignment and action from my peers as well as more senior managers. Even tougher for me was that most of them had far greater technical expertise than I did. In addition to leadership issues, time management had reached a new level of criticality. I was swamped with urgent projects and dramatically compressed time frames. I realized a key learning for me was how to delegate more and empower my team.

David: As I watched Jennifer in our first meeting in well over a year, I was struck by how clear and confident she sounded. She never went off on a tangent, a tendency that had typified our earliest conversations. She was just as engaging, dynamic, and warm as ever, but she was clear and focused. She seemed far more powerful than when I had last seen her. It looked as if she had gained 5 years of seasoning in just 18 months.

Jennifer: The first thing we worked on in that meeting was revising my priority grid to sort out the truly important tasks from the others. I had to raise the bar on who I was willing to annoy and how much. David asked me what percentage of the time I felt stretched and what percentage of the time was I hearing new feedback from my managers or peers instead of the same old feedback. We then jumped into setting long-range goals and priorities and establishing metrics and accountabilities for those goals.

In that very first meeting, we developed a personal model of leadership that made sense for me:

- paint a vision;
- set the strategy to get there;
- communicate, communicate, communicate (to motivate, engage, and guide people);
- build the team (essentially, coach, enable, and empower people to do what they need);
- hold people accountable; and
- measure success.

Like many of the topics we discussed, it looks simple, and I already had a solid foundation for all these tasks. But I had to sharpen my game and rise up to a whole new standard. I have always felt most comfortable leading from a position of expertise and formal authority. David was helping me to see that I could play a leadership role even when I did not know all the details. Instead of me painting the vision and setting the strategy, I learned to follow a process of leadership where my role was to make sure that the vision and strategy got created by the team. I began to see that leadership was less about doing everything with the team and more about building a team that together can do everything.

David: Jennifer, through our previous work together and her own experiences, had learned most of the skills that she needed. By the end of our first meeting, it was clear (thinking in terms of the development pipeline), that there were only a few areas where she needed new capabilities. Most of what she needed was help in thinking through how to attack new kinds of situations. Most of our time together in the first round of coaching had focused on insight (what does it take to really be successful?), building capabilities, and then finding places where she could apply and test those new capabilities in real-world practice. Now I could see that our work needed to shift to a different aspect of insight (what does Jennifer want to accomplish in her leadership role?) and to the next level of real-world practice (how can Jennifer combine her skills in new ways to face ever-changing challenges?). As a result, we redesigned our meeting schedule. Instead of half-day sessions, we agreed to meet every month or two, for no more than 2 hours at a time. During those 2 hours, my role was dramatically different. I might only ask a few questions and make a few suggestions. Sometimes, just being with Jennifer allowed her to step back and work the process by herself. As we work together now, I often feel like I'm working myself out of a job with Jennifer—in fact, that is my ultimate agenda. One of my most important goals is to help the people I work with become more independent learners so they do not need me.

Jennifer: It is interesting that David mentions that. I've worked with a dozen coaches over the years in different programs, and I had my pick of who I could chose to work with this time. I chose David because from the very first moment we met he was different from the others. Most coaches wanted to give me my 360 and then go straight to the development needs, just like I did. David told me to ignore the feedback until I understood where I really wanted to go and what was most important to me. From the very first meeting, I felt like David believed that I could do anything. It took a while to figure out what that was, but then the rest was easier and more valuable.

I know it cannot be easy to see the potential in everyone. It is not easy to believe in the person. David talks about being a great coach, not just settling for being a good coach. Well, there is one way that I saw that come through. David believed in me. He said, "Here you are, Jennifer, now let us look at all that you can do. You are good, but you could be great." He pushed me hard to grow, but he never projected his needs or expectations on me.

I called David back to be my coach because I knew he would push me and he would help me figure out what I needed. Anyone could have done a 360 and taught me some new skills. There are lots of things I could work on, but David always asked what is the absolute best thing and never let me settle for less.

The attitude that David projected in our first meeting was that, even if he just had a 6-month contract with me, he was looking at the long haul. He was not coaching me for where I was right now, but for where I could be someday in the future. He brings incredible patience and respect.

Even now, as David says, he may only ask a few questions or make a few comments in our meetings, but his words resonate at multiple levels. I understand it at one level, and it is useful. But as I think about it, it is richer. His messages tie together and build from one meeting to the next. They make me think. I've worked with coaches who have been very helpful, but the minute I leave the meeting, I'm off to the next thing. They did not make me think. That is why I wanted to work with David again.

ROUND TWO: OUR SECOND COACHING CONVERSATION

David: Jennifer walked into this meeting feeling the weight of the business on her shoulders. These were the days of the technology slowdown, after the Internet bubble imploded, and, as Jennifer said, "The only good news for us is that we're not alone; everyone else is hurting, too." She was involved in another workforce reduction, one that involved shutting down an entire lab. She wanted to talk about how to lead in a tense, difficult environment where the future was uncertain.

Jennifer: My energy was zapped. We had put so much effort into how to handle a series of crises that we had little energy left over for managing the aftereffects. We were having to reprioritize all our projects, and there was this incredible undertow of chaos and uncertainty. With my team, I was focusing on one aspect of the leadership model we had built last time—communicating what was going on. It was hard to paint the vision right now, so I did my best to communicate what I could. I've always been open with my communications, but David suggested I think about three categories:

1. Emphasize what is constant. For example, I helped people see that the foundation of HP's mission and values was a real anchor for us. I talked about how my own mission as a leader, and the principles that I stood for, were not going to change. Finally, our top priority business objectives were not going to change; the need to hit key milestones and deliverables was certain.
2. Communicate clearly what is changing. I tried to lay out a systematic picture of what was changing and why. Instead of a simple message like, "business is bad, so we have to cut back," I tried to show them how specific changes in customer demands and our competition were driving the need to reprioritize certain projects. Even though it was a huge and traumatic change, what we were going through was not entirely random.
3. Be explicit about what is not clear. I also wanted to communicate what I did not know. Rumors often started because people would make up stories to fill the vacuum. By telling people what was constant, what was changing, and what was unknown, I could not alleviate their fears, but I could engender a little more trust and sense of team.

David: We discussed three other important issues. First was the ever-present theme of focusing on top priorities. That would be particularly important now, because in times of crisis it is easy for people to become reactive and therefore scattered. By focusing on a few key issues, she and her team would be more likely to deliver tangible successes that would boost morale. Second was highlighting the opportunity for Jennifer to step up her leadership. She had established herself as a trusted and respected leader, and here was an opportunity to rally people around an agenda. It was the first completely "white space" leadership opportunity she'd had. Third was to explore ways for Jennifer to take care of herself. She was clearly stressed by everything going on around her, and her leadership capacities would begin to suffer if she did not ensure that she was being nourished. Jennifer was quick to see that she needed to take this message to her team as well.

ROUND TWO: OUR THIRD COACHING CONVERSATION

David: Jennifer had just received her annual performance review the week before we met. She received a glowing review overall but was concerned that of the five categories that Xuan examined, not all of them were outstanding. I was amused by the fact that she was unhappy with his ratings but had rated herself lower than Xuan did in every single category. As she said, "I'm a tough grader on myself, but I still want the A from other people."

This became a pivotal conversation for Jennifer. As I listened to her summarize Xuan's feedback and her reactions, it was apparent that Xuan and I saw many of the same issues with Jennifer. He told her, "You always dive for the ball yourself. You take on too much and try to drive everything yourself." He emphasized the need to raise her level of leadership to the next level. From Xuan's perspective, she was doing a great job in her current role and was ready to start preparing for the next level position. Jennifer's reaction was that she still had a lot of work to do at this level. In some ways, this sounded like the Jennifer I had met in our very first meeting years ago—although she was now playing at a much higher level, she still wanted to perfect this game before even considering a move to the next.

Jennifer: I was totally consumed by what was happening around me, and it was out of control. Xuan and David helped me realize that I had gone back to thinking about what was happening next week and next month. I had to move on to start thinking about what was going to happen 2 years from now. I needed a framework for managing year-over-year execution so I could learn how to build an organization, not just a team of people. It was the same old lesson again, just taken to the next level. I hope that I can internalize the lesson this time, that it is not just about continually stretching myself, but about figuring out the next game and learning the new set of rules. I do not have to be perfect at this level before I can advance to the next.

ROUND TWO: ONGOING CONVERSATIONS

David: Throughout 2003, Jennifer and I continued to meet for 2-hour face-to-face meetings approximately every other month. Early in the year, I suggested that we had reached a logical conclusion to our work together, at least until Jennifer's next promotion. She requested that we continue meeting to help make sure she stays grounded in what she has learned. My current coaching with Jennifer is totally different than when we started. Originally, we focused on insight and capabilities. Now, we focus much more on real-world practice and accountability—staying focused on the goal, persisting, applying skills in new situations, and really getting good at using what she has learned.

In our meetings at this point, the chief value is that Jennifer takes time to reflect by talking through her situation and her plans with me—something she might not do if I was not there. Once in a while, I still find myself pushing and challenging her to aim higher. Like anyone operating in such an intense environment, Jennifer can become absorbed in the tactical aspects of her job, so I remind her to stay grounded in her highest priorities. And in other meetings, we just share stories, like good friends, which solidifies the bond we have as well as reinforces the lessons she has learned.

It has been a rich and rewarding journey for both of us, and so we have the opportunity to share some of our insights with others.

LESSONS FOR COACHES AND PARTICIPANTS

Jennifer: Watching what my coach did, and comparing that to what I've seen with other coaches, here is the advice I'd give:

- Take the long view. Even if you just have a 6-month contract, build a foundation that will help that person his or her entire life. Approach your coaching as if you were entering into a long-term commitment, and try to help the person go beyond where that person thinks he or she can go.

- Get to the heart of things. Almost everyone you work with will have complex issues and multiple levels to explore, so you need to be clear on your purpose and stay grounded in what really matters the most. It is easy for me to get distracted with the crisis of the moment, so your role as coach is always to move people closer to the core, to stay connected to the fundamental purpose. You have to be patient with the person's distractions, but you do not have to follow them yourself.
- Be totally committed to the person. My coach had an amazing ability to focus on me. I never felt his ego influencing our agenda. Every time we met, he helped me unfold and reveal something deeper and truer about me.
- Make it real. Even though we spent so much time on insight and reflection, my coach always asked, "So what are you going to do about it?" There was always an emphasis on action. Even though I'm an action-oriented person, I could have spun around in circles waiting for things to crystallize. It seemed like every new insight led to some specific action. And that new action then provided clarification and deepening of the insight.
- Do not sugarcoat things. My coach never bombarded me with feedback; in fact, he would err on the side of not giving me too much of it. I'm sure David saw things the first day he met me that he never mentioned until months later. Still, when I needed to hear something, he held up the mirror and made it so clear that I could not avoid it. Without a hint of judgment or evaluation, he would provide a reflection of what I really needed to hear, at that moment, to continue making progress.
- Make the person work. There were so many times when I wanted my coach to give me a simple answer to my question. I do not think he ever did. He would always share his perspective but only after he asked me the questions to think it through for myself. And it was always worth it, because I learned I could usually find my own way. The times when I could not figure it out for myself, I had a greater appreciation for the answer that he would share. Always, I had to take ownership for the decision myself.

I also learned an important lesson about how to get the most value from coaching:

- Be clear on what you want from your coach and from each meeting. A good coach can help you learn in many ways, but part of the challenge is for you to figure out how you can use your coach to best advantage. That starts with knowing exactly what you want to get from your coaching. It is important to be diligent about your purpose, how you work with your coach, and what you want from each session.

David: Jennifer has reminded me what a joy it is to work with enthusiastic learners. She demonstrates the best qualities of an active, engaged participant. Anyone who wishes to benefit from coaching could emulate her in the following ways:

- Balance skepticism and trust. Jennifer rarely took anything I said at face value. She would question and challenge and debate my suggestions, and yet she always took me seriously. She listened carefully, tested ideas out, and then was willing to go try new things. She was willing to grapple with ideas and figure out what really made sense for her style and her needs.
- Make learning a priority. Jennifer clearly wanted to improve her skills so she could gain new opportunities and make a bigger contribution at work. She had a demanding job when we met, and she has a much larger and much more demanding job today. Yet she always finds time to try new approaches to what she's doing. Jennifer has also made a commitment to coaching and developing others, which is just another way she demonstrates that learning is a priority.
- Balance humility and confidence. This is a hard quality to describe, but Jennifer demonstrates this better than any person I have known. The

humility shows up constantly in Jennifer's willingness to seek advice, to listen to other people's point of view, to be open to changing her own approach. I even suggested to her that at times she may appear naive or inexperienced when she seems so enthusiastically curious about what other people would do without making it clear that she knows what she is doing. Yet she balances this humility and openness with forceful resolve. Jennifer has strong values and strong opinions on many topics. She will not back down from a debate. She has raised issues with senior management that others are reluctant to surface. When she takes on a task, she throws herself into it fully. So that quality of pursuing things with confidence and yet having the humility to listen to others and adapt when necessary has enabled her to strike a harmonious balance between taking strong leadership positions on issues and acting decisively while remaining constantly open to learning.

- If you want to be coached, be coachable.[4] I believe that Jennifer has attracted so many mentors and advocates in her career for the same reasons that I loved working with her. Because she is so warm, enthusiastic, and appreciative, I am even more willing to give of myself for her. Those qualities come naturally to Jennifer, but anyone who actively engages his or her coach and expresses such positive energy and enthusiasm will gain significantly from the effort.

In terms of lessons that might be helpful for other coaches, two things stand out from my work with Jennifer:

- Do not fall in love with your tools. Jennifer needed a certain kind of coaching early in our work and a very different kind of coaching as time went on. I had to adapt my approach to always meet her where she was. The development pipeline is a helpful framework for thinking about the person's needs at different points in time, but even within that, coaches will benefit from a large, flexible tool-kit that offers multiple ways to cultivate insight or provide accountability.
- Be clear about your purpose. Jennifer is such a charming, engaging, and dynamic personality that it would be easy to just follow her lead. I am certain that I could have been helpful to Jennifer had we just worked on the issues that she requested and the topics that she presented. But I have spent a lot of time thinking about my purpose as a coach. Number one is a commitment to helping the person achieve what he or she most values. For Jennifer, that required that I ignore some of what she was asking for and push her to a different realm. At any given moment, it would have been easy to be seduced by the tactical issues and easy answers that Jennifer was searching for. But if I had, I do not think we'd still be working together again 3 years later.

This advice applies on multiple levels: Be clear on your purpose as a coach, your purpose in working with each person, your purpose in each session, and your purpose at each moment. None of these is easy to attain, and I drift all the time.

For Jennifer, I had to be clear on my purpose so we would not skate along from one issue to the next, having a great time but never wrestling with the deeper issues. For other participants, I have to be clear on my purpose or else I'll get bored to tears with how simple and even trivial their issues are. For others, I have to be clear on my purpose or I'll get frustrated because they're not making progress at the speed I think they should. Sometimes I have to remind myself that my purpose is not to have them be ideal coaching clients, but to help them achieve what they most value. And I have to accept them for who they are and work with them at their pace and in their style.

CONCLUSION

David: Over the 3 years that we worked together, I helped Jennifer learn or improve in at least a dozen skill areas: delegating, coaching, prioritization and time management, leadership, communication, net-

[4] This is an adaptation of a quote from Ovid: "If you want to be loved, be lovable."

working, managing upward, influencing, listening skills, organizational politics, stress management, coping with ambiguity, and so forth. Yet that is not what this story is about. The story of Jennifer's transformation is really about one or two simple lessons that she has taken and applied to increasingly greater and more complex challenges. The theme, which she has had to relearn at ever deeper levels, is to be clear and grounded in what is most important and make decisions based on the long-term priorities rather than the pressing needs of the moment. It is a simple lesson, perhaps, but one with profound implications.

Working with Jennifer over an extended period of time has helped me stay grounded in my own highest priorities as well. I am embarrassed to admit how many times I've found myself emphasizing some point to Jennifer about staying focused while thinking, "David, you better listen to yourself." No matter how good, or even great, I ever become as a coach, I always see how much I have to learn from my clients in being a better and more complete person. Jennifer, like other clients of mine, is able to accomplish things in her job that I could never do. I am grateful to Jennifer, and to all my clients, for the opportunity to work with them and for all that they have taught me.

Jennifer: Besides being fun, working on this project allowed me to reflect on what I've learned and see the progress I've made. Overall, I have to admit I'm a real stubborn case. I think David picked me to write about because I was such a challenge. Throughout my career, people have given me great advice, like telling me to be more focused. But just giving the advice—or the feedback or whatever—has never been enough. So to get me to stop and actually change was huge.

Coaching had real value in forcing me to take time to reflect. Momentarily going slow prepared me to go faster and farther in the long run. Finding the right coach has increased my potential to take my career farther than I ever thought possible 3 years ago. Back then, I was stubbornly committed to being good at everything I did. Now I see that being great at the important things feels a heck of a lot better, and that drive has pushed me way past limits that I only thought I had.

EPILOGUE

David: Since September 2004, Jennifer has been working as part of a hand-chosen "war room" operational team to help reposition one of HP's biggest businesses. She is now serving two levels above her previous role, reporting to an executive vice president. Just before the original article on which this chapter was based went to press, she was told that she was being recommended for a role at that level, largely because of her performance on the war room team. This two-level move is striking because it is happening in a static job environment where few people have had opportunities for significant advancement, and even meaningful lateral career moves are scarce.

Jennifer: This latest move was like being put on a rocket. Some of the depth of what I worked on with David has only now become apparent to me. His coaching to take time to think has been essential. There are even more temptations and distractions at this level. The sense of urgency on this project was almost overwhelming, so being able to take control of my time and stay focused on the right process has been the single most influential thing that has contributed to my growth as a leader and enabled the scope of the work that I've been able to accomplish.

References

Druckman, D., & Bjork, R. A. (Eds.). (1991). *In the mind's eye: Enhancing human performance.* Washington, DC: National Academy Press.

Hicks, M. D., & Peterson, D. B. (1997). Just enough to be dangerous: The rest of what you need to know about development. *Consulting Psychology Journal, 49,* 171–193.

Hicks, M. D., & Peterson, D. B. (1999). The development pipeline: How people really learn. *Knowledge Management Review, 9,* 30–33.

Peterson, D. B. (1993). *Skill learning and behavior change in an individually tailored management coaching program.* Unpublished doctoral dissertation, University of Minnesota, Minneapolis.

Peterson, D. B. (2002). Management development: Coaching and mentoring programs. In K. Kraiger (Ed.), *Creating, implementing, and managing effective training and development* (pp. 160–191). San Francisco: Jossey-Bass.

Peterson, D. B. (2003). Apply influence skills. In J. Helsing, B. Geraghty, & L. Napolitano (Eds.), *Impact without authority* (pp. 121–141). Chicago: Strategic Account Management Association.

Peterson, D. B., & Hicks, M. D. (1995). *Development FIRST: Strategies for self-development.* Minneapolis, MN: Personnel Decisions International.

Peterson, D. B., & Hicks, M. D. (1996). *Leader as coach: Strategies for coaching and developing others.* Minneapolis, MN: Personnel Decisions International.

Peterson, D. B., & Hicks, M. D. (1999, April). *From good coach to great coach: Best lessons.* Keynote address at the Coaching and Mentoring Conference, Linkage, Incorporated, Boston.

Peterson, D. B., & Kraiger, K. (2004). A practical guide to evaluating coaching: Translating state-of-the-art techniques to the real world. In J. E. Edwards, J. C. Scott, & N. S. Raju (Eds.), *The human resources program evaluation handbook* (pp. 262–282). Thousand Oaks, CA: Sage.

Peterson, D. B., & Sutherland, E. (2003, April). *Advanced coaching: Accelerating the transition from good to great.* Pre-conference workshop at the annual conference of the Society for Industrial and Organizational Psychology, Orlando, FL.

CHAPTER 36

THE RELUCTANT PRESIDENT

Karol M. Wasylyshyn

The split between what is nourishing at work and what is agonizing is the very chasm from which our personal destiny emerges.

—David Whyte (1994, p. 5)

This engagement began as the grooming of a chief executive officer (CEO) successor candidate whose ambivalence about his new president role was at least matched by the ambivalence of the CEO/owner about the need to have a successor at all. It unfolded successfully with the president taking full command of his leadership challenges and the CEO/owner becoming more resolved about his retirement transition as well as more trusting of his eventual successor. There was also secondary gain for the senior management team as it endorsed and embarked upon key organization development initiatives. What happened in between was a roller coaster ride during which my clinical training was as helpful as extensive experience I had had in business and coaching. Furthermore, on the basis of my experience with other *superkeepers* (a term coined by Berger & Berger [2003]) like the client Frank, this good outcome was influenced by three coaching process or meta principles—traction, trust, and truth-telling—as well as by four methodology factors—a holistic approach, deep behavioral insight, the active involvement of top corporate executives, and sustained relationships. These process and methodology considerations are discussed below after presentation of the case.

THE FACTS—CLIENT, CULTURE, BOSS

The Client

Frank M. had been with Banyun, a privately held employee benefits consulting firm with annual revenue of approximately $50 million, for 9 years when at age 40 he was made president. This unexpected appointment was widely perceived as a major step toward his eventually becoming CEO. In our first meeting, Frank summarized his situation:

> I would have been content to just keep selling, but we were growing fast, things inside were getting more and more chaotic, the CEO had started to worry about perpetuation of the company, and before I knew it, I was president. This ticked off a couple of the other guys—one in particular who really wanted it—but for me, it is a pain. It is next to impossible for me to produce more business, manage my current accounts, and deal with all the infrastructure and people issues crucial for our continued success. John (the CEO) just does not want to spend the necessary time on this; I do not think he sees how complex things have

Reprinted from the *Consulting Psychology Journal: Practice and Research, 57,* 57–70. Copyright 2005 by the American Psychological Association and the Society of Consulting Psychology.

> gotten on the management side. All he wants to do is produce business, and he keeps raising the bar. Somebody's got to get a hold of this thing. It looks like that somebody is me, and I'm taking a financial hit to do it.

Frank had been recruited to Banyun on the basis of his outstanding sales success at IBM. The combination of his potential for ownership, interest in learning Banyun's business, and a move to the East Coast was enticing enough for him to accept the offer and relocate his wife and three children. Within a few years of his hiring, he had become one of the top two business producers at Banyun—along with the CEO. In the midst of a health scare and based on counsel from his legal advisor, the CEO made the impetuous decision to appoint a president. Because he valued sales success above all else and had a relatively good relationship with Frank, he saw Frank as his best choice. Although it was the right timing for appointing a president, John had little appreciation of what it would take to stabilize the firm through its rapid growth and to position it securely for the future. John's answer to any question about strategy was always the same: top-line growth.

The Culture

In this competitive, sales-driven culture, the business producers rapidly fell in and out of favor with the CEO on the basis of their monthly results. This pattern of intermittent reinforcement had begun to create retention risks, another problem with which Frank would have to grapple. But good, bad, or ugly, the culture was *strong,* and there was a lot about it that held appeal. Founded by the CEO's father, the company had long enjoyed a portfolio of prestigious corporate clients and had double-digit growth for several years running. It had a stellar reputation for quality service, customer focus, and integrity. Its employees were well-paid, loyal, and enjoyed the comfort of elegant surroundings. Appearances were paramount to the CEO, and the gestalt at Banyun was Brooks Brothers crisp. The company's success rested solidly on a foundation of excellent people, comprehensive technical training, an adherence to orthodoxy, and strong standards of accountability. For the most part, employees were thriving in this atmosphere of innovation, competition, and an admixture of commitment to work–family integration and reward for beyond-the-beyond heroics.

There was also a darker side to Banyun's culture, manifested by an atmosphere of anxiety among the administrative staff and overt expressions of exasperation from professional and management employees. This was due primarily to the CEO's relentless micromanagement, crude attacks on people, impulsive firings, and obstinacy. For years he had waited to succeed his father, and when he did, his recrudescent narcissism (H. Levinson, 2003) washed over the company in undulating waves of need, self-aggrandizement, and inappropriate displays of power and dominance.

At the same time, the firm's folklore abounded in stories about the CEO's incredible generosity and empathy for employees, especially during times of family illness or death. In summary, a moat of eggshells lay between the splendor of his office and the staff beyond. As one senior manager described it, "As good as this place is to work, you can feel really whiplashed, too." From the mail room to the boardroom, the firm's atmosphere tilted on the axis of the CEO's labile mood.

The Boss

Beneath the surface of this seemingly impeccable gentleman was the wounded heart of an abused and emotionally impoverished child born to privilege but denied the psychological sustenance to thrive as a secure adult. Maintaining control was his leitmotif, and because his locus of control was completely external, those around him were conditioned to provide frequent ego feedings and to avoid hitting the hot buttons of his massive insecurity.

The CEO frequently told employees about childhood traumas he suffered at the hands of his sadistic father. These stories were perceived as manipulative attempts to rationalize his bad behavior; horrifying as they were, they had long ago lost their potential to heal the wounds he inflicted. As Frank put it, "At some point, you have to get over it and move on."

Clearly, the CEO was a formidable challenge in this coaching engagement, a challenge that had to be met lest progress with Frank be sabotaged by John's narcissistic rage, especially as Frank became increasingly effective in his presidential role. I would have to orchestrate a sequence of steps that produced an alliance with John, helped soothe his replacement fears, and reinforced his sense of trust with Frank.

THE PRELUDE

The prospect of executive coaching for Frank was the human resource (HR) director's idea; he had grown weary of the CEO's tendency to complain about Frank and question—in earshot of others—whether he had done the right thing in appointing Frank president. Although the HR director knew the job was a stretch for Frank, he believed Frank was well equipped to meet the demands of the job, and he knew how well respected he was throughout the firm. The HR director was also psychologically sophisticated enough to recognize that John's baseless complaints were a defense against his retirement fears.

With the CEO's agreement, the HR director went on a round of initial screening interviews with prospective coaches. Toward the end of my meeting with him, the urgency and poignancy of the situation tumbled out when he said, "I'm concerned that if Frank and John do not get their relationship right, Frank will leave and that will be a major blow to the company. And as far as working with a coach, Frank's a tough street fighter kind of a guy. He's pragmatic and wants to stay focused on results. He's not into a lot of psychology, and I do not know how he'll do with a female coach." To which I replied, "Let us see what he decides."

The initial meeting with Frank was memorable. Fit, polished, and direct, he got right down to business. He had already met with two other coaches, and I discerned quickly that he was not impressed with what he'd heard so far. In his words, "There are some things I need to learn about doing this job, but I do not think I'm going to learn much from people who haven't led anything or who do not understand the world I operate in. How do people like you do what you do?" In those opening minutes, I gave him a quick summary of my own business background, leadership experiences, companies I had consulted to, and an overview of my coaching model. Then I sat back and listened as he answered my question about what he needed to learn. Frank focused most on staffing, operational issues, and the challenge of managing the CEO. At the end of this 2-hour meeting, he asked me for references. Having anticipated his request, I gave him names of both coached clients and company contacts. A few days later, Frank called to say he was ready to start the coaching. Of note in the phone call was his comment, "I do not want to contemplate my navel, but I think there's probably a connection between things that have happened in my life and what's going on for me at Banyun; so I'm assuming you'll take a good look at everything, right?" Right. In the midst of what adult development theorist D. J. Levinson (1978, p. 60) described as the BOOM effect, that is, "becoming one's own man," Frank was ripe for learning—and change.

THE START-UP

After the introductory conversation with Frank, I facilitated an agenda-setting meeting in the CEO's office. Frank and I joined John and the HR director for a discussion of the coaching methodology, our respective roles, time frame, the boundaries of confidentiality, objectives of the coaching, and how we'd assess progress. We concluded with the selection of a representative group of people—14 in all—for Frank's 360 data gathering.

My initial observations of the CEO tracked with what I had heard from Frank and the HR director. He was a man of enormous energy and passion for his business, accomplished and flawed, commanding and insecure. A tinderbox for whom shame could easily produce an amygdala hijack (Goleman, 1995). A tormented person of dualities that could scuttle an orderly succession, endanger Banyun's future, and continue to erode the morale in the company. I also sensed his impatience with process, so I was succinct:

- Methodology—I would use a four-phase model customized to the needs of this engagement: (a) data gathering, including a development history, a battery of psychometrics,[1] and face-to-face 360 data gathering; (b) feedback, when all the data would be synthesized and used to specify coaching areas; (c) coaching, during which an array of learning resources would be used; and (d) consolidation of coaching gains.
- Roles—The CEO and HR director would be active collaborators with Frank and me, that is, coaching would not be done in a vacuum. Both Frank and I would benefit from collateral information provided by them, and we wanted to make sure they felt in-the-loop.
- Time frame—Approximately 12 to 15 months for the four phases. During the coaching phase, there would be 2-hour monthly meetings plus e-mail and phone consultation as needed.
- Confidentiality—I emphasized that most data would be kept in complete confidence and explained the importance of this for my establishing and maintaining a strong working alliance with Frank. At the same time, it would be critical for us to maintain open lines of communication. I would have at least monthly conversations with them in which we'd gauge progress and momentum, share new observations, and so forth.
- Objectives of coaching—Two areas emerged in this meeting: (a) Frank's forging a stronger, more trusting relationship with the CEO; and (b) his building relationships with others throughout the firm (not just his sales peers and the CEO).
- Assessing progress—I would have a private meeting with the CEO at the 6-month point, a 12-month joint meeting with the CEO and Frank, and quarterly conversations with the HR director. In addition, as indicated above, I would be available to the CEO and HR director on an ad hoc basis.
- Selection of 360 sample participants—This concrete task initiated our four-way collaboration. It also provided some surprises and clues for Frank in terms of whom the CEO viewed as key stakeholders.
- Communication strategy—Because this was the first time Banyun had used an executive coach and because there was a residue of envy and resentment surrounding Frank's appointment as president, I scripted the CEO and HR director. They needed to speak of the coaching as a business resource, an investment in both Banyun's future and in Frank's development as an even more effective leader. We also agreed that I would interview everyone on site, beginning each conversation with a question exploring what he or she understood about my work with Frank. This would give me the opportunity to clarify any misconceptions and amplify the developmental intent of the engagement.

THE WORK

Having grounded the coaching with the agenda-setting meeting, we moved on to complete the data-gathering phase. I took Frank's history in a 3-hour face-to-face meeting and gave him the packet of psychometrics to complete on his own. Frank's early years were a Brothers Grimm tale of meager surroundings and emotional deprivation given his self-absorbed mother, a distant father, and later, an equally distant stepfather. Frank's one emotional anchor during his formative years was his maternal grandmother, who remained a constant source of nurturance and affirmation until she died when he was in college. An outstanding athlete from grade school through college, Frank embarked on an NBA basketball career, but a serious injury ended that pursuit. Through a serendipitous series of events, he wound up in sales, eventually joining IBM, where he surpassed quota after quota

[1] Psychometric battery consisted of Watson–Glaser Critical Thinking Appraisal, Myers–Briggs Type Indicator, the Life Styles Inventory, the NEO PI-R, and the BarOn Emotional Quotient Inventory.

and was well regarded by all who knew him. In his own words, "Sales was great for me from the beginning. You learn your products, know your goals, work harder than most, and you can measure your success. I'm a pragmatist who does not need a lot of love or stroking. I can take a lot, too."

True to the early signal Frank sent about a probable "connection" between his past and the present at Banyun, the synthesis of his history and the psychometric data were pivotal. It revealed a psychological insight that had important implications for both his personal life and leadership of Banyun. This insight was about his sadomasochistic pattern in significant relationships, including his spouse and the CEO. We moved quickly from history to immediate applicability of the insight: His tolerance for others' dysfunctional behavior kept him trapped in draining, toxic relationships that afforded him minimal appreciation, love, or acknowledgment of his accomplishments. Yes, he could "take a lot," but that also meant he had little psychic energy left to invest in his own personal growth and well-being. Moreover, given the leadership demands of his role, he had no time for the larger strategic and operational issues. Knowing I was trained clinically, Frank joked about "getting two for the price of one." I responded by explaining the need to maintain the boundaries of our work and by also indicating my willingness to refer him to a therapist, if he was interested. At a later point in the coaching, Frank did ask for referral to a marital therapist, an intervention that proved helpful. With Frank's permission, I shared relevant information with that clinician.

Based on the feedback, we finalized the coaching agenda. This agenda targeted three strengths to leverage: business development ability, leadership potential, and relationship with the CEO. We also agreed on two areas for development: internal relationship building and people management. These areas fundamentally tracked with what was discussed in the agenda-setting meeting, and Frank saw how they were inextricably linked to each other. Progress in any one area would likely have a positive effect on other coaching objectives. Of note was the fact that most people believed that Frank managed the CEO better than anyone else at Banyun.

To anchor the coaching phase, Frank and I collaborated on the creation of a preliminary action plan, that is, the specific action steps he would take to make headway in the areas identified. The CEO and HR director received copies of Frank's plan, and I urged them to give Frank positive reinforcement whenever they saw him "working" the plan well and to take advantage of their observations to give him constructive criticism when he was not working it well. During the initial months, I interacted most with the HR director, who proved to be a remarkably effective collaborator and who forged a strategic partnership with Frank. Regarding the CEO, once he realized the benefits of Frank's coaching for himself, he became more involved. He acknowledged Frank's progress (to Frank and others), and of greater significance he was better able to express his annoyance or concerns directly to Frank—a behavior that had a positive effect on their relationship. The presence of the CEO's sadistic father and the healing effect of the shift in the John–Frank dynamic enveloped the CEO's comment, "I realize I do not have to worry about Frank blowing up at me when I'm not happy with something he's done."

The coaching was also anchored by the use of a technique I created some years ago—the visual metaphor (see Figure 36.1). This pictorial representation of Frank's current, transitional, and future leadership states—as described by him—was a handy way for us to assess where we were in the coaching. We often referred to it at the outset of a coaching meeting. Frank's metaphor amplified the overarching importance of his managing the relationship with the CEO. In Frame 1 (current state), Frank was in the midst of a major storm. Frame 2 (transitional state) indicated progress. And in Frame 3 (future state), Frank saw himself working collaboratively with the CEO, staying focused on issues critical to the company's future. After a year of coaching, Frank had moved into Frame 2, and by the end of the second year, he was in Frame 3 and working on solidifying that progress. Because he enjoyed movies, I used them as a resource,

FIGURE 36.1. Visual metaphor—a pictorial representation of Frank's current, transitional, and future leadership states, as described by him.

especially during the consolidation phase (e.g., *Gladiator, Hoosiers, Mr. Holland's Opus, The Big Kahuna*, and *Elizabeth*).

Areas for Development

Regarding internal relationship building, Frank learned, primarily from the 360 data, that his results-oriented, no-nonsense approach was fundamentally a strength, though a double-edged one. People wanted more from him as president of the company. He came to appreciate that employees at all levels needed more access to him and to feel they could interact on a broader array of issues, that is, not just client-related problems or opportunities. Using emotional intelligence as a major learning vehicle (Goleman, 1995, 1998), Frank made enormous gains in this area. The coaching helped him generalize his emotional self, a self he had mostly suppressed defensively, across a broader array of situations. Frank's major actions included his (a) displaying greater empathy regarding personnel issues, (b) conveying appreciation for the good work of sales support functions, (c) increasing casual interactions and being more visible throughout the firm, and (d) being more attuned to employees' personal events and acknowledging them with voice or e-mails.

To make headway on the people management development area, we used a results/attitude grid (see Figure 36.2). This grid helped Frank see where his direct reports stood and, more important, what he needed to do developmentally with each of them. This led to key people decisions about which the CEO was especially pleased, for he was harboring unspoken resentment about "bad hires" Frank had made.

RESULTS/ATTITUDE GRID	
1 +R +A	2 -R +A
3 +R -A	4 -R -A

FIGURE 36.2. The results/attitude grid. Quadrant 1: High potentials—what needs to be done to keep them? Quadrant 2: Results lacking—what needs to be done to get results on track? Quadrant 3: Attitude problem—is attitude adjustment possible? If yes, what's the plan? If no, is this person more trouble than he/she is worth? Answer to last question determines course of action. Quadrant 4: Results and attitude problem—is person in wrong job? If so and there is a better job fit in company, such people can move swiftly to Quadrant 1. If not, separation from company is probably best. R = results; A = attitude.

Leveraging Strengths

In some ways, Frank's capitalizing on his strengths proved to be the more demanding part of his coaching agenda. Regarding business development, he persisted in a difficult dialogue with the CEO about the growing demands of the presidential role, that is, how it siphoned time away from his developing new business and how there needed to be a change in his compensation so that he was not so penalized financially for assuming the president role. The time spent on this issue in coaching meetings, as well as the coach's private conversations with the CEO, eventually produced a resolution that was satisfactory to Frank financially and had a positive effect on his overall enthusiasm for the job. He also became more intentional about coaching others' sales success.

It was gratifying for Frank to see leadership potential emerge as a strength from the 360 data gathering. There were a number of coordinated action steps that produced rapid gains in this area. These included his (a) assuming a more forceful role at companywide events when business results and plans for the future were communicated, (b) creating other opportunities to convey strategic plans, and (c) being more involved in the recruitment and assimilation of key people into Banyun. To support Frank's leadership impact further, I introduced him to respected resources in the areas of recruitment, organization development, and leadership development.

Of note, coaching meetings were influenced by my frequent challenge to Frank that "insight is cheap unless you use it." This resulted in his taking a number of courageous steps over the next couple of years, including productive confrontations with chronic cynics at Banyun, the firing of nonperformers, persistence regarding strategic discipline, and censoring people's reflexive tendencies to trash the CEO.

While Frank made enormous headway on his relationship with the CEO, this coaching area would require continued vigilance into the future. We identified four action steps that served him well immediately: (a) increasing daily communication with John, the CEO; (b) having monthly dinner meetings with John; and (c) ensuring that they displayed a united front to employees on all key business matters.

On a deeper level, Frank learned about the pros and cons of working for a narcissistic boss. His reading and our subsequent discussions of Maccoby's (2000) *Harvard Business Review* article was especially helpful. He realized that through it all, there was much he respected in terms of John's risk taking, public visibility, and uncanny "nose for the business" that had propelled the company's growth. Frank also came to better understand—and even anticipate—the CEO's (a) swings between grandiosity and despair, (b) irrational distrust of others, and (c) maddening preoccupation with himself. Moreover, he became attuned to the subtleties and nuances of both his private and public interactions with the CEO. In his words, "I'm a lot clearer about what I'm dealing with and what I need to do to avoid setting him off and to influence a positive atmosphere." Frank's deepened attunement led to actions he would intensify and sustain over time. These included his (a) creating opportunities for the CEO to be more visible both inside and outside the company; (b) working thorny business issues behind the scenes more, thereby avoiding open dissent in the management committee; (c) reinforcing the CEO's better ideas and distracting him from bad ones; and (d) finding ways to give John frank feedback but without threatening the CEO's inflated self-image.

In tandem with Frank's efforts to manage the CEO, I continued to pursue my own agenda with John. Trust was built primarily through my empathy for his concerns. I also made considerable progress on his ability to see Frank as someone who deserved his trust, who was completely committed to the company, and who would be a superb successor when John chose to retire. As time unfolded, I made the most of opportunities to minimize the CEO's worst fears about retirement. I introduced him to the concept of legacy and facilitated his ability to verbalize what this would be for Banyun by the time he retired ("$100 million in revenue"). Furthermore, I heightened his interest in exploring the arts, serving altruistic causes, and possibly using his wealth to fund "naming" opportunities at academic and other organizations. This effort ignited his awareness of the glittering image he could sustain, even after his time at Banyun.

DISCUSSION

Many coaching tools were used to help Frank meet the challenges of the president's job. There were obvious tools, such as a clear coaching agenda, the developmental history, a battery of psychometrics, the customized 360 data gathering, selected readings, the frequency of coaching meetings, a cascade of valuable action steps, and the coaching relationship. There were more creative tools, too, like the visual metaphor, the results/attitude grid for assessing direct reports, and the use of movie scenes to reinforce learning about leadership. But in the end, the success of this work was influenced most by its grounding in the three coaching process (meta principles) and four methodology factors to which I referred in the introduction of this chapter. This approach reflects the integration of my experience in business, clinical training, research, consulting, and assuredly by what hundreds of executive clients have said about what helped them most. This is an approach that can lead to sustained results—with clients who want to learn, have the courage to change, and who perceive the need for change as one of life's continuous gifts.

Here's how these process and methodology considerations played out in the coaching of Frank, who in the end was no longer the "reluctant president."

Three Meta Principles

1. Traction. What I mean by traction in coaching is akin to the interaction between car tires and roads—a gripping of the surface while moving but without slipping. This need to keep moving without slipping is fundamental to effective coaching. The work will falter, drift, or even fail without it.

There were many factors involved in attaining and maintaining traction in Frank's coaching, beginning with my assessment of the "rightness" of the coaching referral. Had this been a certain derailment or no-win scenario, I would have passed or referred it to a colleague with appropriate warnings because I do not think companies should waste money on such coaching agendas (see chap. 8, this volume). Although I had some reservation about Frank's trust in the value of coaching and the climate of the coaching referral, I was swayed by his appetite to learn, willingness to invest sufficient time, and the potential for us to form a strong working alliance. In retrospect, his involvement in the choice of his coach was a key factor in our forming a rapid and strong working alliance.

Finally, because of the size of Frank's 360 sample—14 including the CEO and HR director—his feedback was given in two sessions to help sustain traction. History and psychometric data were discussed in one 3-hour meeting, and the 360 feedback was given in a second 3-hour session that concluded with our final agreement on targeted areas for coaching. Both meetings were held in my office and were audiotaped for his future reference.

2. Trust. This meta principle connotes a reciprocal trusting not just between the coach and coachee but with the two internal collaborators as well—in this case the CEO/boss and the HR partner. As I got to know the CEO, his trust in both me and the value of the coaching grew through the consistency of our conversations and, curiously, through my refusal to take on additional engagements at Banyun. Both Frank and he had invited my participation in other initiatives (e.g., company survey and leadership development program), and they were eager for me to coach other members of the management committee. My instinct to hold a strong boundary and not extend service beyond the initial coaching engagement paid off. Midway in the coaching, the HR director said, "John respects your not getting enmeshed with us like other consultants have. This has helped your trust with him because he does not see you as more interested in getting business than in helping Banyun."

Overall, the HR director served as an objective translator of events in the company, and as such, he was an invaluable source of collateral information. The CEO got increasingly better at expressing his true opinions, venting frustrations, and revealing his concerns about the future, so much so that I had to manage the boundary of our relationship carefully and in a way that was not narcissistically wounding to him.

In addition to my fostering these collaborative working relationships, there were two other key factors that influenced the building of trust: confidentiality and emotional competence. Always central to the issue of confidentiality is the question: Who's the client? Although coaches vary in their perspectives on this question, I've not wavered from mine: The coachee is always the client, and the bill-paying corporate sponsor is just that, the sponsor. As I previously wrote,

> In terms of forming strong connections with clients, coaches who work from a perspective of the *executive as client* (versus the organization as client) are likely to form faster and more trusting coaching relationships. Seasoned coaches discover how to work from this perspective—satisfying both the coached executive and the sponsoring organization. (chap. 8, this volume, p. 82)

Having discussed the boundaries of confidentiality openly in the agenda-setting meeting, I was not compromised later by inappropriate questions regarding information that was off-limits, such as history, psychometric or 360 feedback data, and specific content of coaching meetings. However, to foster the CEO's and HR partner's functioning fully in their roles as collaborators, I remained in frequent contact with them, capitalized on my private time with the CEO, and conveyed thematic material from the 360 data gathering—particularly as it related to Banyun's culture. I also provided my general assessment of how the coaching was progressing and what each of them could do to gain the most mileage from this investment.

Managing the meta principle of trust in coaching relationships also requires the coach to possess a high degree of emotional competence, which is defined as the awareness of and ability to manage one's emotions. I had to censor strong negative feelings about the CEO as well as strong positive feelings about Frank. Obviously, maintaining objectivity was critical. Throughout the coaching I wanted what I taught and modeled in terms of key dimensions of emotional competence—self-awareness, discipline, empathy, and attunement to others—to help accelerate Frank's evolution as a leader.

Finally, as I had anticipated, coach gender was not an issue. It proved to be an asset manifested in numerous ways, including Frank's (a) willingness to be vulnerable, (b) shedding of defenses, (c) exploration of emotions as a leadership asset, and (d) discussion of marital issues as they adversely affected his work-related relationships.

3. Truth telling. I think of the meta principle of truth telling as a double mirror, that is, helping both client and company to see essential truths in the looking glass. Surely I helped Frank see what he needed to see. Through my relationship with the HR director, I helped Banyun see systemic issues that had implications for effective leadership. These findings, based on 360 data, signaled concerns about micromanagement, insufficient strategic planning, lack of managerial bench strength, and the need to develop the next generation of effective leaders. This information influenced two constructive organization development initiatives: a company culture survey and a leadership development program for mid- and senior-level managers.

Four Methodological Factors

1. Holistic approach. Coaching executives from a holistic perspective means the coach has the inclination to get to know his or her client fully—not just through the myopic lens of work. It means the coach has the skill to weave a fuller, more luminous tapestry of the client's life, making the connections that will matter most in the coaching. Working holistically means the coach will have the courage to address critical intersections between work and personal priorities. I refer to this as *work–family integration*, not *work–family balance*, the more common term but a flawed semantic in that it raises an expectation on which it is virtually impossible for most senior executives to deliver.

While I maintained an appropriate boundary between the coaching agenda and issues of significant concern in Frank's private life, my willingness to serve in a triage capacity was helpful and much appreciated by him. Having led him to a competent

1 Describe his strengths.
2 Give an example of when he used these strengths particularly well.
3 What could he improve so he would be even more effective?
4 Give an example of when these limitations were especially apparent.
5 Describe his management style.
6 How does he develop people?
7 How effective is he in getting the right people in the right jobs?
8 How does he relate to others specifically:
Direct reports? Peers? His boss? Clients?
9 How would you describe Banyon's culture?
What works? What doesn't?
10 Compare Frank's leadership style to John's.
11 How does Frank manage his work–family priorities?
12 If you were to offer him one piece of advice—advice that would help make him even more effective than he already is, what would you say?

FIGURE 36.3. Customized interview protocol for 360-degree feedback.

marital therapist, for example, had a palliative effect and minimized his distraction at work.

Finally, coaches working holistically with executives has implications for executive retention. True to the HR director's worst fear, Frank's exasperation—given the dual tensions of managing the CEO and Frank's personal issues—produced thoughts about leaving Banyun. In the safety of the coaching relationship, Frank had a place to vent and to receive guidance that eased his frustration, helped him maintain perspective, and prevented a precipitous decision to resign.

2. Deep behavioral insight. The rapid engagement of senior executives is often the initial challenge in coaching them. Bringing deep insight about behavior to the surface, especially as it relates to leadership, can be especially effective in meeting this challenge. Psychologist coaches, in particular, can tap into a broad armamentarium of tools for this purpose. My "good look at everything" for Frank was accomplished with the taking of a developmental history and a battery of psychometrics. I used the 360 data gathering to surface relevant information about Frank's leadership and to learn more about Banyun's culture (see Figure 36.3, customized interview protocol). And I accelerated rapid engagement by setting two feedback meetings and getting to the first one quickly so we could mine the history and psychometric data for deeper insights.

Frank's recognition of his pattern of sadomasochistic relationships had a lasting impact on him as well as influencing much of what he learned and did throughout the coaching. Finally, his coaching was a carefully sequenced and nuanced process of delivering insight, supporting his courageous efforts to apply the insights, and then consolidating his behavioral gains.

3. Involvement of top executives. Regardless of how secure they may or may not be, senior executives want to know where they stand with top management. And effective executive coaches will find ways to bring this information to their work—without it becoming the raison d'être of the engagement.

In the work with Frank, this methodology consideration was both easy and difficult. It was easy in the sense that the engagement was riveted on his relationship with the CEO. The spigot of information was wide open, and, if anything, I was constantly making choices about the intensity of the water pressure. It was difficult in the sense that coaching meetings could have easily been overwhelmed by the Frank–John relationship agenda—at the expense of Frank's learning and attention to other dimensions of his leadership.

In this sense, the delineation of a full coaching agenda of strengths to leverage and development areas was most helpful. Furthermore, the concrete preliminary action plan helped maintain focus on the broader agenda. As I said to Frank in one coaching meeting, "We do not want our work together to be a microcosm of what goes on at Banyun: total preoccupation with the CEO."

4. Sustained relationships. In my view, the coaching of senior executives is a boundaryless process—not a contained program. The coach does whatever needs to be done and is not trapped in a lock-step, company-endorsed model with a ceiling on engagement length. The coaching of superkeepers like Frank is more relational than transactional. This means that the coaching relationship is likely to be sustained, that is, it can hold value for the executive for a number of years. Specifically, after an initial body of work is completed and progress on goals is achieved, the executive may choose to retain the coach further. This is not a scenario of dependency. Rather, it is the natural evolution of a valued business relationship to one in which the coach becomes a trusted advisor.

This is what occurred after 15 months of coaching Frank. We had accomplished our primary coaching objectives, and I would now, as trusted advisor, be an objective sounding board providing him a safe place to express concerns, test ideas, plan, and discuss people challenges—including the CEO. This relationship would also serve as an antidote to the isolation that often occurs for business people in senior leadership roles. Saporito (see chap. 15, this volume) wrote, "The fact of the matter is, the higher an individual moves in an organization, the less feedback he or she is likely to receive. Senior executives tend to get isolated from real-time, unvarnished feedback about the impact of their individual leadership" (p. 149).

Regarding other sustained interaction, we settled into a productive pattern of my having a June luncheon with the CEO and the three of us sharing a Christmas luncheon at year-end. As enjoyable as these occasions were, they required careful planning in terms of the issues I needed to initiate, punctuate, or illuminate with John. In the relaxed atmosphere of these settings, I made the most headway with the CEO regarding both his retirement fears and his relationship with Frank. In one hyperbolic burst he said, "I would trust Frank with my life."

This shift from coach to trusted advisor warrants our attention because it holds enormous promise, especially for coaches working with top corporate executives. Sheth and Sobel (2002) wrote the following:

> When you have reached the final and most rewarding stage (of a client relationship), you'll become a trusted advisor who consistently develops collaborative relationships with your clients and provides insight rather than just information. At this stage you will have *breakthrough* relationships. Because of the broad, influential role you play and the unusual degree of trust that you develop, these relationships will be of a significantly higher order than the run-of-the-mill associations that so many professionals have with their clients. (p. 14)

CONCLUSION

This case study illustrates how a timely executive coaching engagement helped accelerate the effectiveness and influence the retention of a company's top CEO successor candidate. Using a data-driven and insight-oriented approach, the executive and his coach identified specific coaching objectives with implications for the company's success as well as for the executive's development. The case also represents how coaching at the top can influence organizational development—even in a culture dominated by the needs and whims of a partially dysfunctional CEO.

Finally, this case exemplifies the value of a long-term coaching model, a model that influenced the coach's role shift from coach to trusted advisor. But there are many coaching models for working effectively with senior executives. Rather than exploring or debating the differences among them, there are more compelling questions to consider: What's next for this strong application area within psychology? How will psychologists capitalize on trusted advisor relationships with powerful business leaders? How will we intensify the strategic use of psychology to not only aid business results, but to increase the nourishing and decrease the agonizing effects of the workplace?

References

Berger, L. A., & Berger, D. R. (Eds.). (2003). *The talent management handbook: Creating organizational excellence through identifying, developing, and positioning your best people.* New York: McGraw-Hill.

Goleman, D. (1995). *Emotional intelligence.* New York: Bantam Books.

Goleman, D. (1998, November–December). What makes a leader? *Harvard Business Review,* 93–102.

Levinson, D. J. (1978). *The seasons of a man's life.* New York: Ballantine Books.

Levinson, H. (2003, January). *Recrudescent narcissism: Where did ethics go?* Paper presented at the American Psychological Association Division 13 meeting, Scottsdale, AZ.

Maccoby, M. (2000, January–February). Narcissistic leaders: The incredible pros, the inevitable cons. *Harvard Business Review,* 69–77.

Sheth, J., & Sobel, A. (2002). *Clients for life: Evolving from an expert for hire to an extraordinary advisor.* New York: Simon & Schuster.

Whyte, D. (1994). *The heart aroused: Poetry and the preservation of the soul in corporate America.* New York: Doubleday.

CHAPTER 37

DEVELOPING THE EFFECTIVENESS OF A HIGH-POTENTIAL AFRICAN AMERICAN EXECUTIVE: THE ANATOMY OF A COACHING ENGAGEMENT

Paul C. Winum

"I have a very important coaching assignment for you," she said when I picked up my office phone a few days before the Christmas holiday. Mary[1] was a director of management development for a Fortune 500 consumer products company whom I had met 2 years prior after delivering a presentation at a conference in California. This was the second time she had called with a referral, and I could hear in the tone of her voice that she was quite concerned about this one. Mary went on to recount that a number of serious issues had been raised about the leadership and management style of one of the company's business unit heads, Tom Mackey. Tom was a young executive with a stellar resume and lots of potential who had been recruited from another prominent Fortune 500 company with the intention of placing him into his current role. His unit was responsible for approximately $500 million in annual sales and employed about 1,200 people. He had been in the job for just about a year, and complaints about some of his management decisions and actions had made their way back to corporate headquarters after only a few months. According to the reports Mary had received, Tom was frequently "missing in action," leaving word with his assistant that he was "out in the field." "His team says he schedules too many meetings," she related, "and then either misses them or spends much of the meeting time on his cell phone. He delegates all the work to subordinates and then confronts employees with performance issues in front of others when they fall short of his expectations. Tom is viewed as very political, frequently dropping the names of the senior executives in the company he knows and regularly talks with. He is seen as overly demanding, manipulative, and not particularly smart. He tends to blame others when there is a problem and takes the credit himself for successes. Tom is too proud to ask for guidance or to take feedback from others, and, as a result, he lacks awareness about the impact he is having on his colleagues and has lost the trust and confidence of the business team he has been given to lead," Mary concluded.

Given the litany of concerns that she had conveyed, I asked Mary about the efforts she and others in the company had taken to address the complaints about Tom, including the option of dismissing or reassigning him. "One more thing," Mary said in responding to my question. "Tom is African American, and our company has very few African Americans in executive positions. The senior vice president of human resources, who is also an African American and a mentor to Tom, has insisted that we meet our diversity goals and that we do whatever it takes to support Tom's success, including assigning him a coach. We are very concerned about Tom failing in his executive role and

I gratefully acknowledge the input of Greg Pennington during the design and development phases of this case.
Reprinted from the *Consulting Psychology Journal: Practice and Research*, 57, 71–89. Copyright 2005 by the American Psychological Association and the Society of Consulting Psychology.

[1] All names used to refer to clients in this chapter are fictitious.

potentially leaving the company. That is why I am calling you."

FURTHER EXPLORATION AND CONSIDERATIONS IN RESPONDING TO THE PRESENTING SITUATION

I told Mary that I was honored that she thought of me as a resource for this situation and that I would be happy to partner with her in thinking through the best way to proceed. Following the brief overview of the situation presented by Mary, I began to wrestle with the many complexities and concomitant choices that confront every practitioner who undertakes serious and ethical executive coaching and development work (Kilburg, 1996, 1997, 2002; Schein, 2003). Trying to practice what I preach, I began to inquire into the presenting situation by exploring with Mary some of the key questions recommended by Winum and Blanton (2003) to clarify value and focus when beginning a coaching engagement (see Table 37.1). I posed the following questions to Mary:

TABLE 37.1

Key Questions for Coaches to Ask Referral Sources to Clarify Value and Focus

Question
1. Whose budget will pay for this work?
2. Who will notice if the coaching work is successful?
3. What specifically will be noticed?
4. How will the environment/culture be improved?
5. How will the results of the business unit be impacted?
6. If successful, might there be improvement in any of the following:
a. Retention/morale of employees who work with the coachee?
b. Productivity of the coachee, coworkers, or the business unit?
c. Customer experience and retention?
d. Reduction in any litigation exposure?
e. Time expended by you and others in dealing with the coachee?
7. What would be the impact if there were no change in this situation?
8. Can you arrange access to the coachee's supervisor?
9. What information do you want about progress—when and how?
10. By when do you expect tangible results?

- What kind of feedback had Tom received from his boss about the concerns that had been expressed about him?
- What was Tom's response to any prior feedback to him and to the suggestion that he work with an executive coach?
- Who specifically were the complainants, and to whom were they complaining?
- What were the links in the communication chain in the organization through which concerns about Tom were passed?
- What was Tom's relationship in the organizational hierarchy to Mary, to his boss, to his business unit, and to the senior vice president (SVP) of human resources (HR)?
- Aside from the SVP of HR, how committed were any of the principals to Tom's success?
- What were the business issues and performance imperatives that helped shape the context within which Tom was expected to lead?
- In what ways might racial and diversity issues relate to others' perceptions of Tom's leadership effectiveness?
- What was this business unit's previous history related to the use of executive coaches?
- Was coaching Tom the preferred intervention in this situation, or might it be more useful to offer guidance to Tom's boss or to Mary as an internal resource?
- If the deployment of an external consultant was determined to be a viable option, was I the best person to do the work?

After we covered the questions above, we made a telephone appointment to talk the following day to explore the landscape and various choices in more depth. I also sent Mary the general sequence of steps my firm uses to design individual executive coaching programs (see Figure 37.1). In the interim, I walked down the hall to the office of my colleague Dr. Greg Pennington, seeking his perspectives and counsel on the case. Greg is a clinical psychologist by training with 20 years of postdoctoral experience in organizational consulting. He is also African American with specialized training and interest in diversity issues. In addition, Greg had done some work a few years back for the company

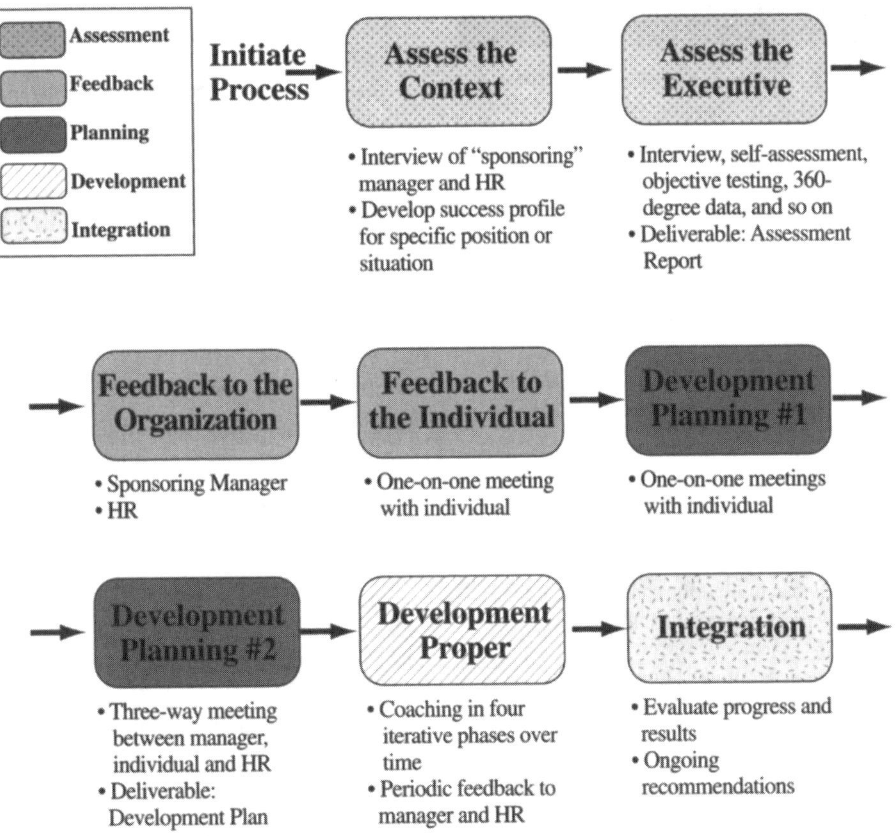

FIGURE 37.1. Coaching delivery: Sequence of key components. HR = human resources.

that Tom was with, and I wanted to get his insights about the culture of the company and to see if he would be willing to take on the work if the client was willing for him to do so. I was glad to have such a capable colleague who could so readily offer a knowledgeable perspective on the case. My goal was to be well prepared for the scheduled call with Mary, and that included lining up alternative consulting resources to maximize the choices for her if an external coach turned out to be what was needed. I was prepared to refer the client to a seasoned colleague in the city where the executive was located, in the event that travel costs and rapid accessibility were important considerations.

Greg recalled his work in the company, and he had met the senior HR executive during that engagement. He conveyed that the company had a fast-paced, performance-driven culture that had invested some time and money in diversity training for key managers a few years prior. He also gave me two books related to racial issues in organizational life (Livers & Caver, 2003; McClenney, 1987) and shared ideas from a presentation he was preparing to deliver at the Midwinter Conference of the Society of Consulting Psychology (Pennington, 2003) on coaching African American senior executives (see Table 37.2). Greg offered to help in any way with the case, either as a shadow consultant (Kilburg, 2002) or by taking the case on directly.

I left my consultation with Greg with a few working hypotheses to explore with Mary. The first hypothesis was that Tom had been placed in a job over his head, without the requisite prior experience or preparation by the company, in order to meet diversity goals that were set at the senior-most levels. If so, this would be consistent with one promotional pattern for minority executives observed by Thomas and Gabarro (1999) and reported in their book *Breaking Through*. This would also suggest that Tom would need some important managerial and leadership skill development to function effectively in the position he had. A

TABLE 37.2

Executive Coaching With African American Senior Executives: Issues and Actions

Issue and action
1. Race matters. The race card is present even if face down. You are more likely to understand its impact if you find ways to raise it as the coach. It is too costly for the executive to play it.
a. Find a way to open this discussion. Most executives will not volunteer it.
b. Understand what behaviors are interpreted differently when demonstrated by Blacks compared with non-Blacks.
2. Rumors of intellectual inferiority flourish. Innate intellectual ability is still the predominant belief in companies and in people. Some people are born smart and some folks are not.
a. Insist on defining behavioral performance indicators in setting goals rather than general attributes and characteristics.
b. Force others to define "strategic thinking," as this is often used as a substitute for questioning innate intellectual ability.
3. Warring souls at peace. Though an executive title and pay provide more options, they do not change one's core identity. You cannot look at a Black person and NOT see the color of their skin. They cannot deny their color, and their self-identity will always include race.
a. Explore the person's activities outside of work. Leverage those interests and skills.
4. Provide more "how to" than "hugs." There is more value in a coach providing directions to navigate the environment than in exploring for insight. Navigation includes mapping the environment, charting paths of least resistance and of impact, and running interference to minimize obstacles.
a. Identify the written and unwritten rules for success in the organization.
b. Ask and answer: Where and how will race be perceived as an obstacle?
5. Race does not matter. Ultimately, executives understand that they must contribute to the bottom line. You must accept the paradox that it is critical to consider race in order to get to the point where race does not matter.

related hypothesis was that Tom understandably might have felt like he was in over his head—felt a bit like an imposter who needed to mask his vulnerabilities, partially because of his own psychological make-up and partially because of the attributes of the company culture that did not encourage exposing weaknesses. A third hypothesis was that to turn the situation and perceptions of Tom around, successful intervention would require attention to the interpersonal field and the communication pipeline that generated and communicated perceptions about Tom throughout the organization.

The next day Mary and I explored the situation involving Tom and the many questions that I posed to her. I learned that Mary and others definitely perceived Tom as being in over his head and as trying to hide that from others. Mary shared the organization chart (see Figure 37.2) identifying the key players in the organizational structure and conveyed her understanding about who was complaining about Tom and how the communication loops worked.

It seemed that Susan (the HR director at the corporate headquarters [HQ]) and Ken (Tom's direct supervisor, who was also located at corporate HQ) had received most of the complaints directly and indirectly from one of Tom's direct reports (his administrative assistant, Kerry) and from two members of his business team (Steve, who reports to Susan, and Diane, who reports to the corporate finance director at HQ). Also, the last company 360-degree feedback survey on Tom (which Mary, Susan, and Ken had all seen and which they shared with me) was replete with numerous disparaging comments to go along with the dismal quantitative ratings. As it turned out, Mary was seeking an executive coach for Tom at Susan and Ken's request, who would be paying the bill. They had discussed the matter at length internally and had already decided on this course of action.

I related the coaching options I was prepared to offer Mary: (a) Greg Pennington, in the event that a race and gender match was desired; (b) a senior colleague from the city where Tom was located to provide geographical convenience; or (c) me. Mary felt that I would be a very good fit with Tom, and she wanted to proceed with her recommendation of me to Susan and Ken. I agreed to take the next step. In my mind, that meant moving my point of contact from a referring professional at company headquarters to the two primary sponsors who were requesting the coaching intervention: Ken (Tom's boss) and Susan (the HR director for field operations).

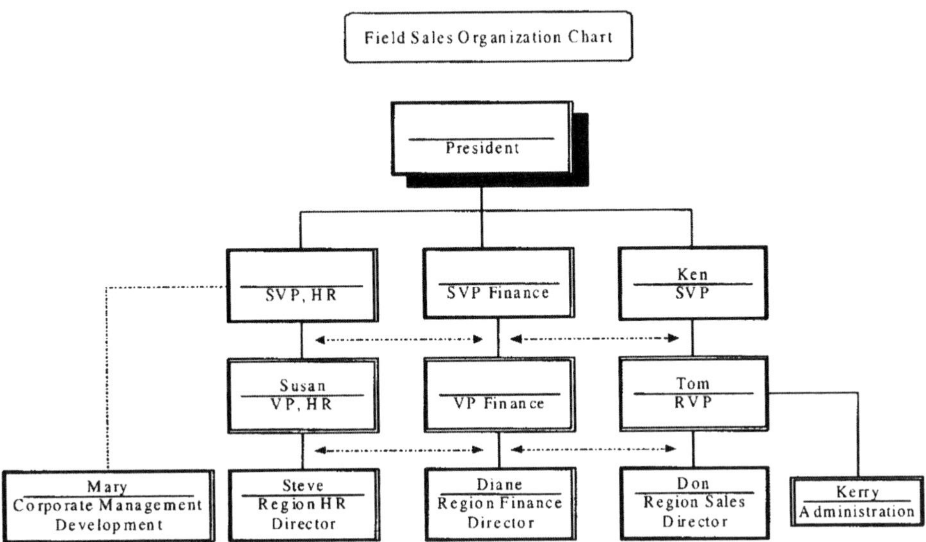

FIGURE 37.2. Field sales organization chart. SVP = senior vice president; HR = human resources; VP = vice president; RVP = regional vice president.

THE PROPOSED COACHING PROGRAM

Mary asked if I could provide an outline for a coaching program with Tom. I understood Mary's need to get something in writing that would outline the scope and costs of the assignment. Before agreeing, I explained the desirability of careful alignment among the principal stakeholders in the coaching context and a thorough assessment before finalizing any coaching plan. To achieve that alignment and assessment, I proposed two meetings. First, I wanted to meet with Ken and Susan to hear their perspectives about the situation directly. Second, I proposed a four-way meeting with Ken (Tom's manager), Susan (the HR director), Tom, and me. The goal for that meeting was to discuss the reasons for establishing a coaching program for Tom and the method, expectations, and reporting parameters for it. After Mary agreed to convey those initial steps to Ken and Susan, I drafted a document summarizing the presenting situation as I understood it, the desired objectives for the coaching work with Tom, success measures, and the 10-step approach I would likely take along with the fee estimate for the work.

The objectives of the proposed coaching program included reference to the benefits or value the organization would gain from the program and were as follows:

1. Significant improvement in Tom's credibility, respect, and effectiveness.
2. Enhanced self-awareness regarding the impact of Tom's decisions and actions on the members of his management team and in the eyes of his boss.
3. Improved morale among the members of his management team.
4. A significant decrease in complaints and concerns expressed to Tom's boss, Ken, and the regional HR director, Steve.

The summary document indicated that the attainment of these objectives would be measured though a 3-month progress check-in with Tom's boss and members of the management team and through a quantitative and interview-based 360-degree feedback process conducted 6 months after the start of the program. In addition, Tom's retention in the role and in the company were set as success measures because these were explicit concerns expressed by Mary in her initial call.

The method and deliverables I outlined in the coaching summary contained the following 10 steps:

1. An initial meeting with Ken, Susan, and me to hear their concerns about Tom and their desired objectives as well as to prepare for a

meeting with Tom to present the coaching program.

2. A four-way conference with Ken, Susan, Tom, and me to establish alignment and clarity about the purpose, method, expectations, and reporting parameters of the coaching program.
3. An individual meeting between Tom and me to begin building our coaching partnership and to conduct an initial assessment of Tom's strengths and development needs.
4. Interviews with selected members of the regional management team to gather perspectives relevant to the coaching objectives.
5. A feedback and developmental planning meeting with Tom to summarize assessment results and to draft an initial development plan.
6. Monthly coaching sessions with Tom conducted in person and supplemented by telephone consultation focused on the execution of his development plan.
7. Bimonthly written progress reports summarizing coaching contacts and agreements sent to Tom, Ken, and Susan.
8. Gauging progress through a custom-designed progress dashboard, a five-question survey to assess perceived progress toward program objectives during and after the program.
9. A final quality and satisfaction check with Tom, Ken, Susan, and Mary about the coaching program.
10. Six- and 12-month follow-up after the completion of the coaching program to determine the sustainability of developmental progress.

Mary presented the proposed coaching program to Ken and Susan, who approved it, and a date was set 2 weeks later to begin implementation of Step 1.

IMPLEMENTATION OF THE COACHING PROGRAM

Step 1: The Initial Meeting With Ken and Susan (February)

At an airline club in the city where Tom worked, I met with Ken and Susan to hear directly from each of them about the circumstances that led to their request to Mary to identify a coach for Tom. I started by asking them to provide some background about Tom's history with the company, the business context within which he was operating, and their concerns regarding his effectiveness as the head of the region. They explained that Tom had been recruited from another large consumer products company, where he had rapidly risen to a senior management role less than 5 years after completing his graduate work in management from a prominent U.S. university. In addition to his prior experience and accomplishments, Tom was an attractive executive recruit because, as an African American, including him in the executive ranks advanced an important company diversity goal. Once on board, he was placed in a developmental role where he could gain exposure to the company's field sales organization personnel. Within a year, he was promoted to the regional vice president's job he now occupied.

The region Tom was asked to lead had a recent history of mediocre performance results. Tom's predecessor had been in his role for more than 10 years and was well liked. When this man retired, Ken saw the opportunity to raise the performance expectations for the region and to put someone in the job who could drive the desired results. Tom was eager to deliver and began his tenure by making some personnel changes that were not at all popular. Soon afterward, complaints about Tom's management style and leadership effectiveness started to find their way to Ken and Susan, much as Mary had related. A principal concern was their perception that Tom seemed more interested in advancing his own career by carefully cultivating relationships with the senior-most executives in the company than in building constructive relationships with his regional management team. According to Ken and Susan, when problems would arise within the region, Tom never accepted responsibility for them but would always attribute the problems to the failure of others to execute their jobs properly. They clearly felt that Tom needed to take ownership of the problems and to concentrate on "managing down" as well as he was "managing up." In their view, he had to repair seriously damaged trust, respect, and credibility in his leadership or the company risked losing key members of his management team.

I reflected my understanding of Ken and Susan's communication and desired objectives back to them, and we agreed upon a plan to implement the coaching steps outlined above. As I inquired about the organizational context into which Tom was placed in the region, it became apparent to Ken and Susan that one factor that was contributing to the dissatisfaction with Tom was that he had been asked to change the status quo and significantly improve bottom-line performance when he was given the assignment. Also, there had not been much ongoing contact between Ken and Tom outside of regular management conference calls involving all of the regional vice presidents. When I asked Ken what he was prepared to do differently to support Tom's improvement, he agreed to increase the frequency of his contact with Tom to permit collaborative discussion about the challenging issues related to the region's change process.

The last agenda item for our meeting was a discussion about how my coaching services would be introduced to Tom. It was clear to me that Ken had not previously communicated his concerns very candidly or directly to Tom, and both Ken and Susan agreed that this would be essential in order for Tom to know exactly where he stood and to engender the appropriate motivation for coaching. We laid out a communication sequence that included a statement by Ken of Tom's value to the company, direct feedback about his performance to date, and the concerns Ken had. The coaching program steps and process would then be explained along with the parameters of confidentiality.

Step 2: The Four-Way Meeting With Tom (February)

We met at a restaurant near Tom's office immediately after our conference at the airport. There, I laid eyes on Tom for the first time. He was a tall, athletically built, impeccably dressed Black man in his early 30s. I made a mental note that there seemed to be tension in all of us, knowing that there would be some difficult things said to Tom that he had not directly been told before. The comfortable setting eased the tension a bit, and reflecting our previous discussion, Ken began with a number of comments about the difficult situation that Tom was presented with in the region. After affirming the company's commitment to Tom, Ken communicated several concerns about Tom's leadership actions that he had directly observed and that had been reported to him by others. Susan added commentary from feedback that had come to her through the HR director in the region. Ken and Susan's comments to Tom conveyed the same content they and Mary had expressed to me earlier but were stated with less negative valence and seriousness than before. It became readily apparent that one area for improvement was the clarity of communication between Ken and Tom. I intervened by asking Ken and Susan to state how serious the situation actually was, forcing them to speak with more candor and directness than before. Tom finally got to hear the depth of the concerns about him and stiffened visibly in his chair. He responded by expressing his appreciation for their frankness and his willingness to address the concerns. Ken then introduced the coaching program, and I provided details about the sequence of steps and about how I envisioned us working together. We all agreed upon my providing regular updates of our work to Tom, Ken, and Susan at least every other month. Tom and I then scheduled two 2-hour blocks of time, one that afternoon and one on the following day to begin the next step of the process.

Step 3: The One-on-One Meeting With Tom (February)

We met in the afternoon at a hotel near his office to respect Tom's request that we not meet in his office. At this point, he wanted to avoid any questions that would arise about my presence at field headquarters. We began by talking about the meeting we had had with Ken and Susan and about the coaching relationship we were embarking upon. I shared some personal and professional biographical information with Tom and related the history of my contacts with Mary, Ken, and Susan. Tom offered some criticism about Ken's lack of communication and candor and wondered if there were political dynamics that might be contributing to perceptions about him. I decided to share my opinion that the company's diversity goals were undoubtedly a factor that influenced Tom's placement in his position and the company's commitment to his success. We then had a candid discussion about how Tom's race might be influencing perceptions of him and his feelings about it. He expressed appreciation for my candor and willingness to discuss the subject of race. I believe that my choice to open that topic with Tom greatly helped to quickly establish rapport, trust, and a working alliance. I pledged to offer Tom whatever I could to help him build his leadership effectiveness.

I spent the rest of the afternoon listening to Tom tell a detailed life and career history. I learned that he grew up in a blended family with nine siblings in a small manufacturing town. He excelled in school subjects and in athletics through dedicated and diligent effort. Working in factories during his high school years, he was introduced to structured approaches to the execution of work and contributed to family finances as well. He was admitted to a top-tier university on a full athletic scholarship and became a starting player on the varsity football team as a freshman. The academic and athletic challenges that Tom took on moving from his small high school and town to a major university were formidable. Tom met the challenges with long hours of hard work, perseverance, and the support of a girlfriend who ultimately became his wife. After college, Tom was recruited by a large consumer products company that trained and placed him in their sales organization. Applying the same relentless drive and structured discipline that had always served him well, Tom was promoted quickly through the ranks to several management positions that usually involved leading others who were significantly older than him. Concurrent with his work, he undertook and completed an MBA degree. After several years, Tom was recruited to a Fortune 100 company, where he worked in sales management before joining his current employer. He then told of his rapid orientation, the assigning of a mentor who was not regarded in particularly high esteem in the company as a whole, and the early experiences of managing his region. He reported having several weak players whom he changed out and having put in some process disciplines to hold people accountable. On the personal front, he was attending to the many details that go along with a cross-country relocation and the move into a new home. Embarrassed about having to spend so much time with these personal matters and not wanting to set a bad example to others, he would sometimes tell his assistant to tell others that he was "in the field" when he was taking care of personal business. When the time came for the annual company 360-degree feedback survey, Tom's management team and direct reports skewered him. A few months later he got the call from Ken to meet with him, Susan, and an executive coach at the restaurant, and our conversation had come full circle.

After Tom finished telling his personal and career history, I reflected on and tried to synthesize both the information I had heard and the perceptions that I had formed during our few hours together. Even though we had already used up the time we had allotted for that afternoon, I asked Tom if he wanted to hear some immediate impressions or to wait until the next day. After such a comprehensive self-revelation, Tom was anxious for some immediate reactions, so I agreed to share my initial assessment. I told Tom that I was genuinely impressed by his journey and felt privileged to now be a part of it. His was a story of persistence, of meeting and overcoming adversity, and of high achievement through a steady, unwavering commitment to the accomplishment of his goals. At the same time, his vocabulary and verbal expression belied his postbaccalaureate education level. Frequently "in over his head," Tom had learned to disguise very understandable knowledge and skill deficits through the bravura that was the default behavior in the male-dominated business and athletic arenas in which he was playing. The accelerated rate of Tom's career had also deprived him of some important developmental experiences that can only come from time in grade. His achievements had been highest in situations where there was a high degree of structure and a focus on the repeated execution of tasks. Now, in a new company with a culture he had not yet learned, he had taken on a senior leadership position with an organization with more than a thousand employees and an annual revenue goal of half a billion dollars. There was a tremendous amount of knowledge about the business that he needed to learn, and his leadership position called for some different skills than the tactical task execution roles he had been in before. He had also been placed in a context that demanded significant organizational change. In his first year, Tom had made several management blunders and, in the eyes of others, tried to pass accountability for these errors to them. While he always did what he believed was needed to improve the performance of his region, he often kept his own counsel and seemed to act without the input or involvement of other key figures in the organization. To make matters worse, he was perceived as a personal pet of the senior HR executive and the president of the company, who were trying to give support to Tom as one of the few members of the executive ranks with minority status. Taken collectively, an underdeveloped skill set, covering mistakes by blaming others, and perceived favoritism by the company's senior-most leaders seemed to me to be a recipe for executive disaster.

My verbal assessment report to Tom was honest, direct, and included mention of strengths and areas for development. He recorded notes of some comments in his electronic organizer. Tom told me that my assessment felt very accurate to him and asked me what the prognosis was for his present situation. I told him that I could not offer an opinion about that before meeting the key members of his management team but that his personal attributes, character, and high level of motivation definitely made him a great candidate for coaching and excellent developmental progress. I stated my willingness to work with him and repeated my pledge to offer anything I could to support his growth as a manager and as a leader. We shook hands and agreed to get together again in the morning to discuss how we would proceed with Tom's development program.

The next morning, I told Tom that I believed that the coaching plan ought to assist him in making a turnaround with his management team in the short term and to support his growth and development as a senior-level leader and manager for the longer term. As a first step to help with the turnaround, we decided that it would be useful for me to spend time alone with the four key members of his management group to solicit their perceptions about Tom as a leader and manager. Doing this would round out my assessment of Tom given that I had already spoken with his boss (Ken) and two peers (Mary and Susan). After these discussions, I would have a better grasp of the landscape within which Tom was operating and could gauge their readiness to accept changes in his behavior. Tom agreed, and we discussed how Tom would introduce me in a way that would be most constructive. We settled on five elements he would communicate to his team:

1. As a result of some feedback he received from Ken and Susan, an executive coach has been offered to assist him in his development as the regional vice president. (This would let his team know that their concerns and complaints had been heard and were being addressed.)
2. Ken and Susan have affirmed the company's commitment to him in his position. (This statement conveys support for Tom from the corporation and that they would be wise to make some effort to work with him.)
3. He was sincerely interested in addressing any concerns about his leadership and was very committed to developing his capability. (This states Tom's commitment to improve and sets an example about the importance of development.)
4. He would need their help both in understanding his strengths and development needs and in getting ongoing feedback. Toward this end, ask them to meet with his coach and share their candid views related to his leadership and development. (This invites his team to become collaborative partners in his development and reflects the reality that he will have a hard time turning things around without their cooperation and support.)
5. Thank them for their assistance and convey awareness of how important they are to the success of the region.

I also asked Tom to send me a copy of his most recent performance review from Ken. Before leaving, I gave Tom several dates on which he could schedule the meetings with me and his key managers and told him I would mail him a written summary of this first stage of our work, with copies to Ken and Susan. When I returned to my office the next day, I constructed a three-page summary describing the highlights of the meetings the day before along with my initial assessment of Tom and the agreements we made about next steps. I sent this to Tom, Ken, and Susan. In the mailing to Tom, I included a copy of Jim Collins's *Harvard Business Review* article (Collins, 2001) about what he calls "Level 5 Leadership" (humility + fierce resolve) and a copy of the *Successful Manager's Handbook* (Personnel Decisions International, 2002), with the suggestion that Tom read the sections on people and self-leadership. A week later, I received a copy of the performance review I asked Tom to send. In general, it indicated satisfactory performance on both business and people objectives. The summary contained many positive comments about Tom's first year as the regional vice president and noted a few areas for improvement, including building team unity and alignment in his management team.

Step 4: My Meetings With Tom's Management Team (March)

Within 3 weeks, I was back into the assignment, this time at the company's regional headquarters, where I was scheduled to meet individually with Diane (finance director), Kerry (administrator), Steve (HR director), and Don (sales director). Each meeting lasted between an hour and an hour and a half. I had prepared a simple structure for each meeting. To begin, I asked each person to state their understanding of the purpose of our meeting as they understood it (so I could gauge the quality of the communication that had taken place between Tom and each of them). Next, I offered some information about my background and the sequence of events to date. Third, I asked each director to provide a brief overview of his or her role and perspectives on the region. Fourth, I invited each director to offer any information that he or she thought was relevant to Tom's leadership/development and asked for elaboration, details, and specific examples from there.

Some initial caution notwithstanding, each of the directors warmed up to the task quickly and freely shared a litany of stories and observations about Tom. From Diane and Steve, most of the comments about Tom were negative: "He was not trustworthy" (with examples cited); "He was most concerned about making himself look good"; and "He came in acting like a know-it-all when he did not know anything" were representative comments. Kerry was more balanced in her perspective, offering contrasts between Tom and his predecessor, whom she also worked for. Don was mostly positive, having been promoted into his current job by Tom. He reported that Tom had made some early mistakes and had shifted the power balance in the management team, taking decision authority in many areas that had previously been delegated. Those moves had not been popular with those who lost power, especially in finance and HR. Don indicated that Tom seemed more comfortable acknowledging what he did not know and had made some good personnel decisions in his organization (e.g., his own promotion to the sales director's position).

I ended each meeting by conveying my appreciation for the comments and assistance that I had been given. I also suggested that Tom's development was something that they might benefit from and that there would be future opportunities for them to contribute to it, planting another seed to enlist their collaboration. I stopped by Tom's office before leaving to let him know the meetings had gone well and to finalize the arrangements for a dinner meeting that night to discuss our next steps. Just as I arrived, he was beginning a conference call with his boss and the other regional vice presidents from across the country. He invited me to listen in on the call, which I did for its full duration—about an hour. I listened for the things that seemed important to Ken and how Tom responded to his boss and colleagues. Most of the talk was about performance to plan. Tom picked his spots to contribute and did so confidently, having moved his region from one of the bottom positions in the ranking to the middle of the pack. He entered certain notes and due dates in his organizer throughout the call. After the call, I offered some immediate positive feedback about how he had handled himself. In an effort to broaden Tom's perspective, I also engaged him in an exercise to identify what Ken's boss was holding Ken accountable for and to consider the implications of that on his interactions with Ken.

Step 5: Generating Tom's Development Plan (March)

At dinner, I summarized the themes from my meetings that day with Tom's team—the prevailing need to build trust, own his previous errors, and generate alignment in a fractionated team—without indicating who had said what. I offered my judgment that these three themes ought to form the central core of his development plan for the next 6 months. I told him that I thought he could make significant improvements in his working partnerships with his business team but that it would be difficult and probably take 6 to 12 months to really turn things around. I recommended three-way conferences with the two of us meeting with each of the directors to redress past missteps and agree upon working guidelines to move forward. I suggested an outline of communication points to make in setting up the three-way conferences, and we agreed that additional developmental action steps could be identified after they were completed. We agreed to arrange the readministration of his company's 360-degree feedback survey and to track his progress through a "progress dashboard" composed of items specifically designed around his development agenda. I shared some ideas about the processes relevant to the leadership of organizational change (Winum, Ryterband, & Stephenson, 1997). We also talked about the readings I had sent Tom. He particularly responded to the idea of leading with humility from the Collins article. Tom shared several insights and showed genuine enthusiasm about the possibility of changing his approach to leading his team and region. From my perspective, a tangible shift was occurring in him. This shift would need to be made in a manner that fit with both the needs of his region and the corporate culture of the organization.

Steps 6 and 7: Implementing the Development Plan (April–October)

Because it was about the time of the year when Tom's company normally executed its 360-degree feedback process, he was able to have the corporate HR department send forms to his raters right away. We decided to hold off on the three-way conferences with his directors until he got his results back. Four weeks later, Tom mailed me his results and we scheduled the three-way conference meetings the next week and time for the two of us to discuss his 360-degree feedback.

Tom's 360-degree feedback results were below the norms for his peer group and company norms in nearly every category but were significantly better than the ratings he had received in his previous feedback survey, especially among his direct reports. Tom was rated highest on items related to valuing diversity, leveraging people with different perspectives, and demonstrating competitive passion. The lowest rated items related to Tom's technical expertise, creating long-term strategies, and being trusted by others he works with. This feedback was consistent with my assessment of Tom as gleaned from the comments of everyone I had spoken with thus far.

Tom and I got together the next week to discuss his 360-degree feedback results and plan for the three-way meetings with his directors. He was pleased with the improved ratings compared with the previous year's survey and accepted that there was still lots of room for improvement. We agreed that the three-way conferences would provide a great opportunity to identify specific ways he could work on his developmental areas.

The meetings began the next morning and went quite well despite some initial apprehension and skepticism. Tom clearly stated his desire to improve his partnership with each director. He conveyed the key messages he had taken from all the feedback he had been given about his leadership impact and extended a genuine apology for mistakes he had made during his first year. He also issued a sincere invitation for additional feedback and recommendations about how he and the regional management team could best move forward.

Tom's apology and ownership of his management missteps were followed by some candid discussion about past issues. The meetings resulted in a number of concrete suggestions and explicit agreements about how Tom and each director would work differently in the future. The theme underlying most of the suggestions and agreements was to increase substantially the frequency of collaboration and communication between Tom and his management team. The goal was for Tom to invite ongoing input from his directors about key issues impacting the region and to proactively share the rationale behind key decisions, especially ones that were likely to be controversial, so that his motivations as a leader could become more transparent.

As Tom and I debriefed the meetings, he conveyed his relief about having the opportunity to discuss issues directly and about identifying specific actions he could take to improve his working relationships with his team. He stated his intention to begin taking immediate action on the agreements reached during the three-way conferences and to keep me apprised as he executed his development plan. Over the course of the next 3 months, Tom and I met twice more and spoke on the phone several times about how things were going. The substance of those contacts was focused on what he was doing differently and how his team and boss were reacting to the changes he was making. When he reported that a difficulty or miscommunication had occurred, we brainstormed ways for Tom to recover and to extract lessons learned that he could incorporate into his future management practices. Twice during this period, I sent brief reports to Ken and Susan updating them about the implementation of Tom's development plan.

Step 8: Gauging Progress (November)

As stated in the initial program outline, a customized progress dashboard was designed and distributed to the four members of the regional management team who were involved in the three-way conferences and to Ken and Susan, the program sponsors. This step occurred 6 months after the three-way conferences when Tom really began executing his development plan. There are four Likert-type items in the progress dashboard that ask observers to compare current perceptions relevant to Tom's development objectives with perceptions of him 6 months earlier. In addition, there was one open-ended question requesting any additional comments relevant to Tom's effectiveness and development as a leader. The request for progress feedback was made via e-mail and offered complete anonymity to observers about their individual responses to encourage candor. Tom was to see only a collapsed norm for each item.

Appendix 37.1 depicts the progress dashboard results with the average ratings of the six observers indicated in parentheses after each item. The ratings across all observers indicate modest improvement in perceptions on all four items compared with 6 months earlier. Responses to the open-ended question included comments that Tom was listening better to his team, noticeably working to be inclusive, and starting to gain some trust among his direct reports. At the same time, several raters remarked that the attainment of trust and credibility among the members of his management team would take time. Tom was encouraged to maintain his efforts and to continue seeking feedback about his impact as a leader.

Steps 9 and 10: The Quality Check and Follow-Up (December–Present)

One year after the initial call from Mary, I sent a formal request for feedback to Tom, Ken, and Susan using the RHR Client Feedback Survey (see Appendix 37.2). This brief survey has 10 items that inquire about satisfaction with services provided, the results of services, and the return on investment realized by the organization. There are both forced-choice and open-ended questions on the survey. All responses indicated agreement or strong agreement with the forced-choice items. The write-in comments were very complementary about expectations being met and the partnership that was established to enhance Tom's effectiveness. A second progress dashboard is scheduled for distribution to the same observer group in April to determine how well Tom's progress has been sustained.

DISCUSSION

This case study underscores several principles that I have found to be critical in most executive coaching and development endeavors. The first of these is that effective executive leadership results from the interaction between the person-specific attributes and capabilities of the executive and the context in which the executive is operating (see chap. 15, this volume). Consequently, to be successful, executive coaches need to focus assessment and intervention efforts on both the attributes and behavioral capabilities of the executive *and* the leadership context. This is especially true in cases where the executive is faltering. In the present case, Tom's initial difficulties and near derailment were certainly impacted by his lack of experience in enterprise-wide change management and also by his inclination to hide his inexperience rather than to openly acknowledge what was all too apparent to those he was responsible for leading. In addition, the change agenda that Tom's boss, Ken, had charged him with leading had not been made explicit to anyone else in the region. Tom had not worked previously within such a strong matrix management structure, and his skill deficits in building alliances with critical team members over whom he did not have direct authority contributed to negative perceptions of him as a leader. To effectively intervene, the coaching program with Tom needed to develop his understanding of the intricate interpersonal and business context he was placed into and to develop insights and greater self-awareness about his leadership actions within that context.

A second coaching principle that this case study reaffirms is the importance of achieving candor and alignment between the individual being coached and key organizational stakeholders regarding the purpose, method, and desired outcomes of the coaching work. Prior to the four-way meeting with Ken, Susan, Tom, and me, Tom did not have a clear understanding about how concerned his superiors were about his leadership performance and how critical it was that he take responsibility for changing the perceptions that had emerged of him as a leader. Not only did the four-way meeting mobilize Tom's attention and motivation, it established an explicit alliance regarding his development and success. This alliance engaged Ken as a partner in Tom's development agenda, resulted in more frequent contact between Tom and Ken, and provided guidelines for ongoing dialogue for them about the leadership challenges in the region. Also, the subject of how Tom's race had influenced his placement into his position and the political implications of his success or failure had never been discussed openly with Tom. I believe that my willingness to do this, at Greg Pennington's suggestion, significantly deepened Tom's trust in me and catapulted our coaching partnership. Furthermore, the three-way conferences that were conducted with Tom's management team included them in the development alliance. The improvement that Tom was able to make regarding his perceived leadership effectiveness was aided by enlisting his colleagues and direct reports as allies in the process.

The use of a progress metric and quality review was very well received by Tom and the executive sponsors of this case, Ken and Susan. They appreciated the identification of specific objectives for the coaching program and a systemic method to determine its effectiveness. Although the tools used were quite simple, they provided some empirical data consistent with recent recommendations in the literature to gauge the impact of consulting services (Kincaid & Gordick, 2003; Winum, 2003; Winum, Nielsen, & Bradford, 2002). Predetermining progress reporting and a timetable for following-up on the work also facilitated adherence, a critical issue in executive coaching discussed by Kilburg (see chap. 22, this volume).

A final lesson that this case teaches is the importance of incorporating proactive developmental support in the career planning and placement of high-potential executives. In their effort to attract and retain individuals with the potential to assume senior leadership positions and to meet organizational diversity goals, companies sometimes place managers and executives in "stretch" jobs that provide exposure to new challenges and opportunities for growth. This was certainly the case with Tom. It would have been very useful for the organization and for Tom to incorporate a well-designed orientation and integration program to support his transition into the company. I made the recommendation to Susan that she take the initiative to develop and champion an on-boarding process for all key hires to support and accelerate their integration and success in the company.

As I reflect on this coaching program, I feel privileged for the opportunity we consulting psychologists have to work with leaders like Tom and to make a tangible impact on their lives and the many people they affect in their executive positions within organizations.

APPENDIX 37.1

Customized Progress Dashboard

Name of Individual:
Date of Feedback:

Please indicate progress made by underlining your response to each of the questions below:

1. Compared with six months ago, has this individual's executive credibility, respect and effectiveness increased (underline 5, 6 or 7), diminished (underline 1, 2 or 3) or remained about the same (underline 4)?

   Diminished 1 2 3 4 5 6 7 Increased (Avg. 5.5)

2. Compared with six months ago, has this individual's self-awareness regarding the impact of his decisions and actions on others increased, diminished or remained about the same?

   Diminished 1 2 3 4 5 6 7 Increased (Avg. 5.5)

3. Compared with six months ago, have favorable perceptions of this individual as a leader and manager within the organization improved, diminished or remained about the same?

   Diminished 1 2 3 4 5 6 7 Improved (Avg. 5.17)

4. Compared with six months ago, has the morale among this individual's direct reports and RBT improved, diminished or stayed about the same?

   Diminished 1 2 3 4 5 6 7 Improved (Avg. 5.67)

Please add any additional comments relevant to this individual's development as a leader and manager in the space below.

- Tom has become a strong leader. He listens well to his team and is gaining their attention and support.
- Has made progress with his team although still has a few gaps to close. It will take time for perceptions of Tom as a leader to really change.
- Much improved focus on his style with no setbacks in the last six months.
- Keep trying daily!
- Rebuilding trust and credibility will take time but he is making progress.
- Continue to seek feedback
- Tom is working hard to be inclusive and beginning to build trust with his team.

Thank you for your responses to these questions! Please return this form directly to:
Paul C. Winum, Ph.D., 1355 Peachtree Street, Suite 1400, Atlanta, GA 30309
Phone (404-870-9160) Fax (404-870-9164) E-Mail (pwinum@rhrinternational.com)

(Appendixes continue)

APPENDIX 37.2

Client Feedback Survey

COMPANY NAME ________________	POSITION (optional) ________________
***DATES OF RHR SERVICES:* February-November 2003**	

SURVEY

	Strongly Agree	*Agree*	*Disagree*	*Strongly Disagree*	*Not Applicable*
1. I am satisfied with the quality of service RHR has provided our organization.					
2. I feel the RHR consultants working with us are true partners with us in addressing our organization's needs.					
3. The services provided by RHR to date have achieved their intended results.					
4. The RHR consultants' level of service met my expectations.					
5. Our organization's overall effectiveness increased as a result of RHR services.					
6. Our company realized a profitable return on our investment in RHR's services to us.					

ADDITIONAL COMMENTS

The primary benefits I expected to be gained from the services delivered by RHR were

____

____

____

Please comment on the benefits you and your organization actually received and their value.

____

____

____

Please offer any recommendation you have about how RHR might enhance the quality and value of its services.

____

____

____

Please provide any other comments you would like to offer regarding the quality or value of your experience with RHR.

____

____

____

Thank you for your participation. Please mail this completed survey to Dr. Patricia Weik, at 220 Gerry Drive, Wood Dale, IL 60191 or at pweik@rhrinternational.com

References

Collins, J. (2001). Level 5 leadership: The triumph of humility and fierce resolve. *Harvard Business Review*, 67–76.

Kilburg, R. R. (Ed.). (1996). Executive coaching [Special issue]. *Journal of Consulting Psychology: Practice and Research, 48*(2).

Kilburg, R. R. (1997). Coaching and executive character: Core problems and basic approaches. *Consulting Psychology Journal: Practice and Research, 49*, 281–299.

Kilburg, R. R. (2002). Shadow consultation: A reflective approach for preventing practice disasters. *Consulting Psychology Journal: Practice and Research, 54*, 75–92.

Kincaid, S. B., & Gordick, D. (2003). The return on investment of leadership development: Differentiating our discipline. *Consulting Psychology Journal: Practice and Research, 55*, 47–57.

Livers, A. B., & Caver, K. A. (2003). *Leading in black and white.* San Francisco: Jossey-Bass.

Lowman, R. L. (2001). Constructing a literature from case studies: Promises and limitations of method. *Consulting Psychology Journal: Practice and Research, 53*, 119–123.

McClenney, E. H., Jr. (1987). *How to survive when you're the only Black in the office.* Richmond, VA: Virginia Carter Printing.

Pennington, G. (2003). *Executive coaching with African American senior executives: Issues and actions.* Presented at the 2003 Midwinter Conference for the Society of Consulting Psychology, Scottsdale, AZ.

Personnel Decisions International. (2002). *Successful manager's handbook* (6th ed.). Minneapolis, MN: Author.

Schein, E. H. (2003). Five traps for consulting psychologists, or how I learned to take culture seriously. *Consulting Psychology Journal: Practice and Research, 55*, 75–83.

Thomas, D. A., & Gabarro, J. J. (1999). *Breaking through: The making of minority executives in corporate America.* Boston: Harvard Business School Press.

Winum, P. C. (2003). Developing leadership: What is distinctive about what psychologists can offer? *Consulting Psychology Journal: Practice and Research, 55*, 41–46.

Winum, P. C., & Blanton, J. (2003). *Key questions for coaches to ask referral sources to clarify value and focus.* Master Coaching Workshop at 2003 Midwinter Conference for the Society of Consulting Psychology, Scottsdale, AZ.

Winum, P. C., Nielsen, T. M., & Bradford, R. E. (2002). Assessing the impact of organizational consulting. In R. L. Lowman (Ed.), *Handbook of organizational consulting psychology* (pp. 645–667). San Francisco: Jossey-Bass.

Winum, P. C., Ryterband, E., & Stephenson, P. (1997). Helping organizations change: A model for guiding consultation. *Consulting Psychology Journal: Practice and Research, 49*, 6–16.

CHAPTER 38

EYE MOVEMENT DESENSITIZATION AND REPROCESSING: FOUR CASE STUDIES OF A NEW TOOL FOR EXECUTIVE COACHING AND RESTORING EMPLOYEE PERFORMANCE AFTER SETBACKS

Sandra Foster and Jennifer Lendl

Every few years, a novel method appears that offers consulting psychologists an innovative tool for enhancing the performance and productivity of workers in the workplace. Such a promising new intervention is the eye movement desensitization and reprocessing (EMDR) method, developed by Francine Shapiro in 1987. EMDR was introduced and first studied as a rapid treatment for anxiety and traumatic stress.

In the first empirical study of EMDR (Shapiro, 1989), victims of sexual assault and Vietnam combat veterans experienced a significant decrease in distressing symptoms—flashbacks, ruminating, sleep disturbances, and uncomfortable physiological arousal—after a single clinical session. Moreover (and relevant to consulting), the participants also described a perceptual shift: the reprocessing component of EMDR. The participants found that they could stop blaming themselves for the traumatic incidents and that they could come to terms with what had happened and move on with their lives, which they did, as indicated by follow-up reports.

Replications of Shapiro's (1989) initial investigation indicated that EMDR was more effective than other treatments in alleviating symptoms of posttraumatic stress disorder (PTSD; Boudewyns, Hyer, Peralme, Touze, & Kiel, 1995; Carlson, Chemtob, Rusnak, & Hedlund, 1995; Vaughan et al., 1994). In two controlled studies (Rothbaum, 1995; S. A. Wilson, Becker, & Tinker, 1995a) comparing EMDR with a waiting-list control condition, EMDR was more efficacious in mitigating the sequelae of traumatic incidents. In a 15-month follow-up study, S. A. Wilson and her colleagues found that 84% of the participants originally diagnosed with PTSD were sufficiently symptom-free to no longer warrant that diagnosis (S. A. Wilson, Becker, & Tinker, 1995b).

How does a method that is apparently effective with PTSD offer consulting psychologists a tool for optimizing performance of people in the workplace? As one of the initial 36 people trained in EMDR in 1990, Sandra Foster believed that layoffs, mergers, and economic downturns affected corporate leaders and their reports in many of the same ways that a critical incident traumatizes a person in a combat situation. On the basis of this assumption, we pioneered efforts to use EMDR to assist our Silicon Valley corporate clients in breaking free of the negative mental and emotional effects of stressful workplace change. We found that EMDR was a promising intervention that could be used in coaching executives and others in business to get past negative thinking and physical distress to reach optimal performance at work. We also found

This chapter was originally presented at the Division 13 meeting convened at the 104th Annual Convention of the American Psychological Association in Toronto in August 1996.

that EMDR could assist sales professionals in moving past procrastination about "cold calling" and in responding more resiliently to rejections.

Although the precise mechanism of EMDR is not yet clear, it appears that this method operates more directly on mental processing than verbal coaching alone can. It is possible that EMDR is one method, among others (e.g., electrical stimulation; Schmitt, Capo, & Boyd, 1986), that is hypothesized to promote "accelerated information processing" (Shapiro, 1995, p. 28). *Information processing,* as cognitive scientists now refer to it, was elaborated on by Freud (1919/1955) and Pavlov (1927) to describe the neurophysiological system that reacts to, stores, and makes meaning of human experiences, including those that are traumatic.

Results of recent research (Charney, Southwick, Krystal, & Deutch, 1994; Southwick, Krystal, Johnson, & Charney, 1992) suggest that trauma may alter multiple neurobiological systems, possibly resulting in neurotransmitter dysregulation. The symptoms of PTSD—flashbacks, nightmares, and intrusive thoughts—may well be the manifestations of unprocessed information that is repetitively stimulated by this dysregulation. Moreover, this pattern appears to inhibit the sufferer's resolution of the event.

Shapiro (1995) suggested that it is possible for such upsetting information to be processed to an "adaptive resolution" (p. 29), leaving a person with affect that is more neutral, accepting, or reconciled and with useful information that can be called on in future situations. Clinical reports and research on the method suggest that EMDR desensitizes traumatic incidents and facilitates the reconstructing of related maladaptive, self-referenced cognitions and that it can do so rapidly. It thus appears that EMDR may be freer of the time constraints of traditional psychotherapy or consultative coaching, which depend on verbal rather than physiologically based interventions.

In speculating how EMDR works, it may be that the eye movements in EMDR trigger a neurological mechanism that activates the accelerated information processing. Recently, Ramachandran (1995) found that involuntary eye movements were triggered by irrigating the left ear canal with cold water, an action that neurologists know will produce a stimulation of the vestibular organ and alter spatial perception. The resulting activation of the right hemisphere by the eye movements allowed Ramachandran's stroke patients to recover temporarily an awareness of their paralysis that had been denied previously. This shifting of a person's view of things may be what occurs in EMDR, along with an unusual access to memories.

As Shapiro (1995) noted, other hypotheses have been proposed to explain how EMDR might set in motion this rapid processing: (a) A dual focus on past events and present stimuli activates the rapid information processing and (b) desensitization is generated by *reciprocal inhibition* (Wolpe, 1982), which is the pairing of a relaxation response with the upsetting stimuli. Indeed, a correlation was found between the participants' physiological responses and their self-reported decreases in subjective distress (D. L. Wilson, Silver, Covi, & Foster, 1996).

The eye movements are the hallmark of EMDR, but they are only one component of a clinical method (Shapiro, 1995) that incorporates eight stages: (a) client history and case formulation; (b) preparation of the client; (c) assessing and delineating the components for reprocessing; (d) desensitization of upsetting material; (e) "installation" (Shapiro, 1995, p. 157) of the new positive cognition; (f) assessing the client's physiological state after the processing; (g) closure of the EMDR session; and (h) reevaluation of intersession emotions, cognitions, and behaviors.

We have used EMDR with more than 50 professionals in several industries. Four case studies are presented to illustrate EMDR as an executive coaching tool, as a means for assisting high-functioning professionals regain their productivity after a critical incident, and as a rapid intervention for treating a professional's performance anxiety.

METHOD

Participants

The participants were a pilot for a prominent U.S. airline, a female tenured professor in her early 50s who had voluntarily resigned her post and was seeking an executive position in the public sector, a former male chief executive officer (CEO) who was underperforming after being forced to resign, and a high-powered female office manager whose productivity and sense of efficacy were impaired after an accident. Three participants were highly functioning professionals who had experienced a perceived setback that had seriously impaired their productivity. They construed the EMDR intervention as coaching to restore their performance to the high level exhibited before the setback. The professor desired a significant career change and sought assistance for her performance anxiety about interviewing.

Measures

The intensity of physical symptoms and negative emotions was assessed at pre- and posttreatment and during the course of the EMDR sessions using Wolpe's (1982) Subjective Unit of Disturbance Scale (SUDS). Participants were asked to rate their distress on this 11-point scale (0 = *no disturbance,* 10 = *the worst disturbance you can imagine*).

Behavioral outcome measures were those that were most pertinent to each participant's goal. For example, for the pilot, the measures included whether he returned to the simulator and was cleared to fly, the number of subsequent months of flying, whether daily management tasks were completed on a specific workday (deeming it a "capably functioning day"), and the percentage of capably functioning days per total workdays each month. For the CEO, the measures included how aggressively and effectively he put together new real estate deals. For the professor, the measures included actually applying for the job about which she sought advice and how capably she handled the job interview.

Procedure

After the basic EMDR protocol, the pilot, the CEO, and the office manager were asked to describe their setback and its subsequent impairment. The professor was asked to describe her concerns about job interviewing. All participants then were prompted to specify the upsetting image and distressing emotions experienced as they recalled the incident or concern. Each was then asked, "What current negative belief about yourself do you think of when you recall this incident (or concern)?" For the CEO, his negative belief was "I'm not intelligent enough [to have prevented my being terminated]."

Once the participant described the incident and elaborated the negative self-referenced belief, each was asked, "How would you prefer to think about this incident now as a new positive belief about yourself?" This last question initiated the cognitive restructuring process, an integral element of EMDR. A rating scale devised by Shapiro (1989) was used to assess the believability of this new belief (1 = *not at all true,* 7 = *totally true*). For the CEO, the new positive cognition was "I'm smart enough for what I need to do for life's decisions"; the initial believability rating was 6.

In accordance with the EMDR protocol, one of us asked each participant to again think of the upsetting incident and negative belief and to "follow my fingers with your eyes" to voluntarily produce the eye movements, or saccades. After a set of saccades, usually 12 to 24 multidirectional eye movements, the participant was asked, "What came to mind just then?" After the first set of saccades, the CEO commented that "I wanted to leave with dignity and I couldn't" as he recalled the circumstances surrounding his departure.

After noting the participant's comments, one of us then asked him or her, in a neutral manner, to "think of that" and had him or her perform another set of eye movements. This process was repeated until the distressing incident or concern was desensitized, which was determined by a SUDS rating of 0 (or as low as the participant believed it could go) and the reconstructing of the negative, self-referenced belief. The believability of the new positive belief was assessed periodically during the latter stages of EMDR. When the participant's rating reached a 7 and felt "totally true," this new positive self-referenced belief was paired with the disturbing incident or concern during a final set of saccades.

In addition, a modification was made to the basic EMDR protocol. After the desensitization and reprocessing of the upsetting incident were complete, each participant was asked to visualize his or her desired outcome. This mental rehearsal of envisioned goals was then "installed" with sets of eye movements.

Case Study Outcomes

The CEO. This 59-year-old man requested coaching, saying he was depressed and underperforming after being forced to resign his position as CEO of a large real estate development firm 4 years earlier. The incident caused him to feel despondent and to doubt his ability to put together the far-reaching deals he had been successful at in the past. He was troubled by nightmares and intrusive thoughts about the way he left his company and reported feeling "stuck and upset" about the actions of the board of directors. He chided himself for not having the wherewithal to prevent his termination.

His initial SUDS rating of 8 had dropped to 6 by the end of the first 120-minute session. The negative belief ("I'm not intelligent enough . . .") had begun shifting to an understanding that his termination was more of a power struggle than an indictment of his abilities. During the processing, he realized that there had been warning signs of difficulties within his organization. (Indeed, after he left, there was an investigation of the company by two federal agencies and costly penalties were assessed.) After two subsequent 90-minute sessions, his SUDS rating had reached 0, and his comment was that the incident and its aftermath felt like "part of the distant past." By the end of Session 3, he felt resolved that he could use this event as an experience that could inform his future decisions. His new positive belief felt "very true" and had a rating of "6+."

In the months after the EMDR intervention, the CEO reported that he had quickened his work pace and was making decisions he had shelved for months. At the time of this writing (15 months after the coaching), he was actively involved in a large deal involving the development of major hotels in several U.S. locations. He was optimistic about the outcome.

The professor. This participant sought coaching for performance anxiety about interviewing the next day. She was tenured at a top university and was well-known in her field. She had never applied for a position after her original "job talk" for her academic position. She earnestly desired to explore life "outside the Ivory Tower" and was seeking an executive position in the public sector. Her self-talk about the process included several negative statements, such as "I'll come across as arrogant," "I'll be ill at ease," and "I'll panic in this unknown situation." A single 120-minute session of EMDR allowed her to process her negative belief of "I'm not in control" and her anxiety about interviewing (a SUDS rating of 5) and change it to the new positive belief of "I can control my emotions" and no anxiety (a SUDS rating of 0).

The next day, she went to the interview. She later reported that she had performed well but had concluded that the position was not the best match for her. The agency notified her that she was the company's second choice and gave her encouraging feedback about her presentation and skills. Without hesitation, she pursued other positions and accepted one that better suited her.

The airline pilot. This 53-year-old pilot with a major U.S. airline was preparing to advance to second-officer grade and to fly an aircraft new to him. He had 26 years of service with his company and sought this advancement as a way of challenging himself. Before an incident during which he got upset and left the simulator, he had experienced 2 years of personal difficulties and was separated from his wife of many years. One of his two children had been using street drugs for some time and could no longer attend college classes or complete his part-time job duties. The pilot requested medical leave, aware that he was too anxious to return to the simulator. The employee assistance program counselor making the referral told us that the pilot would have to retire for medical reasons if he did not pass the proficiency check (PC) by the end of his leave period.

Before the pilot began the performance coaching, we spent 12 hours assisting him in understanding and responding effectively to the immediate crisis of his child's needing drug treatment. Only after this intervention did he report that he could concentrate on preparing for his PC.

He then participated in 7.5 hours of EMDR-integrated performance coaching in five sessions spanning 4 weeks. His initial SUDS rating increased to 10 as he recalled being in the simulator, feeling panicky, and drawing a blank on the information he had to demonstrate. He also noted thinking that the instructor was "disgusted with" him and his performance. His negative beliefs were "I'm unprepared, ... I'm inadequate," and "I'll be fired for incompetence."

During the processing, he realized that he was in fact unprepared because it had been difficult for him to concentrate enough to be able to study. He reported that he understood he had been procrastinating about returning to the simulator because he feared that he would "blow it" again and would be embarrassed about failing the PC. He also realized that he expected a perfect performance and that this unattainable end result contributed to his procrastination.

His new positive belief was "That [the PC] wasn't so bad. I can do it"; the believability rating was 5. His visualization of his desired outcome was seeing himself leaving the simulator, smiling, and knowing with confidence that he had passed and would soon be back in the cockpit. By the end of his last EMDR session, the pilot's SUDS rating had decreased to 4, but his feeling was one of being "enthusiastic" about the PC, "focused and in charge." (In high-performance situations, we have noted that the SUDS rating may not reach 0 at any point because of the consultee's perceived need for alertness and some adrenaline to be present.)

Five days after the final session, the pilot passed his PC, demonstrating outstanding skill according to his evaluator. Another proficiency check was scheduled 4 months later. The participant reported that he did not feel the need to do additional preparation beforehand. His comment about this second successful PC was, "I knocked 'em dead!" At the time of this writing, he had been flying without anxiety or mishap for 11 consecutive months.

The office manager. This 44-year-old woman approached Sandra Foster when she was giving a speech and stated, "I need your help in getting back to what I do well." Three months before, the participant, who had a highly successful work history of office management and professional-practice marketing, had been injured in an accident.

The participant had been traumatized by the accident that injured her head, shoulder, and back. She was taken to an emergency room, treated, and released, but headaches and back pain persisted. More troubling to her was the anxiety she continued to experience and the loss of confidence about her work. She had difficulty concentrating because of intrusive thoughts about the accident. She felt angry that this had happened to her and distraught that she was not performing at her customary high level. After the accident, she became phobic about being in any situation that resembled the accident.

The participant completed the Impact of Events Scale (IES), a self-report measure of PTSD symptom severity, and the State version of the State–Trait Anxiety Inventory, Form Y-1 (STAI). Her pretreatment score on the IES was 54. Horowitz, Wilner, and Alvarez (1979) found an average score of 44 for those who had experienced a traumatic event. The participant's score of 54 thus fell in the severe symptom range. Her pretreatment score on the STAI was 70, indicating serious state anxiety. In studies of the measure reported in the manual (Spielberger, Gorsuch, Lushene, Vagg, & Jacobs, 1983), the mean state score for normal women aged 40–49 years was 36.03 (SD = 11.07).

Her beginning negative belief was "I'm helpless. I can't think"; her initial SUDS rating was 8. At the outset, her new positive belief was "My survival instinct comes to my rescue." During the course of the processing, this belief evolved to "My intellect will see me through and I will be successful"; the final believability rating was 7. As her final SUDS rating fell to 0, she reported feeling "wonderful" about her capabilities.

After 10 hours of EMDR spanning 33 days and five sessions, her score on the IES had dropped to 34. She checked "often" on the IES item, "I avoided letting myself get upset when I thought about it or was reminded of it." Her posttreatment score on the STAI had decreased to 20, indicating she was feeling much calmer and seldom bothered by intrusive thoughts or nightmares. In terms of behavioral outcomes, her percentage of capably functioning workdays had increased from none to 95% at post-treatment. She also spontaneously reported that her headaches were less frequent and less painful by the end of the final EMDR session. Three weeks later, she flew "fairly comfortably" on a commercial flight. Encouraged by this, she made plans for a vacation that entailed both flying and a cruise.

DISCUSSION

Results of the four cases presented here are encouraging and warrant further investigation. Future researchers should include empirical investigations that control for the methodological weaknesses inherent in case studies, particularly experimenter effects and lack of comparison groups. Nevertheless, the data from these and other single-case studies are promising with respect to specific issues that many professionals face: coming back resiliently from business losses, separating personal problems from business challenges, alleviating performance anxiety and fear of cold calling, and enhancing overall performance.

References

Boudewyns, P. A., Hyer, L. A., Peralme, L., Touze, J., & Kiel, A. (1995, August). *Eye movement desensitization and reprocessing and exposure therapy in the treatment of combat related PTSD: An early look.* Paper presented at the 103rd Annual Convention of the American Psychological Association, New York.

Carlson, J. G., Chemtob, C. M., Rusnak, K., & Hedlund, N. L. (1995, June). *A controlled study of EMDR and biofeedback assisted relaxation for the treatment of PTSD.* Paper presented at the Fourth European Conference on Traumatic Stress, Paris.

Charney, D. S., Southwick, S. M., Krystal, J. H., & Deutch, A. Y. (1994). Neurobiological mechanisms of PTSD. In M. M. Murburg (Ed.), *Catecholamine function in posttraumatic stress disorder: Emerging concepts* (Progress in Psychiatry, No. 42). Washington, DC: American Psychiatric Press.

Freud, S. (1955). Introduction to psychoanalysis and the war neuroses. In J. Strachey (Ed. & Trans.), *The standard edition of the complete psychological works of Sigmund Freud* (Vol. 17). London: Hogarth Press. (Original work published 1919)

Horowitz, M., Wilner, N., & Alvarez, W. (1979). Impact of Events Scale: A measure of subjective stress. *Psychosomatic Medicine, 41,* 209–218.

Pavlov, I. E. (1927). *Conditioned reflexes.* New York: Liveright.

Ramachandran, V. S. (1995). Anosognosia in parietal lobe syndrome. *Consciousness and Cognition, 4,* 22–51.

Rothbaum, B. O. (1995, November). *A controlled study of EMDR for PTSD.* Paper presented at the 29th Annual Meeting of the Association for the Advancement of Behavior Therapy, Washington, DC.

Schmitt, R., Capo, T., & Boyd, E. (1986). Cranial electrotherapy stimulation as a treatment for anxiety in chemically dependent persons. *Alcoholism: Clinical and Experimental Research, 10,* 158–160.

Shapiro, E. (1989). Eye movement desensitization: A new treatment for post-traumatic stress disorder. *Journal of Behavior Therapy and Experimental Psychiatry, 20,* 211–217.

Shapiro, E. (1995). *Eye movement desensitization and reprocessing.* New York: Guilford Press.

Southwick, S. M., Krystal, J. H., Johnson, D. R., & Charney, D. S. (1992). Neurobiology of posttraumatic stress disorder. *American Psychiatric Review, 11,* 347–367.

Spielberger, C. D., Gorsuch, R. L., Lushene, R., Vagg, P. R., & Jacobs, G. A. (1983). *Manual for the State–Trait Anxiety Inventory (Form Y).* Palo Alto, CA: Consulting Psychologists Press.

Vaughan, K., Armstrong, M. S., Gold, R., O'Connor, N., Jenneke, W., & Tarrier, N. (1994). A trial of eye movement desensitization compared to image habituation training and applied muscle relaxation in posttraumatic stress disorder. *Journal of Behavior Therapy and Experimental Psychiatry, 25,* 283–291.

Wilson, D. L., Silver, S. M., Covi, W. G., & Foster, S. (1996). Eye movement desensitization and reprocessing: Effectiveness and autonomic correlates. *Journal of Behavior Therapy and Experimental Psychiatry, 27,* 219–229.

Wilson, S. A., Becker, L. A., & Tinker, R. H. (1995a). Eye movement desensitization and reprocessing (EMDR) treatment for psychologically traumatized individuals. *Journal of Consulting and Clinical Psychology,* 63, 928–937.

Wilson, S. A., Becker, L. A., & Tinker, R. H. (1995b). *Fifteen-month follow-up of a controlled study.* Paper presented at the annual meeting of the American Psychiatric Association, Miami, FL.

Wolpe, J. (1982). *The practice of behavior therapy.* Elmsford, NY: Pergamon Press.

CHAPTER 39

EXECUTIVE COACHING FROM THE EXECUTIVE'S PERSPECTIVE

John H. Stevens Jr.

During his 2003 tenure as president of American Psychological Association's (APA's) Division 13 Society of Consulting Psychology, and again as editor of the *Consulting Psychology Journal: Practice and Research*, Richard Diedrich has challenged our propensity for professional insularity and self-reinforcing dialogue by calling for more participation, perspective, and voice from the clients we serve as consulting psychologists (Diedrich, 2003, 2004). Toward that end, client-executives are now not only attending the Division 13 Mid-Winter Conference in greater numbers, but are also participating at those conferences as keynote speakers, panel presenters, and small group discussants. In addition, articles written from the client's perspective have appeared with increased regularity in the *Consulting Psychology Journal* over the past 2 years (see, e.g., Freedman & Stinson, 2004). Client-executives have even become coauthors of articles published in the journal (see, e.g., chap. 35, this volume).

This chapter adds to this professionally important endeavor by eliciting and synthesizing the thoughts and views of seven top management executives from four major business sectors about their real-time experience as recipients of executive coaching.

EXECUTIVE COACHING AS A CONSULTING PSYCHOLOGY SERVICE

Despite the growing popularity of executive coaching and the increasing number of references to it in both the public media and professional literature, there is relatively little empirical research supporting the validity and reliability of coaching interventions with executive clients (chaps. 1 and 7, this volume; Kilburg, 2004; Sashkin, 2005). The recent two-part special issue of the *Consulting Psychology Journal* both highlights this incongruity and presents several practitioner-fashioned coaching models, methods, and approaches (Kilburg, 2004, 2005).

Potentially hampering the development of a scientifically based field of executive coaching is the likelihood that different things happen under the term *executive coaching* at different levels of the organization. Furthermore, the reasons for coaching engagements differ, and any organizationally sponsored "program" of coaching may include executives who are unwilling, unready, or unable to derive benefit from a coaching-type intervention. These factors, and more, potentially give rise to variables akin to "apples and oranges" and may lead researchers to only

Grateful acknowledgement is extended to the seven CEOs and presidents who graciously gave their time and reflections to this chapter. Their insights and perspectives reveal them to be among an elite and special group of business leaders and professionals.
Reprinted from the *Consulting Psychology Journal: Practice and Research, 57,* 274–285.

the most generic conclusions about the efficacy of coaching.

In addition, there remains a great deal of confusion and mystery as to what actually happens behind closed doors when executives engage with a coach. While case study material and narrative approaches have a place in the evolution of our knowledge about executive coaching, most are written from the practitioner's vantage point of what happened, what worked, and what outcomes were achieved (chaps. 6 and 7, this volume; Lowman, 2001). On the other hand, case material anchored in a context other than the consultant's own perspective may give rise to additional insights and knowledge about what actually occurs in a coaching engagement. Lowman (see chap. 7, this volume) argued that, "Adding the perspective of the person being coached is especially useful because what interventionists think may be of importance to a process of change may not be what was viewed as being most helpful by the client" (p. 91).

This convergence of Diedrich's call for more client voice in shaping our professional dialogue and Lowman's argument that the client's perspective may be important to understanding what actually occurs behind the closed doors of a coaching engagement—both proffered as a way to strengthen our theoretical and practice foundations—provided the impetus for this chapter. This chapter provides a glimpse of what executive coaching is for those in the top-most position of an organization as experienced and defined by *them*.

THE PROCESS

Seven top management executives from four major business sectors (industrial manufacturing, financial services, health care, and academia) were invited to share their views and perspectives regarding executive coaching. I interviewed each CEO or president separately over the telephone in a manner that was informal, conversational, and guided by 11 preconstructed questions. Each executive had received the questions well in advance of the telephone interview and was encouraged to use the questions to help stimulate and guide his or her reflections and thoughts but not to be limited by them. Each interview was tape recorded with permission from the executive and was later transcribed.

Three of the seven executives interviewed had at one time been engaged in a coaching relationship with me, each spanning more than 2 years. Two of these three executives and all of the remaining four had had experiences with an executive coach other than me. All seven executives, one of whom was a woman, had engaged with an executive coach during their tenure as CEO or president of their respective organizations. Three of these seven continue to lead and manage their organizations from this top management position, whereas four have respectfully "retired" in the past 18 months into postcareer roles as consultant, not-for-profit board chair, adjunct faculty professor, and stay-at-home granddad.

EXECUTIVE COACHING FROM THE EXECUTIVE'S PERSPECTIVE

The commentary and reflections of the seven CEOs and presidents collected from the guided interviews were reviewed and organized around the 11 interview questions. As much as possible, the actual "voice" of the executive is reflected in the quotations selected and presented under each question below, with only minor editing to improve readability. An effort was made to present relevant and representative quotations for each question rather than provide multiple examples of a common theme. A thematic summary is presented in Table 39.1.

Question 1: What Is Your Definition of Executive Coaching (EC)?

Please consider the following in addition to any other thoughts you have as you formulate your answer:

- What do you think the goal or purpose of EC is (or should be)?
- What kinds of issues or topics does (or should) EC focus on?

> EC should be a voice that brings a perspective that is different from mine and

TABLE 39.1

Summary of Themes by Question (Q)

Q1: Definition/purpose of EC
To help the CEO and/or president . . .
- Gain a deeper, broader, clearer understanding of the issues they contend with in their role;
- Comprehend and cope with increasing degrees of complexity and ambiguity;
- Shape and set the tone or ethos of the organization; and
- Say and do necessary but difficult things in the right way.

Q2: Why engage in EC?
- To have a sounding board that challenges and sharpens one's thinking;
- For self-improvement; to strengthen one's ability to meet the responsibilities of the position; and
- To ameliorate or address potential shortcomings in how one carries out the role of CEO or president.

Q3: "Ingredients" of an effective EC engagement
Coach-centered:
- Interested in the success of the executive and his or her organization; invested in the work;
- Comfortable with and grounded in the executive's contextual framework; highly credible;
- Authentic, genuine, and ethical in personal character; respectful in demeanor; possessing a smart, insightful perspective; and
- Capable of listening to what is said and to what is meant.

Executive-centered:
- Willingness to consider issues from a different point of view;
- Openness to influence; willingness to be helped;
- Capable of trusting another person and engaging in honest, open dialogue; and
- Psychologically mature and healthy.

Content-centered:
- A mutual interest in the relationship and in the value of the work;
- A prevailing climate of trust in the organization; and
- A goal-orientation; clarity around why, what, and how.

Q4: Benefit from EC
- Judgments and actions more measured and considered;
- Better choices and decisions giving rise to more of the right actions;
- Better self-restraint in handling power, status, and adulation;
- More clarity and focus on role responsibility as the anchor for conduct and action; and
- More personal satisfaction from the role of leader.

G5: "Pitfalls" to keep in mind
- Seeing the executive coach as an "answer person";
- Thinking that it's all about "you" rather than you in relation to the organizations' agenda; and
- Engaging with a coach who is ill-prepared for this work or of questionable character.

Q6: Confidentiality
- It is paramount to the relationship and to the success of the endeavor; and
- Having and adhering to clear, professionally crafted guidelines is necessary and important.

Q7: Feedback to the organization
- Appropriate and respectful feedback is necessary and legitimate;
- Parameters should be clarified and agreed to up front;
- The executive coach should not ferry information or messages to or from people; and
- It requires the highest level of skill and sophistication to effectively balance the demands for both confidentiality and feedback.

Q8: All team members in EC
- Executives need to engage willingly and for their own reasons;
- Demanding or forcing them to engage in EC diminishes the potential value of it; and
- Coaching an individual divorced from his or her context delimits EC's effectiveness.

Q9: Considerations regarding team members in EC
- CEO president sets the tone or conditions that influence willingness to participate;
- No standardized approach; one size will not fit all; and
- Make the parameters and process clear up front.

Q10: Training and preparation of the coach
- Needs a theoretically sound foundation in human psychology and social systems;
- Needs a familiarity and comfort with the business environment and context;
- Needs the ability to see and work with organization design/structure problems; and
- Needs to have a real-world understanding.

Q11: Outside or inside coach
- An outside coach has numerous potential advantages and represents a greater potential value to the executive and/or organization; and
- A coach from the inside may be OK only if the organization is very large.

Note. EC = executive coaching; CEO = chief executive officer.

that of others on my team, and should be able to ask questions I hadn't thought of as well as help me think about the complexity of what I am wrestling with as the company's top leader.

What EC focuses on or does should change as the executive matures and develops in his or her role over time. It may start out as, "I've got a problem and I'm not clear on what to do or how to do it," but should eventually move to a deeper sense of what the executive's work really is.

An executive should at some point begin to realize that how he engages with people, how he solves problems, what he writes, and what he says actually creates an ethos for the organization. Coaching can and should help him think clearly about what he is doing and how he is doing it so that he creates the proper ethos for the organization.

EC can help us be more courageous, do and say the things we know we need to, and to find the right way to do it, even when it's uncomfortable for us.

EC is not about getting an answer; it's about getting help to understand what we are dealing with in all of its richness and fullness so that we can make good choices on what to do and how to do it.

EC is not a consultative relationship . . . it's a mutually collaborative relationship. My thought is that in a consulting relationship, it's like "here's my problem, give me some answers." In a collaborative relationship, we are mutually exploring ways to look at a problem, considering options together, and developing potential actions to take.

EC can prompt a pattern of reflection so that the voice of the executive coach becomes like a second inner voice that the executive can listen to or use if he or she wants to, but it takes a while for the executive to incorporate the sensibility and voice of the executive coach.

I really think EC is about seeing the complexities more clearly, considering other perspectives more fully, and bringing together and solidifying all our thinking on a subject so that we can get a handle on it. We can have a lot of ideas and thoughts about something but need help fashioning a sound bite so that the problem becomes comprehensible without critical omissions.

The higher up in an organization one gets, the more executive-level work really, truly becomes two things . . . exercising good judgment for the sake of the company and interacting with people in a way that is successful . . . that's what EC should be focused on . . . helping me with those two things, my real job, so to speak.

Question 2: What Might Prompt an Executive to Engage in an EC relationship?

As president, it is too easy to get people to simply agree with you. To have an ongoing dialogue with someone who can challenge me to ask myself, "Do I have the right motives, do I have the right perspective, am I taking into account things I don't know, am I challenging myself adequately, am I looking at the issue in the right way, and so forth?" is what I want from an executive coach.

For me, it's really the recognition that in my role (as CEO), everybody I'm working with has an agenda, and that I too have an agenda. And those agendas can get in the way of clear-headed thinking . . . clear-headed thinking that serves the company agenda. The benefit of EC is being in a relationship with somebody where their agenda is to help me gain clarity in my thinking.

I am not looking for an "expert" with answers. I'm looking for somebody who has the skill set and capacities to help me focus in a clear and appropriately detached way so that clarity emerges in my own thinking about the work I'm doing, the direction I'm going, and the relationships I have.

There has to be the interest and willingness to take a hard, honest look in the mirror and to want to strengthen one's capacity for the job of leading the company. You can't believe that you are already the best you'll ever be.

The impetus for EC will most likely come from the governing body or board. Remember . . . executives have inflated egos, and I believe that they will not generally or readily recognize the opportunity for self-improvement. There may be some that will, but I don't think the numbers are large in my view.

I just don't see how anyone can do executive-level work without getting outside help, but I know that EC is not on most people's radar screens.

Question 3: What Are 2–3 Essential "Ingredients" That Underlie an Effective EC Engagement?

The executive coach has to be smart and have enough experience and background to understand the pressures, challenges, and responsibilities we face. And they have to be good listeners . . . they have to listen really, really well, not only to what I say but to what I mean.

I think the EC relationship is a helping relationship, but the executive really has to want to be helped to go beyond what he or she thinks already. The executive can't believe that he or she is the only one with a valid or correct view of a situation.

There's the intelligence and demeanor of the coach . . . but there especially needs to be a mutual interest in the relationship and in the value of the outcome, including a shared belief that the organization and the executive are worthwhile to work with. The coach can't come in and think, "Oh, this organization stinks, it's not a sexy place, this guy's a loser . . . I'm not too interested." That doesn't work.

The executive has to be willing to entertain the possibility that their situation is something other than the way that they have defined it. The perception of the executive could be misplaced or distorted. That's what the coach is there to do . . . help refocus that perception so that issues can be looked at and understood in a different light.

I'm looking for someone who understands our challenges and barriers and reality and can work within that reality to help us find answers to our issues. I don't want someone who idealizes how things should be and then becomes critical or judgmental but, rather, someone who works within our constraints and within our reality, however imperfect our world may be.

It would be the ability of the person to present him- or herself authentically because it's the person . . . their heart, their soul, their spirit . . . that I'm interested in. While there are a lot of smart people in the world, I'm looking for somebody who can interact with me in that way on that level, and who has the capacity to do that with others in my organization as well.

If the lieutenants don't trust the CEO, then efforts to engage them in an EC relationship are likely to be stonewalled or at least nonproductive.

There should be a goal-orientation or focus to the discussion to help keep clear what we are trying to do or striving for. For us executives to painfully go through a good helping process, we need to be anchored in, "Here's where we are, here's what we are trying to do, and here's where we're going."

I think that a previous experience with getting help does influence the executive's willingness to engage in an EC relationship. Whether it was with a pastor, social worker, or counselor . . . it makes a difference. If you think you are totally self-sufficient, it's hard to engage in or get benefit from executive coaching. There is also the possibility that some people may have had a bad experience with getting help and therefore are unwilling to accept coaching help.

I wonder if an important part about effective coaching isn't also appropriately managing expectations in all directions about what ultimately can be accomplished.

Question 4: For You, What Has Been Most Useful (or Valuable) From EC?

Coaching helped me to see beyond myself and what I was doing . . . and that is the most important thing to me about being a good leader . . . to understand that it is not all about "you."

Coaching helps me to go beyond what I think I know, and that's really important because that enables me to be more considered in my work as the leader of this organization.

The process of talking out loud offered the opportunity for reflection; you get to hear your own voice in a fuller dimension. In addition to hearing the coach's voice, I could hear myself better.

Being reminded that I was the one responsible . . . and being reminded of what I was responsible for. It was kind of like being held accountable, but without the negative judgment of a boss.

EC helped my work as president become more meaningful to me and to the organization in the sense that it (my work) made a greater difference.

EC helped me check my perceptions and alter my judgments about how I viewed issues. Then I had the choice to soften or modify my position or to change my approach.

I think that in many organizations, people don't really talk to each another . . . they just move through their day. When they do talk, it is simply a transaction. EC gives people a chance to really talk about what they think and feel relative to the work they do and the meaning of it; it certainly did that for me.

Sometimes things you said would not immediately affect the way I was thinking about something. Sometimes I even disagreed with what you said. However, over time, rolling around in my mind was your perspective, your point of view, your comments, and eventually I got around to looking at the issue differently. Many times it even happened that I then changed my view or changed what I was initially going to do. I found that most helpful, as I think back to our work together.

EC helped me sort out my own reactions to things so that I'd make a more measured and informed response rather than an impulsive or emotional one. I then could say what needed saying in a way that wasn't a personal attack on someone because I was using my role responsibilities in the organization as my anchor, not my personal feelings about the issue or the person.

When coaching is done successfully, my view is more robust and encompassing, what becomes important shifts, and my capacity for making sense of complex, ambiguous affairs expands. Then my choices and decisions are better, and the right actions follow. That should be among our goals as company leaders . . . to have that happen for ourselves and to help that happen for others.

Question 5: What Are 2–3 "Pitfalls" That Executives Should Keep in Mind When Considering Whether or Not to Participate in an EC Relationship?

They should remember that the executive coach is not an answer person, or a friend, and doesn't solve problems. The executive coach is not Dear Abby . . . the executive needs to figure out how to solve the problem him- or herself.

The client isn't me. The client is the company and its agenda. The executive coach is here to help me serve that agenda in the role I have to the best of my God-given ability.

Don't just assume that the caliber of available coaches is always good. There are a lot of people calling themselves executive coaches who are really unfit professionally, morally, and ethically to do this work. The coach is in a very powerful role; he or she needs to have their own internal guidance system so that they don't cross the line . . . and it is a very thin line between good and bad coaching.

Question 6: What Is the Nature and Scope of Confidentiality in an EC Engagement?

My thought is that confidentiality is the foundation upon which an EC relationship is based. Without confidentiality, the whole process does not work . . . it falls apart.

Confidentiality has to be at the absolute highest level, and you (the coach) really only get one shot at that. If at any point I tell you something and somehow it leaks out and I find out, we're done . . . absolutely done . . . you don't get a second chance. And you will never be back to where you were.

Confidentiality means that the executive coach should not be carrying messages for anyone up or down the organization . . . not from the CEO and not to the CEO. The coach is not a communication link.

There are, I think, special circumstances when the coach should be released from confidentiality. I'm sure that your own professional psychology association has a Code of Ethics that contains guidelines about honoring, preserving, and breaching confidentiality. That's part of why I trust someone with your background in this type of work.

Question 7: What Should the Nature and Extent of Feedback to the Organization Be When Executives Are Engaged in EC?

I do think that coaches have some responsibility to the organization to report back. If we're having an organizational issue that we are trying to solve, and some senior managers are not working in concert with our effort . . . that is, they are not representing the president's message or position the right way, we ought to know that . . . that's what we are paying for.

I think there needs to be some way of structuring feedback to the organization so that it doesn't become personal or awkward for people and still protects the confidentiality of any uncensored discussion the coach had with people.

I think there needs to be a balance between what managers think they can do in an autonomous way and what they need to do to reach our company goals or to go in the direction that the president wants. If that is out of balance, then the president needs to know that. Hence, there needs to be some channel of appropriate and respectful feedback about what is perceived or thought about elsewhere in the organization.

Who invited the coach to the table? If it was the Board, then the coach needs to say up front to the Board that the engagement is between the executive and the coach, and then try to define the scope and limits of feedback to them up front about the executive . . . and the executive needs to know what the parameters and expectations are before engaging with the coach.

The coach has to be very skilled and alert so to avoid being trapped in the middle and/or manipulated into being a messenger between parties, especially when it's the Board and the CEO. That's why I think this whole notion of executive coaching, for me, requires very talented and uniquely prepared individuals. Everybody is putting it on their resume now, and I'm going, "Wait a minute, this is a lot harder and more complicated than you think."

Question 8: How Important (or Useful) Is It for All Members of an Executive Team to Be Simultaneously Engaged in EC? Why?

If you have some members of an executive team who don't want to participate, or are unwilling to participate, then I'm not sure it's worth forcing them . . . they'll just go through the motions and nothing worthwhile will happen.

I think that it tells you something about your team members to the extent they are not willing to engage with an executive coach.

One of the challenges that hadn't occurred to me before is how difficult it must be to coach someone in isolation, divorced from firsthand knowledge of the context the person is in, and seeing the rest of the organization and the peers and colleagues and subordinates and superiors, and so on solely through the eyes of that individual.

I would think that the hardest thing to pull off in a coaching context is where a coach "parachutes" into an issue and is dealing with one individual executive and has to learn about and sort though the biases, the blinkers, the blind spots, and the prelims the individual is seeing with. I have to wonder given the impediments and inhibitions that that puts on effectiveness, whether that is even ever worth doing . . . which is a thought that hadn't occurred to me before.

Question 9: What Parameters or Conditions Need to Be Considered When Executives From the Same Team Are Engaged in EC?

I don't think you can take a standard formula and apply it to each person. Each person is going to need their own strategy and structure around which to be engaged in EC. They are likely to move along at their own pace as well and may want different things from the EC relationship. Different things will work for different people; one size will not fit all.

The degree of respect, the degree of trust, the degree of fellowship among members of the group will influence people's readiness and willingness to participate in EC.

The president should not be inquiring about them, like asking the coach, "What did they say?" or asking them how come they are not meeting with you (the coach) more regularly.

There needs to be a nondefensive attitude by the CEO. Not everyone is going to be pleased by everything the CEO does. This may come out in their coaching sessions. The CEO can't give undue concern to this.

The CEO has to trust the process, trust the executive coach, and make it easy and OK for people to participate (in EC), or perhaps to not participate.

Define the roles and the process up front. I think they are different for a coaching engagement with an individual versus a team. Just think of the complexity involved regarding confidentiality when engaging a team . . . it is immense. So, the rules have to be different and clearly explained up front.

I think as the senior person who understands and values the EC process, I need to make sure that people don't somehow feel unfairly punished if they have chosen not to engage in EC. Everyone grows and moves at their own pace . . . I have to help them find something to help move them developmentally forward that fits where they are at the moment.

Question 10: How Important (or Relevant) Is It That an Executive Coach Be Trained in Business? . . . in Psychology? . . . in Human Resources? . . . in Some Other Discipline? Why?

Any one who has a theoretically sound framework for understanding human beings in relationship could potentially offer something useful because business organizations are social systems with a business agenda.

I think that it is very difficult for most human resources people to have a full picture; they mostly get to view only a very thin slice of an organization. That would hamper them as executive coaches. They could coach around specific issues, though, like handling a problem employee.

I think that executive coaches could be trained in any number of things, but they need to have a solid theoretical framework for and an interest in the psychology of organizations and the psychology of people.

I think the training should be in psychology, sociology, anthropology, OD [organizational development] . . . those disciplines. I can even imagine that if you were well trained in theology and clergy, you could probably figure out how to do EC within reason, provided you were familiar with business-type organizations.

Behavioral science is where the foundations need to be because this is about human beings and social systems, not about business per se. But they need to understand what a business organization is about and the demands on the business organization leadership.

If they understand human development and how people evolve and adapt as conditions change, they'd be in a good place for this type of work. I don't think an MBA helps you much with this stuff.

There are enough people in every industry that have been trained up the wazoo on the specific aspects of a business or industry . . . full of answers for both good questions and bad questions. But EC is not about delivering answers . . . it's about figuring out what are the right questions, and how do they get asked, and of whom. And it's about how do we best engage in dialogue around those questions. That's the mindset needed for this kind of work for EC to be most helpful.

Being trained in people dynamics is good, but if you only see the interactional, people side of an issue, you may miss the possibility that the more salient and more important issue is the poorly conceived or dysfunctional organizational design . . . the structure people are working in may need fixing.

The professional discipline matters, but so does having an understanding of real-world issues. I can tell you about people who have PhDs that still don't understand how to change a flat tire. The executive coach should have his or her own track record of experience in a real-world environment.

One's formal training is a lesser issue, in my view. The perspective the coach has, his or her philosophical make-up, and the moral and social skills of that person are the more important issues. Relative to being trained in business . . . one needs to have exposure or understanding, not of a particular industry, but of what the business environment is like.

Question 11: How Critical (or Essential) Is It That an Executive Coach Be Someone From "Outside" the Organization Versus Someone From "Inside" the Organization? Why?

I think it should be someone from the outside because of the neutrality the person would bring. It would have to be a pretty large organization for it to be someone from the inside.

Although it's harder to be objective the longer you (the outside coach) are involved with a particular institution, there is something potentially valuable about the outside coach having experienced a lot of other companies, organizations, and institutions . . . like your perspective on the issues and traits in common. While they can all still be fairly distinct, they are probably not unique.

You (the outside coach) don't have a stake in the outcome. If the organization is not doing well, you are not responsible for making it better. You are there to help the people there make it better. And that's a very important distinction.

There is also the issue of confidentiality. I do think it is easier to keep some level of confidentiality if it's an outside person.

I do think that sometimes chief executives need to rely on wisdom from outside because there isn't always a lot of objective wisdom inside the organization at every moment. When you are in it, you very often can't see it . . . objectively, or otherwise . . . also, there are blind spots . . . lots of them for lots of reasons, and inside people no matter how well intended can't see them either.

If the person is inside, eventually that person becomes imbued with the same way of thinking about things as the people they're trying to be helpful to. So I am biased toward someone from the outside, who theoretically brings a fresh, uninfected perspective with a capacity to be less attached to a particular outcome . . . a managed objectivity, so to speak.

I thought this was a trick question . . . so I'll answer it very clearly . . . always outside. If you are inside an organization, I don't care who you are or how you are, you have a clouded perception, or rather a contaminated perception, because you are part of that context. The value of the outside coach is that he or she has clearer vision and is better able to say the unsayable.

THEMATIC SUMMARY

There were a number of shared themes in the commentary and thoughts of these seven executives relative to each question. These themes are presented in Table 39.1 in descending order of frequency and/or emphasis for each question.

It seems reasonable to conclude from the comments quoted earlier and the shared themes presented in Table 39.1 that these seven top-level executives consider executive coaching to be a unique process wherein something is not done *to* them, nor is something done *for* them. To these seven CEOs and presidents, executive coaching is a helping process wherein something is done *with* them in a way that also *enables* them to better meet their role obligations and responsibilities.

There was also a great deal of agreement among these seven executives that this process occurs within a unique and personalized relationship that is forged on the sacrosanct foundations of confidentiality, mutual interest, and mutual respect. To them, executive coaching is an intimate exchange of views and perspectives with a uniquely prepared and professionally anchored person that aims to strengthen an executive's ability to think and act in a clear-headed, well-considered way in the service of the mission and purpose of their organization.

IMPLICATIONS AND THOUGHTS FOR DISCUSSION

This glimpse into executive coaching as experienced and defined by these seven top-level executives aligns well with a view of the executive coach as confidant, sounding board, and trusted advisor. For them, the helping process as represented by executive coaching is not focused on fixing, ameliorating, or healing personality deficiencies or behavior deficits but, rather, on helping successful, healthy individuals more fully meet and carry out their role responsibilities as defined by their position and status in an organization.

There is no doubt that a fair number of people holding highly responsible positions in an organization could use help to resolve personal issues that delimit their potential effectiveness or need help to modify ingrained behavioral habits and styles that result in suboptimal performance in their role. "Coaching" has emerged over the past 25 years as a more acceptable intervention than "counseling" in the business world for these situations (see chaps. 9 and 13, this volume), even though they may be, in many cases, indistinguishable in practice.

Given the potential for confusion regarding the intent behind an executive coaching engagement, and the implications that this confusion may have for studying the efficacy of executive coaching, perhaps some thought and discussion should be given to the terminology or labels used. For example, *leadership consultation* or *leadership coaching* may better denote what these seven CEOs and presidents described as executive coaching. Likewise, *developmental coaching* or *performance coaching* might better denote an effort to help an executive address elements in his or her personality or behavior that hamper his or her effectiveness and/or an effort to strengthen one's readiness for the challenges and demands of a different or higher organizational position. Or, perhaps *manager development coaching* versus *leader development coaching* might be considered to help distinguish an effort intended to strengthen one's managerial skills (e.g., delegation) versus his or her leadership skills (e.g., securing people's commitment, not just their compliance). With more front-end clarity regarding the intent of the coaching engagement, including the goals or outcomes desired and the expectations of those involved, perhaps more descriptive precision could be attained in the labels or terminology used. This, in turn, might contribute to developing a better classification system or model of coaching as a multidimensional intervention process or activity.

These seven executives also made clear their view that the coaching process occurs within the context of a "helping relationship" and acknowledged two critical variables for a successful helping experience: (a) the openness and willingness of the executive to be influenced by the coach and (b) the coach's wise and ethical use of this influence-power. Two articles appeared in the *Harvard Business Review* within the past 3 years warning business executives not only of the potential misuse and abuse of this influence-power by the coach, but also of the potential dangers of engaging a well-intended but ill-prepared "coach" naive to the notions and challenges inherent in managing a successful coaching relationship (Berglas, 2002; Sulkowicz, 2004).

The professionally prepared and ethically anchored consulting psychologist potentially represents a lower level of risk in this regard than other executive coaching practitioners and may have the added advantage of being formally trained in recognizing and managing boundary, transference, and dependency issues and so forth that are inherent in an effective helping relationship. Perhaps ongoing and advanced training in recognizing, avoiding, and resolving the inherent ethical dilemmas associated with the acquisition and use of influence-power and in the recognition and management of underlying dynamic and relational issues could help to further distinguish consulting psychology as a preferred background for this kind of work.

The seven CEOs and presidents also suggested that the credibility of the coach, and hence their willingness to listen and be influenced by him or her, was in large measure dependent on how grounded and familiar the coach was with their "reality" and the challenges they faced as business professionals leading a business organization. Their comments give credence to what Diedrich and Kilburg wrote in their forward to the 2001 *Consulting Psychology Journal* special issue on executive coaching: "Psychologists who coach executives . . . must have an in-depth feel for the lives that these most competent, ambitious, and talented people lead and how to successfully intervene with them" (see chap. 5, this volume, p. 63).

Coaching executives clearly requires a demonstrable understanding of business, organizations, management, leadership, economics, and the impact of world events on these and other arenas composing the executives' field of play. Perhaps a more formal or deliberate opportunity for training in these areas should be considered by the mid-winter conference program planning chairs and/or the continuing education chairs of Division 13, particularly with the beginning, entry-level, or less seasoned division members in mind.

These views also give legitimacy to Diedrich's (2003, 2004) call for more participation, perspective, and voice from the clients we serve as consulting psychologists. Increasing and broadening the dialogue with executive-level leaders at the Division 13 Mid-Winter Conference and encouraging their voice in the form of articles published in the *Consulting Psychology Journal* can only strengthen the familiarity that consulting psychologists have for the reality and challenges that client-executives face as business professionals and organization leaders.

IN CLOSING

This chapter has provided a glimpse into what executive coaching is for those in the topmost position of an organization as experienced and defined by them. Although their perspectives and comments cannot and should not be overgeneralized, there is potentially considerable food for thought concerning the preparation for and practice of executive coaching. Perhaps others will be inspired to extend or sharpen the thoughts and issues reflected here, or at the very least perhaps they will take up the challenge of listening to our clients and allowing them to help influence and shape our knowledge and practice as consulting psychologists.

References

Berglas, S. (2002, June). The very real dangers of executive coaching. *Harvard Business Review,* 87–92.

Diedrich, R. C. (2003, August). *Let's talk with our clients.* Division 13 presidential address presented at the 111th Annual Convention of the American Psychological Association, Toronto, Ontario, Canada.

Diedrich, R. C. (2004). In the eye of the CEO. *Consulting Psychology Journal: Practice and Research, 56,* 129–131.

Freedman, A. M., & Stinson, G. H. (2004). Herding cats: Lessoned learned from managing and coordinating organization development consultants. *Consulting Psychology Journal: Practice and Research, 56,* 44–57.

Kilburg, R. R. (Ed.). (2004). Trudging toward Dodoville—Part I: Conceptual approaches in executive coaching [Special issue]. *Consulting Psychology Journal: Practice and Research, 56*(4).

Kilburg, R. R. (Ed.). (2005). Trudging toward Dodoville—Part II: Conceptual approaches in executive coaching [Special issue]. *Consulting Psychology Journal: Practice and Research, 57*(1).

Lowman, R. L. (2001). Constructing a literature from case studies: Promise and limitations of the method. *Consulting Psychology Journal: Practice and Research, 53,* 119–123.

Sashkin, M. (2005, February). *Coaching for leadership development: Basic aims, contextual guidelines, and essential elements.* Keynote address presented at the Mid-Winter Conference of the Society of Consulting Psychology, San Antonio, TX.

Sulkowicz, K. J. (2004, February). Worse than enemies: The CEO's destructive confidant. *Harvard Business Review,* 64–71.

Index

ABCDE model, 169–171
Abilities, 124
Absolute thinking, 169, 170
Acceptance
  of coaching, 279, 280
  organizations at, 261
Accountability, 98, 273
Action (AFT component), 178
Action frame, 176, 177
Action frame theory (AFT), 175–182
  components of, 176–179
  core of, 176, 177
  illustration of usefulness of, 175–176
  and Kilburg's three foci of executive coaching, 179–180
  stages of, 181–182
Action research, 110
Action step, 110
Active exclusion, 259
Active experimentation, 125
Addictions, 252–253
Adherence. *See* Intervention adherence
Adherence protocol, 247–251
Adhocracy, 225
Adult development, 52, 95, 283–289
  case examples, 285–288
  in late midlife, 286–287
  in midlife, 284–285
  stages of, 284
"Advantaged group," 259
Adventurous character structure, 297
Advising, 209
Affection, 96
Affirmative action, 258
African American executive case study, 389–404
African American executives, issues with, 392
AFT. *See* Action frame theory
Age differences, 51
Aggression, 96, 97
Alice's Adventures in Wonderland (Lewis Carroll), 67
Ambivalent attachment style, 195–196
American Psychological Association (APA), 42, 56
American Society for Training and Development, 48
Analogy, 307
Anger management, 171
Antisocial personality disorder, 297
APA. *See* American Psychological Association
Applegate, J., 306
Applied psychology, 4–5
Approachability, 325
Argyris, Chris, 110n, 326
Arthur Anderson, 5
Asking questions, 304
Assessing coaching engagements, 87–88
Assessment
  of executive, 35, 96–97, 151–152, 181
  of goal/problem, 110
Assessment tools, 214
Attachment styles, 192, 195–196
AT&T Corporation, 5, 6
Attentional and Interpersonal Style, 276
Attribute listing, 306–307
Attunement to others, 85
Austin, N. K., 103–104
Authenticity, 311
Authority
  executive, 96
  formal, 225
Avoidant attachment style, 195
Awareness
  and duration of coaching process, 50
  of issues, 250
  self-, 57, 116, 312, 314–315
  and self-efficacy, 49

Bacon, Sir Francis, 305
Barriers to inclusion, 259
BASIC I.D., 275–280
Beck, A., 292, 295
Beckhard, Richard, 104
Behavior
  continuities of, 97
  role, 98
Behavioral approach, 47–48
Behavioral requirements, 150–151
Behavior change, 55
  impact on organization of individual, 116
  models of, 167–168
  study focusing on, 84
  sustainability of, 49–50, 87–88
  sustained, 82
Behavior modification, 250
Behavior therapy, 7
Belief systems, 169–171
Benne, K. D., 230
Berglas, S., 82
Blackwell, B., 244
Bluck, S., 70
Bolman, L. G., 229
Boundaries
  coaching vs. therapy, 269, 270
  establishing, 117
Brainstorming, 305–306
Bray, D. W., 6
Brouwer, P. J., 329
Bruner, J., 69

Bug list, 306
Business
  knowledge/expertise in, 32–33
  as public service, 312–313
Business-linked executive development, 149–155
  case study, 152–155
  dynamics of, 149–150
  model for, 150–152
Business simulations, 6

California Personality Inventory (CPI), 296
Career coaching, 34
Carroll, Lewis, 67
Case study(-ies)
  of airline pilot, 410–411
  of CEO, 410
  of coaching up, 8–13
  competitive senior executive, 118–122
  of culture change, 264–265
  of demoralized operations director, 241–243
  of Frank, 377–388
  of Gloria and Anne, 343–355
  of Henry, 137–141
  of Howard, 152–155
  of HP manager, 125–128
  of Jennifer, 357–375
  of Ms. L., 278–280
  of office manager, 411–412
  of professor, 410
  of retiring executive, 99–102
  of Ted, 145–147
  of Terry, 333–342
  of Tom, 389–404
Case study method. *See also* Narrative mode
  applications/limitations of, 76
  as basis for theory, 76–77
  conditions for, 77
  Lowman's framework for, 66
  and modernist science, 71
  presentation styles of, 70
  self-report, 74
  standards for, 76
  value of, 66, 73–74, 331–332
Catastrophizing, 169
CBC. *See* Cognitive–behavioral coaching
CCL. *See* Center for Creative Leadership
Center for Creative Leadership (CCL), 6, 7
Center for Minority Health (CMH), 344
Change
  ABCDE model of, 169–171
  sustained behavior, 324
Change leadership, 35
Change management, 35
Character, 291–296
  empirical studies of, 293–295
  as term, 291
  theoretical perspectives on, 291–293
Character (Gail Sheehy), 291
Character structure(s), 296–301
  adventurous, 297
  case example, 300–301
  conscientious, 298–299
  dramatic, 297–298
  leisurely, 298
  self-confident, 296–297
  vigilant, 299
Checklists, 277
Chesler, Mark, 259
Client feedback survey, 400, 404
Client's past, 269, 271
Cloninger, Robert, 293
CMH (Center for Minority Health), 344
Coaching. *See also specific types of coaching, e.g.:* Executive coaching
  acceptance of, 279, 280
  forms of, 34
  origins of, 31
Coaching, therapy compared with, 267–274
  and confidentiality, 272–273
  and contracting, 272
  and control, 271–272
  differences, 268
  legality/accountability issues, 273–274
  and red flags for non-therapists, 270–271
  and relationship with clients, 268–269
  and supervision, 274
  taboos, 269–270
  and therapist-turned-coach awareness, 271
  training, 274
Coaching agenda, 84
Coaching agreement, 249
Coaching contract, 146
Coaching effectiveness model, 245–248
Coaching Experience Survey, 49
Coaching sessions, 85
Coaching tools, 85–86
Coaching up, 8–13
Cognitions, 275, 278
Cognitive–behavioral coaching (CBC), 162–164
Cognitive–behavioral therapy, 157–164
  assumptions of, 157–158
  categories of, 158
  efficacy of, 161–162
  executive coaching applications of, 158–162
  recommendations for, 163–164
  strengths of, 162
  weaknesses of, 162–163
Cognitive complexity, 252
Cognitive-restructuring therapies, 158
Collaborative process, 80
Comfort around top management, 325
Commitment
  to contract for coaching, 110
  contracts for establishing, 212–213
  inspiring, 124, 128
  lack of, 251–252
  to path of progressive development, 246–247
Communication
  deep interpersonal, 311, 314–315
  executive, 312
  management roles using, 313–314
Communication style, 49
Company House, 217, 218, 220, 221, 223, 229
Compassion, 294, 325
Competence standard, 75–76
Conditions (AFT component), 176, 177
Confidentiality
  in coaching vs. therapy, 272–273
  executives' perspectives on, 419
  and external coaching, 51, 83
  and internal coaching, 212
  preserving, 118
  as skill of psychologists, 45
Conflict resolution, 35
Conflicts of interest, 83
Conflict theory, 189, 192–194
Confrontation, fear of, 171
Conscientious character structure, 298–299
Consequence (AFT component), 179
Consolidation phase, 115
Constructive–developmental theories, 218–219
Constructivism, 69, 71
Consultants, 104
Consulting, 134
Consulting Psychology Journal, 7–8, 17, 43, 323, 413
Continuing development, 116

Continuing support, 116–117
Continuities of behavior, 97
Continuous improvement, 110
Contracting, 212–213, 272
Control issues, 150, 271–272
Conversation, 268
Cooperativeness, 294
Coping-skills therapies, 158
Core competencies, 324–326
Core irrational beliefs, 169
Corporate management assessment center, 6
Counselors, 104
Countertransference, 270
Cowell, J., 41, 48–49
CPI (California Personality Inventory), 296
Creative problem solving, 303–309
  attribute listing in, 306–307
  and coach as teacher, 304
  generating options in, 305–306
  Idea Checklist in, 306
  and marketing value of coaching, 307–308
  metaphorical approaches to, 307
  morphological synthesis in, 307
  psychologists' role in, 308
  research on, 303–304
  role of questions in, 304–305
  and scientific method, 305
  stating problem in, 305
  teaching approaches to, 304
Creativity, 325
Credentials of coaches, 44–45, 55, 81–82, 319
Credibility, 210
Critical mass, organizations at, 260–261
Cronshaw, Steven, 175–176, 181, 182
Cultural differences, 51
Culture
  organizational, 84, 224
  personal, 224
Culture change, 257–265
  case study, 264–265
  focus areas for coaches, 263–264
  leading change, 262–263
  organizational imperative for diversity/inclusion, 257–259
  outsider's perspective, 262
  partnering with leaders, 261–262
  partnership competencies, 262
  path from exclusion to inclusion, 259–261
  safe learning environment, 263
Customer focus, 325

Dashboard, progress, 400, 403
Data gathering, 43, 114, 115
Deal, T. E., 229
Dealing with paradox, 325
Decision making, 98, 227
Deep insight, 386
Deep interpersonal communication, 311, 314–315
Defensiveness, 252–254
Defensive reasoning, 326
Demands, 169
Dependency, 96, 270
Development
  continuing, 116
  mind-set for ongoing, 130
  personal, 116
Developmental coaching, 34, 217–234, 423
  as EC role, 108–109
  First Company House in, 224–228
  model of, 219–224
  personal culture in, 224
  professional agenda in, 223–224
  Second Company House in, 228–232
  self in, 221–223
  work context in, 223
Developmental conflicts, 192–194
Developmental counseling, 17, 40, 57
Developmental level, 52, 53, 55
Developmental planning, 152
Developmental Structure/Process Tool, 53
Development Dimensions International, 6
Development phase, 115–116
Development Pipeline, 359–360
Development planning, 34, 181–182
Development plans, 212–213
Diedrich, Richard, 43, 89, 413
Direct analogy, 307
DISC model, 333, 334
Disorganized attachment style, 185, 186
Disseminator role, 227
Disturbance handler, 227
Diversity
  definition of, 258
  lack of consideration of, 51
  organizational imperative for, 257–259
  tolerance vs. inclusion, 258
Dodo bird, 74
Dodo bird hypothesis, 67
Dodoville, 67–69, 71, 74
Dominance, 296
Doyle, Marilyn, 113

Dramatic character structure, 297–298
Drucker, P., 304, 305
Drug/biology modality, 275–276, 278
Duality, 269

EC. *See* Executive coaching
Educational background of coaches, 55
Education of client, 250
Educators, 104
Ego, 292
Ego ideal, 96–98
Ellis, A., 168–170
EMDR. *See* Eye movement desensitization reprocessing
Emotional competence, 84–85
Emotional pain, 312, 314, 315
Emotions, identifying, 10–11
Empathy, 144, 294
Empirically validated therapies, 67–68
Empirical research, 47–54
  on character, 293–295
  by Foster and Lendl, 47
  by Garman, Whiston, and Zlatoper, 54
  by Gegner, 49–50
  by Hall et al., 50–51
  by Judge and Cowell, 48–49
  by Laske, 51–54
  by Olivero et al., 47–48
  of schemas, 295–296
  summarized by Kampa and White, 65
Encouragement, 250
Enhanced feedback, 108*n*
Entrepreneur role, 227
Environment
  for learning, 263
  shaping, 125, 128
Equifinality principle, 68
Erikson, Erik, 283–284
Ethics Code (of APA), 75–76
Exclusive clubs, 259–260
Executive assessments, 6
Executive coaches
  business experience/knowledge of, 82
  characteristics/style of, 33
  credentials/experience of, 48, 81–82
  effective, 32–33, 325
  factors in choosing, 45, 81–82
  personal characteristics of, 82–83
  preparation for, 36
  prerequisites for, 32–33
  psychology background of, 82
  references of, 82

Executive coaches (*continued*)
selecting, 36–37
as teachers, 304
Executive coaching (EC), 133–141
basic definition of, 31–32
case study, 8–13, 137–141
for change leadership/management, 35
competence standard for, 75–76
components of, 25
conceptual approach to, 23–28
for conflict resolution/mediation, 35
as consulting psychology service, 413–414
consulting vs., 134
definitions of, 8, 28, 31–32, 41–42, 56
effectiveness of, 49–54
as emerging competency, 61–64
evolving practice theory for, 110–111
for executive assessment/ development/succession planning, 35
executive focus for, 24
focus of engagements, 84–85, 96
goals of, 25, 26
history of, 3–7
implementing, 135–137
indicators of successful, 66–87
key stakeholders in, 32
Kilburg's three foci of, 24, 179–180
knowledge required for, 63, 95
lack of data about, 66, 68
lack of scientific base for, 74–75
levels of, 134
literature on, 7–8
literature review on, 21–23
mediated focus for, 24
methods/techniques of, 25–27
negative outcome factors, 27–28
as ongoing process, 133
in organizational context, 134–135
for organizational values/vision/ mission/strategy, 35
as partnership, 33–34
by PDI, 129
for performance management, 35
personal/career/performance coaching vs., 34
positive psychology approach to, 65
process of, 56–57, 110
psychotherapy vs., 44
purpose of, 42–43
reasons for seeking, 159
recipients of, 55, 56
scope of, 161
stages of, 43
standards for, 42, 56
structured approach to, 32
system focus for, 24
for team-building, 35
techniques/methodologies for, 43–44
therapeutic interventions vs., 158–159
working definition of, 28
Executive Coaching (Kilburg), 46
Executive coaching model, 80–81
Executive coaching roles, 103–111
clarification of, 105
as coaches, 104–110
common elements in, 110
as consultants, 104
for development, 108–109
evolving practice theory for, 110–111
for executive's agenda, 109–110
for performance, 106–107
situational aspect of, 103–104
for skills, 105–106
Executive Coaching With Backbone and Heart (O'Neill), 46
Executive communication, 312
Executive development programs, 5–7
Executive focus, 24, 179, 180
Executives
assessment of, 96–97
coaching as perk for, 81
interviewing, 97–98
reaction to ideal of working with coach, 80–81
as recipients of coaching services, 45–46, 48–49
successful, 96
typology for assessing, 87–88
unique needs of, 160–161
Executive's agenda, 105, 109–110
Executives' perspective, 413–424
on confidentiality in EC, 419
on definition of EC, 414, 416
on essentials of effective EC engagement, 417–418
on executive team in EC, 420–421
on feedback to organization with EC, 419–420
importance of, 414
on motivation to use EC, 416–417
on outside vs. inside coaches, 422
on pitfalls of EC, 419
summary of themes by question, 415
on training of coach, 421–422
on value derived from EC, 418–419
Executive vice president (EVP), 283
Experience of coaches, 55, 81–82, 95
Experts, coaches as, 104
External coaches/coaching
definition of, 12
executives' perspectives on, 422
and internal coaching, 210
literature on, 51
pros/cons of, 83
roles of, 104
External support, 116
Eye movement desensitization reprocessing (EMDR), 40, 47, 54, 407–412
case study outcomes, 410–412
measures used in study, 409
participants in study, 408–409
procedure, 409
stages of, 408

Fact gathering, 115
Failure, fear of, 125
Fantasy analogy, 307
Fear
of confrontation, 171
of failure, 125
Feedback, 43–44, 49, 51, 116. *See also* 360-degree feedback
in action frame theory, 181, 182
asking for, 130
in developmental planning, 152
enhanced, 108n
objective, 160
to organization, 419–420
Feedback debriefing, 34
Filipczak, B., 321
First Company House, 217, 218, 224–228
First-order coaching, 224–227, 229–230
Flexibility, 117, 231, 269
Forgetfulness, 250
Formal authority, 225
Formal coaching, 104n
Fosdick, Harry Emerson, 315
Foster, Sandra, 47
Frankl, Viktor, 293
Frito-Lay, 308
Functional job analysis, 176

GAPS (goals, abilities, perceptions, and standards), 124, 128
Garman, Andrew N., 54
Gegner, C., 49–50
Gender differences, 51
Generating options, 305–306

Gilmore, David, 285
Gioia, D. A., 228–229
Global evaluations of human worth, 169
Goals, 124, 251
Goleman, D., 324
Grant, Joseph M., 316

Haber, R., 220, 221, 224
Habermas, T., 70
Habits, breaking, 125
Hall, D. T., 50–51
Hardiman, Rita, 259
Hargrove, R., 7, 46–47
Hay/McBer Executive 360, 143–144
Health status, 312, 313, 315
Herd effect, 306
Histrionic personality disorder, 298
Holistic approach, 114, 144–145, 160–161, 385–386
HR. *See* Human resources
Hudson Institute, 7
Human resource frame, 229, 231, 232
Human resources (HR), 50, 209

ICF. *See* International Coaches Federation
Idea Checklist, 306
Implementation phase, 115, 152
Inclusion
  barriers to, 259
  definition of, 258
  organizational imperative for, 257–259
  path from exclusion to, 259–261
Inclusive organizations, 261
Individual change, 123–130
  case study, 125–129
  coaching strategies for, 123–125
  coaching tips for, 129–130
  executive coaching for, 129
  and impact on organization, 116
  intensive coaching for, 128, 129
  targeted coaching for, 128, 129
Industrial Revolution, 4
Influence, 104
Information processing, 408
Inquiry, 144
Insight
  building, 124
  translating, into action, 130
Integrity
  as core competency, 325
  of relationships, 98
Intellectual horsepower, 325
Intensive coaching, 128, 129
Internal coaches
  backgrounds of, 208
  effective, 211
  executives' perspectives on, 422
  literature on, 51
  networks of, 80
  pros/cons of, 83–84
  role of, 104, 208–209
  team builders/trainers vs., 209
Internal coaching, 207–214
  advising vs., 209
  assessment tools for, 214
  and confidentiality, 212
  contracting issues with, 212–213
  definition of, 208–209
  and external coaching, 210
  general expectations/program design for, 211–212
  mentoring vs., 209–210
  selection/training issues with, 210–211
  setting/logistics of, 213–214
  sponsor roles with, 213
Internal collaborators, 80
International Coaches Federation (ICF), 41, 42, 56, 89
Interpersonal savvy, 325
Interpretations in coaching work, 198–202
Intervention adherence, 241–254
  case study, 241–242
  developing protocol for, 248–251
  literature on, 243–245
  model of, 245–248
  problems contributing to nonadherence, 251–254
Interview protocols, 85–86, 386
Involuntary eye movements, 408
Involvement of top executives, 386–387
Irrational elements, 169
Iterative approach, 143–147
  case study, 145–147
  focus of, 144
  holistic, 144–145
  principles of, 143
  tips for, 145

Jackson, Bailey, 259
Job context, 181
Judge, W. Q., 41, 48–49

Kaleel Jamison Consulting Group, 257
Kampa, S., 65, 237
Kegan, R., 222
Kets de Vries, M., 296
Kiel, Fred, 113, 167
Kilburg, Richard, 17, 18, 40–41, 44, 46, 73, 74, 89, 93, 167, 179–180, 237, 304, 324, 333
Knowledge requirements, 44, 45, 51, 63, 82, 95
  in business, 32–33
  in psychology, 32
KRW, 113
Kuhn, T. S., 3

Landmark events, 283
Laske, Otto, 19, 51–54, 92
Late midlife, 286–287
Lazarus, Arnold A., 275, 276
Leader development coaching, 423
Leadership, paradox of, 263
Leadership coaching, 423
Leadership development, 6, 61
Leadership Development Plan, 152
Learning, increased, 55
Learning Community Behaviors, 264–265
Learning process, 143
Learning styles, 86
Legacy coaching, 34
Legislation, 273–274
Leisurely character structure, 298
Lendl, Jennifer, 47
Levinson, Harry, 18–19, 167
Lewin, Kurt, 5, 110*n*, 230
Licensing accountability, 273
Life coaching, 34, 63
Life span development, 217
Listening, 325
Literature review, 39–57
  databases used for, 40
  on definition of EC, 21–23
  on empirical research, 47–54
  and evolution of wisdom of coaching, 7–8
  on history of executive coaching, 40–41
  on intervention adherence, 243–245
  linking empirical studies to practice articles, 54–55
  on practice, 41–47
Loevinger, J., 219
Logicoscientific mode, 66–67, 69–70, 75
Loneliness, 314
"Looking Glass," 6
Looped feedback, 144
Low frustration tolerance, 169
Lowman, Rodney L., 6, 66, 331

Macik-Frey, Marilyn, 93
Managed care, 272–273
Management, as art form, 313
Manager development coaching, 423
Managerial consultation, 4–5
MAP (master action plan), 84
Marketing, 279, 307–308
Master action plan (MAP), 84
Masterful Coaching (Hargrove), 46–47
McAdams, D. P., 70
MCI, 313
Meaningfulness, 286–287
Meaning making, 221–222
Means (AFT component), 177, 178
Media perceptions of executive coaching, 319–322
Mediated focus, 24, 180
Mediation, 35
Meichenbaum, D., 245, 248–250
Mental health problems, 252–253
Mentoring, 209–210
Meta-analytic studies, 67–68
Metaphorical approaches, 307
Midlife transition, 283–289
Millier, Jennifer, 357–375
Millon, Theodore, 295
Millon Clinical Multiaxial Inventory—III, 295
Mintzberg, H., 225–227, 312, 313
Modernist science, 66–67, 71
Mold, H. P., 7
Momentum, maintaining, 117–118
Monitor role, 227
Morphological synthesis, 307
Motivation
  assessing, 252
  building, 124
  for change, 129–130
  for engaging in EC relationship, 416–417
  of learner, 304
  learning influenced by, 143
Multimodal therapy, 275–280
  and acceptance of coaching, 279, 280
  case study, 278–280
  and coaching vs. therapy, 278
  interventions used with, 276
  Lazarus model of, 275–276
  and new markets, 279
  shifting perspectives and value of, 277
  shortcomings of, 277–278
  and 360-degree feedback, 277
  value added with, 276–277
Multirater feedback systems, 6
Multisystems view, 117
Mundane, managing the, 125
Myers–Briggs Type Indicator, 276

Napoli, D. S., 5
Narcissistic personality disorder, 297
Narrative mode, 69–71
The Nature of Managerial Work (Mintzberg), 312
Negative coaching outcomes, 27–28
Negotiator role, 227
Newly assigned leader coaching, 34

Objectivity, 45
Object relations theory, 189–190, 192, 195–196
Obsessive–compulsive personality disorder, 299
OD. *See* Organization development
Olivero, G., 47–48
O'Neill, M. B., 46
Ontic–developmental stages, 52–54, 219
Openness, 98
Organizational context, 134–135
Organizational culture, 84, 224
Organizational environment, 247–248, 253–254
Organizational imperatives, 150
Organizational support, 125
Organization development (OD), 6, 343–344
Organizations
  at acceptance, 261
  at critical mass, 260–261
  diversity/inclusion as mandate of, 257–259
  feedback to, 419–420
  inclusive, 261
  individual change and impact on, 116, 160
  success factors for roles within, 150
  symbolic difference, 260
  values/vision/mission/strategy of, 35
Organization sponsors, 80
Osborn, A., 305–306
Osborn–Parnes Creative Problem Solving Program, 308
Outcome criteria, 76
Outcome study of executive coaching, 79–89
  demographics, 79–80
  executives' reaction to idea of coaching, 80–81
  external coaching, 83
  factors in choosing coach, 81–82
  focus of coaching engagements, 84–85
  indications of successful coaching, 86–87
  internal coaching, 83–84
  personal characteristics of coaches, 82–83
  sustainability of learning/behavior change, 87–88
  tools for, 85–86

Paradigmatic mode, 69–71
Paradigms, new or modified, 3
Paradox of leadership, 263
Paranoid personality disorder, 299
Partnerships
  coaching success through, 33–34
  competencies of, 262
  forging, 123–124, 128
  with leaders for culture change, 261–262
Passive–aggressive personality disorder, 298
Passive exclusion, 259
Pastoral counseling, 315
"The Path From a Monocultural Club to an Inclusive Organization" (Path model), 259–261
Path of progressive development, 246–247
PDG (Personal Development Guide), 151
PDI. *See* Personnel Decisions International
Pennebaker, James, 315
Perceptions
  of executive coaching, 54
  of media, 319–322
  of other people, 124
Perfectionism, 171
Performance coaching, 34, 106–107, 423
Performance issues, 171
Performance management, 35
Persistence, 125, 128
Personal analogy, 307
Personal characteristics of coaches, 82–83
Personal coaching, 34
Personal culture, 224
Personal development, 116
Personal Development Guide (PDG), 151
Personality, 291–292
Personal lives of executives, 50

Personnel Decisions International (PDI), 6, 7, 17, 43, 123, 357, 398
Peters, T. J., 103–104
Peterson, David, 7, 357–375
Planning, developmental, 152
Planning phase, 115
Political frame, 229–232
Political savvy, 325
Positive psychology, 66
Positive response bias, 76
Positivist approach to scientific inquiry, 66–67, 75
Postmodernism, 69
Posttraumatic stress disorder (PTSD), 407
Practice, timing of, 125
Practice literature, 41–47
  on credentials of coaches, 44–45
  on definitions/standards, 41–42
  on distinguishing coaching and psychotherapy, 44
  on purpose of executive coaching, 42–43
  recent books, 46–47
  on recipients of services, 45–46
  on techniques/methodologies, 43–44
Practice theory, 110–111
Preferential-style thinking, 170
Preliminary action plan, 84
Premack principle, 276
Premature termination, 244–245
"Presence," 46
Primary referrals, 88
Priority grid, 364–365
Problem, stating the, 305
Problem solving, creative. *See* Creative problem-solving
Problem-solving therapies, 158
Professional agenda, 223–224
Professional agenda interview, 52
Professional coaches, 32, 35
Professional House, 217, 218, 220–223
Professionalism, 83
Profile of Success, 150–151
PROFILOR, 126
Progress dashboard, 400, 403
Psychoanalytic theory, 96
Psychodynamic approaches, 185–204
  applications of, 190–191
  case study, 185–187
  coaching methods in, 196–202
  conflict theory in, 189, 192–194
  definition of, 188
  key propositions of, 188–189
  limitations of, 202–203
  object relations theory in, 189–190, 192, 195–196
  purposes of, 191
Psychological study, 135–136
Psychologists
  as coaches, 45, 54, 55
  innovation fostered by, 308
Psychology, knowledge and expertise in, 32
Psychometric battery, 84, 86, 115, 135
Psychotherapy, 27
  avoiding, 95–96
  executive coaching vs., 44
PTSD (posttraumatic stress disorder), 407
"Pure-hearted" principles, 294

Qualitative inquiry, 70
Questions
  asking, 304
  role of, 304–305
Quick, James Campbell, 93

Rational–emotive behavior therapy (REBT), 157, 167–172
  ABCDE model of change, 169–171
  applications for, 171–172
Reciprocal inhibition, 408
Reeducation, 230, 232
Referrals
  danger signals requiring, 270
  to treatment resources, 251, 252
Referral sources, 390
Referred power, 114
Relapse prevention, 244
Relationship coaching, 34
Relationship traction, 85
Relationship with client, 268–269
Relationship with coach, 85, 95–96, 247, 387
Reluctant president case study, 377–388
Reminders, 250
Resistance, planning for, 117
Resource allocator, 227
Responsibility, 49, 296
Result (AFT component), 179
Results/attitude grid, 382
Reversibility, 277
Rewards, 251
RHR. *See* Rohrer, Hibler, and Replogle
RHR International, 17, 40
Rimmer, Eric, 113
Rogers, Carl, 124
Rohrer, Hibler, and Replogle (RHR), 5
Role behavior, 98
Role fitting, 97
Rosenzweig, S., 67

Saccades, 409
Sadomasochism, 253
Schein, E., 5
Schema model, 292
Schema Questionnaire, 295–296
Schemas
  and character, 292–293
  in cognitive restructuring, 158
  empirical studies of, 295–296
Schizoid personality disorder, 295
Schizotypal patients, 295
Scientific inquiry on coaching, 66–71
  empirical, 66–68
  lack of, 67
  logical/modernist approaches to, 66–67, 69–70
  meta-analytic, 67–68
  narrative approach, 69–71
Scientific method, 305
Scott, Walter Dill, 4
Secondary referrals, 88
Second Company House, 217, 218, 228–232
Second-order coaching, 224, 229–230, 232
Seeking permission, 196, 197
Self, in developmental coaching, 218–223
Self-acceptance, 170
Self-awareness, 57, 116, 312, 314–315
Self-confident character structure, 296–297
Self-control therapy, 158
Self-determination, 293
Self-directedness, 293–294
Self-disclosure, 269
Self-efficacy, 49, 57, 293
Self-esteem, 143, 293–294
Self-knowledge, 325
Self-management, 85
Self-observation, 85
Self-regulation, 250
Self-reports, 74
Self-transcendence, 294–295
Self-understanding, 116
Seligman, M. E. P., 65
Semantics, 82
Senior executive coaching, 113–122
  approach to, 113–115
  business-linked, 149–155
  case study, 118–122
  guidelines for, 117–118

Senior executive coaching (*continued*)
  key issues with, 116–117
  program structure for, 115–116
Senior executives, involvement of, 386–387
Senior vice president (SVP), 283
September 11, 2001, terrorist attacks, 289
Sequestered schemas, 292
Setting-the-foundation stage, 150–151, 181
17-factor model, 23–24
Shadow consultants, 253, 254
Shapiro, Francine, 407, 408
Sheehy, Gail, 291
Simple structure organizations, 225
Sims, H. P., Jr., 228–229
16 Personality Factor Questionnaire (16PF), 276
Skills
  building, 124–125, 128
  coaching for, 105–106, 159
Social acceptance, 143
Social action, 176
Social anxiety, 161
Soft skills, 285
SO SMART, 84–85
Specificity, 144
Sperry, Len, 7
Spokesman role, 227
Sponsor roles, 213
Stake, R. E., 70–71
Stakeholders, 32
Stambaugh, Jan, 125–128
Standards, organizational, 124
Standards for executive coaching
  core competencies, 324–326
  issues with, 56
  lack of, 41–42
  need for, 323–327
  Triple T proficiency model, 326–327
Stating the problem, 305
Storytelling, 197
Stress, 160, 162
Stress inoculation training, 158
Structural frame, 229–231
Subjective Unit of Disturbance Scale (SUDS), 409
Subject–object interview, 52–53
Subject–object relations, 222
Successful Manager's Handbook (Personnel Decisions International), 398
Success profiles, 108
SUDS (Subjective Unit of Disturbance Scale), 409
Superkeepers, 377
Supervising consultants, 253
Supervision for coaching, 274
Sustained behavior change, 324
Sustained relationships, 387
SVP (senior vice president), 283
Symbolic difference organizations, 260
Symbolic frame, 229, 231, 232
System focus, 24, 179, 180
Systems-oriented approach, 32, 114–115, 117
Systems thinking, capacity for, 53

Talent agents, 125
Targeted behavioral coaching, 34
Targeted coaching, 128, 129
Teal, T., 324
Team-based approach, 114, 123
Team builders, 209
Team-building, 35
Team coaching, 34
  guidelines for, 329–330
  parameters for, 420–421
  simultaneous, 420
Tertiary referrals, 88
Therapy, coaching vs. *See* Coaching, therapy compared with
Thompson, Dale, 7
360-degree feedback
  adoption of, 6
  for assessment of individual, 151–152
  description of, 136
  and executive's reaction to EC, 80–82
  Hay/McBer Executive, 143–144
  interview protocol for, 386
  and multimodal therapy, 277
  pitfalls of, 233
  PROFILOR survey, 126
Tobias, L. L., 40, 326, 327
"Tokens," 260
Tolerance, 258
Traction, 384
Trainers, 104
Training
  as coaching proficiency, 327
  executives' perspectives on, 421–422
  importance of, 274
Transference, 96, 269
Transfer-of-training problem, 7
Transformational coaching, 46
Transformative coaching, 53–54
Trauma, 407, 408
Triple T proficiency model, 326–327
Trust, 83, 123–124, 127–128, 325, 384–385
Truth telling, 385
Turk, D. C., 245, 248–250
201 Great Ideas for Your Small Business (Applegate), 306
Type A behavior, 160, 162
Typology for assessing coaching engagements, 87–88

Vaill, Peter, 110n
Video coaching, 34
Vigilant character structure, 299
Visual metaphor, 381–382

Wampold, B. E., 66, 67
Washington State, 273–274
Wasylyshyn, Karol M., 19, 76, 93
Westin, D., 188, 189
"What?" questions, 305
Whiston, Deborah L., 54
White, Randall P., 65, 91, 237
"Why?" questions, 305
Whyte, David, 377
Williams, Kathryn, 113
Witherspoon, Robert, 91
Work context, 223

Xerox, 313

Young, P., 295

Zlatoper, Kenneth W., 54

About the Editors

Richard R. Kilburg received his Ph.D. in clinical and community psychology from the University of Pittsburgh in 1972. He attended a postgraduate program in mental health administration at the Community Psychiatry Laboratory at Harvard University and obtained a masters degree in professional writing from Towson University in 1992. He has held positions in the Department of Psychiatry of the University of Pittsburgh as an assistant professor; as the director of the Champlain Valley Mental Health Council, a community mental health center in Burlington, Vermont; and in the American Psychological Association's offices of Professional Affairs and Public Affairs. He also has been in private practice as a clinician and consultant. Currently, he is the senior director of the Office of Human Services at Johns Hopkins University, a multiprogram service component of the human resources department that meets the developmental needs of the faculty and staff of the university. He has published widely in the fields of management, professional impairment, and executive coaching. He has edited four special issues of the *Consulting Psychology Journal: Research and Practice* devoted to executive coaching. His four previous books are *Professionals in Distress: Issues, Syndromes, and Solutions in Psychology*; *How to Manage Your Career in Psychology*; *Executive Coaching: Developing Managerial Wisdom in a World of Chaos*; and *Executive Wisdom: Coaching and the Emergence of Virtuous Leaders.* He was the founding president of the Society of Psychologists in Management, and he is a fellow of Division 13, the Consulting Psychology Division of the American Psychological Association. He is the recipient of the 2002 Distinguished Contribution to Psychology in Management Award given by the Society of Psychologists in Management and of the 2005 Harry and Miriam Levinson Award given by the American Psychological Foundation. He has one son, Benjamin, and currently lives in Towson, Maryland.

Richard C. Diedrich completed both his PhD and AM in educational psychology at the University of Chicago and earned his AB at Ripon College. He has more than 35 years of experience as a consultant and trainer with business and industry as well as with a range of educational institutions and bureaus. Dr. Diedrich was employed by RHR International for 19 years; during that time he managed the Boston office for 12 years. He worked as a senior consultant with the Hay Group for 10 years. He taught at the University of Chicago and was on the faculty at Purdue University. He has also held positions as a school psychologist and director of research for suburban Chicago public schools, and he served as a commissioned personnel psychologist with the U.S. Army for 2 years. He is currently a consulting psychologist in independent practice. Dr. Diedrich was president of the Society of Consulting Psychology (Division 13) in 2002–2003, has been editor of the *Consulting Psychology Journal* for the past 9 years, and is a fellow of the American Psychological Association.